# REINVENTING FRENCH AID

Laure Humbert explores how humanitarian aid in occupied Germany was influenced by French politics of national recovery and Cold War rivalries. She examines the everyday encounters between French officials, members of new international organizations, relief workers, defeated Germans and displaced persons (DPs), who remained in the territory of the French zone prior to their repatriation or emigration. By rendering relief workers and displaced persons visible, she sheds lights on their role in shaping relief practices and addresses the neglected issue of the gendering of rehabilitation. In doing so, Humbert highlights different cultures of rehabilitation, in part rooted in pre-war ideas about 'overcoming' poverty and war-induced injuries and, crucially, she unearths the active and bottom-up nature of the restoration of France's prestige. Not only were relief workers concerned about the image of France circulating in DP camps, but they also drew DP artists into the orbit of French cultural diplomacy in Germany.

LAURE HUMBERT is Lecturer in Modern History at the University of Manchester.

# REINVENTING FRENCH AID

The Politics of Humanitarian Relief in French-Occupied
Germany, 1945–1952

LAURE HUMBERT
*University of Manchester*

# CAMBRIDGE
## UNIVERSITY PRESS

University Printing House, Cambridge CB2 8BS, United Kingdom

One Liberty Plaza, 20th Floor, New York, NY 10006, USA

477 Williamstown Road, Port Melbourne, VIC 3207, Australia

314–321, 3rd Floor, Plot 3, Splendor Forum, Jasola District Centre, New Delhi – 110025, India

79 Anson Road, #06–04/06, Singapore 079906

Cambridge University Press is part of the University of Cambridge.

It furthers the University's mission by disseminating knowledge in the pursuit of education, learning, and research at the highest international levels of excellence.

www.cambridge.org
Information on this title: www.cambridge.org/9781108831352
DOI: 10.1017/9781108916981

© Laure Humbert 2021

This publication is in copyright. Subject to statutory exception and to the provisions of relevant collective licensing agreements, no reproduction of any part may take place without the written permission of Cambridge University Press.

First published 2021

A catalogue record for this publication is available from the British Library.

Library of Congress Cataloging-in-Publication Data
Names: Humbert, Laure, 1985– author.
Title: Reinventing French aid : the politics of humanitarian relief in French-occupied Germany, 1945–1952 / Laure Humbert.
Description: 1 Edition. | New York : Cambridge University Press, 2021. | Includes bibliographical references and index.
Identifiers: LCCN 2021002778 (print) | LCCN 2021002779 (ebook) | ISBN 9781108831352 (hardback) | ISBN 9781108932776 (paperback) | ISBN 9781108916981 (epub)
Subjects: LCSH: World War, 1939–1945–Civilian relief–Germany (West) | Refugees–Government policy–France–History–20th century. | International relief–Germany (West) | Humanitarian assistance–Germany (West) | World War, 1939–1945–Refugees–Germany (West) | Refugee camps–Germany (West)–History–20th century. | France–Foreign relations–Germany. | Germany–Foreign relations–France.
Classification: LCC D809.G3 H86 2021 (print) | LCC D809.G3 (ebook) | DDC 363.34/9880943409044–dc23
LC record available at https://lccn.loc.gov/2021002778
LC ebook record available at https://lccn.loc.gov/2021002779

ISBN 978-1-108-83135-2 Hardback

Cambridge University Press has no responsibility for the persistence or accuracy of URLs for external or third-party internet websites referred to in this publication and does not guarantee that any content on such websites is, or will remain, accurate or appropriate

In loving memory of Thomas Hartley 1983–2011

# CONTENTS

*List of Figures* viii
*Acknowledgements* x
*Note on the Text* xii
*List of Abbreviations* xiii

Introduction  1

PART I  The Politics of Relief  35

1  The Politics of Immigration: Unwanted Wartime Collaborators or Ideal White Settlers?  37

2  In the Shadow of Nazi Occupation: Making and Overseeing Displaced Persons' Camps  77

3  The Politics of Neutrality: Repatriating and Screening DPs in the Early Cold War  137

PART II  Reconstructing the Body, Rehabilitating the Mind?  197

4  The 'Broken' DP: 'Remaking' the Minds and Bodies of Refugees  199

5  'Rehabilitation' through Work? Vocational Training and DP Employment  248

6  Transforming DPs into French Citizens? The Resettlement of DPs in France  293

Conclusion: Reinventing French Aid?  325

*Select Bibliography*  334
*Index*  353

# FIGURES

I.1 Historical organization chart of the direction PDR (1945–1955). Reproduced by kind permission of Cyril Daydé.  23
1.1 'Pierre, also called "Bamboula", born in Heidelberg, will someone adopt him?', in Haut Commissariat de la République française en Allemagne, Service des Personnes Déplacées, *Sept ans d'activité en faveur des personnes déplacées en zone française d'occupation, 1945–1952*, rapport dactylographié et illustré [undated], [Bibliothèque du Ministère des Affaires Etrangères, Direction des Archives], p. 99.  50
1.2 'The "*Malgré-nous*" of the Balkans', *L'Est Républicain*, 31 August 1949.  75
2.1 UNA, UNRRA, S-0421-0063-05, 'The medical doctor J. Bierlaire, Team, 579, examining with the DP doctor Endre a DP patient. DP Miss Guterbaum is working the switchboard', Medical Service Team 579, photo album, Ravensburg, 10 July 1946, p. 8.  129
2.2 UNA, UNRRA, S-0421-0063-05, 'The medical officer J. G. G. Bierlaire giving a vaccination to a DP', Medical Service Team 579, photo album, Ravensburg, 10 July 1946, p. 11.  130
2.3 UNA, UNRRA, S-1058-0001-01, 'This French girl welfare officer wears the croix de guerre for her experiences in the French maquis' [undated].  131
2.4 UNA, UNRRA, UNA, S-1058-0003, A UNRRA director, a Frenchman, Mr Rodie who was a leader in the French underground movement and escaped after eleven months in a German concentration camp.  131
3.1 'Changes in DP and refugee numbers since 8 May 1945 in the French zone', in HCRFA, Service des Personnes Déplacées, *Sept ans d'activité en faveur des personnes déplacées en zone française d'occupation, 1945–1952*, rapport dactylographié et illustré [undated], pp. 32–33.  138
3.2 (a and b)  UNA, UNRRA, S-0419-0005-02, Convoi de rapatriement Yougoslave, depart Tuttlingen, 26 May 1947.  140
3.3 UNA, UNRRA, S-0421-0039-07, Repatriation propaganda poster 'Poland is calling you. They are waiting for you'. On the man's backpack and woman's card it reads 'Food for 120 days'. UNRRA Team 676, Konstanz. Kindly translated by Katarzyna Nowak.  176

## LIST OF FIGURES

3.4  UNA, UNRRA, S-0420-0005-05, 'What every repatriate should know – Poland is awaiting you (plural you)'. Map of the new Poland and UNRRA's repatriation speech to Polish DPs, 9 November 1946. Kindly translated by Katarzyna Nowak.   177

4.1  (a and b) UNA, UNRRA, S-1021-0085-04, Visit for young mothers, medical centre, Freiburg.   213

4.2  UNRRA, S-0433-0002-01, Maison d'enfants d'Haldenhof, Überlingen.   220

4.3  UNA, UNRRA, S-1021-0085-04, UNRRA Team 572, The children's meal, Centre Sanitaire Infantile, Mooswaldkopf [undated].   221

4.4  UNRRA, S-0421-0023-09, 18 April 1946, Team 572, Gutach. 'Today is Thursday. The Polish school is unfortunately closed, but we had the luck to surprise the young pupils, who, under the direction of their Polish teacher are learning gardening. These out-of-school occupation seem to please them very much.'   222

4.5  'No it is not a vocational school. But the young gardeners are still concerned about the weather'. HCRFA, Service des Personnes Déplacées, *Sept ans d'activité en faveur des personnes déplacées en zone française d'occupation, 1945–1952*, rapport dactylographié et illustré [undated], [Bibliothèque du Ministère des Affaires Etrangères, Direction des Archives], p. 96.   223

4.6  UNA, UNRRA, S-0418-0005-04, UNRRA Team 211, Child's drawing, Centre de Schwenningen, Latvian colony, Kračevskis Zīmēšana [undated].   227

4.7  UNA, UNRRA, S-0420-0001-02, Improvised Toys, published by arrangement with the Nursery School Association of Great Britain.   228

4.8  UNA, UNRRA, S-1021-0085-08, Lindau's toy-making workshop, UNRRA Team News, vol. 1, no. 13, 15 June 1946.   229

4.9  UNA, UNRRA, S-0421-0031-02, Exposition, Lithographs by V. K. Jonynas, November 1946, Freiburg.   241

5.1  UNA, UNRRA, S-0421-0031-01, Exhibition, 'Art and Work', 2–16 June 1946.   249

5.2  UNRRA, S-0421-0023-09, 18 April 1946, Team 572, Durand, Gutach, UNRRA Store.   277

5.3  MAE, HCRFA, PDR9/102, Photographs taken in the Freiburg School, Section dessin de bâtiment [undated].   288

5.4  MAE, HCRFA, PDR9/102, Photographs taken in the Freiburg School, Section peinture [undated].   289

6.1  'Emigration of DPs from the French zone', in Haut Commissariat de la République française en Allemagne, Service des Personnes Déplacées, *Sept ans d'activité en faveur des personnes déplacées en zone française d'occupation, 1945–1952*, rapport dactylographié et illustré [undated], [Bibliothèque du Ministère des Affaires Etrangères, Direction des Archives], p. 54.   303

# ACKNOWLEDGEMENTS

Many people contributed to the completion of this book. I would particularly like to thank Martin Thomas for his supervision, knowledge and unflinching support during and after the completion of my PhD thesis and Peter Gatrell for sharing his considerable expertise on refugee history since my arrival at the University of Manchester. My thanks, too, to Sharif Gemie and Fiona Reid, who put me on the trail of refugees' history, to Richard Overy, who acted as a second supervisor to my PhD thesis and to Patricia Clavin and Richard Toye for their critiques as viva voce examiners. Friends and colleagues commented helpfully on draft chapters and key arguments developed in this book. In particular, I owe gratitude to Antoine Burgard, Daniel Cohen, James Connolly, Eleanor Davey, Alex Dowdall, Jean-Marc Dreyfus, Charlotte Faucher, Christian Goeschel, Craig Griffiths, Frances Houghton, Jo Laycock, Penny Summerfield, Alexia Yates and Bertrand Taithe. Research was undertaken with financial support from the Arts and Humanities Research Council. Additional research funding was provided by grants from the Royal Historical Society and the Society for the Study of French History.

I would also like to thank the staff at the United Nations Archives in New York and the French Diplomatic Archives at La Courneuve, in particular Cyril Daydé, who allowed me to reproduce the historical chart of the direction PDR. I am also grateful to Lelde Kalmite, who shared information about her father's artwork. I wish to express my gratitude to Corine Defrance, who invited me to present my research in Paris, Greg Burgess for allowing me to see the manuscript of an article ahead of its publication, Camilo Erlichman and Christopher Knowles for organizing 'the Allied Occupation of Germany Revisited' in 2016, and everyone who gave feedback on my work at conferences I attended. I would also like to thank the many colleagues who have encouraged the writing of this book at different stages, in particular Alison Carrol, Ludivine Broch, Marie-Luce Desgrandchamps, Eloise Moss, Ana Carden-Coyne, Pierre Fuller, Peter Jackson, Sasha Handley, Jessica Pearson, Sarah Roddy, and Julie-Marie Strange. I have also benefitted greatly from discussion with Kasia Nowak, Margot Tudor, Jennifer Chapman, and my undergraduate students at the University of Manchester. Thanks also go to the anonymous reviewers of the book manuscript at Cambridge University Press for their support and feedback, and the editorial team for their guidance.

Finally, I owe a great debt of thanks to my family and friends for their unconditional support and love. To Gabriel, Anne-Claire, John, Joy, Marie-Laure, Camille, Hélène, Bérengère, Noémie B, Noémie G, Guillaume, Matthieu, Louis, Andrew, Lubi, Alix, Susana, Heike, Simon, Alex, Chrissy, Claire, Emme, Daryl, Joe, Will, Ninette, Goeff, Magdelena, Dylan, Antoine, Lucy, Eleanor, Pierre, Charlotte, Frances, James, Martina, Eloise, Craig, Aidan: big thanks! Special thanks also go to my parents-in-law, Peter and Margaret, my grandparents, papi Roger, mamie *Dédette*, Mãezinha and Paizinho, my great uncle and aunty, Alain and Françoise, uncles and aunty, tontons Jo, Avelino and Casimira, my parents, Maria and Yves, my sister, brother and brother-in-law, Hélène, Mat and Tom. Lastly, thanks to my husband David, who helped me battle on with the book and introduced me to the delights of being a mum to our much-loved Antoine.

# NOTE ON THE TEXT

All translations from French and German are mine unless otherwise stated. Every effort has been made to trace the copyright owners of material reproduced in this book, and I invite anyone who has further information to contact me.

# ABBREVIATIONS

| | |
|---|---|
| AMGOT | Allied Military Government of Occupied Territories |
| CFLN | Comité français de Libération nationale (French Committee of National Liberation) |
| CPDR | Commissariat des Prisonniers, Déportés et Réfugiés (November 1943–September 1944) (Commissariat for Prisoners, Deportees and Refugees) |
| GFCC | Groupe français du Conseil de Contrôle (French group in the Allied Control Council) |
| GMZFO | Gouvernement Militaire de la Zone Française d'Occupation (Military Government of the French Zone of Occupation) |
| HCRFA | Haut-Commisssariat de la République Francaise en Allemagne |
| ILO | International Labour Organization |
| INED | Institut National d'études démographiques |
| IRO | International Refugee Organization |
| MMLA | Mission Militaire de Liaison Administrative |
| MPDR | Ministère des Prisonniers, Déportés et Réfugiés (September 1944–November 1945) |
| MRP | Mouvement républicain populaire (Popular Republican Movement) |
| ONI | Office National d'Immigration |
| ORT | Organisation Reconstruction Travail |
| PCIRO | Preparatory Commission of the International Refugee Organization |
| RPF | Rassemblement du peuple français (Rally of the French People) |
| SFIO | Section Française de l'Internationale ouvrière (French Socialist Party) |
| SHAEF | Supreme Headquarters Allied Expeditionary Force |
| UNAF | Union Nationale des Associations Familiales (National Union of Familial Associations) |
| UNRRA | United Nations Relief and Rehabilitation Administration |

# Introduction

Several human silhouettes emerge on the corner of each street. They begin to shout with joy. Then, men and women, as if responding to a signal, spring forth from all over the place. Poles, Russians, Czechs, and French as well, all welcome us in their own language, greeting us after the fashion of their homeland. We thought we were entering an enemy town, but it is Babel that receives us as liberators. This war is rich in paradoxes.[1]

Describing the constant stream of Displaced Persons (DPs) roaming the devastated cities of Germany and acclaiming the French liberating troops in April 1945, French war correspondent James de Coquet evoked the Tower of Babel. This biblical image is a recurring trope in diaries, memoirs, and novels of the post-war years.[2] The defeated Reich that the victors encountered in spring 1945 was a bewildering patchwork of people belonging to countless nationalities and moving in every conceivable direction. Millions of those uprooted by war – former soldiers and prisoners of war (POWs), forced labourers, and survivors of death and work camps, alongside Eastern European refugees – were on the move. 'Through a singular paradox, racism has made of Germany the crossroads of all human races', observed Coquet. 'The war has exploded all the millennial divisions and we are witnessing the most extraordinary human flux that history has ever experienced.'[3] Poles, Estonians, Lithuanians, Latvians, French, Italians, Belgians, Dutchmen, Ukrainians, Russians, Yugoslavs, and others competed with German locals for sparse food and accommodation. Victims lived amidst their former oppressors, deportees cohabited with those who had voluntarily gone to Germany, former elites shared houses with 'ordinary' peasants, and millions of children wandered around searching for lost family members.

---

[1] James de Coquet, *Nous sommes les occupants* (Paris: Librairie Arthème Fayard, 1945), p. 115.
[2] François Cochet, 'Des retours "décalés". Les prisonniers de guerre et les requis du travail', in Christiane Franck (ed.), *La France de 1945. Résistances, retours, renaissances* (Caen: Presses universitaires de Caen, 1996), pp. 141–152, 147.
[3] De Coquet, *Nous sommes les occupants*, p. 141.

In early 1945, the Allies were confronted with a humanitarian disaster of staggering proportions. The presence of nearly 11 million DPs in Germany presented the liberators with a colossal logistical challenge.[4] In the three Western zones, the Allies encountered nearly 6 million civilian foreign workers, two million prisoners of war, and 700,000 surviving concentration camp prisoners.[5] All these uprooted people needed to be registered, dusted with DDT, fed, clothed, housed and, above all, repatriated to their countries of origin. Yet, means of transportation, food and clothing were insufficient. Basic services, such as running water, electricity and heating utilities, had ceased to function. The only thing that still seemed to flow was alcohol. 'Madness reigns amongst the soldiers' observed French relief worker Eliane Brault, describing soldiers 'swimming in wine'.[6] While all four occupiers (the Americans, the British, the Soviets, and the French) faced enormous obstacles in establishing law and order and reassembling DPs to facilitate their repatriation, the French faced especially difficult challenges. France itself was emerging from four years of German occupation and had lacked time to prepare for the chaos and destruction brought on by Nazism.

Charged by the Supreme Headquarters of the Allied Expeditionary Forces (SHAEF) with establishing camps, categorizing DPs, and arranging interim provision for them in what would become their occupation zone, French military authorities also needed to provide assistance for more than a million Frenchmen, prisoners of war (POWs), labour conscripts, and political and racial deportees, still held in Germany prior to organizing their repatriation.[7] These included around 800,000 French POWs, captured by the Wehrmacht during the fall of France in 1940 and approximately 600,000 industrial and agricultural workers, who spent their war years in German factories and farms.[8] Finally, 86,827 deportees arrested by 'measures of repression' were

---

[4] 6.5 million DPs were to be found in the three Western zones and 4.5 million in the Soviet zone. Corine Defrance, Juliette Denis and Julia Maspero, 'Personnes déplacées en Allemagne occupée et guerre froide: une introduction', in Corine Defrance, Juliette Denis and Julia Maspero (eds.), *Personnes déplacées et guerre froide en Allemagne occupée* (Frankfurt am Main: Peter Lang, 2015), pp. 11–36, 12.

[5] [Figures of August 1944] Ulrich Herbert, *Hitler's Foreign Workers. Enforced Foreign Labor in Germany under the Third Reich*. Translated by William Templer (Cambridge: Cambridge University Press, 1997), p. 1.

[6] Eliane Brault, *L'épopée des AFAT* (Paris: Editions Pierre Horay, 1954), p. 209.

[7] According to Herbert, there were 1.3 million Frenchmen in Germany in August 1944. Herbert, *Hitler's Foreign Workers*, p. 1.

[8] Estimated numbers vary between 600,000 and 650,000. Bernard Garnier, Jean Quellien and Françoise Passera, *La main d'œuvre française exploitée par le IIIe Reich* (Caen: Centre de Recherche d'Histoire Quantitative, 2003), p. 11; On the history of the Service du Travail Obligatoire, see Helga Bories-Sawala, *Dans la gueule du loup. Les français requis du travail en Allemagne* (Villeneuve d'Ascq: Presses Universitaires Septentrion, 2010); Patrice Arnaud, *Les STO. Histoire des Français requis en Allemagne nazie 1942–1945* (Paris:

interned in concentration camps and 75,721 persons considered Jewish by French and German laws were sent to their death.[9] Whereas the vast majority of POWs and labour conscripts were eager to return home, fewer deportees had survived the monstrous Nazi camps. Sixty per cent of deportees by various measures of repression and, only three per cent of those deported on racial grounds survived.[10] The fast and orderly repatriation of French *Absents*, as the Ministry of Prisoners, Deportees, and Refugees [PDR] under Henri Frenay called them, represented a critical domestic challenge for the new Republican elite seeking to establish its authority, and prove its legitimacy, to a nation left profoundly divided by the war.[11]

For French observers arriving in Germany in the spring of 1945, the sight of these columns of refugees evoked memories of the French Exodus in 1940: 'One felt an intense joy retracing the routes of 1940, but [this time] in the opposite direction', noted Coquet.[12] Relishing *les voluptés de la revanche* (the pleasures of revenge), Coquet nevertheless admitted that the desolation and destruction of Germany, and the human distress accompanying it, were more shockingly tragic than the equivalent scenes in France during the summer of 1940.[13] He was right; the number of uprooted people struggling to survive in

---

CNRS Éditions, 2010); Raphaël Spina, *Histoire du STO* (Paris: Perrin, 2017). On the history of French Prisoners of War, Yves Durand, *Les Prisonniers de guerre dans les Stalags, les Offlags et les Kommandos* (Paris: Hachette, 1994); Raffael Scheck, 'Collaboration of the Heart: The Forbidden Love Affairs of French Prisoners of War and German Women in Nazi Germany', *The Journal of Modern History*, vol. 90, no. 2 (2018), pp. 351–382.

[9] La Fondation pour la mémoire de la déportation, *Le Livre-Mémorial des déportés de France arrêtés par mesure de répressions et dans certains cas par mesure de persécution, 1940–1945* (Paris: Tirésias, 2004).

[10] By the middle of October 1945, an estimated 1.3 million French citizens had returned home: 895,000 from the American zone, 270,000 from the British zone, 215,000 from the Soviet zone and 170,000 from the French zone. In total, 2.2 million people were repatriated to France. Jean-Marc Dreyfus, *Ami, si tu tombes* (Paris: Perrin, 2005), p. 37.

[11] See, for example, Marie-Anne Matard-Bonucci and Edouard Lynch, *La Libération des camps et le retour des déportés* (Bruxelles: Complexe, 1995); Christiane Franck (ed.), *La France de 1945. Résistances, retours, renaissances* (Caen: Presses Universitaires de Caen, 1996); Megan Koreman, 'A Hero's Homecoming: The Return of the Deportees to France, 1945', *Journal of Contemporary History*, vol. 32, no. 1 (1997), pp. 9–22; Pieter Lagrou, *The Legacy of Nazi Occupation: Patriotic Memory and National Recovery in Western Europe, 1945–1965* (Cambridge: Cambridge University Press, 2000); Annette Wieviorka, *1945. La découverte* (Paris: Seuil, 2015).

[12] De Coquet, *Nous sommes les occupants*, p. 56; Also see Jacques Notin, *Les vaincus seront les vainqueurs* (Paris: Perrin, 2004), p. 128. On the history of the French 'exodus' see, for instance, Hanna Diamond, *Fleeing Hitler: France 1940* (Oxford: Oxford University Press, 2007); Nicole Dombrowski Risser, *France under Fire: German Invasion, Civilian Flight and Family Survival during World War Two* (Cambridge: Cambridge University Press, 2015).

[13] De Coquet, *Nous sommes les occupants*, p. 130.

defeated Germany far outweighed those caught up in the French Exodus five years earlier.[14] More importantly, the Allied invasion of Germany was accompanied by a monstrous explosion of violence and by the horrific discovery of the Nazi concentration camps. On entering Germany in the spring of 1945, French liberating soldiers, repatriation officers, and relief workers had to adjust to a new and strange realm of experiences, which shattered all previous norms.

This book follows the journeys of French relief workers in the German ruins, examining how they encountered DPs of multiple nationalities and negotiated daily life. French field workers worked for a plethora of international, governmental, and voluntary agencies involved in the care of refugees, including the United Nations Relief and Rehabilitation Administration (UNRRA), created in 1943 to bring aid and relief to peoples and countries devastated by war. French relief workers had very different professional backgrounds and wartime experiences. Some were drawn to relief work by their Catholic faith, while others were former military officers. Some were well-trained anti-Nazi resisters, while others were former collaborators. Their stories thus provide a fascinating lens through which to examine how French wartime experiences of collaboration, 'cohabitation' or resistance influenced the subsequent French post-war occupation of Germany.

Despite significant Allied efforts to equip relief workers with basic training in refugee relief and UNRRA's attempts at coordinating the work of voluntary organizations, few field workers had received adequate preparation for the situation they encountered. Sonia Vagliano, a French resister who had joined de Gaulle in London during the war, was only 23 when she entered Buchenwald in April 1945. Having followed the invading army ever since the Normandy landings in June 1944, she had witnessed considerable human distress. However, in her memoirs she described the harrowing experience of confronting Buchenwald.[15] The Allies found 21,000 survivors in Buchenwald, including 2,700 French survivors. In seeking a way to express her feelings, she turned to metaphor, drawing a comparison between the sight of the camp and Hieronymus Bosch's tormented artwork:

> I am not certain about how I feel, but I would never have thought that I could one day wish to find myself again in Verviers in the cold, under the bombs and everything ... At least, there, it was normal, human ... Here, it is a nightmare, all these people are grotesque, it is Bosch's hell ...

---

[14] Lagrou, *The Legacy of Nazi Occupation*, p. 81; Sharif Gemie and Fiona Reid, 'Chaos, Panic and the Historiography of the Exode', *War and Society*, vol. 26, no. 2 (2007), pp. 73–98, 74.

[15] François Cochet and Yves Durand, 'Le rassemblement 'européen' dans l'Allemagne de 1945', in Antoine Fleury and Robert Frank (eds.), *Le rôle des guerres dans la mémoire des Européens* (Berne: Peter Lang, 1997), pp. 95–110, 100.

Perhaps, I'll be woken ... and they will all have disappeared up in smoke through the chimney.[16]

The sight of German desolation recalled the apocalypse. Olga Jungelson, later known as Olga Wormser-Migot, the historical adviser for Alain Resnais' 1955 film *Nuit et Brouillard* (Night and Fog), worked for the French Ministry of Prisoners, Deportees and Refugees. In May 1945, she was sent to Bergen-Belsen with a list of 1,200 names of French deportees.[17] She related in similar terms her first encounter with survivors in Bergen-Belsen and its profoundly important emotional impact: 'For a month, after my return, it was impossible to readapt. I relived the days in Germany. My life was at the Orsay station [and] the Hotel Lutetia.'[18] In this luxury Parisian hotel, the former headquarters of German intelligence situated on Boulevard Raspail, French deportees were registered, fed, clothed, screened, and, above all, provided with administrative papers.[19] Between April and August 1945, the Lutetia welcomed between 18,000 and 20,000 deportees, representing more than a third of the returning deportees. French repatriation officers and relief workers working with Nazi victims in Germany and France had no guidelines to help them understand their grief or cope with it. They faced their distress before psychiatrists had constructed theories of 'traumatic witnessing' and over-identification.[20] Although no French relief workers were clinically diagnosed with any kind of traumatic conditions, some suffered from compassion fatigue and were left with psychological scars, resulting from the unsatisfying experiences that leave many relief workers as much 'soiled as ennobled'.[21]

In this book, I examine these complicated encounters between French officials, members of new international organizations, relief workers, DPs, and defeated Germans in the territory of the French occupation zone. I focus, in particular, on the close relationships between French citizens and the sizeable group of DPs, who remained in the zone prior to their repatriation or emigration in a third country. DPs only comprised one, yet significant, strand of this bigger demographic upheaval. Their lives were regulated by a multitude of actors belonging to different entities, such as the French state, international organizations, and private charities. This book disentangles the different scales of regulation and control of DPs' lives, from the treatment of

---

[16] Sonia Vagliano-Eloy, *Les demoiselles de Gaulle, 1943–1945* (Paris: Plon, 1982), p. 227.
[17] Sylvie Lindeperg, *Nuit et Brouillard. Un film dans l'histoire* (Paris: Odile Jacob, 2007), p. 21.
[18] Quoted in ibid., p. 22.
[19] Olga Wormser-Migot, *Le retour des déportés. Quand les Alliés ouvrirent les portes* (Bruxelles: Editions Complexe, 1985).
[20] Lisa H. Malkki, *The Need to Help. The Domestic Arts of International Humanitarianism* (Durham, NC: Duke University Press, 2015), p. 56.
[21] Ibid., p. 75.

DPs on the ground to the level of diplomatic negotiations and international laws. This multi-scale investigation transcends state-centred approaches that currently dominate the historiography of DPs in the French zone.[22] This view from above has left little room for the endeavour of international organizations or the everyday encounters between relief workers and DPs. By rendering mid- and ground-level relief workers visible, this book shed lights on their crucial role in shaping relief and encampment practices. This book also goes beyond most studies of post-war humanitarianism, which centre overwhelmingly on the perspectives of American and British relief workers.[23] In doing so, it reveals that approaches to the DP question were intrinsically linked to how French policy-elites and administrators tried to rebuild France, guarantee its security, and reconstruct its relations with its wartime Allies after 1945. It also illuminates how French politicians and officials diverged from front-line aid workers in their conceptualization of the significance of the DPs for French humanitarianism and in the solutions they advanced to repair the injuries of displacement. Crucially, it highlights different cultures of relief and rehabilitation and understandings of DPs' needs in the French zone, in part rooted in pre-war ideas about 'overcoming' poverty and war-induced injuries in the French domestic context.

As they tried to reckon with the aftermath of war and genocide, French occupation officers and relief workers exchanged ideas about how best to heal the physical and mental wounds of DPs. Relief workers were convinced of their ability to 'positively' reshape the lives of DPs and transform their ways of being and thinking. DP camps became thus sites of experimentation, where relief workers attempted to propose a new organization of DPs' intimate life. Camps did not simply function as device of containment and enclosure. They were also spaces of unique cultural encounters, where knowledge about the 'refugee' population was created and where gender, ethnic and social identities

---

[22] Andreas Rinke, *Le Grand retour – Die französische Displaced Person-Politik (1944–1951)* (Frankfurt am Main: Peter Lang, 2002); Julia Maspero, 'La question des personnes déplacées polonaises dans les zones françaises d'occupation en Allemagne et en Autriche: un aspect méconnu des relations franco-polonaises (1945–1949)', *Relations internationales*, vol. 138 (2009), pp. 59–74.

[23] For recent attempts at 'de-centring' the history of UNRRA, see Jessica Reinisch, 'Internationalism in Relief: The Birth (and Death) of UNRRA', *Past and Present*, supplement 6 (2011), pp. 258–289; Charles Wesley Sharpe, 'The Origins of the United Nations Relief and Rehabilitation Administration, 1939–1943', PhD thesis, University of Pennsylvania (2012); Jessica Reinisch, '"Auntie UNRRA" at the Crossroads', *Past and Present*, supplement 8 (2013), pp. 70–97; Rana Mitter, 'Imperialism, Transnationalism, and the Reconstruction of Post-war China: UNRRA in China, 1944–1971', *Past and Present*, supplement 8 (2013), pp. 51–69; Laure Humbert, 'The French in Exile and Post-war International Relief, c. 1941–1945', *The Historical Journal*, vol. 61, no. 4 (2018), pp. 1041–1064.

were profoundly remade.[24] DPs were offered educational, cultural and occupational opportunities in tandem with physical treatments, medical screening, gymnastic exercises, and sport. Through these activities, relief workers strove to heal, discipline, and remake DPs' bodies and minds. Their approaches to relief work were underpinned by gendered assumptions, racial prejudices and the received wisdom of the superiority of certain ethnic groups over others.

DPs had different ethnic origins, nationalities, gender, ages, social backgrounds and wartime trajectories. French military estimates suggest that, in the territories which, in July 1945, became part of the French occupation zone, there were approximately 514,000 DPs before the German capitulation.[25] French and Soviet nationals, who formed the two largest DP groups, were repatriated first. Despite logistical and transport difficulties, repatriation rates were surprisingly high. By the middle of September, nearly 300,000 'foreign' DPs had been repatriated from the French zone. After the mass repatriation of French and Soviet nationals, the largest single group comprised those claiming Polish citizenship (78 per cent), although a significant minority of DPs hailed from the Baltic States. In October 1945, the number of DPs dropped to approximately 75,000, of which roughly 35 per cent were located in the Northern region of the zone (Saar, Rhineland-Palatinate), with the remaining 65 per cent in the Southern region (Baden, Württemberg).[26] A report produced by the High Commission of the French Republic in Germany in 1952 observed that 'one would need as many definitions [of DPs] as nationalities', highlighting that, in the French zone alone, one could find 35 different 'nationalities' (understood as both state citizenship and ethnic membership).[27] These included Poles, Soviet POWs, Ukrainians, Hungarians, Romanians,

---

[24] Daniel Cohen, *In War's Wake: Europe's Displaced Persons in the Postwar Order* (Oxford: Oxford University Press, 2011), pp. 58–78.
[25] MAE, HCRFA, PDR6/467, GMZFO, Réponse aux chiffres demandés par Berlin, 18 January 1947; Others estimates are lower. A undated note for M. Rivain maintains that there were 475,000 DPs in the zone in May 1945. PDR6/869, Note pour M. Rivain, Directeur du Cabinet de l'Ambassadeur de France HCRFA [undated].
[26] In 29 November 1945, French authorities estimated that there were 75,282 DPs in the French zone, with 26,026 living in the Northern part of the Zone and 49,256 in the Southern part. [MAE, HCRFA, PDR6/467, Compte-rendu d'activité de la troisième section pendant le mois de Novembre, 29 November 1945.] But the evidence suggests that the DP population was only exhaustively listed in the spring and summer of 1947, revealing the presence of nearly 5,000 DPs. PDR6/467, Nombre total de DP recensés en ZFO [undated]; Copie de la Lettre du Général d'armée Koenig à Secrétaire d'Etat aux Affaires Allemandes et Autrichiennes, 28 July 1948.
[27] HCRFA, Service des Personnes Déplacées, *Sept ans d'activité en faveur des personnes déplacées en zone française d'occupation, 1945-1952*, Rapport dactylographié et illustré [undated], [Bibliothèque du Ministère des Affaires Etrangères, Direction des Archives], p. 9.

Yugoslavs, Czechs, stateless, Lithuanians, Estonians, Latvians and Jews, all presenting different reasons for their exile in Germany. Amongst them, some DP groups were considered by French administrators and relief workers as more valuable than others. Considered as potential 'future' citizens for France, they received better treatment and opportunities.

Despite historians' rediscovery of the 'DP story' since the late 1980s, the French zone has remained understudied, for France was a second-rank occupying force, one whose zone and DP population was significantly smaller, and its wider political influence more limited than those of its Western Allies.[28] Created out of areas formerly allocated to the British and American zones, the French zone bordered France and included the Saar, the Rhineland-Palatinate, and the south-western parts of Baden and Württemberg (separately, it also included the northwest section of Berlin).[29] And yet, the French zone offers an ideal site in which to trace how relief approaches and practices were coloured by domestic concerns, with France facing specific material constraints resulting in part from its experiences of Nazi occupation. In the French zone, DPs were often perceived through the prism of French wartime experiences. Yet, DPs' wartime experiences were complex affairs, fitting uneasily into publicly acceptable categories of good and evil, resisters and collaborators. Indeed, the amalgamation of various groups of persons with radically different

---

[28] The literature on DPs is vast. See for example: Wolfgang Jacobmeyer, *Vom Zwangsarbeiter zum heimatlosen Ausländer: Die Displaced Persons in Westdeutschland, 1945-1951* (Gottingen: Vandenhoeck & Ruprecht, 1985); Mark Wyman, *DPs: Europe's Displaced Persons, 1945-1951* (Ithaca, NY: Cornell University Press, 1998); Atina Grossmann, *Jews, Germans, and Allies: Close Encounters in Occupied Germany* (Princeton, NJ: Princeton University Press, 2007); Ben Shephard, *The Long Road Home: The Aftermath of the Second World War* (London: Vintage, 2011); Tara Zahra, *The Lost Children: Reconstructing Europe's Families after World War II* (Cambridge, MA: Harvard University Press, 2011); Cohen, *In War's Wake*; Anna Holian, *Between National Socialism and Soviet Communism: Displaced Persons in Post-war Germany* (Ann Arbor: University of Michigan Press, 2011); Pamela Ballinger, 'Impossible Returns, Enduring Legacies: Recent Historiography of Displacement and the Reconstruction of Europe after World War II', *Contemporary European History*, vol. 22, no. 1 (2013), pp. 127-138; Peter Gatrell, *The Making of the Modern Refugee* (Oxford: Oxford University Press, 2013). On DPs in the French zone: Rinke, *Le Grand retour*; Maspero, 'La question des personnes déplacées polonaises dans les zones françaises d'occupation en Allemagne et en Autriche'; Laure Humbert, 'French Politics of Relief and International Aid: France, UNRRA and the Rescue of Eastern European Displaced Persons in Post-war Germany, 1945-1947', *Journal of Contemporary History*, vol. 41, no. 3 (2016), pp. 606-634.

[29] British forces controlled the industrial Rhineland and the Ruhr, and the Americans ruled southern Germany, Bavaria and two enclaves on the North Sea. The French zone, whose borders were only delimitated on 29 June (North of the zone) and 4 July (South), was considerably smaller than the other zones and made little political, geographical, or economic sense.

wartime experiences within the 'DP category' stands in sharp contrast to the development of a 'hierarchy' of victims in France, with resistance fighters and political deportees topping the scale of probity.[30]

The history of French encounters with DPs was certainly shaped by domestic concerns, but it was not only a Franco-DP story. It involves the emerging mandates of the United Nations and the politics of the Soviet Union and the newly Communist Eastern European states from which many of the DPs hailed from. The presence of this group of DPs in the French zone provoked diplomatic tensions between the French occupying forces and Eastern European countries, in addition to constituting a source of social problems and welfare dilemmas. Both the Soviet Union and new communist authorities in Eastern and Central Europe were demanding the repatriation of their nationals. On the international scene, discussion about the voluntary or forced repatriation of Eastern European DPs was central to creeping Cold War tensions among the occupiers, causing friction between the Western Allies and the Soviet Union and hastening the demise of the wartime alliance.[31]

In the context of the nascent Cold War, French repatriation policies were shaped by the contradictory demands of the French labour market, the necessity to maintain reciprocal arrangements with the Soviet Union and a desire to adopt a position of 'disinterested bystander' between East and West. In marked contrast to its Western Allies, French decision makers had to comply with what Catherine Gousseff has described as a *politique du donnant-donnant* (reciprocal giving) with the Soviet Union in order to guarantee the return of French internees and the repatriation of the *Malgré-nous* – POWs from Alsace-Lorraine who had been forcibly enrolled in the Wehrmacht and captured by the Red Army.[32] Yet despite these reciprocal

---

[30] See Chapter 3.
[31] Cohen, *In War's Wake*, p. 19; Guy S. Goodwin-Gill, 'Different Types of Forced Migration Movements as an International and National Problem', in G. Rystad (ed.), *The Uprooted. Forced Migration as an International Problem in the Post-war Era* (Lund: Lund University Press, 1990), pp. 15–45, 22–30.
[32] Catherine Gousseff, 'Des migrations de sorties de guerre qui reconfigurent la frontière: ouverture et refermeture de l'URSS avant la guerre froide (1944–1946)', in Sophie Coeuré et Sabine Dullin (eds.), *Frontières du communisme* (Paris: La Découverte-Recherche, 2007), pp. 428–442, 433. Also see Pavel Polian, 'Le rapatriement des citoyens soviétiques depuis la France et les zones françaises d'occupation en Allemagne et en Autriche', *Cahiers du Monde russe*, vol. 41, no. 1 (2000), pp. 165–190; Catherine Klein-Gousseff, *Retour d'URSS. Les prisonniers de guerre et les internés français dans les archives soviétiques, 1945–1951* (Paris: CNRS Éditions, 2001); Gäel Moullec, 'Alliés ou ennemis? Le GUPVI-NKVD, le Komintern et les "Malgrés-nous." Le destin des prisonniers de guerre français en URSS (1942–1955)', *Cahiers du monde russe*, vol. 42, no. 2–4 (2001), pp. 667–678. Jacques Bariéty and Corine Defrance, 'Les missions de la France Libre en Union Soviétique et les "Malgré-nous" (1942–1944)', *Revue d'Allemagne et des Pays de Langue Allemande*, vol. 39, no. 4 (2008), pp. 533–550.

arrangements with the Soviet Union, DPs constituted for French leaders an enticing demographic opportunity to replenish a French population diminished by two world wars and a declining birth rate.

French attempts to transfer DPs to France were not a charitable enterprise: French planners were mainly interested in healthy and diligent workers able to work in specific fields, notably in French mines and agriculture. But, the question of DP emigration defied consensus in France. Communist decision makers and their ideological fellow travellers on the French Left, particularly numerous within the Ministry of Labour and, to a lesser extent, the newly created Office National d'Immigration (ONI), were strongly opposed to the recruitment of what they regarded as fascist DPs and 'war collaborators'. There was more at stake than this political and ideological opposition emerging from within the Ministry of Labour. Beneath the surface of what was ostensibly a political and ideological opposition lay a labyrinth of economic fears, a traditional protectionist reflex, as well as a raft of moral and cultural concerns about the 'assimilability' and 'desirability' of DPs. Population experts and policymakers were obsessed with the issue of assimilation. They evaluated the cultural and economic desirability of DPs in terms of nationality, politics, gender, class, religion, profession and age, and their assessments varied widely. Arguments over the recruitment of DPs therefore sat at the juncture of several critical debates about French post-war politics of migration and France's diplomatic strategies in the context of the nascent Cold War.

'Caring' for DPs thus became a political and moral project, overseen by the French state, international organizations and occupation authorities. Solutions to the DP problem reflected contradictory assessments of France's economic, labour, and security needs. At the national level, debates about whether DPs should be transferred to France as migrant workers or repatriated to their countries of origin were linked to discussion about France's labour needs and diplomatic relations with the Soviet Union and Eastern European authorities. At the level of the military government in the zone, the issue of the transfer of DPs in France was as cultural in focus as economically determined. French administrators tried to sell France as a welcoming and exciting destination to DPs. After 1947 and the launch of the French recruitment scheme, occupation officials engaged in a fierce competition with other national recruiting missions, including Australia and Britain, to promote the French way of life. French occupation officials, many of whom were Gaullists, were particularly concerned about the image of France circulating in DP camps. They often associated the encouragement of DP immigration with French patriotism. For them, the issues posed by the recruitment of DPs were far greater than a problem of satisfying manpower needs. Their anxieties about DPs' reluctance to come to France were tied to the reformulation of French identity and the restoration of French prestige in post-war Germany.[33]

During the period under consideration, French Foreign Ministry staff, occupation authorities, and French relief officials were particularly sensitive to issues of prestige and the manner in which France was represented internationally. In the spring of 1945, French military reports stressed the importance of the presence of French relief worker' teams, in Germany for reasons of national prestige.[34] In May 1945, a French commandant deplored, for instance, the integration of French female relief workers from the Mission Militaire de Liaison Administrative (MMLA) teams into the UNRRA. According to him, female relief workers in 'French uniform [...] constitut [ed] the best of all propaganda for our country'.[35] Such reports revealed the paradoxical coexistence of insecurity about French influence in Germany and an underlying and enduring confidence amongst some political leaders, diplomats, occupation officials, and relief workers in France's cultural, medical, and humanitarian 'superiority'.[36]

Significantly, France was a victor of the last hour and considered by most Germans to be victory's opportunist.[37] In less than a year, the French went from the status of being occupied by the Nazis to being occupiers of Germany, and from the status of relief recipient to that of relief providers on the international stage. This affected not only the French self-perception but also how Germans, British, and American occupiers thought about them.[38] As French sociologist Edgar Morin observed in 1946, 'France remained, for Germans, the nation that gave them *a coup de pied de l'âne* [a cowardly kicking]. Nothing seemed more petty and insulting than the presence of

---

[33] Their efforts were part of broader efforts to sell France in the German ruins. Karen Adler, 'Selling France to the French: The French Zone of Occupation in Western Germany, 1945–c.1955', *Contemporary European History*, vol. 21, no. 4 (2012), pp. 575–595.

[34] SHD, 8 P 23, Rapport secret du capitaine P. Gerbault, chef de la Section G-5 de la MFL, 22 April 1945.

[35] SHD, 8 P 23, Lettre du Commandant P. Sorbac chef de la MMFL G-5 à M. le Lieutenant Colonel, chef de la MMFL, 12th AG, 4 May 1945.

[36] On a French captain's assessment of French influence within the nascent UNRRA, see for instance, MAE, HCRFA, PDR 1/18, Compte-rendu de Mission du Capitaine Mussinger, 27 June 1945. On the belief in the superiority of French culture, see, for instance, Riccarda Torriani, 'Nazis into Germans: Re-education and Democratisation in the British and French Occupation Zones, 1945–49', PhD thesis, University of Cambridge, 2005; Riccarda Torriani, '"Des bédouins particulièrement intelligents"? La pensée coloniale et les occupations française et britannique de l'Allemagne (1945–1949)', *Histoire et Sociétés. Revue européenne d'histoire sociale*, vol. 17 (2006), pp. 56–66.

[37] Edgar Morin, *L'an zero de l'Allemagne* (Paris: Editions de la cité Universelle, 1946), p. 52.

[38] Jessica Reinisch, *The Perils of Peace. Public Health Crisis in Occupied Germany* (Oxford: Oxford University Press, 2013), p. 281.

French troops in their territory'.[39] German perceptions of French occupiers were further shaped by the myth of *Erbfeindschaft* (hereditary enmity), the collective memories of the destruction of south-western Germany in the seventeenth century by Louis XIV, the struggles with Napoleon and the behaviour of French troops during the occupation of the Rhineland after 1919.[40] It was in fact the third time that the French occupied German territories since the French Revolution. Humanitarian efforts must thus be understood within the larger context of debates about the restoration of French prestige and justification of French actions in Germany.[41]

Humanitarian aid became a component of French efforts at restoring France's international prestige against the backdrop of increasing anxieties about its international standing.[42] Not only were occupation officers concerned about the image of France circulating in DP camps, but French occupation authorities drew a number of DP artists into the orbit of French cultural diplomacy. For French occupiers, exhibiting French cultural richness was considered as a way to express and project French political power.[43]

---

[39] Morin, *L'an zero de l'Allemagne*, p. 52.

[40] Michael Rowe, 'France, Prussia, or Germany? The Napoleonic Wars and Shifting Allegiances in the Rhineland', *Central European History*, vol. 39, no. 4 (2006), pp. 611–640; Rainer Hudemann, 'France and the German Question, 1945–1949: On the Interdependence of Historiography, Methodology and Interpretations', in Frédéric Bozo and Christian Wenkel (eds.), *France and the German Question, 1945–1990* (New York: Berghahn, 2019), pp. 17–34.

[41] To be sure, the notion of 'prestige' is a very difficult concept to define and analyze. Considered by some scholars as an 'illusion', it is perceived by others as a crucial tool of foreign policy. International Relations theorists define it as a relational concept, which depends on a community's shared beliefs about a state's capacity and the perceptions of other states with regards to this ability to exercise power. Yet, as René Girault and Robert Frank have demonstrated, it is very difficult for historians to access policy-elites' *intimate* perceptions of French power. Jonathan Mercer, 'The Illusion of International Prestige', *International Security*, vol. 41, no. 4 (2017), pp. 133–168; Yuen Foong Khong, 'Power as Prestige in World Politics', *International Affairs*, vol. 95, no. 1 (2019), pp. 119–142. I would like to thank Charlotte Faucher for her insightful comments. Faucher, *Projecting France. The Making of French Cultural Diplomacy in Britain, 1870–1945* (Oxford: Oxford University Press, forthcoming).

[42] Robert Frank, 'Conclusions', in René Girault and Robert Frank (eds.), *La puissance française en question (1945–1949)* (Paris: Publications de la Sorbonne, 1988), pp. 463–468.

[43] See, for example, Richard Gilmore, France's Postwar Cultural Policies and Activities in Germany, PhD dissertation, University of Geneva, 1971; Jérôme Vaillant, 'Aspects de la politique culturelle de la France en Allemagne 1945–1949', in Henri Ménudier (ed.), *L'Allemagne occupée, 1945–1949* (Bruxelles: Complexe, 1990), pp. 201–220; Stefan Zauner, *Erziehung und Kulturmission: Frankreichs Bildungs-Politik in Deutschland, 1945–1949* (Munich: Oldenbourg Verlag, 1994); Defrance, *La politique culturelle de la France sur la rive gauche du Rhin*; Mombert, *Jeunesse et livre en Zone française d'occupation 1945–1949*; Torriani, 'Nazis into Germans'.

A number of Baltic DPs, often acquainted with French 'high culture', were offered opportunities to work in French cultural institutions, such as the French institute in Mainz, or open their own.[44] The Department of Cultural Affairs encouraged DP art exhibitions and concerts, which bolstered not only DP art and cultural traditions, but also French influences. In their work, DP artists praised French intellectual and art traditions, including Voltaire, Rousseau, Delacroix, Cézanne, Baudelaire, Debussy, Rodin or Matisse.[45] DP exhibitions reinforced the idea of France as a 'protector' of small nations and the image of Paris as 'the Mekka [sic] for all painters' in the word of a DP artist.[46]

By examining how a small number of DPs were drawn into French cultural policies in French-occupied Germany and how French relief workers tried to sell 'France' as a welcoming destination to DPs, this book unearths the active, and often bottom-up, nature of the reaffirmation of French national identity and reassertion of its international influence in the aftermath of Vichy and Nazi occupation. French relief officials believed in French cultural superiority and understood relief as a vehicle for restoring French prestige. For them, humanitarian work reflected both France's renewed sense of responsibility and the country's self-interested concern for its image abroad. This book does not argue, however, that the French succeeded in their efforts at 'rebranding' France as a welcoming nation in the aftermath of Vichy. Presenting France as a hospitable and humanitarian nation proved challenging. Over the course of the occupation, the UNRRA and (later) the IRO became an important forum for DPs to raise concerns about French provisions of aid and to publicize French failures.[47] Further, despite French officials' efforts to publicize the attractions of France, DPs proved understandably cautious about emigrating to what they regarded as an impoverished and, for some, a quasi-Communist country.

My purpose in entitling this book *Reinventing French Aid* is thus threefold. First, I wish to emphasize the acute uncertainties that marked the history of the administration of DPs in the French zone. In 1945, it was neither clear to French occupation officials nor relief workers what post-war France would

---

[44] The DP Ratermanis worked as professor of French Literature in the French Institute in Mainz. HCRFA, Affaires culturelles, 62, Fiche: M. Ratermanis, signé R. Schmittlein, 6 December 1948.

[45] UNA, UNRRA, S-0418-0002-04, Résumé de l'art Estonien.

[46] UNA, UNRRA, S-0418-0003-08, Semaine de Culture des DPs à Wurzach, 3–10 November 1946. Introduction by Janis Kalmite.

[47] See, for instance, the numerous complaints of the Polish Committee of Ravensburg in UNA, UNRRA, S-0421-0061-07;S-0432-0001-05, Edmond Szente Gutch à Monsieur Durand, Directeur du Team 572, 28 October 1946; S-0421-0031-07, Compte-rendu de la réunion des Employment Officers (Gutach), 25–27 November 1946; MAE, HCRFA, 2Bad/39, [A2.301/1], Rapport Affaires administratives, partie personnes déplacées, 24 July 1946.

look like or where 'non-repatriable' DPs would end up. Nobody knew how long DPs' life in limbo would last or how to handle the emotional consequences of surviving Nazi terror and genocide. Very few people had anticipated the problems that would arise when trying to establish DPs' legal identities and provide professional certificates, 'translatable' in different countries. And yet, these uncertainties also gave rise to visionary aspirations around individual and collective reconstruction. Second, the term 'French' calls attention to the fact that these aspirations were coloured by domestic concerns. This book argues that the history of DPs should be connected to the key themes of French post-war history. In the French zone, discussions about how best to serve the interests of DPs resonated with broader national debates about the immediate past and the fate of France after Vichy and the 'reintegration' of French *Absents*. Third, in choosing 'reinventing', I suggest that historians need to be attentive to the element of change and continuity in the history of post-war humanitarian organizations. Building on recent historical scholarship, I reveal the fragmentation of visions for relief work within international organizations, beyond their claims to the embodiment of a 'new humanitarianism'.[48] For all their insistence on novelty and the 'modernization' of relief, this book argues that UNRRA and the International Refugee Organisation [IRO] welfare programmes were enacted in the French zone in ways that reveal the persistence of conservative social ethics.

This is not the familiar story of relief work in the aftermath of the Second World War. While existing scholarship has suggested that new international organizations brought a 'psychological Marshall Plan' to post-war Europe, I argue that the influence of the psy-sciences in shaping discussions over the rehabilitation of DPs was more limited.[49] Histories of refugee and child welfare, notably by Tara Zahra, have illuminated the growing influence of psychology on the treatment of refugees in post-war Europe. In the United States and Britain, the 1940s marked a key moment, in which exiled continental analysts and native psychologists connected mental health to broader issues of reconstruction and citizenship.[50] The child-survivor was especially

---

[48] Silvia Salvatici, 'Help the People to Help Themselves': UNRRA Relief Workers and European Displaced Persons', *Journal of Refugee Studies*, vol. 25, no. 3 (2012), pp. 452–473.

[49] Tara Zahra, '"The Psychological Marshall Plan": Displacement, Gender and Human Rights after World War II', *Central European History*, vol. 44, no. 1 (2011), pp. 37–62.

[50] Mathew Thomson, *Psychological Subjects: Identity, Culture and Health in Twentieth-Century Britain* (Oxford: Oxford University Press, 2006); Mathew Thomson, *Lost Freedom: The Landscape of the Child and the British Post-war Settlement* (Oxford: Oxford University Press, 2013); Michal Shapira, *The War Inside: Psychoanalysis, Total War, and the Making of the Democratic Self in Post-war Britain* (Cambridge: Cambridge University Press, 2013).

singled out for attention by psychologists and education specialists.[51] A number of British and American relief workers certainly approached refugee welfare armed with the psychoanalytic theories and practices of social work prevalent in the United States and the United Kingdom at mid-century. However, the overwhelming majority of French relief workers relied on different perceptions of social work rather than psychological expertise. Most of them had, in the words of an American worker working in the French zone, 'never heard of Freud'.[52] At the micro-level of the field, relief workers did not wholeheartedly embrace the norms and international standards established by 'refugee experts'. The connections between 'expert' discourses and everyday practices were far from straightforward. In the French zone, the emphasis was mainly placed on vocational rehabilitation, the re-education of mothers and rest in the countryside as a means to improve mental and physical health. The range of treatment offered was influenced by various pre-war ideas about 'overcoming' poverty and war-induced injuries, including the inter-war 'practical education', social hygiene crusade and vocational training movement. These influences remain largely hidden in the history of the rehabilitation of DPs in the aftermath of the Second World War.

This is not either the familiar story of the French zone. Traditionally, the history of the French zone has been examined from the perspective of French occupiers and occupied Germans, be they generals, civilian administrators or French and German intellectuals working for a Franco–German rapprochement. This book presents a more international picture, in which foreign DPs competed with Germans for the favour of French occupiers and Allied relief workers. Overall, there is much to be gained by paying greater attention to the presence of the DPs and international organizations in this landscape. Most obvious, perhaps, examining French close encounters with DPs and international actors forces us to reconsider the view that French occupiers were harsh occupiers and nothing else. Early scholarly work on the French occupation zone focused on the severity of the occupation, including French plans to dismember Germany, take revenge for German war crimes and resort to obstruction in the Allied Control Council (the quadripartite body in Berlin).[53] Since the 1980s and the opening of the occupation archives in

---

[51] Ivan Jablonka (ed.), *L'enfant Shoah* (Paris: Presses Universitaires de France, 2014); André Rosenberg, *Les enfants dans la Shoah. La déportation des enfants juifs et tsiganes de France* (Paris: Les editions de Paris, 2013), pp. 435–470.

[52] UNRRA, S-1021-0085-02, Elise Zach, Informal welfare report, Freiburg, 16 June 1947. Freud's influence on French psychiatry was relatively limited. Elisabeth Roudinesco, *La bataille de cent ans: Histoire de la psychanalyse en France*, vol. 1, 1885–1939 (Paris: Seuil, 1986); Gregory M. Thomas, *Treating the Trauma of the Great War. Soldiers, Civilians and Psychiatry in France, 1914–1940* (Baton Rouge: Louisiana State University Press, 2009), p. 159.

[53] German historians tended to present the French as harsh occupiers?, 'industrial cannibals' who exaggeratedly requisitioned German clothes and raw materials, undertook

Colmar in 1986, the historiography of the French zone has undergone a significant revision.[54] The end of the Cold War has witnessed the emergence of more balanced analyses, which emphasize that the French occupation programme contained important and successful policies for German renewal, reform and democratization, including the early reopening of universities and an important reform of the German social security system, which went far beyond the achievements of the British and American military governments in this domain.[55] Yet, these more nuanced historical accounts have tended to focus on political history, neglecting people's daily experiences of occupation and gendered encounters in the zone.[56] As a result, we know little about how French occupiers, defeated Germans and surviving DPs, divided by memory and wartime experience, negotiated daily life and interacted with each other.[57]

At the political level, approaches to the DP question were closely related to the ways in which French policymakers mobilized both to reconstruct the French nation and administer their zone. French occupation policies were determined by three key priorities: 'grandeur', security and coal.[58] The work of French policy-elites and top-level occupation officials was shaped by

excessive, frenzied industrial removals and imposed a draconian food policy on the German population under their control. 'Industrial cannibalism' was a phrase used by Werner Abelshauser in 'Wirtschaft und Besatzungspolitik in der französischen Zone 1945–1949,' in Claus Scharf and Hans-Jürgen Schröder (eds.), *Die Deutschlandpolitik Frankreichs und die Französische Zone 1945–1949*, quoted in Martial Libéra, *Un Rêve de Puissance: La France et le Contrôle de l'économie Allemande (1942–1949)* (Bruxelles: Peter Lang, 2012), p. 27; For an early criticism of these views, see Frank Roy Willis, *France, Germany and the New Europe 1945–1967* (Stanford, CA: Stanford University Press, 1967).

[54] Rainer Hudemann, 'Revanche ou parternariat' A propos des nouvelles orientations de la recherche sur la politique française à l'égard de l'Allemagne après 1945', in Gilbert Krebs and Gérard Schneilin (eds.), *L'Allemagne 1945–1955. De la capitulation à la division* (Asnières: Publication de l'Institut d'Allemand, 1996), pp. 127–152; 'L'occupation française après 1945 et les relations franco-allemandes', *Vingtième Siècle. Revue d'histoire*, vol. 55, no. 3 (1997), pp. 58–68.

[55] Hudemann, 'France and the German Question, 1945–1949'.

[56] An important exception is Ann-Kristin Glöckner, 'Shared Spaces: Social Encounters between French and Germans in Occupied Freiburg, 1945–1955', in Camilio Erlichman and Christopher Knowles (eds.), *Transforming Occupation in the Western Zones of Germany. Politics, Everyday Life and Social Interactions, 1945–1955* (London: Bloomsbury, 2018), pp. 191–210. It is also worth mentioning that the topic of gender is attracting new scholarly attention: Anne-Laure Briatte is currently working on the German mothers of 'occupation children' fathered by French soldiers and Stefanie Siess on social representations in ego-documents from the French zone. Karen Adler is writing a book provisionally entitled *France in Germany: A Social and Cultural History of Occupation*.

[57] My approach draws on Grossmann's work *Jews, Germans, and Allies*.

[58] Marie-Benédicte Vincent, 'Introduction. La denazification de l'Allemagne en zone françaised'occupation: Quelles spécificités?', in Sebastien Chauffour, Corine Defrance,

contradictory assessments of what constituted France's main threats.[59] The French were obsessed by the eternal 'German problem', responsible for three wars against France in 1870, 1914 and 1939. In this respect, France's position was markedly different from the other western occupying powers. Just as in 1919, French policies towards their former enemy were strongly determined by France security's needs. Unlike in the aftermath of the First World War, however, French policy-elites and occupiers were also preoccupied by the Soviet threat and committed to transform German society, by scrapping its expansionist and aggressive character.[60] The democratization of Germany was thus put at the forefront of French security policies.[61] In addition, the French Foreign Office initially hoped to encourage autonomist and separatist tendencies in the Rhineland and the Ruhr and transform the Saar, with its highly significant coal and steel industry, into an independent state orientated towards France.[62] The detachment of the Rhineland, largely supported by a French Germanophobic public opinion, was unacceptable to the British, Americans and Soviet occupiers. By contrast, the Allies approved the Saar's economic union with France and in November 1947, the Saar Constitutional Assembly ratified a new constitution, which conferred on the Saarland a new elected and autonomous government under the control of France.[63]

These two interrelated issues of the Saar and the Rhineland illuminate the complexity of French security policies towards their former enemy. Ever conscious of Germany's physical proximity, French attempts to secure the political or economic detachment of the Ruhr and Rhineland region as well as measures taken to ensure German industrial disarmament were devised to prevent Germany from regaining its economic power and thereby its military potential.[64] Yet while French political and security strategies favoured

Stefan Martens and Marie-Bénédicte Vincent (eds.), *La France et la dénazification de l'Allemagne après 1945* (Bruxelles: Peter Lang, 2019), pp. 11–30.

[59] Geneviève Maelstaf, *Que faire de l'Allemagne? Les responsables français, le statut international de l'Allemagne et le problème de l'unité allemande (1945–1955)* (Paris: Direction des Archives, Ministère des Affaires Etrangères, 1999).

[60] On French security policies in the era of the First World War, see Peter Jackson, *Beyond the Balance of Power: France and the Politics of National Security in the Era of the First World War* (Cambridge: Cambridge University Press, 2013).

[61] This was already to some extent the case in the aftermath of the First World War. Jackson, *Beyond the Balance of Power.*

[62] Rainer Hudemann and Raymond Poidevin (eds.), *Die Saar 1945–1955. Ein Problem der europäischen Geschichte – La Sarre 1945–1955. Un problème de l'histoire européenne* (Munich: Oldenbourg Verlag, 1992); Rainer Hudemann, Burkhard Jellonnek and Bernd Rauls (eds.), *Grenz-Fall. Das Saarland zwischen Frankreich und Deutschland 1945–1960* (St. Ingbert: Röhrig Universitätsverlag, 1997); Bronson Long, *No Easy Occupation. French Control of the German Saar, 1944–1947* (New York: Camden House, 2015).

[63] Pierre Gerbet, *Le relèvement, 1944–1949* (Paris: Imprimerie Nationale, 1991), p. 100.

[64] Reinisch, *The Perils of Peace*, p. 292.

decentralization, if not dismemberment, French economic priorities privileged a unified administration of Germany. Debates about the retraining of DPs were also shaped by contradictory assessments of France's security needs: on the one hand, retraining DPs to work and repairing the injuries of displacement was deemed essential to support French governmental policies to transfer DPs to France. On the other hand, by reeducating DPs, the French ran the risk of leaving a highly trained and productive labour force in Germany, if DPs refused to emigrate in France. The development of a skilled and specialist labour force was seen as a potentially dangerous economic asset for a future newly independent Germany.

Any attempt to grasp the complexities of French policy towards Germany during the early years of the Provisional Government and the Fourth Republic thus requires a sound understanding of both the international and domestic contexts.[65] It also necessitates a multi-scale analysis of the DP question, which engages with governmental actors in Paris, experts (economists, demographers, medical professionals) who acquired outsized authority in post-Liberation France, private actors (French businessmen who hoped to profit from the German market) and occupation officials in the zone.[66] This book is firmly rooted in an important recent trend in the historiography, which provides a richer and more nuanced understanding of the considerable regional variation in French policies and their contingency in relation to wider post-war political goals. Dietmar Hüser has developed the concept of a 'double-game French policy', with French authorities officially formulating maximalist negotiation positions towards their Allies and publicly defending a severe policy to respond to the expectations of the French public while, in practice, implementing a more nuanced one.[67]

The history of Franco-DPs close encounters is a reminder that the French were not solely harsh and exploitative occupiers: French relief workers often jumped into the task of reconstructing DPs' lives with vigour and energy. French practices towards DPs are in fact deeply implicated in the mixed record of the French zone: DP camps were both sites of violent discipline, but also spaces of valuable educational opportunities and exchange across cultures.[68] There were in fact important tensions between the utilitarian (turning DPs

---

[65] Dietmar Hüser, *Frankreichs "doppelte Deutschlandpolitik".Dynamik aus der Defensive-Planen, Entscheiden, Umsetzen in gesellschaftlichen und wirtschaftlichen, innen- und aussenpolitischen Krisenzeiten 1944–1950* (Berlin: Duncker und Humblot, 1996); Talbot Imlay, 'A Success Story? The Foreign Policies of France's Fourth Republic', *Contemporary European History*, vol. 18, no. 4 (2009), pp. 499–519.

[66] Herrick Chapman, *France's Long Reconstruction: In Search of the Modern Republic* (Cambridge, MA: Harvard University Press, 2018).

[67] Hüser, *Frankreichs 'Doppelte Deutschlandpolitik'*.

[68] Jordanna Bailkin, *Unsettled. Refugee Camps and the Making of Multicultural Britain* (Oxford: Oxford University Press, 2018).

into productive future citizens) and recreational (providing southing and restful activities) roles of rehabilitation, between the disciplinary (controlling DPs' bodies) and empowering nature (encouraging DPs' expression and initiatives) of relief activities.

In the eyes of some relief workers, DP living conditions were more pleasant in the French zone, where DPs enjoyed more privacy, than in the British and American zones, where they were regrouped in large military caserns and barracks.[69] The smaller number of DPs in the zone largely prevented the population regime adopted in the British and American zones, which concentrated DPs in large settings in the vicinity of ruined cities.[70] On the whole, the French zone accommodated fewer Germans (5.8 million inhabitants in January 1946) and DPs than the other zones.[71] In the North of the zone, liberated by the Americans, authorities regrouped DPs in large military caserns and barracks, clearly separating DP spaces from their local German surroundings. In the South, by contrast, the French Army either reassembled DPs in smaller and more varied camps or left them in German households [chez l'habitant]. By June 1947, in the overall zone, 10,347 DPs lived outside camps and 29,814 inside camps of various sites.[72] For French relief workers, small camps and private accommodations guaranteed more 'normal' and 'safer' conditions for DPs. French home-grown experiences of deportation and labour conscription had spawned anxieties about the effects of camp-life on personal morality.[73]

This book complicates this view of small dwelling and private accommodations as more 'curative' than large camps. On the one hand, despite overcrowding, constant noise and the lack of privacy, DPs could imprint their own identities and impose individuality on the physical spaces of large DP camps. Large camps brought different classes of DPs together, who prior to the war would certainly not have mixed, and thus afforded new class, gender and cultural encounters.[74] On the other hand, DPs could feel more vulnerable and

---

[69] UNA, UNRRA, S-0438-0005-02, S. M. Chabanne, 'Rapport et suggestions pour la réorganisation de la Zone française', 6 November 1945.
[70] René Ristelhueber, Au secours des réfugiés. L'oeuvre de l'Organisation Internationale pour les Réfugiés (Paris: Plon, 1951), p. 118.
[71] Malcolm Proudfoot, European Refugees, 1939–1952 (London: Faber and Faber, 1957), p. 192.
[72] Julia Maspero, 'Sur les traces des camps de personnes déplacées dans les anciennes zones françaises en Allemagne et en Autriche: une mémoire effacée ou déplacée?', in Jean-Frédéric de Hasque and Clara Lecadet (dir), Après les camps. Traces, mémoires et mutations des camps de réfugiés (Paris: Academia Harmattan, 2019), pp. 171–198, 174.
[73] Lagrou, The Legacy of Nazi Occupation, pp. 148–149.
[74] Katarzyna Nowak, 'Voices of Revival. A Cultural History of Polish Displaced Persons in Allied-Occupied Germany and Austria, 1945–1952', PhD thesis, University of Manchester, version submitted in July 2018.

isolated 'chez l'habitant' and could be subjected to harsher work conditions. The requisition of German private spaces to house DPs caused great tensions not only between French occupiers and German landlords, but also amongst the French occupiers.[75] In towns, German local inhabitants often resented the sharing of their domestic spaces with French occupiers and DPs.[76] Requisition inscribed in the private sphere defeat and foreign occupation.[77] Tensions over room allocations formed an important axis of political protest amongst DPs, but also between DPs, defeated Germans and French occupiers.

The French zone had suffered less war damage, particularly when compared to the Soviet and British zones. With the exception of the Saar, France's zone was predominantly rural with only a handful of large towns, which, by German standards, had suffered relatively little physical destruction. The town centres of Koblenz, Ludwigshafen, Mainz and Saarbrücken (the Saar's capital) had suffered greatly, but the surrounding countryside was almost untouched. Some areas, such as the town of Tübingen, had undergone little bombardment, but living conditions remained difficult and the countryside hosted homeless German civilians from heavily bombed urban areas.[78] Public health was significantly better than in the other zones. Tellingly, German mortality in the zone was lower than mortality in France itself.[79] The zone also accommodated fewer German refugees from the East of the Oder-Neisse line. In August 1945, at Potsdam, the Allies decided to sanction the principle of population transfer for German refugees.[80] These included 'National Germans'

---

[75] See, for instance, UNA, UNRRA, S-0438-0005-02, Report, welfare officer, Southern district, 8 June 1946 or S-0421-0040-05, Bauche à Lavau, 29 June 1946.

[76] According to French regulations, houses belonging to former members of the Nazi Party were supposed to be requisitioned first, but this was not always the case in practice. Glöckner, 'Shared Spaces', p. 202.

[77] Anne Duménil, 'L'expérience intime des ruines: Munich, 1945-1948', in Bruno Cabanes and Guillaume Piketty, *Retour à l'intime au sortir de la guerre* (Paris: Tallandier, 2009), pp. 101-115, 107; Jennifer Evans, *Life among the Ruins – Cityscape and Sexuality in Cold War Berlin* (London: Palgrave, 2009); Margarete Myers Feinstein, 'All Under One Roof: Persecutees, DPs, Expellees and the Housing Shortage in Occupied Germany', *Holocaust and Genocide Studies*, vol. 32, no. 1 (2018), pp. 29-48, 31; Bettina Blum, 'My Home, Your Castle': British Requisitioning of German Homes in Westphalia', in Erlichman and Knowles (eds.), *Transforming Occupation in the Western Zones of Germany*, pp. 115-132.

[78] According to French official figures, the zone accommodated between 300,000 and 400,000 German evacuees in October 1945. The majority of them lived in the Rhineland (140,000) and Württemberg (131,000), the rest in Baden (84,500), the Palatinate (45,000) and the Saar (2,500). MAE, HCRFA, PDR6/467, GMZFO, Direction générale des affaires administratives, Direction des Personnes Déplacées, statistiques générales, 30 October 1945. Also see: Gerhard Junger, *Schicksale 1945. Das Ende des II. Weltkrieges im Kreis Reutlingen* (Reutlingen: Oertel and Spörer, 1991), pp. 113-114.

[79] Reinisch, *The Perils of Peace*, pp. 273-274.

[80] Several terms were used to describe these expulsions (including the German word *Vertreibung* 'expulsion' and the Czech word *Odsun* meaning transfer) and these

(*Reichsdeutsche*), groups who had lived in the areas east of the Oder-Neisse line which were part of Germany on 31 December 1937, and refugees of 'Ethnic German origin' (*Volksdeutsche*) – Germans who had lived as minority groups in foreign countries.[81] The French, who had not been invited to the Potsdam Conference, deferred the notification of a clear position on the issue, as some considered them unnecessary mouths to feed.[82] For all that, civilian life in the French zone was still impaired by chaos and disruption. Despite being the most rural, the French zone was far from self-sufficient. Resources were scarce, transportation facilities limited and French occupation officials, as well as the French public, were unwilling to meet the additional costs of reconstruction.

DPs' lives were further complicated by the administrative confusion that characterized the French occupation regime. Coordination between Parisian ministries and the administration of the zone was inadequate.[83] French occupation personnel was both too numerous and too heteroclite.[84] In practice, the

---

German refugees. There is an extremely abundant literature on this topic. For an analysis of the different terms and historical interpretations Alfred J. Rieber, 'Repressive Population Transfers in Central, Eastern and South-Eastern Europe: A Historical Overview', *Journal of Communist Studies and Transition Politics*, vol. 16, no. 1 (2000), pp. 1–27. Ian Connor, *Refugees and Expellees in Post-war Germany* (Manchester: Manchester University Press, 2007), pp. 20–22. The first post-war German census carried out in October 1946 registered 5,645,000 expellees from the former eastern regions of the Reich. In addition, around 3 million Germans were expelled from Czechoslovakia (mainly from the Sudetenland). On the French zone see Andrea Kühne, *Entstehung, Aufbau und Funktion der Flüchtlingsverwaltungim Württemberg-Hohenzollern 1945–1952* (Sigmaringen: Jan Thorbecke Verlag, 1999), pp. 33–34.

[81] The term *Volksdeutsche* was invented in 1938 by the German government. Doris L. Bergen, 'The Nazi Concept of *Volksdeutsche* and the Exacerbation of Anti-Semitism in Eastern Europe, 1939–1945', *Journal of Contemporary History*, vol. 29, no. 4 (1994), pp. 569–582.

[82] The French were also initially opposed to the transfer between zones of expellees, but they were forced to reconsider their position by the Americans. Mathias Beer, 'Die französische Besatzungszone in Deutschland als Aufnahmegebiet für deutsche Flüchtlinge und Vertriebene nach dem Zweiten Weltkrieg', in Detlef Brandes, Holm Sundhaussen and Stefan Troebst (eds.), *Lexikon der Vertreibungen. Deportation, Zwangsaussiedlung und ethnische Säuberungim Europa des 20. Jahrhunderts* (Vienne: Böhlau, 2010), pp. 252–255. This did not mean – as some scholars have claimed – that the French were unanimously opposed to the principle of transfer of population, however. In fact, if de Gaulle had obtained the detachment of the Rhineland, 7 million Germans would have been compelled to leave. Gousseff, 'L'Est et l'Ouest entre consensus et divergence face aux DPs d'Allemagne', p. 44.

[83] Julia Wambach, 'Vichy in Baden-Baden – The Personnel of the French Occupation in Germany after 1945', *Contemporary European History*, vol. 28, no. 3 (2019), pp. 319–341.

[84] Sylvie Levèvre, *Les relations économiques franco-allemandes de 1945 à 1955. De l'occupation à la coopération* (Vincennes: Institut de la gestion publique et du développement économique, 1998).

administration of the zone was managed by two parallel and competing organizations in Baden-Baden: the 'civil cabinet' under General Koenig, former administrator in the Ruhr in 1923 and hero of the French Resistance in Bir-Hakeim in 1942, and the military government headed by the administrator Emile Laffon, a left-leaning and brilliant lawyer, until his resignation on 14 November 1947. The administrative structure of the zone was very hierarchical. Laffon was installed in Baden-Baden and was represented in each of the four provinces by a *Délégué Supérieur* [Superior Delegate]. And yet, regionally and locally, each *Délégué supérieur* retained considerable room for manoeuvre.[85] Joseph Rovan, who had survived the Dachau concentration camp and worked in the French Bureau of Popular Culture, described the zone as a 'group of autonomous principalities placed under the direction of a weak central government'.[86] Indeed, each of the French administrative districts often pursued its own autonomous policy.

This inherent tension between Baden-Baden's top-down assertiveness and regional contestations profoundly shaped the implementation of French occupation policies. It also influenced the treatment of DPs in the zone. In this complex administrative environment, the coordination of DP policies remained difficult, despite the creation of the Service Prisoniers, Déportés and Réfugiés (PDR) in August 1945 as part of the Direction Générale des Affaires administratives, under the authority of General Administrator Laffon (Fig. I.1). The Central Direction of the PDR Service was installed on 20 September in Rastatt.

In each region, a chef de section PDR was attached to the *Délégué Supérieur*. Further, the PDR organization was often at loggerheads over how to administer DPs with the French UNRRA headquarters, established in the autumn of 1945.

The PDR service began working in Baden-Baden on 11 August 1945, two months before UNRRA set up its regional headquarters.[87] According to the PDR director, the military government had nothing to gain from the presence of UNRRA, standing only to lose sovereign control in key areas.[88] The Military Governor Koenig was equally hostile to the signature of the agreement with UNRRA, given that, in his own words, 'UNRRA provided no material supplies' and that was likely to 'take control of DP centres at a time when the DP problem was expected to have almost ceased to exist in the zone'.[89] In this

---

[85] See, for instance, UNA, UNRRA, S-0421-0028-05, J. Rozale, *Mise au travail obligatoire des DPs à Singen*, 3 July 1946.
[86] Gerbet, *Le relèvement*, p. 90.
[87] MAE, HCRFA, PDR1/33, Note de service, 10 August 1945.
[88] MAE, HCRFA, PDR1/18, Poignant, Note pour le Ministre, 28 July 1945.
[89] MAE, HCRFA, Bonn 159, Général de Corps d'Armée à Novateur, [Probably January 1946].

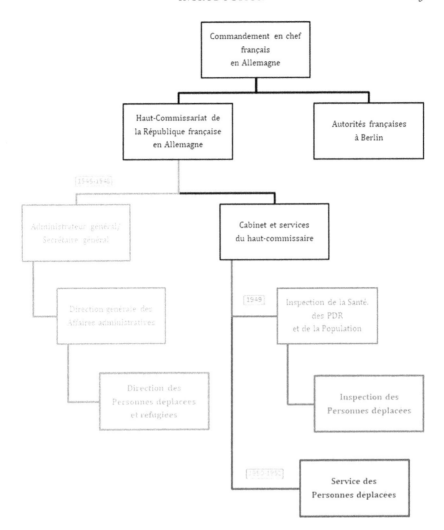

**Fig. I.1** Historical organization chart of the direction PDR (1945–1955). Reproduced by kind permission of Cyril Daydé, 'Les personnes déplacées et réfugiées en zone française d'occupation d'après les archives diplomatiques françaises. Fonds d'archives et méthodes de recherche', in Defrance, Denis, Maspero (eds.), *Personnes déplacées et guerre froide en Allemagne occupée*, pp. 349–367, 365.

characterization, UNRRA merely signified another unwanted layer in a policy-making process that was already more than complicated enough. From its beginning to its end, the history of PDR-UNRRA relations (at the level of authorities in the zone) was punctuated by innumerable petty administrative and personal quarrels.[90] It was not until 18 February 1946 that the transfer of responsibilities from the PDR service to UNRRA staff was officially agreed. As this delay implies, the transfer proved a difficult, messy affair, occurring at a time when UNRRA's own existence was increasingly questioned internationally. Tensions were particularly acute in the Southern part of the Zone, in the Baden Württemberg area, where DPs remained under PDR control until late 1945.

There was more at issue in the conflict between the PDR and UNRRA that a bureaucratic jostling for authority: conflicting interests and various strands of humanitarianism coexisted within UNRRA. This book unearths significant cultural differences between French UNRRA officials, many of whom were former military officers, who thought that organizing DPs camps required military discipline and order, and the attitudes of the majority of relief workers on the ground. The French Director of UNRRA headquarters envisioned humanitarian aid in highly traditional ways. He attempted to run his administration in a military manner.[91] Field workers, by contrast, brought in with them a variety of perspectives and placed a greater emphasis on vocational rehabilitation, the re-education of mothers and rest in the countryside as a means to improve DPs' mental and physical health.

French relief workers promulgated a highly gendered vision of relief that centred on helping DP mothers to care *for* (nurturing) their children, and DP fathers to care *about* (breadwinning) their children. They insisted that DPs should conform to particular domestic arrangements and gendered norms. DP mothers, in particular, were to be 'retrained' into methods of childcare. French relief workers also brought with them a specific set of assumptions and experiences, based on pre-war ideas about the 'return to the countryside', the inter-war 'social hygiene' crusade, the development of 'agricultural colonies' for psychiatric patients in the French Empire and the professional reorientation movement, which framed how they approached rehabilitation.[92] Confident in the 'therapeutic' nature of open-air homes and gardening, French relief workers sent, for instance, a number of DP children to spend days in the fresh in the Black Forest. Yet, the temporary placement of children in these houses in the Black Forest caused grave anxieties amongst a number of DP parents and DP children, who found these temporary separations emotionally

---

[90] UNA, UNRRA, S-0412-0012-05, Monthly report, French Zone of Occupation for the month of October 1945, 7 November 1945.

[91] UNA, UNRRA, S-0417-0002-02, Le Général de Corps d'Armée F. Lenclud à tout le personnel UNRRA en Zone d'Occupation Française, 18 February 1946.

[92] On the history of occupational therapy and rehabilitation, see, for instance, Ana Carden Coyne, 'The Art of Resilience. Veteran Therapy from the Occupational to the Creative, 1914–1945', in Leo Van Bergen and Eric Vermetten (eds.) *The First World War and Health. Rethinking Resilience* (London: Brill, 2020), pp. 39-70.

difficult. The placement of DP children in open-air homes thus reveals the tensions between the 'disciplinary' and 'therapeutic' nature of rehabilitation.

Unearthing specific ways of understanding DP needs in the French zone, based on pre-war ideas about 'overcoming' poverty and rehabilitating 'indigenous' patients, is not to say that there was a coherent 'French' approach to DP rehabilitation. Rather, this book suggests that reconstructing DP bodies and minds meant different things, at different times, to different actors: much depended on context. In France, the years after the Second World War were marked by profound social and cultural transformation in the ways French pedagogues, social workers and psychologists thought about the proper shape of family, motherhood and fatherhood.[93] Debates about how best to administer and rehabilitate DPs developed in parallel with anxieties about juvenile delinquency and the 'dysfunctional family'.[94] The war had wrecked parental authority and, in particular, the image of the father, damaged by the shameful defeat, the dishonourable captivity and the acceptance of foreign occupation.[95] In the French Empire, the rise of juvenile delinquency was not attributed to the absence of father, but instead to the increased mobility of children, who left their homes to find work in urban centres.[96] This book therefore brings to the fore these anxieties and explores the myriad voices adopted by relief workers and occupation officials in their dealings with DPs. It shows, in particular, that welfare discussion amongst relief workers reflected both the strength of the ideals of the nuclear family and anxieties about its fragility. These discussions also revealed the continued importance of religious faith and morality amongst French relief workers, many French social workers coming from the traditions of 'social Catholicism' and the 'popular education' movement. Both DP elites and relief workers drew heavily on Christian faith and values to 'regulate' DP mothers' life and combat immoral DP behaviours.

---

[93] Zahra, *Lost Children*; Sarah Fishman, *From Vichy to the Sexual Revolution Gender and Family Life in Postwar France* (Oxford: Oxford University Press, 2017), pp. 15–16; Daniella Doron, *Jewish Youth and Identity in Postwar France. Rebuilding Family and Nation* (Bloomington: Indiana University Press, 2015); Ludivine Bantigny, 'La jeunesse, la guerre et l'histoire (1945–1962)', in Ludivine Bantigny (ed.), *Jeunesse oblige* (Paris: Presses Universitaires de France, 2009), pp. 153–166; Shannon Fogg, *Stealing Home. Looting, Restitution, and Reconstructing Jewish Lives in France, 1942–1947* (Oxford: Oxford University Press, 2017).

[94] Sarah Fishman, *The Battle for Children World War II, Youth Crime and Juvenile Justice in Twentieth Century France* (Harvard: Harvard University Press, 2002); Richard Ivan Jobs, *Riding the New Wave. Youth and the Rejuvenation of France after the Second World War* (Stanford, CA: Stanford University Press, 2007); On fears in the French Empire see, for example, Jessica Pearson-Patel, 'From the Civilizing Mission to International Development: France, the United Nations, and the Politics of Family Health in Postwar Africa, 1945–1960', PhD dissertation, University of New York (2013), p. 286.

[95] Bantigny, 'La jeunesse, la guerre et l'histoire (1945–1962)', p. 159.

[96] Pearson-Patel, 'From the Civilizing Mission to International Development', p. 290.

The history of welfare programmes in the French zone may seem like a marginal tale within the broader story of twentieth-century humanitarianism, but it is illuminating for what it teaches us about the transformation of humanitarian practices in the wake of the two world wars. The Second World War was not a radically 'modernising' moment in the history of humanitarianism.[97] To be sure, the war saw an explosion of private organizations, American funds and expert discourses about the 'rehabilitation' of DPs. These internationally minded experts shared a sense of professional mission and a belief in the importance of training and skills in shaping post-war humanitarianism.[98] But, their views did not represent the perspectives of those working at all levels of international organizations. In the French zone, UNRRA was placed under the supervision of a French general, who drew upon French military discourses of efficiency, discipline and practices of military relief predating the war.[99] This book thus complicates theories of 'modern humanitarianism', which tend to present it as a specific and coherent discourse and set of practices emerging in the aftermath of the First World War.[100]

After the First World War and Russian Civil War, humanitarianism became intimately connected with international peace making. Scholars have recently crowned the period of the early 1920s as marking a key 'turning point' in the history of humanitarianism, with the appearance of new actors and discourses. According to such narratives, philanthropists and missionaries were progressively superseded by experts, physicians, engineers, who relied on scientific approaches to international relief aid and mobilized mass media to raise awareness and attract funds from the European and American publics.[101] In

---

[97] Cohen *In War's Wake*, p. 66.
[98] See, for example, Reinisch, 'Internationalism in Relief', pp. 258–289; '"Auntie UNRRA" at the Crossroads', pp. 70–97.
[99] Bertrand Taithe, *Defeated Flesh: Welfare, Warfare and the Making of Modern France* (Manchester: Manchester University Press, 1999); Adam J. Davis and Bertrand Taithe, 'From the Purse and the Heart: Exploring Charity, Humanitarianism and Human Rights in France' *French Historical Studies*, vol. 34, no. 3 (2011), pp. 413–432; Silvia Salvatici 'Fighters without guns': humanitarianism and military action in the aftermath of the Second World War', *European Review of History*, vol. 25, no. 6 (2018), pp. 957–976; Andrew Arsan, Laure Humbert and Benjamin Thomas White, 'Military force, humanitarian action, and French power in the world', Panel for the Society for the Study of French History 2017.
[100] Bruno Cabanes, *The Great War and the Origins of Humanitarianism, 1918–1924* (Cambridge: Cambridge University Press, 2014); Keith Watenpaugh, *Bread from Stones. The Middle East and the Making of Modern Humanitarianism* (Oakland: University of California Press, 2015). For a critical analysis of this strand of literature, see Bertrand Taithe, 'The "Making" of the Origins of Humanitarianism', *Contemporanea*, vol. 18, no. 3 (2015), pp. 489–496.
[101] Cabanes, *The Great War and the Origins of Humanitarianism*, pp. 1–17.

this context, humanitarian aid became a permanent, transnational, neutral and secular regime for tackling the *root causes* of human suffering. This narrative is problematic, not least because it is partial. It has resulted in an incomplete picture of humanitarianism, disregarding deeper continuities and blurring the links between official and non-official aid.[102] In the French zone, the French UNRRA headquarters thought that its staff represented the interest of the French state and its concern for its image abroad.

By focusing on the intersections between 'military' and civilian approaches to relief within humanitarian organizations, this book also sheds new light into the gendering of humanitarian leadership roles as masculine, since despite the fact that many women participated in relief operations, few had positions of power at the headquarters and district level in the zone. UNRRA male and often military officials believed that the presence of female relief workers in DP camps was good for DPs' re-education and morale, but insisted on an image of familial bond between sexless 'relief' mothers and children.[103] In practice, however, the evidence reveals a much more diverse set of practices and a more fluid gender culture. The context of occupation suspended some of the expectations of 'respectable femininity'. Some female relief workers gave instructions to DPs, had an important purchasing power and acquired independence. This was resented by some of their male colleagues. By examining these gendered tensions, this book reveals the persistence of a maternalist discourse, which presented women as natural carers. It also illuminates how relief workers tried to re-inscribe old conceptions of manliness and femininity onto DPs. In the French zone, educational programmes reinforced the association of femininity with caring, domesticity and motherhood. A gendered analysis of relief in the French zone thus reveals deep anxieties about women's greater political and social agency following the defeat of 1940 and foreign occupation. These concerns must be placed in the wider context of the search for 'gender peace', that is to say attempts for the restoration of traditional gender roles in response to the chaos of war, defeat and foreign occupation. The French defeat of 1940 initiated a painful process of social disruption and ideological revaluation, which had repercussions beyond the metropolitan borders.

---

[102] See, for example, Johannes Paulmann, 'Conjunctures in the History of International Humanitarian Aid during the Twentieth Century', *Humanity: An International Journal of Human Rights, Humanitarianism and Development*, 4, 2 (2013), pp. 215–238; Glen Peterson, 'Colonialism, Sovereignty and the History of the International Refugee Regime', in Matthew Frank and Jessica Reinisch (eds.), *Refugees in Europe 1919–1959: A Forty Years' Crisis?* (London: Bloomsbury, 2017), pp. 213–228.

[103] Georges Woodbridge, *UNRRA: The History of the United Nations Relief and Rehabilitation Administration*, vol. 2 (New York: Colombia University Press, 1950), p. 470.

This book draws on a rich and diverse base of archival research, comprising documents from the UNRRA and IRO archives in New York and Paris, reports from the French occupation zone and Foreign Ministry materials, in addition to records from the French national and military archives, private papers, records from the International Tracing Service (ITS), films, photographs and newspapers. Historical accounts of DP life in the French zone, as in the other Western zones, are abundant.[104] DPs' health, fitness and calorie intake were methodically examined and voluminously documented by doctors and nutritionists, their wartime experiences thoroughly scrutinized by legal experts, their language abilities and professional aptitudes tested by technical instructors and educators.[105] This wealth of historical sources presented an important methodological challenge. The sum of these reports contributed to the construction of what Daniel Cohen has termed a 'refugee nation', an abstract group of dispossessed people united by a need for special care.[106] In the first instance, this 'refugee nation' was constructed by relief workers who produced reports and monitored DPs' lives. It was then shaped by archivists, who selected and catalogued these records, removing material in the process, thereby forging archival silences.

In her work on colonial archives, Ann Stoler has invited historians to consider archives both as sites of knowledge retrieval but also of knowledge production and foundations of historical authority and state power.[107] Following her lead, we should consider aid agencies' records as both the product of humanitarian bureaucratic machines, but also as 'technologies' that could strengthen the power of an organization. The documents considered here were often written by relief workers, who wanted to report on how they *successfully* delivered aid. The historian has to pick their way through the layers of self-promotion and propaganda and read relief workers' report along the grain to recover DPs' agency. It is notable that relatively few reports mentioned errors and failures on the part of relief workers. In November

---

[104] Atina Grossmann, 'Entangled Histories and Lost Memories. Jewish Survivors in Occupied Germany, 1945-1949', in Avinoam Patt and Michael Berkowitz (eds.), *We Are Here: New Approaches to Jewish Displaced Persons in Postwar Germany* (Detroit, MI: Wayne State University Press, 2010), pp. 14-30, 17.

[105] The UN archives also hold an enormous volume of weekly reports written by field workers. The 'series PDR' of the French Occupation Zone archives, as well as the archives of Henri Frenay's Ministry PDR, the archives of the *Comité d'histoire de la Seconde Guerre Mondiale* (deposited in the French National Archives) and the French military archives (in Vincennes) also contain an large quantity of official reports documenting the different aspects of DP life in the French zone.

[106] Daniel Cohen, 'Naissance d'une nation: Les personnes déplacées de l'après-guerre, 1945-1951', *Genèses*, vol. 38 (2000), pp. 56-78.

[107] Ann Laura Stoler, *Along the Archival Grain: Epistemic Anxieties and Colonial Common Sense* (Princeton, NJ: Princeton University Press, 2009).

1945, for instance, UNRRA Director of the DP Operation Frederick Morgan wrote to the French UNRRA Director General Lenclud that he was satisfied that the situation in the French zone was 'not nearly so bad as one might have been led to believe from the many disjointed and irresponsible statements that one has heard in the past from all kinds of sources'.[108] These negative statements about UNRRA are often absent from the organization's own records, but abound in the archives of the French zone.[109] By destabilizing the official 'humanitarian discourse', this book highlights the active agency of DPs in negotiating the aid that was provided to them, even though French relief workers and occupiers gave them little say over how 'aid' was delivered.

While reports from aid agencies can yield valuable new insights into relief workers' everyday encounters with DPs, they can also impoverish and curtail historical understanding. Drawing solely on these documents can indeed bias the interrogations and introduce effects of 'invisibility' or 'overestimation'.[110] Aid reports are often silent about German inhabitants and surroundings, neglecting the tensions between DPs and German residents.[111] Few relief workers referred to antisemitic violence, although such hostility existed. In July 1946, for instance, an antisemitic incident occurred in the youth Jordanbad camp.[112] In November 1948, a representative of the American Joint Distribution Committee also reported that 'Lettish DPs' provoked Jews in a restaurant in Ummendorf. 'After some shouts of "Heil Hitler" [...] a row broke out between Jews and Lettish DPs'.[113] Such tensions are also concealed in humanitarian photography. Humanitarian photographs depicted relief work as spatially contained and set off from the German population.[114] And yet, in what scholars have called the 'society of collapse', which was marked by

---

[108] UNA, UNRRA, S-0417-0001-01, Frederick Morgan to Lenclud, 25 November 1945.

[109] On a positive statement of UNRRA activities, see UN, UNRRA, S-0417-0001-03, Rapport succintsur les activités de UNRRA en zone Française depuis le 18 février 1946, 31 July 1946.

[110] Dzovinar Kévonian, 'La Cimade et les réfugiés: organisation privée et processus de légitimation dans l'espace international, 1945–1951', in Dzovinar Kévonian, Geneviève Dreyfus-Armand, Marie-Claude Blanc-Chaléard, *La Cimade et l'accueil des réfugiés: Identités, répertoires d'actions et politique de l'asile, 1939–1994* (Nanterre: Presses Universitaires de Nanterre, 2013), pp. 101–121; Watenpaugh, *Bread from Stones*, p. 24.

[111] Reinhold Adler, 'Der schwierige Weg zur Normalität Die UNRRA in Biberach und Umgebung 1945 bis 1947', *Heimatkundliche Blatter fur den Kreis Biberach*, vol. 30 (2007), pp. 36–57, 35.

[112] UNA, UNRRA, S-0421-0011-07, Rapport à M. le Directeur du UNRRA Team 209 de la part de M. Parades, Chef du centre Jordanbad, 16 July 1946.

[113] JDC Archives, Records of the Geneva Office of the American Jewish Joint Distribution Committee, GER.347, H. Laufer, Letter from AJDC French Zone/Germany to Rosalie Westreich, Incidents at Biberach, 2 November 1948.

[114] Lisa Smirl, *Spaces of Aid. How Cars, Compounds and Hotels Shape Humanitarianism* (Chicago: University of Chicago Press, 2015), p. 42.

a rise in criminality, DPs were repeatedly accused of being a drain on Germany's resources.[115] For most Germans, DPs were 'privileged' and living a 'comfortable life' amidst an environment of scarcity.[116] As Jean Lucien Estrade, former governor of the military government in Tuttlingen recalled, DP status was very sought after and enviable.[117] This hostility towards DPs draws out continuities in 'patterns of thought' that were internalized in the Nazi era about 'Slavic subhumans'.[118] Another important silence concerned the ways DPs' wartime experiences were recounted and rewritten. While acknowledging suffering, relief workers often tended to focus on individual reconstruction and DPs' futures.[119] Certainly, these silences are important and should be regarded as positive statements. They indicate what mattered for high officials and relief workers.

These sources reveal a great deal about the mundane life of relief workers and occupation officials. Humanitarian work offered an opportunity for travelling, adventure and escapism after years of rationing and privation. Questions of diet and material entitlement sustained relief workers' attention. The immediate post-war years were dominated by a 'culture of scarcity' in France, which created widespread resentment towards the Provisional Government (then the Fourth Republic) and little empathy for 'Hungry Germans'.[120] In France, peace did not end day-to-day life privation. While the government continued to resort to a rationing system and price controls, French citizens engaged in widespread food protests and demonstrations.[121] In this context, empty stomachs and cupboards bare of food impacted on collective mentalities, influencing in turn French official policies towards its

---

[115] Rainer Schulze, 'Growing Discontent: Relations between Native and Refugee Populations in a Rural District in Western Germany after the Second World War', in Robert Moeller (ed.), *West Germany under Construction: Politics, Society, and Culture in the Adenauer Era* (Ann Arbor: University of Michigan Press, 1997), pp. 53–72.

[116] Atina Grossmann, 'Grams, Calories, and Food: Languages of Victimization, Entitlement, and Human Rights in Occupied Germany, 1945-1949', *Central European History*, vol. 44, no. 1 (2011), pp. 118-148, 129.

[117] Jean-Lucien Estrade, *Tuttlingen April 1945–September 1949 Die französische Militärregierung in Tuttlingen* (Tuttlingen: D. Gagstatter, 1986), p. 31.

[118] Jan-Hinnerk Antons, 'Displaced Persons in Postwar Germany: Parallel Societies in a Hostile Environment', *Journal of Contemporary History*, vol. 49, no. 1 (2014), pp. 92-114, 93.

[119] Antoine Burgard, 'Une nouvelle vie dans un nouveau pays. Trajectoires d'orphelins de la Shoah vers le Canada (1947–1952)', PhD thesis, Université du Québec à Montréal/ Université Lumière Lyon 2, September 2017, p. 192.

[120] Megan Koreman, *The Expectation of Justice: France, 1944–1946* (Durham, NC: Duke University Press, 1999).

[121] Dominique Veillon, *Vivre et survivre en France 1939–1947* (Paris: Payot, 1995); Fabrice Grenard, *La France du marché noir (1940–1949)* (Paris: Payot, 2008), p. 238.

former enemy.[122] Whilst relief workers often attributed themselves a rich diet, much of the DPs' bitterness coalesced around material entitlements and food rations. DPs resented the control of their daily life by relief workers. They perceived the refugee regime as disempowering and patronising.[123] DPs' petitions about the insufficient quantity, inadequate composition or simply bad quality of the rations distributed were numerous. By contrast, in the spa town of Baden-Baden, some French occupation officials lived a life of luxury, which led some contemporaries, particularly on the French left, to label Baden-Baden a 'little Vichy'.[124] In this context, defeated Germans and DPs bemoaned their losses and miserable living conditions and envied the French occupiers and relief workers.

Overall, the discourse and visual strategies of relief workers were very assertive: they claim to represent the views of the refugees, in a way preventing DPs from speaking for themselves about their experiences. As with many humanitarian archives, these records tend to flatten the historical experience of the peoples towards whom its policies were directed.[125] DPs are often either represented as victims or future migrants. DPs' personal files reflect both DPs' presentational strategies (including how they adapted their answers according to what they believed was expected from them) and relief workers' perceptions of them. In their reports, many relief workers unthinkingly replicate the inequalities of power between relief 'providers' and 'recipients'. They tell us not what everyday encounters with DPs were like, but what they looked like to them. The historian has thus to be sensitive to the paternalist assumptions embedded in official documents: relief workers' reports tend to focus on the minority of male DPs who were drunk, violent or who engaged in black-market activities, and the minority of female DPs who did not carry out their 'motherly duties'.

Taken as a whole, though, this material offers access to the ways in which French relief workers experienced certain aspects of the daily life of the occupation. PDR and UNRRA correspondences reveal the centrality of language in shaping encounters on the ground.[126] While DPs were often

---

[122] Dietmar Hüser, 'Ventres creux, mentalités collectives et relations internationales – la faim dans les rapports franco-allemands d'après guerre', in Francine-Dominique Liechtenhan and Brad Abrams (eds.), *Europe 1946: Entre le deuil et l'espoir* (Bruxelles: Editions Complexe, 1996), pp. 142–164.
[123] Nowak, 'Voices of Revival', p. 109.
[124] Adler, 'Selling France to the French', p. 584.
[125] Watenpaugh, *Bread from Stones*, p. 23.
[126] On the broader issue of languages at war and peace see, for instance, Hilary Footitt, 'War and Culture Studies in 2016: Putting "Translation" into the Transnational?', *Journal of War and Culture Studies*, vol. 9, no. 3 (2016), pp. 209–221.

multilingual, relief workers often only spoke French, German or English.[127] Miscommunications between French liaison officers, relief workers and repatriation officers were frequent. Eastern European repatriation officers often displayed resentment towards French liaison officers, whom they suspected of behind-the-scenes machinations in French. The French were equally suspicious of the members of the repatriation missions. Both sides were, to a large extent, dependent on their interpreters. Finally, these reports also provide routes into the gendered aspects of the occupation, operating as an archive of unexpected facets of the occupation, such as romance and sexual relationships between French, Germans and DPs.[128] The defeats of 1940 in France and 1945 in Germany caused important disruptions in perceptions of sexuality and gender norms, with the Allied occupation putting tremendous strain on relations between German men and women. The UNRRA was part of this disruptive process. Histories of gender and sexuality in defeated Germany focus overwhelmingly on the American zone.[129] And yet, in the French zone French female UNRRA workers' sexual conduct faced sharp scrutiny from UNRRA's military and conservative headquarters.

Finally, for a minority of French relief workers who had been active participants in the Resistance against the Nazi occupiers, these sources constitute an especially interesting site through which to trace issues of revenge and mourning. Jacqueline Lesdos, a nurse from the resistance *Combat* movement who worked with DPs in the American zone, found it extremely difficult to forge strong bonds with her American co-workers. While she forged powerful emotional bonds with the DPs, she did not connect with her US co-workers.[130] In July 1945 she discovered that the Nazis had killed her brother. While she could not help but hate Germans, she was horrified at the sight of young American soldiers 'fraternizing' with German women. In a very moving letter

---

[127] 'I found that Americans [...] could usually speak only American. The English were slightly, but not much better. The French, to my surprise, were almost equally unilingual', UNA, UNRRA, S-1021-0085-02, report signed B. H. Roberts, [1947?].

[128] Laure Humbert, 'When Most Relief Workers Had Never Heard of Freud. UNRRA in the French Occupation Zone, 1945–1947', in Sandra Barkhof and Angela K. Smith (eds.), *War and Displacement in the Twentieth Century: Global Conflicts* (London: Routledge, 2014), pp. 199–223.

[129] Petra Goedde, *GIs and Germans: Culture, Gender and Foreign Relations, 1945–1949* (Yale: Yale University Press, 2003); Elizabeth Heineman, *What Difference Does a Husband Make? Women and Marital Status in Nazi and Post-war Germany* (Berkeley: University of California Press, 2003); Maria Höhn, *GIs and Fräuleins: The German-American Encounter in 1950s West Germany* (Chapel Hill: University of North Carolina Press, 2002); Grossmann, *Jews, Germans, and Allies*; Heide Fehrenbach and Timothy Schroer, *Recasting Race after World War Two: Germans and African Americans in American-Occupied Germany* (Boulder: University Press of Colorado, 2007).

[130] AN 72/AJ/1968, Jacqueline Lesdos, *Souvenirs personnels*, p. 16.

written to her mother, she related her visit in April 1946 to Neuengamme camp, where her brother had been murdered:

> Standing next to the grave, I hated, and hated so fiercely. Instead of this banal inscription, I would have wanted to read on the cross 'to the victims of the German people who have left all these horrors occurring on their soil'. No one people deemed civilized would have accepted the effects of a dictatorship so abominable had this people not been characterized by their attachment to discipline ...[131]

Jacqueline Lesdos resigned in July 1946, convinced that she could not 'rehabilitate DPs' as she was so devastated by her brother's death. She strongly empathized with the DPs. 'In every one of them, I could see my suffering brother ... They could feel it.'[132] In the absence of a body to bury, she seemed to have invested DPs' bodies with her own pain.[133] In 1945, the troubled legacies of collaboration and resistance were felt deeply between those who had collaborated and those who had resisted. French relief workers were anything but united amongst themselves. This book demonstrates that, depending on their assigned tasks, political orientation and wartime experiences, French occupation officials and UNRRA humanitarian actors often constructed very different interpretations of the DP situation.

*Reinventing French Aid* falls into two parts. Part 1 anchors the history of French DP administration within the field of international history and French domestic politics. It demonstrates that humanitarian aid was influenced by the dynamics of French politics of national recovery and the rivalries of the Cold War. Particular attention is paid to the debates about the transfers of DPs to France; the emergence of different cultures of encampment in the zone and the tensions around the repatriation and screening of DPs. Chapters 1–3 reveal that approaches to DPs reflected contradictory assessments of France's economic, labour and security needs and bring to light the power of local administrators to reinterpret and shape emigration and repatriation policies on the ground. Part 2 interrogates how relief workers attempted to reconstruct DPs' bodies and minds in the French zone and maps out different cultures of 'rehabilitation' in the French zone. Chapters 4–6 reveal that the French often understood the work of rehabilitation in paternalistic terms and adopted a genuinely civilizational posture: the relationship between relief workers and

---

[131] AN 72/AJ/1968, Jacqueline Lesdos, Lettre explicative pour maman, Darmstadt, 19 April 1946.
[132] AN 72/AJ/1968, Jacqueline Lesdos, *Souvenirs personnels*, p. 22.
[133] Bruno Cabanes and Guillaume Piketty, 'Introduction', in Bruno Cabanes and Guillaume Piketty (eds.), *Retour à l'intime au sortir de la guerre* (Paris: Tallandier, 2009), pp. 11–33, 24.

DPs was informed by ideas about 'French' superiority. Ultimately, this book takes the line that genuine belief in France's goodness – and that 'what was good for France was good for the world' – could blind officials and relief workers to the inherent self-interest of their policies and their deeply embedded hierarchical assumptions.

# PART I

The Politics of Relief

# 1

## The Politics of Immigration
### Unwanted Wartime Collaborators or Ideal White Settlers?

In the aftermath of the Second World War, DPs constituted an enticing demographic opportunity to replenish a French population diminished by two world wars and a declining birth rate.[1] French attempts to transfer DPs to France were not a charitable enterprise: French planners were mainly interested in healthy and diligent workers able to work in specific fields, notably in French mines and agriculture.[2] Put simply, a number of French policy elites were eager to transform Europe's post-war refugee crisis into an economic and demographic opportunity. But, the question of DP emigration defied consensus in France. Communist decision makers and their ideological fellow travellers on the French Left, particularly numerous within the Ministry of Labour and, to a lesser extent, the newly created Office National d'Immigration (ONI), were strongly opposed to the recruitment of what they regarded as fascist DPs and 'war collaborators'. Thus, despite the early high hopes attached to the transfer of fit and industrious DPs to France and the intense diplomatic negotiations surrounding this, it was not until April 1947 that a coordinated and significant

---

[1] The past decade has witnessed the rise of an impressive new historiography concerning the resettlement of DPs. See, in particular, Andreas Rinke, *Le Grand retour – Die französische Displaced-Persons-Politik (1944–1951)* (Frankfurt am Main: Peter Lang, 2002); Paul-André Rosental, *L'intelligence démographique: sciences et politiques des populations en France (1930–1960)* (Paris: Odile Jacob, 2003), pp. 109–112; Daniel Cohen, *In War's Wake: Europe's Displaced Persons in the Postwar Order* (Oxford: Oxford University Press, 2012); Sylvia Salvatici, 'Le gouvernement anglais et les femmes réfugiées d'Europe après la Seconde Guerre mondiale', *Le mouvement social*, vol. 225, no. 4 (2008), pp. 53–63; Tara Zahra, *The Lost Children: Reconstructing Europe's Families after World War II* (Cambridge, MA: Harvard University Press, 2011), pp. 146–172; Ruth Balint, 'Industry and Sunshine: Australia as Home in the Displaced Persons' Camps of Postwar Europe', *History Australia*, vol. 11, no. 1 (2014), pp. 102–127; Julia Maspero, 'Quand la politique française d'immigration rencontre la question DP en Allemagne occupée. Entre préoccupations nationales et diplomatiques au début de la guerre froide, 1945–1948', in Corine Defrance, Juliette Denis and Julia Maspero (eds.), *Personnes déplacées et guerre froide en Allemagne occupée* (Frankfurt am Main: Peter Lang, 2015), pp. 155–175.

[2] Alexis Spire, 'Les réfugiés, une main-d'œuvre à part? Conditions de séjour et d'emploi, France, 1945–1975', *Revue européenne des migrations internationales*, vol. 20, no. 2 (2004), pp. 13–38.

recruitment scheme was launched in the French zones of Germany and Austria, quickly followed in the summer of 1947 by equivalent efforts in the British and American zones. These initiatives, however, did not put an end to the (often) intense institutional infighting between the Ministries of Foreign Affairs, Labour, Population and Interior and the occupation authorities in the zones over the resettlement of DPs in France. Crucially, this chapter demonstrates that the selection of DPs triggered extensive controversies about how far DPs could or should be assimilated into the nation state and about the presumed superiority or inferiority of various categories of DPs and refugees.

The multiple contradictions in French policies illustrate France's conflicting interests. On the one hand, DPs promised a temporary solution to France's growing demand for workers and a potentially valuable 'blood transfusion' able to counter the menace of long-term stagnation threatening the French nation.[3] De Gaulle himself had identified population growth and immigration as critical policy priorities in the spring of 1945.[4] Introducing young and robust elements from Europe into France's flagging population might go some way to reinvigorating the nation. On the other hand, recruiting DPs on a large scale was a risky diplomatic venture, particularly for those hailing from the territories annexed by the Soviet Union after 1939. Both the Soviet and new communist Polish authorities were demanding the repatriation of their nationals. As far as the recruitment of 'German expellees' was concerned, France was compelled to comply with the demands of British and American occupiers, who thought that German manpower was essential for the industrial reconstruction of Germany. Resettling DPs and German expellees in France was also a perilous domestic political enterprise in the pro-communist context of the post-war Liberation, since the Communist Party presented DPs as 'war collaborators'. After the trauma of war and foreign occupation, the issue of collaboration was a particularly efficient political weapon for French communists. The sense of guilt deriving from the Occupation, the fact that the Communist Party – *the party of the 75,000 martyrs* – emerged from the war draped in national colours, and the catastrophic post-war financial and economic situation all came together to place the communist citadel in a paramount position in French intellectual, political and cultural life.[5] There was more at stake than this political and ideological opposition emerging from within the Ministry of Labour. Beneath the surface of what was ostensibly a

---

[3] On immigration as a blood transfusion, see Elisa Camiscioli, *Reproducing the French Race: Immigration, Intimacy and Embodiment in the Early Twentieth Century* (Durham, NC: Duke University Press, 2009), pp. 83–91.

[4] Charles de Gaulle, *Discours et messages* (Paris: Plon, 1970), p. 530.

[5] Pierre Milza, 'L'année 1947 dans les combats culturels de la guerre froide', in Serge Berstein and Pierre Milza (eds.), *L'année 1947* (Paris: Presses de Sciences Po, 2000), pp. 411–436, 413.

political and ideological opposition to the entry of allegedly 'anti-communist' DPs lay a labyrinth of economic fears, a traditional protectionist reflex, as well as a raft of moral and cultural concerns about their 'assimilability' and 'desirability'. Population experts and policymakers were obsessed with the issue of assimilation. They evaluated the cultural and economic desirability of DPs in terms of nationality, politics, gender, class, religion, profession and age, and their assessments varied widely. Arguments over the recruitment of DPs therefore sat at the juncture of several critical debates about French postwar politics of migration and France's diplomatic strategies in the context of the nascent Cold War.

Multiple factors thus slowed the recruitment of DPs. The diplomatic risk of antagonizing the Polish government played a decreasing role in French calculations, even before the final eviction of the communists from the tripartite coalition in office in May 1947.[6] But factors more closely associated with the French labour market were influential, including employers' reluctance to offer DPs work contracts, the housing shortage and trade unions' efforts to screen foreign migrants as they threatened French workers' leverage in the labour market.[7] The disputes over the transfer of DPs to France must be situated within this extraordinary context of the immediate post-war years, which saw a rapid proliferation of institutions in charge of population planning and migration control.[8] Trade union representatives enjoyed unprecedented access to immigration control by dint of their presence on the Board of Directors of the ONI. Not only did workers' representatives gain unparalleled representation; their expectations of democratic decision-making and free collective bargaining in the workplace were equally unprecedented.[9] Alongside DPs' racial or ethnic traits, trade unionists paid attention to DPs' wartime experiences, the strength of their nationalist sentiments and their professed willingness to 'assimilate' in France. Contradictory perceptions of DPs stemmed from Cold War tensions as well as conflicted memories of the interwar years and the wartime experiences of collaboration and resistance.[10]

---

[6] Maspero, 'Politique française d'immigration', pp. 155–175.
[7] Herrick Chapman, *France's Long Reconstruction: In Search of the Modern Republic* (Cambridge, MA: Harvard University Press, 2018), pp. 41–74.
[8] The provisional government created a new Ministry of Population and Public Health, which replaced the former Ministry of Health. This was quickly followed by a decree in March 1945 establishing a Consultative Committee on Population and the Family, which was originally created in 1939 but subsequently suppressed by Vichy. Six months later, in October 1945, the Institut national d'études démographiques (INED) was founded.
[9] Léon Gani, *Syndicats et Travailleurs immigrés* (Paris: Éditions Sociales, 1972); Adam Steinhouse, *Workers' Participation in Post-Liberation France* (London: Lexington Books, 2001), p. 200.
[10] Peter Lagrou, *The Legacy of Nazi Occupation: Patriotic Memory and National Recovery in Western Europe, 1945–1965* (Cambridge: Cambridge University Press, 2000), p. 6.

Despite this radical institutional redesign of the mechanisms of immigration control, scholars have highlighted continuities between the practices and discourses of the Vichy government and the Republic that followed it.[11] Openly racially motivated initiatives became increasingly indefensible in the wake of Vichy and the use of ethnic or racial criteria was officially banned in the 2 November 1945 ordinance, which equipped France with a comprehensive juridical system to control immigration flows. Yet, the practices of flattening individuals into hermetic and hierarchical groups continued to influence French immigration policies. Racial hierarchies were incorporated in a language of economic productivity, psychological stability, reward for wartime service, and cultural assimilability. In this context, some refugees, notably the Banatais, held a special grip on the French post-war imagination, particularly in the French occupation zones and in the recently recovered regions of Alsace and Lorraine. In Alsace–Lorraine, the regional press campaigned for the admission of Banatais, whose wartime experience was used as a means of rehabilitating the memory of the *Malgré-nous*. A number of observers saw a connection between their own experience of forced incorporation into the German army and that of the Banatais, and, as a result, the Alsatian press labelled them the *Malgré-nous des Balkans* in a play on the Alsatian label *Malgré-nous* or *in spite of ourselves*, which was used to describe those Alsatians and Lorrains forcibly conscripted into the German army. In the French occupation zones of Germany and Austria, Banatais elites presented Banatais refugees as 'ideal migrants'. They reclaimed, in particular, their eighteenth-century French roots, their ancestors having been transferred from Alsace–Lorraine to colonize the Banat by Empress Maria Theresa. Their reclamation of Frenchness was in part driven by their efforts to downplay their participation in Nazi's war crimes and conceal that they had benefited from Hitler's racial policies in Central Europe. The Banatais' story simultaneously epitomized the contradiction of French immigration discourses and the role of migrants themselves in making a positive case for their admission in France.

## Facing a Demographic Emergency

After the First World War, France attracted over a million foreign migrants, who were willing to fill vacant positions in often unattractive and low-paid

[11] Patrick Weil, *La France et ses étrangers* (Paris: Calmann-Lévy, 1991); Maxim Silverman, *Deconstructing the Nation: Immigration, Racism and Citizenship in Modern France* (New York: Routledge, 1992); Vincent Viet, 'La politique de l'immigration entre main d'oeuvre et population', in Berstein and Milza (eds.), *L'année 1947*, pp. 461–475, 462; Karen Adler, *Jews and Gender in Liberation France* (Cambridge: Cambridge University Press, 2003); Maud S. Mandel, *In the Aftermath of Genocide: Armenians and Jews in Twentieth Century France* (London: Duke University Press, 2003), pp. 60–61.

occupations.[12] In 1945, France faced a huge labour shortage again. Reverting to the practice adopted after the First World War, French officials attempted to attract single men to work for short periods of time. In contrast to the 1920s, though, France also hoped to facilitate the entry of *assimilable* foreigners on a long-term basis in order to transfuse fresh blood into its flagging population. Anxious debates about manpower requirements were aggravated by a lingering fear of demographic decline dating from the 1880s, an anxiety that was fuelled by the losses France experienced during the two world wars.[13] This long-running demographic obsession nurtured French aspirations to recruit *assimilable* migrants, judged capable of producing French offspring and being transformed into French citizens. From a demographic and socioeconomic standpoint, DPs constituted an unmatched reservoir of white, European, young, healthy and malleable workers.[14] It was estimated that approximately three-fifths of the DP population was aged between eighteen and forty-five; men were more numerous than women.[15] Collectively, DPs were seen as a potential solution to counter the menace of long-term demographic stagnation threatening the French nation.

European DPs were therefore central to French post-war population politics and discussions about their transfer to France began remarkably early on in the spring of 1945.[16] Anticipating that some DPs, notably those who had voluntarily collaborated with the Nazis, would refuse to return home for fear of retaliation or legal punishment, French authorities engaged in negotiations with their Western Allies.[17] As a member of the Military Mission for German Affairs stated, France needed 'to act quickly' to 'avoid international complications' with the Soviet Union and Eastern European governments.[18] As will become clearer in Chapter 3, the repatriation of French citizens held captive in

---

[12] Mary Dewhurst Lewis, *The Boundaries of the Republic: Migrant Rights and the Limits of Universalism in France, 1918–1940* (Stanford: Stanford University Press, 2007), p. 248.

[13] Rosental, *L'intelligence démographique*, pp. 101–117. Also see Hervé Le Bras, *Marianne et les lapins. L'obsession démographique* (Paris: Hachette, 1991).

[14] MAE, HCRFA, DGAP, 116, Rapport pour la réunion interministérielle des Affaires Allemandes et Autrichiennes du 7.11.1945, 31 October 1945.

[15] MAE, HCRFA, PDR6/869, Note pour M. Rivain, Directeur du Cabinet de l'Ambassadeur de France, HCRFA [undated].

[16] A series of conferences took place in Paris with the representatives of the Direction Générale de la Famille, Ministère du Travail, Ministère de l'Agriculture, the Foreign Office and representatives of UNRRA. UNRRA, S-0523-0645, Dr. W. Langrod to Miss M. L. Gibbons, 27 June 1945.

[17] CAC, Versement 770623, article 83, Raymond Bousquet pour le Ministre des Affaires Etrangères à Ministre du Travail et de la Sécurité Sociale, Emploi en France des travailleurs yougoslaves recrutés en Allemagne, 15 June 1945.

[18] MAE, HCRFA, AP 116, Le Commandant Domergue, Chef des Services Centraux De la Division Travail à Ingénieur en Chef du Génie Maritime Ziegel, 27 June 1945; MAE, HCRFA, PDR1/14, Report, 28 August 1945, p. 11.

the territories ruled by the Soviet Union depended, in part, on the swift repatriation of Soviet nationals. Moreover, the French worried that other European countries might act first, taking 'the cream of the crop' from DP camps. In May 1945, the French government approached UNRRA with an enquiry as 'to the possibility of the immigration of foreign workers from Germany to France'.[19] In June, Gaston Palewski, the director of de Gaulle's personal cabinet, initiated a recruitment operation 'in close liaison with the Army and the Secret Services'.[20] The Military Mission for German Affairs engaged in discussions with SHAEF authorities in the field and the UNRRA European Regional Office.[21] Furthermore, Minister of Labour, Alexandre Parodi, posted a formal request with SHAEF's Major General, Lewis, for the admission of 20,000 miners, 10,000 agricultural workers and 5,000 builders to France, all to be selected from existing DP workers.[22]

These early negotiations were soon echoed at the diplomatic level by the French Foreign Minister, Georges Bidault. On 20 July 1945, Bidault approached both the Military Governor of the British zone, Marshal Montgomery, for the recruitment of a batch of DPs residing in the British zone and the Governor of the American zone, General Eisenhower, for a similar number to be gleaned from the American zone. Three days later, Bidault followed up his initial requests with a letter to General Fraser, the French UNRRA delegate. In these requests, the entry of these workers was considered a 'temporary measure, for the duration of their contracts, namely 6, 9 or 12 months'. The possibility of a longer stay was, however, left open.[23] In the summer of 1945, French authorities seemed, therefore, well on their way to completing the prompt recruitment of DPs. A team of doctors and representatives of the coal industry, the Ministry of Labour and the Ministry of Agriculture were sent to the American zone to prospect DP camps and assess DPs' professional ability, health and physical aptitude.[24] On 15 August, General Eisenhower further authorized the recruitment of 35,000 Polish

---

[19] UNRRA, S-0523-0645, Dr. Langrod to Miss M. L. Gibbons, 'Admission of non French nationals into France for employment. Statement up to the date of the new French request', 19 September 1945.
[20] Rosental, *L'intelligence démographique*, pp. 110–111.
[21] MAE, HCRFA, AP 116, Résumé de la conversation du 11 juillet 1945 entre le Lt-Cl. Szimanski, Détachment SHAEF et le Commandant Domergue; UNRRA, S-0523-0645, Letter from Dr. W. Langrod to Miss M. L. Gibbons, 10 October 1945.
[22] CAC, Versement 770623, article 83, Ministre du Travail et de la Sécurité Sociale à Monsieur le Major General Lewis, chef de la mission de SHAEF, 3 July 1945.
[23] CAC, Versement 770623, article 83, Copy, Ministry of Foreign Affairs, signed Bidault, 20 July 1945.
[24] MAE, HCRFA, AP 116, Rapport confidentiel sur le recrutement des ouvriers polonais en zones Française, Anglaise et Americaine, Dumergue, 16 January 1946.

DPs.[25] Lastly, on 28 August 1945 Bidault enjoined the Military Governor of the French zone, General Koenig, to comply with a policy that he summarized in the following terms: 'Not impeding in any way, and even, insofar as we can, facilitating the repatriation of persons who expressed the desire to do so', but 'taking full account of the economic and demographic necessities of our country in our attitude towards healthy and usable elements that, for some reason, refuse to return home'. Bidault nevertheless introduced a word of caution: 'It is obvious that this second course of action must not appear overtly in the current discussions in Berlin.'[26]

## Diplomatic Strategies in the Context of the Nascent Cold War

Bidault's official injunction illustrates vividly the ambiguities of French policy. Almost from its inception, a number of French officials sought ways to balance the demands of Eastern countries under communist domination with France's pressing labour needs. Yet recruiting DPs, particularly Soviet DPs, was a risky diplomatic venture. Soviet nationals, unlike other DPs, could be forced to return home under the Franco-Soviet Agreement of June 1945.[27] There nevertheless remained considerable confusion regarding DPs hailing from territories annexed by the Soviet Union during the war, notably Eastern Poland and the Baltic states, who objected to repatriation on the ground that the land of their birth had been transformed by a communist takeover. This helps explain why the efforts of the Ministry of Foreign Affairs and occupation authorities in the zones were, in 1946, mainly concentrated on the recruitment of Polish nationals.

Negotiations with Polish authorities proved a particularly difficult affair, occurring at a time when French authorities were maintaining a diplomatic link with both the representatives of the Polish government of London and the communist government of Lublin and then Warsaw. As Julia Maspero has demonstrated, a confusing dialogue between French occupation authorities and representatives of both the London and Warsaw governments lasted until the autumn of 1946 in the French zones.[28] While publicly affirming their commitment to DPs' prompt repatriation to the Warsaw missions, French occupation officials strove, behind the scenes, to recruit the healthiest DPs for

---

[25] MAE, HCRFA, AP 116, Le Ministre Plénipotentiaire Secrétaire Général pour les Affaires Allemandes et Autrichiennes à le Général de Corps d'Armée Koenig, 19 October 1945 [signé de Leusse].

[26] MAE, HCRFA, ADM 40, Copie Télégramme confidentiel, Ministre des Affaires Etrangères à Général Koenig, 28 August 1945.

[27] See Chapter 3.

[28] Julia Maspero, 'La question des personnes déplacées polonaises dans les zones françaises d'occupation en Allemagne et en Autriche: un aspect méconnu des relations franco-polonaises (1945–1949)', *Relations internationales*, vol. 138 (2009), pp. 59–74.

the reconstruction of France.[29] In the spring of 1946, the Warsaw government accepted, in principle, an agreement for the recruitment of DPs from the French zone in compensation for the departure of Polish miners from France.[30] A significant number of Polish workers residing in France did indeed decide to return to Poland between 1945 and 1948, the Liberation prompting a 'fever of return in the Polish mining communities'.[31] In total, France signed three diplomatic agreements with Poland (on 20 February and 28 November 1946, and on 24 February 1948), permitting the return of Polish workers from France to Poland.[32] The return of these Polish workers led the Warsaw government to envisage an agreement on the transfer of Polish DPs to France. Yet, in the spring of 1946, the Warsaw government backtracked and refused to sign a formal agreement with French authorities. Frustrated and eager to accelerate the process of the transfer of Polish DPs to France, the French Foreign Office announced that the French government would carry out its operation without formal approval from the Warsaw government on 30 July 1946.[33] Meanwhile, in Germany, the Central Polish DP committee for the Southern Zone lobbied French authorities to open its doors to Polish DPs. They wrote to Koenig to celebrate the Fourteenth of July and remind France of its tradition of hospitality, recalling the welcome of 'their ancestors' in 1830 and 1863.[34]

French diplomats' efforts to recruit Polish DPs were not solely motivated by French manpower needs in the context of the establishment of the Monnet Plan and the impending repatriation of German POWs.[35] These were also shaped by the necessity of reducing the 'economic burden' of the administration of DPs in the zone and the conviction that German overpopulation constituted an inherent security threat to Europe.[36] In French diplomatic

---

[29] MAE, HCRFA, Direction générale des Affaires politiques, 116, Note de l'Administrateur Général à l'attention de Directeur Général de l'Economie et des Finances et Directeur du Travail, 25 September 1945.

[30] Maspero, 'Politique française d'immigration', p. 161.

[31] Dariusz Jarosz and Maria Pasztor, *Conflits Brûlants de la guerre froide. Les relations franco-polonaises de 1945 à 1954* (Paris: Lavauzelle, 2005), p. 19; CAC, Versement 770623,83, Monsieur R. Poignant, mémoire de stage, L'immigration polonaise dans le Pas-de-Calais, Section Sociale, Mars 1948, ENA, Promotion Nations Unies, 1–107, p. 72.

[32] Janine Ponty, 'Les rapatriements d'ouvriers polonais (1945–1948)', *L'impact de la Seconde Guerre mondiale sur les relations franco-polonaises* (Paris: INALCO, 2000), pp. 125–137, 128.

[33] Maspero, 'Politique française d'immigration', p. 162.

[34] HCRFA, Ambassade de Bonn, 148, Comité Polonais Central pour la Zone Sud à Général Koenig, Fribourg, 14 July 1946.

[35] Vincent Viet, *La France immigrée. Construction d'une politique, 1914–1997* (Paris: Fayard, 1998), p. 147.

[36] MAE, HCRFA, PDR3/5, Situation démographique de la Zone Française d'Occupation en rapport avec les transfers de population, le rapatriement des prisonniers de guerre et des

negotiations with British and American policymakers, the question of the recruitment of Polish DPs was linked to that of German workers. For many French officials, German overpopulation was a root cause of Nazi expansionism. In the zone, French occupation authorities further dreaded that the intermingling of various ethnicities might serve as a breeding ground for rebellion. By the end of the summer of 1945, they grew increasingly frustrated with the delays of the transfer of these DPs.[37] Yet, the dissension between ministers in France in 1946 hampered the launch of the recruitment of DPs.

Immigration policy involved several administrative entities, each driven by their own rationale. In the case of DPs, the Ministry of Foreign Affairs and the military government had their own rationales, which were strongly influenced by France's security needs and the economic imperatives of reducing the costs of their administration in the zone. Alexis Spire has distinguished three other such 'rationales' at work at the national level regarding immigration: Firstly, a demographic rationale was promoted by the Ministry of Population and focused on the search for *assimilable* migrants in order to repopulate France. Secondly, a 'police rationale' was embodied by the Ministry of Interior, which sought to ensure that migrants posed no threat to public order. Finally, a 'manpower rationale' operated within the Ministry of Labour, which tried to reconcile the (often-contradictory) needs of the French economy with the necessity of safeguarding the interests of the existing French national workforce.[38]

## Obsession Assimilatrice

Debates over the recruitment of DPs pointed to what Paul-André Rosental has famously termed France's *obsession assimilatrice*. This obsession went hand in hand with an identity-related nationalism, which justified all sorts of ethnic taxonomy.[39] Deep-seated anxieties about France's demographic decline inspired population experts to establish a pseudo-scientific hierarchy of foreigners, in which some ethnicities were judged 'more' capable of producing French offspring and being transformed into French citizens. Long-held assumptions about the racial inferiority of non-whites and fears about miscegenation continued to influence population discourses among the important

---

réfugiés, le recrutement de main d'oeuvre pour la France [undated; 1947?]; MAE, Affaires Economiques et financières, Affaires Allemandes et autrichiennes, 1944–1949, 131, Note sur le Problème démographique allemand, Direction générale des affaires administratives et sociales, 8 February 1947.

[37] MAE, HCRFA, PDR1/14, Report, 28 August 1945, p. 11.
[38] Alexis Spire, *Etrangers à la carte. L'administration de l'immigration en France (1945–1975)* (Paris: Grasset, 2005), p. 140.
[39] Rosental, *L'intelligence démographique*, pp. 111–112.

pro-familialist and natalist lobby within the Ministry of Population and the newly created *Institut National d'Etudes démographiques* (INED). Created in October 1945 and closely linked to the Ministry of Population, the INED became the key instrument of 'populationist' research and policy, placing scientists and scientific planning at the centre of government thinking. INED demographers and population experts evaluated the cultural and economic desirability of migrants in terms of age, gender, profession, race and class, with some groups being deemed more culturally close to 'Frenchness' than others.[40]

George Mauco, the secretary of the Consultative Committee on Population and the Family, was arguably the most important proponent of a 'radical' *ethno-racialisante* policy of selection, based on the idea that some migrants were unassimilable (Jews and Arabs in particular). His views echoed the scientific racism of the Vichy years.[41] According to him, parents shaped children's subconscious at a young age, making it almost impossible for children to escape their 'ethnic determination'. Such discourses were reminiscent of late-nineteenth-century theories that nations were the products of a process of heredity, fixing certain psychological characters in a group of people.[42] Mauco was not alone in attributing negative psychological characteristics to migrants. *Enarque* Robert Poignant, for instance, also observed that one should not underestimate the *emotional element* in the Polish character: 'In the Polish soul, feelings of anger, enthusiasm, attachment and depression reach levels that we [as French] do not know.'[43] Eastern European DPs, like Jewish DPs (mainly from Poland), did not rank highly in this *ethno-racialisante* hierarchy of desirability. Germans, on the other hand, were rated amongst the most desirable candidates for immigration to France, alongside

---

[40] Alexis Spire, 'Un régime dérogatoire pour une immigration convoitée. Les politiques françaises et italiennes d'immigration/emigration après 1945', in *Studi Emigrazione/Migration Studies*, vol. 146 (2002), pp. 309-323; Amelia Lyons, *The Civilizing Mission in the Metropole. Algerian Families and the French Welfare State during Decolonization* (Stanford, CA: Stanford University Press, 2013), p. 35.

[41] On Georges Mauco and his role in the Consultative Committee see notably Patrick Weil, 'Racisme et discrimination dans la politique Française de l'immigration', pp. 77-102; Weil, 'Georges Mauco, expert en immigration: Ethnoracisme pratique et antisémitisme fielleux', in Pierre-André Taguieff (ed.), *L'antisémitisme de plume 1940-1944* (Paris: Berg International, 1999), pp. 267-276; For a recent reappraisal of Mauco's role see Greg Burgess, 'The Demographers' Moment: Georges Mauco, Immigration and Racial Selection in Liberation France, 1945-1946', *French History and Civilization*, vol. 4 (2011), pp. 167-177.

[42] Glenda Sluga, *The Nation, Psychology, and International Politics, 1870-1919* (Basingstoke: Palgrave Macmillan, 2006), p. 66.

[43] CAC, Versement 770623,83, Monsieur R. Poignant, mémoire de stage, L'immigration polonaise dans le Pas-de-Calais, Section Sociale, Mars 1948, ENA, Promotion Nations Unies, 1-107, p. 37.

'Nordic' migrants such as Scandinavians, Finns, Danes, Irish, English, Belgians and Swiss nationals.[44]

If this right-wing racism and radical demographic injunctions were progressively swept away within the Ministry of Population, demographers continued to exert pressure to take 'the human factor' into account informally. Patrick Weil has demonstrated how a handful of councillors of states, who were former resistance fighters, managed to remove ethnic selection from the official entry criteria for migrants in the ordinance passed on 2 November 1945.[45] Yet ethnic origins were incorporated into a sophisticated language of economic productivity (which took into account migrants' health, age and professional qualifications), gender (the Ministry of Population advocated the entry of more single male workers to compensate for the excess of French women of marriageable age) and psychological stability.[46] Just as unmarried mothers were offered little, if any, opportunity to emigrate, people aged over forty-five had little prospect of passing through the screening of labour migrants. Young people with elderly dependents were also advised to separate from them, a suggestion that, quite understandably, revived traumatic memories of wartime separations.

In a report entitled *Des Français pour la France* (French for France), pediatrician Robert Debré and population expert Alfred Sauvy argued that France could not rise from the destruction 'with the weakness of the elderly'; it needed instead the *élan de la jeunesse* to undertake bold reforms.[47] But, this youth needed to be controlled and, as far as migrants were concerned, carefully selected. Debré and Sauvy included ethno-racial categorizing as a criterion for selecting migrants, as well as age and professional skills. Debré and Sauvy's report has been extensively studied as it contained ethnic stereotyping and prejudices, informed in part by memories of the sometimes-difficult integration of migrant workers during the interwar years.[48] According to them, 'Slavic people' – by which they meant Czechs, Serbs, Poles and Hungarians – were fairly well integrated into French society. '*Assimilation* with its share of intellectual and physical adaptation came easily', although Polish life continued to be determined by Polish priests, nuns, teachers, societies, sports and national food.[49] In general, pro-natalists tended to value pious Polish Catholic sentiments and their strong sense of family and

---

[44] Rosental, *L'intelligence démographique*, Note 40, pp. 311–312.
[45] Patrick Weil, *La France et ses étrangers. L'aventure d'une politique de l'immigration de 1938 à nos jours* (Paris: Folio, 2004), pp. 75–81.
[46] Rosental, *L'intelligence démographique*, p. 114.
[47] Robert Debré and Alfred Sauvy, *Des Français pour la France. Le problème de la population* (Paris: Gallimard, 1946), p. 9.
[48] Ibid., p. 93.
[49] Ibid., pp. 227–228, 94.

prolific birth rates. But Polish migrants' ostentatious demonstration of their Catholic devotion in the interwar years contributed to their stigmatization by French miners' groups in the north-east of France.[50] While left-leaning French workers saw themselves as anti-clerical and *militant* (political activists), they associated Polish workers with employers and malign clerical influence.[51] Dispersion of Polish migrants within the territor was thus considered essential to their assimilation. 'Nothing is more unfortunate ... than these colonies of Poles in the North or East of France.'[52]

In summary, Population and Public Health Minister Robert Prigent endorsed the selection of healthy, young and 'culturally assimilable' candidates among DPs. Former member of *Jeunesse Ouvrière Chrétienne* (JOC), a Catholic workers' youth movement, Prigent was convinced that Polish DPs could help restore France's 'abandoned villages and revive dying lands'.[53] He saw Polish DPs as a long-term demographic solution, which might offset the depopulation of the French countryside (*les campagnes françaises*).[54] His views were reminiscent of interwar theories on agricultural colonization, which championed the entry of migrant families, which would be settled in rural areas either as tenant farmers or landowners instead of the recruitment of single male workers on temporary work contracts.[55] Rural life was preferable for the integration and *assimilation* of Polish workers when compared to an urban and industrialized environment.[56] From a demographic standpoint, DP and German children were the most valued of all, their youth promising better prospects for seamless integration into French society.

## The 'Value' of DP Children

Tara Zahra has shown that French planners viewed Europe's refugee children as a rich 'human treasure', easily transformable into French citizens.[57] Not only did

---

[50] Gérard Noiriel, *Le creuset français. Histoire de l'immigration XIXe-XXe siècle* (Paris: Seuil, 1988), pp. 166–167.

[51] Janine Ponty, *Polonais méconnus. Histoire des travailleurs immigrés en France dans l'entre-deux-guerres* (Paris: Publications de la Sorbonne, 1988), p. 153. On how the presence of Polish priests could be an obstacle to assimilation, see Marion Fontaine, 'La Polonité face à la sécularisation dans le monde minier lensois', Patrick Weil (ed.), *Politiques de la laïcité en France au XXe siècle* (Paris: PUF, 2007) pp. 327–351.

[52] Debré and Sauvy, *Des Français pour la France*, p. 231.

[53] Cohen, *In War's Wake*, p. 104.

[54] CAC, Versement 770623, article 83, Le Ministre de l'Agriculture au Ministre du Travail, 23 August 1945.

[55] Ponty, *Polonais méconnus*, p. 241.

[56] Spire, *Etrangers à la carte*, p. 140.

[57] Zahra, *Lost Children*. Also see Fabrice Virgili, *Naître ennemi. Les enfants de couples franco-allemands nés pendant la Seconde Guerre mondiale* (Paris: Payot, 2009); Rainer Gries, 'Les Enfants d'Etat' Französische Besatzungskinder in Deutschland', in Barbara-

the French implement a plan to 'repatriate' all children born to French–German couples in wartime and occupied Germany, but a number of them also tried to transfer Polish and Belgian 'abandoned children' to France.[58] These plans to solicit the emigration of German children contrasted sharply with the treatment of half-German children in the aftermath of the First World War, who were often considered scarred by the traits of their 'barbaric' German fathers.[59] Yves Denéchère argues that French authorities established a policy of 'abandon/ adoption' in their zone, their goal being to monitor the abandonment by their German mothers of any children with French fathers and to organize their subsequent adoption in France.[60] This policy also applied to babies born out of union between German women and French occupation soldiers. This phenomenon constituted the 'first great movement of adoption in France', preceding those following the Korean and Vietnam wars.

French efforts to transport orphans and abandoned children from Germany to France were, in part, motivated by humanitarian considerations. Promises of a more just society were born of the resistance, and invocation of children's suffering was powerful.[61] Popular representation of the arrival of the 'Buchenwald boys' to France, half of the one thousand Eastern European Jewish teenagers found when the camp was liberated, illustrates vividly the potency of this egalitarian and humanitarian rhetoric. In the French press, it was interpreted as a sign of the return of French liberal and republican political values after the trauma of the Holocaust, even though reports often stripped it of its Jewish specificity.[62]

---

Stelzl-Marx and Silke Satjukow (eds.), *Besatzungskinder: Die Nachkommen alliierter Soldaten in Österreich und Deutschland* (Vienna: Böhlau Verlag, 2015), pp. 380–407; Katherine Rossy, 'Faceless and Stateless: French Occupation Policy toward Women and Children in Postwar Germany (1945-1949)', in Philip E. Muehlenbeck (ed.), *Gender, Sexuality and the Cold War. A Global Perspective* (Nashville: Vanderbilt University Press, 2017), pp. 15–34.

[58] Translation, Tracing of Children, Ministry of Prisoners of War, Deportees and Refugees, Direction of Captivity, Paris, 27 September 1945, 82516961/64, ITS Digital Archives.

[59] Ruth Harris, '"The Child of the Barbarian": Rape, Race and Nationalism in France during the First World War', *Past and Present*, vol. 141, no. 1 (1993), pp. 170-206.

[60] Yves Denéchère, 'Des adoptions d'Etat: les enfants de l'occupation française en Allemagne', *Revue d'Histoire Moderne et Contemporaine*, vol. 57, no. 2 (2010), pp. 159-179; 'Vers une histoire de l'adoption internationale en France', *Vingtième Siècle. Revue d'Histoire*, vol. 102, (2009), pp. 117-129. Anne Laure Briatte is currently undertaking a research project on the lives of these German mothers. ('The damages of military occupation through the lens of gender. The lives of mothers of "children of the occupation" in the French zone of occupation.')

[61] Daniella Doron, 'Lost Children and Lost Childhood. Memory in Post-Holocaust France', in Seàn Hand and Steven Katz (eds.), *Post-Holocaust France and the Jews 1945-1955* (New York: New York University Press, 2015), pp. 85–117, 88.

[62] Daniella Doron, *Jewish Youth and Identity in Postwar France. Rebuilding Family and Nation* (Bloomington: Indiana University Press, 2015), pp. 43–44.

*Pierre, dit Bamboula, né à Heidelberg, quelqu'un l'adoptera-t-il?*

**Fig. 1.1** 'Pierre, also called "Bamboula", born in Heidelberg, will someone adopt him?', in Haut Commissariat de la République française en Allemagne, Service des Personnes Déplacées, *Sept ans d'activité en faveur des personnes déplacées en zone française d'occupation, 1945–1952*, rapport dactylographié et illustré [undated], [Bibliothèque du Ministère des Affaires Etrangères, Direction des Archives], p. 99. Note: This is a highly racialized term and it is not my intent to cause offence by including it. Nevertheless, I have left the term attached to the original photograph in order to illustrate the racial elements of French post-war policies of adoption.

Transferring children was not only a selfless humanitarian gesture, however: in general, only healthy and psychological stable children were admitted and white children were more likely to be transferred to France than the so-called 'coloured-mixed' children. The resettlement of children born out of union between French colonial occupation soldiers and German women met serious reservations in France, as this official publication and the denigrating nickname suggest (Fig. 1.1).

This 'adoption' policy provoked understandable anxieties among Allied child welfare specialists, who feared that the French were proposing an 'extremely flexible interpretation of national status' and what it meant to be 'of French heritage'.[63] A child specialist pointed out that 'in addition to French children, or part French children, there is some indication that the French are moving children of other nationalities into France for adoption'; Polish and

---

[63] Confidential report on conferences on unaccompanied children held in Berlin March 15–22 1946, Eileen Blackey, Child Care Consultant, pp. 5–6, 6.1.2, 82489046 – 47, ITS Digital Archives.

Belgian children were mentioned particularly in this respect.[64] The activities of Anne Marie de la Morlais, who worked for the PDR service in Berlin as a welfare worker, wrought tensions between UNRRA and French authorities:

> Madame de la Morlais reports that there are 4,000 French children in Berlin and approximately 100,000 French children still in Germany. This, of course, is interpreting a French child to be any child with even a small percentage of French blood. Madame de la Morlais has set up what amounts to a flourishing social agency in Berlin. She has 600 cases of German girls, wives of Frenchmen, who are in Berlin with their children. These mothers will be permitted to go to France [...]. She is very active in contacting all German officials and German institutions to determine the whereabouts of any French children. Apparently, she has become quite well known in Berlin and not infrequently German girls with illegitimate children come to her to give up the children. If she finds abandoned children on the streets or in parks, or if on a visit to a hospital she finds children who are not getting proper care [...] she removes the child and sees to it that he gets proper care, with the idea, of course, that he will eventually go to France.[65]

The chosen children were issued with new French 'certificates of origin' to replace their German birth certificates. These new certificates erased all record of the children's origins and birthplace. The infants were then given new French names and assigned to French adoptive families.[66] Estimated numbers of such children who were 'repatriated' to France for adoption vary between 384 and 961.[67]

The need to 'depopulate' Germany, combined with the belief that young Germans could easily be assimilated into France, prompted the transfer of German children to France. This was also the case for German adults. After the Second World War, German migrants were often considered as desirable migrants because of their perceived work ethic. In diplomatic negotiations, Raymond Bousquet, a representative of the French Foreign Office, repeatedly explained to his British counterparts that the Germans were better workers

---

[64] UNRRA Central Headquarters for Germany, Minutes of Inter-zonal conference on Child Search and repatriation–16–18 October 1946, p. 10, 6.1.2, 82489967, ITS Digital Archives.
[65] Confidential report on conferences on unaccompanied children held in Berlin, 15–22 March 1946, Eileen Blackey, Child Care Consultant (p. 7), 6.1.2, 82489048, ITS Digital Archives.
[66] After the creation of the Federal Republic of Germany, French authorities' desire to prevent problems from cropping up in the future led to the removal of the administrative traces of this policy from German archives. Denéchère, 'Des adoptions d'Etat'.
[67] Denéchère, 'Des adoptions d'Etat'; Tara Zahra, '"A Human Treasure": Europe's Displaced Children between Nationalism and Internationalism', *Post-war Reconstruction in Europe. Past and Present*, vol. 210, supplement 6 (2011), pp. 332–350, 339.

than the Slavs, who were difficult to assimilate.[68] According to British sources, he even argued that, 'from a security point of view', it was preferable to leave badly assimilated Poles in Germany than to transfer them to other Western countries. He recommended the installation of Slavs in Germany near the French frontier and the emigration of Germans to France.[69] The British diplomat Sir George Rendel doubted whether this proposal would add to European security, especially considering the ways in which the *Volksdeutsche* had served before the war as an outpost for Nazi infiltration.[70] Yet, for some French observers, the perceived productivity of German refugees outweighted the issue of their wartime past. These ambiguities of the French position are vividly illustrated in the debates over the recruitment of Banatais.

### Banatais Politics: De-Germanizing and Re-Frenchifying Refugees?

In the post-war era, Banatais elites tried to shift between German and French identities: their reclamation of Frenchness was in part driven by their efforts to conceal their collaboration with the Nazis. Many Banatais bore physical evidence of their collaboration with the Nazi regime: an SS tattoo, received upon their first enlistment, which indicated their blood group.[71] A French security report noted that '[t]here is almost no family without at least one member that participated in SS organisations'.[72] As with other expellees' organizations in post-war Germany and Austria, Banatais often accentuated the mistakes of the post–World War One settlement, by presenting themselves as victims of the Treaty of Trianon, while downplaying and relativizing their participation in Nazi Germany's crimes.[73] They invoked the Francophile activities of the Banatais delegation at the Paris Peace Conference in 1919, which lobbied for the creation of an autonomous Lorrainer province ('Neu-Lothringen') under the protection of the French state. They also insisted on to the work of Etienne Frecôt, president of the *Association des descendants*

---

[68] NA, FO/945/470, Note of informal discussion in the office of Monsieur Bousquet, Ministry of Foreign Affairs, on the subject of German emigration, on 30 April 1947.
[69] NA, FO/945/470, Minutes of Anglo-French discussions on the recruitment in the British and French Zones of Austria and Germany of DP for work in France and in the UK, meeting held at the Quay d'Orsay, 28 April 1947.
[70] Ibid.
[71] AN, F/7/16116, Note d'information sur l'immigration des 'Banatais' en France, 23 November 1948; MAE, Haut Commissariat de la République Française en Autriche, AUT, PDR3/99, Note sur la mission de M. Taddei en Autriche, 30 August 1948.
[72] AN, F/7/16116, Note d'information sur l'immigration des 'Banatais' en France, 23 November 1948.
[73] MAE, HCRFA, AP 116, *DP Express,* 22 September 1945; For other expellees' organizations, see Pertti Ahonen, *After the Expulsion: West Germany and Eastern Europe 1945–1990* (Oxford: Oxford University Press, 2003), p. 46.

*d'anciens colons français du Banat* in the interwar period.[74] In a leaflet entitled 'Is the Banatais a National-Socialist?', the author wrote that the majority of ordinary Banatais did not participate in and profit from the persecution and deportation of Jews, but, on the contrary, provided their Jewish neighbours with essential food, including butter, meat, eggs and cheese. The report reads: 'I would not go as far as claiming that they did it for their love of the Jews, Banatais were indifferent to them, but because they needed to sell off their products.'[75] In 1946, jurist Emil Botis published *Recherches sur la population Française du Banat*, in which he pointed out that the behaviour of the majority of Banatais was not worse than that of the majority of French people, as even in France some people succumbed to Nazi antisemitic propaganda.[76]

Banatais representatives invoked French loyalties, based on the fact that their ancestors from Alsace–Lorraine had colonized the Banat in the eighteenth century at the desire of Empress Maria Theresa. Banatais intellectuals used the disciplines of geography, biology, sociology and history to buttress pseudo-scientific claims of their French origins.[77] Botis rejected, for instance, the common definition of ethnicity based on the mother tongue and common assimilation of the Banatais into the *Swabian* ethnic group.[78] According to him, Hungarian and Serbian intellectuals included anyone 'speaking German under this label'.[79] He claimed that the Banatais borderland was denied its *Wilsonian* right to national self-determination after the First World War.[80] In 1919, the Allies had insisted on the principle of self-determination for a settlement in Eastern Europe, but this principle was not systematically applicable in a region characterized by centuries of migrations and intermixing of ethnic groups.[81] For Botis, Banatais identity remained (almost) unconquered, even though the Banatais lost their French mother tongue as a result of the

---

[74] MAE, AUT, PDR 3/99, Traduction: Retour des Banatiens dans leur pays d'origine, en France, Bureau Central du Comité des Français du Banat [Translation of a document dating from 11 August 1948 and signed by J. Lamesfeld]; [Traduction de l'Allemand] Le Banatien est il national-socialiste?; Emil Botis, *Recherches sur la population Française du Banat* (Timisoara: unknown publisher, 1946), p. 34; J. Lamesfeld, *Von Osterreich nach Frankreich. Die Banater Aktion und Robert Schuman* (Salzburg: Donauschwäbische Verlagsgesellschaft, 1973), p. 38.
[75] MAE, AUT, PDR3/99, Traduction de l'Allemand, Le Banatien est il national-socialiste?
[76] Botis, *Recherches sur la population Française*, p. 40.
[77] Emmerich Reitter, 'Considérations générales sur le problème des minorités allemandes du Sud-Est européen et spécialement la question des Alsaciens et Lorrains du Banat', 1945; Botis, *Recherches sur la population Française*; Série d'articles publiés dans les dernières nouvelles du Haut Rhin.
[78] Botis, *Recherches sur la population Française*, p. 16.
[79] Ibid., p. 16.
[80] Ibid., p. 6.
[81] Peter Jackson, *Beyond the Balance of Power: France and the Politics of National Security in the Era of the First World War* (Cambridge: Cambridge University Press, 2013).

German 'drive to the East' and Austro-Hungarian efforts to Magyarize the inhabitants of this region. Yet, except from the distant memory of a French past in the north-western region of the Banat, very few French traces remained except in their cuisine habit: they still cooked '*calete*' (from the French *galette*) and ate frogs.[82] Moreover, contrary to the claims made by Banatais elites to French authorities, far from all the refugees from Banat were infused with strong pro-French sentiments. The response of ordinary Banatais to emigration in France often stands in stark contrast to their elites' campaign to be transferred to the old 'motherland'.[83]

Many French occupation officials were aware that some of the Banatais had enthusiastically collaborated with the Nazis and that their claims to Frenchness were now tentative at best.[84] Nevertheless, French officials offered them support and advocated their transfer to France. In a telegram dating from June 1946, General Koenig spat out his real opinion: 'These people are *sagouins* [filthy pigs] who only remember France because they are expelled from the Banat. Yet, it is expedient to support them so I give 5,000 marks for the Munich Council.'[85] General Koeltz expressed similar views, arguing that it was 'a well-known fact that these elements were in previous generations the pioneers of Germanism in the Balkans'.[86] Despite that admission, many believed that it was important to give them a special status of 'French from the Banat' to set them apart from the rest of the DP population. General Administrator Emile Laffon recognized that the Banatais' political sentiments were profoundly Nazi, but that, their dubious past notwithstanding, they constituted a particularly 'advanced' and skilful population who had

[82] Smaranda Vultur (ed.), *Germanii din Banat prin povestirile lor* (Paideia: Bucuresti, 2000), pp. 249, 253; quoted in Irina Martin, *Contested Frontiers in the Balkans. Habsburg and Ottoman Rivalries in Eastern Europe* (London: IBT Tauris, 2013), p. 145.
[83] AN, F/7/16116, L'inspecteur de Police Villeneuve en Autriche à Monsieur le Commissaire de Police G. Alexinsky, délégué du Ministère de l'Intérieur, 8 December 1948.
[84] See for instance: CAC Fontainbleau, Versement 770623, 83, Lettre de Corps d'Armée Koeltz à Général de Corps d'Armée Koenig, 3 November 1945; L'administrateur Général Laffon à Secrétaire Général du Comité Interministériel pour les Affaires Allemandes et Autrichiennes, 19 November 1945; Lettre du Sous-Secrétaire d'Etat, Commissaire aux Affaires Allemandes et Autrichiennes à Général Koenig, 25 August 1946. As Mirna Zakic has recently demonstrated, '[t]here [was] no evidence of marked individual or group dissent with Nazi policies within the Banat *Volksdeutsche* community during the war'. In fact, the 'Documents indicative of some individual *Volksdeutsche*'s ambivalence toward or distaste for those policies which directly benefited the *Volksdeutsche* community were produced after the war, and usually involved implicit or explicit exculpation. Mirna Zakić, 'The Price of Belonging to the Volk: Volksdeutsche, Land Redistribution and Aryanization in the Serbian Banat, 1941–1944', *Journal of Contemporary History*, vol. 49, no. 2 (2014), pp. 320–340, 323.
[85] MAE, Bonn, 152, Fiche d'instance, population du Banat de Temesvar, 5 June 1946.
[86] MAE, Bonn, 152, Général de Corps d'Armée Koeltz au Général de Corps d'armée Koenig, 3 November 1945.

transformed the Banat into the granary of Central Europe.[87] He further argued that Banatais should be distinguished from other *Volksdeutsche*, as the majority of them resisted Nazi temptations in the interwar years and only succumbed to Nazi propaganda in the wartime period, due to the Nazis' violent coercive methods.[88] For Koeltz, it was, however, necessary to re-educate and denazify the Banatais before accepting them in France.[89] Specialists also recognized the necessity to prepare their 'welcome' in France – through press campaign recalling their French origins.[90]

Refugees from the Banat, who had fled the advancing Red Army or had been evacuated by the Nazis, were often described as more productive and highly skilled, whether because of superior training or innate ability, than supposedly 'lazy' Polish and Ukrainian DPs. In August 1946, French authorities estimated that there were 22,000 refugees who claimed to be 'French from the Banat' in Austria and 11,000 in Germany, including 8,800 in the American zone and 2,300 in the British zone.[91] The exact number of these French Banatais is, however, very difficult to assess. Banatais were not recognized as an official national or ethnic group by the Allied authorities and therefore did not appear as such in the statistics produced by them or by UNRRA.[92] Banatais committees tended to further exaggerate figures.[93] These Banatais elites presented Banatais refugees as 'ideal migrants'. They portrayed themselves as healthy, hard-working and culturally and economically valuable migrants.[94] They boasted specifically

---

[87] CAC Fontainbleau, Versement 770623, 83, Administrateur Général Laffon à Secrétaire Général du Comité Interministériel pour les Affaires Allemandes et Autrichiennes, 19 November 1945.

[88] Ibid.

[89] CAC Fontainbleau, Versement 770623, 83, Général de Corps d'Armée Koeltz à Général de Corps d'Armée Koenig, 3 November 1945.

[90] MAE, NUOI, 297, L'émigration des Alsatiens et Lorrains du Banat de Temesvar, 29 March 1947.

[91] CAC Fontainbleau, Versement 770623, 83, Données statistiques actuelles sur la population du Banat, 14 August 1946.

[92] Banatais were either registered according to their previous state citizenship or counted as *Volksdeutsche*.

[93] In January 1946, Banatais elites estimated that there were between 30,000 and 100,000 Banatais in Austria. MAE, HCRFA, AP 116, Rapport préliminaire sur les Alsaciens-Lorrains du Banat de Temesvar actuellement en Bavière et en Autriche, 4 January 1946; In September 1945, they claimed that there were between 40 and 60,000 *Banatais* in postwar Germany and Austria; CAC Fontainbleau, Versement 770623, 83, Bureau des Lorrains et Alsaciens du Banat, au Haut Commandement Militaire Français, Munich, 20 September 1945; Also see AN, F/7/16116, Note de Renseignements concernant le 'Comité des Français du Banat' dont le siege se trouve à Colmar, 19, Grand' rue, transmise le 10 Janvier 1951, à Monsieur le Directeur de la réglementation, Ministère de l'Intérieur.

[94] CAC Fontainbleau, Versement 770623, 83, François Pfeiffer, Memoire au sujet de la culture du chanvre et de son élaboraiton; Dr. Emeric Reitter, Le rôle des Colons Alsaciens et Lorrains dans l'évolution agricole en Banat.

about their high moral standards and law-abiding nature. A leaflet read: 'The Banater woman can be considered as a true example of high morality. Conjugal infidelity is almost unknown, illegitimate children seen as scandalous. A *fiancée* who has lost her virginity cannot wear a bridal crown. These are, of course, old-fashioned views, but there are important to our people.'[95] While highlighting the high morality of Banatais woman, they insisted on the working ethos of Banatais men. They often recalled the gigantic efforts produced by their ancestors to turn infertile soil into productive soil, notably the work of the Comte Claude Florimont Mercy in the eighteenth century.[96] Yet the biography of this comte Mercy was also used during the Nazi occupation as an example of a *Lorrainer* who had championed German culture in the Banat.

Banatais elites' lobbying activities must be understood in the dire context of the post-war period.[97] Refugees from the Banat arrived to overcrowded and war-ravaged territories and faced the resentment of the local population, which was understandably reluctant to share their scarce resources with foreigners.[98] The situation was arguably worst in Austria, where the majority of the Banatais had settled temporarily. Austria's status as a victim of Nazi aggression absolved its government of the legal and financial obligations towards them which were imposed on Germany by the Potsdam Agreement.[99] As a result, the government had no obligation to shelter *Volksdeutsche* and provide them with basic social rights. Moreover, the Potsdam Agreement did not regulate the status of German refugees from Yugoslavia, Romania and Bulgaria, who therefore could not be 'repatriated' to Germany like other *Volksdeutsche*. To make things worse, they ranked lower in post-war Austrian ethnic taxonomies than Sudeten Germans and expellees from the Bohemian lands.[100]

In response to this situation, Banatais representatives created committees and tried to construct a common and binding identity. This reclamation of Frenchness was perhaps a way to normalize conditions and relieve refugees from monotonous daily life. Peter Gatrell has argued that, throughout the twentieth century, 'refugees have helped to fashion themselves by recourse to history', i.e. refugees use the past to express their predicament and articulate

---

[95] MAE, AUT, PDR3/99, Traduction de l'Allemand, Le Banatien est il national-socialiste?
[96] CAC Fontainbleau, Versement 770623, 83, 'Recolonisation' in *DP Express*, 22 September 1945; Données statistiques sur la colonisation du Banat au XVIII siècle', 15 August 1946.
[97] Lamesfeld, *Von Osterreich nach Frankreich*, p. 8.
[98] Ahonen, *After the Expulsion*, p. 24; Zahra, 'Prisoners of the Postwar: Expellees, Displaced Persons and Jews in Austria after World War II', *Austrian History Yearbook*, 41 (2010), pp. 191–215, 194.
[99] Zahra, 'Prisoners of the Postwar', p. 194; Lamesfeld, *Von Osterreich nach Frankreich*, p. 38.
[100] Zahra, 'Prisoners of the Postwar', p. 200.

their collective action.[101] Throughout history, the Banatais developed multi-layered identities.[102] In the post-war era, they were able to shift between French and German identities depending on circumstances. But these efforts also represented an astute political and diplomatic action, enabling them to downplay their own participation in the Nazi war for *Lebensraum*. Two Banatais committees became particularly prominent in the immediate post-war months. In Bavaria, Dr Emmerich Reitter, a former lawyer and member of the Romanian parliament, and his son-in-law, Dr François Buding, created the Group for Alsatians and Lorrainers of the Banat [*Groupe des Alsaciens et des Lorrains du Banat*].[103] In June 1945, in a memorandum to the French government, Reitter insisted: 'We do not want to form a national minority in France, but *really* we want to get our French citizenship back with all its obligations and rights.'[104] In Austria, Johann Lamesfeld, a former civil servant, created the Committee for the French of the Banat [*Comité des Français du Banat*], later renamed Central Committee for Alsatians and Lorrainers of the Banat [*Comité Central des Alsaciens et Lorrains du Banat*].[105] In his published memoirs, Johann Lamesfeld recounted his journey from his village, Blumenthal (Maşloc) in the Romanian Banat, to Austria with his horse, cattle and family, and his fears of deportation to the Soviet Union. Having heard about the activities of the Romanian Senator Reitter in Germany, he decided to create a committee to protect his countrymen from robbery and kidnapping.[106]

Despite evidence of complicity with the crimes of the Third Reich, Banatais elites gained the favour of several French occupation officials, who invoked leniency towards them.[107] The French diplomat Jacques Tarbé de Saint-Hardouin highlighted that Reitter's attempts to *re-Frenchify* Banatais were

---

[101] Peter Gatrell, *The Making of the Modern Refugee* (Oxford: Oxford University Press, 2013), p. 12.

[102] Adriana Babeți and Cécile Kovácsházy (eds.), *Le Banat, un Eldorado aux confins*, Cultures d'Europe centrale, hors-série N. 4 (2007).

[103] CAC Fontainbleau, Versement 770623, 83, Lettre du Commandant P. Sorbac, à Monsieur le Colonel, chef de la MMFL, 15 September 1945.

[104] For Austria: MAE, AUT, PDR 3/99, Traduction, Dr. Emmerich Reitter, Des Alsaciens et des Lorrains du Banat, Circulaire, 15 January 1946; For Germany: MAE, Bonn 152, A. Poignant, Note relative aux Souabes du Banat, 3 January 1946.

[105] AN, F/7/16116, Note de Renseignements concernant le 'Comité des Français du Banat' dont le siège se trouve à Colmar, 19, Grand' rue, transmise le 10 Janvier 1951, à Monsieur le Directeur de la réglementation, Ministère de l'Intérieur.

[106] Lamesfeld, *Von Osterreich nach Frankreich*, p. 12. In the Romanian Banat, his fellowmen in age of work were deported to the Soviet Union; In the Yugoslav Banat, they were interned in camps irrespective of their ages or whether they were guilty of crimes. Martin, *Contested Frontiers in the Balkans*, pp. 143–144.

[107] MAE, HCRFA, Ambassade de Bonn, 152, R. A. Lebon, Chief French Liason Officer, Note 'Banat de Temesvar' [undated].

tendentious.[108] Yet, Banatais' displays of devotion and allegiance to France's campaign fitted into the vision of France (as *historical land of asylum, espoir des petites nations*) French officials wanted to promote. French Foreign Ministry staff and occupation officials, many of whom were Gaullists, were particularly sensitive about issues of prestige and the manner in which France was represented internationally. During a visit of the Funk-Kaserne, a French observer noted 'how it was moving for him to hear in Munich, the cradle of Nazism, these children reading seriously the French language and welcoming me with a heartfelt *Marseillaise*'.[109] Banatais were drawn into the orbit of French cultural diplomacy in Germany and Austria.[110] In reinventing their *Frenchness*, Banatais were promoting France in the Third Reich's ruins. Banatais' campaign fitted with the French strategy of cultural expansion, 'French radiance' (*rayonnement culturel*), a substitute for France's faded political and diplomatic weight in the international arena.[111] Although Banatais received more financial and material help from French authorities than other DP groups, their transfer to France was, however, put on hold until 1947, like that of the DPs. On the domestic front, as Interior Ministry official Pages later explained, 'it seemed difficult to imagine that the French government could explain [in such a way that it would be understood to the French population] that there were different kinds of SS and that the Banatais were flawless SS'.[112] Ministerial infighting was also to play a critical role in blocking their recruitment. In order to fully grasp the reasons behind the delays that affected the launch of the Banatais' and DPs' recruitment schemes, we need to return to the results of the October 1945 election at the Constituent Assembly.

## Unwanted 'Fascists'

By the end of October 1945, French occupation authorities were pressing for the recruitment of DPs. Diplomatic concerns, combined with a fear that refugees would soon be attracted to more 'attractive countries' (such as America or Canada) and anxieties about German overpopulation, fostered a sense of emergency. The Inter-ministerial Committee for German Affairs was

---

[108] CAC Fontainebleau, Versement 770623, 83, J. Tarbé de Saint Hardouin à Laffon, 23 November 1945.
[109] MAE, Bonn 152, Banat de Temesvar, à l'usage des journalistes [undated].
[110] On fundings, CAC Fontainebleau, Versement 770623, 83, Lettre du Commandant P. Sorbac à Monsieur le Colonel Chef de la MMFL, 15 September 1945.
[111] Corine Defrance, *La politique culturelle de la France sur la rive gauche du Rhin 1945–1955* (Strasbourg: Presses Universitaires de Strasbourg, 1994); Eric Dussault, 'Politique Culturelle et Dénazification dans la zone d'occupation française en Autriche (Tyrol et Vorarlberg) et à Vienne de 1945 à 1955', *Guerres mondiales et conflits contemporains*, vol. 221, no. 1 (2006), pp. 83–92.
[112] AN, F/7/16116, Pages, Note pour Monsieur le Ministre de l'Intérieur, 16 October 1948.

also concerned by the economic burden imposed by DPs on the French administration.[113] In the field, however, the progress of the French prospecting mission was slow, its members being allegedly more interested in tourism than in assessing the 'value' of DPs.[114] The majority of French inspectors touring DP camps did not speak German or Polish; in return, DPs were extremely mistrustful of them and tended to refuse answering questions about the pre-war profession.[115] Frustrated with this situation, the military government of the zone contacted the provisional government asking it to accelerate the recruitment of DPs. 'Any further delay,' Koenig noted, 'would represent a considerable number of working hours lost for our national economy'.[116] Despite Koenig's injunction, the transfer of DPs was abruptly stopped by the Ministry of Labour at the end of November.

On 21 November 1945, the Ministry of Labour came under the sway of communist trade unionists. Gaullist Minister Alexandre Parodi was replaced by Ambroise Croizat, a former metal worker, trade unionist and long-serving communist organizer. Communist participation in the resistance had given the party an aura of legitimacy that was confirmed by the result of the election of October 1945. Communists were at the forefront of those for whom the Liberation meant the inauguration of a purged republic. The Ministry of Labour, which had been severely affected by the *épuration* [purges] and was staffed by a new political class forged by the resistance, was to play a critical role in opposing the transfer of DPs to France.[117] In contrast to departments such as the Ministries of Industry and Agriculture, which were considered to be 'technical', the Ministry of Labour portrayed itself as a primarily *social* institution, one that was particularly committed to developing privileged relations with the trade unions.[118] A May 1946 British Foreign Office report picked up this point:

---

[113] MAE, HCRFA, Ambassade de Bonn, 258, Note du Commandant Domergue, Paris, 28 December 1945; Affaires Economiques et financières, Affaires Allemandes et autrichiennes, 1944–1949, 131, Note relative au recrutement de la main d'oeuvre parmi les 'personnes déplacées', Commissariat Général aux Affaires Allemandes et Autrichiennes, 7 March 1946.

[114] MAE, HCRFA, Direction générale des Affaires politiques, 116, Le Général, Commandant en Chef en Allemagne à Monsieur le Secrétaire Général au Comité Interministériel pour les Affaires Allemandes et Autrichiennes, 12 November 1945.

[115] MAE, HCRFA, Direction générale des Affaires politiques, 116, Note, Recrutement pour la France des 'Displaced Persons' se trouvant en Allemagne, Mission Militaire pour les Affaires Allemandes, 24 June 1945, p. 4.

[116] MAE, HCRFA, PDR6/847, Général de Corps d'armée Koenig à Président du GPRFA, 30 November 1945.

[117] Jean-Pierre Le Crom, 'L'épuration administrative du Ministère du Travail à la Libération', in Chatriot, Join-Lambert and Viet (eds.), *Les politiques du Travail*, pp. 103–120, 119.

[118] Lucie Tanguy, 'Institutionnalisation de la formation syndicale et politique sociale du ministère du Travail (1950–1970)', in Chatriot, Join-Lambert and Viet (eds.), *Les politiques du Travail (1906–2006)*, pp. 479–493, 483; Alain Chatriot, 'L'introuvable

The Ministers of Reconstruction, Industrial Production and Labour are all Communists. Moreover, the Communist sympathies of the majority of French trade unions make it necessary for the French government to be very careful of accepting refugees whose political outlook is likely to give rise to conflict with French workers and therefore to industrial trouble. This applies particularly to dissident Poles and Yugoslavs.[119]

The Ministry of Labour favoured the entry of migrants from North Africa, Poland and especially Italy over DPs.[120] In both Berlin and Baden-Baden, French authorities expressed frustration at the fact that, after so much effort spent in negotiating with the Western Allies, the Ministry of Labour could suspend the recruitment of DPs arbitrarily. This seemed all the more absurd since the Ministry was at the time planning direct negotiations with the Warsaw government to launch a recruitment scheme in Poland. But, from a communist point of view, those Eastern Europeans who refused to return to their Soviet-annexed homeland were intrinsically undesirable.[121]

This change of policy within the Ministry of Labour meant that a few thousand already selected DPs, including miners, were left in limbo in camps while awaiting a decision. On 28 December 1945, Berlin Administrator Commandant Domergue vehemently complained about it: 'We can indeed recall the influence that Polish and Italian priests and schoolteachers had on their fellow workers [...] and the way they combated very effectively our influence. Tomorrow trade-unionist leaders will replace these priests; admittedly, they will defend the democratic conceptions in place in Eastern Europe, but they will also remain closely tied to their governments.'[122] As Domergue's report makes clear, communist decision makers and their ideological fellow travellers on the French Left feared the excessive influence of Polish priests on Polish DPs. These fears were partly rooted in memories of the interwar years, when Polish communities isolated themselves from French mining communities in Northern France. Supported by miners' employers, Polish priests established many parishes. After the trauma of collaboration and fascism, perceptions of Polish Catholic sentiments and their supposed allegiance to right-wing views acquired more sinister undertones. Life in DP camps also

---

démocratie sociale: débats intellectuels, luttes politiques, acteurs sociaux et administratifs, 1944–1950', pp. 385–401, 396.

[119] NA, FO 371/57711/0017, 218/8/46, Letter from Duff Cooper to Sir George Rendel, Paris, 21 May 1946.

[120] MAE, HCRFA, Direction générale des Affaires politiques, 116, Annexe I, Note du Commandant Domergue, 16 January 1946.

[121] MAE, HCRFA, Ambassade de Bonn, 258, Note du Commandant Domergue, Paris, 28 December 1945.

[122] Ibid.

encouraged the revival of nationalism. DP leaders named camps after national heroes, promoted folk traditions, traditional literature and religious activities, fostering a 'long-distance nationalism' with characteristics redolent of the Vichy regime.[123]

A significant political and ideological opposition to fascist DPs also emerged from within the newly created ONI.[124] Created in November 1945, the ONI was vested with sole control over the recruitment and entry of foreigners into France. On 26 March 1946, the ONI was placed under the joint supervision of the Ministry of Labour and the Ministry of Population and was entrusted to Bernard Auffray, an ardent defender of Spanish refugees and exiles from Central Europe. Under his leadership, the ONI recruited numerous trade unionists to its staff. Within the ONI, trade unionists advocated a thorough screening of migrants to protect the national workforce and guarantee full employment. They feared that DPs, like foreign migrants in general, undermined the labour market by accepting inferior wages and more limited social protection. Despite the commensurately large reconstruction demands, fears of unemployment, fuelled by the memories of the economic crisis of the 1930s, combined with the food and housing shortage shaped anti-immigration attitudes.[125] A quarter of the housing stock had been destroyed during the war, and post-war reconstruction initially prioritized the rebuilding of ports, railways and roads, rather than new housing stock.[126] This opposition emerging from within the ONI was particularly visible at the end of 1947, when the first recruiting ONI mission was sent to Germany. ONI agents distinguished themselves by their discourteous, condescending attitudes towards DPs. The searing memories of collaboration, combined with recollections of previous waves of Polish migrants and the alleged influence of their priests, exacerbated negative perceptions of allegedly *fascist* and *conservative* DPs.

## 'Unprofessional' Migrants

While many trade unionists feared the arrival of what they regarded as anti-communist reactionaries, some employers were apprehensive about the professional values of refugees, particularly Polish refugees. They were anxious that camp life had had devastating effects on their morality and work ethic. As

---

[123] See Chapter 4.
[124] See Chapter 6.
[125] Louis Chevalier, 'Bilan d'une immigration', *Population*, vol. 5 (1050), pp. 129-140, p. 132; Jean-Pierre Le Crom, 'Les années "fastes" de la *Revue française du Travail (1946-1948)*', *Revue française des affaires sociales*, vol. 4, no. 4 (2006), pp. 25–43, 33.
[126] Robert Gildea, *France since 1945* (Oxford: Oxford University Press, 2009), p. 95.

early as February 1945, during an inter-ministerial meeting held at the Ministry of Labour, the Labour Inspector of Limoges complained about Polish 'lack of will' and their uncooperative 'frame of mind', deploring the Polish workers' refusal to work because they lacked clothes and shoes. He further added that most of them had large families, with too many 'children and pregnant women', or, in other words, *inaptes au travail*.[127] In Lorraine, local authorities deplored the involvement of Polish refugees in alcohol trafficking and black-market activities with American soldiers stationed in the Meuse region.[128] In October 1945, the Minister of Agriculture voiced French farmers' concerns about the instability of Polish manpower.[129] He explained that most rural employers were not willing to pay for the introduction of DPs, anticipating trouble in placing DPs in suitable employment if the government failed to pay the necessary introductory fees.[130] French farmers tended to prefer German POWs to Polish workers, as they were less costly, appeared more disciplined and, perhaps more importantly, did not need lodging. POWs could also be replaced if they fell ill.

The correspondence between various regional labour offices and the Ministry of Agriculture reflects widespread anxiety about Polish apathy, lack of work ethic and propensity to theft.[131] According to the Ministry of Agriculture, the problems that these refugees posed were not technical (i.e. due to their lack of training) but, rather, were 'psychological'.[132] Many post-war observers feared that camp life and forced idleness had devastating moral effects on DPs, transforming labour conscripts into anti-social, sexually perverted and unstable elements.[133] René Mayer alleged, for example, that camp life catalyzed the development of an 'appalling mentality'. 'One can say that the majority of Poles have lost the habit of work and that

---

[127] CAC, Versement 770623, article 83, Compte-rendu de la réunion interministérielle du 24 février 1945.

[128] CAC, Versement 770623, article 83, Monsieur Keller, Contrôleur de la Main d'Oeuvre (en mission à Verdun) à Chef du Bureau de la main-d'oeuvre étrangère, 24 April 1945.

[129] CAC, Versement 770623, article 83, Ministre de l'Agriculture au Ministre du Travail, 23 August 1945; This can be compared to the opposition of local government officials to the Algerian migrant population. Lyons, *The Civilizing Mission in the Metropole*, pp. 31–32.

[130] CAC, Versement 770623, article 83, Ministre de l'Agriculture au Ministre du Travail, 1 October 1945.

[131] CAC, Versement 770623, article 83, Procès Verbal de la Commission régionale de Main d'Oeuvre du 9 mai 1945; Monsieur Keller, Contrôleur de la Main d'Oeuvre à Chef du Bureau de la main-d'oeuvre étrangère, 24 April 1945.

[132] CAC, Versement 770623, article 83, Ministre de l'Agriculture au Ministre du Travail, 23 August 1945.

[133] MAE, HCRFA, Direction générale des Affaires politiques, 116, Général de Corps d'armée, Koenig à Président du GPRF, 16 November 1945.

it would be dangerous to introduce them into France prior to their re-education [...].¹³⁴ In fact, the attitude of the Ministry of Agriculture was at this point highly ambiguous: on the one hand, it urged the Foreign Minister to 'go along' with the recruitment; on the other hand, it cast doubts on the professional value of Polish workers.

The recruitment of DPs also elicited opposition from French administrators in Germany. In Germany, rumours about a characteristically Polish lack of discipline and unwillingness to work circulated. Stereotypes of Polish and Ukrainian refugees as morally lax, natural criminals and black marketers were commonplace. Observers singled out DP idleness, drunkenness, loose sexual behaviour, evasion of work and violence.¹³⁵ A military official, working in Ravensburg, lamented that there were many criminals among the DP population, which was a widespread prejudice among Germans and Allied occupiers more broadly.¹³⁶ According to him, DPs were more inclined to theft and black marketeering than the surrounding German population. 'Thinking only about robbing, committing crime without a moment of hesitation, the transfer of these foreigners to France could cause nothing but an outbreak of criminality.'¹³⁷

Even within the *Quai d'Orsay*, some well-placed government officials agreed with local residents that Polish refugees did not fit in France. In January 1946, a Foreign Ministry memorandum stated bluntly: 'currently, it does not appear possible to recruit a stable and good-quality workforce amongst Displaced Persons [...]. Nevertheless, in the case of a rapid demobilization of prisoners of war and as a consequence of a severe workforce crisis, France could envisage the use of DPs for temporary work.'¹³⁸ Immigration discourses about the relative aptitudes for work and reproduction revealed the persistence of ethnic prejudices and latent eugenic rationales in post-Liberation France. In the French zone, some local officials tended to downplay the productive value of Poles, while singling out the commendable traditions, strong work ethic,

---

[134] MAE, HCRFA, Direction générale des Affaires politiques, 116, GMZFO, Note pour Monsieur le Directeur du travail, 27 March 1946.

[135] See, for instance, MAE, HCRFA, Ambassade de Bonn, 258, Général de Corps d'Armée Koeltz à Administrateur Général, LR/MS N.949/PDR, 18 December 1945.

[136] On German fears of Polish DPs in the French zone, see notably Jürgen Wolfer, *Ein hartes Stück Zeitgeschichte: Kriegsende und französische Besatzungszeit im mittleren Schwarzwald. Zwischen 'Werwölfen', 'Kränzlemännern' und 'schamlosen Weibern'* (Hamburg: Verlag Dr. Kovac, 2012), p. 165.

[137] MAE, HCRFA, Direction générale des Affaires politiques, 116, Note du Cabinet et Travail, 15 February 1947.

[138] MAE, Affaires Economiques et financières, Affaires Allemandes et autrichiennes, 1944–1949, 131, Note pour Monsieur Bousquet, Directeur Général des Affaires Administratives et sociales au MAE, GFCC/N.2613/PDR, 4 January 1946.

exemplary hygiene and stronger sense of community of the Baltic refugees.[139] Not only were Baltic DPs deemed 'honest' and 'clean', but they were regarded as polyglot. 'Baltic people rapidly assimilate foreign languages; there are many interpreters among them. Each one of them has the command as well as his mother tongue, of a second or third language: Russian, German, English or French (there was a French high school in Riga).'[140]

French authorities were not alone in favouring the entry of Baltic DPs over Polish DPs.[141] The British government also initially 'opted for' Baltic DPs, linking racial and gender criteria in their recruitment scheme in order to present it in a favourable light to British employers. Its first recruitment scheme, tellingly named the 'Balt Cygnet Scheme', was aimed at Baltic women recruited to supply domestic staff for hospitals and sanatoria in Britain. Baltic women were judged to display the highest moral standards. If, from an *ethinicisant* point of view, Baltic refugees were deemed more easily 'assimilable' than Poles their staunch anti-communism foreshadowed, however, other assimilation problems in France. Unlike others, most notably Poles, many Baltic DPs were neither forced labourers nor former concentration camp inmates but had fled westward in 1944 as the Soviet Army advanced. Because their countries no longer existed as independent states but only as Soviet republics, they spent considerable efforts preserving their nationality, their particularism and their language.

If Baltic DPs topped French charts of probity, Jewish DPs were deemed difficult to assimilate. Despite hosting several post-war European Zionist organizations and allowing the transit of migrants to Palestine through French territory, French authorities showed little interest in Jewish DPs as migrant workers.[142] France was not the only country to display prejudice and discrimination towards Jewish migrants.[143] New World countries were equally

---

[139] MAE, HCRFA, Direction générale des Affaires politiques, 116, Direction du Travail, Section Main d'œuvre, PDR, Recrutement pour la France, [10 February 1946], GMZFO, Note pour Monsieur le Directeur du travail, 27 March 1946.

[140] CAC, Versement 770623, article 172, Note sur les 'Personnes Déplacées' Baltes dans les camps de l'UNRRA en Allemagne, 12 February 1947.

[141] Diana Kay and Robert Miles, *Refugees or Migrant Workers? European Volunteer Workers in Britain 1946-1951* (New York: Routledge, 1992); Linda McDowell, 'Workers, Migrants, Aliens or Citizens? State Constructions and Discourses of Identity among Post-war European Labour Migrants in Britain', *Political Geography*, vol. 22 (2003), pp. 863-886; Linda McDowell, *Hard Labour. The Forgotten Voices of Latvian Migrant Volunteer Workers* (New York: Routledge, 2005); Salvatici, 'Le gouvernement anglais et les femmes réfugiées d'Europe'.

[142] Julia Maspero, 'La politique française à l'égard de l'émigration juive polonaise de l'immédiat après-guerre', in *Bulletin du Centre de recherché français à Jérusalem*, [en ligne] 22 (2011), mis en ligne le 25 mars 2012, consulté le 3 Octobre 2012. http://bcrfj .revues.org/6513.

[143] Anne Grynberg, 'Des signes de resurgence de l'antisémitisme dans la France de l'après-guerre (1945-1953)', *Les cahiers de la Shoah*, vol. 5, no. 1 (2001), pp. 171-223. Also see

hostile. In Australia, for instance, Jews were considered undesirable because they were deemed 'clannish, aggressive and cosmopolitan', a group which did not assimilate easily and whose loyalty would always be suspect.[144] As Elisa Camiscioli argues in her work on labour power and the racial economy in interwar France, '[s]kills, productivity and even brute strength have always been ideologically inflected categories, subject to the perceived influence of gender, race, and nation'.[145]

In summary, despite the early high hopes attached to the recruitment of DPs and the intense diplomatic negotiations surrounding it, DPs' transfer to France was put on hold in 1946 and the early months of 1947. By the summer of 1946, only 3,000 DPs had arrived in France.[146] Several reasons can account for this: over the summer of 1946, repatriation operations were intensified in the French zone. And, although DPs represented the most 'open' source of migrants, the recruitment of DPs elicited opposition from different quarters in metropolitan France. The searing memories of collaboration, combined with recollections of previous waves of Polish migrants and the alleged influence of their priests, exacerbated negative perceptions of allegedly *fascist* and *conservative* DPs. While many trade unionists feared the arrival of what they regarded as anti-communist reactionaries, many employers were apprehensive about the professional value of DPs. Overall, French public opinion was hostile to the entry of foreign migrants. In 1947, an investigation by INED revealed that only 33 per cent of the French population were in favour of the entry of foreign migrants.[147] Yet, by the beginning of 1947 France desperately needed workers to realize the Monnet Plan.[148] For their part, government officials increasingly realized that France could not afford to *faire la fine bouche* [be fussy].[149] The National Assembly evidently agreed, particularly having approved the Monnet

---

Pierre Birnbaum, Un mythe politique: 'la République juive' de Léon Blum à Pierre Mendès France (Paris: Fayard, 1988); Richard C. Vinen, 'The End of an Ideology? Right-Wing Antisemitism in France, 1944-1970', The Historical Journal, vol. 37, no. 2 (1994), pp. 365-388.

[144] Suzanne D. Rutland, '"The Unwanted." The Story of Survivor Jewish Migration to Australia, 1945-1954', in Johannes-Dieter Steinert and Inge Weber-Newth (eds.), Beyond Camps and Forced Labour (Osnabrück: Secolo, 2005), pp. 123-132, 129.

[145] Camiscioli, Reproducing the French Race, p. 52.

[146] Spire, 'Les réfugiés une main d'oeuvre à part?'.

[147] AN, AJ/43/1269, Prof. J. Ray, 'Les problèmes actuels de l'immigration face à l'opinion publique française', in Pages documentaires. Un problème social: emigration et immigration, April-May 1950, pp. 261-277, 263-264.

[148] MAE, Affaires Economiques et financières, Affaires Allemandes et autrichiennes, 1944-1949, 131, Ministre des Affaires Etrangères à Monsieur Henri Bonnet, Ambassadeur de France à Washington, projet du 6 février 1947, p. 8.

[149] MAE, HCRFA, PDR6/822, Compte-rendu concernant le voyage effectué du 13 février au 2 mars 1947 en zone UK – USA et Française d'Allemagne par la Mission Française de recrutement de travailleurs personnes déplacées, 1 March 1947.

Plan on 14 January 1947. As a result, in February 1947 France declared itself prepared to take in 50,000 DPs, to help 'rectify [the] serious manpower situation'.[150] By this point, the impending Liberation of German POWs (a requirement reiterated by the American authorities on 3 December 1946), coupled with the prospect of a worsening economic crisis due to the severe winter weather, jeopardized the implementation of the Monnet Plan.[151] The communist Ministry of Labour Croizat was also becoming increasingly isolated within the government. Given the persistence of restrictions and privations, a growing hiatus between workers and the Communist Party was emerging.[152]

## The Requirements of the Monnet Plan

By early 1947, the attempted recruitment of Italian migrants had produced meagre results. It proved unexpectedly costly as well. Polish workers settled in France were also returning home under the agreements on voluntary repatriation that were newly signed by the Polish government.[153] Although the American authorities accepted the principle of transforming POWs into free workers, 'skilled and untrained volunteer miners [were] most urgently required' for the Monnet Plan.[154] Fifty-six thousand German Prisoners accounted for 20 per cent of French coal production at the time.[155] Their imminent departure was paralleled by a significant reduction in the imported coal supplies from the Ruhr. Ambassador to Paris Alfred Duff Cooper informed the British government that, although Amboise Croizat anticipated 'difficulties with the trade unions', he was disposed to consider the recruitment of DPs.[156]

For French diplomats, the question of the recruitment of DPs was inherently linked to that of German migrants. British and American officials required France to accept the principle of accepting DPs before negotiating

---

[150] NA, FO/945/470, Inward telegram from Lubecke to Control Office and 8 other addressees, CCG 02996, 18 February 1947.

[151] MAE, Affaires Economiques et financières, Affaires Allemandes et autrichiennes, 1944–1949, 131, Résumé des propositions continues dans la communication sur les prisonniers de guerre, 4 février 1947. Also see Claude d'Abzac-Epezy, 'La France face au rapatriement des prisonniers de guerre allemands', *Guerres mondiales et conflits contemporains*, vol. 233, no. 1 (2009), pp. 93–108, 94.

[152] Philippe Buton, 'L'éviction des ministres communistes', in Serge Berstein and Pierre Milza (eds.), *L'année 1947* (Paris: Presse de Sciences Po, 1999), pp. 339–355, 340–341.

[153] Ponty, 'Les rapatriements d'ouvriers polonais.'

[154] NA, FO/945/470, Inward telegram from Lubecke to Control Office and 8 other addressees, CCG 02996, 18 February 1947.

[155] MAE, Affaires Economiques et financières, Affaires Allemandes et autrichiennes, 1944–1949, 131, Ministre des Affaires Etrangères à Monsieur Henri Bonnet, projet du 6 février 1947, p. 8.

[156] NA, FO/945/470, Télégramme from Paris to Foreign Office, 7 February 1947.

the recruitment of German workers.[157] They lamented the fact that France refused to accept Polish DPs, while striving to recruit Germans.[158] During informal negotiations at the *Quai d'Orsay*, an American official observed: 'If the manpower situation in France is so critical, why on earth are you sending back thousands of Polish workers to Poland? [...] And why are you refusing the DPs that we are offering to you?'[159] The representative of the Ministry of Foreign Affairs, Bousquet, responded by stating that France considered the recruitment of DPs an 'indispensable supplement' to meet the requirements of the Monnet Plan, and the recruitment of German labour to be a form of compensation for the loss of German POWs.[160] American authorities seemed immune to this line of argument. They insisted that the French government placed them in a very difficult situation in relation to their British Allies:

> [O]n one hand, the government has committed itself to you to authorize in its zone the recruitment of German migrants for France; on the other hand, it has committed itself to Great Britain, by virtue of the Byrnes-Bevin agreements, to retain all the material and human resources of the American zone for the bi-zonal economy [...]. Yet, the exportation of German workers will put a strain on the economic recovery [...] and will aggravate the manpower crisis which is already severely affecting industries in the two zones.[161]

Admittedly, there were divergences of views between experts in the French Foreign Office.[162] But for the Foreign Minister Bidault, France needed to both recruit German workers and avoid the growth of the German population: 'there should be no transfers of German population beyond those already agreed at Potsdam, [...] transfers specified by Potsdam should now stop, [...] emigration of Germans should be encouraged and [...] the settlement of displaced persons in Germany should be forbidden.'[163]

---

[157] NA, FO/945/470, Minutes of Anglo-French discussions on the recruitment in the British and French Zones of Austria and Germany of DP for work in France and in the UK, meeting held at the Quay d'Orsay, 28 April 1947.

[158] CAC, Versement 770623, article 172, Note d'information, Conversation du capitaine Martin-Siegfried avec le commandant Negrie, 18 April 1947.

[159] Ibid.

[160] MAE, HCRFA, PDR6/822, Secrets notes on Conference held at French Ministry of Foreign Affairs, between US and IGCR representatives and members of the French government on recruitment of labour from Germany for France, 31 March 1947, p. 1.

[161] CAC, Versement 770623, article 172, Note d'information, Conversation du capitaine Martin-Siegfried avec le commandant Negrie, 18 April 1947.

[162] In his memoirs, Massigli has described the moral and organizational crisis of the Department. Pierre Grosser, 'L'entrée de la France en guerre froide', in Serge Berstein and Pierre Milza (eds.), *L'année 1947* (Paris: Presses de Sciences Po, 2000), pp. 167–188, 187.

[163] NA, FO/945/470, Note of informal discussion in the office of Monsieur Bousquet, Ministry of Foreign Affairs, on the subject of German emigration, on 30 April 1947.

By the spring of 1947, French diplomats feared losing valuable labourers to Belgium or Britain. Since the spring of 1946, Belgian and British recruitment missions had been scouting DP camps for robust, young workers. French authorities, particularly interested in young DP miners, were worried that none would be left.[164] Furthermore, in June, members of the US Congress even threatened to withdraw Marshall Plan assistance from 'any European nation refusing to open its borders to a reasonable number of DPs'.[165] In summary, the requirements of the Monnet Plan, combined with the pressures of the British and American Allies, added impetus to the recruitment.

## A Parliamentary Mission in Germany

In February 1947, a parliamentary mission toured DP camps in Germany to assess the DP population. This parliamentary mission originally comprised two representatives of the Ministry of Foreign Affairs, three representatives of the Ministry of Labour, a CGT representative, a *Confédération Générale de l'Agriculture* (agricultural trade union) representative, an interpreter and an ONI representative who was charged with assessing the professional aptitudes and ethnic backgrounds of DPs.[166] They were soon to be joined by a representative of the *charbonnages de France* (National Coal Board), a representative of the French Confederation of Christian Workers (CFT) and a representative of the Ministry of National Economy.[167] Quite remarkably, the Ministry of Population had no representative in the parliamentary information mission. Upon its arrival, two radically opposed views divided the delegation. For the representatives of the Ministry of Labour and the CGT, DPs were 'fascists': 'the fact that they did not want to be repatriated to their own countries proved that they had collaborated with the enemy.'[168] For the representatives of the Ministry of Agriculture, the Ministry of the National Economy and the *Houillères*, there were certainly collaborators among DPs but these were *lampistes* (low-rank subalterns), and, besides this, France, given its desperate manpower situation, could not afford 'to be fussy'.[169]

---

[164] NA, FO/945/470, Inward Telegram from Lubbecke to control office, 18 February 1947.
[165] Cohen, *In War's Wake*, p. 106.
[166] MAE, HCRFA, PDR6/822, Télégramme Roger Bloch pour Baden (Cabinet), 4 February 1947.
[167] CAC, Versement 770623, article 172, Rapport commun établi par les membres de la mission d'information sur le problème des personnes déplacées des trois zones d'occupation en Allemagne (9 au 23 février 1947), [2 May 1947].
[168] MAE, HCRFA, PDR6/822, Compte-rendu concernant le voyage effectué du 13 février au 2 mars 1947 en zone UK – USA et Française d'Allemagne par la Mission Française de recrutement de travailleurs personnes déplacées, 1 March 1947.
[169] Ibid.

THE POLITICS OF IMMIGRATION 69

Clearly, this issue of collaboration revived painfully fresh memories. For those who had been persecuted during the Occupation, the prospect of recruiting 'collaborators' was unacceptable. 'Hence DPs were asked insidious questions about their wartime activities and about their reasons for refusing repatriation (Ministry of Labour and CGT leanings).'[170] The most *irreductible* opponent to the recruitment of these *fascist* refugees, CGT representative Doutre, had been deported to Dachau. '[He] nevertheless seemed moved every time that he encountered political deportees. Two of them in Schömberg (French zone) were deported to Dachau like he was.'[171] The February 1947 parliamentary mission concluded in favour of recruitment, despite recognizing the difficulties of obtaining precise and accurate information about DPs' wartime activities. Its report mentioned the existence of an incomplete 'Fichier Berlin', providing a list of individuals who had voluntarily worked for the Germans. The mission recommended not overestimating the importance of collaborators among DPs:

> These elements are a tiny minority. Alongside leaders who exert a massive influence in a *milieu d'oisifs* often gullible, there is a mass of individuals – for the most part young – that French life will be able to mould [...]. This is essentially a safety question that the Ministry of Interior, which is not represented in our Mission, will have to solve.[172]

The 'Fichier Berlin' was in practice almost inapplicable.[173]

From a moral standpoint, according to this report, Baltic DPs topped the scale of probity, ahead of Yugoslavs, Hungarians and Poles:

> If one can make a generalization on a question as delicate as this one, the different authorities concurred in admitting that, from a moral point of view, the Baltic people are at the top, followed by the *Banatais*, the Yugoslavs, the Ukrainians and then the Poles. It is nevertheless believed that the former, who in the months following the Liberation proved to be undisciplined, underwent a remarkable recovery.[174]

As we have seen, racial hierarchies were incorporated in a language of economic productivity, psychological stability and cultural assimilability. Alongside DPs' racial or ethnic traits, attention was paid to their ability to speak French, their professional skills, age, wartime experiences and professed

---

[170] Ibid.
[171] Ibid.
[172] CAC, Versement 770623, article 172, Rapport commun établi par les membres de la mission d'information sur le problème des personnes déplacées des trois zones d'occupation en Allemagne (9 au 23 février 1947), [2 May 1947], p. 13.
[173] AN, F/7/16116, Note d'information, a/s de l'immigration en France des ressortissants du Banat, 6 May 1949. See Chapter 6.
[174] CAC, Versement 770623, article 172, Rapport commun établi par les membres de la mission d'information sur le problème des personnes déplacées, p. 14.

willingness to 'assimilate' in France. The report also insisted on the need to select DPs who had been persecuted by the Nazis – arguing that this would both hasten their assimilation and do them a humanitarian service – who had worked or had relatives in France or had lost all their families and ties with their countries of origin.[175] In practice, the French recruitment scheme rarely did justice to the suffering of the war's various victims. The closer scrutiny of DPs' health, professional skills and ethnic origins shows that DPs were treated above all as a large migrant group upon whom France could call for its own needs. They were to be admitted within the streams of foreign workers, and their legal status was fixed to their work and residence permits.

The mission still specified that DPs had to be 'rehabilitated' and 're-educated', pointing to their 'gregarious instinct' and irrational fears of official forms and enquiries.[176] Agricultural trade unionist René Massot reached the same *paternalistic* conclusion: DPs were not intrinsically bad, but care was needed when reintegrating them into normal work and family conditions. '[T]heir tragic existence in the last several years should help us to understand and excuse some of [our] grievances.'[177] Anxieties about the lasting effects of camp life on the morality of these former victims of the Nazi regime were further aggravated by concerns about their nationalist sentiments. As a result of their prolonged life in camps, DPs were regarded as having fallen prey to a variety of social and mental maladies. The most frequent diagnosis was that DPs suffered from 'apathy'.[178] The 1947 parliamentary mission further recommended breaking up DP communities, by encouraging their settlement throughout French territory.[179]

> We noticed the power that certain leaders often exercised [over DPs]. It will be essential to curtail this in order to prevent the formation of communities [...] which represents a security risk and a threat to smooth assimilation. We must not lose sight of the fact that DPs are not voluntary emigrants prepared to accept a foreign civilization with alien habits, but refugees whose gazes remain fixed on their homelands, and therefore try to recreate its *ambiance* while waiting the time to return home.[180]

---

[175] Ibid., p. 8.
[176] CAC, Versement 770623, article 172, draft report.
[177] CAC, Versement 770623, article 172, Rapport sur les possibilités de recrutement parmi les 'personnes déplacées' en Allemagne, question vue sous l'angle special agricole [undated].
[178] Edward A. Shils, 'Social and Psychological Aspects of Displacement and Repatriation', *Journal of Social Issues*, vol. 2, no. 3 (1946), pp. 3–18; H. B. M. Murphy (ed.), *Personnes déplacées, recueil d'études sur la psychologie des réfugiés, leur santé mentale et les problèmes de leur réinstallation* (Paris: UNESCO, 1955); Gatrell, *The Making of the Modern Refugee*, p. 104.
[179] CAC, Versement 770623, article 172, Rapport commun établi par les membres de la mission d'information sur le problème des personnes déplacées, p. 15.
[180] Ibid., p. 14.

## Launching the Recruitment

Following this report, in March 1947 the Inter-ministerial Economy Committee finally approved the recruitment scheme.[181] On 15 April 1947, the Minister of Population sent a letter of protest to the Minister of Foreign Affairs, recalling that, according to the decree of 24 December 1945, 'all the questions regarding immigration and population were within his remit'.[182] Despite this apparently unequivocal statement, he had not been consulted concerning the draft agreement to be signed with the American and British authorities, and the draft agreement did not take into account demographic considerations regarding the origins of DPs.[183] Without doubt, the Ministry of Population was progressively erased from the decision-making process. On 4 June 1947, when plans for the recruitment of DPs were finally implemented, the resulting initiatives were entrusted to an ONI delegation, directed by Mr Hornez, representative of the Ministry of Labour.[184] Once again, the Ministry of Population was not represented. In addition, 'the requirement that each entrant possess a work permit from the Ministry of Labour meant that immigration which did take place under the auspices of the ONI would necessarily be tied to the domestic employment scene and not to long-range demographic considerations'.[185]

French authorities eventually signed agreements for the recruitment of DPs with the American, the British and the Inter-Governmental Committee on Refugees' authorities on 10 June 1947.[186] For its part, the Polish government finally accepted the transfer of DPs to France under certain conditions.[187] These agreements concerned only non-German DPs, but several letters were exchanged on the same day rendering the terms of this agreement applicable to the recruitment of *Reichsdeutsche* and *Volksdeutsche* in the British and

---

[181] MAE, HCRFA, PDR6/849, Administrateur general Laffon à Gouverneurs, délégués supérieurs pour les GM du Bade, Wurtembourg, de l'état Rhéno-Palatin, 27 March 1947.
[182] CAC, Versement 770623, article 172, Ministre de la Santé Publique et de la Population à Ministre des Affaires Etrangères, Direction Générale des Affaires Administratives et Sociales, 15 April 1947.
[183] Ibid.
[184] CAC, Versement 770623, article 172, Décision relative à l'organisation du recrutement des travailleurs en Allemagne et en Autriche, Ministre du Travail et de la Sécurité Sociale, 4 June 1947.
[185] Gary Freeman *Immigrant Labor and Racial Conflict in Industrial Societies: the French and British Experience, 1945-1975* (Princeton, NJ: Princeton University Press, 1979), p. 71 quoted in Silverman, *Deconstructing the Nation*, p. 39.
[186] NA, FO/945/470, Telegram from the British Embassy, Duff Cooper, N.523, 12 June 1947.
[187] Maspero, 'Politique française d'immigration', p. 167.

French zones of Austria.[188] An annex to the British agreement stipulated that 2,000 DPs would be recruited in the French zone by British authorities and 14,000 DPs in the British zone by French authorities.[189] British, for instance, required France to accept one DP or *Volksdeutsche* with their family for each German recruited. According to the terms of the agreements, American and British authorities had to pay the entire maintenance expenses of the selection centres involved. They also had to provide DPs with footwear and clothing. In practice, due to financial difficulties, the British authorities did not follow this requirement to the letter.[190] The agreement further stipulated that miners' families could join them after sixty days, and families of other workers after ninety days. Once DPs were in possession of work contracts, they were to receive a residential permit and a temporary labour permit. They were to be paid at the same rate as French workers and were entitled to join the trade union of their choice. The following DPs were to be returned to the American zone: 'DPs who have rescinded their contract for a valid reason, DPs who have not the aptitude to work in France, DPs who by action or propaganda become a danger to public order.'[191]

The official launch of the scheme revived public debates about collaboration with the Nazis in France. This did not apply solely to Eastern European DPs; it also affected Italian migrants. In a press conference on 27 March 1947, responding to the *Confédération française des travailleurs chrétiens* (CFTC) concern that the CGT was carrying out 'political recruitment' in Italy, Ambroise Croizat argued that no 'political selection' should take place and that choices about which migrants to accept should not take into account their political or religious views, with the sole exception of those 'who compromised themselves either in carrying out fascist activities or in voluntarily collaborating with the Nazis'.[192] Yet, for some trade-unionists DPs had betrayed their own country and collaborated with the Nazis. The *fédération du sous sol* (a mining federation), for instance, published an article condemning the extension of the recruitment to the American zone, and affirming that certain recruits had swastika tattoos.[193] By contrast, journalists in Alsace and Moselle organized a campaign for the recruitment of Banatais, rehabilitating the memory of their wartime past.

---

[188] NA, FO/945/470, Telegram from the British Embassy, Duff Cooper, N.523, 12 June 1947.
[189] NA, FO/945/470, Telegram to MacVittie, PW/DP Division, 24 July 1947.
[190] NA, FO/945/470, Letter to Colonel Logan-Gray, Allied Commission for Austria, 18 June 1947.
[191] NA, FO/945/470, Agreement between the French government and the IGRC regarding the recruitment and the establishment in France of DPs originally in the American zones of Germany and Austria.
[192] Gani, *Syndicats et Travailleurs immigrés*, p. 34.
[193] Ibid., pp. 28–29.

## Les Malgré-nous des Balkans

The campaign of support for the Banatais must be understood in the specific context of auto-justification, which followed the trauma of annexation and collaboration with the Nazis. The 'return' of Alsace–Moselle in 1945 is commonly presented as less complicated than the return of Alsace in 1918, the local population embracing its French nationality and citizenship more wholeheartedly than in the aftermath of the previous conflict.[194] Nonetheless, despite the eventual successes of the reintegration of Alsace into France, historians have demonstrated that the reconstruction of post-war Alsace was at times painful and that the memory of the wartime experience was profoundly problematic.[195] The Banatais held up a mirror to the way that the people of Alsace–Lorraine framed their own wartime suffering: Banatais' wartime experiences were used as a means of rehabilitating the memory of their Alsatian brothers who were also 'forcibly enrolled' by the Germans. In February 1947, the *Dernières nouvelles du Haut-Rhin* published a series of articles on the Banatais written by Maxime Felsenstein, the *rédacteur en chef*, comparing their situation to that of the *Malgré-nous* who were forcibly enrolled in the Waffen-SS. 'There were thus 30,000 former compatriots of the Alsatian and the Lorrainers who experienced, despite the distance, the separation and the centuries, the same tragic fate as their brothers in the land. *Dramatique pendant de l'Histoire.*'[196]

In the same vein, in August 1948 *L'Est Républicain* published an investigation about 'our cousins from the Banat of Temesvar' carried out by Sacha Simon. He presented France as their 'second homeland', the country of their ancestors.[197] As these examples suggest, perceptions of DPs were closely related to individual and community memories of France's own wartime experiences. On 22 November 1947, the appointment of the Lorrainer Robert Schuman as President du Conseil generated much enthusiasm in the Banatais milieu.[198] Referring to him as 'Unser Freund' in his memoirs, the

---

[194] Elizabeth Vlossak, *Marianne or Germania. Nationalizing Women in Alsace, 1870–1946* (Oxford: Oxford University Press, 2010), p. 288.

[195] Marc Lienhard, 'Méandres de la mémoire: les Alsaciens sympathisants et collaborateurs du régime nazi', in Jean Pierre Rioux (ed.), *Nos embarras de mémoire. La France en souffrance* (Paris: Lavauzelle, 2008), pp. 119–129; On the return of French Jews in Strasbourg, see Mandel, *In the Aftermath of Genocide*, p. 58.

[196] CAC Fontainbleau, Versement 770623, 83, Tirage à part de l'enquête sur les Alsaciens et Lorrains du Banat, Maxime Fels, publiée dans les 'Dernières Nouvelles du Haut-Rhin', du 8 au 14 février 1947.

[197] Sacha Simon, 'Nos cousins du Banat de Temesvar', in *L'Est Républicain*, 30–31 August and 1 September 1948.

[198] AN, 3AUT/99, Helmut Kuhn à Bernhard Schelp, Commentaires sur l'émigration des Banatois en France, 2 September 1948, Kematen.

Banatais representative Lamesfeld was very gratified to receive an official invitation to travel to Paris to meet French officials in April 1948.[199] In his memoirs, he recalls a warm welcome and pleasant conversation with Schuman, *homme de l'Est* [man from the East], with whom he could converse in a Lorrainer dialect similar to his own.[200] In practice, the recruitment of Banatais generated nothing but disappointment:

> Disappointment as a result of the impossibility of realizing their project of group settlement in France. Disappointment at the way their emigration was carried out; when the head of a household left, other members of the family waited one hundred and twenty days before being able to join him [...]. Disappointment for the PDR Direction which could not obtain from the *métropole* the advantages that the Banatais were expecting. Disappointment for the Banatais themselves who, lulled into unmet promises, abandoned their hope of being one day admitted to France and then refused the offers that were made to them.[201]

## Conclusion

In the philo-communist context of the Liberation, the recruitment of DPs defied consensus and elicited opposition from different quarters. On the one hand, Eastern Europeans were often perceived as culturally more *assimilable* than North African colonial migrants. On the other hand, communist decision makers and their ideological fellow travellers on the French Left – particularly numerous in the Ministry of Labour and the ONI – opposed the recruitment of those they regarded as fascist DPs and wartime collaborators. Despite widespread scepticism, the recruitment scheme was cautiously implemented in April 1947.[202] This was partly the result of an urgent need for manpower to enact the Monnet Plan and partly a consequence of wider diplomatic bargaining to secure the entry of German migrants. It was also shaped by nagging worries about German overpopulation and the inherent security threat that this posed to Europe. These initiatives, however, did not put an end to the disagreements over the resettlement of DPs. As this chapter demonstrates,

---

[199] Lamesfeld, *Von Osterreich nach Frankreich*, p. 20.
[200] Ibid., p. 21; On Schuman's defence of Alsatian and Lorrainer particularism see Raymond Poidevin, *Robert Schuman Homme d'Etat 1886–1963* (Paris: Imprimerie Nationale, 1986), pp. 58–81.
[201] HCRFA, Service des Personnes Déplacées, *Sept ans d'activité en faveur des personnes déplacées*, p. 45.
[202] UNRRA, S-0417-0003-03, Lettre du General de Corps d'Armée Lenclud à Mrs les Field Supervisors et Directeurs de Teams, 9 April 1947.

Fig. 1.2 'The "*Malgré-nous*" of the Balkans', *L'Est Républicain*, 31 August 1949.

opposition to the recruitment went beyond the limited circles of communist trade unionists and labour experts of the Ministry of Labour and the MRP-dominated Ministry of Population. The resettlement of DPs triggered wider controversy about how far DPs could or should be assimilated into the nation state and about the relative superiority or inferiority of certain ethnic groups. While Baltic and Banatais DPs tended to top the scale of probity, stereotypes of Polish and Ukrainian DPs as morally lax and more inclined to theft remained relatively widespread. Yet, if DPs undoubtedly faced discrimination with *ethnicisant* overtones, the 'ethnic discourse' surrounding them was never entirely coherent. Indeed, the issue of wartime collaboration, as well as the strength of their nationalist sentiments, blurred these ethnic taxonomies. As the example of the Banatais illustrates, a number of French officials, trade union leaders and other social commentators projected their own wartime experiences onto DPs. While communists acted with exaggerated ferocity against DPs, perhaps in an attempt to purge the memory of the years 1939–1941, Alsatians projected their own memories of 'forced enrolment' onto DPs (Fig. 1.2).

Although the Ministry of Labour 'officially' rallied to the DP scheme in the spring of 1947, anti-DPs attitudes persisted at lower administrative tiers within the Ministry and the ONI. As will be explained in Chapter 6, most of the ONI field agents working in Germany were hostile to the entry of what they regarded as anti-communist and reactionary migrants. Little wonder that, by December 1947, the recruitment scheme had yielded meagre results: only 6,625 DPs had entered France.[203] Paradoxically, when France was finally *ready* to recruit DPs – in 1948 – many refused to emigrate to what they regarded as a quasi-*communist* country.

---

[203] Chevalier, 'Bilan d'une immigration', p. 134.

# 2

# In the Shadow of Nazi Occupation

## Making and Overseeing Displaced Persons' Camps

As they entered German territories in the spring of 1945, French occupiers were emerging from four years of Nazi occupation and the divisive experiences of resistance, collaboration, labour conscription and deportation.[1] France was the only Western occupier that had not only experienced Nazi occupation but whose government had actively collaborated with the Nazis and provided a large 'labour force' to the Third Reich.[2] In addition to reassembling 'foreign' DPs in the territories under French control to facilitate their repatriation, French occupation officials had to provide assistance to around 1.7 million Frenchmen and women held captive in Germany. These included a million French POWs captured in June 1940, half a million workers from the *Relève* and the *Service du Travail Obligatoire* (Service for Labour Conscripts) and around 50,000 political and racial 'deportees', survivors of concentration camps and commandos.[3] The fast and orderly repatriation of these *Absents*, as the Ministry of Prisoners, Deportees and Refugees Henri Frenay called them, posed a critical domestic challenge for the new republican elite seeking to establish its authority and prove its legitimacy to a nation left profoundly divided by the war.[4] In numerical terms, the repatriation of French *Absents*

---

[1] Denis Peschanski, *Vichy 1940–1944: Contrôle et exclusion* (Brussels: Éditions Complexe, 1997); Denis Peschanski, *La France des camps. L'internement, 1938–1946* (Paris: Gallimard, 2002).
[2] During the Second World War, France was numerically the third country providing workers after the Soviet Union and Poland. Raphaël Spina, *Histoire du STO* (Paris: Perrin, 2017), p. 16. On the history of STO, see also Helga Bories-Sawala, *Dans la gueule du loup. Les français requis du travail en Allemagne* (Villeneuve-d'Ascq: Presses Universitaires du Septentrion, 2010); Patrice Arnaud, *Les STO. Histoire des Français requis en Allemagne nazie 1942–1945* (Paris: CNRS Éditions, 2010).
[3] Annette Wieviorka, 'Preface', in Alain Navarro, *1945. Le retour des Absents* (Paris: Stock, 2015), pp. 8–9. On the history of French POWs, see Yves Durand, *Les Prisonniers de guerre dans les Stalags, les Oflags et les Kommandos* (Paris: Hachette, 1994); Raffael Scheck, 'Collaboration of the Heart: The Forbidden Love Affairs of French Prisoners of War and German Women in Nazi Germany', *The Journal of Modern History*, vol. 90, no. 2 (2018), pp. 351–382.
[4] Megan Koreman, 'A Hero's Homecoming: The Return of the Deportees to France, 1945', *Journal of Contemporary History*, vol. 32, no. 1 (1997), pp. 9–22, 21; Christiane Franck

was an undeniable success. By the end of September, the French authorities had 'successfully' repatriated around 1.3 million French citizens. In political terms, however, the results were more mixed. The French press and Communist Party cast aspersions on Frenay's management of their return.[5] Furthermore, by the end of September, some French families still eagerly awaited news of their loved ones, in particular of Alsatian and Lorrainers, conscripted into the German army and captured by the Red Army during the war.[6] Others longed for the return of dead bodies, buried in Germany, to begin the bereavement process. In the French zone, while the repatriation of Soviet and French DPs was nearly completed, the repatriation of Polish DPs had not started and DP camps thus needed to be prepared for the forthcoming winter.[7] In this chapter I ask, in what ways did divisive experiences of 'deportation' and returns shape how DP camps were made and managed in the French zone. Were the needs of 'foreign DPs' considered as similar to that of French *Absents*? Why were there so many tensions between the French Prisoners, Deportees and Refugees (PDR) organization and the United Nations Relief and Rehabilitation Administration (UNRRA) over the administration of DP camps? And, finally, how far were debates about the making and overseeing of DP camps connected to broader domestic discussions about coming to terms with the past?

Drawing on field reports and correspondence between UNRRA, the Ministry of PDR and organization PDR and the Ministry of Foreign Affairs, this chapter moves past existing political and cultural histories of the return of French *Absents* and administration of 'foreign' DPs in the zone. The existing

---

(ed.), *La France de 1945. Résistances, retours, renaissances* (Caen: Presses Universitaires de Caen, 1996); Pieter Lagrou, *The Legacy of Nazi Occupation: Patriotic Memory and National Recovery in Western Europe, 1945–1965* (Cambridge: Cambridge University Press, 2000).

[5] Annette Wieviorka, *Déportation et Génocide: Entre la mémoire et l'oubli* (Paris: Hachette, 2003), p. 101; Christophe Lewin, *Le retour des prisonniers de guerre français: Naissance et développement de la F.N.P.G., 1944–1952* (Paris: Publications de la Sorbonne, 1986), p. 59; Henri Frenay, *La nuit finira* (Paris: Robert Laffont, 1973), pp. 511–512; Robert Belot, 'La résistance française non-communiste et l'image de l'URSS: Henry Frenay et le mouvement Combat', in Georges-Henri Soutou and Emilia Robin-Hivert (eds.), *L'URSS et l'Europe de 1941 à 1957* (Paris: Presses Universitaires de la Sorbonne, 2008), pp. 245–285.

[6] Catherine Klein-Gousseff, *Retour d'URSS. Les prisonniers de guerre et les internés français dans les archives soviétiques, 1945–1951* (Paris: CNRS Éditions, 2001); Gäel Moullec, 'Alliés ou ennemis? Le GUPVI-NKVD, le Komintern et les "Malgré-nous". Le destin des prisonniers de guerre français en URSS (1942–1955)', *Cahiers du monde russe*, vol. 42, nos. 2–4 (2001), pp. 667–678; Jacques Bariéty and Corine Defrance, 'Les missions de la France Libre en Union Soviétique et les "Malgré-nous" (1942–1944)', *Revue d'Allemagne et des pays de langue allemande*, vol. 39, no. 4 (2008), pp. 533–550.

[7] MAE, HCRFA, PDR6/467, Graphique concernant le rapatriement de Personnes Déplacées en Zone Française d'Occupation [undated].

historiography has rightly emphasized the cultural and social impacts of home-grown experiences of deportation on the post-war domestic memorial and political landscapes. Peter Lagrou has demonstrated that large-scale deportation spawned anxieties about the effects of camp life on the morality of individuals, the French authorities being alarmed by the lax moral standards of French labour conscripts.[8] Likewise, drawing on the archives of the French Foreign Ministry and the Ministry of Prisoners, Deportees and Refugees (PDR), Andreas Rinke has contextualized the DP problem within the broader framework of French repatriation efforts.[9] His study offers keen insights into French internal political tensions and the diplomatic constraints under which the French government and the Ministry of PDR operated. However, these studies rely overwhelmingly on official discourses and governmental sources. In doing so, the scholarship marginalizes both the role of wartime experiences in shaping relief workers' everyday activities and the views of relief workers who were not top-level officials. This chapter offers depth and balance to these high-policy-focused accounts, rendering mid- and ground-level relief workers visible and bringing their role in shaping relief and encampment practices to light. As it will demonstrate, DP policies were not solely determined in Washington (UNRRA's Division of Welfare and Repatriation), London (UNRRA's European Regional Office) or Paris and Baden-Baden (capital of the French zone), but were also heavily dependent upon how local agents interpreted and implemented official instructions in the field. In doing so, this chapter provides a more nuanced, grassroots-level picture of French DP administration and policies, examining critical tensions that existed between various actors in charge of DPs in the French zone.

Assessing everyday administrative practices challenges us to consider the attitudes of UNRRA relief workers and PDR officers towards DPs and the ways they imagined DP spaces as both site of discipline and/or valuable education and recuperation. It also prompts us to examine how the physical environment of DP camps gave rise to specific kinds of interactions between DPs, Germans and relief workers.[10] In so doing, this chapter makes three arguments. First, it highlights diverse cultures of encampment in the zone. Relatively large numbers of DPs lived in smaller camps and private accommodations in the zone. Discussions about the 'curative' effects of small dwellings for DPs amongst field workers were interconnected to broader debates about the effects of camp life in France. While relief workers in the field congratulated themselves on their advancement of more individualistic and effective

---

[8] Lagrou, *The Legacy of Nazi Occupation.*
[9] Andreas Rinke, *Le Grand retour – Die französische Displaced Persons-Politik (1944–1951)* (Frankfurt am Main: Peter Lang, 2002).
[10] Jordanna Bailkin, *Unsettled. Refugee Camps and the Making of Multicultural Britain* (Oxford: Oxford University Press, 2018), p. 9.

solutions for DPs than their British and American counterparts, this chapter nuances the view that small camps and private accommodations necessarily led to more 'normal' and 'safer' conditions for DPs. Second, this chapter traces significant difference in culture between French UNRRA officials, who believed in French cultural superiority and understood relief as a vehicle for restoring French prestige, and the attitudes of the majority of relief workers on the ground. For the former, many of whom were former military officers, approaches to the DP question were closely related to the ways in which policy elites and occupation officers mobilized to reconstruct the image of the French nation and bolster its prestige in Allied-occupied Germany. For them, humanitarian work reflected both France's renewed sense of responsibility and the country's self-interested concern for its image abroad. Relief workers on the ground, by contrast, brought in more varied perspectives on relief work, which in turn changed as their interactions with DPs evolved. UNRRA was presented as an exercise of international cooperation, but the majority of its personnel in the French zone were of French origin.[11] Third, this chapter shows that DP spaces created unique intimate interactions and frictions between French volunteers, international relief workers, and DPs from various ethnicities, classes, and generations.[12] These relationships were influenced by the structure of occupation. Relief workers possessed a variety of material advantages over the local population and DPs: a minority used these to buy entertainment and goods on the black market, or engage in 'illicit' sexual liaisons.[13] French occupation officials and UNRRA authorities condemned such behaviours, particularly 'transgressive' relationships occurring between 'female' relief workers and male DPs. Official concerns about 'professional misbehaviours' reflect the search for a gender peace and restoration of traditional gender roles in response to the chaos of war, defeat and foreign occupation.[14] These professional misbehaviours were all the more condemned that DP camps

---

[11] UNA, UNRRA, S-0412-0012-05, C. Mercier, Monthly report (October 1945) DP operation French Zone, 7 November 1945.

[12] Bailkin, *Unsettled*, p. 11.

[13] On consumerism in the French zone, see Karen Adler, 'Selling France to the French: The French Zone of Occupation in Western Germany, 1945–c.1955', *Contemporary European History*, vol. 21, no. 4 (2012), pp. 575–595; On how some German women became involved with French men for food or other necessities, see Ann-Kristin Glöckner, 'Shared Spaces: Social Encounters between French and Germans in Occupied Freiburg, 1945-1955', in Camilio Erlichman and Christopher Knowles (eds.), *Transforming Occupation in the Western Zones of Germany. Politics, Everyday Life and Social Interactions, 1945–1955* (London: Bloomsbury, 2018), pp. 191–210.

[14] Claire Miot 'Sortir l'armée des ombres. Soldats de l'Empire, combattants de la Libération, armée de la Nation : la Première armée française, du débarquement en Provence à la capitulation allemande (1944-1945)', PhD thesis, Ecole normale supérieure Paris-Saclay (2016), p. 642.

had a public face. DP spaces welcomed officials from other zones and were the objects of international scrutiny. In this context, it was feared that relief workers' deviant behaviours could damage the international reputation of France.

## Repatriating French Citizens

From the beginning of the French occupation, a number of French occupiers and members of the French PDR organization looked suspiciously at the installation of UNRRA in the zone. Describing his uphill battle to gain acceptance within the French zone, the French UNRRA Director General Lenclud gloomily noted in October 1946 that, since his appointment as director of the zone a year earlier, UNRRA had developed within a 'poisoned atmosphere', its administrative structure challenged from all sides.[15] To a degree he was right: the administrative conflict between the PDR service and UNRRA HQ preceded the signature of the 18 February agreement in 1946, which formalized the relations between UNRRA and French authorities in the zone, and lasted until the termination of UNRRA in June 1947. An UNRRA memorandum described the resultant problem: 'Relations with the PDR have always been very difficult due to the fact that the PDR did the job before UNRRA' and 'wanted the whip hand'.[16]

To understand the difficult implementation of UNRRA HQ in the French zone, it is essential to grasp French grievances about the ways in which the organization allegedly failed to facilitate the repatriation of French nationals in the spring of 1945. In fact, the organization PDR inherited some of the personnel of the administrations initially set up to repatriate French nationals in the resistance capital of Algiers in 1943. It is impossible to understand cultural reflexes within this organization without taking account of this basic fact.[17] From the start, some French military viewed with a jaundiced eye the creation of an international (civilian) organization. Amongst them, Henri Frenay, the head of the Commissariat for Prisoners, Deportees and Refugees, created in Algiers in November 1943, expressed concerns about Allied planners' sluggishness in making provision for the rapid repatriation of European DPs.[18] Frenay's Commissariat (and then Ministry) and UNRRA planners

---

[15] UNA, UNRRA, S-0417-0001-03, Lenclud, Confidential replies to questionnaire attached to letter 6300/CC/DAC/ADM dated 23.9.1946, 4 October 1946, p. 2.
[16] UNA, UNRRA, S-0412-0012-05, Monthly report, French Zone of Occupation for the month of October 1945, 7 November 1945.
[17] Rinke, *Le Grand retour*.
[18] MAE, Alger, CFLN, 634, Rapatriement des PDR et transports de populations à prévoir après l'armistice; 690, Télégramme Frenay à Diplofrance Washington, N. 1153, 4 May 1944.

viewed the organization of repatriation in very different terms.[19] From the beginning, the PDR conceived repatriation as a military matter.[20] French PDR staff had misgivings about the international composition of UNRRA teams and advocated the creation of more homogeneous, nationally based relief teams instead.[21] For PDR officers, the formation of French relief teams with a 'psychological knowledge of their countrymen' seemed more appropriate in order to provide the necessary support to DPs than the constitution of teams whose members often lacked any command of DPs' languages or even a working knowledge of German.[22] The French also came out in favour of more substantial recruitment of female personnel, resorting to cultural stereotypes that women shared inherent nurturing qualities and were more likely to empathize with deportees.[23]

If anything, the late deployment of ill-equipped UNRRA teams in the field (the first UNRRA teams only left England on 17 March 1945), as well as their initial mismanagement of DP camps, proved sceptical French planners right. The liberation of Bergen-Belsen was a great disappointment for Frenay's Ministry, the British military having underestimated the incidence of typhus and having failed to take effective measures on time.[24] The initial period, in which UNRRA operated under its November 1944 agreement with the Supreme HQ Allied Expeditionary Force (SHAEF), left an impression of pervasive chaos, inefficiency and ineptitude. The London office failed either to establish an effective field operation in France and Germany or to institute a successful working relationship with the military.[25] It was an inauspicious beginning for what was heralded as a new type of international organization. UNRRA's absence from what was, in the eyes of many French people, their

---

[19] Laure Humbert, 'The French in Exile and Post-war International Relief, c. 1941–1945', *The Historical Journal*, vol. 61, no. 4 (2018), pp. 1041–1064.

[20] François Cochet, *Les exclus de la victoire. Histoire des Prisonniers de guerre, déportés et STO 1945–1985* (Paris: Kronos, 1992), p. 109.

[21] AN, F/9/3153, Procès Verbal de la Conférence tenue le 5 avril 1945 sous la présidence de Monsieur Frenay.

[22] SHD, 8 P 22, Letter from C.G. First Army to C.G. Twelfth Army group (lettre remise le 11 février 1945); 8 P 33, Commandant P. Sorbac chef de la MMFL G-5 à Colonel, chef de la MMFL, 12th AG, 4 May 1945.

[23] AN, F/9/3286, UNRRA, Standing Technical Sub-Committee on Displaced Persons for Europe, draft report of the 18th meeting, 8 May 1945. And AN, F/9/3110, Note sur le recrutement des équipes féminines françaises, Paris, 6 February 1945.

[24] Annette Wieviorka, 'French Internees and British Liberators', in Jo Reilly, David Cesarani, Tony Kushner and Colin Richmond (eds.), *Belsen in History and Memory* (London: Frank Cass, 2001), pp. 125–133; Paul Weidling, '"Belsenitis": Liberating Belsen, Its Hospitals, UNRRA and Selection for Re-emigration 1945–1948', *Sciences in Context*, vol. 19, no. 3 (2006), pp. 401–418.

[25] Ben Shephard, *The Long Road Home: The Aftermath of the Second World War* (New York: Alfred A. Knopf, 2011), p. 137.

paramount domestic challenge significantly undermined the organization's credibility amongst a number of French officials. In the summer of 1945, Frenay concluded bitterly that '[o]n the whole, UNRRA teams arrived once the battle was over'.[26] In August 1945, he urged the Ministry of Foreign Affairs to put a brake on UNRRA's activities in the French zone, where there were fewer than a hundred UNRRA relief workers in place.[27]

Yet, Frenay himself, and his handling of repatriation, were criticized by the French press. The Communist Party orchestrated a violent campaign against him, dubbing him l'obligé or le protégé de Pucheu (a notorious Vichy collaborator) and casted aspersions on his administration of the ministry. Frenay found himself accused of supporting René Hardy, a former member of the resistance suspected to have betrayed Jean Moulin.[28] Furthermore, he was charged with handing over Spanish deportees to Franco and neglecting Jewish children survivors. These accusations regarding Frenay's wartime conduct revealed not only the profound divisions in a society coming to terms with its recent past, but also the ways in which the issue of repatriation exacerbated such tensions.[29] The analysis of French archives of the Mission Française de Rapatriement (MFRA), the forerunner of the PDR service established in the summer of 1944, revealed strong rivalries between resistance fighters and former Vichytes. Like the rest of French occupation personnel, French repatriation officers had often been hastily recruited in Paris in autumn 1944. The MFRA had inherited the administrative structure of the 'Maison des Prisonniers' set up by the Vichy regime. For many former members of the resistance, those who had not fought in it did not deserve the status of 'rescuers'.[30]

These tensions over the repatriation of French nationals were closely linked to the struggle over how to understand the recent experiences of occupation, collaboration, resistance and persecution. For many former participants in anti-Nazi resistance, their work with DPs marked a continuation of their wartime fight and they found it difficult to cooperate with former Vichyites. In June 1945, Lieutenant D'Astier de la Vigerie, who had been a leading figure

---

[26] MAE, HCRFA, PDR1/18, Henri Frenay, Note à l'attention de Monsieur Kaepplin, Paris, 31 July 1945; NUOI, 7, Note pour le Ministre, Affaires Économiques, 18 August 1945, p. 5.

[27] UNA, UNRRA, S-0425-0007-04, Confidential report, UNRRA II French corps area, Situation report, 8 August 1945, p. 4.

[28] Wieviorka, Déportation et Génocide, p. 101; Lewin, Le retour des prisonniers de guerre français, p. 59.

[29] Koreman, 'A Hero's Homecoming', pp. 9–22; Robert Belot, Henri Frenay: De la Résistance à l'Europe (Paris: Seuil, 2003); Lewin, Le retour des prisonniers de guerre français.

[30] See, for instance, Eliane Brault, L'épopée des AFAT (Paris: Éditions Pierre Horay, 1954), pp. 202–203.

of the resistance, was uncompromisingly critical of the French officers of the Special Mission of Repatriation and Information. In a report sent to Frenay, he underlined the degree of animosity between serving French repatriation officials in occupied Germany and revealed the lines of disagreement between former resisters and erstwhile Pétainists: 'They live in the most incredible opulence, enjoying the highest comforts, possessing the fullest luxuries. They spend their time drinking, throwing parties and screwing [baiser] [...] They are incompetent, and, moreover, Pétainist, never ceasing to criticise the actions of the Government of the Republic and in particular those of the Minister of Justice and of your minister [PDR].'[31] French officers also took different approaches to responding to those people from Alsace-Lorraine, who had collaborated with the Germans. While de la Vigerie complained about the misbehaviours of some French officials, staff from the service for Alsatians and Lorrainers complained that French repatriation officials failed to understand the specificities of these regions' wartime experiences. They ignored the dialects of Alsace or Lorraine and the complex history of the three departments, annexed by the Germans in 1940. In their dealings with French nationals enrolled in the Wehrmacht, these repatriation officers made major blunders. Worst, though, they often proved incapable of distinguishing a German from an Alsatian.[32] The return of people from Alsace-Lorraine was a complex problem: thousands of young men needed to be screened, as amongst these mobilized persons, 'some were volunteers and even Nazi propagandists'.[33] After the mass repatriation in the spring and summer of 1945, a considerable number of Alsatians remained in Germany, in particular, in the Soviet zone, where Soviet officials pursued a policy of 'benevolent abandonment'.[34]

In the summer of 1945, the repatriation of most French nationals (except those from Alsace-Lorraine) was completed, yet the work of French repatriation officers was not over. The search for information about Frenchmen presumed dead or missing continued, and the repatriation of Polish DPs had not yet started. While the administration of the zone was transferred from the troops of the First French Army to the military government, the mission of the repatriation corps was entrusted to the PDR service.[35] Both

---

[31] MAE, HCRFA, PDR1/16, Lieutenant d'Astier de la Vigerie à Ministre des Prisonniers de Guerre et des déportés politiques, 15 June 1945.

[32] MAE, HCRFA, PDR1/14, Colonel Demay à Chef de la Division 'Personnes Déplacées', 17 September 1945.

[33] Instruction on the Search of Alsatians and Lorrains, Godechevre, 14 January 1946, 6.1.1, 82517003, ITS Digital Archives.

[34] MAE, HCRFA, PDR1/18, Organisation de la division des personnes déplacées dans les organismes de contrôle en Allemagne, 13 June 1945.

[35] Marie Thérèse Chabord, 'Les organismes français chargés des prisonniers, déportés et réfugiés (Alger 1943 – Paris 1945)', *Revue d'histoire de la deuxième guerre mondiale*, vol. 42 (1961), pp. 17–26; Cyril Daydé, 'Les personnes déplacées et réfugiées en zone

transfers proved equally difficult. The handover of power from the invading troops of the French First Army to the military government, staffed by civilians in uniform, was a complex and messy affair. General Administrator Laffon recalled that [he] 'took control of an imprecise inheritance, ill-defined and by no means inventoried', with a considerable proportion of untrained staff.[36] The administration of the zone only became fully operative ten days later, on 26 July.[37] In this context, the installation of the PDR Direction was strenuous, due to the scarcity of material, personnel, and financial resources.

The PDR organization began working in Baden-Baden on 11 August 1945, two months before UNRRA set up its regional HQ.[38] In September, the service was moved from Baden-Baden, the capital of the zone, to a castle in Rastatt, 12 km north of Baden-Baden.[39] The setting of the castle of Rastatt, where the trials of German officials in the French zone later took place, provided the PDR Direction with a majestic, but rather unpractical and uncomfortable, working environment.[40] The implementation of French administrative services in hotels and castles was part of French occupiers' strategy to demonstrate their status as the new rulers, through the 'symbolic' occupation of high-profile and luxurious spaces.[41] Unlike the town of Rastatt, badly damaged by Allied bombings, the castle and its park remained intact. The PDR organization occupied fifty-one rooms, but the lodging of its personnel was particularly deficient: unlike those French administrators hosted in the comfortable hostels of Baden-Baden, in Rastatt the PDR director Alfred Poignant shared an apartment with a German family.[42] With the occupation of the castle of

---

française d'occupation d'après les Archives diplomatiques françaises. Fonds d'archives et méthodes de recherche', in Corine Defrance, Juliette Denis and Julia Maspero (eds.), *Personnes déplacées et guerre froide en Allemagne occupée* (Frankfurt am Main: Peter Lang, 2015), pp. 349–367.

[36] MAE, HCRFA, Ambassade de Bonn 43, Administrateur Général, Adjoint pour le GMZFO à Général de Corps d'Armée Commandant en Chef Français en Allemagne, 17 September 1945.

[37] Sylvie Lefèvre, *Les relations économiques franco-allemandes de 1945 à 1955. De l'occupation à la coopération* (Paris: Comité pour L'histoire Économique et Financière de la France, 1998), p. 68.

[38] MAE, HCRFA, PDR1/33, Note de service, 10 August 1945; Andrea Kühne, *Entstehung, Aufbau und Funktion der Flüchtlingsverwaltung in Württemberg-Hohenzollern, 1945–1952* (Berlin: Franz Steiner Verlag, 1999), p. 41.

[39] *Sept ans d'activité en faveur des personnes déplacées*, p. 6.

[40] Yvelines Pendaries, *Les Procès de Rastatt (1946–1954)* (Bern: Peter Lang, 1995), pp. 141–142.

[41] This was an attitude that was also prevalent in the British zone: Bettina Blum, 'My Home, Your Castle: British Requisitioning of German Homes in Westphalia', in Erlichman and Knowles (eds.), *Transforming Occupation in the Western Zones of Germany*, pp. 115–132, 121.

[42] MAE, HCRFA, Ambassade de Bonn 148, Laffon à Général d'Armée Commandant en chef français en Allemagne, 26 November 1946.

Rastatt, the authority of French occupiers and PDR officers was nevertheless expressed in an inanimate architectural symbol of power to both defeated Germans and DPs.[43]

The PDR service was first directed by General Kaepplin, who suffered from health problems and was soon replaced by his *Sous-directeur* Alfred Poignant in the winter of 1945.[44] Poignant was an *agrégé d'allemand*, who had taught in Berlin in the early 1930s and then worked at the *Lycée français* in Algiers.[45] His superiors described him as a skilled pedagogue.[46] He joined the international service of the PDR Ministry in July 1944. In December he became 'chef d'Etat-Major de la Mission Française de Rapatriement en Allemagne'.[47] As the head of the French repatriation mission, Poignant had shown '[a] great deal of dynamism, method and rigour' and a 'deep knowledge of Germany'.[48] For all his previous experiences and profound knowledge of Germany, Poignant was in charge of an organization, which was significantly understaffed for the task ahead.[49] In addition to administrating DPs, the organization had to gather information about French and Allied men presumed missing or dead and make provision for the approximately 330,000 German civilians expected to return to the French zone. They also dealt with the exhumation and transfers of French corpses to France and the pilgrimage of French families coming to visit tombs of French dead buried in Germany, before their corpses were repatriated to France.[50]

---

[43] In Rastatt itself, there were not many registered DPs: around 350 Polish DPs were settled in a military casern. UNA, UNRRA, S-0438-0005-02, S. M. Chabanne to Lenclud, Rapport et suggestions pour la réorganisation de la Zone Francaise, 6 November 1945.

[44] HCRFA, Ambassade de Bonn 148, Fiche pour le Général, signé chef du Cabinet civil R. de Varreux. Objet: Nomination de M. Poignant comme Directeur des Personnes Déplacées. 11 January 1946; Général de Corps d'Armée Koenig à Roger Kaepplin, 12 January 1946.

[45] MAE, HCRFA, PDR3/237, Note pour Directeur de l'Administration Générale, sous-direction du personnel, 27 August 1947; AN, F/17/28771, Dossier Personnel Alfred Poignant, Notice individuelle, destinée à l'inspection générale, Année 1937–1938 (date de l'inspection 23 mai 1938, pris connaissance, 15 Novembre 1938).

[46] AN, F/17/28771, Dossier Personnel Alfred Poignant.

[47] MAE, HCRFA, Bonn 148, Fiche pour le General, 11 January 1946.

[48] AN, F/17/28771, Dossier Personnel Alfred Poignant.

[49] MAE, HCRFA, Bonn 148, Fiche pour le Colonel Vrinat, Attributions et activité de la Direction des Personnes Déplacées, 10 December 1946.

[50] MAE, HCRFA, Bonn 148, Général d'armée Koenig to Roger Kaepplin, 12 January 1946; Fiche pour le Colonel Vrinat, 10 December 1946. In total, according to the PDR official report, 18,532 corpses were transported from 1947 to 1949. Service des Personnes Déplacées, *Sept ans d'activité en faveur des personnes déplacées en zone française d'occupation, 1945–1952*, rapport dactylographié et illustré [undated], [Bibliothèque du Ministère des Affaires Etrangères, Direction des Archives], pp. 6; 87–91. Jean Marc Dreyfus is currently working on a project on the French search mission for the corpses of French deportees in Germany.

By the end of October 1945, when UNRRA HQ was set up in the zone, the PDR organization controlled the majority of DP camps in the Southern part of the French zone (Baden Württemberg) and, many within its ranks, looked suspiciously at this international organization, which had not provided enough assistance for the repatriation of French citizens.[51] At the same time, the arrival of UNRRA HQ brought administrative confusion in the field. The PDR Director Poignant never entirely accepted UNRRA's authority over what he regarded as his private fiefdom. According to him, the Foreign Ministry agreed to UNRRA's involvement for 'high political reasons', but DPs did not benefit from its presence. 'UNRRA has no supplies, no personal files, no transport resources, no means of communications,' he hissed.[52] There were fewer than a hundred UNRRA relief workers in the zone.[53] Most UNRRA teams were located in the Northern part of the zone (Rhineland-Palatinate; Saar), regions liberated by the US army.[54] Only four UNRRA teams (Freiburg, Biberach, Wangen and Rottweil) operated in the South, the territory of Württemberg, which had been freed by the First French Army.[55] Often isolated, many UNRRA workers felt neglected and had the 'unfortunate impression' 'that nobody [was] interested in their work'.[56] In Wangen, the UNRRA Director commented that 'our chief problem [...] seems to be WAITING. Waiting is worse than working; but for the sake of the DPs we must try to be patient'.[57] In the context of the escalating rivalry between the PDR service and UNRRA headquarters, UNRRA officials nevertheless insisted that they were doing *more* for DPs than the PDR administration, notably by providing recreational and educational activities.[58] In spite of the administrative difficulties that they encountered, UNRRA officials saw themselves as undertaking a different project than their PDR counterparts, presenting DP camps as sites of valuable recuperation rather than simply discipline. In this

---

[51] UNA, UNRRA, S-0438-0005-02, S. M. Chabanne to Lenclud, Rapport et suggestions pour la réorganisation de la Zone Francaise, 6 November 1945.
[52] MAE, HCRFA, PDR1/18, Poignant, Note pour le Ministre, 28 July 1945.
[53] UNA, UNRRA, S-0425-0007-04, Confidential report, UNRRA II French corps area, Situation report, 8 August 1945, p. 4.
[54] UNA, UNRRA, S-0436-0059-02, Field Report No. 2, District Director UNRRA, XXIII Corps Area, 12 June 1945; S-0436-0059-08, Bryce Ryan, Director Team 17 to Mr Guy Drake-Brockman, UNRRA Team 17, 17 June 1945.
[55] UNA, UNRRA, S-0425-0007-09, List of teams in the First French area, Field Supervisor: Mr Moreland, 5 August 1945.
[56] Ibid.
[57] UNA, UNRRA, S-0421-0086-02, A. Aley, Weekly report No. 2, week ending 8 September 1945. On the First French Army in Southwest Germany, see Miot 'Sortir l'armée des ombres'.
[58] UNA, UNRRA, S-0417-0001-03, Rapport succint sur les activités de l'UNRRA en ZFO depuis le 18 février 1946, 31 July 1946, p. 5.

context, DP spaces varied greatly in the French zone both in terms of how and by whom they were administered, but also in relations to their physical environment.

## Making DP Camps

After the Liberation, DPs were hastily regrouped in improvised camps of various sizes to facilitate the maintenance of law and order, the provision of basic services such as food and medical care and the screening and repatriation of DPs. Camps were spread across the zone, with a clear divide between the North, liberated by the Americans, and the South, set free by the French. In the North, the American military authorities regrouped DPs in large military caserns and barracks, clearly separating DP spaces from their local German surroundings. In the South, by contrast, the French Army either reassembled DPs in smaller and more varied camps or left them in German households [*chez l'habitant*]. DP sites thus differed widely in terms of their physical environment and openness to the surrounding local communities.

In the eyes of some relief workers, DP living conditions were more pleasant in the South, where DPs enjoyed more privacy, than in the North, where DPs tended to be regrouped in large military settings.[59] In his history of the International Refugee Organisation, French diplomat René Riestuehlber argued that DP conditions were on the whole more 'normal' in the French zone than elsewhere in Germany. '[I]n the French zone, the small number of refugees, the methods adopted and the local conditions have prevented a regime of population concentration in the vicinity of ruined cities. The impression that dominates is that of people dispersed within pleasant countryside [campagne riante] and picturesque villages.'[60] The objective of the next section is to complicate this claim. On the one hand, despite overcrowding and the lack of privacy, DPs could imprint their own identities and impose individuality on the physical space of large DP camps.[61] The DP camp of Gneisenau was, for instance, re-baptized with 'great fanfare' 'Gniezno' by its Polish inhabitants in January 1946.[62] Gniezno was the capital of Poland in the legend of Lech, the mythological founder of Poland. On the other hand, DPs could feel more vulnerable and isolated 'chez l'habitant'. The requisition of German private spaces to house DPs caused great tensions not only between

---

[59] UNA, UNRRA, S-0438-0005-02, S. M. Chabanne, 'Rapport et suggestions pour la réorganisation de la Zone française', 6 November 1945.

[60] René Ristelhueber, *Au secours des réfugiés. L'oeuvre de l'Organisation Internationale pour les Réfugiés* (Paris: Plon, 1951), p. 118.

[61] Bailkin, *Unsettled*, p. 25.

[62] UNA, UNRRA, S-1021-0085-05, W. J. Faucette, Directeur UNRRA Team 20, Autonomous camp government, 31 March 1947.

French occupiers and German landlords, but also among the French.[63] In towns, German local inhabitants often resented the sharing of their domestic spaces with French occupiers and DPs.[64] Requisition inscribed in the private sphere defeat and foreign occupation.[65]

When the French authorities took control of the overall zone in the summer of 1945, there were approximately 150,000 registered DPs: 110,000 were registered in the South of the zone, including 55,000 Russians, 27,000 Poles and 9,000 Yugoslavs.[66] In November 1945, the number of DPs dropped to 75,282 DPs living in camps, of which roughly 35 per cent were located in the Northern region of the zone (Saar, Rhineland-Palatinate), with the remaining 65 per cent in the Southern region (Baden, Württemberg).[67] In addition, around 20,500 DPs lived in private accommodation, 7,500 in the North (Palatinate, Saarland, Rhineland) and 13,000 in the South (Baden, Württemberg).[68] In the autumn of 1945, the French zone comprised 44 DP camps, including 5 in the Rhineland, 7 in the Palatinate, 2 in the Saar, 11 in the Baden and 19 in the Württemberg areas.[69] In the North, the largest DP communities were concentrated in Landstuhl (5,500), Lebach (4,500), Niederlahnstein (3,100), Gneisenau (2,850) and Pirmasens (2,600).[70] In the Baden area, the most numerically important groups of DPs resided in

---

[63] See, for instance, UNA, UNRRA, S-0438-0005-02, Report, welfare officer, Southern district, 8 June 1946 or S-0421-0040-05, Bauche à Lavau, 29 June 1946.

[64] According to French regulations, houses belonging to former members of the Nazi Party were supposed to be requisitioned first, but this was not always the case in practice. Glöckner, 'Shared Spaces', p. 202.

[65] Anne Duménil, 'L'expérience intime des ruines: Munich, 1945-1948', in Bruno Cabanes and Guillaume Piketty (dir), *Retour à l'intime au sortir de la guerre* (Paris: Tallandier, 2009), pp. 101–115, 107; Jennifer Evans, *Life among the Ruins – Cityscape and Sexuality in Cold War Berlin* (London: Palgrave, 2009); Margarete Myers Feinstein, 'All Under One Roof: Persecutees, DPs, Expellees and the Housing Shortage in Occupied Germany', *Holocaust and Genocide Studies*, vol. 32, no. 1 (2018), pp. 29–48, 31; Blum, 'My Home, Your Castle', pp. 115–132.

[66] MAE, HCRFA, PDR1/15, Note pour Kaeppelin, 3 August 1945.

[67] On 29 November 1945, the French authorities estimated that there were DPs in the French zone, with 26,026 living in the Northern part of the Zone and 49,256 in the Southern part. [MAE, HCRFA, PDR6/467, Compte-rendu d'activité de la troisième section pendant le mois de Novembre, 29 November 1945.] But the evidence suggests that the DP population was only exhaustively listed in the spring and summer of 1947, revealing the presence of nearly 5,000 DPs. [PDR6/467, Nombre total de DP recensés en ZFO [undated]; Général d'armée Koenig à Secrétaire d'Etat aux Affaires Allemandes et Autrichiennes, 28 July 1948.]

[68] MAE, HCRFA, PDR6/467, 3eme section, 1er bureau, Effectif des Personnes Déplacées, 15 October 1945.

[69] *Sept ans d'activité en faveur des personnes déplacées en zone française d'occupation*, p. 6.

[70] UNA, UNRRA, S-0438-0005-02, Population DP en Zone Française d'Occupation (Zone Nord) [undated; 30 October 1945].

Mulheim (4,040), Freiburg (2,900) and Offenburg (2,700). In the Württemberg area, the largest DP communities lived in Ravensburg (5,000), Wangen (4,200), Rottweil (3,700), Balingen (2,770), Saulgau (2,700), Biberach (2,600) and Friedrichaffen (2,200).[71] While some camps were tightly controlled, with armed guards at the perimeters, other spaces were more open to the local surroundings. These different physical settings informed how DPs and relief workers thought of themselves and each other. As UNRRA Team Director Jean Gerbier observed when he arrived in Lindau 'DPs were unaware of their rights – and their duties – nearly all of them were DPs without even knowing it'.[72] In his area, DPs were scattered across twenty-nine villages and the UNRRA team was installed in several town-centre buildings. If, as Jean Gerbier observed, 'for the last seven months UNRRA's activities revolved around the word "camp"' [elsewhere in Germany], most UNRRA teams in his region had no camps.[73] In the French zone, unlike in the two other Western zones, the refugee camp was not a standardized and generalizable technology of power in the management of mass displacement.[74]

For DPs who lived in large military structures in the North of the zone, overcrowding, unpleasant smell and constant noise were common problems. In the North, American efforts to manage the post-war disruption had hinged on the use of large military structures (Landstuhl, Lebach, Gneisenau, Homburg, Augusta, Niederlahnstein, Feyen and Pirmasens). Men and women were mixed together in military blocks and barracks, which were often in poor conditions, with broken roof and missing windows.[75] These spaces bore the marks of war.[76] Near Koblenz, for instance, DPs had been regrouped in three military caserns formerly belonging to the Wehrmacht: Augusta (made of six blocks in good conditions but without central heating), Gneisenau (where not a single building in the camp had escaped artillery fire) and Niederlahnstein (where the living conditions were fairly good despite the damage on the roof caused by bombing).[77] The SHAEF *Guide to the Care of Displaced Persons in*

[71] UNA, UNRRA, S-0438-0005-02, Population DP en Zone Française d'Occupation (Zone Sud), 30 October 1945.
[72] UNA, UNRRA, S-1021-0085-08, Jean Gerbier, Rapport sur les activités de l'UNRRA dans le cercle de Lindau (Bavière) 30 octobre 1945 – 30 avril 1947, 8 May 1947, p. 3 bis.
[73] UNA, UNRRA, S-0421-0053-04, Le chef du détachement UNRRA à Direction UNRRA Wangen, 13 November 1945.
[74] Liisa Malkki, 'Refugees and Exile: from "Refugee Studies" to the National Order of Things', *Annual Review of Anthropology*, vol. 24 (1995), pp. 495–523; Bailkin, *Unsettled*, p. 6.
[75] *Sept ans d'activité en faveur des personnes déplacées en zone française d'occupation*, p. 16.
[76] UNA, UNRRA, S-0438-0005-02, R. le Goff, Rapport du service 'Welfare' sur le district Nord, 31 March 1946, p. 5.
[77] MAE, PDR6/493, Rapports d'Inspection médicale, November 1945; UNA, UNRRA, S-1021-0085-05, W. J. Faucette, Directeur UNRRA Team 20, Autonomous camp government, 31 March 1947.

*Germany* had prescribed that national groups should be housed together, families maintained intact, and single men and single women separated.[78] This bureaucratic ideal was rarely fulfilled. In Niederlahnstein, 3,100 Polish DPs lived in badly damaged barracks, whose capacity was of 2,000 inhabitants.[79] In Feyen, near Trier, DPs slept in corridors, cellars and attics.[80] In some military caserns, ethnic groups lived in close proximity with one another. The military casern of Pirmasens hosted, for instance, 2,785 DPs, including 3,679 Poles, 50 Romanians, 24 Spaniards and 24 Czechs in October 1945. Composed of 9 blocks of barracks and 27 blocks of small family dwellings, the casern had suffered from 'extensive damage by bombing'.[81] DPs helped repairing the facilities.[82] According to a relief worker, DPs preferred the family dwellings over the barracks, as they allowed a small amount of privacy.[83] On the whole, DPs had little control over the choice of their roommates.[84] In Landstuhl, for instance, Ukrainian DPs felt isolated amongst the majority of the Polish DP population.[85] For DP priests, this close proximity encouraged immoral behaviour and 'unacceptable' intimate relations between young men and women.[86] It was also detrimental to DP mental health as the constant and inescapable noise in these overcrowded camps constituted a heavy charge for DP nervous systems, already affected by years of captivity and encampment.[87]

Tensions over room allocations formed an important axis of political protest amongst DPs.[88] In the military structure of Landstuhl, while the UNRRA team was housed very comfortably, 5,500 DPs lived in barracks planned for 2,500 inhabitants in October 1945.[89] Earlier that year, the UNRRA director commented on this striking contrast. '[The UNRRA team] ha[s] excellent food, superb beds, plenty of service, and very fine friends among the Poles and the military. And I personally at least am paid a good salary. But quite a number of us didn't come to Europe with the idea of being the United Nations first pensioners.'[90] As this quote reveals, DP built

---

[78] Malcolm Proudfoot, *European Refugees, 1939–1952* (London: Faber and Faber, 1957), p. 163.
[79] UNA, UNRRA, S-0438-0005-02, Visit to Camp at Niederlahnstein, 28 September 1945.
[80] UNA, UNRRA, S-0438-0005-02, Visit to the PDR Centre at Treves, 29 September 1945.
[81] UNA, UNRRA, S-0421-0081-02, H. N. Nevins, UNRRA team report, 31 October 1945.
[82] UNA, UNRRA, S-0421-0059-02, J. Castillo à Directeur du District Nord, 6 March 1946.
[83] UNA, S-0421-0059-01, Mr Truchet du team 61 au sujet du choix d'un camp en vue de passer l'hiver, 11 July 1945.
[84] Walczewski, *Destin tragique des polonais déportés en Allemagne*, p. 64.
[85] UNA, S-0421-0045-04, Directeur Team 2 Landstuhl à Direction Générale UNRRA, 25 April 1947.
[86] Walczewski, *Destin tragique des polonais déportés en Allemagne*, p. 85.
[87] Ibid., p. 87.
[88] UNA, UNRRA, S-0438-0005-02, Visit to Camp at Niederlahnstein, 28 September 1945.
[89] UNA, UNRRA, S-0438-0005-02, Visit to the Camp at Landstuhl, 1 October 1945.
[90] UNA, UNRRA, S-0436-0059-08, Report from Bryce Ryan, Director Team 17 to Guy Drake-Brockman, 17 June 1945.

environment embodied social structures and created a clear divide between UNRRA workers and DPs and between different groups of DPs. Within camps, relief workers were easily recognizable because they were dressed in khaki-coloured uniforms, which even DPs employed by UNRRA were required to wear. In Landstuhl, for instance, DPs working for UNRRA represented a 'class of privileged DPs', who benefited from better housing conditions than the rest of the DP population.[91] Not only were they lodged more comfortably, but they also had access to recreation facilities unlike other DPs. The UNRRA mess was supposed to be a 'foyer' for all DPs to play cards and table tennis, but was in effect used for marriages and parties organized by small groups of DPs.[92] In Landstuhl, as in many other camps, the allocation of housing inscribed in the private sphere privilege and power. The architecture of camps governed DPs' inclusion or exclusion in the aid system.

These military caserns were aimed at instilling a sense of discipline, hygiene and community, by isolating residents from local population. Yet, these aims were not easily achieved due to overcrowding, the lack of soap and the porosity between DP and German spaces. In January 1946, a medical inspection of the casern of Trier-Kemmel revealed, for instance, that the camp was overpopulated, the rooms extremely dirty, the camps deprived of electricity, DPs stealing light bulbs. 'Plundering has become the general rule.'[93] Most military caserns had clearly demarcated boundaries separating DP space from the German surroundings. In her work on DP spaces in the American zone, Anna Holian argues that confined spaced served a political purpose, separating 'those who belonged in Germany from those who belonged elsewhere.'[94] According to her, American authorities developed a policy of 'divided jurisdiction' that established DP camps as spaces of exception to avoid tensions and revengeful acts against the German population. This clear divide did not always appease the resentment of local German inhabitants who lived nearby. Following well-established antisemitic and racist stereotypes, many Germans associated DPs with rampant criminality and illicit trade activities.[95] DP camps were regarded as potential sources of social unrest and breeding grounds for infectious diseases.[96] In Landstuhl, for instance, DPs were

---

[91] UNA, UNRRA, S-0421-0042-01, Lettre à Monsieur le directeur UNRRA Team 2, 7 June 1947.
[92] UNA, UNRRA, S-0421-0042, 03, Rous, Principal Welfare to de Fos, 4 October 1946.
[93] UNA, UNRRA, S-0433-0002-03, De Cilleuls, rapport d'inspection, 17 January 1946 (pp. 25–28).
[94] Anna Holian, 'The Ambivalent Exception: American Occupation Policy in Postwar Germany and the Formation of Jewish Refugee Spaces', vol. 25, no. 3 (2012), pp. 452–473, 458.
[95] Laura Hilton, 'The Black Market in History and Memory: German Perceptions of Victimhood from 1945 to 1948', *German History*, vol. 28, no. 4 (2010), pp. 479–497.
[96] Andreas Rinke observes that the criminality rate was lower in the French zone than in the other Western zones. He speculates that this stemmed from France's 'harshness' and the strict attitude of French occupation officials. *Le Grand retour*, p. 298.

accused of contributing to the rise of criminality and 'polluting' the water of the town.[97] DPs were commonly associated with filth and diseases by their German neighbours. Although camps were often imagined to emphasize the differences between those who lived inside and outside, they were in close physical interactions with the village and town which they were part of.[98] Even when DP camps had clearly demarcated boundaries, close physical interactions between DPs and local inhabitants still occurred. In Pirmasens, for instance, after a fusillade occurring in the vicinity of the camp, a German woman was found 'lying' in the bedroom of a DP by the police.[99] DPs were clearly separated in the realms of administration from Germans, but DP camps were not hermetically enclosed 'parallel societies', totally separated from German society in spatial terms.[100]

DP spaces aimed at fixating DP population in specific and confined locations. DP camps contained all the essential elements of collective life, including schools, churches, libraries and sport facilities.[101] Yet, DPs' movement in and out of camps was never fully controlled. In September 1945, the French military government strictly restricted DPs' freedom of movement and prevented them from moving more than 5 km from their place of residence without the authorization of the camp Director.[102] DPs profoundly resented this restriction. In Biberach, a relief worker from the Jewish Relief Unit noted: '[t]he reasons why people are complaining [...] are the following: the small food rations, the impossibility of moving about for more than 5 kilometres

---

[97] UNA, UNRRA, S-0421-0041-04, Dr Rellay à Administrateur Reclus, 10 February 1947.
[98] Bailkin, *Unsettled*, p. 134.
[99] UNA, UNRRA, S-0421-0059-03, P. Le Bouty, Compte-rendu Fusillade entre la police allemande et trois DP du camp de Pirmasens, 15 April 1946.
[100] Jan-Hinnerk Antons, 'Displaced Persons in Postwar Germany: Parallel Societies in a Hostile Environment', *Journal of Contemporary History*, vol. 49, no. 1 (2014), pp. 92–114. On the historic triangle of Germans, Jews, Allies also see Frank Stern, 'The Historic Triangle: Occupiers, Germans and Jews in Postwar Germany', in Robert Moeller (ed.), *West Germany under Construction: Politics, Society and Culture in the Adenauer Era* (Ann Arbor: University of Michigan Press, 1997), pp. 199–230; Atina Grossmann, *Jews, Germans and Allies: Close Encounters in Occupied Germany* (Princeton, NJ: Princeton University Press, 2007); Margarete Myers Feinstein, *Holocaust Survivors in Postwar Germany, 1945–1957* (Cambridge: Cambridge University Press, 2010).
[101] Julia Maspero 'Sur les traces des camps de personnes déplacées dans les anciennes zones françaises en Allemagne et en Autriche: une mémoire effacée ou déplacée?', in Jean-Frédéric de Hasque and Clara Lecadet (dir.), *Après les camps. Traces, mémoires et mutations des camps de réfugiés* (Paris: Academia Harmattan, 2019), p. 175.
[102] MAE, HCRFA, PDR6/467, Commandant en Chef Français en Allemagne, Note de Service concernant la discipline et le contrôle de la circulation des personnes déplacées, 27 September 1945.

without an official laissez-passer pass, the hopelessness of the emigration situation, still being forced to live in a camp fourteen months after the liberation.'[103] In Gailingen, the UNRRA Director vehemently remonstrated against the ban imposed on Jewish DPs for crossing the Swiss border to celebrate Purim with the Jewish community of Diessenhofen: 'Our DPs, are not Germans, but the victims and survivors of German savagery. Isn't it, thereby, at least shocking, if not scandalous to refuse to them what one permits to the others?'[104] If these measures limited DP movement, they did not prevent them from travelling. DPs changed residence and travelled frequently across and beyond the zone. For some DPs, travelling was essentially a matter of breaking free after years of forced immobility and deprivation of most elementary freedom; for others, it was motivated by an urge to find remaining parents in Germany.[105]

At the border of the French and American zones, according to an official report, 'on the bridges over the Rhine, papers were only cursorily checked by the Americans and not at all by the French'.[106] On 29 July 1946, DPs' freedom of movement was further limited. A French instruction stipulated that DP could not go out of the local area (*cercle*) without the authorization of the PDR officer and that only the French Superior Delegate could authorize a journey outside of the French zone.[107] Despite the French authorities' attempts at controlling DPs' movement, the evidence suggests that many DPs travelled illegally in the zone, for DPs used various strategies to bypass French control. For instance, in August 1946, UNRRA team director reported the 'mysterious' journeys of a Polish Jews in and out of his camp in Gailingen without ID card and resident permit.[108] Relief workers were aware of the numerous illicit movements that took place across the zone. The French authorities struggled, in particular, to police Jewish DP movements, for Zionist organizations used various strategies to hide DPs and French official instructions were contradictory.[109] The French zone was host to only a small number of Polish Jewish DPs fleeing Poland.[110] Far from Germany's eastern borders, the zone offered fewer

---

[103] WL, HA6 B-2/1, Report Nr. 2 Jewish Relief Unit, Biberach, July 30 1946, Dixi Heim.
[104] UNA, UNRRA, S-0421-0038-06, Schutterle, chef détachement UNRRA (Team 676) Gailingen à Field Supervisor, 12 March 1947.
[105] *Sept ans d'activité en faveur des personnes déplacées en zone française d'occupation*, p. 22.
[106] MAE, HCRFA, PDR6/467, Extrait du Rapport Mensuel Mois de Décembre Délégation de Rhénanie [undated, probably December 1945].
[107] *Sept ans d'activité en faveur des personnes déplacées en zone française d'occupation*, p. 22.
[108] UNA, UNRRA, S-0421-0039-03, Jacque Bauche to Lieutenant Jousse, 29 August 1946.
[109] David Lazar, *L'opinion française et l'Etat d'Israël, 1945–1949* (Paris: Calmann-Lévy, 1972); Catherine Nicault, *La France et le sionisme, 1897–1948. Une rencontre manquée?* (Paris: Calmann-Lévy, 1992).
[110] This was particularly the case in the French sector in Berlin.

material resources than the American zone.[111] But many Jewish DPs transited through the French zone and French sector in Berlin.[112] French official instructions concerning Jewish DPs were contradictory, shaped by a variety of changing factors.[113] Efforts to accommodate Jewish organizations' demands were highly significant, Zionists enjoying considerable political support in the French press and among the new Republican elite. Yet the French authorities remained uncomfortable with the idea of not satisfying British requirements, before the UN partition decision of 29 November 1947 led to an easing of immigration restrictions to Palestine. Relief workers were aware of the numerous illicit movements that took place across the zone. Despite the French authorities' important efforts at policing and restricting DPs' circulation in the zone, controlling their movement was never fully successful.

In the South, a relatively large proportion of the DP population was dispersed throughout the countryside and lived outside camps, in requisitioned hotels, houses and inns. The physical structure of DP camps varied greatly: DP camps included a former Hitler Youth school (Calw), a prison camp (Schömberg), monasteries (Reute, Blönried, Weingarten and Inzigkofen), castles (Isny, Wurzach), a former internment camp (Villingen), large stone buildings (Ebingen, Tuttlingen), clusters of wooden huts (Tübingen, Freudenstadt and Kisslegg), requisitioned hotels (Konstanz) and private houses (Freiburg, Rottweil, Emmendingen).[114] Some DPs were also accommodated in the remnants of former concentration camps, in particular the sub-camps of the Natzweiler-Struthof complex (Frommern).[115] Conditions varied accordingly. In Schömberg they were dire. DPs lived in a prisoners' camp in the vicinity of a factory devoted to the extraction of shale oil. They suffered from cold, muddy surroundings and air pollution.[116] The castle of Wurzach, which had served as a POW camp during the war, bore little resemblance with Schömberg' prisoners camp.[117] There was a high level of cultural activity, Baltic DPs organizing concerts and traditional folkloric

---

[111] Wiener Library, H46A-3/2, Letter from W. Heim, UNRRA SP 50386, BPM 510, Haslach, Germany, 20 May 1946.

[112] Thomas Albrich, *Exodus durch Österreich. Die jüdischen Flüchtlinge, 1945–1948* (Innsbruck: Haymond Verlag, 1987); Idith Zertal, *From Catastrophe to Power. The Holocaust Survivors and the Emergence of Israel* (Oakland: University of California Press, 1998); Rinke, *Le Grand retour*; Julia Maspero, 'French Policy on Postwar Migration of Eastern European Jews through France and French Occupation Zones in Germany and Austria', *Jewish History Quarterly*, vol. 2 (2013), pp. 319–339.

[113] HA6B-2/1, Detailed report of activities of M. F. Mandelbaum, 4 September 1946.

[114] UNA, UNRRA, S-0417-0001-08, UNRRA HQ – French zone, Reply to Questionnaire dated 23 April 1946, No. 98/06, Secret, pp. 7–10.

[115] UNA, UNRRA, S-0433-0002-03, De Cilleuls, rapport d'inspection, 21 February 1946, p. 55.

[116] UNA, UNRRA, S-1021-0085-02, Evacuation du camp de Schömberg [undated].

[117] On the history of this castle during the war, see Gisela Rothenhäuser, *Reaching across the Barbed Wire. French PoWs, Internees from the Channel Islands and Jewish Prisoners*

dances.[118] The Latvian artist Kalmite painted and exhibited his missed homeland. His daughter, born in Wurzach, believes that Kalmite's identity as an artist was forged during his time in Wurzach through his close interactions with other members of the Latvian diaspora and encounters with the physical environment of the castle.[119] In Munderkingen (near Ehingen), 45 DPs lived in a eighteenth-century house with decorated ceiling and marquetry doors.[120] In the town of Ravensburg, the majority of the 3,000 DPs lived in private houses. The Ravensburg DP centre consisted of a building, located in the town centre, in which the team had organized an UNRRA store and several workshops.[121] The material experiences of DPs thus diverged significantly in the South of the zone. Smaller 'spaces' tended to be seen as more 'homelike' than larger ones, but none were ever considered as 'home' by relief workers and DPs alike.[122]

Cohabitation with Germans in private houses aroused tensions, especially when people had to live together in relatively small spaces. In the winter of 1945, some agricultural DP workers who lived in German housing moved to camps in the hope of finding more comfortable living conditions.[123] The situation was particularly tense in towns, where many DPs experienced difficult and even abusive relationships with their German landlords. In Freiburg, there was great competition over accommodation between the DP population, local students, the claims of the Regional Military Government and their families, and the German administration.[124] Germans, French occupiers and DPs were forced to live together in close proximity as neighbours.[125] A group of 3,500 DPs was originally accommodated in the Vauban Camp. The UNRRA team lived within the same camp, but it soon moved outside the camp. The Vauban Camp was also dismantled and its inhabitants either transferred to other camps or requisitioned houses.[126] In Freiburg, like in other towns, the

---

*from Bergen-Belsen in Schloss Wurzach (1940–1945)* (Jersey: Channel Island Publishing, 2012).

[118] UNA, UNRRA, S-0421-0086-01, Welfare report for Kreis Wangen, Team 210, 4 October 1945, Grace Gavey.

[119] Lelde Kalmite, Ilze Arajs, *Two Generations of Art in Emigration – The Kalmite Story*, exhibition catalogue (2016).

[120] UNA, UNRRA, S-0438-0005-02, O. Despeigne, Ehingen, 25 June 1946.

[121] UNA, UNRRA, S-0417-0004-14, Dorothea Greene, Ravensburg, Team UNRRA 579, [August 1946?].

[122] Bailkin, *Unsettled*, p. 70.

[123] UNA, HCRFA, S-0438-0009-05, Réunion des Welfare Officers du District Sud des Teams de l'Est, 15–16 Janvier 1946, Wangen.

[124] UNA, UNRRA, S-0438-0005-02, Report, welfare officer, Southern district, 8 June 1946.

[125] On Franco–German relationships in Freiburg, see on the ways in which 'shared' spaces were connected to question of power in the French zone, see Glöckner, 'Shared Spaces', pp. 202–203.

[126] UNA, UNRRA, S-1021-0085-06, E. J. Bastiaenen, Historique du Centre DP de Fribourg [undated], p. 7.

UNRRA director had to frequently intervene to protect DPs, who were subjected to growing pressure on the part of French occupation authorities to abandon their lodging.[127] In Konstanz, the UNRRA director also battled with the local military government to relocate Polish DPs evicted to the profit of Germans.[128] In June 1946, PDR officers put posters up threatening DPs that they will lose all DPs' privileges and have to pay for their rents if they could not show a work certificate that stipulates that they were at work.[129] DPs' close integration within German spaces neither guaranteed their inclusion nor altered their sense of being cut off from German society.[130]

On the whole, PDR or the French UNRRA headquarters prided themselves in having devised a more individualist and suitable solution for the DPs in their care and, thereby, hastening their return to some sense of 'normality'.[131] In December 1945, when the UNRRA team arrived in Gutach, they found around 500 DPs scattered in twenty villages in the surrounding area.[132] There, DPs were fed by the local German authorities and lived either *chez l'habitant* or in requisitioned hotels. The UNRRA Director organized a mess and a medical service in the Gutach village. He also established a small school and a transit camp to host DPs coming from Haslach.[133] The rest of his DPs lived in requisitioned hotels and private lodgings:

> In spite of great difficulties, it is my opinion that the organisation of centres such as ours is very interesting, and that the results approach more closely the aims of UNRRA than those achieved in a camp. A camp is much easier to run, but the overcrowded condition in which the DPs are forced to live is not to be recommended either from the point of view of health or morale.[134]

To be sure, by June 1946, after the mass repatriation of Soviet and Polish DPs, the majority of the 28,048 DPs in UNRRA Southern district lived in individual lodgings or in small groups of 50–100 persons, in large houses, hotels and inns.[135] A year later, by June 1947, in the overall zone, 10,347 DPs lived

---

[127] Ibid.
[128] UNA, UNRRA, S-0421-0039-03, Jacques Bauche à Pourchet, 24 August 1946.
[129] UNA, UNRRA, S-0421-0040-05, Bauche à Thomasset, 21 June 1946.
[130] See Chapter 5.
[131] For the PDR, see, for instance, *Sept ans d'activité en faveur des personnes déplacées en zone française d'occupation*, p. 27.
[132] UNA, UNRRA, S-0419-0001-07, UNRRA team report no. 5, Pierre Durand, 5 April 1946.
[133] UNA, UNRRA, S-0421-0035-01, Pierre Durand, Notice sur l'organisation du centre de Gutach, 9 March 1946.
[134] UNA, UNRRA, S-0412-0012-05, Pierre Durand, 'Report on the organization of the Centre of Gutach', 9 March 1946.
[135] UNA, UNRRA, S-0438-0005-02, Report of welfare officer, Southern District, 8 June 1946.

outside camps and 29,814 inside camps of various sites.[136] In August 1946, an UNRRA welfare officer acknowledged after visiting Konstanz: 'we are progressively moving DPs towards a normal life. In fact, they are fed by the German economy and we have to ensure that, through a system of vouchers, the DP housewife could get her milk from the dairyman, her bread from the baker and the rest of her provisions in an UNRRA store.'[137] These claims cut the story short, however. DPs did not necessarily enjoy more 'privacy' and 'normal' conditions in the South of the zone than elsewhere, as they could be subjected to pressures and threats from their German neighbours or French 'benefactors'. Further, from the perspective of the administrators, the fact that many DPs lived in private accommodation complicated the provision of basic services such as food and medical care. Transport was a nightmare. Vehicles in the French zone were in short supply, petrol even more so and the roads were atrocious.[138]

Dispersal also hampered the development of recreational activities and the organization of cultural events. Some welfare officers were disappointed to be marooned in rural areas having imagined being in charge of social activities within a large camp. In Emmendingen, UNRRA Team 576 Director Dalichampt reported that most new welfare employees attached to his team were unhappy. As he conceded, being a part of his team, 'entails the major inconvenience of being a *travail de détail* of rural social work, admittedly interesting but rather unrewarding and not producing impressive results', when compared to the cultural events organized in huge camps.[139] He urged UNRRA authorities to inform all new recruits that the French zone did not have 'model camps with between 5,000 and 10,000 DPs, like they were told [was the case] in the theoretical training classes'.[140] According to UNRRA Director Jean Gerbier, DPs living in private accommodation were uninterested in communal recreational activities anyway. 'The reason behind this is not only transport and communication difficulties. It stems from the fact that private life is a much more normal way of life than camp life. Hence, DPs behave as free and independent men, that is to say, if we dare say it, in a more selfish manner.'[141]

---

[136] Maspero 'Sur les traces des camps de personnes déplacées dans les anciennes zones françaises en Allemagne et en Autriche', pp. 171–198, 174.
[137] UNA, UNRRA, S-0421-0031-12, G. Loustalot, Rapport mensuel sur le centre de rassemblement de Constance, 25 August 1946.
[138] UNA, UNRRA, S-1021-0085-02, Report signed by Miss Roberts [undated].
[139] UNA, UNRRA, S-0421-0015-06, Marcel Dalichampt à Germaine Loustalot, 12 February 1946.
[140] Ibid.
[141] UNA, UNRRA, S-1021-0085-08, Jean Gerbier, Rapport sur les activités de l'UNRRA ...', p. 15.

This discourse about 'DP housing' revealed specific transformations in thinking about the effects of camp life occurring in the French domestic setting in the aftermath of war.[142] The home-grown experiences of deportation and labour conscription spawned anxieties about the effects of camp life on the morality of individuals. French political leaders were alarmed by the lax moral standards of French labour conscripts and feared that they had been contaminated by the promiscuity in Nazi work camps.[143] Further, the wartime separation of spouses triggered widespread discussion about the rise of deviant behaviours and divorce amongst French *Absents*.[144] In post-war France, these fears persisted and shaped some of the discussions about DPs' housing. French observers warned that camp life catalyzed the development of an appalling mentality, the overwhelming majority of Polish DPs having lost the habit of work.[145] Likewise, the PDR Director argues that placing DPs in large camps, as it had been done in the US zone, left a detrimental impression on Poles.[146] The return to 'marital order' and domestic life was seen as a political and moral priority both in France and in the French occupation zone. In this context, relief workers tended to view small camps and private accommodations as 'curative': they provided a 'refuge' from the risks of close proximity and immorality. In reality, however, small settings or private accommodations neither necessarily guaranteed safer nor more comfortable or 'recuperative' conditions.[147]

## Overseeing DP Camps

The effectiveness of camp administration suffered a great deal as a result of the tensions that existed between the PDR organization and UNRRA. The problem of DP accommodation did not rank highly amongst the Military Government's priorities. As a result, both organizations were threatened with a reduction of their staff and criticized for costing too much. Further, jurisdictional boundaries

---

[142] Leora Auslander has demonstrated that the Provisional Government made an extraordinary, albeit short-lived, effort to reunite returnees with their possessions, 'offering those who would recuperate nothing the opportunity to mourn by narrating their losses'. Leora Auslander, 'Coming Home? Jews in Postwar Paris', *Journal of Contemporary History*, vol. 40, no. 2 (2005), pp. 237–259, 256. Also see Shannon Fogg, *Stealing Home: Looting, Restitution, and Reconstructing Jewish Lives in France, 1942–1947* (Oxford: Oxford University Press, 2017).
[143] Lagrou, *The Legacy of Nazi Occupation*, pp. 148–149.
[144] Sarah Fishman, *Femmes de prisonniers de guerre (1940-1945)* (Paris: L'Harmattan, 1996), p. 230.
[145] MAE, HCRFA, DGAP, 116, Note pour Monsieur le Directeur du travail, 27 March 1946.
[146] PDR6/1017, Le Sous-Directeur de la Direction PDR à Monsieur le Directeur Général Adjoint des Affaires Administratives, 7 September 1945.
[147] For further reflection on DP spaces and mental health, see Chapter 4.

between them remained unclear and contested, before the signature of the Franco-UNRRA agreement on 18 February 1946.[148] The 18 February agreement was not only tardy, it was also profoundly confusing.[149] As in the two Western zones, the French authorities kept overall responsibility for the repatriation, control and movement of DPs, while UNRRA was in charge of the administration of the camps, tracing, statistical surveys, sanitary and welfare services.[150] The agreement granted PDR officers the right to check for fraud and other irregularities in DP camps' administration, but it did not allow them to *intrude* on administrative matters.[151] In theory, UNRRA directors were thus responsible for the internal organization of their camp, PDR officers were in charge of external problems (including policing and control) and Military Government liaison officers retained responsibility for the definitive categorization of DPs by nationality and, therefore, for repatriation.[152] In practice, the division between responsibilities did not always work out so neatly. PDR officers also derided the February 1946 agreement as a deeply unfair economic bargain, as French occupation authorities were responsible for providing the supplies, including food, that UNRRA then distributed.[153] According to the calculation of Administrator General Laffon, a DP cost an average of 360 marks a month with UNRRA in 1946. Without it, a DP would have cost an average of 60 marks or less. This meant that for 51,000 DPs (from January to June) one would have saved 18,360,000 marks for six months.[154]

The geographical distance that separated the head offices of the PDR organization and UNRRA administration rendered effective communication

---

[148] UNA, UNRRA, S-0417-0010-09, E. J. Bastiaenen, Historique du centre DP de Fribourg, vingt-deux mois au service de l'UNRRA en Zone Française d'Occupation, 1 June 1947, p. 1.

[149] Prior to this date: UNA, UNRRA, S-0417-0001-02, No. 5310DGAA/Dir PDR du Général Commandant en Chef Français en Allemagne en date du 30 Novembre 1945 et par lettre No. 5540 DGAA/Dir PDR de l'Administrateur Géneral pour le Gouvernement militaire de la zone Française en date du 24 décembre 1945; Lettre de l'Administrateur Général Laffon à Mr. Le Général de Corps d'Armée F. Lenclud, 12 January 1946; UNA, S-0417-0001-02, accord fixant les responsabilités respectives du directeur général de l'UNRRA et du général commandant en chef français en Allemagne dans la zone française d'occupation en Allemagne, copie.

[150] Silvia Salvatici, 'Fighters without Guns: Humanitarianism and Military Action in the Aftermath of the Second World War', *European Review of History*, vol. 25, no. 6 (2018), pp. 957–976.

[151] *Sept ans d'activité en faveur des personnes déplacées en zone française d'occupation, 1945–1952*, p. 15.

[152] UNA, UNRRA, S-0438-0005-02, R. le Goff, Rapport du service Welfare sur le District Nord de la ZFO, à la date du 31 mars 1946, pp. 1–27, 3.

[153] MAE, HCRFA, Bonn 159, Copie rapport confidentiel Laffon à Koenig, 7. [July 1946?]; MAE, HCRFA, ADM 40, Laffon à Général d'Armée Koenig, N. 15339, 29 July 1946.

[154] MMAE, HCRFA, ADM 40, L'administrateur Général Laffon à Monsieur le Général d'Armée, N. 15339, 29 July 1946, pp. 4–5.

between them harder still. In February 1946, UNRRA Zone HQ was moved from Rastatt (also home to the PDR Direction) to Haslach, some 75 kilometres from Baden-Baden. Originally, Lenclud had wished to be installed in Durlach, near Karlsruhe, which was of easy access to Baden-Baden and to UNRRA Central HQ in Bad Arolsen.[155] Yet he did not receive permission from the US Authorities and had to set up the HQ in Haslach instead. Haslach was an unpractical location. It could take up to 10 days – partly due to delays in postal communication, difficulties in using the telephone line or shortages of fuel – for team reports to travel from the field to UNRRA HQ.[156] Cumbersome administrative machinery, combined with extremely poor transport and communication facilities, not only impeded the growth of more harmonious relations between UNRRA HQ and its field staff.[157] It also affected the work of voluntary organizations, which struggled to obtain the adequate 'laissez passer' and permissions to carry on their activities.[158]

The administrative structure of control in DP camps was complex and the strata of power multi-layered. To make things worse, UNRRA's administrative structure was incoherent until it was eventually adapted to the zone on 22 July 1946.[159] Prior to June, UNRRA's subdivision into two district sectors was at odds with German administrative practices and with the five administrative divisions recognized by the French.[160] In June 1946, the Northern and Southern districts were replaced by three Supervisors' offices, in Neustadt, Freiburg and Tübingen.[161] UNRRA's administrative effectiveness in the French zone only really made itself felt in the summer of 1946, by which time its termination was being contemplated in London and Washington. This complex administrative structure made the implementation of directives difficult to put in effect in a uniform manner across the zone; it also required relief workers to fill in double forms and respond to the injunctions of two administrations.

---

[155] UNA, UNRRA, S-0417-0001-04, Lettre de Général de C. A. Lenclud à Monsieur Le Général de Corps d'Armée, 16 January 1946.
[156] UNA, UNRRA, S-0417-0004-09, Mr E. P. Moreland to General Lenclud, Retablissement de la discipline, 18 Janvier 1946; S-0433-0002-06, R. P. Duby, District medical officer à Monsieur le Géneral de C. A. Lenclud, 4 March 1946.
[157] Note to Miss de la Pole, M. Linden, 21 September 1945, 6.6.1, 82502529-30, ITS Digital Archives.
[158] American Jewish Joint Distribution Committee, 1945–1954 Geneva Collection, Ger.65, Letter from Melvin S. Goldstein to Emigration Department, 28 February 1947.
[159] UNA, UNRRA, S-0417-0001-03, Rapport succint sur les activités de UNRRA en Zone Française depuis le 18 février 1946, 31 July 1946.
[160] MAE, HCRFA, ADM 40, Letter N. 5310 (30 November 1945) and N. 5540 (24 December 1945) from General Laffon to General Lenclud.
[161] UNA, S-0417-0001-04, Lenclud à Laffon, réorganisation du dispositive de UNRRA en ZOF, 1 August 1946.

Both the PDR organization and UNRRA central administration imposed strict accounting rules and standards of monthly reporting. They required field workers to report statistics on each camp's demographic situation, the general state of health and nutrition, the provision of welfare service. In conformity with the 18 February agreement, UNRRA's accounts, as well as registration lists, were subject to merciless scrutiny by the PDR, which was ever ready to dramatize UNRRA's failings and shortcomings. According to the PDR organization, a number of UNRRA teams were in a state of 'absolute chaos', with no control and monitoring of the distribution of supplies. In September 1946, for instance, the director of the PDR service complained about the administration of UNRRA team 676 in Konstanz, which showed a gap of 27 DPs between the theoretical headcount and the number of DPs receiving food rations cards.[162] Incorrect head counting led to wasteful handling of goods.[163] Some UNRRA team directors threatened to resign if criticisms continued. As the director of UNRRA in the zone admitted 'the DPs [were] not, and [could not] be submitted to frequent and regular roll-calls as in the case of soldiers'.[164]

Some scholars have interpreted this insistence on the bureaucratic and regimented management of DP camps as evidence of a new professional and bureaucratic form of delivering aid.[165] But this argument ignores important continuities in humanitarian practices. As Sarah Roddy, Julie-Marie Strange and Bertrand Taithe suggest, the roots of humanitarian accountability lie in the late-Victorian and Edwardian Britain, when the private charitable sector developed and delivered accountability and monitoring in cooperation with the press to advertise and authenticate its legitimacy.[166] UNRRA's administration inherited and redeployed a number of these older auditing and accounting practices. Yet behind this insistence on transparency and efficient delivery of aid, however, fraudulent practices and erroneous reports abounded. Some were certainly the result of carelessness on the part of UNRRA workers. Others were linked to the complexity of the task confronting relief workers and difficulties of controlling DPs.

---

[162] UNA, UNRRA, S-0417-0010-07, Lettre du Directeur des Personnes Déplacées à Monsieur le Général de Corps d'Armée Lenclud, 14 September 1946.

[163] UNA, UNRRA, S-0417-0010-07, E. Begleiter (team 591) to Mr Schutterle, Field Supervisor, 20 July 1946.

[164] UNA, UNRRA, S-0417-0001-03, Replies to questionnaires attached to letter 6300/CC/DAC/ADM dated 23.9.1946.

[165] Daniel Cohen, *In War's Wake: Europe's Displaced Persons in the Postwar Order* (Oxford: Oxford University Press, 2011), p. 77.

[166] Sarah Roddy, Julie-Marie Strange and Bertrand Taithe, 'Humanitarian Accountability, Bureaucracy and Self-regulation: The View from the Archive', *Disasters*, vol. 39, no. 2 (2015), pp. 188–203; 'The Charity-Mongers of Modern Babylon: Bureaucracy, Scandal and the Transformation of the Philantropic Marketplace, c. 1870–1912', *Journal of British Studies*, vol. 54 (2015), pp. 118–137.

In the summer of 1946, complaints about UNRRA's lack of accountability, inefficient political and moral screening, involvement in illegal trafficking, poor professional standards and excessive costs found their way into the Ministry of Foreign Affairs.[167] Things soon escalated further and reached UNRRA Central Administration.[168] In September, the French UNRRA Director Lenclud compiled a thirteen-page report responding point by point to the PDR's criticisms concerning the lack of professionalism among UNRRA staff, their alleged involvement in the black market, the statistical inaccuracies evident in UNRRA accounting, their inefficient screening and their general tactlessness. He accused the PDR in return of having hired unsuitable individuals.[169] He noted that three UNRRA officials from the Pirmasens team were dismissed because of their alleged involvement in the trafficking of goods destined for DPs. Other PDR officials implicated in this affair were still in office. In addition, he recorded somewhat defensively that '[t]he UNRRA field supervisor in the Province of Baden, was arrested, [...] following complaints lodged by the UNRRA Director and this is a most outstanding example of the severity of the UNRRA administration in matters of integrity.'[170] Finally, his response to the allegations made about UNRRA's disproportionate cost was that 'it costs France nothing'.[171]

Despite Lenclud's defence of the organization, occupation officials continued to demand the dismantlement of the organization, deemed according to the administrator general Laffon 'completely irresponsible and costly'.[172] Laffon argued that the DP situation was much better in those regions where UNRRA was not present as the majority of DPs in these areas were working. Speaking from the perspective of Saarland, Gilbert Grandval concurred. He believed that UNRRA workers were too concerned with cultivating their popularity among DPs and insufficiently attentive to restabilizing law and order and preventing stocks of food, cigarettes, medical materials and drugs being looted.[173] The Superior Delegate of Württemberg was of the same opinion, claiming that UNRRA was 'an enterprise of idleness', which did not

---

[167] MAE, HCRFA, Bonn 159, Note pour Monsieur de Varreux [undated].
[168] UNA, UNRRA, S-0417-0001-01, copie, Lenclud to Lt. General Sir Frederick Morgan, 11 August 1946.
[169] UNA, UNRRA, S-0417-0001-03, Confidential Letter from Lenclud to Koenig, 4 October 1946 [in response to the letter N. 6300/CC/DAC/ADM, 27.09.1946], p. 4.
[170] Ibid., p. 4.
[171] Ibid.
[172] MAE, HCRFA, Ambassade de Bonn 148, Lettre de l'administrateur général Laffon, adjoint pour le Gouvernement Militaire de la Zone d'occupation Française à Monsieur le Général d'Armée Koenig, 25 November 1946.
[173] MAE, HCRFA, ADM 40, Le Colonel Grandval, Gouverneur de la Sarre à l'Administrateur Général, Adjoint pour le Gouvernement Militaire de la Zone Française d'Occupation, Sarrebruck, 13 November 1945.

encourage DPs to work.[174] So embittered did this UNRRA–PDR conflict become that, at the end of 1946, the Paris authorities opened a confidential investigation into it. The resultant report signed by Roger Bloch, undersecretary of state and commissar for German and Austrian Affairs, concluded that it was essentially a trifling argument between incompatible personalities.[175]

These tensions were not simply a matter of clashing personalities, however. Within DP camps, PDR officers and UNRRA camp authorities strove to instruct DPs about discipline, hygiene and the principles of hard work. But living conditions in occupied Germany and the own behaviour of some relief workers threw these ideals of discipline and hard work into disarray. Like many French occupiers, relief workers were eager to demonstrate their status as the new rulers. They displayed their power not only through instructing official orders, but also symbolically through their military credentials and material entitlements. For all UNRRA HQ's insistence on military efficiency, however, the organization rapidly acquired a bad reputation for its amateurism and the indiscipline among its ranks. Instead of conducting 'exemplary' lives, too many UNRRA staff seemed to indulge in a life of vice and pleasures.

## Cultures of Military and Civilian Relief

At the centre of UNRRA's difficulties in the zone was a fascinating paradox: UNRRA HQ was placed under the supervision of a French general, General Lenclud. Yet the organization suffered from a deep division between its military and masculine head, and its civilian and more feminized field staff. While at the high level of the administration UNRRA planners celebrated international work and promoted new approaches to refugee relief, Lenclud envisioned humanitarian aid in highly traditional ways.[176] He attempted to run his administration in a military manner. According to him, military discipline was the 'cornerstone of [the organisation's] mission'.[177] Lenclud was a career army officer and graduate of France's elite Saint-Cyr military academy whose family had suffered a great deal during the war. One of his

---

[174] UNA, UNRRA, S-0417-0001-04, Lettre confidentielle de G. E. McCandlish, chef de cabinet à Assistant Director, Haslach, 23 janvier 1947.

[175] MAE, Bonn 159, Lettre du Sous-secrétaire d'Etat, Commissaire Général aux Affaires Allemandes et Autrichiennes à Monsieur le MAE, Service des Affaires sociales. N. 1708/SOC, Paris, 3 December 1946.

[176] Silvia Salvatici, '"Help the People to Help Themselves": UNRRA Relief Workers and European Displaced Persons', *Journal of Refugee Studies*, vol. 25, no. 3 (2012), pp. 428–451.

[177] UNA, UNRRA, S-0417-0002-02, Le Général de Corps d'Armée F. Lenclud à tout le personnel UNRRA en Zone d'Occupation Française, 18 February 1946.

sons was killed by the Germans, another had been held hostage.[178] His appointment by de Gaulle in October 1945 was certainly honorific.[179] Lenclud enjoyed a good personal relationship with General Koenig, although Koenig expressed some reservation about the organization.[180] His HQ was a socially and politically conservative group, in part constituted of retired Armistice officers (that is to say officers who had continued to serve the Vichy regime) and of respected and decorated resisters. The Medical Zone officer, the Médecin-Genéral Jean Lambert des Cilleuls, had, for instance, continued to work for the Vichy regime in the South of France, before his retirement in April 1943.[181] General dit Lizé de Marguerittes, by contrast, appointed on 16 May 1946 as UNRRA liaison officer, was a prestigious General, and a decorated member of the resistance. Formerly military commander in Baden-Baden, 'he made a name for himself [amongst the French administration] due to his extreme severity, adopting an uncompromising position on [questions of] behaviour and disciplinary issues'.[182] These French military officers, often at the end of their military careers, were presided over by an international organization, whose norms and policies were established for the most part in London and Washington. These French UNRRA military officials found it difficult to adjust to their status of non-combatants and their uniform without *galons*. Lenclud resented the fact that UNRRA personnel had to wear a kakhi uniform without being able to display military grades. As a result, UNRRA high-civil servants could be mistaken with second-class soldiers of the occupation troops. This uniform without *galons* made it more difficult, according to him, to establish links between UNRRA, occupation troops and German Bürgermeister.[183]

The role of the French military elite has been extensively documented in the historiography of the French zone, a number of French military commanders having commanded colonial divisions during the war.[184] Their vision of French German policy was rooted in an approach to occupation that looked back to an era of French predominance. Amongst these commanders, General Joseph Goislard de Monsabert, Supreme Commander of the Occupation

---

[178] MAE, HCRFA, Bonn 160, Koenig à Ambassadeur Ponsot, organisation internationale des réfugiés, N. 2739/CC/CAC, 6 June 1947.

[179] Ibid.

[180] See, for instance, MAE, HCRFA, Bonn 160, Lettre du General Koenig à Général de Corps d'Armée Lenclud, N. 4359/CC/CAC/ADM [undated, June 1947?].

[181] A. Camelin, 'Le médecin-Général Jean Lambert des Cilleuls', éloge prononcé à la Société Française d'histoire de la médecine.

[182] UNA, UNRRA, S-1021-0084-11, Histoire de l'UNRRA, Relations avec les autorités militaires en zone française, by Mr G. Sebille [June 1947?], p. 4.

[183] UNA, UNRRA, S-0417-0001-01, Lettre du Général Lenclud à Monsieur le Lieutenant Général Sir Frederick Morgan, 21 February 1946.

[184] Marc Hillel, *L'occupation Française en Allemagne* (Paris: Balland, 1983), pp. 151–180.

Troops, drew in significant ways on practices and discourses elaborated in colonial Morocco. He was influenced by Marshal Hubert Lyautey's theory of 'pacification' designed to bring peace among the Moroccan population in the inter-war years.[185] A common historiographical judgment is that French occupation policies were dominated by two conflicting approaches in 1945 and the early months of 1946 – a military understanding of national security issues and a more democratic desire to re-educate Germans.[186] What is less known, however, is how the conservative social and religious backgrounds of senior officers shaped French politics of DP administration and the international organization of relief in the zone. At the Liberation, the size of the French Army was significantly reduced and 16,700 military officers were dismissed.[187] This reduction of military staff in the wake of war was not in itself unusual, but it was unprecedented in its scale and nature.[188] In this context of purges, the demobilizing French Army regarded UNRRA as 'a dumping-ground for their surplus personnel'.[189] UNRRA was 'inundated with a stream of officers, boasting numerous honours and years' experience'.[190] A number of politically compromised officers were removed (sometimes only for a limited period of time) and sent to Germany in conformity with a policy of removal for upper-echelon civil servants who were particularly competent, but had adopted politically condemnable stances under the Vichy regime.[191]

UNRRA HQ's fixation on military credentials is indicative of some of the difficulties that French professional officers faced when confronting the legacies of the defeat of 1940. Lenclud attached enormous importance to questions of hierarchy, decorum, politeness and manners. He was openly condescending towards both the PDR Director and its Administration.[192] He insisted that the high-ranking French military officers working for UNRRA had far better credentials (and social backgrounds) than those of

---

[185] Drew Flanagan, 'La juste sévérité: pacifier la zone française en Allemagne occupée, 1945–1949,' in James Connolly, Emmanuel Debruyne, Élise Julien, and Matthias Merlaien (eds.), *Occupations en territoire ennemi: Expériences, transferts, héritages (1914–1954)* (Lille: Presses Universitaires du Septentrion, 2018), pp. 205–216.

[186] Rainer Hudemann, 'Le général Koenig commandant en chef français en Allemagne (1945–1949)', p. 86.

[187] Ibid., pp. 239–262, 240.

[188] Claude d'Abzac-Epezy, 'Fin de guerre, épurations et dégagements des cadres: l'exemple de l'armée française à l'issue de la seconde Guerre Mondiale', in Jacques Frémeaux and Michèle Battesti (eds.), *Sortir de la guerre* (Paris: Presses de L'université Paris-Sorbonne, 2014), pp. 239, 241.

[189] UNA, UNRRA, S-1021-0031-07, History of UNRRA, Personnel Division [undated].

[190] Ibid.

[191] Martial Libéra, *Un Rêve de Puissance: La France et le Contrôle de l'économie Allemande (1942–1949)* (Frankfurt am Main: Peter Lang, 2012), p. 312.

[192] UNA, UNRRA, S-0417-0001-03, Confidential letter (translation) from Lenclud to Monsieur le General d'Armée Koenig, 4 October 1946, p. 4.

the PDR: 'If an impartial comparison should be made at each level between the UNRRA officials and the PDR officials it would easily be established that the honour and advantage would go to UNRRA. We have within our ranks: One Général de Corps d'Armée (four stars) – one Brigadier General – One General Medical Corps – five senior officers of the General Staff.'[193] Ever obsessed with questions of prestige and reputation, Lenclud logged a formal complaint against PDR Director Poignant whom he claimed had 'unjustly' criticized three UNRRA team directors of honourable families and impeccable military pedigree. Exasperated, he asked the military government for 'moral reparation' in February 1947, notably for Major Evans, heir of an old and honourable English family, a 'brilliant air officer during the First World War'.[194] At the lower level of the hierarchy, some UNRRA directors used the same military language, negotiating their legitimacy through their military pedigree.[195]

The highly militarized nature of the French UNRRA HQ was not specific to the French zone. Across the three Western zones, a number of UNRRA high officials were generals and expressed views of relief work firmly embedded in militaristic, patriarchal and national frameworks. These military men included the Director of UNRRA's Displaced Persons Operation in Germany, the British Lieutenant General Sir Frederick Morgan. Yet in France and in the French occupation zone, the experience of the defeat of 1940 enhanced officers' feeling of isolation within French society, while aggravating civilian contempt for military virtues.[196] If Lenclud drew upon French military discourses of efficiency, discipline and practices of military relief predating the war, his understanding of his mission ran against the realities of operational life, for far more time was spent on disciplining the workforce than anticipated. Such tensions between military ethos (saturated with notions of discipline and efficiency) and civilian mobilization were not new. The Franco-Prussian war in the late nineteenth century was an important step in the long-term militarization of civilian relief agencies.[197] In 1945, in the wake of another conflict, these tensions

---

[193] UNA, UNRRA, S-0417-0001-03, Lenclud, Confidential replies to questionnaire attached to letter 6300/CC/DAC/ADM dated 23.9.1946, 4 October 1946, p. 13. Also see MAE, HCRFA, Bonn, 159, undated UNRRA Report.
[194] UNA, UNRRA, S-0417-0001-04, Copie, Lenclud à Général d'Armée Koenig, 17 March 1947.
[195] UNA, UNRRA, S-0421-0039-03, Lettre de Bauche à Pourchet, 29 July 1946.
[196] Robert Paxton, *Parades and Politics at Vichy* (Princeton, NJ: Princeton University Press, 1966), p. 430. On civilian experiences of displacement during the war see, for example, Nicole Dombrowski Risser, *France under Fire. German Invasion, Civilian Flight and Family Survival during World War Two* (Cambridge: Cambridge University Press, 2012).
[197] Bertrand Taithe, 'The "Making" of the Origins of Humanitarianism?' *Contemporanea*, vol. 18, no. 3 (2015), pp. 489–496, 490; Bertrand Taithe, *Defeated Flesh: Welfare, Warfare and the Making of Modern France* (Manchester: Manchester University Press, 1999), p. 156.

resurfaced in new ways, as French humanitarian military officials strove to design relief policies worthy of their status of 'victors' and re-inscribe older gendered and class-based ordering of society onto DPs.

## Smuggling and Trafficking

Despite UNRRA HQ' insistence on military prestige and discipline, imposing norms of personal and professional morality onto relief workers proved very difficult. On the one hand, UNRRA often offered extremely high wages to people who had just experienced four years of hardship and privation, making low-price black-market luxury goods understandably tempting. On the other hand, employment with UNRRA was meant to be temporary.[198] In November 1945 UNRRA had a total of 244 workers in the French zone.[199] The February 1946 accord prompted sharp increases in staff. By then, the organization counted 321 'class I' personnel, a figure which rose to 579 by July, alongside a further 142 'class II' and 82 'class III' staff.[200] Class II personnel were considered as 'local employees' and paid (in Reichsmarks) considerably less than class I personnel. A number of French nationals were hastily recruited as Class II with the promise that they would become class I.[201] In January 1946, Lenclud enjoined his subordinates to bring his staff into line: 'it is no longer permissible for orders not to be followed or for reports not be sent'.[202] The main issue was, however, that UNRRA's work had developed late in the zone, and 'was expanding at a time when elsewhere there was contraction'.[203] Transfers from one team to another were frequent. UNRRA personnel thereby lived in a state of 'perpetual instability', which created frustration and discouragement.[204] In the summer of 1946, Lenclud deplored a 'combative spirit' [esprit combatif] among the UNRRA personnel.[205]

---

[198] UNA, UNRRA, S-1021-0031-07, History of UNRRA, Personnel Division [undated].

[199] UNA, UNRRA, S-0417-0001-06, Monthly reports for November, signed Lenclud, 4 December 1945.

[200] Class I personnel were those hired internationally, class II personnel were local employees and class III personnel were volunteers attached to private voluntary relief organizations, supervised but not in the paid employ of UNRRA. MMAE, HCRFA, PDR 3/16, Etat numérique du Personnel UNRRA dans la zone française, 28 June 1946; UNA, UNRRA, S-0417-0001-03, Rapport succint sur les activités de UNRRA en Zone Française depuis le 18 février 1946, Haslach, 31 July 1946.

[201] UNA, UNRRA, S-0433-0001-04, Robert Duby, Medical Officer à General des Cilleuls, Haslach, 28 August 1946.

[202] UNA, UNRRA, S-0417-0004-09, General Lenclud to Mr E. P. Moreland, District Director, Ebingen, 18 January 1946.

[203] UNA, UNRRA, S-1021-0085-02, Report signed by Miss Roberts [undated], p. 3.

[204] UNA, UNRRA, S-0421-0024-05, Compte-rendu d'inspection du team 573 de Müllheim, 8 August 1946.

[205] UNA, UNRRA, S-0417-0004-09, Lenclud à Moreland, 26 June 1946.

Disciplining this workforce was a serious matter for Lenclud's HQ.[206] UNRRA Assistant Director bemoaned the 'poor quality' of some recruits and the 'anarchy' that prevailed in some areas.[207] French UNRRA authorities also complained about the misbehaviour of 'low-grade' inspector personnel sent by UNRRA Central HQ to field.[208] Complaints about professional misconduct ranged from accusations of smuggling family members into DP camps, use of international telephone lines for private matters, absence without leave and the failure to apply UNRRA's own directives to serious misdemeanours such as black marketeering and thefts.[209] Relief workers' misbehaviours had negative effects onto DPs. In Kaiserslautern, for instance, Baltic DPs complained that UNRRA employees were using Red Cross parcels to feed their own families rather than DPs.[210] A local observer in the Rhineland captured the mood: 'Overall, UNRRA employees do not work to death. Their work is not monitored; everyone does what they fancy doing.'[211] Cases of professional misconduct were not confined to lower-level staff, for some UNRRA officials postponed meetings to go 'hunting wild boar'.[212] In September 1946 a scandal broke out after a Field Supervisor was discovered using envelopes emblazoned with a swastika for his daily correspondence.[213] UNRRA workers were also involved in large-scale trading for the sake of profit and power: food, cigarettes and medical supplies were stolen from the organization and sold on the black market.

UNRRA relief workers' involvement in black-market activities not only seriously tarnished the reputation of the organization: it also undermined relief workers' authority over DPs. The institution of black markets flourished

---

[206] UNA, UNRRA, S-0421-0042-04, G. Drake-Brockman, District Director to Field Supervisor Koblenz Area, All teams, Lack of discipline UNRRA personnel, 15 January 1946; UNA, UNRRA, S-1021-0084-10, General Marchal, History of the DP Operation in Germany, ERO Technical Instructions No. 72 [1947?].

[207] UNA, UNRRA, S-0417-0004-09, Schurmans à Moreland, 3 June 1946.

[208] UNA, UNRRA, S-0417-0001-01, Lenclud à Chief of Operations, CHQ, 24 August 1946.

[209] UNA, UNRRA, S-0421-0042-04, G. Drake-Brockman, District Director to Field Supervisor Koblenz Area, All teams, Lack of discipline UNRRA personnel, 15 January 1946; UNA, UNRRA, S-0421-0038-01, Lt. Col. Mercier, à Field supervisors et Directeurs du District Nord, 15 February 1946. UNA, UNRRA, S-0417-0010-07, Lt. Colonel. M. Pichot à Dalichamp, 17 February 1947; Lt. Colonel. M. Pichot à Directeur du Team 20 Coblence, 14 February 1947; S-0417-0004-9, Directeur du District Sud à Directeur de la Zone Française, 19 June 1946.

[210] UNA, UNRRA, S-0421-0038-02, Les réfugiés du camp des Baltes de Kaiserslautern en Palatinat à Directeur de l'UNRRA, 9 August 1946.

[211] MAE, HCRFA, PDR 3/25, Rapport secret sur la situation d'UNRRA en Rhénanie-Hesse Nassau, Coblence, 9 July 1946, p. 2.

[212] UNA, UNRRA, S-0417-0004-09, Schurmans à Moreland, 3 June 1946.

[213] UNA, UNRRA, S-0417-0001-07, Général de Marguerittes dit Lizé à Bureau du Directeur, 27 September 1946.

in Allied-occupied Germany as a mixture of shortages, rationing and price controls created powerful incentives to direct scarce resources away from 'official' markets.[214] Black-market activities acquired a symbolic dimension for UNRRA HQ, which was strict on disciplinary matters, and defeated Germans, who laid considerable blame on DPs, considered as 'the king of the black market'.[215] Most of the German population was involved in some sort of illicit trading to obtain food and basic commodities that were not available through the legal distribution systems.[216] Yet, there was a moral gradation between black, grey and white markets, in other words between what was seen as more or less immoral by occupation officials, relief workers and Germans alike. French occupation officials and UNRRA authorities certainly tried to curb black-market activities amongst their staff but imposing norms of professional conduct took time.[217] In January 1946, UNRRA fieldworkers were arrested in Freiburg for trafficking cigarettes.[218] Six months later, a Field Supervisor was arrested for trafficking and purloining a variety of goods for which he eventually received a six-month conditional sentence.[219] In November 1946, UNRRA HQ issued administrative order 86 which stipulated that any UNRRA employee who was found trading UNRRA or rationed goods would immediately be fired.[220] Despite this instruction, black-market activities continued regardless. In March 1947, UNRRA Protective Officer Lefebvre reported seventeen new cases involving organization staff, including four thefts and two whole fieldwork teams placed under investigation. Moreover, a substantial wine trafficking operation was also discovered in the North of the zone in which several UNRRA officers were implicated.[221] Consequent arrests

---

[214] On the black market in the French zone, Rainer Hudemann, *Sozialpolitik im deutschen Südwesten zwischen Tradition und Neuordnung, 1945–1953: Sozialversicherung und Kriegsopferversorgung im Rahmen französischer Besastzungspolitik* (Mainz: Von Hase & Koehler Verlag, 1988); Jürgen Wolfer, *Ein hartes Stück Zeitgeschichte: Kriegsende und französische Besatzungszeit im mittleren Schwarzwald. Zwischen 'Werwölfen', 'Kränzlemännern' und 'schamlosen Weibern'* (Hamburg: Verlag Dr. Kovac, 2012), pp. 323–327; As far as UNRRA policy was concerned: S-0417-0010-07, Traduction de l'ordre administratif No. 86 du CHQ du 9.11.1946, 21 November 1946.

[215] Wolfer, *Ein hartes Stück Zeitgeschichte*, p. 324. Also see, for instance, German complaints in Tübingen. MAE, HCRFA, PDR6/487, L'administrateur Lucien Léon à Directeur des Personnes Déplacées, 28 April 1947.

[216] Hilton, 'The Black Market in History and Memory', p. 496.

[217] UNA, UNRRA, S-0421-0042-04, Koenig, Note de Service, 1 February 1946.

[218] MAE, HCRFA, PDR6/560, Procès Verbal, Compagnie de Fribourg, Brigade de Rastatt, 28 January 1946.

[219] UNA, UNRRA, S-0417-0002-10, Lefebvre à General de C. A. Lenclud, 24 March 1947.

[220] UNA, UNRRA, S-0417-0010-07, Traduction de l'Ordre Administratif No. 86 du CHQ du 9.11.46, 21 November 1946.

[221] Ibid.

tarnished UNRRA's reputation.[222] As PDR Officer Muller observed, criminal proceedings revealed 'the emptiness that existed behind the great UNRRA façade', the anarchic and self-interested behaviour of UNRRA staff conflicting with the occupation administration's ideals.[223]

Crucial for UNRRA HQ was not only the ways DPs' lives were regulated and policed, but also the manner in which France was represented internationally. UNRRA opened French administration to international scrutiny. French UNRRA HQ was deeply anxious about the information that circulated within the organization about conditions and practices in the French zone. On many occasions, the UNRRA HQ complained about the violence committed by French and German police against DPs notably on the ground of black-market activities. In February 1947, for instance, UNRRA authorities protested against a harsh police search conducted at six a.m. in the Hindenburg Kaserne in Tübingen.[224] The cigarettes distributed by UNRRA were confiscated and several DPs arrested for illegal possession of clothes, photographic film, bikes and tyres.[225] According to the UNRRA Director, these search operations were conducted with the 'usual brutality of Germans'.[226] From General Lenclud down, many UNRRA officials expressed concern about such incidents, fretting that cases of brutal treatment were jeopardizing France's image in Germany.[227] Lenclud noted, for instance, 'I feel a profound aversion to inform UNRRA's higher hierarchy of incidents which might damage the good reputation of our country.'[228] Field Supervisor Rodie also lamented that the French were more severe towards DPs than towards Germans, while an important number of these DPs belonged to Allied nations who had fought for the liberation of Europe and in some cases France.[229] For him, this was not only an inhuman policy but also an anti-national one.[230] In March 1947, the combined pressure from UNRRA and the desire to prevent ugly

---

[222] UNRRA personnel were put on trial in the tribunals of the military government, and not military courts UNA, UNRRA, S-0417-0011-03, Note pour le Colonel Pichot, 4 July 1946.
[223] MAE, HCRFA, PDR3/237, Administrateur de 4ème classe Muller (PDR) à Administrateur Général, 1 October 1946.
[224] UNA, UNRRA, S-0419-0001-07, Similar police search in Niederlahnstein in May 1947 [Report by J. Casier].
[225] UNA, UNRRA, S-0419-0001-06, Délégué de Cercle à Roquet Field Supervisor, No. 1758/PDR/RD/MS, 18 February 1947.
[226] UNA, UNRRA, S-0419-0001-06, Fabry à directeur Général de la ZFO à Haslach, Team 589 Reutlingen, 5 February 1947.
[227] UNA, UNRRA, S-0419-0001-07, R. Lavigne, Area Team Director à Directeur Général d'UNRRA en ZFO, fouille au camp de Niederlahnstein, 21 May 1947.
[228] UNA, UNRRA, S-0419-0001-06, Lenclud à Général d'Armée Koenig, 10 February 1947.
[229] UNA, UNRRA, S-0419-0001-06, E. Y. Rodie, Field Supervisor à Direction de la Zone, Arrestation de DP, 31 December 1946.
[230] Ibid.

confrontations between DPs and Germans pushed Laffon to issue an order forbidding German police to intervene in DP camps.[231]

Professional misbehaviour, smuggling and trafficking were certainly perpetrated by both sexes, albeit in greater numbers by men – at least, of those who were caught. Yet for a woman to use commodities to buy entertainment or engage in illicit traffic during a period when the ideology of women's role was still intimately entwined with domesticity and family life was seen as a 'betrayal' of their nature. In the French zone, relief workers drew heavily on Christian faith and values to 'regulate' DPs' life and organize relief. Many (female) French field workers came from middle-class backgrounds and the traditions of social Catholicism.[232] Illicit practices challenged Christian conceptions of femininity, which revolved around notions of the virgin, single and professional female social worker entirely dedicated to a superior moral and Christian cause.[233] Christian concerns about the 'transgressive' behaviour of female workers responded to fears about women's greater political and social agency following the vote in 1944, as well as anxieties about the changing nature of the profession of social worker. Catholic and military officials feared that the role of social worker had attracted women for the wrong reasons, among which, the desire for independence, the job's snobbish *caché*, and a heightened (and, it was implied, undeserved) standing in the adult world.[234]

## French UNRRA Volunteers

The majority of UNRRA relief workers in the zone were French or francophone.[235] Although French was not recognized as an official language of UNRRA, the working language was French in the zone and most of the communication between the HQ and the teams occurred in French, thus avoiding translations, except for instructions emanating from the high level of the organization. Relief workers without the command of the French language lived in a state of isolation. An UNRRA Welfare supervisor noted

---

[231] MAE, HCRFA, PDR 6/556, L'administrateur Laffon à Délégué Général pour le GM du Land Rhéno-Palatin, Section des PD, 5 March 1947.

[232] Geneviève Perrot, 'Les savoirs en service social avant 1950', *Vie Sociale*, vol. 3, no. 3 (2008), pp. 33–43.

[233] Lae, *Une fille en correction*, p. 83.

[234] Cyril Le Tallec, *Les assistantes sociales dans la tourmente, 1939–1946* (Paris: L'Harmattan, 2003), pp. 19, 207. On the crisis of the profession also see Armelle Mabon-Fall, *Les assistantes sociales au temps de Vichy* (Paris: L'harmattan, 1995), pp. 23–29. On UNRRA – see, for instance, UNRRA, S-0438-0005-01, O. Despeigne, Report Reutlingen, Team 589, 23 June 1946.

[235] In the autumn 1945, British and American personnel were progressively replaced by French and Belgian staff. UNA, UNRRA, S-0425-0007-04, Rhatigan to Stallabrass, Neustadt, 25 August 1945.

that the 'Army surrounding us' only spoke the 'the sweet language of our France'.[236] In October, 66 per cent of UNRRA personnel were French.[237] In February 1946, the proportion rose to 78 per cent for the Southern district.[238] For UNRRA experts who visited the zone or UNRRA relief workers transferred to this 'French enclave', this often came as a surprise. Those who came from the US zone and were used to its comfort, living conditions in the zone came as a shock.[239]

French UNRRA relief workers' backgrounds were extremely heterogeneous. In October 1946 an article in *Ici-Paris* examined worsening suicide rates following the French defeat in 1940. It detailed the story of a beautiful young Parisian woman, of Iranian origin, who, after several suicide attempts, decided to join UNRRA. 'Out of desperation, she just signed up to be an UNRRA interpreter. She is going to Germany, fully contented, as she was told that she is sixty-five times more likely to be the victim of a terrorist attack.'[240] Without doubt, this story was anecdotal. Yet the evidence suggests that, in some case, enrolment with UNRRA was driven by escapism. A number of methodological challenges must be confronted when assessing the motivations and social, educational and cultural backgrounds of French UNRRA workers. It remains impossible to gather systematic information about UNRRA recruits in post in the zone, UNRRA staff personal files being closed for historical research. However, some team reports and personal evaluations offer clues about the diversity of French men and women's social circumstances. Admittedly, these evaluations are incomplete records and the details vary widely. These documents were either created by UNRRA supervisors to assess the performance of UNRRA workers or by UNRRA field workers to show that they were successfully administering and rehabilitating DPs. When used cautiously, however, these sources still offer unparalleled evidence of the discrepancy between the military background of the French UNRRA HQ and the formal training of French UNRRA field workers.

Although the professionalization of international relief work was among its main objectives, UNRRA largely disregarded the question of standard qualifications during the recruitment of French workers. While it imposed rigorous entry requirements on American recruits (candidates had to be between 30 and 55 years of age with a minimum of five years' experience in social

---

[236] UNA, UNRRA, S-0417-0011-01, G. Loustalot à Mr Lecomte de Nouye, [7 February 1946?].

[237] UNA, UNRRA, S-0412-0012-05, C. Mercier, Monthly report (October 1945) Displaced Persons operation French Zone, 7 November 1945.

[238] UNRRA, S-0417-0010-09, Nominal Role, Southern French zone, District HQ, 28 February 1946.

[239] UNA, UNRRA, S-0417-0011-01, G. Loustalot à Lecomte de Nouye [7 February 1946?].

[240] UNA, UNRRA, S-0417-0002-01, Médecin Général des Cilleuls à Général de Corps d'Armée Lenclud, 17 October 1946; *Ici-Paris*, 1–8 October 1946.

work in government or voluntary agencies as well as having the required professional qualifications), a number of French recruits had neither impressive educational backgrounds nor professional experience in relief work.[241] By 1945 the professionalization of the domestic position of *assistante sociale* (female social worker) was far from complete. Indeed, the legislation governing this new professional corps was only implemented in April 1946. Faced with a severe shortage of social workers during the war, the French authorities had recruited many staff lacking proper training. Even among those with specialist qualifications, there was a rift between those with 'medico-social' backgrounds and those who had been trained in 'pure social work'.[242] The number of social and humanitarian workers expanded significantly during the Vichy period, as the number of civilian war victims multiplied.[243] UNRRA recruiters could not ignore the profound impact of the war and its legacy in France.

The high demand for social workers in France forced UNRRA to ease its requirements regarding age and professional experience. The Chief of the UNRRA Mission in France blamed the Ministry of PDR for picking the best candidates.[244] Another significant problem was that French UNRRA workers were usually selected by British and American recruiters unfamiliar with the French education system.[245] Welfare supervisor Germaine Loustalot, who had participated to the recruitment, recalled:

> The atmosphere in which this recruitment was carried out was very unusual. People with goodwill and zealous people came to us. They belonged to the resistance. Many of their former companions in arms were in Germany, in the concentration camps. They wanted to join them, to alleviate their pain and, in some way, to finish the struggle that they had started together. The war was at its height. There were also people coming to us, whose main motivation was to go, to go anywhere, to do anything, at any price. Above all, they wanted to go. And, finally, there was the mass of those who did not know what to do, Business and Industry were not working, and were attracted by UNRRA's high wages [...].[246]

---

[241] Laura Megan Greaves, 'Concerned Not Only with Relief': UNRRA's Work Rehabilitating the Displaced Persons in the American Zone of Occupation in Germany, 1945–1947, PhD dissertation, University of Waterloo, Ontario, Canada, 2013, p. 91.

[242] Henri Pascal, *La construction de l'identité professionnelle des assistantes sociales. L'association nationale des assistantes sociales (1944–1050)* (Paris: Presses de l'EHESP, 2012), pp. 23–24.

[243] Jean-Pierre Le Crom, *Au secours Maréchal ! L'instrumentalisation de l'humanitaire (1940–1944)* (Paris: Presses Universitaires de France, 2013), p. 256.

[244] UNA, UNRRA, S-1021-0031-02, A.2, Relations with Governments [undated].

[245] UNA, UNRRA, S-1021-0031-07, History of UNRRA, Personnel Division [undated].

[246] UNA, UNRRA, S-1021-0084-14, Germaine Loustalot, Training Center Director, 'Rapport sur la partie psychologique des questions personnel', 20 May 1947.

Loustalot explained that former tramway conductors, attracted by UNRRA's relatively well-paid posts, were recruited as 'cooks' while young untrained women were recruited as nurses.[247] Not only was the recruitment system haphazard, but salaries and grades varied arbitrarily.[248] A number of Frenchmen, in particular, resented the fact that their wages were considerably lower than those of their American, and to a lesser extent, British co-workers.[249] UNRRA introduced perceived status differences that were not based upon training, ability or experience, but rather on the relative position of particular personnel within the organization's pay grades. This sense of injustice was intensified by the fact that most of the British and Northern American recruits could not speak German.[250] 'We have recruited in haste' observed Loustalot. 'This haste was completely uncalled for; In three case out of four [...] the recruits remained during long and tedious weeks in transfer centres in France or Germany; some have waited up to four or five months before being deployed with their teams!!!'[251] It was also something of a paradox that a considerable number of French candidates were rejected by UNRRA recruiters on the ground that they lacked English-language skills. At the higher level of French UNRRA HQ, however, as we have seen, no one used English.[252]

The French authorities soon became aware that many unsuitable candidates were being recruited by UNRRA.[253] In early April 1945, concerns erupted that French welfare recruits were too young and inexperienced compared to their counterparts from Belgium and Holland.[254] Large numbers of doctors were transferred to UNRRA bypassing formal interview selection.[255] Between 85 and 90 per cent of the French UNRRA (male) doctors were compelled to work for the organization because they were still on Army active service.[256] Some resented this position, not least because, as a result of their mobilization, they earned less than an internationally recruited UNRRA nurse.[257] The

---

[247] Ibid.
[248] UNA, UNRRA, S-1021-0031-07, Draft, History of UNRRA, Personnel Division [undated], p. 15.
[249] UNA, UNRRA, S-1021-0031-07, History of UNRRA, Personnel Division [undated].
[250] AN, F/9/3289, Copie d'une lettre de Jacques Franck [undated].
[251] UNA, UNRRA, S-1021-0084-14, Loustalot, 'Rapport sur la partie psychologique'.
[252] UNA, UNRRA, S-0417-0011-01, G. Loustalot à Mr Lecomte de Nouye, [7 February 1946?].
[253] MAE, HCRFA, PDR1/18, Lieutenant Wagner, Compte rendu de visite (Granville) du 29 mai 1945, 30 May 1945.
[254] MAE, HCRFA, PDR1/18, Compte rendu mission Commandant Merpillat/Capitaine Dissard, Centre d'instruction de Granville, 27 April 1945.
[255] AN, F/9/3309, Compte-rendu de la réunion UNRRA du 23 mars 1945.
[256] UNA, UNRRA, S-1448-0000-0014, M. T. Morgan to Head of Mission, 4 April 1945.
[257] MAE, HCRFA, PDR 1/18, Compte-rendu de Mission du Capitaine Mussinger, 27 June 1945.

French UNRRA Health Director later lamented that certified doctors were rejected, while not-yet-graduated doctors were hired.[258] Reflecting on UNRRA's humanitarian wage hierarchy, an UNRRA supervisor highlighted the necessity to adopt standardized wages: 'I do not personally believe that any international organization will achieve good international relationships amongst its own staff unless the pay and conditions for all are equal and unless the staff itself is picked in such a way to ensure that the individual members of it can comprehend the meaning and substance of international work.'[259] In spite of UNRRA's clear professionalization and internationalist ambitions, its wage rates were profoundly unfair, tending to reinforce national and gender inequalities.

The majority of new UNRRA staff had been recruited in Paris in autumn 1944. Others came to Germany with the French Red Cross.[260] A number of French recruits attended a short training program organized in Granville, a small town in north-western France. There, enthusiastic instructors attempted to kindle the 'sacred flame' of UNRRA's mission.[261] As French UNRRA relief worker Jacqueline Lesdos observed in her memoirs, this training was undoubtedly idealistic and *grandiloquent*: But weren't we in the period of the necessary large enthusiasms?[262] UNRRA recruits were given a 'Memorandum of the Provisional Conditions of Employment on Field Service', explaining the organization's purpose and the scope of its activities. Recruits were told that they constituted a 'body of truly international servants' devoted to the interests of the forty-four nations that had created it. Their aim was to help people to help themselves 'without discrimination as to race, creed or political belief'.[263]

Historians are divided in their assessment of this training: the base was poorly located, some of the lectures dull and the lack of guidance about field conditions made the stress laid on theory seems out of place.[264] Yet UNRRA

---

[258] UNA, UNRRA, S-0433-0003-07, Medecin Général des Cilleuls à Général de Corps d'Armée Lenclud, 3 April 1946.
[259] UNA, UNRRA, S-1021-0031-07, History of UNRRA, Personnel Division [undated].
[260] UNA, UNRRA, S-0433-0003-07, E. Hollard Zone Personnel Officer à Monsieur le Directeur Team 15 Lebach, 29 August 1946.
[261] See, for example, Captain Laveissiere eagerness to instill a 'flame of enthusiasm'. According to him, repatriation was an 'act of good faith requiring a lot of love'. MAE, HCRFA, PDR 1/18, Adieu à Mr Arnold-Forster par E. Laveissiere, 30 June 1945.
[262] AN, 72/AJ/1968, Jacqueline Lesdos, *Mais qu'est ce que l'UNRRA*, p. 3.
[263] AN 72/AJ/1968.
[264] Georges Woodbridge, *UNRRA: The History of the United Nations Relief and Rehabilitation Administration* (New York: Colombia University Press, 1950), vol. 2, p. 484; Shephard, *The Long Road Home*, pp. 139–142; Susan Armstrong-Reid and David Murray, *Armies of Peace: Canada and the UNRRA Years* (Toronto: University of Toronto Press, 2008), pp. 163–165; Salvatici, 'Help the People to Help Themselves', p. 431.

recruits seemed to have welcomed the cosmopolitan mixtures of nationalities and the food diet.[265] The centre was directed by the American Patterson and the instruction team led by Briton Arnold Forster, a Francophile instructor and skilled pedagogue. Among the instructors was the French captain Laveissiere, who had previously worked at the Mission Française de Rapatriement and fully embraced the 'Forsterian spirit' – 'UNRRA is an administration that does not employ civil servants, but rather apostles'.[266] A number of French observers lamented the domination of 'Anglo-Saxon' methods and resorted to essentialist, preconceived and simplistic assumptions about their *liberal* approaches.[267] They focused on national stereotypes and peculiar traits that the British and Americans were reported to have possessed. British methods were 'baffling', recalling the 'constitutional British empiricism'.[268] While the teaching staff was mainly constituted of British personnel, the majority of recruits were French: 'In conclusion, the background element is French: French is the most spoken language, the majority of the recruits are French, French temperament dominates. The superior and managerial element is British: way of life, bilingual conferences, managerial staff.'[269] If this report tended to reflect a preoccupation with national stereotypes, disregarding other possible facets of humanitarian methods, the evidence suggests a certain degree of acculturation. Lectures were delivered in French and English, but some key documents (including the SHAEF guide for displaced persons) remained in English.[270] UNRRA recruits were introduced to UNRRA's mission, the issue of registration, welfare and DP health and psychology.[271]

While the French were fairly poorly represented at the high level of the administration, they represented the single largest group of Continental European Employees up to May 1946, with 23.7 per cent of UNRRA total employment, as recruitment in France began earlier than elsewhere.[272] By far,

---

[265] Sharif Gemie, Fiona Reid, Laure Humbert, *Outcast Europe: Refugees and Relief Workers in an Era of Total War 1936-1948* (London: Bloomsbury, 2011), pp. 152–159.
[266] MAE, HCRFA, PDR1/18, Adieu à Mr Arnold-Forster par F. Laveissiere, 3 June 1945.
[267] MAE, HCRFA, PDR 1/18, Compte-rendu de Mission du Capitaine Mussinger, 27 June 1945.
[268] Ibid.
[269] Ibid.
[270] MAE, HCRFA, PDR1/18, Lieutenant Wagner, Compte rendu de visite (Granville) du 29 mai 1945, 30 May 1945.
[271] Lectures about the 'psychology of the deportee' were presented by Captain Merpillat and Françoise Dissard. Françoise Dissard had an impressive background: after completing her thesis in law on the reform of hospitals in the seventeenth century, she graduated as a nurse. During the war, she worked as a professor of law and social economy in a social-worker school before joining the *Mission de Rapatriement en Allemagne*. MAE, HCRFA, PDR 1/31, Curriculum Vitae de Françoise Dissard.
[272] UNRRA, S-1021-0078-06, A statistical analysis of Class I Employees in the Displaced Persons Operation, Germany, March 1945 to May 1946.

the greater part of the total number of employees served in the British and American zones. In the French zone, some French recruits had exceptional language skills and educational backgrounds. For instance, Suzanne Balasko-Moreau was forty-three when she joined UNRRA in January 1946. Hired to be a 'translator', she was then re-designated as a Welfare Assistant. Holder of the highest teaching qualification in France, the *agrégation*, she spoke fluent French, Spanish, English, Italian and Portuguese, her language skills refined during 1941–1944 when she had worked in a camp for British women and children in Troyes.[273] Other evidence suggests she was atypical. The backgrounds of French UNRRA welfare or assistant welfare officers working in the Southern District are, in this respect, revealing. In January 1946, the welfare department only numbered nineteen woman welfare officers, two Belgians, one American and sixteen French. Among the French, three were qualified nurses, three had a *baccalauréat*, three were *assistantes sociales*, three held no qualifications, one was a *surintendante*, one had a Red Cross diploma and two failed to provide information about their educational backgrounds.[274] Their field supervisor often complained about their casualness and lack of conscientiousness, lamenting that they were exasperatingly over-confident for their ages.[275] Yvonne Florence Renée Blaise was a typical example. She joined UNRRA in April 1946 at the age of twenty-six as an Assistant Welfare Officer, receiving £600 a year. She had no social work background, but a *baccalauréat* in History and Philosophy.[276] In her personal evaluation, her female supervisor noted that she was good but 'a little bit too self-confident'.[277] Her colleague 'Miss Boute' 'placed the interest of her love affairs above the interest of her work, and for that she [was] criticized by everyone'.[278] While feminine desires for relief service abroad were complex, this comment, formulated by a female supervisor on an evaluation questionnaire, revealed that (female) relief superiors were complicit in reinforcing stigmatization of female sexuality and a conservative vision of femininity.

The French personnel recruited by UNRRA had strikingly different middle-class backgrounds, work experience and motivations. UNRRA male workers'

---

[273] UNA, UNRRA, S-0438-0004-05, Fiche de renseignements, Suzanne Balasko-Moreau.
[274] UNA, UNRRA, S-0420-0001-02, Liste du Personnel Welfare District Sud de la Zone française, 2 January 1946.
[275] UNA, UNRRA, S-0438-0004-05, Confidentiel, Problèmes courants rangés par teams, 23 July 1946.
[276] UNA, UNRRA, S-0438-0004-05, Fiche de renseignements, Yvonne Florence Renée Blaise [undated].
[277] UNA, UNRRA, S-0438-0004-05, Confidentiel, Problèmes courants rangés par teams, 23 July 1946.
[278] UNA, UNRRA, S-0438-0004-05, R. le Goff, District Welfare Officer to Mademoiselle Muller, 11 May 1946.

backgrounds were equally diverse. Some were demobilized soldiers.[279] Others were former POWs, while others had remarkable resistance credentials. UNRRA Director Marcel Dalichampt was, for instance, forty when he joined UNRRA. According to his immediate superior, captivity had left him very 'mature' in attitude, and thus better equipped to understand DPs' emotional needs.[280] His colleague, fellow UNRRA Director Gadras, was a former social worker previously responsible for a large-scale wartime relief scheme for French refugees that involved supervising twenty-three 'departments' in the South of France, totalling nearly seventy social workers.[281] Captain Raymond and UNRRA Team Director Vincent had also worked for the Foreign Refugees Service in France.[282] Another UNRRA Director, Jacques Bauche, was awarded the prestigious 'compagnon de la Libération' status in recognition of his resistance work.[283] Bauche had joined the Naval Free French forces in June 1940, participating in the Dakar operation in September 1940, the Gabon campaign in November and then the Eritrean and Syrian campaign in early 1941. Finally, some had backgrounds in business, industry or state administration. In Lindau, Jean Gerbier organized his team along commercial managerial lines, his aim being to obtain 'a peak efficiency in the [...] customers' (the DPs) satisfaction'.[284] UNRRA teams thus brought men of various professional backgrounds closer together.

Some French males resented the higher salaries of British and American recruits, but on the whole, UNRRA offered extremely high wages at a time when both shortages and inflation plagued the economy in France. While some former resistance recruits were driven by patriotic duty and the need to alleviate the suffering of their brothers in arms, others were attracted by what was perceived at the time to be a 'fashionable profession'. Being an *assistante sociale* was considered to be *chic* and *à la mode* among young French bourgeois women.[285] The profession of *assistante sociale* was nonetheless in crisis,

---

[279] See, for instance, the case of Army officer Massip who had worked previously with the service PDR. UNA, UNRRA, S-0417-0004-12, From Mr E. P. Moreland, District Director to General Lenclud, Directeur de la Zone Française d'occupation, 7 January 1946.

[280] UNA, UNRRA, S-0421-0029-04, Germaine Loustalot, Personel Evaluation of Marcel Dalichampt, 28 February 1947.

[281] UNA, UNRRA, S-0425-0007-05, Mr J. M. Gadras, Director UNRRA team 96 Karlsruhe to Mr Alex. E. Squadrilli, 19 October 1945.

[282] UNA, U NRRA, S-0421-0018-08, Team 583 UNRRA C. J. Vincent à Poignant [25 April 1946?].

[283] Vladimir Trouplin, *Dictionnaire des compagnons de la Libération* (Paris: Elytis, 2010), pp. 82–83.

[284] UNA, UNRRA, S-1021-0085-08, Jean Gerbier, 'rapport sur les activités de l'UNRRA dans le cercle de Lindau...', 8 May 1947, p. 6.

[285] Le Tallec, *Les assistantes sociales dans la tourmente*, pp. 19, 207; Mabon-Fall, *Les assistantes sociales au temps de Vichy*, pp. 23–29.

as it was feared that the profession had attracted women for the wrong reasons, including a desire for independence and standing in the world. Parallel to these anxieties were real cases of relief workers' inexperience, incompetence and trafficking, which worried the UNRRA officials as it could potentially damage France's reputation.

## The Gender Politics of a Male-Dominated Organization

The study of UNRRA correspondence reveals significant continuities in discourses about women social politics and respectable femininity, as well as deep anxieties about women's greater political and social agency following the defeat of 1940 and foreign occupation.[286] French UNRRA HQ had a traditional view of relief work, focusing on restoring a conception of gender roles based on a clear differentiation between men and women's position within the aid system. Since the seventeenth and eighteenth centuries, even in paternalistic societies in which the public sphere was often confined to men, missionary philanthropy and charitable organizations created spaces and significant social roles for women.[287] In times of war, women's aid was particularly appreciated because it eased the strains put on soldiers and freed men for combat. Yet, women legitimized their public activities using the qualities that were attached to their gendered role in the private sphere, including altruism, care, virtue and morality. These qualities of 'respectable femininity' were the foundation of the maternalist discourse that underpinned many public and international commitments by women in France and Europe in the late nineteenth and early twentieth centuries.[288]

In the aftermath of the Second World War, gender discrimination continued at the official and unofficial level. Women's humanitarian role was still seen by a number of French male doctors as auxiliary: women were expected to be empathic, well presented and maternal figures. At a welfare officers' meeting in August 1946, Zone medical Officer General Des Cilleuls described the welfare service as a benevolent and feminine addition to the Health Service, which was usually entrusted to men. His imagery was telling: '[t]he Welfare Service was born out of the Health service as Eve was created out of

---

[286] Dolores Martin-Moruno, 'L'humanitaire au féminin. Florence Nightingale, Valérie de Gasparin et Clara Barton', in *Humanitaire et Médecine. Les premiers pas de la Croix-Rouge (1854-1870)* (Genève: Genège humanitaire, centre de recherches historiques, 2013), pp. 37-64, 39.

[287] Adam J. Davis and Bertrand Taithe, 'From the Purse and the Heart: Exploring Charity, Humanitarianism and Human Rights in France', *French Historical Studies*, vol. 34, no. 3 (2011), pp. 413-432, 422.

[288] Glenda Sluga, 'Women, Feminisms and Twentieth-Century Internationalism', in Glenda Sluga and Patricia Clavin (eds.), *Internationalisms: A Twentieth-Century History* (Cambridge: Cambridge University Press, 2016), pp. 61-84.

Adam's rib and from this couple emerged a spiritual guardian called Relief.'[289] According to him, Welfare Officers had to perform stereotypically feminine tasks such as working with children, assisting male doctors and distributing clothing. He insisted on female relief workers' moral mission, for being a relief worker was not solely seen as delivering effectively but also as having a positive morale influence on DPs. The virtues of patience, discretion and adequate presentation, considered as feminine characteristics of the nurses, were exalted in UNRRA's zone training, while poor moral attitudes were considered as a 'betrayal' of their position.[290] This revealed the persistent masculinism of military medicine within humanitarian aid.

In this context, French female UNRRA workers' sexual conduct faced sharp scrutiny from UNRRA's military and conservative HQ, but also from their immediate (female) supervisors. At the upper-level and mid-level of UNRRA hierarchy, officials worried about independent French women exerting sexual agency and seeking illicit sexual liaisons with German men or DPs, sometimes with the insidious implication that French UNRRA women were complicit in their own disgrace. Discourses about UNRRA women's misbehaviour encapsulated many fears about the disruptive effects of war and its ability to erode differences between men and women. In the inter-war years, despite the strong 'women at home' ideology, right-wing movements, including the Croix de Feu and left-wing parties, mobilized women who could express their nurturing nature in their social action. This large inter-war mobilization of women perpetuated stereotypes of women as 'natural caregivers'.[291] Even the Communist Party shifted from an egalitarian dismissal of biological essentialism to a discourse based upon women's supposed 'caring nature' in the 1930s.[292]

UNRRA HQ's anxieties over female immoral behaviour illuminate the search for a 'gender peace' and restoration of traditional gender roles in response to the chaos of war, defeat and foreign occupation. A number of scandals confirmed catholic fears that members of the *assistance sociale* would transgress traditional morality and be exposed to the 'horror and vice' of DP life.[293] In the summer of 1946, one such scandal broke in Gutach. The UNRRA Welfare Officer was found guilty of having an affair with a former SS member

---

[289] UNA, UNRRA, S-0438-0009-04, Conférence des Welfare Officers de la Zone Nord, 9 et 10 aout 1946, programme du samedi 10 aout, p.18.
[290] UNA, UNRRA, S-0433-0002-06, De Cilleuls, Conference medicale du 14 Juin 1946.
[291] Caroline Campbell, 'Building a Movement, Dismantling the Republic: Women, Gender, and Political Extremism in the Croix de Feu/Parti Social Français, 1927–1940', *French Historical Studies*, vol. 35, no. 4 (2012), pp. 691–726, p. 693.
[292] Caroline Campbell, 'Gender and Politics in Inter-war and Vichy France', *Contemporary European History*, vol. 27, no. 3 (2018), pp. 482–499.
[293] Le Tallec, *Les assistantes sociales dans la tourmente*, p. 18.

disguised as a DP.[294] The Team director reported that the ex-SS man 'was seen at [her] place at hours when he was not supposed to be there, or in other words, at hours when a DP *n'avait rien à faire* at a Welfare Office'.[295] As a result of this scandal, the team Director received an official reprimand for failure to screen the supposed DP properly. The Welfare Officer was reassigned to another team.[296] Another of her team colleagues meanwhile became pregnant and married a DP.[297] Over the spring of 1946 several more 'scandalous' pregnancies were unearthed in the French zone. UNRRA HQ was concerned about relief workers who flaunted their sexuality and seemed more interested in their own material pleasures and gratification than administering DPs. In Landstuhl, the Welfare Field Supervisor found a young member of the team four months pregnant and in floods of tears. The father of her child was a member of the team who had a German mistress. The Welfare Supervisor's solution was pretty straightforward: 'For her, for UNRRA, for the profession of *assistante sociale* she must leave us.'[298] But much the same thing happened in nearby Kandel. She therefore urged UNRRA HQ to devise a series of rules for women in the field: 'These women should neither be allowed to live in the camp nor in private accommodation near the camp. Furthermore, they should be <u>absolutely forbidden</u> to have anything to do with the Mess [...] They do a few favours, gain some sense of authority and soon no one in the team dares utter a word of blame.'[299] The Southern District Welfare Officer recalled that the consequent difficulties were so widespread that she spent more time 'on the problems of UNRRA [women staff] than on those of the Displaced Persons properly so-called'.[300] An UNRRA Welfare Supervisor believed that 'unlike their Anglo-American sisters, [the] girls from France were not ready to live the mixed life that was offered to them.' Employment with UNRRA afforded them access to an unbelievable bounty of goods:

> We have to remember that these women found themselves alone in teams of more than fifteen persons; they were in a hostile land, withdrawn, without intellectual resources and they did not necessarily speak the common language of the community. Working hours were long, very long. Mental fatigue, physical exhaustion and loneliness were their daily lot. We should not forget another important factor: we had just experienced four years of severe rationing, with almost complete suppression of

---

[294] UNA, UNRRA, S-0421-0034-06, Fiche de renseignement.
[295] UNA, UNRRA, S-0421-0025-07, Durand à Général Lenclud, 9 September 1946.
[296] UNA, UNRRA, S-0421-0026-01, A. L. Weicheldinger, Zone Personnel Officer à Field Supervisor No. 2, 9 December 1946.
[297] UNA, UNRRA, S-0421-0034-06, Fiche de renseignement [undated].
[298] UNA, UNRRA, S-0438-0003-03, R. Le Goff, lettre manuscrite, 18 February 1946.
[299] Ibid.
[300] UNA, UNRRA, S-1021-0085-02, Miss Roberts, Southern District Welfare Officer, report [undated].

alcohol, tea, coffee; Overnight, we had access to a rich and abundant food with coffee. Admittedly, this was very pleasant. But, it created an overheated and nervous atmosphere. The sum of all these factors, combined together, meant that many of the young recruits, some were not even twenty-one-years old, did not cope, the consequences of this being at times tragic.[301]

Not equipped to cope with the pressures brought to bear on them in the field, some resigned while others succumbed to the temptation of black marketeering or, even worse, 'immoral' sexual behaviour. The behaviours of these women profoundly worried their French superiors who feared that their actions threatened France's prestige.

These discussions about feminine 'respectability' were certainly an expression of wider domestic anxieties about women's changing role in French society. Scholars of post-war France have demonstrated how the 'language of virility' was omnipresent in 1945.[302] The French defeat of 1940 had initiated a painful process of social disruption and ideological revaluation of heterosexual norms, French men losing very temporarily their social and sexual prerogative.[303] The experiences of defeat and captivity threatened masculine authority, exacerbating soldiers' feeling of de-masculinization, fears of adultery and anxieties that war had reversed gender hierarchies, women taking advantage of the exceptional circumstances of war to free themselves from traditional morality.[304] This was also made manifest in the challenge posed by the male military German occupiers and (later) by American troops.[305]

---

[301] UNA, UNRRA, S-1021-0084-14, Germaine Loustalot, 'Rapport sur la partie psychologique des questions personnel', 20 May 1947.

[302] Julian Jackson, *Living in Arcadia. Homosexuality, Politics and Morality in France from the Liberation to Aids* (Chicago: Chicago University Press, 2009), pp. 40–41; Michael Kelly, 'The Reconstruction of Masculinity at the Liberation', in H. R. Kedward and Nancy Wood (eds.), *The Liberation of France* (Oxford: Berg, 1995), pp. 117–288; Fabrice Virgili, *Shorn Women: Gender and Punishment in Liberation France* (Oxford: Berg, 2002). On the sexual crimes committed by the First French Army in the French zone, in particular, see Miot 'Sortir l'armée des ombres', pp. 622-655.

[303] Mary Louise Roberts, 'Beyond "Crisis" in Understanding Gender Transformation', *Gender and History*, vol. 28, no. 2 (2016), pp. 358–366; Roberts, *What Soldiers Do: Sex and the American GI in World War II France* (Chicago: Chicago University Press, 2013).

[304] Cabanes and Piketty, *Retour à l'intime*, p. 19; Mary Louise Roberts, *Civilization without Sexes: Reconstructing Gender in Postwar France, 1917–1927* (Chicago: University of Chicago Press, 1994); Laura Lee Downs, *Writing Gender History* (London/New York: Bloomsbury, 2010), pp. 97–99; Christopher E. Forth and Bertrand Taithe (eds.), *French Masculinities: History, Culture and Politics* (London: Palgrave-Macmillan, 2007); special issue in *Modern and Contemporary France* 'Gender, Politics and the Social in Historical Perspective: Essays in the Honour of Siân Reynolds', vol. 20 (2012).

[305] Recent research on daily life in the French occupation zone and gendered German–French encounters in Freiburg has revealed that French women found it more difficult to adapt to the situation of occupation than French men. Ann-Kristin Glöckner, 'German–French Encounters in the City of Freiburg under French Occupation 1945–1949', paper

Research in UNRRA archives revealed that for a number of French UNRRA officers, material goods, as much as military insignia, were seen as symbols of virility and power. In the secluded and mundane French community of occupied Germany, material entitlements became intertwined with contested recognition of authority.[306] Epitomizing frustrations among French male UNRRA staff was their inability to carry a gun or wear military insignia. As early as February 1945 French Liaison Officers raised this issue, 'It seems utterly impossible for them to go to Germany without carrying a firearm.'[307] In Landstuhl, an American UNRRA Director concurred: 'the ability to carry a gun and a military symbol is significant in dealing both with other military units and with German supply sources.'[308] As Ryan's statement implies, this problem was neither specific to the French zone nor to French recruits. Malcolm J. Proudfoot, an army officer in charge of refugee relief operations and the author of a detailed study on the topic published in 1957, noted indeed that in the three Western zones 'the civilian and the soldier were as oil and water, and dependence on the military was resented to the end.'[309] It remains a feature of modern humanitarian intervention, UN field workers sometimes showing signs of an inferiority complex towards military actors.[310] Arguably, though, the institutional rivalry between the PDR administration and UNRRA, when combined with gender anxieties deriving from the war, significantly aggravated these problems of status among relief workers in the French zone.[311] French officials frequently complained that UNRRA Directors were assigning themselves military grades without authorization.[312] Gender tensions were, in this sense, bound up with broader questions of national identity and efforts to come to terms with the recent past.[313]

presented at 'The Allied Occupation of Germany revisited', German Historical Institute, 29–30 September 2016.

[306] Adler, 'Selling France to the French', pp. 575–595, 576.

[307] AN, F/9/3309, L'officier de rapatriement Olivier Gobert à l'officier de rapatriement Pouzadoux, 3 February 1945.

[308] UNA, UNRRA, S-0436-0059-08, report from Bryce Ryan, Director Team 17 to Guy Drake-Brockman, Landstuhl, 17 June 1945.

[309] Proudfoot, *European Refugees*, p. 236.

[310] Sandra Whitworth, *Men, Militarism and UN Peacekeeping. A Gendered Analysis* (London: Lynne Rienner Publishers, 2004), p. 151.

[311] As Karen Adler has demonstrated in her work on the French occupation zone, '[t]he French military in post-war Germany was very different from the army which had just helped to win the war – or believed it had.' Adler, 'Selling France to the French', p. 576.

[312] UNA, UNRRA, S-0421-0042-04, Lettre de l'Etat Major Zone Française à Messieurs les Directeurs de District, 12 January 1946. Also see S-0421-0033-03, A. Thomasset à Messieurs les Directeurs des Teams 572–576, 13 February 1946.

[313] Karen Adler, 'Reading National Identity: Gender and "Prostitution" during the Occupation', *Modern and Contemporary France*, vol. 7, no. 1 (1999), pp. 47–57.

## Relief Work as a Vehicle for the Restoration of French Prestige?

While inadequate training and incompetence was frequently discussed amongst UNRRA and PDR officials, public statement was made praising the professionalism and efficiency of UNRRA relief workers. UNRRA spent great efforts and resources in developing its public relation strategies, through films, photography and DP exhibitions. DP spaces were not isolated encampments: they had a public face. In many DP camps, exhibitions were organized by DPs and relief workers and attended by a diverse audience of French occupation officials and international UNRRA experts.[314] These exhibitions aimed to display DPs' artistic and creative talents and showcase the efforts, resolve and skills of industrious DP men and women. Photographs and 'picture stories' were also taken by relief workers and sent to UNRRA public relation office, showcasing the successes of rehabilitation and reconstruction.[315] Before the eyes of the viewers, readers or visitors, relief workers were turned into 'professional', empathic and disciplined staff and, DPs into healthy, well-nourished and satisfied relief 'recipients'. This publicity was underpinned by the need to maintain public confidence in UNRRA's work. Throughout its existence, UNRRA was highly criticized by occupation officers across the three Western zones for its lack of effective response to the problem of DPs across Europe and North America.[316]

In the aftermath of the Second World War, public relations were granted greater significance by Western governments and newly created UN agencies alike.[317] Both the PDR and UNRRA archives contain numerous photos

---

[314] See, for instance, UNA, UNRRA, S-0421-0031-06, Compte-rendu de la réunion du 7 Mars 1946 du Comité Artistique, Fribourg, 9 March 1946; UNRRA, S-0421-0031-09, Rapport sur la fête du 16 Décembre 1945, 19 March 1946; S-0438-0008-02, Rapport de la conférence des welfare officers du district sud, 22 and 23 January 1946; S-0418-0003-08, Semaine de Culture des DPs à Wurzach, 3–10 November 1946, Prospectus. Introduction by Janis Kalmite; S-UNA, UNRRA, S-0421-0031-02, Fribourg, Exposition, V. K. Jonynas, November 1946.

[315] For instance, UNRRA, S-0421-0023-09, 'La journée du jeudi 18 avril 1946 au team 572', par Pierre Durand, Gutach. This is an eleven-page photo album of the UNRRA team of Gutach, composed of thirty-three photos. It is a 'picture story' – a sequence of shots accompanied by captions. The text is written in both French and English; it is signed by the French director of the team (Pierre Durand) and the translation by J. N. Russell on 27 April 1946. This illustrated story documents the life of the UNRRA team on Thursday, 18 April 1946, from 8:30 and the inspection of the team transport to 7:30, during the changing of the Polish Guard.

[316] MAE, HCRFA, ADM 40, L'Administrateur Général Laffon à Monsieur le Général d'Armée, Commandant en Chef Français en Allemagne, 16 November 1946.

[317] Mark Alleyne, *Global Lies? Propaganda, the UN, and World Order* (Basingstoke: Palgrave Macmillan, 2003); Tom Allbeson, 'Photographic Diplomacy in the Postwar World: UNESCO and the Conception of Photography as a Universal Language, 1946–56', *Modern Intellectual History*, vol. 12, no. 2 (2015), pp. 383–415; Alexander

depicting life in DP camps.[318] Since the late nineteenth century, photography was used by humanitarians to draw attention to human suffering, bear witness and raise funds, but the Second World War gave a renewed impetus to humanitarian photography.[319] DPs were central to UNRRA visual discourses of 'new beginnings', which emphasized a break with the Nazi period.[320]

The visual discourse that emerged in the French zone resembled the narrative produced in the two other Western zones. We find similar types and scenes fixed again and again by the camera's lens. These include: well-ordered teams running camps in a military manner, well-stocked stored, idyllic settings (notably in the Black Forest) and a very gendered reading of rehabilitation. UNRRA images do not focus on distress, starving babies and suffering bodies, but on the contrary highlighted how DPs were sufficiently fed and successfully rehabilitated both physically and spiritually.[321] Photographers contributed to shape (very optimistic) gendered visual discourses. DP 'girls' were typically portrayed carrying out feminine activities (sewing, taking care of children ...) and DP men masculine activities (repairing trucks, guarding camps ...).[322] While photographs taken in the French zone were certainly part of this wider public relations' efforts on the part of the international organization, they also reflected French efforts at projecting a new vision of France as a 'humanitarian

---

Medcalf, 'Between Art and Information, 1948-1970', *Journal of Global History*, vol. 13 (2018), pp. 94-120.

[318] The photo albums that I uncovered can be broadly divided into three distinct groups: the albums found in the archives of international organizations (the United Nations Relief and Rehabilitation Administration and the International Refugee Organisation), the photo albums made by the French vocational service (the Formation Professionnelle Accélérée) and available in the archives of the French occupation zone (PDR9), the photos taken by the French Prisoners, Deportees and Refugees' service and published in Haut Commissariat de la République française en Allemagne, Service des Personnes Déplacées, *Sept ans d'activité en faveur des personnes déplacées en zone française d'occupation, 1945-1952*, rapport dactylographié et illustré, [undated], [Bibliothèque du Ministère des Affaires Etrangères, Direction des Archives].

[319] Nicolas Bouvier and Michèle Mercier (eds.), *Guerre et humanité. Un siècle de photographie. Les archives du Comité international de la Croix Rouge* (Genève: Editions d'Art Alberta Skira, 1995), p. 8; Paul Betts 'The Polemics of Pity. British Photographs of Berlin, 1945-1947', in Johannes Paulmann (ed) *Humanitarianism and Media. 1900 to the Present* (London: Berghahn, 2018), pp. 126-150, p. 126; Heide Fehrenbach and Davide Rodogno, 'Introduction', in Heide Fehrenbach and Davide Rodogno (eds.), *Humanitarian Photography: A History* (Cambridge: Cambridge University Press, 2015), pp. 1-21, 6.

[320] Alleyne, *Global Lies?*; Allbeson, 'Photographic Diplomacy in the Postwar World', pp. 383-415.

[321] Silvia Salvatici, 'Sight of Benevolence. UNRRA's Recipients Portrayed', in Fehrenbach and Rodogno (eds.), *Humanitarian Photography*, pp. 200-222, 200-201.

[322] See, for instance, UNRRA, S-0421-0023-09, 'La journée du jeudi 18 avril 1946 au team 572', par Pierre Durand, Gutach.

nation' against the backdrop of increasing anxieties about its international standing.

Relief work was understood by some PDR and UNRRA officials as a vehicle for the restoration of French prestige. In the spring of 1945, French military officials stressed the importance of the presence of French relief worker teams in Germany for reasons of national reputation.[323] In a report addressed to the military government, the French UNRRA HQ also noted that the 'work of UNRRA specialised personnel, social workers, doctors and nurses, whose PDR service is deprived of, benefit French propaganda'.[324] This report illuminates the widening of the notion of 'propaganda' beyond the cultural sphere and the active, and often bottom-up, nature of the reaffirmation of French national identity in post-war Germany. For French UNRRA officials, humanitarian publicity material was not so solely considered as a means to communicate internationalist ideals but also regarded as a way to project a new vision of France's as a 'humanitarian nation'. For instance, the French medical director des Cilleuls wanted to ensure a prestigious place for French doctors in UNRRA and asked his staff to provide good material, worthy of France's tradition of social and medical progress, to UNRRA Public Information service.[325]

Responding to des Cilleuls' demands, the UNRRA medical team of Ravensburg produced, for instance, an album in July 1946, with captions written in both English and French.[326] The front cover represented a general and peaceful view of Ravensburg taken 'from the Veitburg', with no sign of war or displacement. Containing twenty-four pages, this album opened with an image of the medical office installed in a rich villa and a presentation of the team (the male doctor is in the centre surrounded by a *female* chief nurse and a *female* DP secretary). This was followed by a graph of the weekly consultations and a presentation of the services offered, including treatment with X-ray screening and vaccinations. The posed, scripted and highly staged form of these images is used to construct an idealized image of medical international cooperation: the dentist is Hungarian, the ophthalmologist and gynaecologist are Lithuanian, the nurses are Polish and the chief secretary stateless. Photographic sequences focused on the collective efforts of the medical team: the camera was positioned at the level of the observation seats. Patients and medical staff were all in the frame: no one was left out. This album

---

[323] SHD, 8 P 23, Rapport secret du capitaine P. Gerbault, chef de la Section G-5 de la MFL, 22 April 1945. For further analysis of this point, see book's introduction.
[324] Ibid.
[325] UNA, UNRRA, S-0433-0002-06, Conférence médicale du 14 juin 1946.
[326] UNA, UNRRA, S-0421-0063-05, UNRRA, Medical Service Team 579, Ravensburg, 10 July 1946.

demonstrated that expensive devices had been made available to DPs and that considerable efforts were being placed in the training of DP aid-nurses, with an image of a classroom with *female* DP learning human anatomy. The caption reads in an imperfect English 'it was supposed that the knowledge, acquired by an attentif learning, should give a chance to the DP's to be able to continue or to develop their studies at a school of their homeland'.[327] Although this album was made a year after the liberation, there are very few traces of the physical and psychological scars of the war. All together, the photographs emphasized the central role of France and French doctors in UNRRA's internationalist project. They emphasized France's 'special' mission and integrated it into a universal pictorial language that traversed national, linguistic and ideological barriers between people (Figs. 2.1 and 2.2).

UNRRA images were highly selective and erased important distracting details about the heterogeneity of the French UNRRA staff and the micropolitics of relief analyzed in this chapter. They often focused the viewer's attention on French wartime underground activities and decorations. These two portraiture-style photos, for instance, stand out: they differed from the other snapshots because of their composition and photographic artistry. Both are looking away from the camera (Figs. 2.3 and 2.4).

The role of photographs in constructing the 'myth of the Resistance' has been examined in relation to the Liberation of Paris, but not in regards to the French zone.[328] The French press coverage of UNRRA's activities was very limited. It is nevertheless striking that the importance of the French resistance was replicated in the historiography of UNRRA. According to UNRRA official historian Woodbridge, the employment of French nationals was often a 'reward for wartime services in the underground movements'.[329] This view stands in sharp contrast with early impression of the French occupation zone as a 'refuge' for wartime collaborators.

The French zone rapidly acquired (at least in the French press) an image of 'little Vichy' in Baden-Baden, the zone being portrayed as a refuge for wartime collaborators. As we have seen, some civil servants benefited from a 'policy of éloignement'.[330] In the autumn and winter of 1944–1945 many French collaborationists sought refuge in Germany, Pétain's administration having fled to Sigmaringen castle.[331] A few, like other European collaborators, certainly tried

---

[327] Ibid., p. 22.
[328] Catherine E. Clark, 'Capturing the Moment, Picturing History: Photographs of the Liberation of Paris', *The American Historical Review*, vol. 121, no. 3 (2016), pp. 824–860.
[329] Woodbridge, *UNRRA*, vol. 1, pp. 251–252.
[330] Jacques Tarbé de Saint-Hardouin, *Quatre années de politique française en Allemagne (8 mai 1945–12 aout 1949)*, p. 54.
[331] André Brissau, *Pétain à Sigmaringen* (Paris: Librairie Perrin, 1966); Jean Paul Cointet, *Sigmaringen* (Paris: Perrin, 2003); Henry Rousso, *Un château en Allemagne: La France de Pétain en exil, Sigmaringen 1944–1945* (Paris: Fayard, 2012); Christine Sautermeister,

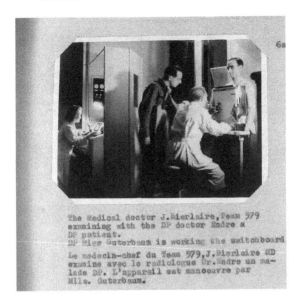

Fig. 2.1 UNA, UNRRA, S-0421-0063-05, 'The medical doctor J. Bierlaire, Team, 579, examining with the DP doctor Endre a DP patient. DP Miss Guterbaum is working the switchboard', Medical Service Team 579, photo album, Ravensburg, 10 July 1946, p. 8.

to hide among the vast group of DPs, under false identities. Others found themselves amongst prisoners of war in Poland, where they fabricated false documents and engaged in criminal activities.[332] A Commission of Inquiry sent to investigate conditions in the French zone reported in April 1946 that thirteen of the zone's highest-ranking officials were implicated in the Vichy regime.[333] These images of a 'little Vichy' in Baden-Baden remind us to be cautious when assessing the broader significance of these UNRRA photographs and avoid attributing more weight to these sources than they had. It is very difficult to assess how widely these UNRRA photographs were circulated and exhibited in France and abroad. But the absence of information about the circulation of these images does not diminish their value: they offer

---

*Louis-Ferdinand Céline à Sigmaringen. Novembre 1944 à mars 1945. Chronique d'un séjour controversé* (Paris: Gallimard, 2013).

[332] MAE, Pologne 1944–1949, 82, Direction D'Europe, s/Direction de l'Europe Orientale, Le Ministre des Affaires Etrangères à Ministre des Anciens Combattants et Victimes de la guerre, 6 March 1946.

[333] Frank Roy Willis, *France, Germany and the New Europe 1945–1963* (Stanford: Stanford University Press, 1965), p. 35; Julia Wambach, 'Vichy in Baden-Baden – The Personnel of the French Occupation in Germany after 1945', *Contemporary European History*, vol. 28, no. 3 (2019), pp. 319–341.

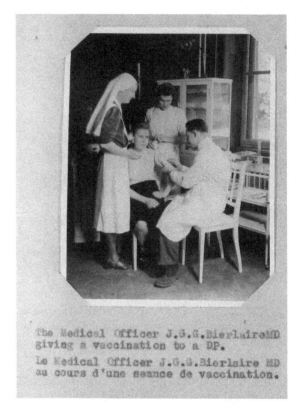

**Fig. 2.2** UNA, UNRRA, S-0421-0063-05, 'The medical officer J. G. G. Bierlaire giving a vaccination to a DP', Medical Service Team 579, photo album, Ravensburg, 10 July 1946, p. 11.

a lens onto French-specific efforts at selling the 'Resistance' and rebuilding a specific image of France in the aftermath of the defeat and Nazi occupation of France. These UNRRA photographs served as powerful symbol of a specific political culture and values that arose during the resistance period.

The importance of restoring French prestige and power is a common theme in the historiography of the zone.[334] What is less known, however is how far relief workers and DPs participated in this enterprise and how DPs were drawn into the orbit of French cultural diplomacy, at a time when France's position was threatened and the Americanization of Germany feared. In the aftermath of the First World War, art exhibitions had already been used by the

---

[334] See, for instance, Corine Defrance, *La politique culturelle de la France sur la rive gauche du* Rhin (Strasbourg: Presses Universitaires, 1994).

Fig. 2.3 UNA, UNRRA, S-1058-0001-01, 'This French girl welfare officer wears the croix de guerre for her experiences in the French maquis' [undated].

Fig. 2.4 UNA, UNRRA, UNA, S-1058-0003, A UNRRA director, a Frenchman, Mr Rodie who was a leader in the French underground movement and escaped after eleven months in a German concentration camp.

French during the occupation of the Rhineland to serve Paul Tirard's policy of 'pacific penetration'.[335] According to Christina Kott, the fact of exposing one's art and classifying the enemy's art constituted an act of symbolic

---

[335] Paul Tirard, *L'Art français en Rhénanie pendant l'Occupation, 1918–1930* (Coblence: Haut Commissariat de la République Française dans les Provinces du Rhin, [1930?]).

sovereignty.[336] In the aftermath of the Second World War, French occupation and UNRRA officials drew a number of DP artists, in particular Baltic DPs, into the orbit of French cultural diplomacy. They encouraged DP art exhibitions and concerts, which bolstered not only DP art and cultural traditions, but also French ones. These DP exhibitions and concerts served several purposes: For DP artists, cultural productions could help them continue their national struggle in exile and reclaim a sense of identity in a context marked by lingering suspicions about collaboration during the German occupation of the Baltic States.[337] For some relief workers, artistic expression had a therapeutic value.[338] Since the late nineteenth century, occupational therapy, which aimed at encouraging creativity and spontaneity through the teaching of handicrafts, was used in mental asylums and soldiers' hospitals across Europe to heal physical and psychological wounds.[339] For French occupiers, exhibiting French cultural richness in the zone was considered as a way to express French political power.[340]

Baltic DPs found an enthusiastic supporter in the military government in the person of Raymond Schmittlein, an early Gaullist who was put in charge of educational reforms in the French zone.[341] Schmittlein had lived in Lithuania and Latvia between 1934 and 1940 working as a professor and as a foreign correspondent for the Havas news-agency. He became a staunch defender of

[336] Christina Kott, *Préserver l'art de l'ennemi? Le patrimoine artistique en Belgique et en France occupée, 1914–1918* (Frankfurt am Main: Peter Lang, 2006).

[337] Inta Gale Carpenter, 'Folklore as a Source for Creating Exile Identity among Latvian Displaced Persons in Post-World War II Germany', *Journal of Baltic Studies*, vol. 48, no. 2 (2017), pp. 205–233. Some concerts were organized by DP committees during national holidays. See, for instance, UNA, UNRRA, S-0421-0031-01, Concert pour la fête nationale lithuanienne, Colonie Lithuanienne de Fribourg, 16 February 1947.

[338] See, for instance, WL, HA5-4/3, Welfare Division, *Report on Psychological Problems of Displaced Persons*, 1 June 1945, pp. 1–41, 36.

[339] Ana Carden-Coyne, 'Butterfly Touch: Rehabilitation, Nature and the Haptic Arts in the First World War', *Critical Military Studies*, published online first (2019), available at www.tandfonline.com/doi/pdf/10.1080/23337486.2019.1612151?needAccess=true (last consulted on 10 August 2019).

[340] See, for example, Richard Gilmore, France's Postwar Cultural Policies and Activities in Germany, PhD dissertation, University of Geneva, 1971; Jérôme Vaillant, 'Aspects de la politique culturelle de la France en Allemagne 1945–1949', in Henri Ménudier (ed.), *L'Allemagne occupée, 1945–1949* (Bruxelles: Complexe, 1990), pp. 201–220; Stefan Zauner, *Erziehung und Kulturmission: Frankreichs Bildungs-Politik in Deutschland, 1945–1949* (Munich: Oldenbourg Verlag, 1994); Defrance, *La politique culturelle de la France sur la rive gauche du Rhin*; Mombert *Jeunesse et livre en Zone française d'occupation 1945–1949*; Riccarda Torriani, 'Nazis into Germans: Re-education and Democratisation in the British and French Occupation Zones, 1945–49', PhD thesis, University of Cambridge, 2005.

[341] UNRRA, S-0438-0009-01, World Student Relief, Report on visit to French zone from Yngve Frykholm, Franlgen, 8 June 1946; Corine Defrance Raymond Schmittlein (1904–1974): médiateur entre la France et la Lituanie *Cahiers Lituaniens*, No. 9 (2009). Text kindly shared by Corine Defrance

Baltic DPs.[342] Exhibitions of Baltic art did not simply involve an imposition of French culture but were developed from interactions with Baltic artists. Schmittlein helped establish the Baltic Fine Art School in Freiburg, entrusting it to his friend Jonynas, a Lithuanian artist who had exhibited his work in Paris in the inter-war years.[343] Exhibitions and leaflets were produced and circulated boasting both French intellectual and art traditions, including Voltaire, Rousseau, Delacroix, Cézanne, Baudelaire, Debussy, Rodin, Matisse and Esthonian art.[344] These exhibitions reinforced the idea of France as a 'protector' of small nations and the image of Paris as 'the Mekka [sic] for all painters' in the words of a DP artist.[345] French occupation officers and relief workers valued DP art not only for its therapeutic value but also for its 'propaganda' benefits: exhibiting DP art became an important tool to position France as an important actor in post-war internationalism.

## Conclusion

In his remarkably perceptive documentary film on the return of French *Absents*, Henri Cartier-Bresson captured the raw horror that Allied liberators encountered at the Liberation. 'Each building site was a penal colony, each worker a slave, each soldier a prison guard or a torturer. This was Germany, yesterday.' The collapse of Germany was accompanied by a humanitarian disaster of staggering proportions. Nazi victims surfaced from factories, concentration camps, streets or hiding places. Having longed for home and fantasized about those they had left behind for years, most sought to return swiftly. Some began their journey immediately after the Liberation, on foot or by any borrowed means of transport. Others expected justice and the punishment of traitors and collaborators prior to their repatriation. Former collaborators rubbed shoulders with anti-Nazi activists. Cartier-Bresson, who had himself been held captive during the war, powerfully captured the experiences of 'life after death' for former captives in the first days following their Liberation.[346] He filmed the return by plane of French deportees and their

---

[342] UNRRA, S-0438-0009-01, World Student Relief, Report on visit to French zone from Yngve Frykholm, Franlgen, 8 June 1946; Corine Defrance 'Raymond Schmittlein (1904–1974): médiateur entre la France et la Lituanie' *Cahiers Lituaniens*, No. 9 (2009). Text kindly shared by the author.
[343] Robert Marquant, 'Raymond Schmittlein 19 juin 1904–29 septembre 1974', in Manfred Heinemann (ed.), *Hochschuloffiziere und Wiederaufbau des Hochschulwesens in Westdeutschland 1945-1952, die französische Zone* (Hildesheim, 1991) quoted in Defrance 'Raymond Schmittlein (1904–1974)'.
[344] UNA, S-0418-0002-04, Résumé de l'art Estonien.
[345] UNA, S-0418-0003-08, Semaine de Culture des DPs à Wurzach, 3–10 November 1946, Prospectus. Introduction by Janis Kalmite.
[346] Richard Bessel and Dirk Schumann (eds.), *Life after Death* (Cambridge: Cambridge University Press, 2003).

arrival in Le Bourget, an airport in the North East of Paris, evoking their joy at drinking their first glass of French wine in years. After the *mal du pays* [homesickness], French returnees suffered on arrival, the *mal du retour*, a sadness created by recollections of those who did not survive. Cartier-Bresson's film encapsulates the transition from 'extreme violence' to the long slow adjustment to peacetime. It shows columns of refugees moving Westwards and Eastwards. It was no coincidence that Cartier-Bresson's film ended with scenes of joyous, tearful reunions in a Paris railway station. In 1945, for French officials and the majority of French people the headline story was French *Absents*' homecomings and family reunions. UNRRA is not mentioned once in his film, and neither is the problem of those DPs who refused to return 'home'. And yet, although Henri Cartier-Bresson's film is silent about the fate of DPs who could not or did not want to return 'home', his account is nevertheless pivotal to the story told in this chapter. French domestic wartime experiences coloured how French occupation officials and relief workers perceived DPs in the French zone. They influenced how the French constructed certain categories of DPs as 'deserving' victims in opposition to 'unworthy' one, potential valuable future citizens in opposition to undesirable one. They also shaped the manner in which French officials and relief workers attempted to transform DPs' ways of being and thinking. Crucially, they informed how field workers organized and oversaw DP spaces. Discussions about the 'curative' effects of small dwellings for DPs were, for instance, interconnected to broader debates about the effects of camp life in France, originating in French home-grown experiences of deportation.

As a result, in the French zone, 'DP spaces' varied greatly in terms of their physical environment, openness to the surrounding local communities and levels of regulation. Within these spaces, a wide spectrum of interactions took place between relief workers and DPs, which ranged from violent punishing to romantic love. For the officials examined here, organizing DPs' camps required military discipline and order. They sought to re-inscribe older gendered and class-based ordering of society onto DPs.[347] For relief workers on the ground, however, DP spaces were not simply sites of discipline: they were also spaces of valuable education and recuperation. These tensions between various approaches to relief were highly gendered. UNRRA officials believed that the presence of women in DP camps was good for DPs' re-education and morale, but insisted on an image of familial bond between sexless 'relief' mothers and children.[348] Some UNRRA women

---

[347] See Chapter 4.
[348] Woodbridge, *UNRRA*, vol. 2, p. 470.

certainly embraced this view. When the UNRRA Welfare Officer Vatin-Pérignon, wife of the former head of the Civil Cabinet of Marshall Lyautey in Maroc, defended her achievement with DPs, she reported that her best achievement was the fact that 'All [DPs] called me *Maman* [Mummy].[349] In practice, however, the evidence reveals a much more diverse set of practices and a more fluid gender culture. The context of occupation suspended some of the expectations of 'respectable femininity'. Some female relief workers gave instructions to DPs and acquired an important purchasing power and independence. Others engaged in romantic relationships with DPs. This was resented by some of their male colleagues.

The allegedly 'transgressive' and immoral conducts of a minority of female relief workers were not only the subjects of criticisms amongst French occupation and PDR officials. It also tarnished UNRRA's reputation in DP elites' eyes. DPs neither wholeheartedly accepted relief workers' authority nor did they unquestionably embrace the built environment in which they were placed.[350] They also condemned relief workers' mundane life and desire to enjoy themselves. Significantly, Ignacy Walczewski, secretary of the Catholic Church for Polish DPs in Germany, wrote that relief workers often regarded DPs as 'colonizer looked down on indigenous population'.[351] Yet for all their sense of cultural superiority, their own behaviour was morally condemnable. DP religious elites reproved, in particular, the 'bad examples' that some female relief workers were giving to DPs when having affairs outside of the bond of marriage.[352]

French officials' anxieties about female relief workers' transgressive behaviours were tied to the reformulation of French identity and the restoration of French prestige in post-war Germany. Relief officials realized that the presence of women was good for French propaganda, but insisted that they led an exemplary life. The ways DP camps were organized and overseen were not for DPs' sake alone, but also for the public to appreciate. In many DP camps, exhibitions were set up to display DPs' artistic and creative talents and showcase the efforts, resolve, skills and exemplary work of French field workers. Photographs and 'picture stories' were also taken by relief workers and sent to UNRRA's public relations office, showcasing the successes of rehabilitation and reconstruction. For French UNRRA officials, humanitarian publicity material was not solely considered as a mean to communicate internationalist ideals but also regarded as a way to project a new vision of

---

[349] UNA, UNRRA, S-0438-0003-03, M. Vatin-Pérignon à Doctoeur Général des Cilleuls, 20 January 1946.
[350] Bailkin, *Unsettled*, p. 25.
[351] Walczewski, *Destin tragique des polonais déportés en Allemagne*, p. 80.
[352] L'aumônier du centre de Biberach quoted in ibid., p. 128.

France as a 'humanitarian nation' against the backdrop of increasing anxieties about its international standing. They emphasized France's 'special' mission and tried to integrate it into a universal pictorial language that traversed national, linguistic and ideological barriers. Yet, as we will see in the next chapter, French relief officials did not succeed in imposing their sanitized and idealized visions of aid.

# 3

# The Politics of Neutrality

## Repatriating and Screening DPs in the Early Cold War

At a time of utter destruction and ruins across Germany, when railway, port and road networks were in pieces, official statistics, reports and photographs presented the repatriation of DPs as an unprecedented technological and logistical achievement. During the months immediately after the war, millions of DPs were successfully and safely transported back to their countries of origin. In the French zone, 'Western' and Soviet nationals were repatriated first, followed by Yugoslavs and Poles.[1] In total, by the end of 1945, 417,240 DPs and POWs had been repatriated.[2] According to French official figures, these included 102,160 Soviet DPs, 14,727 Polish DPs, 13,187 Yugoslav DPs, 1,788 Czech DPs, 16,000 Dutch DPs and 2,000 Austrians.[3] These figures certainly need to be viewed with caution, as there were significant differences between Western and Soviet counts.[4] Nevertheless, by the end of 1945, the French authorities estimated that the mass repatriation of Soviet citizens and Western nationals was finished.[5]

The logistical and technological 'success' that repatriation came to symbolize had two sides: on the one hand, a well-orchestrated operation in the eyes of Western occupiers and field workers; on the other hand, a political failure for Soviet and Eastern European leaders who lamented the non-return of many of their own citizens, who refused to be repatriated to Communist-led countries and became servants of the capitalist system. In July 1947, the Soviet

---

[1] The repatriation of Polish DPs was slower due to shortages in trains and the restrictions imposed by the Allied Council in Berlin. By the end of 1945, 14,727 Polish DPs had been repatriated. In 1946, 20,750 and in 1947, 5,778 DPs were repatriated. HCRFA, Service des Personnes Déplacées, *Sept ans d'activité en faveur des personnes déplacées en zone française d'occupation, 1945–1952*, rapport dactylographié et illustré [undated], pp. 19–20.

[2] MAE, HCRFA, PDR6/467, Personnes Déplacées rapatriés (ex-prisonniers de guerre et civils) depuis la fin des hostilités au 1er mars 1948 par semestre.

[3] MAE, HCRFA, PDR6/467, Réponse aux chiffres demandés par Berlin [probably 18.1.1947].

[4] Kaja Kumer-Haukanõmm, 'The Repatriation of Estonians, 1945–1952', in Corine Defrance, Juliette Denis and Julia Maspéro (eds.), *Personnes déplacées et guerre froide en Allemagne occupée* (Bruxelles: Peter Lang, 2015), pp. 97–114, 99.

[5] MAE, HCRFA, PDR6/947, Note pour le Colonel de Villeneuve, 29 December 1945.

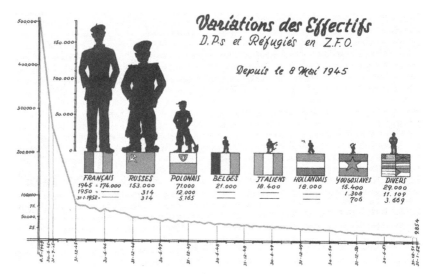

Fig. 3.1 'Changes in DP and refugee numbers since 8 May 1945 in the French zone', in HCRFA, Service des Personnes Déplacées, *Sept ans d'activité en faveur des personnes déplacées en zone française d'occupation, 1945-1952*, rapport dactylographié et illustré [undated], pp. 32-33.

authorities claimed that 9,805 Soviet DPs still resided in the French zone, including 753 Russians, 2,731 Ukrainians from Galicia, 903 Estonians, 2,666 Latvians and 2,752 Lithuanians.[6] Yet, as we will see, the repatriation of DPs was neither – as often implied – simply a matter of successful transportation nor only a matter of failed 'return politics' in the context of the nascent Cold War. Rather the picture is more complicated: repatriation was characterized by an extremely complex power structure which oversaw the channelling and regulating of different kinds of returns and the screening of distinct groups of DPs (Fig. 3.1).

The aim of this chapter is to examine the complexities of the power structure that governed the repatriation and screening of DPs in the French zone, behind the sanitized images of repatriation, produced by international organizations and occupation authorities. Repatriation became a 'success' story via the circulation of defined images, which were put in motion with the help of official publications, newspapers and photographs. Although shot by different kinds of photographers, 'repatriation' photographs often shared a visual vocabulary of composition and framing. They aimed at conveying a

[6] MAE, HCRFA, PDR6/1033, Secret, Griefs invoqués contre la Zone Française d'Occupation, Lettre N. 1518 du Général Yourkine [probably July 1947].

sense of order and efficiency.[7] On 26 May 1947, for instance, UNRRA relief workers registered 110 'last-minute repatriation volunteers', including 67 men, 17 women and 26 children in Tuttlingen, a small town in the Württemberg area, before their departure to Yugoslavia in May 1947.[8] A photo album containing thirteen images of this convoy was compiled, picturing the joy of these women and men leaving behind the tragedy of the war and returning 'home'. The photographer of these shots is unknown, but captions beneath the photographs provided some information about the events depicted. The train left Tuttlingen at 11:30 on 26 May and comprised ten wagons. Each repatriate received seven-day food rations for the journey and sixty-day food rations for beginning their future lives in Yugoslavia. The convoy arrived on 28 May in Yugoslavia at the camp Jesenice. This album is characteristic of the visual 'iconography of repatriation' created by UNRRA. Like many other captions appearing in the British and American zones, the photographs of the Tuttlingen album helped construct the discourse of an organization effectively bringing DPs back to their countries of origin, while carefully hiding the politics behind this process.[9] UNRRA photographs concealed the divisions at play when they were shot. In this album, eight images depicted smiling, well-fed and well-clothed repatriates in front of train wagons decorated with large bunches of flowers (Fig. 3.2). One of the wagons was adorned with a portrait of Tito.

The stories told by these images are, of course, incomplete. These shots did not record the incident preceding the departure of the train, when two Yugoslav DPs fled the convoy, stealing personal objects and American blankets.[10] They also masked the difficulties of the return, whereby repatriation rarely (if ever) equalled homecoming.[11] Finally, these images were silent about DPs' opposition and resistance to repatriation, which was common, carefully

---

[7] Silvia Salvatici, 'Sights of Benevolence. UNRRA's Recipients Portrayed', in Heide Fehrenbach and Davide Rodogno (eds.), *Humanitarian Photography: A History* (Cambridge: Cambridge University Press, 2015), pp. 200–222; Laura Briggs, 'Mother, Child, Race, Nation: The Visual Iconography of Rescue and the Politics of Transnational and Transracial Adoption', *Gender & History*, vol. 15, no. 2 (2003), pp. 179–200.

[8] MAE, HCRFA, PDR6/740, Gouverneur Délégué Supérieur pour le Gouvernement Militaire du Wurtemberg à Administrateur Général Adjoint pour le GMZFO, 9 June 1947.

[9] UNA, UNRRA, S-0419-0005-02, Convoi de rapatriement Yougoslave, depart Tuttlingen, 26 May 1947.

[10] MAE, HCRFA, PDR6/740, Gouverneur Délégué Supérieur pour le Gouvernement Militaire [GM] du Wurtemberg à Administrateur Général Adjoint pour GMZFO, 9 June 1947.

[11] Laura Hammond, 'Examining the Discourse of Repatriation: Towards a More Proactive Theory of Return Migration', in Richard Black and Khalid Koser (eds.), *The End of the Refugee Cycle?* (London: Berghahn, 1999), pp. 227–244.

**Fig. 3.2 (a and b)** UNA, UNRRA, S-0419-0005-02,
Convoi de rapatriement Yougoslave, depart Tuttlingen, 26 May 1947.

erasing any sign of Yugoslav anti-repatriation activities in the French zone.[12] Repatriation officers regularly complained that the French zone was a refuge for anti-repatriation propaganda. Mlle Raudseps, the UNRRA secretary pictured above, for instance, was suspected of anti-Soviet repatriation activities.[13] She was a Baltic DP who had studied in France prior to the war, was sent to Germany as a forced labourer and became a member of the Baltic Committee of Tuttlingen after the war.[14] Overall, these photographic representations reinforce a particular narrative about UNRRA, featuring some of the key elements examined in the previous two chapters: UNRRA's insistence on military efficiency and the logistics of aid; the gendered nature of relief work – Monsieur Riotte was the *male* Chief of the transit camp, and Mlle Raudseps the *female* secretary; the 'objective and neutral' nature of its work; and, finally, the emphasis on the successes of 'rehabilitation' prior to the repatriation of DPs. There is no mention of the PDR organization and the micro-politics of relief described in the previous chapter. Instead, UNRRA is the sole 'competent' organization in charge of repatriation. In sum, these images conceal any signs of brutality, resistance, prejudice and politics, giving instead the impression of a united and happy family.

Analyzing the production and circulation of these repatriation images reveals the important role of photography in the construction of UNRRA's image of 'humanitarian neutrality'. Photographs of repatriated DPs were central to cultural and political depictions of 'new beginnings' and visual discourses which emphasized a break with Nazism. As David Forsythe suggests, humanitarian neutrality is a matter of constructed image.[15] These photographs conveyed a vision of progress and apolitical aid. Yet, the issue of repatriation was central to creeping Cold War tensions among the occupiers, 'repatriation officers' and DPs. The fact that so many similar shots were taken thus presents a paradox: despite important public relation efforts and the circulation of many photographs about repatriation, UNRRA failed to maintain its neutral image in Germany. At the level of high politics, as

---

[12] In the summer of 1946, a political incident occurred in the Yugoslav DP camp of Kisslegg, in the Kreis of Wangen following the display of the monarchic flag. Concerned about the potential diplomatic implications that this might have with the new Yugoslavian authorities, the French authorities recommended 'immediate intervention' and some sanctions. MAE, HCRFA, PDR6/740, Le Gouverneur, délégué supérieur pour le GM du Wurtemberg à l'Administrateur Général, 10 March 1947; MAE, HCRFA, PDR6/740, Télégramme signé Laffon, 26 July 1946.

[13] MAE, HCRFA, PDR6/984, Représentant de l'Etat Major des Armées d'Occupation Soviétiques en Allemagne à Colonel Cherifi, 25 November 1947.

[14] On Austra Raudseps' background see MAE, HCRFA, PDR6/984, Rapport concernant la propagande antisoviétique contre le rapatriement, 29 December 1947.

[15] David P. Forsythe, 'On Contested Concepts: Humanitarianism, Human Rights, and the Notion of Neutrality', *Journal of Human Rights*, vol. 12, no. 1 (2013), pp. 59–68, 66.

repatriation caused friction between the Western Allies and the Soviet Union, UNRRA became increasingly seen as an instrument of the West. At the lower level of everyday encounters between occupiers, repatriation officers and DPs, UNRRA field workers were slower to subscribe to the emerging Cold War paradigm.[16] Yet, their presence contributed to exacerbate conflicts between PDR and Eastern European officials about who should be forcedly repatriated and who should not, who should be entitled to aid and who should not.

As the challenges of working with UNRRA's photographs of returning DPs indicate, it is essential to map the complex and muddy 'politics of neutrality' occurring behind such sanitized visions of repatriation. To accomplish this analysis, this chapter delves beneath the level of national government and policy to reconstruct the ways in which repatriation was put into practice. While recognizing the importance of diplomats and national politicians in formulating repatriation and screening policies, it illuminates how repatriation and screening also crucially depended on how French administrators and members of international organizations reinterpreted and implemented these instructions in the zone. The impact of UNRRA has notably been neglected in the historiography of repatriation in the French zone.[17] The prevailing view is that French policy was essentially pro-Soviet during this period, France facing specific material constraints resulting in part from its experiences of Nazi occupation and the presence of French citizens in the Soviet Union. From a Soviet perspective, recent studies have downplayed the influence of central policy and the capacity of the Soviet state to control repatriation, particularly during the first chaotic months after the Liberation.[18] Building

---

[16] Daniel Cohen, *In War's Wake: Europe's Displaced Persons in the Postwar Order* (Oxford: Oxford University Press, 2011), p. 19. On how relief workers were slow to subscribe to the emerging Cold War paradigm, Jesssica Reinisch 'Auntie UNRRA' at the Crossroads', *Past and Present*, vol. 218, no. 8 (2013), pp. 70–97.

[17] Pavel M. Polian (translated by Christine Colpart), 'Le rapatriement des citoyens soviétiques depuis la France et les zones françaises d'occupation en Allemagne et en Autriche', *Cahiers du Monde russe*, vol. 41, no. 1 (2000), pp. 165–189; Andreas Rinke, *Le Grand retour – Die französische Displaced Person-Politik (1944–1951)* (Frankfurt am Main: Peter Lang, 2002), pp. 340–349; Julia Maspero, 'La question des personnes déplacées polonaises dans les zones françaises d'occupation en Allemagne et en Autriche: un aspect méconnu des relations franco-polonaises (1945–1949)', *Relations internationales*, vol. 138 (2009), pp. 59–74; Histories of UNRRA focus overwhelmingly on the British and American zones, at the exception of George Woodbridge, *UNRRA: The History of the United Nations Relief and Rehabilitation Administration* (New York: Columbia University Press, 1950); Reinhold Adler, 'Der schwierige Weg zur Normalität Die UNRRA in Biberach und Umgebung 1945 bis 1947', *Heimatkundliche Blatter fur den Kreis Biberach*, vol. 30 (2007), pp. 36–57.

[18] Seth Bernstein, 'Ambiguous Homecoming: Retribution, Exploitation and Social Tensions during Repatriation to the USRR, 1944–1946', *Past and Present*, vol. 242, no. 1 (2019), pp. 193–226.

on these recent works, this chapter acknowledges that French officials were remarkably reluctant to openly confront Soviet Repatriation Officers in 1945–1946, to be sure. But it argues that contradictory instructions and jurisdictional disputes between French authorities and UNRRA opened spaces for DP leaders hostile to repatriation to make claims of their own and to develop strategies to avoid forced repatriation, hiding under false identities or taking up job opportunities offered by French occupiers. By highlighting these discrepancies between official policies and practices, this chapter demonstrates that historians of post-war humanitarianism need to pay more attention to the dynamic relationship between prescription and practice, diplomats and occupation officials, experts and field workers.

UNRRA's official stance on repatriation was inconsistent. In August 1945, UNRRA Resolution 71 stipulated that UNRRA's primary task was to promote repatriation. The organization was itself to exist only as a temporary agency. Yet UNRRA officials did not devise clear instructions about how that policy was to be applied in the field, the policy of each military government having precedence on the issue. During the course of 1946, UNRRA's official position gradually shifted towards more encouragement for repatriation. At the same time the organization carried out a vast screening operation to determine who was/was not eligible for help. In each zone, however, the degree to which these pro-repatriation measures and screening policies were applied depended considerably upon national policies and individual officials. In the French zone, contradictory instructions from the Foreign Ministry and UNRRA headquarters engendered differences in implementation. The result was that some groups fell within the remit of the DP category in the British and American zones but not in the French zone (and vice versa). Crucially, this chapter highlights the vicissitudes of repatriation and screening, repatriation incentives and screening policies being highly contingent on changing circumstances, institutional rivalries, local realities and DPs' nationality. In doing so, this chapter puts forward new ways of thinking about the history of repatriation, screening and 'humanitarian' neutrality in the aftermath of the Second World War.

## Deserving and Undeserving Recipients of Aid

Histories of humanitarianism have demonstrated that throughout the nineteenth and twentieth centuries, humanitarian aid has always been highly selective, humanitarian organizations constructing categories of 'deserving' victims in opposition to 'unworthy' ones. Much of the argument in the existing literature has been over the relative importance of inter-state agreement over the definition of 'deserving' victims and the significance of individual rights in conceptualizing 'refugees' in inter-war Europe.[19] For some scholars, the First World War represented a key moment in shaping understanding of 'human dignity' in Europe, legal scholars in the League of Nations insisting on the 'humanitarian rights' of certain groups of victims.[20] For others, by contrast, in the interwar years, understanding of why certain categories of people should or should not receive aid largely depended on their ethnicity, religion, citizenship and utility to state, rather than the concept of 'human dignity'.[21] These tensions between individual rights and a definition of refugee based on an individual's membership in a specific group persisted in the immediate aftermath of the Second World War.

At the level of inter-state policies, debates about who should be included and excluded from the DP category occurred during a period of transition in the definition of refugee, in the context of the drafting of the Universal Declaration of Human Rights, which announced the refugee status of 1951 based on the concept of 'fear of persecution'.[22] In this respect, the period marked a crucial shift away from notions of citizenship (the protection of refugee was predicted on an individual's membership in a specific group) to individual human rights in Western Europe. In 1946, the definition of 'refugee' was changed to include both persons unable and those *unwilling* to receive state protection.[23] At the level of the field, however, the determination of those who were (or not) entitled to stay in Germany, receive international aid and emigrate to a third country depended on DPs' wartime experiences, pre-war citizenship, ethnicity, gender, age and perhaps most importantly utility to the French state.

DPs' wartime experiences were complex affairs, fitting uneasily into publicly acceptable categories of good and evil, resisters and collaborators. The amalgamation of various groups of persons with radically different wartime experiences within the 'DP category' stands in sharp contrast to the development of a 'hierarchy' of victims in France.[24] The Supreme Headquarters Allied

---

[19] Barbara Metzger, 'The League of Nations, Refugees and Individual Rights', in Matthew Frank and Jessica Reinisch (eds.), *Refugees in Europe 1919–1959: A Forty Years' Crisis?* (London: Bloomsbury, 2017), pp. 101–119.

[20] Bruno Cabanes, *The Great War and the Origins of Humanitarianism, 1918–1924* (Cambridge: Cambridge University Press, 2014).

[21] Keith David Watenpaugh, *Bread from Stones. The Middle East and the Making of Modern Humanitarianism* (Oakland: University of California Press, 2015).

[22] Dzovinar Kévonian, 'Deux siècles de réfugiés: Circulations, Qualifications, Internationalisation', *Pouvoirs*, vol. 44, no. 1 (2013), pp. 17–32.

[23] Andrew Paul Janco, '"Unwilling": The One-Word Revolution in Refugee Status, 1940–1951', *Contemporary European History*, vol. 23, no. 3 (2014), pp. 429–446.

[24] François Cochet, *Les exclus de la victoire: histoire des Prisonniers de Guerre, Déportés et STO* (Paris: Kronos, 1992); Pieter Lagrou, *The Legacy of Nazi Occupation: Patriotic Memory and National Recovery in Western Europe, 1945–1965* (Cambridge: Cambridge University Press, 2000).

Expeditionary Force's definition of 'displaced persons' was deliberately inclusive and did not reflect the diversity of DPs' lived experiences. In Allied terminology, 'displaced persons' were originally defined as civilians who found themselves 'outside the national boundaries of their country by reason of the war' and were in need of repatriation.[25] This definition aimed primarily at differentiating civilian DPs from POWs. When planning for the repatriation of refugees, Allied planners, and notably the British and Americans who thought first and foremost about providing for their own citizens, lumped together all civilians who needed to be repatriated under the broad category of DPs while, in effect, insisting that POWs held priority over DPs. With the exception of the Channel Islands, their territories had not been invaded and their civilian population had not been displaced outside their territories. The war remained a classical war in which armies fight and take prisoners.[26] But, for French planners the distinction between civilian DPs and POWs was incongruous, as a French volunteer who arrived in 1942 to replace a POW under the 'Relève' scheme had priority over a 1944 deportee interned in a concentration camp.[27] Further, this inclusive definition of DPs stood in sharp contrast with the formation of a hierarchy of victims in France, occurring in the midst of the intense political conflicts that followed the Liberation.

In the mythology of resistance and martyrdom that emerged, resistance fighters and resistance deportees topped the scale of probity.[28] The differences between survivors of concentration camps and death camps faded away.[29] POWs were, to a large extent, 'excluded' from the myth of national heroism, while forced labourers were as a whole suspected of collaboration, guilty of having in one way or another contributed to the Nazi war efforts.[30] As Camille

---

[25] The SHAEF Outline Plan of 3 June 1944 was the first Allied document to describe a DP policy. In this Plan, DPs were defined as: 'civilians outside the national boundaries of their country by reason of the war, who are (1) desirous but unable to return home, or find homes without assistance; (2) to be returned to enemy or ex-enemy territory' FO 1052/10, ' SHAEF Planning directive: refugees and DPs (DPs)', 3 June 1944, p. 1. This plan was significantly revised in April 1945. The revised SHAEF Plan (known as Administrative Memorandum No. 39) expanded the definition in a number of ways: it introduced the criterion of nationality (distinguishing between United Nations DPs, enemy DPs and ex-enemy DPs) and specified that only UN DPs qualified for assistance. 'Administrative Memorandum No. 39 (Revised-16 April 1945)', in Malcolm Proudfoot, *European Refugees, 1939–1952* (London: Faber and Faber, 1957), p. 445.

[26] Annette Wieviorka, *Déportation et génocide. Entre la mémoire et l'oubli* (Paris: Hachette, 2003), p. 42.

[27] Rinke, *Le Grand retour*, p. 26.

[28] Jean Marc Dreyfus, 'Conflit de mémoires autour du cimetière de Bergen-Belsen', *Vingtième Siècle. Revue d'Histoire* (2006), pp. 73–87.

[29] Jean-Marc Dreyfus, *Amis, si tu tombes* (Paris: Perrin, 2005), pp. 80–81.

[30] Tensions crystallized around the battle ('querelle du titre') between the *Fédération Nationale des Déportés du Travail* and survivors of concentration camps around the title

Fauroux demonstrates, this hierarchy of victims, reflected in the creation of distinctive administrative categories at the Liberation, was highly gendered. At its bottom was the category of 'female volunteers', which embodied national indignity.[31] The formation of this hierarchy of victims and 'moral economy of gratitude' created resentments and bitterness among various groups, even resistance fighters, who received the honour of the nation and were celebrated as national heroes. Free French fighters, for example, felt that they were not sufficiently praised in comparison with First World War veterans.[32]

The undistinctive 'DP' category posed challenges to the black and white demarcation of collaboration and resistance. For British and American military planners, isolated as they were from direct experience of civilian population transfers, the tracing and categorization of DPs in Germany was, in some respects, an arid bureaucratic exercise. For French military and PDR planners, by contrast, repatriating and tracing civilians was less dispassionate. This fundamental disjuncture in the perception of the DP problem: immediate and personal for the French; a matter of logistics for the British and Americans, was a source of significant conflict between them. French military authorities opposed, in particular, the principle of prioritizing the repatriation of POWs over that of DPs. After the liberation of Buchenwald in April 1945, the French secured a relaxation in the Allied policy of absolute priority for the POWs.[33] The same month, SHAEF also introduced a criterion of nationality (understood as state citizenship) in the definition of 'DPs' and specified that only UN DPs qualified for assistance. UN DPs (nationals of Allied countries) were separated from enemy DPs (nationals of Germany, Austria and Japan) and ex-enemy DPs (nationals of Italy, Finland, Romania, Bulgaria and Hungary). By establishing this distinction, Allied authorities sought to clearly separate winners from losers.[34]

The Allies initially adopted a collective definition of 'DPs' based on national affiliation (as understood as both state citizenship or ethnic membership, notably for Jewish DPs) rather than on notions of persecution. Significantly,

---

'déportés du travail'. Spina, 'La France et les Français devant le Service du Travail Obligatoire', pp. 1107–1123; Olivier Lalieu, 'Le statut juridique du déporté et les enjeux de mémoire, de 1948 à nos jours', in Tal Bruttmann, Laurent Joly and Annette Wieviorka (eds.), Qu'est ce qu'un déporté? Histoires et mémoires des déportations de la Seconde Guerre mondiale (Paris: CNRS Éditions, 2009), pp. 333–350, 334.

[31] Camille Fauroux, 'L'étiquette infamante de volontaire'. Genèse administrative d'une catégorie de l'histoire de l'occupation', Revue d'histoire moderne et contemporaine, vol. 2, no. 66 (2019), pp. 96–115.

[32] Guillaume Piketty, 'From the Capitol Hill to the Tarpeian Rock? Free French Coming out of War', European Review of History, vol. 25, no. 2 (2018), pp. 354–373.

[33] Wieviorka, Deportation et genocide, p. 84.

[34] Between National Socialism and Soviet Communism: Displaced Persons in Post-war Germany (Ann Arbor: University of Michigan Press, 2011), p. 44.

they refused to assist the millions of German 'expellees' who lost their homes in the east. This notably included the civilians who fled westwards as the Red Army advanced and those expelled from their homes east of the Oder-Neisse, the 13 to 15 million German-speaking inhabitants of Poland, Czechoslovakia, Hungary, Yugoslavia, Russia and the three Baltic countries. In practice, however, the division between DPs and refugees did not always work out so neatly. Some 'ex-enemy' nationals hid under false identities, and others married and acquired 'new' nationality to avoid repatriation or retribution.[35] This was in particular the case of Soviet nationals who did not want to return to Soviet-annexed countries but could in theory be forcedly repatriated.

## The Geopolitical Contexts of Repatriation

Debates over forced repatriation revealed the very complex and uncomfortable position of the Western Allies, stuck between the principles that they had begun to make during the war and the post-war realities.[36] In marked contrast to the aftermath of the First World War, which witnessed the development of minority protection under the League of Nations system, peacemakers insisted on the necessity of creating nationally and ethnically homogeneous nation states. In this context, it was essential to return each citizen to their own nation.[37] Yet for many people the issue of 'return' was not straightforward. Baltic DPs claimed that they had no 'homeland' to return to; the new shape of the eastern borders of Poland also meant that Ukrainians depended on the Soviet Union. These DPs held state citizenship, but they strongly refused to return to their countries of origin and rejected the Soviet Union's state protection. The result of the discussion about who should or should not be repatriated at the UN was the emergence of the principle of 'voluntariness' as an important new norm for repatriation.[38]

---

[35] On the fluidity of DP identities, see Adam Seipp and Andrea Sinn, 'Landscapes of the Uprooted: Displacement in Postwar Europe', *Holocaust and Genocide Studies*, vol. 32, no. 1 (2018), pp. 1–7; Margarete Myers Feinstein, 'All under One Roof: Persecutees, DPs, Expellees, and the Housing Shortage in Occupied Germany', *Holocaust and Genocide Studies*, vol. 32, no. 1 (2018), pp. 29–48.

[36] Gousseff, 'L'Est et l'Ouest entre consensus et divergence face aux DPs d'Allemagne', in Defrance, Denis and Maspéro (eds.), *Personnes déplacées et guerre froide en Allemagne occupée*, p. 38.

[37] On forced deportations and minority protection in the aftermath of the First World War, see Eric D. Weitz, 'From the Vienna to the Paris System: International Politics and the Entangled Histories of Human Rights, Forced Deportations and Civilising Missions', *The American Historical Review*, vol. 113, no. 5 (2008), pp. 1313–1343. On the aftermath of the Second World War, see, for example, Jessica Reinisch and Elizabeth White (eds.), *The Disentanglement of Populations. Migration, Expulsion and Displacement in postwar Europe* (London: Palgrave Macmillan, 2011).

[38] Katy Long, *The Point of No Return: Refugees, Rights and Repatriation* (Oxford: Oxford University Press, 2013), p. 52.

At the war's end, the largest single group of DPs were Soviet nationals. Unlike other DPs in the three Western zones, Soviet citizens could be forced to return home. This Soviet exception was agreed at the Yalta Conference, where American, British and Soviet authorities concluded secret agreements for the reciprocal exchange of liberated civilians and POWs.[39] At Yalta, the Allies also promised that Soviet citizens would be sent eastwards first. Two factors underpinned this reciprocal agreement: the need to consolidate an alliance with the Soviet Union in order to defeat Japan, and the necessity to secure the release of Western POWs held captive in areas under the Red Army's control. The definition of a 'Soviet citizen' remained vague, and the status of DPs hailing from territories annexed by the Soviet Union during the war, notably eastern Poland and the Baltic States, unclear.[40] This confusion stemmed from the peculiar status of Baltic DP citizenship, as British and American authorities recognized *de facto* but not *de jure* the annexation of the Baltic States by the Soviet Union.[41] In this context, Baltic DPs could refuse Soviet citizenship on the grounds that the annexation had not been officially recognized and bypass these repatriation agreements. Although America and Britain never repudiated these elements of the Yalta accords, military officials progressively undermined these repatriation agreements, notably by limiting Soviet repatriation officers' access to DP camps. In the American zone, for instance, the military command secretly agreed to exclude Baltic DPs from the forced repatriation process on 18 May 1945.[42] On 4 September, General Eisenhower went further, confining forced repatriation to three categories of people: (i) Soviet citizens who had been captured in German uniform, (ii) those who had joined in the Red Army on or after 22 June 1941 and who were not subsequently discharged and (iii) those who had voluntarily rendered aid to the enemy. The situation was more complex in the French zone and remained confused at least until December 1945, when the French Foreign Office sent clearer instructions to the zone.

---

[39] Anna Holian, *Between National Socialism and Soviet Communism: Displaced Persons in Post-war Germany* (Ann Arbor: University of Michigan Press, 2011), p. 38; Ulrike Goeken-Haidl, *Der Weg zurück. Die Repatriierung sowjetischer Kriegsgefangener und Zwangsarbeiter während und nach dem Zweiten Weltkrieg* (Essen: Klartext Verlag, 2006), pp. 126–134.

[40] Kim Salomon, *Refugees in the Cold War. Toward a New International Refugee Regime in the Early Postwar Era* (Lund: Lund University Press, 1991), pp. 101–102; Juliette Denis, 'Complices de Hitler ou victimes de Staline? Les déplacés baltes en Allemagne de la sortie de guerre à la guerre froide', *Le Mouvement Social*, vol. 244, no. 3 (2013), pp. 81–98; Kumer-Haukanõmm, 'The Repatriation of Estonians', pp. 102–107; Gousseff, 'L'Est et l'Ouest entre consensus et divergence face aux DPs d'Allemagne', pp. 50–51.

[41] Denis, 'Complices de Hitler ou victimes de Staline?', p. 87.

[42] Ibid., p. 86.

At the heart of France's contradictory policies was the problem of French citizens held captive in the Soviet Union. In their dealings with Moscow, French decision makers had to comply with what Catherine Gousseff described as a *politique du donnant-donnant*, always making concessions in order to guarantee the return of French internees and *Malgré-nous* ['in spite of ourselves'].[43] *Malgré-Nous* were POWs from Alsace-Lorraine who had been forcibly enrolled in the Wehrmacht and captured by the Red Army. For most of the period between 1944 and 1946, French discussions on the repatriation of Soviet nationals were restricted by this question. Indeed, French–Soviet bilateral negotiations on repatriation began months before the Allied negotiations in Yalta due to the large numbers of French citizens in the Soviet Union and the presence of Soviet citizens in liberated France. Repatriation started before the signing of official agreements, with the liberation of 1,500 *Alsaciens-Lorrains* held in the Soviet camp at Tambov on 7 July 1944.[44] A gentleman's agreement regarding repatriation was subsequently reached between the French Foreign Ministry and the Soviet ambassador in October 1944, the point at which Moscow officially recognized the Provisional Government. An inter-ministerial commission was also established to coordinate repatriation plans, bringing together representatives from various French ministries, including the PDR and the War, the Interior, the Finance and the Foreign Ministries.[45] An estimated 93,918 Soviet citizens were in French territory, a figure that prompted security fears among the French authorities.[46] These included soldiers who had fought in the Wehrmacht's Vlasov Army and forced labourers of the Todt Organization, plus several escapees who had

---

[43] Catherine Gousseff, 'Des migrations de sorties de guerre qui reconfigurent la frontière: ouverture et refermeture de l'URSS avant la guerre froide (1944–1946)', in Sophie Coeuré et Sabine Dullin (eds.), *Frontières du communisme* (Paris: La Découverte-Recherche, 2007), pp. 428–442, 433. Also see Polian, 'Le rapatriement des citoyens soviétiques'; Catherine Klein-Gousseff, *Retour d'URSS. Les prisonniers de guerre et les internés français dans les archives soviétiques, 1945–1951* (Paris: Editions du CNRS, 2001); Gaël Moullec, 'Alliés ou ennemis ? Le GUPVI-NKVD, le Komintern et les "Malgrés-nous". Le destin des prisonniers de guerre français en URSS (1942–1955)', *Cahiers du monde russe*, vol. 42, no. 2–4 (2001), pp. 667–678; Rinke, *Le Grand retour*, pp. 236–237; Jacques Bariéty and Corine Defrance, 'Les missions de la France Libre en Union Soviétique et les "Malgré-nous" (1942–1944)', *Revue d'Allemagne et des Pays de Langue Allemande*, vol. 39, no. 4 (2008), pp. 533–550.

[44] Klein-Gousseff, *Retour d'URSS*, p. 18.

[45] MAE, Europe, URSS (1944–1960), 68, Point de la question des ressortissants soviétiques au 1er Novembre 1945, activité du Ministère de la Guerre au Profit de la Mission Militaire Soviétique pour le Rapatriement des citoyens soviétiques libérés dans les territoires de l'Ouest de l'Europe. [Probably November 1945]. For a broad summary of Soviet DPs in France see Georges Coudry, *Les camps soviétiques en France. Les 'russes' livrés à Staline en 1945* (Paris: Albin Michel, 1997).

[46] MAE, Europe, URSS (1944–1960), 65, Note A.S Problèmes à résoudre pour l'"hebergement et l'entretien des ressortissants soviétiques se trouvant en France, 14 October 1944.

joined the French resistance.[47] Repatriation to the Soviet Union of members of each of these groups began in November 1944.[48] During the same period, the French signed a bilateral agreement with the government of the Czechoslovak Republic on repatriation.[49] These agreements preceded the signing of the Franco–Soviet treaty on 10 December 1944, a military alliance mainly designed to contain the resurgence of German power.[50]

Despite the pro-Soviet orientation of French foreign policy during this period, the issue of forced repatriation and those to whom the measure applied was divisive. In the winter and spring of 1945, as the French Foreign Office was developing its position on forced repatriation, several ministers wanted to avoid compulsory repatriation, for three main reasons: the respect for French liberal traditions, the expectation that any war criminals and collaborators should face trial and the lack of consensus over the definition of a 'Soviet citizen'.[51] The Ministry of Justice focused, in particular, on former soldiers from the Vlasov Army who were known to have committed crimes on French soil.[52] Opposition to forced repatriation also reflected a long-standing tradition of presenting France as the cradle of the rights of man.[53] In the wake of the defeat and Vichy, the reassertion of asylum was seen as a fundamental feature of French cultural identity and a way to recover lost prestige.[54] The situation was particularly confused for Eastern European nationals who originated from territories unattached to the Soviet Union prior to 1 September 1939. The key aspect of this problem was that France did not formally recognize the annexation of the territories, although it did not contest it

---

[47] Klein-Gousseff, *Retour d'URSS*, p. 20.
[48] Polian, 'Rapatriement des citoyens soviétiques', p. 174.
[49] UNRRA, S-0523-0012, Bilateral Agreement between the Government of the Czechoslovak Republic and the Provisional Government of the French Republic on Repatriation, translation of official French text, 21 November 1944.
[50] Jean-Rémy Bezias, *Georges Bidault et la politique étrangère de la France, Europe, Etats-Unis, Proche-Orient, 1944–1948* (Paris: L'harmattan, 2006), p. 163.
[51] MAE, Europe, URSS (1944–1960), 67, Note du jurisconsulte du department, 20 September 1945.
[52] MAE, Europe, URSS (1944–1960), 67, Note de la Direction des Unions pour la Direction d'Europe, 13 September 1945.
[53] Antoine Fleury, 'Droits de l'homme et enjeux humanitaires', in Robert Frank (ed.), *Pour l'histoire des relations internationales* (Paris: Presses Universitaires de France, 2012), pp. 453–469.
[54] See, for example, Cohen, *In War's Wake*, p. 16; Greg Burgess, 'Remaking Asylum in Postwar France, 1944–1952', *Journal of Contemporary History*, vol. 49, no. 3 (2014), pp. 556–576, 558; Jéremy Guedj, 'La France et l' "institution" des réfugiés, de l'urgence à la normalization (1946–1951)', in Aline Angoustures, Dzovinar Kévonian and Claire Mouradian (eds.), *Réfugiés et apatrides. Administrer l'asile en France (1920–1960)* (Rennes: Presses Universitaires de Rennes, 2017), pp. 115–125, 118.

either.⁵⁵ As a result, even within the Ministry of Foreign Affairs there were considerable debates over the issue of forced repatriation. The *Direction des Unions* considered that it would be inopportune to grant asylum to Soviet citizens, even those originating from the Baltic States, as these candidates were suspected of collaboration with Germany.⁵⁶ There were indeed significant numbers of DPs who had engaged in anti-Soviet activities in collaboration with German forces, and who feared reprisal upon return. Instead, in a letter dated 29 May 1945, Foreign Minister Georges Bidault was inclined to adopt a favourable position with regard to Baltic DPs because of the former warm relations between France and the Baltic States.⁵⁷ Eventually, the necessity of avoiding any confrontation with the Soviet Union prevailed in June 1945, and the French policymakers dropped the requirement for considering cases on an individual basis.⁵⁸ This was soon supplemented by an official accord on repatriation, concluded between Paris and Moscow on 29 June 1945.

French policy regarding forced repatriation was shaped by a variety of factors. Efforts to placate the Soviet authorities were highly significant, motivated by the paramount imperative of securing the release of French POWs held on Soviet territory and maintaining the Franco–Soviet alliance established in December 1944. The agreement on 29 June was, in some respects, more radical than the bilateral agreements concluded by the British and American authorities at Yalta.⁵⁹ Within it, France committed itself to repatriating all Soviet citizens, including those who were likely to be prosecuted for their collaboration with the Nazis.⁶⁰ Yet, the French authorities remained uncomfortable with the very idea of forced repatriation and sought means of adapting, or circumventing, their agreement with Moscow.⁶¹ As a result, French policy in the zone was highly fluid in the summer and autumn of 1945. These ambiguities were evident from the very outset of the discussions about repatriation at the UN. They were given potent expression by the French delegation at UNRRA's Third Council in London in August 1945.

---

[55] MAE, Europe, URSS (1944–1960), 67, Note de la Direction d'Europe, rapatriement des citoyens soviétiques se trouvant sous le contrôle des autorités françaises, Londres, 17 September 1945.
[56] MAE, Europe, URSS (1944–1960), 65, Note Direction des Unions, 26 January 1945.
[57] MAE, Europe, URSS (1944–1960), 87, Georges Bidault à M. Bonnet, Ambassadeur de France à Washington, 29 May 1945.
[58] MAE, Europe, URSS (1944–1960), 68, Direction des Unions, L'accord de rapatriement franco-soviétique et le droit d'asile, 20 March 1946.
[59] Polian, 'Le rapatriement des citoyens soviétiques', p. 170. Jean-Noel Grandhomme, 'Tambov et autres camps. Le lent retour d'URSS des "Malgré-nous" d'Alsace-Lorraine (1944–1955)', *Revue d'Allemagne et des Pays de Langue Allemande*, vol. 39 (2008), pp. 551–568.
[60] Polian, 'Le rapatriement des citoyens soviétiques', p. 170.
[61] MAE, Europe, URSS (1944–1960), 67, Ministère des Affaires Etrangères à Berthelot, Secrétaire Général pour les Affaires allemandes et autrichiennes, 11 September 1945.

## The Politics of Neutrality: France, UNRRA and the Problem of Repatriation

Appreciating the role of UNRRA in shaping repatriation discourses and practices is integral to understanding the ambiguities of French policies. According to some scholars, France was the Soviet Union's most pliant Western government, with the French implementing a more draconian forced repatriation policy than their Western allies.[62] Pavel Polian highlights the role of the Soviet government in the process of repatriation and how it brought pressure to bear on the French government. According to him, Soviet authorities were satisfied with the work carried out by French administrators with regard to the repatriation of Soviet nationals and 'anti-Soviet' elements.[63] Further, repatriation persisted far longer in the French zone in Germany (until 1952) than in the other Western zones.[64] Other historians place greater emphasis on differences between the policies France adopted at home and in its occupation zones in Germany and Austria.[65] Indeed, until 1946 Soviet complaints focused more on France and the French zone in Austria than on the zone in Germany, as the methods employed in the French zone were less brutal than those employed in France.[66]

The role of UNRRA in assisting repatriation offers a study in paradox. At the high level of the organization, UNRRA's first director General Herbert Lehman strongly opposed forced repatriation. Until his resignation on 31 March 1946, UNRRA teams were, in theory, committed only to voluntary

---

[62] Mark Elliott, 'The Soviet Repatriation Campaign', in Wsevolod Isajiw, Yory Boshyk and Roman Senkus (eds.), *The Refugee Experience. Ukrainian Displaced Persons after World War Two* (Edmonton: Canadian Institute of Ukrainian Studies Press, 1992), pp. 341–359; Nikolai Tolstoy, *Victims of Yalta* (London: Hodder and Stoughton, 1977); Wolfgang Jacobmeyer, *Vom Zwangsarbeiter zum heimatlosen Ausländer: Die Displaced Persons in Westdeutschland, 1945–1951* (Gottingen: Vandenhoeck & Ruprecht, 1985), pp. 142–143. On broader discussions of Soviet Repatriation and Allied policy see Julius Epstein, *Operation Keelhaul: The Story of Forced Repatriation from 1944 to the Present* (Old Greenwich, CT: The Devin-Adair Company, 1973); Nicholas Bethell, *The Last Secret: Forcible Repatriation to Russia, 1944–1947* (London: Andre Deutsch, 1974).

[63] Polian, 'Le rapatriement des citoyens soviétiques', p. 178.

[64] Ibid.

[65] Georges Coudry suggests that the methods employed in the French zone were less brutal than those employed in France. Mark Wyman also argues that 'France allowed the Soviets to conduct manhunts for Soviet citizens on French soil for months, [but] the French Army of Occupation in Germany was much less cooperative'. Mark Wyman, *DPs: Europe's Displaced Persons, 1945–1951* (New York: Cornell University, 1998), p. 65. Georges Coudry, 'Le rapatriement des ressortissants soviétiques de 1945 à 1947, avatars de la réciprocité', *Guerres mondiales et conflits contemporains*, no. 177 (1995), pp. 105-129, p. 129.

[66] Coudry, 'Le rapatriement des ressortissants soviétiques de 1945 à 1947, avatars de la réciprocité', p. 129.

repatriation. UNRRA Resolution 71 testified to UNRRA's efforts to encourage repatriation; yet, UNRRA officials never devised clear instructions about how this resolution was to be applied in the field. The result was greater leeway for individual interpretation.[67] At the lower level of the zone, UNRRA depended on the military government, PDR officers and national repatriation mission. Within the French Foreign Office, a number of diplomats hoped that cooperation with UNRRA would facilitate French administrators' work with Eastern European missions and the transfers of DPs to France on a temporary basis. Instead, the presence of UNRRA largely complicated French PDR actions in the zone. Several reasons account for this: the lack of a clear and consistent message from UNRRA's central headquarters until the spring of 1946, the subsequent delays in implementing a pro-repatriation policy and the bitter personal and administrative conflicts between the organization PDR and UNRRA Headquarters. For instance, in July 1946 the French UNRRA headquarters circulated Bulletin 19, which contradicted French official policy regarding DPs hailing from the territories annexed by the Soviet Union during the war.[68] Still, in November 1946, UNRRA director of the zone General Lenclud remained unsure whether the Soviet mission could order the forced repatriation of her citizens.[69]

The history of UNRRA in the French zone illustrates the power of local administrators in reinterpreting and shaping policies on the ground, raising important questions about the limits of 'neutral' and 'impartial' humanitarian aid. It also reveals the discrepancies between French public position at the UNRRA Council in London in the summer of 1945 and French UNRRA HQ's attitudes in Germany. At UNRRA's Third Council, held at the County Hall in Westminster, the French delegation was directed by René Massigli, a firm advocate of alliance with Great Britain and France's wholehearted commitment to what would become the 'Western' Bloc.[70] Massigli's delegation endorsed British and American rhetoric about individual freedom and democratic rights, but was also anxious not to alienate Eastern delegations.[71] A note

---

[67] Susan Armstrong-Reid and David Murray, *Armies of Peace: Canada and the UNRRA Years* (Toronto: University of Toronto Press, 2008), p. 59; Woodbridge, *UNRRA*, vol. 2, p. 518.

[68] MAE, HCRFA, PDR6/979, Administrateur Général Laffon à Directeur de l'UNRRA, 6 August 1946.

[69] MAE, HCRFA, PDR6/979, Lenclud à l'Administrateur Général, 1 Novembre 1946.

[70] MAE, NUOI, 7, Note 71, Résolution adoptee par le conseil de l'UNRRA le 18 aout 1945 à la majorité de 24 voix contre 4. On Massigli, Raphaële Ulrich-Pier, *René Massigli (1888-1988) Une vie de diplomate Tome II* (Paris: Peter Lang, 2006), pp. 882–887, 937, 974; MAE, NUOI, 7, Note de la Direction des Conventions Administratives, Réunion à Londres du Conseil de l'UNRRA. Problème des personnes déplacées, 16 August 1945.

[71] MAE, NUOI, 7, Note Direction des Conventions Administratives, 16 August 1945, p. 5; Note Affaires Economiques, 'Troisième session du Conseil de l'UNRRA' [undated].

from the *Direction des Conventions Administratives* indicates how important it was to avoid public statements that might anger the Soviet Union, although the French diplomatic services had prepared resolution projects stipulating that DPs (including those who refused repatriation) should be given UNRRA's assistance without their government's consent.[72] The French delegation welcomed the vote of Resolution 71, which stipulated that UNRRA could extend relief 'on a purely temporary basis' pending DPs' repatriation.[73] It also provided that UNRRA would not assist those DPs who had collaborated with the enemy or had committed crimes against the interests of UN nationals. The French delegation applauded this resolution because it left the door open for emigration to France.[74] Indeed, it enabled the French to oppose potential Russian or Polish protests concerning the entry of DP manpower on the grounds that this was done on a temporary basis and under the supervision of an international organization.[75] A memorandum shows that the French delegation wished that this resolution had gone even further in favour of resettlement in a third country.[76]

Publicly, the French delegation adopted the position of a 'disinterested bystander' between East and West, hoping to assume the role of mediator between America and the Soviet Union and hide behind the discourse of neutral humanitarianism.[77] This discursive strategy was consistent with the main orientation of French foreign policy at the time. Behind the scenes, the evidence suggests that French diplomats sought ways to balance the demands of the Soviet Union with France's liberal traditions and labour needs. A few weeks after the Third UNRRA Council, the French Foreign Ministry stated that forced repatriation should be applied only to those who hailed from territories belonging to the Soviet Union on 3 September 1939 until this would be clarified further later.[78] This was the position of the *Direction d'Europe* within the Quai d'Orsay.[79] On 15 October 1945, a telegram was sent to the French zone. Referring to the Polish–Soviet border agreement dated 16 August 1945, it stipulated that Polish DPs who had originated from territories

---

[72] MAE, NUOI, 7, Note Direction des Conventions Administratives, 16 August 1945, p. 4.
[73] Resolution 71: Functions of the Administration with Respect to Displaced Persons, Woodbridge, *UNRRA*, vol. 3, pp. 142–143.
[74] MAE, NUOI, 7, Note Direction des Conventions Administratives, 17 August 1945, pp. 2–3.
[75] Ibid.
[76] MAE, PDR1/18, Rapport sur le rapatriement ou le non rapatriement des personnes réfractaires, discuté à la 3ème réunion du Conseil de l'UNRRA (Londres, Aout 1945).
[77] MAE, NUOI, 7, Note pour le Ministre, Affaires Économiques, 18 August 1945, p. 6.
[78] MAE, Europe, URSS (1944–1960), 67, Ministère des Affaires Etrangères à Berthelot, Secrétaire Général pour les Affaires allemandes et autrichiennes, 11 September 1945.
[79] MAE, Europe, URSS (1944–1960), 68, Direction des Unions pour la Direction d'Europe, 6 November 1945.

attached to the Soviet Union since 3 September 1939 had the right to choose whether or not to be repatriated.[80] The official French position remained confused for Baltic and Ukrainian DPs during the autumn of 1945. There were approximately 6,000 Baltic DPs in the French zone, and the overwhelming majority of them resided in the Württemberg area (5,658).[81] The exact number of Ukrainians is unknown.[82] Ukrainians tended to be registered according to their last-known citizenship or were classified as stateless in official records.[83] Some claimed Polish nationality in order to avoid forced repatriation. Until December 1945, official instructions about whether or not Ukrainian and Baltic DPs could be forcibly repatriated were contradictory.

In September 1945, the Latvian delegate to the League of Nations Julijs Feldmans reported to the French Foreign Office the kidnapping of seven Latvian refugees by Soviet authorities in Radolfzell, a village near Konstanz.[84] Faced with uncertainty regarding their fate, a number of Baltic DPs fled from the French zone, seeking refuge in the American zone.[85] This escape did not necessarily offer the prospect of better protection. A number of Estonian DPs seeking sanctuary in the American zone were handed over to the French, before being delivered to the Soviet authorities and repatriated to Soviet-occupied Estonia.[86] Faced with mounting requests from local administrators and unsure of the correct course of action to take, the General Secretariat for German and Austrian Affairs urged the Foreign Ministry to send more precise instructions in November 1945.[87] Within the Quai d'Orsay, the *Direction des Unions* disagreed with the *Direction d'Europe* over their interpretation of the 29 June Franco–Soviet agreement. As we have seen, for the *Direction d'Europe* forced repatriation should be applied only to those who hailed from territories belonging to the Soviet Union on 3 September 1939.

---

[80] MAE, HCRFA, PDR6/741, Administrateur Général à Général de Corps d'Armée, N.2765DGAA/PDR, 26 November 1945.
[81] MAE, HCRFA, PDR6/727, État-numérique des Baltes, 26 December 1945.
[82] Bohatiuk argues that there were 19,026 Ukrainians in March 1946. On 1 August 1948, Ukrainians numbered 3,271. 'The Economic Aspects of Camp Life', in Isajiw, Boshyk and Senkus (eds.), *The Refugee Experience*, pp. 69–89, 85.
[83] UNA, UNRRA, S-0421-0029-03, Directeur du District Nord à Monsieur le Directeur de team, critique rapport 83, 8 July 1946.
[84] MAE, URSS 1944–1949, 483, J. Feldmans, délégation Permanente de Lettonie auprès de la Société des Nations, 29 September 1945.
[85] Rinke, *Le Grand retour*, pp. 146–147. Some tried to come back to the French zone in October 1946 as the US denied them the status of DPs as they had arrived in Germany after August 1945. UNA, UNRRA, S-0432-0004-01, Lettre de A. J. Pouzenc, Area Employment Officer à Director Field Operations, 7 October 1946.
[86] Kumer-Haukanõmm, 'The Repatriation of Estonians', p. 111.
[87] MAE, Europe, URSS (1944–1960), 68, Lettre du Ministère plénipotentiaire, secrétaire Général pour les Affaires Allemandes et Autrichiennes à Ministre des Affaires Etrangères, 9 November 1945.

According to the Direction des Unions, however, France could legitimately oppose the repatriation of Baltic DPs who left their countries at the time of its annexation by the Soviet Union; in other words, before 3 August 1940 for Lithuanian DPs, 6 August for Estonian and Latvian DPs, and 27 June for DPs hailing from Bessarabia and Bukovina.[88] But, this affected only a tiny minority; for the rest, it 'appeared difficult to find irrefutable legal argument'.[89] Admittedly, the jurist of this department had demonstrated that *repatriation*, unlike *population transfer*, did not entail *un caractère de contrainte*.[90] But, France's overarching interest, according to the Direction des Unions, was to present a more nuanced stance on 'individual freedom of choice' with regard to the Soviet Union in order to avoid an open clash.[91]

On 20 December 1945, the Foreign Ministry reached a compromise between these contradictory positions, advising Laffon that Baltic DPs should not be forcefully repatriated but conceding that Soviet repatriation officers should be granted access to DP camps to encourage them to return home.[92] France's official position thus shifted before the adoption of the 12 February 1946 landmark resolution at the UN. This change was based on the assumption that those who left their countries before annexation by the Soviet Union were not covered by the agreement and that those who became Soviet citizens after the annexation should not be repatriated because repatriation, unlike population transfer, was optional.[93] This was also the case for Polish citizens originating from east of the Bug River and established in France. As Adolphe Lesur notes, 'contrary to common belief, [French] reserves and opposition to Soviet manoeuvring are obvious. This is amply demonstrated in French diplomatic archives for the period of autumn 1944–spring 1946, thus **before** the 12 February 1946 UN resolution defending DPs' rights'.[94]

The passing of a 12 February 1946 UN General Assembly resolution provided French authorities with an irrefutable legal argument against forced repatriation. This landmark resolution officially recognized DPs' right to

---

[88] MAE, HCRFA, PDR6/1017, Note Concernant le rapatriement des Baltes en URSS, 17 August 1945.

[89] MAE, Europe, URSS (1944–1960), 67, Direction des Unions, Note, 14 September 1945.

[90] MAE, Europe, URSS (1944–1960), 87, Direction des Unions, Note pour la Direction des Conventions Administratives, 10 November 1945.

[91] MAE, Europe, URSS (1944–1960), 68, note de la Direction des Unions, 28 November 1945.

[92] MAE, HCRFA, PDR6/947, Ministre Plénipotentiaire, Secrétaire Général pour les Affaires Allemandes et Autrichiennes à Monsieur l'Administrateur Général Laffon, N. 3824 Pol 5001, 20 December 1945.

[93] Ibid.

[94] Adolphe Lesur, 'Le droit d'option nationale des citoyens polonaise établis en France, nés à l'est du Bug: les positions méconnues du Gouvernement provisoire de la République française d'après les archives du Quai d'Orsay (octobre 1944–février 1946)', *Revue des études slaves*, vol. 75 (2004), pp. 321–332.

asylum, stating that no refugees or DPs who 'expressed valid objections to returning to their countries of origin ... shall be compelled to return to their countries of origin'.[95] But, this repatriation policy was not uniformly applied, disagreement over the question lasting until the spring of 1946 amongst French authorities in Germany.[96] As a result, it was only on 17 June 1946 that Emile Laffon sent clear instructions to the five superior delegates concerning the repatriation of Soviet citizens hailing from the territories annexed by the Soviet Union after 1 September 1939.[97] According to his telegram, the repatriation of nationals from the territories belonging to the Soviet Union before 1939 was compulsory as they fell within the remit of the Franco–Soviet agreement. DPs who were not Soviet citizens before September 1939, however, could refuse repatriation if they provided sufficient evidence that they feared 'persecution'.[98] Prior to that, decision-making was fractured and bent to changing circumstances.

## Negotiating Repatriation with Soviet Repatriation Officers in the Field

In the French zone, repatriation was negotiated at many levels of social exchange, both in the frequent encounters between PDR officials and repatriation officers and locally in the ways UNRRA team directors and local administrators interpreted official instructions and interacted with repatriation officers and DPs. Local authorities and DPs established repatriation practices along quite different lines than those set by official policy. UNRRA team directors implemented directives based on their own understanding of what was being asked of them.[99] In May 1945, for example, an UNRRA director and welfare officer reported placing a Russian family 'threatened' by Russian officers on a farm remote from their DP camp in Kaiserslautern.[100] Other local administrators and relief workers ascribed false identities to DPs, issuing certificates of statelessness to Soviet citizens, including to Soviet Army officers who had fought in the Vlasov Army and served the Germans, thus protecting a number of DPs from forced repatriation.[101] By contrast, some

---

[95] Cohen, *In War's Wake*, p. 26.
[96] MAE, HCRFA, Bonn 257, Télégramme Novateur à Contrôle Berlin et Cigogne, signé de Leusse, 21 April 1946.
[97] MAE, HCRFA, PDR6/1017, Télégramme signé Laffon, Délégations Supérieures, 17 June 1946.
[98] On the appearance of the term 'persecution' in the refugee definition in April 1946, see Janco, '"Unwilling"', p. 438.
[99] UNA, UNRRA, S-0421-0052-01, Jean Gerbier à Rodie, 24 September 1946.
[100] UNA, UNRRA, S-0436-0059-04, C. J. Taylor and John N. Wiley, Welfare report, Kaiserslautern, 14 May 1945.
[101] UNA, S-0417-0001-07, Général de Marguerites à Direction de la Zone, 29 August 1946.

local officials deployed the threat of repatriation to remove foreigners who posed a security threat.

From the outset, French approaches to repatriation were highly ambiguous. While repatriation raised serious concerns for some officials, for others, as they were bombarded with alarming reports concerning rampant DP criminality, repatriation, whether voluntary or forced, appeared an expeditious solution to the DP problem. Memories of the Vlasov Army, coupled with alarming complaints from local Germans, encouraged the belief that they had to get rid of DPs as quickly as possible. In Münsingen, for example, a PDR official put it bluntly: DPs' looting economically weakened the country and created a general feeling of insecurity harmful to the prestige of France.[102] In the sole Kreis of Solgau, French officials reported five accusations of murder, two rapes, fourteen armed burglaries, thirty-eight thefts and four cases of slander.[103] But, attitudes towards DPs were not monolithic. Contrary to these observers, others considered it remarkable 'that retaliation was so insignificant and incidents so limited' after the unprecedented and extraordinary level of atrocity and brutality committed against them.[104] In August 1945, many considered the repatriation of Soviet citizens as completed. For them, Soviet repatriation officers were staying only to kidnap Baltic and Ukrainian DPs and to carry out ideological and political propaganda amongst Germans.[105]

After the mass repatriation of the summer of 1945, French administrators' overarching aim was to reduce the number of DPs, but neither Koenig, Laffon nor Poignant were in favour of forced repatriation.[106] Yet, they were aware of the necessity of honouring the Franco–Soviet agreement and maintaining cordial relations with Soviet officers. By the end of October 1945, more than 90,000 Soviet DPs had been repatriated from the French zone; yet, an important number of Soviet repatriation officers remained in the zone to search for DPs who were reluctant to be repatriated.[107] They employed both legal and illegal practices, including deception, kidnapping, bribery and threats, to force

---

[102] MAE, HCRFA, PDR 6/1066, Le Capitaine Vuillemin, Note de service, N.304/PDR, Münsingen, 26 July 1945.
[103] MAE, HCRFA, PDR6/978, Fiche concernant le comportement des prisonniers et déportés russes. On German perceptions of DP criminality in the French zone see for example Rinke, *Le Grand retour*, p. 232.
[104] MAE, HCRFA, PDR6/1066, Rapport du Colonel Jacquot au sujet du camp russe de Stetten, 2 August 1945.
[105] MAE, HCRFA, PDR6/727, Administrateur Général Laffon à Général Délégué supérieur pour le GM du Bade, 12 November 1945.
[106] MAE, HCRFA, PDR6/956, Note pour le Colonel de Villeneuve, 29 Decembre 1945; PDR6/1017, Poignant à Administrateur Général Adjoint pour le GM, 3 October 1945.
[107] MAE, HCRFA, PDR 1/86, Télégramme pout M. le Général de C. A. Koeltz, signé Sabatier, 12 October 1945; PDR6/1017, Général Koenig à Monsieur le Président du Gouvernement Provisoire de la République Française, 6 May 1946.

DPs to return home.[108] In Neustadt, Soviet officers encouraged French PDR officers to drink by using Russian women as 'honey traps' during Franco–Russian dinners so that the officers would later facilitate repatriation.[109] Forged letters allegedly written by relatives were distributed to convince DPs of safe conditions in the Soviet Union.[110] Soviet officers also circulated leaflets, journals and films aimed at cultivating homesickness.[111] If DPs arrived in transit camps a little too undecided about repatriation, they were kept in a drunken state until their train's departure.[112]

Although most French officials watched the harsh methods employed by Soviet officials with mounting unease, they were all too aware that the prompt repatriation of French nationals largely depended on the preservation of cordial relations with them.[113] If they despaired at the behaviour of the members of the Soviet repatriation mission, they were also remarkably reluctant to openly confront them and reduce the number of *laissez-passer* granted to them.[114] They worked hard to maintain the Franco–Russian friendship, officially celebrating the October Revolution and Armistice Day with their Soviet counterparts.[115] Complaints about the Soviet mission ranged from accusations of running over a German cyclist to black-market activities, requisition of goods without permission, abduction of German citizens and rape.[116] In December 1945, Koenig officially and 'categorically' asked the Soviet marshal Zhukov to reduce the number of Soviet officers in the

---

[108] Marta Dyczok, *The Grand Alliance and Ukrainian Refugees* (London: Palgrave Macmillan, 2000), pp. 5, 52–53.
[109] MAE, HCRFA, PDR 6/947, Lieutenant Touzerie à Capitaine Laugeois, 17 September 1945.
[110] Ibid.
[111] Dyczok, *The Grand Alliance*, p. 54.
[112] MAE, HCRFA, PDR6/984, Rapport concernant la propagande antisoviétique contre le rapatriement, 29 December 1947.
[113] MAE, HCRFA, PDR 6/947, Rapport confidentiel, Lieutenant Rétrain, Officier de Liaison auprès de l'E.M. du 2ème C. A. à Capitaine Laugeois, Chef de la MMAA, Délégation des PDR, PC, 21 August 1945; PDR6/727, Administrateur Général Laffon à Général Délégué supérieur pour le GM du Bade, 12 November 1945.
[114] MAE, HCRFA, PDR6/947, Chef d'escadron Ventrillard à Colonel Commandant les Prévôtés des Troupes d'Occupation, 31 August 1945; MAE, HCRFA, PDR6/1017, Rapport du Lieutenant Retrain, 17 December 1945. UNA, UNRRA, S-0421-0088-01, Lettre du chef du Détachement UNRRA de Wangen au Directeur UNRRA Kreis Wangen et Lindau, Perquisition des Missions Soviétiques au restaurant UNRRA, 27 December 1945.
[115] MAE, HCRFA, PDR6/956, Lieutenant Levy à Officier de Contrôle de 3eme classe, Stetten, 19 November 1945.
[116] See, for example, MAE, HCRFA, PDR6/956, Sous-Directeur des Personnes Déplacées à l'Administrateur Général, 15 December 1945; Capitaine Buonsolzzi à officier de Securité-Air Baiersbronn, 5 January 1946; PDR6/1017, Rapport du Lieutenant Retrain, 17 December 1945; PDR6/978, Rapport Rapatriement des ressortissants russes, 25 January 1946; Commandant Roche à Colonel Poignant, 20 December 1945.

French zone and allow the entry of French officers into the Soviet zone.[117] Yet, soon afterwards the PDR Direction backed down and postponed the decision to limit the number of Soviet officers allowed in the zone.[118]

French reservations about Soviet manoeuvring were apparent from the outset in their attitudes towards Ukrainian DPs.[119] In October 1945, after visiting Tübingen, a French official reported that all Ukrainians firmly refused to be repatriated. These Ukrainians came from western Ukraine and had either been born or resided in Polish territory prior to 1939. DPs' opposition was 'poignant and dramatic', with some shouting 'Shoot us here'.[120] In the previous month, in September 1945, Laffon had issued an instruction for Ukrainian DPs, stipulating that 'Ukrainian nationality did not exist'. Those who claimed Ukrainian nationality were either Soviet citizens (those who held this citizenship on 1 September 1939), Polish citizens (those who held this citizenship on 1 September 1939) or stateless (those who held a Nansen passport). According to this instruction, Soviet citizens needed to be repatriated, irrespective of their personal desires. Ukrainians who claimed Polish citizenship could not be repatriated against their will, and stateless (persons) enjoyed a special status assigned to them by the quality of statelessness.[121] In October, Laffon affirmed that, while France opposed forced repatriation, it had to resign itself to allowing Soviet officers to *faire le tri* as far as those DPs formerly residing to the east of the Curzon Line were concerned.[122] In other words, France had no choice but to grant Soviet officials wide access to – and control over – Soviet nationals. For Laffon, forced repatriation was nevertheless 'an anti-liberal solution that repelled all Frenchmen, and, at their head, the government'.[123] Three months later, another search was carried out at the

---

[117] MAE, HCRFA, PDR6/956, Le Sous-Directeur des Personnes Déplacées à Monsieur l'Administrateur Général, 15 December 1945.

[118] Ibid.

[119] Violent confrontations occurred between Soviet Officer and Ukrainian DPs in the summer of 1945 in Landstuhl. See Goeken-Haidl, *Der Weg zurück*, p. 248.

[120] MAE, HCRFA, PDR 6/947, Sous-Directeur des Personnes Déplacées à Administrateur Général, 3 October 1945. On Ukrainians' fears of repatriation see Ivan Z. Holowinsky, 'DP Experience, Personality Structure and Ego Defence Mechanisms: A Psychodynamic Interpretation', in Isajiw, Boshy and Senkus (eds.), *The Refugee Experience*, pp. 480–488, 483–484.

[121] MAE, Europe, URSS (1944–1960), 80, Administrateur Général Laffon à Ministre Plénipotentiaire, Secrétaire Général pour les Affaires Allemandes et Autrichiennes, 15 September 1945.

[122] The Curzon Line was a demarcation line between Poland and Soviet Russia that was proposed during the Russo–Polish War of 1919–1920 and became (with few changes) the Soviet–Polish border after the Second World War. It was named after the British Foreign Secretary Curzon. MAE, PDR6/947, Laffon à Koenig, 16 October 1945.

[123] MAE, HCRFA, ADM 40, Administrateur Général Adjoint pr GMZFO à Général de Corps d'Armée, 10 October 1945.

Hindenburg Kaserne near Tübingen by a hastily formed Franco-Russian commission constituting two Russian officers and three French administrators. This created another movement of panic amongst Ukrainian DPs. Initially, the commission followed Laffon's instruction. Yet, in the middle of the operation, a French Captain informed the Russian commandant that DPs' former citizenship had to be determined according to the Polono-Russian frontiers of 1939 and not the Curzon Line. DPs hailing from the territories between the two frontiers were granted the 'right to choose'.[124]

As time went by, Soviet authorities expended efforts on convincing DPs to return to their homelands disproportionate to the very small number of DPs that actually returned.[125] Soviet officers remained in Germany not only to return the maximum number of DPs to the Soviet Union but also to cover Moscow's espionage activities in the nascent West.[126] French officials, however, grew increasingly more frustrated at the lack of a reciprocal arrangement for French repatriation officers in the Soviet zone. In December 1945, PDR director Poignant instructed a Commandant to search out DPs who were resisting repatriation.[127] In February 1946, Laffon reiterated that Soviet officers had the right to ask for the list of Soviet citizens living in the zone, to visit (accompanied by a French officer) Polish and Ukrainian camps, and to regroup Soviet DPs in Stetten, Tübingen and Langenargen. Litigious cases were submitted to a newly created Commission [*Commission Mixte des Nationalités*].[128] French reports suggest that this commission tended towards liberal findings, granting the majority of DPs the 'right to choose' on the basis of the 12 February UN Resolution.[129] Furthermore, Poignant developed close personal relations with Soviet officers sympathetic to France. In July 1946, he deplored the departure of a female mission interpreter, noting: 'There is every reason to believe that ... her dismissal is as much due to her liberal views as to her sincere attachment to France'.[130] A month later, the Soviets stopped

---

[124] MAE, HCRFA, PDR6/978, Chef d'Escadron Courtois à Gouverneur, Délégué Supérieur pour le Gouvernement Militaire du Wurtemberg, 17 January 1946.

[125] Juliette Denis, ' « Ils sont rentrés dans leur patrie » : L'URSS face aux personnes déplacées et aux rapatriés lettons, 1946-1950' in Defrance, Denis and Maspero (eds). *Personnes déplacées et guerre froide en Allemagne occupée*, pp. 135–154, 136.

[126] Elliott, 'The Soviet Repatriation Campaign', pp. 341–359, 346.

[127] MAE, HCRFA, PDR 6/947, Sous-Directeur des Personnes Déplacées à l'Administrateur Général, 13 December 1945.

[128] MAE, HCRFA, PDR 6/947, Administrateur Général Laffon à Gouverneurs, Délégués Supérieurs pour le Gouvernement Militaire du Würtemberg, Bade, Palatinat, Sarre, 22 February 1946.

[129] MAE, HCRFA, Bonn 152, Fiche pour Hamonic, 10 July 1946.

[130] MAE, HCRFA, Bonn 152, Secret, Directeur des Personnes Déplacées à Directeur Général des Affaires Administratives, 25 July 1946.

French prospections in the Soviet zone on the grounds of serious shortcomings in the French zone.[131]

PDR and UNRRA correspondences reveal the centrality of language in shaping Franco–Soviet encounters on the ground. Miscommunications between French liaison officers, UNRRA relief workers and Soviet officers were frequent.[132] Soviet officers often displayed resentment towards French liaison officers, whom they suspected of behind-the-scenes machinations. In February 1946, for instance, Soviet officials lodged a formal complaint against the French liaison officer for being 'far too sly' (*malin* in French).[133] Earlier, however, they had shown themselves extremely amicable to him, even lending him a Soviet car. As a result, some French officials (including the security chief of Lindau) accused him of being pro-Soviet and totally devoted to the Soviet mission.[134] The French were equally suspicious of the members of the Soviet mission.[135] Indeed, both sides were, to a large extent, dependent on their interpreters. UNRRA liaison officer General de Margueritles postponed contacting the Soviet mission until late July 1946 as the mission spoke only Russian and the French interpreter was absent.[136] Mistrustful of French liaison officers, the Soviet repatriation mission did not always follow the necessary procedures before visiting a camp, whereby they had to inform local military authorities and ensure they were accompanied by a French liaison officer.[137]

Local authorities often lacked the language skills necessary to read official documents and understand communications between Soviet officers and DPs.[138] In Villingen, for instance, a French official reported that he received around twenty visits from Soviet officers, but only one was accompanied by a French liaison officer. He regretted that they were unable to understand each other without the aid of translators.[139] During one such visit, a Polish DP handed over a list of the Polish inhabitants of the camp to one of the Soviet

---

[131] MAE, HCRFA, PDR6/978, Le général de Brigade, entretien avec le General Davidof et Monsieur Poignant, 4 September 1946.
[132] See, for example, MAE, HCRFA, PDR6/979, Enquête sur les déclarations du citoyen soviétique Bilyk.
[133] MAE, HCRFA, PDR6/978, visite du Lt-Colonel Panzireff, 28 February 1946.
[134] MAE, HCRFA, PDR6/978, Lettre Confidentielle du Commandant Roche à Colonel Poignant, 27 February 1946.
[135] See, for example, MAE, HCRFA, PDR 6/947, Lieutenant Touzerie à Capitaine Laugeois, 17 September 1945.
[136] UNA, UNRRA, S-0417-0001-07, Translation, Liaison Officer to the Director of the French Zone, 27 July 1946.
[137] MAE, HCRFA, PDR6/1017, Délégué de Cercle à Wangen à M. le Chef de la Mission de Liaison auprès de la Mission soviétique de rapatriement, 3 April 1947.
[138] See, for example, MAE, HCRFA, PDR6/947, Le capitaine Evrad à monsieur le Commandant Spitz, 28 August 1945.
[139] MAE, HCRFA, PDR6/1017, St Lieutenant Brunet à Directeur des 'Personnes Déplacées', Villingen, 30 July 1946.

officers. With the help of his secretary, this official tried to explain that he was not allowed to consult this list. During a second visit, his interpreter translated several paragraphs of the official instructions issued by Laffon. Although he claimed that he fully trusted both interpreters, he could not verify that his statements were perfectly translated. He was therefore surprised when he was accused of 'misconduct, lack of politeness and bad presentation'.[140] The inability to understand Russian could have had an even more sinister outcome. In February 1947, a rebellion broke out during the transport of Soviet DPs from the Brombach disciplinary camp to the American–Russian border point in Hof, where there were supposed to be repatriated. The French gendarme reported: 'We had no Russian translator and thus it was easy for inmates to plot a rebellion without our knowledge.'[141] A Soviet DP died during this altercation.

Tensions between the Soviet mission and French authorities also stemmed from conflicting definitions of 'war criminals', 'traitors' and 'quislings'. In accordance with the February 1946 UN resolution, all three categories could be forcedly repatriated.[142] Yet, this could only occur following a measure of extradition and after gathering sufficient evidence that the DP hailed from a country 'in war against Germany' and had committed a 'war crime' or act of treachery.[143] The Soviet interpretation of 'war crimes' was far more expansive than that of the French. The French Foreign Office did not consider a 'war crime' a common law crime or crime of collaboration, while the Soviet Union did not distinguish between different infractions 'against the homeland'.[144] In September 1946, for instance, a dispute emerged around the case of an orthodox DP priest born in the eastern region of Poland in 1905 (attached to the Soviet Union) and a DP UNRRA mess officer born in Vilna in 1927, both accused by the Soviet mission of collaborationist activities in the 'Rada of Byelorussia'.[145] According to Soviet officials, the priest had denounced Soviet citizens to German authorities and declared the 'independence' of the Church

---

[140] MAE, HCRFA, PDR6/1017, Délégué du Gouvernement Mlilitaire pour le Cercle d'Offenbourg, Robert Pierre, 29 July 1946.

[141] MAE, HCRFA, PDR6/1017, Rapport du gendarme Paul Marchand détaché au camp disciplinaire de Brombach, 24 February 1947.

[142] MAE, HCRFA, PDR6/979, Commissaire Général aux Affaires Allemandes et Autrichiennes à l'Administrateur Général, 18 February 1947.

[143] MAE, HCRFA, PDR6/979, Commissariat Général aux Affaires Allemandes à l'Administrateur Général Adjoint, 10 February 1947.

[144] MAE, HCRFA, PDR6/987, Compte rendu de la Conférence Interministérielle du 24 Juin 1947 à Paris.

[145] Later the Foreign Office established that only Soviet citizens could be subjected to forced repatriation. MAE, HCRFA, PDR6/947, Le Ministre des Affaires Etrangères, Rapatriement des ressortissants soviétiques résidant dans les zones d'occupation françaises en Allemagne et en Autriche, 28 June 1947.

of Belarus and its separation from the Moscow Patriarchy.[146] The second DP was accused of conducting spy activities to the Reich's profit and having helped prepare the German attack against the Soviet Union.[147] Both DPs were interrogated by a commission composed of two Soviet officers and a French Commandant and his attaché on 16 November 1946. For the first DP, UNRRA claimed that there was confusion due to having a similar name to a DP who had lived in the Kreis of Wangen and had disappeared. During his interview, the priest refuted the Soviet allegations and claimed that he was 'deported to Prague, and then to Ravensburg and finally in Wangen'. The second DP admitted to be a former colonel in the tsar's army, but refuted any involvement in the German administration. He provided details about his activities as a school teacher during the war. The commission was less convinced by his testimony, as he acted strangely and spoke with tears in the eyes.[148] The commission concluded that both should be liberated but that one should be kept under surveillance.

Faced with mounting criticism from the Soviet delegation at the Allied Council, the French delegate affirmed that France maintained a policy of 'absolute neutrality'.[149] For each litigious case (if Soviet authorities claimed that DP were traitors or were hiding under wrong state citizenship), thorough investigations were conducted and submitted to the *commission mixte des nationalités*.[150] In the summer of 1947, French officials also reminded their Soviet counterparts that DPs had to be 'Soviet' and on the UN list of war criminals to be handed over to Soviet authorities.[151] Despite these efforts, UNRRA reproached PDR officers for failing to protect DPs. On several occasions, UNRRA director Lenclud protested against the illegal arrests of Ukrainian and Baltic DPs.[152] These detentions and subsequent expulsions were not the result of PDR instructions, however. Rather, they demonstrated the difficulties that the PDR experienced in controlling Soviet repatriation officers and implementing a centralized plan for regulating repatriation.[153]

---

[146] MAE, HCRFA, PDR6/979, Traduction du texte original russe – annexe 2, 7 January 1947.
[147] Ibid.
[148] MAE, HCRFA, PDR6/979, Contrôle des ressortissants soviétiques internes au camp de Brombach à la demande la mission soviétique, 16 November 1946.
[149] MAE, HCRFA, PDR6/1017, Procès verbal de l'entretien officiel qui a eu lieu le 31 July 1947 in Berlin.
[150] Ibid.
[151] Ibid.
[152] MAE, Bonn 148, Général de Corps d'Armée Lenclud à Commandant en chef Français en Allemagne, 4 January 1947. Also see UNA, UNRRA, S-0420-0001-03, Rapport sur la campagne de propagande en faveur du rapatriement de printemps des DPs de toutes nationalités par Odette Despeigne, Zone Repatriation Officer, p. 10.
[153] Laffon insisted on the necessity of refuting in the most formal way possible UNRRA's accusation that the staff of the military government was not taking all necessary precautions prior to accepting the arrest requests made by the representatives of foreign

PDR personnel confronted a zone riddled with differing local arrangements, making the implementation of a coherent policy very arduous. In April 1946, disagreement between the PDR organization and the general director of justice over the condemnation of a Baltic DP to forced repatriation after the theft of a bicycle highlighted the lack of uniformity in the zone.[154] The dispute demonstrates that repatriation measures were, on occasion, harnessed to local policing priorities, with local officials deploying the threat of repatriation to remove foreigners who posed a security threat. The zone's internal administrative dynamics gave local officials leeway to use repatriation – and, equally importantly, the threat of repatriation – to control the DP population. In Horb, for instance, the UNRRA director complained about the French official brutal methods, whereby he exerted 'strong pressure on DPs' by letting them know that those who refused repatriation would lose their nationality and be 'Germanized'.[155] In Reutlingen, the UNRRA team director also complained about the 'climate of panic' created by the local military government against DPs (citing requisitions, arrests and expulsions).[156] As we have seen, on 17 June 1946, Laffon instructed his personnel that, although the Franco–Soviet agreement remained in force, France would comply with the UN 12 February Resolution, making only compulsory the repatriation of DPs along the pre September 1939 borders.[157] But, in July 1946, a French UNRRA director asked UNRRA headquarters to intervene to put a stop to a Soviet manhunt in Biberach that, he said, was reminiscent of practices that 'we had hoped would have been ended forever'.[158] 'These unfortunate people are arrested everywhere, in fields where they have worked as peasants for four years, in DP camps, even in the private home of an UNRRA officer where they worked as a domestic servant.'[159]

## Between Policy and Practice: The Repatriation of Polish DPs

As in many other aspects of French occupation policy, a study of repatriation reveals the gap in perceptions between authorities in Paris and authorities in

---

missions. MAE, HCRFA, PDR6/979, l'Administrateur Général Laffon à Monsieur le Général d'Armée, 21 January 1947.

[154] MAE, HCRFA, PDR6/727, Copie Directeur des Personnes Déplacées à Directeur Général de la Justice, 29 April 1946.
[155] UNA, UNRRA, S-0421-0037-01, Lettre de E. Begleiter à Moreland, Team 591, 2 April 1946.
[156] UNA, UNRRA, S-0438-0007-02, Fabry à Directeur Général de la Zone Française à Haslach, 3 March 1947.
[157] UNA, UNRRA, S-0421-0025-07, signé Laffon, Télégramme Nr. 15029 DGAA/Dir. PDR, 17 June 1946.
[158] UNA, UNRRA, S-0421-0003-01, J. J. de Marnhac à Général directeur de la zone française, Biberach, 3 July 1946.
[159] Ibid.

Berlin, Baden-Baden, Rastatt (PDR) and Haslach (UNRRA). Administrative inconstancy was not solely evident in the repatriation of Soviet citizens. It was also clearly apparent in the preparation for the repatriation of Polish DPs, during which a number of French military and PDR authorities maintained close, albeit ambiguous, ties with Polish officials who were hostile to repatriation until the spring of 1946. Unlike for Soviets, there was no repatriation agreement for Polish DPs, but rather a 'good-will understanding'.[160] As with the Soviet Union, this understanding was animated by the principle of reciprocity and the necessity of guaranteeing the return of French internees held in Poland.

After the creation of the communist-led Polish Committee of National Liberation (PKWN) in July 1944, two competing 'national' delegations represented Poland: the Lublin Committee (PKWN) and the Polish government-in-exile in London. The return of French citizens held captive in Poland was given top priority. This meant cooperating with the PKWN, which controlled the majority of the Polish territory.[161] Also important was the need to please the Soviet Union. In December 1944, the recognition de facto of the PKWN was a condition of the signing of the Franco–Soviet agreement. As a result, France was the first Western power to build official relations with the PKWN, which was installed by the Soviets.[162] At the diplomatic level, France officially recognized the PKWN and broke ties with the London government at the end of June 1945, a month before the signing of the Protocol of Potsdam on 1 August 1945, which officially recognized the PKWN on the international stage.

On the ground, in contrast, French authorities maintained contacts with representatives of the London mission both in France and in the French zone.[163] While authorities in Paris ostensibly severed diplomatic ties with representatives of the Polish government-in-exile and strengthened relations with the Lublin Committee, UNRRA and PDR archives reveal that London officers continued to operate in the zone until the autumn of 1946. As Julia Maspero has demonstrated, this allowed French PDR authorities to pursue a 'double game' in the zone, maintaining representatives of the Polish government-in-exile in London in the zone far longer than their British and American allies in order to promote the recruitment of DPs for France.[164] In

---

[160] MAE, NUOI, 294, Compte-Rendu de la Délégation française au comité spécial des réfugiés et Personnes Déplacées, présidée par M. Fouques Duparc, 3 April 1946.

[161] Dariusz Jarosz et Maria Pasztor, *Conflits brûlants de la guerre froide, les relations franco-polonaises de 1945 à 1954* (Paris: Lavauzelle, 2005), p. 35.

[162] Bezias, *Georges Bidault et la politique étrangère de la France*, p. 160.

[163] Paweł Sękowski, 'Les Polonais en France dans l'immédiat après-guerre (1944–1949)', PhD thesis, University of Paris 4 (2015).

[164] Maspero, 'La question des personnes déplacées polonaises', p. 73.

the spring of 1946, the PDR directorate even organized a meeting between representatives of the London government and those of the officially recognized Warsaw government.[165] As might be expected, collaboration between the two missions proved impossible. On 31 March, the French military government relinquished its cooperation with the London mission and ceased sending official instructions to its representatives.[166]

In June 1946, in response to a protest from the official Polish mission, Poignant affirmed that the London mission had been dismantled in the zone.[167] The presence of its officers, however, continued to be tolerated *à titre privé*.[168] If French authorities were less despondent about the behaviour of the official Polish repatriation mission than the Soviet mission, they still believed that the mission was too numerous and occasionally negligent.[169] At the height of the repatriation of Polish DPs in the spring of 1946, a number of repatriation officers asked, for instance, for the right to go to France for their 'Easter holidays'.[170] Overall, the repatriation of Polish DPs suffered long delays, although these cannot be imputed solely to the repatriation mission. This helps to explain the initial cooperation with representatives of the London mission.[171]

Crucially, the French were dependent on the Allied Control Council for the transport of DPs, which limited the number of trains departing from the French zone.[172] An agreement was signed on 20 September 1945 to organize the repatriation of Polish DPs from the American and French zones.[173] Nevertheless, the repatriation began only in mid-November 1945. In November 1945, there was an estimated 59,973 Polish DPs in the various Kreis of the zone.[174] The first wave of repatriation occurred soon afterwards,

---

[165] MAE, HCRFA, Bonn 152, Directeur des Personnes Déplacées à Administrateur Général Adjoint, 16 February 1946.

[166] MAE, HCRFA, PDR3/88, Général d'Armée Koenig à Colonel de la Mission Polonaise de Berlin, 25 June 1946.

[167] MAE, HCRFA, Bonn 148, Fiche pour le Général, 2 August 1946.

[168] MAE, HCRFA, PDR3/88, Général d'Armée Koenig à Colonel de la Mission Polonaise de Berlin, 25 June 1946.

[169] Ibid. The list of accredited representatives is, however, smaller. MAE, HCRFA, PDR3/100, Liste des Membres des missions et organismes étrangers de rapatriement à la date du 1er avril 1947.

[170] Ibid.

[171] MAE, HCRFA, PDR1/86, Conférence du 12 Octobre 1945 présidée par le Colonel Poignant à l'Hotel Stéphanie.

[172] MAE, HRCFA, PDR1/86, L'OR 3 (Commandant) de Rosen Délégué de la Division Personnes Déplacées à Général de Corps d'Armée Koeltz, 11 September 1945.

[173] MAE, Y Internationale 604, Directoire des Prisonniers de guerre et des personnes déplacées, Procès Verbal de la Septième Réunion tenue à Berlin, 19 October 1945; dixième séance, 26 November 1945.

[174] MAE, HCRFA, PDR6/471, Weekly reports, 8–15 November 1945.

with 13,700 Polish DPs repatriated between 16 November and 13 December 1945.[175] Trains with 40 carriages were directed towards Dziedzice, at the Polish–Czech border, through the American zone and through Czechoslovakia.[176] Each train contained a French armed guard and a chef, with 14-day rations for Polish DPs and 18-day rations for the crew.[177] Subsequently, 8,541 Polish DPs left the zone between 13 December 1945 and 21 March 1946.[178] The repatriation slowed down during the winter due to the bad weather conditions. Despite being limited by the lack of available boxcars, repatriation rates rose substantially in the spring of 1946, with 3,064 (March), 6,107 (April), 8,679 (May) and 2,859 (June) Polish DPs repatriated.[179]

In comparison to the British and American zones, these rates were in relative terms considerably higher.[180] But these figures masked a more complex reality. Repatriation was highly contingent on where DPs lived and whether UNRRA relief workers were cooperating with anti-repatriation DP leaders. Indeed, a number of UNRRA directors continued to cooperate with London officers. In August 1946, UNRRA liaison officer Général de Marguerittes informed the director of team 206 that he needed to cease his official relations with Lieutenant Kosinski, officer of the ex-mission of London.[181] A few months later, an UNRRA director reported that a former London liaison officer remained in the Gneisenau camp and exerted a strong influence over the remaining Polish DPs.[182] In December 1946, the Polish repatriation mission remonstrated against 'anti-repatriation' DP leaders who were allegedly protected by UNRRA in the Landstuhl DP camp.[183] In sum, at least until the spring of 1946 French authorities maintained contact with DP leaders who were hostile to repatriation. UNRRA authorities were aware of

---

[175] MAE, HCRFA, PDR 6/741, Administrateur général Laffon à Général de Corps d'armée, 19 December 1945.
[176] MAE, HCRFA, PDR1/86, Sous-Directeur des Personnes Déplacées à Administrateur Général Adjoint pour GMZFO, 12 November 1945.
[177] MAE, HCRFA, PDR 1/86, Télégramme signé Koeltz, 9 November 1945.
[178] MAE, HCRFA, PDR6/809, Laffon à Koenig, 28 March 1946.
[179] MAE, HCRFA, PDR6/764, chef de la Division du Mouvement à Directeur des Personnes Déplacées, signé Maillot, 15 April 1946.
[180] On 30 September 1945, the British zone accommodated 510,328 Polish DPs and the American zone 253,981 DPs. In total, 318,883 Polish DPs were repatriated from the British zone and 186,102 Polish DPs from the American zone from 1 November 1945 to 30 June 1947. Woodbridge, *UNRRA*, vol. 2, p. 518; Proodfoot, *European Refugees*, Table 14, pp. 238–239.
[181] UNA, UNRRA, S-0417-0001-08, Général de Marguerittes dit Lizé à Directeur du Team 206, 2 August 1946.
[182] UNA, UNRRA, S-0420-0005-06, Chef de Cabinet G. E. McCandlish à le Commandant G. Sebille, Haslach, 2 October 1946.
[183] UNA, UNRRA, S-0417-0002-03, Chef de la Mission Polonaise de Rapatriement à Général Lenclud, 7 December 1946.

this 'double-game' policy.[184] This was not specific to Polish DPs. In May 1946, Colonel du Plessis de Grenedan working for the PDR reported that he welcomed 'unofficial' DP delegates to hear about their needs and mentality, including a Yugoslav representative named Pauer, an 'enemy of the Belgrade regime'.[185] Yet, UNRRA received the greatest proportion of criticism from Eastern European authorities for accommodating DP leaders hostile to repatriation.[186]

## UNRRA: The Limits of Neutrality

Eastern European official repatriation missions repeatedly accused UNRRA of protecting war criminals, particularly those with stateless status, while also fostering anti-repatriation propaganda.[187] In January 1946, the Polish government lodged a complaint with UNRRA's European Regional Office concerning the anti-repatriation activities of London-affiliated representatives at the Trier camp.[188] Six months later, the Yugoslav military delegation complained that UNRRA continued to work with royalist committees in Biberach, Ravensburg and Lindau.[189] In Kisslegg, both the republican and royal flags were flying above the camp until the military government of Wangen took down the royalist flag. Although the Royal Yugoslav Committee was dissolved after this incident, protests against UNRRA did not stop. Three months later, a Soviet officer officially protested against the anti-repatriation attitudes of the Biberach, Pirmasens and Lindau UNRRA teams.[190] For its part, UNRRA reproached the Polish and Soviet repatriation missions for their remoteness from DP camps and their consequent failure to build 'intimate contacts with their fellow compatriots'.[191] UNRRA director Lenclud decried such 'double standards', responding vigorously to attacks on the organization.[192]

---

[184] UNA, UNRRA, S-0417-0001-03, Rapport remis à Marguerittes, 9 August 1946, p. 7.
[185] MAE, HCRFA, PDR6/740, Le Colonel du Plessis de Grenedan à Commissaire en Chef Raulin, Directeur du Cabinet Particulier, 29 May 1946.
[186] MAE, HCRFA, PDR6/1017, Le Directeur des Personnes Déplacées à Administrateur Général Adjoint, 14 June 1947.
[187] UNA, UNRRA, S-0417-0001-07, Général de Marguerittes dit Lizé, Mission Soviétique, 29 August 1946. For Polish Mission, see for instance, note, Général de Marguerittes dit Lizé, 3 August 1946.
[188] UNA, UNRRA, S-0420-0001-04, F. E. Morgan to Director French zone, 4 January 1946.
[189] MAE, HCRFA, PDR6/740, Délégation Militaire à Directeur de la Direction des Personnes Déplacées, 3 August 1946.
[190] MAE, HCRFA, Bonn 150, Directeur des Personnes Déplacées à Directeur Général des Affaires administratives, 11 October 1946.
[191] UNA, UNRRA, S-1021-0084-12, Historique, G. Sebille, 7 May 1947.
[192] UNA, UNRRA, S-0417-0001-03, Confidential letter (translation) from General de Corps d'Armée F. Lenclud, Director UNRRA French Zone to Monsieur le General d'Armée, French Commander in Chief, Germany, 4 October 1946.

So, why did UNRRA attract so much criticism? If Eastern European governments increasingly saw UNRRA as an instrument of the West, it was in part because, at UNRRA's upper echelons, there was minimal agreement regarding the extent to which repatriation should be prioritized.[193] UNRRA was predominantly financed by the United States and its director was openly hostile to forced repatriation.[194] On 28 March 1946, after prolonged and acrimonious debates at UNRRA's Fourth Council meeting in Atlantic City, a conciliatory gesture towards Eastern European governments was made in the form of Resolution 92. It required the administration 'to remove any handicaps in the Assembly Centres to the prompt repatriation of displaced persons ... wishing to be repatriated'.[195] This resolution called for the complete registration of all DPs in these assembly centres, with accurate information about those displaced nationals willing to return to their homeland being expected to speed up the repatriation process.[196] A series of tough new measures were also sanctioned by the Council to remove obstacles to repatriation and reduce the number of camp inhabitants. These included the removal of camp leaders and UNRRA personnel known to oppose repatriation.[197] But, even then, the degree to which these pro-repatriation measures were applied depended considerably upon individual officials and varied significantly from one camp to another.

In the French zone, UNRRA headquarters were slow to send clear instructions to its field workers. The slowness with which UNRRA headquarters were put in place, coupled with the bureaucratic competition between PDR and UNRRA officers, created a great deal of administrative confusion. Requests about eligibility and repatriation procedures abound in UNRRA archives.[198] It was only in April 1946 that official instructions were circulated that clearly defined the respective responsibilities of UNRRA and the PDR in preparing repatriation convoys. The PDR organization ordered carriages, planned the journey and provided medical supplies. UNRRA relief workers then organized the different carriages and ensured that there were enough food, drinkable water, beds, American Red-Cross parcels. UNRRA staff then prepared DPs' boarding, arranged a medical visit and delousing for each DP and drew up a

---

[193] Woodbridge, *UNRRA*, vol. 2, p. 470.
[194] Lehman's successor, Fiorello La Guardia, expressed a marked inclination for shifting UNRRA's focus away from welfare work towards repatriation. Armstrong-Reid and Murray, *Armies of Peace*, p. 183.
[195] UNA, UNRRA, S-0420-0006-02, UNRRA, European Regional Office, Order No. 40, Removal of DP Leaders impeding repatriation, 12 September 1946.
[196] UNA, UNRRA, S-0412-0012-04, Bulletin Général N. 18, application de la Résolution 92, 12 July 1946.
[197] Armstrong-Reid and Murray, *Armies of Peace*, p. 183. For the French zone, UNA, UNRRA, S-0421-0025-07, Réunion des Directeurs de Team, 25 September 1946.
[198] See, for instance, UNA, UNRRA, S-0421-0052-01, J. Gerbier, Note, 23 November 1945.

list of repatriates. The PDR was ultimately responsible for boarding.[199] Crucially, some UNRRA instructions contradicted French official policy. As mentioned previously, in July 1946 the French UNRRA headquarters circulated Bulletin 19, which stipulated that Soviet citizens hailing from territories under Soviet control before 1939 could be forcedly repatriated. This contradicted official French policy, which, following the UN resolution of 12 February 1946, condemned forced repatriation for DPs hailing from these territories, except if they were quislings and traitors.[200] As a result of these delays and confusing instructions, some team directors believed that they were entitled to mention emigration opportunities to DPs, thereby creating conflicts with Eastern European repatriation missions.[201]

Laffon also reproached UNRRA officials for failing to understand the 'delicacy' of French policy. He seized upon the fact that UNRRA's director of the Southern district publicly informed his teams that French authorities intended to recruit Polish personnel as foreign auxiliaries. In tandem with public statements that the French were committed to encouraging repatriation, French officials allowed some Eastern Europeans to enlist in the French Foreign Legion to fight in Indochina, thereby avoiding repatriation.[202] For French occupation officials, tactless and insensitive UNRRA workers caused unfortunate diplomatic incidents by leaking confidential information.[203] The employment of Polish DPs in the *Compagnie de Groupements Auxiliaires Etrangers* (GAE) exemplified French ambiguities.[204] GAE companies were set up in March 1946 to watch over German POWs.[205] These groups were themselves composed of former Polish, Hungarian and Yugoslav POWs, and, in August 1946, they employed nearly 2,000 DPs, organized into 14 separate 'companies' whose DP members received the same salaries and social benefits as French soldiers.[206] According to the PDR service's official history, the GAE,

---

[199] MAE, HCRFA, PDR6/1017, Directeur des Personnes Déplacées à Général de Corps d'Armée Lenclud, 27 April 1946.
[200] MAE, HCRFA, PDR6/979, Administrateur Général Laffon à Général de Corps d'Armée, Directeur de l'UNRRA, 6 August 1946.
[201] UNA, UNRRA, S-0417-0003-05, Translation, Screening, 4 March 1947.
[202] MAE, HCRFA, Bonn, 150, Général d'Armée Koenig à Administrateur général adjoint, 4 June 1946.
[203] UNRRA, S-0421-0029-02, R. Schurmans, Acting Director Team 576 à Mr. Moreland, District Director, 14 January 1946.
[204] MAE, HRCFA, Bonn 150, Général d'Armée Koenig à Général Adjoint, 4 June 1946; Lettre secrète du Général de Division Noiret à Monsieur le Général d'Armée, Commandant en Chef Français, GFCC N.1699/PDR, 16 December 1947.
[205] MAE, HRCFA, PDR6/799, Le Directeur des Personnes Déplacées à Délégation supérieures de Bade, Palatinat, Sarre, Rhénanie et Wurtemberg, 27 May 1946. [Projet de lettre.]
[206] MAE, HCRFA, Direction générale des Affaires politiques, 117, Fiche pour l'ambassadeur de France, 10 December 1946. N.9.926 CC/CAM/G.

thanks to their military discipline, enjoyed 'terrific success' among DPs.[207] The PDR organization did not see GAE employment as a hindrance to repatriation as DPs could revoke their work contract eight days before the departure of a repatriation train.[208] Yet, GAE employment was a recurrent source of tension with Eastern European governments, which suspected that these paramilitary units provided cover for former collaborators.[209]

Lenclud broke the UNRRA's 'neutrality' principle by openly denouncing this French authorities' 'double-game' policy and highlighting considerable regional variations. On several occasions, he criticized the PDR's unorthodox methods, deploring that the PDR's overarching goal was 'to repatriate the DPs as quickly as possible' by 'stick[ing] bayonets in their behinds'.[210] For instance, on 7 and 8 June 1946 announcements were published in various German newspapers in Mülheim, Münsingen and Baden for a new regulation to be applied as of 20 June, and informing Polish DPs that 'all the advantages which they have heretofore enjoyed will no longer be accorded to them'. These notices invited Poles to take the last repatriation trains, which were due to leave on 25 June.[211] UNRRA voiced loud complaints about the threatening character of these notices, an impression enhanced by the fact that they were written in German. 'UNRRA is the sole administration for centres, and consequently is alone qualified to notify the displaced persons of all decisions concerning them', commented Lenclud.[212] He continued:

> Whereas the necessity for repatriation has not escaped us, and we have brought all possible aid to this operation, which is one of UNRRA's primary missions, the pressure exerted on the Poles, the threat of depriving them of their status of DPs and of their nationality, is not in keeping with the neutrality that UNRRA imposed upon itself in this matter ... The effect produced on the Poles was deplorable and yet did not have the desired effect, since the train which left Mülheim on 5th June contained only 515 persons, and that which left Munsingen on 7th June 563 persons, despite the threats of the DP officers and the German officials.[213]

---

[207] *Sept-ans d'activité en faveur des personnes déplacées*, p. 28.
[208] MAE, HCRFA, PDR6/740, Le Général d'Armée Koenig à Commissaire Général aux Affaires Allemandes et autrichiennes, 21 April 1947.
[209] MAE, HCRFA, Bonn 152, L. de Rosen, Note pour Monsieur le Général Koenig, 21 April 1947. [Réclamations de la Mission Militaire Yougoslave: 21 novembre 1946, 12 Mars 1947]; PDR3/4, Quatrième conférence des Affaires administratives entre le GFCC et le GMZFO, Berlin, 27 June 1947.
[210] UNA, UNRRA, S-0417-0001-03, Confidential letter (translation) from Général de Corps d'Armée Lenclud to Général d'Armée, 4 October 1946, p. 12.
[211] UNA, UNRRA, S-0417-0001-01, translation of copy of letter, Letter 218/11 from G. Lenclud to Administrateur General, 19 June 1946.
[212] Ibid.
[213] Ibid.

THE POLITICS OF NEUTRALITY 173

The fact that these notices were directed solely at the Poles also created tensions between Poles and DPs of other nationalities, as well as between Poles and Germans.[214] It seems beyond question that, in this instance, local officials in Mülheim, Münsingen and Baden went too far and condoned forcible repatriation, establishing practices along quite different lines than those intended by French authorities.[215]

While UNRRA officials vehemently challenged the PDR over its use of unorthodox methods and for condoning forcible repatriation, the PDR accused UNRRA of preventing repatriation and creating unnecessary conflicts.[216] On 23 May 1946, for instance, Laffon passed on to UNRRA Director Lenclud a protest letter written by twenty-three Polish DPs from the Schiltach (Gutach) centre in which they complained about the difficulties that they encountered owing to repatriation.[217] Cited in this affair, the UNRRA Director argued that this petition was mainly the result of the manoeuvring of a dishonest DP.[218] But, in July 1946 Laffon reiterated his criticism that UNRRA was not putting enough effort into repatriation despite the instructions that they received from UNRRA headquarters in the French zone.[219] As a result, the French PDR service and Laffon's civil cabinet concluded that 'repatriation was carried out without UNRRA's help'.[220]

Lack of coordination between the two competing administrations was particularly glaring in the organization of the Polish repatriation centre in Villingen. In September 1946, Lenclud opposed Laffon's decision to install the transit centre in a former stalag in the town.[221] According to him, French authorities were transporting DPs in conditions 'often inferior to those of animals'.[222] In September 1946, the UNRRA welfare officer observed that the

---

[214] Ibid.
[215] It stirred indeed a wide range of protests amongst UNRRA relief workers. See, for instance, S-0421-0033-03.
[216] On the issue of neutrality see, for example, UNA, UNRRA, S-00417-0003-04, Télégramme UNRRA HQ Paris à UNRRA HQ Haslach, 18 June 1947.
[217] UNA, UNRRA, S-0421-0033-03, Administrateur Laffon à Général de Corps d'Armée Lenclud, 23 May 1946.
[218] UNA, UNRRA, S-0421-0033-03, Durand à Thomasset, 14 June 1946.
[219] MAE, HCRFA, ADM 40, Administrateur Général Laffon à Général d'Armée, Commandant en Chef Français en Allemagne, N. 15339, 29 July 1946, p. 8; Also see letter N. 15243, 16 July 1946; MAE, HCRFA, PDR 3/12 l'Administrateur General Laffon à Monsieur le Général de Corps d'Armée, Directeur Général de l'UNRRA pour la ZFO, N. 15086, 25 June 1946.
[220] MAE, HCRFA, Bonn 159, Général d'Armée Koenig à Commissaire Général aux Affaires Allemandes et Autrichiennes, 16 August 1946.
[221] UNA, UNRRA, S-0420-0004-02, Général de Corps d'armée Lenclud à Adiministrateur general adjoint, 2 September 1946.
[222] UNA, UNRRA, S-0417-0001-03, Confidential letter (translation) from General de Corps d'Armée Lenclud to General d'Armée, 4 October 1946, p. 11. On this issue also see: MAE, HCRFA, PDR6/741, Rapport du Lieutenant Brunet relatif au départ d'1 train de rapatriement à destination de la Pologne et de la Tchécoslovaquie en date du 31 aout

sight of the camp provoked physical revulsion in her: 'I arrived in Buchenwald in April 1945; apart from the corpses on the floor, the camp was clean and *fleuri* [dressed with flowerbeds]. Here, I did not know where to start.'[223] The camp rapidly acquired a terrible reputation, although evidence suggests that conditions within it progressively improved.[224] The lack of UNRRA support for these repatriation efforts not only angered French authorities, but also exasperated UNRRA's field workers themselves. In March 1947, an UNRRA team director reported:

> The problem ... is the following: disembarking living beings, gathering them, taking them on board, and, during these operations, maintaining adequate living conditions. The way in which these different categories of civilized people are crammed together in barracks and cattle trains is absolutely disgusting; one cannot help but wonder if it was necessary to go to so much effort to rehabilitate these uprooted people if all such efforts finally ended with such an appalling conclusion. It is outrageous to see young soldiers travelling in luxurious carriages while the elderly, pregnant women and babies are pitifully set up.[225]

## UNRRA Repatriation Propaganda Campaign (Autumn 1946–Spring 1947)

Problems were exacerbated by a time lag: UNRRA headquarters placed stronger emphasis on repatriation at a moment when the PDR deemed mass repatriation completed. The implementation of UNRRA Resolution 92, which was designed to speed up the repatriation process, was delayed in the French zone. It was only in the summer of 1946 that the French UNRRA headquarters sent clear instructions, highlighting the need to encourage repatriation. This plan was elaborated in close collaboration with the repatriation service of the American zone.[226] At a welfare officers' meeting in mid-August, however, UNRRA officials realized that the majority of their personnel ignored it.[227] The UNRRA repatriation propaganda campaign was sophisticated. On 24 September 1946, Lenclud sent a letter to all his field supervisors and team directors urging them to use 'psychological ingenuity' to convince Poles to

---

1946, 2 September 1946; S-0420-0006-03, Médecin Général des Cilleuls, Zone Medical Officer à Monsieur l'Assistant Director, Haslach, 14 January 1947.

[223] UNA, UNRRA, S-0421-0028-08, Rapport Loustalot N. 1, 25 October 1946.

[224] UNA, UNRRA, S-0417-0003-07, Sebille, Assistant Director à Field Supervisors, 29 October 1946.

[225] UNA, UNRRA, S-0420-0006-03, Dalichampt, Directeur du team 577 à Monsieur le Directeur UNRRA – Zone Française, Villingen, 26 March 1947.

[226] UNA, UNRRA, S-0417-0003-06, Note repatriation, 9 April 1947.

[227] UNA, UNRRA, S-0438-0009-03, Conférence des Welfare Officers de la Zone Nord, 9–10 August 1946.

return home. 'Our mission and our duty forbid us from using any other means than persuasion.'[228] Several official bulletins containing information about conditions in Communist Poland were circulated, educating DPs about the agrarian reform and the new, more inclusive, education system.[229] Team directors were asked to regroup DPs who were willing to be repatriated. Yugoslavs were to be sent to the Tuttlingen centre, Czechs/Slovaks to Calw, Italians to Liebenau, Hungarians to Blönried, Soviets to Immendingen and Poles to Villingen.[230] UNRRA also implemented the Sixty-Day Ration Scheme (derisively dubbed 'Operation Grubstake' by the United States Army, and 'Operation Carrot' by the British).[231] Repatriation posters with the slogan 'Poland calls you' were circulated, repatriation committees were created, sixty-day ration exhibitions were organized and clothes were distributed to those willing to be repatriated (Fig. 3.3).[232] To cap it all, on 24 September 1946 Lenclud issued a declaration to all Polish DPs encouraging them to return to their homeland.[233]

UNRRA Department of Field Operations also provided information in response to questions known to concern Poles within the camps. Practical questions were answered: 'How do I get work?' 'Do I have to pay for tools?' 'Can I be sure that my children will have the opportunity to attend school?' 'Is there a plan to establish collective farms?'[234] In Freiburg, for instance, despite the fact that most DPs were living in private accommodation, UNRRA organized regular meetings with DP representatives, and translated into Polish information originally sent in French by the headquarters. Several conferences and two permanent exhibitions (one in Freiburg and one in Emmendigen) were also arranged in which maps of Poland were prominently displayed (Fig. 3.4).[235]

Equally important were the efforts to improve relationships with Soviet officials and suppress anti-repatriation activities. According to the PDR

---

[228] UNA, UNRRA, S-0417-0003-07, General F. Lenclud à Messieurs les Field Supervisors, 24 September 1946.
[229] UNA, UNRRA, S-0412-0012-04, Bulletin General N. 21, 18 July 1946; Bulletin General N. 31, 2 September 1946.
[230] UNA, UNRRA, S-0421-0078-08, Le Gouverneur, Délégué Supérieur pour le GM du Wurttemberg à Messieurs les Délégués de cercles de la Direction régionale, 8 November 1946.
[231] Woodbridge, UNRRA, vol. 2, p. 515.
[232] UNA, UNRRA, S-0420-0006-01, Confidentiel, Field Supervisor P. L. Roquet à Monsieur le Directeur du team, instruction pour le rapatriement, 13 October 1946.
[233] UNA, UNRRA, S-0417-0002-03, Proclamation de F. Lenclud à tous les Polonais, 24 September 1946.
[234] UNA, UNRRA, S-0420-0005-05, 'What every returning should know' sent by Carl Martini, Department of Field Operations to UNRRA Headquarters, French zone – Haslach, 5 November 1946. On UNRRA repatriation campaign in the French zone, see also S-0417-0003-04.
[235] UNA, UNRRA, S-0420-0005-05, E. J. Bastienen, directeur du team 206 Fribourg à UNRRA CHQ, Fribourg, 7 January 1947.

**Fig. 3.3** UNA, UNRRA, S-0421-0039-07, Repatriation propaganda poster 'Poland is calling you. They are waiting for you'. On the man's backpack and woman's card it reads 'Food for 120 days'. UNRRA Team 676, Konstanz.
Kindly translated by Katarzyna Nowak.

organization, in order to accelerate repatriation, UNRRA resorted to Soviet men whose 'political opinions were totally different from that of the organization'.[236] In the autumn of 1946, during a cordial meeting between UNRRA and Soviet officials in UNRRA's American headquarters, Lenclud invited the Soviet repatriation mission's General Davydof to come to Haslach in order to develop strategies to curb anti-repatriation propaganda and improve the screening of war criminals and quislings. Lenclud also assured the Soviets that the work of a number of UNRRA teams, including Pirmasens and Biberach, would be investigated. In this context, the case of the tsarist general Alexis Lampe received increased attention. Lampe worked for UNRRA in Lindau. He was accused of abusing the DP system to flee repatriation by delivering false 'stateless' identity papers and acting as director of the *Croix-Rouge des apatrides*.[237]

---

[236] MAE, HCRFA, PDR6/978, Directeur des Personnes Déplacées à Directeur Général des Affaires Administratives, 26 July 1946.

[237] MAE, HCRFA, PDR6/1017, Directeur des Personnes Déplacées à Directeur Général des Affaires administratives, Compte-rendu de la conférence du 8 otobre 1946 au HQ Central de l'UNRRA pour l'Allemagne relative au rapatriement des citoyens

## THE POLITICS OF NEUTRALITY

Fig. 3.4 UNA, UNRRA, S-0420-0005-05, 'What every repatriate should know – Poland is awaiting you (plural you)'. Map of the new Poland and UNRRA's repatriation speech to Polish DPs, 9 November 1946. Kindly translated by Katarzyna Nowak.

Finally, harsh measures were taken against DPs circulating anti-repatriation propaganda.[238] At the Polish Lycée of Schwenningen, three professors were dismissed by UNRRA authorities for circulating anti-repatriation propaganda.[239] The DP committees in Horb were also dismantled for engaging in black-market activities and anti-repatriation propaganda.[240] Admittedly, the

---

soviétiques. On Lampe's background, see PDR6/979, Renseignements généraux sur le Général de brigade Alexis Lampe de l'Etat-Major général de l'Armée Impériale Russe.

[238] UNA, UNRRA, S-0412-0012-05, French zone, Zone Director's report – October 1946, No. 455.

[239] UNA, UNRRA, S-0420-0004-04, Chef de la Mission Polonaise de Rapatriement à Commandant Sébille, 10 December 1946; Also see MAE, HCRFA, PDR6/863, Edward Korczynski à Directeur du Field Operation, 30 December 1946.

[240] UNA, UNRRA, S-0420-0006-01, Rapport Paul Bayle, Team 588, à Directeur Zone, 3 December 1946.

significance of these efforts should not be underestimated. Yet UNRRA repatriation programme was implemented late, when 'mass repatriation' was considered completed by French authorities.[241] Furthermore, it was by no means uniformly applied. In its monthly report of October 1946, the French UNRRA headquarters lamented the fact that its 'personnel in the field were slow in appreciating the importance that UNRRA attached to repatriation'.[242] Confusion and disquiet persisted in the field until 1947. On 17 January, an UNRRA Team Director protested that he had yet to receive basic information about repatriation contained in Resolution 92 of March 1946. He also queried an instruction sent by Laffon on 2 October 1946 mentioning emigration: were DPs to be recruited or repatriated?[243] By early 1947, most UNRRA directors considered mass repatriation completed due to the rumours about emigration that were circulated by the Intergovernmental Committee for Refugees and the PDR.[244]

Increasingly aware that the 'DP system' allowed a number of 'real-life villains' to be turned into 'deserving victims', UNRRA carried out a vast screening operation alongside this intensive repatriation campaign.[245] UNRRA's aim was to evict non-eligible DPs from its care, including DPs charged with having collaborated with the enemy. This screening operation was mandated under the organization's order 52. While the filtering of war collaborators was the responsibility of the military government of each zone, UNRRA teams verified that DPs met the organization's eligibility requirements. In the French zone, the determination and verification of DP status was carried out solely by UNRRA, 'without the intervention of the military authorities'.[246] These screening operations targeted, in particular, German-speaking inhabitants of Poland, Czechoslovakia, Hungary, Yugoslavia and the three Baltic countries, who were charged collectively with treason by the Allies and were not eligible for UNRRA assistance. In the French zone, Bulletin 19, dating from July 1946, determined the different categories eligible for UNRRA assistance. These included UN nationals from Continental Europe, the

---

[241] MAE, HCRFA, PDR6/978, Directeur des Personnes Déplacées à Directeur Général des Affaires Administratives, 25 July 1946.
[242] UNA, UNRRA, S-0412-0012-05, French zone, Zone Director's report – October 1946, No. 455.
[243] UNA, UNRRA, S-0420-0005-05, J. J. de Marnhac, Directeur Team 209 à UNRRA Zone Headquarters, Rapatriement, Biberach, 17 January 1947.
[244] UNA, UNRRA, S-0417-0003-05, Screening, 4 March 1947.
[245] See, for example, Gerald Steinacher, *Nazis on the Run: How Hitler's Henchmen Fled Justice* (Oxford: Oxford University Press, 2012); Suzanne Brown-Fleming, *Nazi Persecution and Postwar Repercussions: The International Tracing Service Archive and Holocaust Research* (London: Rowman & Littlefield, 2016), pp. 211–218.
[246] UNA, UNRRA, S-0417-0003-05, Translation, Screening, 4 March 1947.

*persecutee*, the stateless, Italians, repatriated DPs who had returned to Germany, Allied POWs and ex-Wehrmacht members, if they did not originate from enemy or ex-enemy nations and had been forcedly enrolled.[247] Screening operations really gathered pace from August 1946 onwards.[248] These were carried out in two stages. First, DPs were screened by a local Screening Consulting Commission, headed by the UNRRA team director (or another Class I official) and the welfare officer, who checked their identity papers and statements. The role of this commission was purely 'consultative', its aim being to 'do the groundwork for the Zone Permanent Screening Commission'.[249] Secondly, if their cases were deemed difficult, they were deferred to a Permanent Screening Commission.[250]

## Between Protection and Exclusion: UNRRA Screening Operation

The search for war collaborators and quislings amongst the DP population emerged as part of the wider politics of retribution after the war. Just as German civil servants were asked by the occupiers to fill in political questionnaires, DPs (with the exception of Jewish DPs) were required to answer screening questions. As Daniel Cohen suggests, the Allies shared the view that there was a 'collaborationist component' amongst the DP population.[251] At UNRRA's higher echelons, some groups were seen as particularly suspicious: former residents of the Baltic States, Yugoslavs, including many 'post-hostilities refugees', and Soviet Ukrainians.[252] UNRRA Eligibility and screening policies were complex and, at times, inconsistent across the three zones.[253] In the areas bordering the American zone, French authorities were confronted with DPs who, having been rejected by screening teams in the French zone, were accepted in the American zone (and vice versa).[254] The classification of

---

[247] MAE, HCRFA, PDR6/861, Bulletin Général No. 19, Détermination du droit à l'assistance UNRRA, 11 July 1946.
[248] See, for instance, MAE, HCRFA, Bonn 159, Poignant, Note pour Hamonic, 6 July 1946.
[249] UNA, UNRRA, S-0417-0003-05, Translation, Screening, 4 March 1947.
[250] MAE, HCRFA, PDR6/861, Bulletin Général No. 19, Determination du droit à l'assistance d'UNRRA, 11 July 1946.
[251] Cohen, *In War's Wake*, p. 38. Also see Brown-Fleming, *Nazi Persecution and Postwar Repercussions*, pp. 211–218.
[252] UNA, UNRRA, S-0139-0034-08, Rhea Radin, Report and Recommendations on UNRRA Programme for Displaced Persons in Germany.
[253] On the differences between the three Western zones, UNA, UNRRA, S-0139-0034-08, Report and Recommendations on Programme for Displaced Persons in Germany, 11 September 1946; Lowell Rooks to John Hilldring, 24 January 1947.
[254] UNA, UNRRA, S-0417-0003-06, Général de Corps d'Armée Lenclud, Projet de Révision de l'Ordre 52 sur le droit à l'assistance UNRRA, 24 December 1946.

ex-enemy and neutral countries also varied. In the British zone, Finland was classified as an enemy state, while in the American and French zones it was considered a 'neutral' state.[255] In the French zone, PDR authorities were also particularly careful about the handful of DPs who demanded they be 'repatriated' to South and Central America, in particular Guatemala.[256]

In the field, establishing DPs' identity and nationality was especially difficult for those who came from multi-ethnic and border regions with multiple languages. Often, it was not clear whether the 'nationality' of a DP was defined by pre-war citizenship, post-war borders or ethnic membership. Most historical accounts of these supranational *épurations* (purges) focus on their improvised and imperfect nature.[257] Many SS members, Nazi war criminals and 'ordinary collaborators' escaped retribution through the DP system.[258] Many other DPs became innocent victims of the Allies' desire to sort the villains from the good. The procedures were complex, with UNRRA personnel having to comply with the different rules of military government in each zone. Furthermore, there were important differences between DPs' real identities and their identities on paper. Relief workers who carried out these operations knew very little about Eastern European minorities, including their languages and dialects, and the animosities between different ethnic groups.[259] The Allies' imperfect knowledge of the complex composition of the DP population was aggravated by the tendency among DPs to lie and withhold information.[260] DPs singled out screening officers for their naivety, stupidity or base motivation' and learned how to craft acceptable answers to obtain DP status.[261] For example, Latvian publications encouraged DPs to stress that

---

[255] UNA, UNRRA, S-0417-0003-06, Lenclud, Projet de Révision de l'Ordre 52 sur le droit à l'assistance UNRRA, 24 December 1946.

[256] MAE, HCRFA, PDR6/768, Note pour le Colonel du Plessis, 7 August 1946.

[257] See, for example, Cohen, *In War's Wake*.

[258] Brown-Fleming, *Nazi Persecution and Postwar Repercussions*, p. 212; Jan-Hinnerk Antons, 'Britisher Umgang mit militanten Antikommunisten, Kollaborateuren und mutmasslichen Kriegsverbrechern unter osteuropäischen DPs', in Defrance, Denis and Maspero (eds.) *Personnes Déplacées et guerre froide en Allemagne occupée*, pp. 61–75. For a case in the French zone, MAE, HCRFA, PDR6/740, l'Administrateur Général Laffon à Monsieur le Général de Corps d'Armée, Situation d'un ressortissant Yougoslave ex SS, 18 April 1947.

[259] Cohen, *In War's Wake*, pp. 35–57; Denis, 'Complices de Hitler ou victimes de Staline?', pp. 88–92.

[260] UNA, UNRRA, S-0417-0002-03, J. Frans, Rapport sur le contrôle des operations de screening effectuées par les commissions consultatives des teams en exécution des paragraphes 25 à 28 du bulletin général, No. 19 du 11 juillet 1946.

[261] Inta Gale Carpenter, 'Folklore as a Source for Creating Exile Identity among Latvian Displaced Persons in Post-World War II Germany', *Journal of Baltic Studies*, vol. 48, no. 2 (2017), p. 221.

they feared reprisals if they returned to Soviet-occupied Latvia. They were told to evoke memories of the 'Baigais gads', 'the year of horror', of the Soviet occupation of 1940–1941.[262] Displacement allowed some DPs to reinvent themselves and reimagine their past.[263] DPs understood that having a clean past was a pre-condition to start a life anew in the camp.

In the French zone, the study of DP screening draws out an interesting parallel with French approaches to the denazification of Germans, but also with the process of French ethnic purge of Alsace at the end of the First World War.[264] Influenced by their experiences of the war, including the forced enrolment of French Alsatian and Lorrainers in the Wehrmacht, a number of French relief workers wanted to place much greater emphasis on individual circumstances, rejecting the classification of whole group (such as Baltic Germans) as collaborators. Instead of following the initial instructions established by American authorities in 1945, the French military government implemented a denazification policy that was more sensitive to individual situation, often resorting to personalized interviews. A study of screening in the French zone is thus revealing for several reasons. First, the archival records of UNRRA leave no question that there were variations between UNRRA central headquarters, French UNRRA headquarters and the authorities in the zone. UNRRA instructions contradicted official French policy. Laffon commented on the errors in UNRRA Bulletin 19, including its vague and erroneous definitions of stateless DPs and *Volksdeutsche*. According to Laffon, the Potsdam agreement recognized as *Volksdeutsche* only German minorities from Poland, Czechoslovakia, Austria and Hungary.[265] Secondly, contradictory instructions engendered differences in implementation. In the Northern sector of the zone, the UNRRA zone screening officer complained that PDR orders prevailed over UNRRA instructions.[266] The PDR were, for instance, opposed to assisting DPs who had returned to the zone after being repatriated.[267] They were also in favour of providing assistance to Hungarian DPs. According to UNRRA Bulletin 19, Hungarians were 'ex-enemy' nationals and,

---

[262] Ibid., p. 222.
[263] Nowak, 'Voices of Revival', p. 103.
[264] Clemens Vollnhals (ed.), *Entnazifizierung. Politische Säuberung und Rehabilitierung in den vier Besatzungszonen 1945–1949* (Munich: Deutscher Taschenbuch Verlag, 1991); Corine Defrance and Ulrich Pfeil, 'L'Allemagne occupée en 1946', *Guerres mondiales et conflits contemporains*, vol. 4 (2006), pp. 47–64.
[265] MAE, HCRFA, PDR6/979, Administrateur Général Laffon à Général de Corps d'Armée, 6 August 1946.
[266] UNA, UNRRA, S-0417-0002-03, J. Frans, Rapport sur le contrôle des opérations de screening effectuées par les commissions consultatives des teams en exécution des paragraphes 25 à 28 du bulletin général, No. 19 du 11 juillet 1946.
[267] UNA, UNRRA, S-0417-0003-07, Carl Martini, Note pour Monsieur Lenclud [undated].

as a result, were not entitled to assistance.[268] PDR authorities, however, adopted a benevolent attitude towards them, for several reasons. French authorities maintained close ties with Hungarian military leaders hostile to their repatriation as they were grateful for the protection that Hungarian officials had offered to French POWs during the Nazi years.[269] Poignant singled out the contribution of the comte André Szechenyi for his protection of French prisoners.[270] Other reports suggest that a Hungarian military chief had refused to fire his guns when the French First Army arrived.[271]

Screening policies were thus ambiguous, inconsistent and sensitive to changing circumstances. In Lindau, Jean Gerbier made great efforts to ensure that he was complying with UNRRA directives, but in September 1946 he was reprimanded by UNRRA headquarters staff for providing unauthorized assistance to Hungarian DPs. In his response to the complaint, he asked: 'Why is one blamed for commendable intentions? A simple intervention of our superiors would have prevented this.'[272] Gerbier's frustrated response demonstrates the difficulties, despite the best of intentions, of maintaining neutrality. Administrative confusion was also clearly evident in the screening of Romanian DPs. In October 1946, following UNRRA Bulletin 19, eighteen Romanian DPs were expunged from the DP list in Villingen on the grounds that ex-enemy nationals were not entitled to UNRRA assistance. A month later, a new instruction was circulated, which resulted in their being granted DP status in February 1947.[273] This was not specific to the French zone. In September 1946, a UNRRA official noted that, in all three Western zones, UNRRA was asked to care for persons who could 'in no way be considered eligible for UNRRA care'.[274] One could also point out that, in the French zone, the situation of DPs' dependent family was clearly determined only in February 1947, when it was decided that spouses and parents of DPs who did not meet individually the required criteria would not be granted DP status, except on a temporary basis.[275]

In addition to particularly contradictory and confusing instructions, DPs rarely held personal identification papers, which offered clear proof and

---

[268] MAE, HCRFA, PDR6/861, Bulletin General No. 19, Détermination du droit à l'assistance d'UNRRA, 11 July 1946.
[269] Sept-ans d'activité en faveur des personnes déplacées, p. 12. Also see Fejérdy, 'La place de la Hongrie dans la politique étrangère de la France entre 1944 et 1949'.
[270] MAE, HCRFA, PDR6/717, Attestation, N. 25542 DGAA/Dir PDR, 13 November 1946.
[271] MAE, HCRFA, PDR6/717, Compte-rendu de mission, 5 May 1946.
[272] UNA, UNRRA, S-0421-0052-01, Jean Gerbier à Rodie, 24 September 1946.
[273] MAE, HCRFA, PDR6/863, General de Corps d'Armée Lenclud à Administrateur Général, 18 March 1947.
[274] UNA, UNRRA, S-0139-0034-08, Rhea Radin, Report and Recommendations on UNRRA Programme for Displaced Persons in Germany.
[275] UNA, UNRRA, S-0417-0003-06, Eligibility, 9 April 1947.

straightforward recognition of their status. In Kaiserslautern, Keipert Tuba was born Iranian and was married to a German national. Yet, she had no papers to prove her Iranian nationality.[276] Identity documents that established belonging to the *Volkslisten* were utilized to differentiate Germans from DPs.[277] Quite paradoxically, racial criteria used by Nazi Germany, rather than citizenship, served as the defining test. For Allied nationals, several different documents were used to establish whether DPs had 'volunteered' to go to Germany or had been forced to do so, including *Fremdenpass, Arbeitsbuch* (Labour book), *Arbeitskarte* and *Kennkarte* (set up by the Germans for parts of Poland).[278] The forgery of personal documents was also important and several trafficking operations of false identity papers were dismantled.[279] Facing scrutiny of their past, many DPs erased any traces of collaboration.[280] In Laupheim, a Yugoslav DP denounced another DP who had lied to the UNRRA screening commission and used a knitting needle to burn a tattoo of his blood type onto his left arm.[281] Denunciations and accusatory rumours were widespread in DP camps.[282] Some DPs certainly resorted to denunciation as a means of gaining power and possible revenge against adversaries.

In this context, screening was highly contingent on where DPs lived and who they knew.[283] There is compelling evidence that the personal and political views of the interviewer of the local screening commission shaped the outcome of the interviews. A Chinese national, studying in the University of Tübingen, was granted DP status even though he had never left Germany. Heinz Lo was born in Germany to a German mother, who lived in the American zone, and a Chinese father, who lived in 1945 in China. Neither Heinz nor his mother had been persecuted by the Nazis. He nevertheless passed the screening

---

[276] UNA, UNRRA, S-0421-0038-02, Triage des DPs au Team UNRRA 675 de Kaiserslautern.
[277] Paul Lenormand, 'Les déplacées tchécoslovaques en Allemagne et en Autriche', p. 124.
[278] UNA, UNRRA, S-0139-0034-08, General remarks, background of the work done in the selection office of the Deutsches Museum, Munich.
[279] MAE, HCRFA, PDR6/740, Le Secrétaire Général à Général d'Armée, Arrestation en Zone Américaine du ressortissant yougoslave, 13 May 1948.
[280] See, for instance, the case of Yugoslav DP Inre Bosnaj, who was a sous-officer in the Waffen SS and later admitted in the DP centre of Niederlahnstein. MAE, HCRFA, PDR6/740, Général d'Armée Koenig à Directeur de la Commission Préparatoire de l'OIR, Cas du ressortissant yougoslave Inre Bosnaj, 22 September 1948.
[281] MAE, HCRFA, PDR6/740, Procès Verbal de la Gendarmerie Nationale, Brigade de Biberachander riss, 23 September 1947.
[282] Carpenter, 'Folklore as a Source for Creating Exile Identity', p. 277.
[283] Latvian and Lithuanians DPs registered in Polish DP camps were, for instance, less subjected to screening than those residing in other camps. Denis, 'Complices de Hitler ou victimes de Staline', p. 89.

commission's scrutiny on the grounds that he wanted to return to China. The governor of the Württemberg area, however, opposed this decision.[284]

In Kaiserslautern, 229 DPs were screened by the UNRRA team director, its welfare officer and DP leaders: 141 obtained full 'DP status', 23 DPs were excluded and 65 were registered as 'doubtful cases'. Among those excluded, some were Hungarian DPs, others were stateless people who *voluntarily* went to Germany during the war and, finally, some were Baltic *Volkdeutsche*. The 'doubtful cases' included DPs enrolled in the Wehrmacht and Baltic DPs who had fled the advancing Red Army.[285] These results, at least on paper, conformed to the eligibility regulations laid down by UNRRA. But, this was not always the case. In Koblenz, for instance, Polish commanders seemed to conduct the screening operation. According to an UNRRA screening officer, these DP representatives excluded DPs based on their own prejudices.[286] This was not the only case of blatant partiality. In Freiburg, the UNRRA Director followed 'his personal feelings' rather than strictly adhering to UNRRA's rules. 'There is every reason to believe that he acted as a dictator', commented one of his supervisors.[287] The same occurred in Gutach and in Ravensburg, where 'The director ... continued to follow the old ways of a PDR officer; he did not read the General Bulletin 19 and retained the spirit of a security officer, seeing in each DP who did not share his sympathies a suspect'.[288]

UNRRA bureaucracy was hierarchical. Its policies and directives, however, were continually altered, reinterpreted, mediated and not always enforced. From the perspective of the DPs, screening was seen as profoundly arbitrary and brutal.[289] In Tübingen, some DPs refused to present themselves to the screening commission.[290] For Rozītis, who has examined Latvian novels

---

[284] MAE, HCRFA, PDR 6/768, Le Gouverneur, Délégué Supérieur pour le Gouvernement Militaire du Wurtemberg à l'Administrateur Adjoint pour le Gouvernement militaire, 10 April 1947.

[285] UNA, UNRRA, S-0421-00038-02, Directeur du team UNRRA 675 à Directeur de la Direction Générale UNRRA pour la ZFOA, Triage DPs au camp de Kaiserslautern, 26 August 1946.

[286] UNA, UNRRA, S-0417-0002-03, J. Frans, Rapport sur le contrôle des opérations de screening effectuées par les commissions consultatives des teams en exécution des paragraphes 25 à 28 du bulletin général, No. 19 du 11 juillet 1946.

[287] Ibid.

[288] Ibid.

[289] See, for example, Juris Rozītis, *Displaced Literature. Images of Time and Space in Latvian Novels Depicting the First Years of the Latvian Postwar Exile* (Stockholm: Stockholm University, 2005), pp. 100–101; Tomas Balkelis, 'Living in the Displaced Persons Camp: Lithuanian War Refugees in the West, 1944–1954', in Peter Gatrell and Nick Baron (eds.), *Warlands. Population Resettlement and State reconstruction in the Soviet-East European Borderlands, 1945–1950* (New York: Palgrave Macmillan, 2009), p. 28.

[290] UNA, UNRRA, S-0417-0001-07, Compte-rendu d'inspection, Field Supervision No. 3, 10 January 1947.

written in DP camps, DPs had little respect 'for the authorities or administrative order that prevail[ed] in and defin[ed] th[eir] [social] space'.[291] DPs were often scathing about the capacity and ethics of UNRRA relief workers. They often appear in Latvian novels as incompetent, prejudiced and 'petty-minded' individuals with unaccustomed power.[292] There were few mechanisms in place to protect DPs either against the arbitrary power of relief workers or against false denunciation; however, evicted DPs were given the opportunity to appeal to a UNRRA 'Commission d'Appel'. Sebille and Frans, zone screening officers, directed this commission.[293] By January 1947, 1,006 DPs had been excluded, and 62 granted DP status again.[294] Amongst those rejected, 40 per cent originated from enemy or ex-enemy countries, 22 per cent were considered *Volksdeutsche*, 18 per cent were UN nationals who resided in Germany before the war, 10 per cent were UN nationals who had not been displaced during the war and 10 per cent were ex-Wehrmacht members and German Balts.[295] In some cases, the commission faced tragic dilemmas. One Polish DP was in Germany before the start of the war and '[d]espite his very bad health state, the appeal commission, which complied with UNRRA rules, was forced to maintain his exclusion'.[296] Unlike him, some DPs were successful in their appeals. Ladislas Bocz, a Hungarian DP, was reintegrated as a *persecutee*. Interned in Hungary in October 1944 for 'political reasons', he was evacuated to Germany in January 1945.[297] A DP family from Bialystok was also reintegrated into the DP category. The daughter served as a translator, as the family spoke only Russian. They were reintegrated on the grounds that 'it was almost certain that the family was inscribed on the Volklist III or IV'.[298]

After these preliminary screening operations, the Permanent Screening Commission toured individual DP centres. By March 1947, it had visited 43 teams and 24 detachments; that is to say, 67 centres comprising a total DP population of 37,128. Of the population screened, 15.7 per cent were judged to be suspicious:

---

[291] Rozītis, *Displaced Literature*, p. 102.
[292] Ibid., p. 111.
[293] MAE, HCRFA, PDR6/863, UNRRA, G. Sébille à Monsieur les Directeurs de team, 3 February 1947.
[294] MAE, HCRFA, PDR6/863, Resultats du triage UNRRA à la date du 1 Janvier 1947.
[295] Ibid.
[296] MAE, HCRFA, PDR6/863, Décision concernant des appelants du team 589, Reutligen, 14 December 1946.
[297] MAE, HCRFA, PDR6/863, Décision concernant des appelants du team 511, 17 December 1946.
[298] MAE, HCRFA, PDR6/863, Décision concernant un appellant du team 581 Leutkirch, 17 December 1946.

1,182 (i.e. 3.2%) DPs were excluded;
1,217 DPs were put forward for exclusion;
2,826 DPs were submitted as doubtful cases.[299]

For some UNRRA field workers, UNRRA's rigid policy meant that it came to be regarded as 'an administration, which no longer wishes to do anything for the DPs'.[300] It is nevertheless worth noting that the number of DPs excluded in the French zone was considerably lower than in the British and American zones. Admittedly, screening operations were eventually abandoned in the American zone due to widespread criticism.[301] By then, of some 320,000 DPs screened by the US army in cooperation with UNRRA, 12.3 per cent were declared ineligible for DP status. In the British zone, 10.4 per cent were disqualified. By contrast, only 2.8 per cent of those screened were deprived of their DP status by UNRRA officials working in the French zone.[302]

Crucially, a number of French officials wanted to place much greater emphasis on individual circumstances. The study of DP screening draws out an interesting parallel with French approaches to the denazification of Germans. In the first phase of denazification, the French applied sanctions on a smaller portion of the German population, but with more severity.[303] Instead of following the initial instructions established by American authorities in 1945, the French military government implemented a denazification policy that was more sensitive to individual situations.[304] Similarly, French screening authorities thought that DPs should only be accused individually of collaboration and should be given the opportunity to defend themselves. For them, holding a contract of voluntary work did not mean that an individual was a volunteer, they advocated a more nuanced position. In this respect, French field screening officers demonstrated a much greater awareness of the complexity of Nazi labour and racial policies in Occupied Europe than some legal advisers working in UNRRA's higher echelons.[305] Reflecting on his experience as a zone screening officer and member of the Appeal Commission, Frans suggested modifying order 52. He had interviewed 4,982

---

[299] UNA, UNRRA, S-0417-0001-06, Translation, Zone Director's monthly narrative report to the chief of operations, February 1947, 7 March 1947, p. 3; S-0417-0003-05, Translation, Screening, 4 March 1947.
[300] Ibid.
[301] Cohen, 'Between Relief and Politics', p. 446.
[302] Cohen, *In War's Wake*, p. 40.
[303] On denazification in the French zone, Sébastien Chauffour, Corine Defrance, Stefan Martens and Marie-Bénédicte Vincent (eds.), *La France et la dénazification de l'Allemagne après 1945* (Bruxelles: Peter Lang, 2019).
[304] Vollnhals, *Entnazifizierung*. Defrance and Pfeil, 'L'Allemagne occupée en 1946', pp. 47–64.
[305] See, for example, UNA, UNRRA, S-0517-0117, Prof. Franklin, Legal Adviser South Eastern Europe, Criteria for Determining Collaborators, 7 March 1946.

THE POLITICS OF NEUTRALITY                187

DPs, and, of them, had to evict 148 *Volksdeutsche*. The interviews revealed that many were forced to sign their *Einbürgerung*. For him, even if one cannot ignore the behaviour of those who went to Germany to find a cure for National Socialism and then returned to Poland or the Baltic countries as dictators, one should not condemn a group as a whole. 'Belgium, France, Luxembourg, almost as a whole, Holland, Italy, Denmark all had amongst their nationals some who were listed on the Volkslistes, some who were enrolled in the Wehrmacht, and a portion (fortunately small) who behaved anti-patriotically.'[306]

Drawing on these suggestions, French UNRRA zone director Lenclud sent recommendations to UNRRA central headquarters. He insisted on the necessity of a uniform interpretation of order 52 in the three Western zones and of circulating more documentation on screening. The determination of nationality by liaison officers requires an excellent understanding of national and international legislation, territorial clauses of international treaties and both historical and geographical knowledge. Some groups did not fit easily into the categories elaborated by UNRRA. For instance, there were a number of Romanians who, after 23 August 1944, when the pro-Nazi regime was overturned, took arms against the Germans and were imprisoned in Germany.[307] Similarly, UNRRA policies were too vague regarding individual situations of Italians. Given that there were young Italians from the Tyrol area who were forcedly transferred to Austria and incorporated into the Reich, the French insisted that ex-members of the Wehrmacht should receive UNRRA assistance if they presented an individual attestation that there were neither collaborators nor Volklist category I nor had voluntarily enrolled in the Wehrmacht.[308]

Finally, French officials suggested clarifying the definition of *persecutee*. Considerably more DPs were included in the *persecutee* category in the French zone (including Berlin): in December 1946, 1,127 were categorized as such within the French zone, compared to 742 in the American zone and none at all in the British. The reason was simple: the French PDR applied this category to a number of Germans who were persecuted by the Nazis even if they had not been displaced by war.[309] Persecution was understood as a compensation for moral wrong suffered at the hands of the enemy.[310] For UN nationals, Italians and stateless people, the definition of moral wrong was

---

[306] UNA, UNRRA, S-0417-0003-06, Etude de Frans, Screening Officer, December 1946.
[307] UNA, UNRRA, S-0417-0003-06, Lenclud, Projet de Révision de l'Ordre 52 sur le droit à l'assistance UNRRA, 24 December 1946.
[308] Ibid.
[309] UNRRA, S-0417-0003-06, Mercier, Eligibility, 9 April 1947; S-0417-0003-05, Screening, 4 March 1947.
[310] UNA, UNRRA, S-0417-0003-06, Lenclud, Projet de Révision de l'Ordre 52 sur le droit à l'assistance UNRRA, 24 December 1946.

expansive. They received compensation just for being displaced outside national boundaries due to war. For ex-enemies, enemies or neutral nationals, the criteria were much stricter. They needed to have been victims of measures that personally affected them, their family or their ethnic group. Furthermore, these measures had to be motivated by race, religion or pro-Allied or anti-Nazi activities. The French UNRRA headquarters insisted in particular on the necessity of defining clear criteria for German Jews or gypsies applicable in the three zones.[311] In the French zone, in order to obtain the status of *persecutee* one needed to (i) have been detained in a prison or a concentration camp for a minimum of six months, (ii) have suffered corporal punishment leading to a disability, (iii) be under 18 and have lost one parent, (iv) be the widow of a *persecutee* or (v) be over 60 and have lost all family due to war persecutions.[312]

In sum, the projects of screening DPs faced a battery of challenges, including the lack of uniformity in how UNRRA general policies were 'translated' in the three Western zones, the absence of training for relief workers, the tendency of DPs to withhold information and craft 'acceptable answers', and, finally, the inconsistencies between the PDR and UNRRA instructions. Delays in the implementation of UNRRA screening also meant that the organization was focusing on repatriation and the eviction of DPs when the PDR began to publicize information on emigration, giving the impression that UNRRA was an 'administration which no longer wishes to do anything for the [DPs]'.[313] In this context, DPs found ways to quietly resist UNRRA power and discipline. To varying degrees, the constraints and stigmas of 'collaborators' placed by UNRRA on DPs galvanized resistance and, as the Cold War developed, helped DPs to redefine themselves as 'freedom fighters'.[314]

## The Challenge of DPs' Politics

In the autumn of 1946, the Yugoslav National Committee wrote to French authorities to remind them of the 'generous' French hospitality from which their fathers benefited during the First World War.[315] They also evoked their brotherhood in arms. Major Stanojevich Bora, an officer of the Royal Yugoslav Army, wrote, for instance, to General Koenig to offer his services to his 'second

---

[311] Ibid.
[312] UNA, UNRRA, S-0417-0003-06, Mercier, Eligibility, 9 April 1947.
[313] UNA, UNRRA, S-0417-0003-05, Screening, 4 March 1947.
[314] Carpenter, 'Folklore as a Source for Creating Exile Identity'; Arta Ankrava, 'From Displaced Persons to Exiles: Nationalism, Anti-Communism, and the Shaping of Latvian American Diaspora', PhD thesis, University of Minnesota, 2016.
[315] MAE, HCRFA, PDR6/740, Comité National Yougslave, signé Radj. Popovic, 14 October 1946.

fatherland', insisting on the fact that during the First World War, he had fought as a *poilu d'Orient*.[316] Unlike Yugoslav DPs who boarded the train home in May 1947, former Yougoslav officers of the Royal Army decided to resist repatriation and sought ways to find support amongst French officials. Despite their efforts, in December 1946 French authorities refused to give official accreditation to the Yugoslav National Committee in the zone.[317] This was typical of the ambivalence of French authorities. The development of anti-repatriation activities was a constant concern; yet, as we have seen, the PDR maintained informal contacts with many DP leaders who were hostile to repatriation.

At first glance, French authorities seemed to have taken an unequivocally hard line against DP anti-communist leaders. On 2 October 1945, the dissolution of all DP committees that had not received an official recognition was ordered.[318] And, on 1 February 1946 the War Ministry issued an order banning all 'Polish groups'.[319] Conferences and public events were absolutely forbidden, as were anti-repatriation activities.[320] In 1946, for instance, the United Lithuanian Relief Fund of America mourned the fact that there was no Lithuanian newspaper in the French zone.[321] Despite the strict official ban on anti-repatriation propaganda and the various restrictions imposed on DP committees by French authorities, the evidence suggests that anti-repatriation activities flourished. The development of these activities was not specific to the French zone. Nationalism played a central role in DP camps across the three Western zones. Camp life catalyzed the development of a 'long-distance nationalism' among DPs, who maintained strong emotional ties with their home countries.[322] DP nationalism provided a communal means of overcoming the test of displacement and of coping with the sense of depersonalization, homelessness and social downgrading that was exacerbated by life in the

---

[316] MAE, HCRFA, PDR6/740, Major Stanojevich Bora de l'Armée Yougoslave au Général Koenig relative à une demande de function dans la ZFO, 19 October 1946.
[317] MAE, HCRFA, PDR6/740, administrateur Général Laffon à Général d'Armée, Cabinet Civil, 27 December 1946.
[318] UNA, UNRRA, S-0417-0001-07, Compte-rendu d'inspection, Field Supervisor N.3, Haslach, 13 December 1946.
[319] MAE, HCRFA, Bonn 148, Fiche pour le Général, 2 August 1946.
[320] MAE, HCRFA, PDR6/1017, Le Directeur PDR à Administrateur Général Adjoint pour le GM, 14 June 1947; Compte-rendu de l'entretien officiel qui a eu lieu à Berlin-Karlshorst entre les autorités soviétiques et le chef de la division française des personnes déplacées, 31 July 1947.
[321] CAC, Versement 770623, article 172, Dr. J. B. Koncius, Mémorandum de l'United Lithuaniam Relief Fund of America, concernant la situation des DPs ressortissants des Pays Baltes, en particulier des Lithuaniens, 26 August 1946.
[322] Tara Zahra, 'Lost Children: Displacement, Family and Nation in Postwar Europe', *Journal of Modern History*, vol. 81, no. 2 (2009), pp. 45–81, 50.

camps.[323] Authoritarian and fascist personalities often played a crucial role in shaping DP politics.[324]

The French zone was not the centre of DPs' politics. In marked contrast to the American zone and, to a lesser extent, the British zone, DPs had minimal room to engage in associational life or to develop cultural activities in the French zone. The French zone lacked large urban centres, it had fewer major DP camps and its authorities offered DPs considerably less material support. Crucially, DP freedom of movement was strictly limited.[325] Yet, anti-repatriation activities emerged in several DP camps throughout 1946.[326] Posters and proclamations encouraging DPs to accept repatriation offers were torn down in Balingen, Rotweil and Villingen in December.[327] Letters from deportees in Siberia were distributed.[328] In Mülheim, nine Polish DPs previously repatriated to Poland were discovered promulgating anti-repatriation propaganda.[329] Although French authorities refused to authorize the publication of DP newspapers, anti-Soviet DP newspapers, printed in the American zone, were circulated widely through the German post.[330] Relief goods were also distributed by anti-repatriation relief organizations, such as the Polish mission of the Vatican, 'apostle of the non-return to Poland', to promote resistance to repatriation.[331]

As we have seen, repatriation missions repeatedly blamed UNRRA for accommodating DPs who carried out anti-repatriation propaganda. Faced with such attacks, in May 1946 UNRRA carried out a large-scale repatriation poll. Conducted in the three Western zones, the poll was the first (and last) systematic sounding of the DP population. It asked DPs three questions:

---

[323] Balkelis, 'Living in the Displaced Persons Camp', pp. 25–47, 42.
[324] Anna Holian, 'Anticommunism in the Streets: Refugee Politics in Cold War Germany', *Journal of Contemporary History*, vol. 45, no. 1 (2010), pp. 134–161.
[325] A circular dated 27 September 1945 prevented them from moving more than 5 km from their place of residence. UNA, UNRRA, S-0421-0062-02, Groupements Nationaux à Monsieur le Directeur de l'UNRRA, Ravensburg.
[326] In Rottweil, for instance, the Polish Committee was dissolved *pour des raisons diplomatiques* after publishing a political note in September 1946. UNA, UNRRA, S-0421-0072-05, chef de Bataillon Garnier Dupre à Thery, 2 September 1946.
[327] UNA, UNRRA, S-0417-0001-07, Field Inspection, Haslach, 6 December 1946.
[328] UNA, UNRRA, S-0421-0041-05, Lettre ouverte à La Guardia d'un déporté Polonais dans le camp de concentration No. 285 à Borowiczy dans l'URSS!
[329] UNA, UNRRA, S-0417-0001-07, Compte-rendu d'inspection, Haslach, 13 December 1946.
[330] MAE, PDR6/984, Rapport du Gouverneur Délégué supérieur pour le GM du Wurtemberg à Tübingen à l'Administrateur Général Laffon, 29 October 1947.
[331] UNA, UNRRA, S-0438-0003-03, Lettre de De Fos à Directeur de District, Visite du capitaine Lipski, 5 June 1946. Also see Lettre du Directeur du District à General Directeur General d'UNRRA en zone Française d'Occupation, Mission Polonaise du Vatican, 13 June 1946.

'What was their nationality? Did they want to return home? And, if not, why not?' Answers were submitted anonymously. Undoubtedly, we must apply appropriate scrutiny to the information contained in this poll. This poll was 'recognized administratively from its inception as misleading. In many camps the answers were completely stereotypical, and in several instances team personnel found letters issued to displaced persons instructing them how to vote'.[332] Overall, the results revealed not only a 'broad popular opposition to repatriation' but also the extent to which opposition had come to be defined in political terms.[333] While the poll does not present a comprehensive picture of DP opinion regarding repatriation, it provides insight into the differences between the three Western zones in relation to how DPs presented their reasons for refusing repatriation. In the French zone, out of 31,232 DPs from the major groups (the Balts, Poles, Russians, Yugoslavs and Jews) interrogated, 3,845 said yes to repatriation, 19,210 said no and 8,177 refused to participate. In total, 61.5 per cent of the population interrogated said no, a figure considerably lower than in the British (79.3 per cent) and American (88 per cent) zones.[334] Abstention was also considerably higher in the French zone. Furthermore, if one examines only the figures relating to Polish DPs (who did not have the same anti-repatriation drive as the Balts or Jews), one finds that they were even lower. Out of 26,154 interrogated, 7,276 did not participate, 3,768 said yes and 15,110 said no. In total, 57.8 per cent refused repatriation, as opposed to 76.2 per cent in the British zone and 84.4 per cent in the American zone.[335]

From an UNRRA perspective, nevertheless, these results tended to suggest that collective resistance to repatriation was weaker in the French occupation zone, with Polish DPs placing greater emphasis on economic factors than on political motives. For UNRRA officials, this difference stemmed from the fact that many Poles in the French zone worked within the German economy. 'They therefore enjoyed greater economic security.'[336] The greater proportional integration of DPs within the German economy was paralleled by a greater integration of students into German universities.[337] But, the relative weakness of the *political explanation* can also be traced back to four other factors: delays in the repatriation process in the French zone (which meant that more DPs in favour of repatriation might not have had the opportunity to

---

[332] UNA, UNRRA, S-0139-0034-08, Report and Recommendations on Programme for Displaced Persons in Germany, 11 September 1946, p. 7.
[333] Holian, *Between National Socialism*, p. 84.
[334] UNA, UNRRA, S-0417-0002-03, Confidential, Results of Repatriation Poll of Displaced Persons in UNRRA Centers, Annex V, 1–14 May 1946.
[335] Ibid.
[336] Holian, *Between National Socialism*, pp. 84–85.
[337] UNA, UNRRA, S-0438-0009-01, 'World Student Relief', Visit to French Zone from Yngve Frykholm, Franlgen, 8 June 1946.

be repatriated); DP elites' awareness that French authorities were more hostile to their *constructed* 'anti-communist' and 'national' identities (DPs were less likely to be seen as 'Cold War heroes' in the French zone); the (relative) absence of activists and political leaders able to construct this 'broad consensus' among the mass of DPs in the French zone; and DP leaders' appreciation that they needed to remain discreet if they wanted to preserve the unofficial protection that PDR officials granted them.

In the French zone, like elsewhere, DP anticommunism was, at least, not initially a 'mass movement', and DPs were not all infused with strong anti-communist sentiments. Reasons for refusing repatriation varied greatly among individuals and over time. They were shaped by DPs' past experiences and by the post-war context, by the perceived political and economic conditions in their countries of origins, by conditions of DP life in the zone and, later, by opportunities (or supposed opportunities) for emigration. Historians are divided in their assessments of the importance of the *political explanation* (or, in other words, the 'anti-communist explanation') for non-Jewish Polish and Ukrainian DPs' refusal to accept repatriation offers.[338] Wolfgang Jacobmeyer argues that many Poles lacked the ability to make politically informed decisions, suggesting that they were primarily driven by concerns about material security and fear of punishment.[339] Dyczok estimates that 30–40 per cent of Ukrainian DPs were political refugees who made a conscious decision to leave their homes and that 60–70 per cent were forced labourers.[340] Other historians, on the contrary, maintain that Poles, Ukrainians and Russians were categorically opposed to communism.[341] Holian is more nuanced; she suggests that the DP *political explanation* reflected DP elites' efforts to build a consensus against repatriation. They created a 'global framework for individual concerns, one that edited out "merely" personal or economic considerations as well as politically problematic ones such as fear of retaliation for collaboration'.[342]

Behind this consensus, most DPs were less certain about their decision. In the French zone, a small number of Polish Ukrainians wanted to return to Poland (but not to the territories under direct Soviet control).[343] But, for others, repatriation could signify an important drop in the availability of education and healthcare. UNRRA certainly provided fairly generous aid and income-generating opportunities, and better healthcare and education

---

[338] Ibid., p. 86.
[339] Jacobmeyer, *Vom Zwangsarbeiter zum heimatlosen Ausländer*.
[340] Dyczok, *The Grand Alliance*, p. 77.
[341] Anna D. Jaroszynska-Kirchmann, *The Exile Mission* (Athens: Ohio University Press, 2004); Wyman, *DPs: Europe's Displaced Persons*.
[342] Holian, *Between National Socialism*, pp. 87–88.
[343] MAE, HCRFA, PDR6/978, Rapport du Commandant Roche, Recensement des ressortissants soviétiques dans le Kreis Ehingen, 10 May 1946.

than they had known before and could expect if they returned home.[344] In certain camps DPs learned new skills and developed new social networks. Personal matters could get in the way, too. A local repatriation poll was conducted in the winter of 1947. Out of 230 Polish DPs interrogated, 56 responded positively to the question 'would you like to return to Poland?' To the question 'why haven't you returned already?', 22 answered that they were pregnant and waiting for the end of the winter, 7 (ex-POWs) that they did not have adequate clothes, 7 that they were waiting for the end of UNRRA, 11 that they were waiting for news from Poland and 9 that they were waiting for the result of the elections in Poland.[345] In Mülheim, some Polish DP farmers explained that they refused repatriation during the winter as the land could not be cultivated.[346]

For Baltic DPs, things were obviously different. A French official reported that 100 per cent of Baltic DPs were hostile to repatriation as long as their country was occupied by Soviet troops.[347] Fears of deportation in Siberia were expressed very strongly, although they were often exaggerated.[348] On 10 March 1947, a firestorm of protest erupted among Baltic DPs at the opening of the Moscow Conference.[349] In several camps, Latvian, Lithuanian and Estonian DP committees announced the start of a hunger strike to protest against the Soviet occupation of their countries. Various Baltic committees issued letters in which they argued that all totalitarian regimes, more precisely the Nazi and communist ones, were similar. In a letter infused with human rights rhetoric, the Reutlingen Lithuanian committee lamented that their tragedy was their *holocauste à l'hôtel de la liberté*.[350] They compared their condition of victimhood to that of the Jewish DPs.[351] Such discourses were

---

[344] Hammond, 'Examining the Discourse of Repatriation', p. 231.
[345] UNRA, UNRRA, S-0417-0002-03, Mercier, Field Inspector, Etude sur le rapatriement Polonais, 30 January 1947.
[346] UNRA, UNRRA, S-0417-0001-07, Mercier, Compte rendu d'inspection, 13 December 1946.
[347] MAE, HCRFA, PDR6/984, Rapport concernant la propagande antisoviétique contre le rapatriement, 29 December 1947.
[348] See, for example, PDR6/979, Lieutenant Cerise, Compte-rendu de réunions à Ravensburg et Weingarten pour le rapatriement des citoyens soviétiques, 2 December 1946. On cleansing see, for instance, Olaf Mertelsmann and Aigi Rahi-Tamm, 'Cleansing and Compromise. The Estonian SRR in 1944–1945', *Cahiers du monde russe*, vol. 49, no. 2-3 (2008), pp. 319–340.
[349] United Nations Archives (UNA), UNRRA, S-0419-0003-02, Président du Comité Lithuanien à Tübingen à Direction de l'UNRRA, team 589, 10 March 1947; Lettre des Délégués de la Colonie Lithuanienne de Ravensburg à Capitaine Massip, Directeur de l'UNRRA Team 579, 10 March 1947.
[350] UNA, UNRRA, S-0419-0003-02, President du Comité Lithuanien de Reutlingen, Silverstras Balciunas à Direcreur de l'UNRRA, Team 589, 10 March 1947.
[351] Ibid.

common amongst Baltic DPs, who resented the West for its 'empty talk' and were gravely disappointed by the lack of Western support for their cause after the declaration of the Atlantic Charter.[352]

It is hardly surprising that the most visible protests were organized by Baltic DPs.[353] Unlike other DP groups, and notably Poles, many Baltic DPs were neither forced labourers nor former concentration camp inmates. Instead, many had fled westwards in 1944 as the Soviet Army advanced.[354] The overwhelming majority of them lived in the Württemberg area and were intellectuals who came to Germany after June 1940.[355] Soviet authorities repeatedly complained about the activities of Baltic committees, which were particularly active in the Württemberg area and were the refuge of 'war criminals'.[356] On 4 June 1947, during a meeting between the PDR administration and Soviet repatriation officers, Soviet general Bassilov stated that Baltic war criminals had organized numerous committees – described as 'veritable laboratories of anti-repatriation propaganda' – notably in Ravensburg, Freiburg and Tübingen.[357] The most active committee was located in Ravensburg, where DP elites maintained close contacts with the Latvian Committee of Detmold in the American zone. In response to Soviet complaints, the PDR authorities spent considerable resources and efforts on searching for war criminals and on limiting, as much as possible, the circulation of DPs between the French and the American zones. The leadership cadres of the anti-communist DP movement certainly included individuals who had collaborated with the Nazis. This was also arguably the case in the

---

[352] Carpenter, 'Folklore as a Source for Creating Exile Identity'.
[353] Juliette Denis, 'Identifier les "éléments ennemis" en Lettonie. Une priorité dans le processus de resoviétisation (1942–1945)', *Cahiers du monde russe*, vol. 49, nos. 2–3 (2008), pp. 297–318.
[354] On Baltic DPs see notably Thomas Lane, *Victims of Stalin and Hitler: The Exodus of Poles and Balts to Britain* (New York: Palgrave Macmillan, 2004); Balkelis, 'Living in the Displaced Persons Camp'; Angelika Eder, 'Perspectives of Displaced Persons in West Germany after 1945. A Comparison of Jewish, Baltic and Polish Non-Repatriates', in Johannes-Dieter Steinert and Inge Weber-Newth (eds.), *Beyond Camps and Forced Labour* (Osnabrück: Secolo, 2005), pp. 79–89; Laura Hilton, 'Cultural Nationalism in Exile: The Case of Polish and Latvian Displaced Persons', *The Historian*, vol. 71, no. 2 (2009), pp. 280–317; Purs, 'How Those Brothers in Foreign Lands Are Dividing the Fatherland: Latvian National Politics in Displaced Persons Camps after the Second World War,' in Gatrell and Baron (eds.) *Warlands*, pp. 48–66.
[355] MAE, PDR 6/727, Baltes dans les cercles de Ravensbourg, Friedrichshaffen, Saulgau, Wangen, 1 December 1945.
[356] Criticisms formulated by the General Davydov in October 1946. MAE, HCRFA, PDR6/1017, Le Directeur des Personnes Déplacées à l'Administrateur Général, Demande de la Mission Soviétique relative à l'activité des Comités Nationaux Baltes, 14 June 1947.
[357] MAE, HCRFA, Bonn 150, Rapport de l'Administrateur Général Laffon sur la conférence du 4 juin relative au rapatriement des ressortissants soviétiques se trouvant dans la zone française d'occupation en Allemagne, N. 10887, 6 June 1947.

French zone. In early 1947, for instance, French authorities arrested a Lithuanian DP Sakalauskas, as a war criminal.[358] Reflecting on Lithuanian DP politics, Tomas Balkelis concurs, arguing that Lithuanian DP elites made 'a strenuous effort to forge "a single national community" from a mass of disorganised and socially stratified refugees'.[359] In doing so, they attempted to create a positive image of themselves in the West and 'to preserve (or construct) a sense of collective worth'. Aldis Purs comes to the same conclusion in his analysis of Latvian national politics: 'Latvian DP identity became cemented and "packaged" as national identity for Allied consumption.'[360] What concerned French authorities was that, not only were these committees hostile to the Soviet Union, but they were also unfavourable to France.[361] All of their activities were taking place when such political activities were technically forbidden in the French zone (as in the other zones), something that the Council of Foreign Ministers reiterated in April 1947.[362]

## Conclusion

This chapter began with a public relations story about a successful repatriation convoy produced by UNRRA. It ends with the challenges posed by DP politics to the organization, with Eastern European missions accusing UNRRA of protecting anti-communist DP leaders and facilitating the development of anti-repatriation activities. Along the way, this chapter illuminated the tensions between the ways UNRRA and the PDR envisaged repatriation and revealed discrepancies between official instructions and practices in the field. UNRRA was enmeshed in a complex nexus of international and national considerations, receiving instructions on repatriation and screening elaborated in Washington, London and Bad Arolsen (American zone) as well as policy directives from Paris and Baden-Baden. At the higher level of the French Foreign Office and UNRRA administration, decision-making was fractured and bent to changing circumstances until the spring of 1946. As a result, the vertical transfers between this international organization and the national organization were not linear.[363] Problems were exacerbated by a time

---

[358] HCRFA, PDR6/1017, Le Directeur des Personnes Déplacées à Monsieur l'Administrateur Général, Demande de la Mission Soviétique relative à l'activité des Comités Nationaux Baltes, 14 June 1947.
[359] Balkelis, 'Living in the Displaced Persons Camp', p. 42.
[360] Purs, 'How Those Brothers in Foreign Lands Are Dividing the Fatherland', p. 55.
[361] MAE, HCRFA, PDR6/1017, Le Directeur des PDR à Administrateur Général, 14 June 1947.
[362] Holian, *Between National Socialism*, p. 52.
[363] Aline Angoustures and Dzovinar Kévonian, 'Conclusion', in Aline Angoustures, Dzovinar Kévonian and Claire Mouradian (eds.), *Réfugiés et apatrides. Administrer l'asile en France (1920–1960)* (Rennes: Presses Universitaires de Rennes, 2017), p. 279.

lag: UNRRA headquarters placed a stronger emphasis on repatriation in the summer of 1946, at a time when French authorities deemed mass repatriation completed.

At the heart of France's contradictory policies over the repatriation of 'Soviet citizens' was the problem of French citizens held captive in the Soviet Union, a situation which initially forced the French to make concessions in its dealings with the Soviet Union. Yet, the French authorities remained uncomfortable with the very idea of forced repatriation, and sought means of adapting, or circumventing, their agreement with Moscow. Similar ambivalence existed in French policies towards the repatriation of Polish DPs, with the PDR maintaining relations with DP leaders who were hostile to repatriation until the spring of 1946. Contradictory instructions from the Foreign Ministry and UNRRA central headquarters engendered differences in implementation. The history of UNRRA in the French zone illustrates the power of local administrators to reinterpret and shape policies on the ground. It also shows the centrality of the relationship between PDR and UNRRA local officers. PDR personnel confronted a zone riddled with differing local arrangements, making the implementation of a coherent policy very arduous. Repatriation measures were, on occasion, harnessed to local policing priorities, with local officials deploying the threat of repatriation in order to remove foreigners who posed a security threat.

Integrating the history of UNRRA and the PDR with the historical literature of forced repatriation provides other insights. An analysis of the PDR and UNRRA correspondence draws out the centrality of language in shaping Franco–Soviet encounters on the ground. It also reveals important discrepancies across the three Western zones. Far from being uniformly enforced across the three Western zones, UNRRA policies were continually altered, reinterpreted and mediated. In doing so, this chapter has mapped the combination of international influence and profound localism that characterized the work of UNRRA in the French zone. Finally, it has argued that the history of UNRRA in the French zone exemplified the difficulty, if not the impossibility, of sustaining 'impartial' and 'neutral' relief work during peacetimes. Both French authorities and UNRRA headquarters affirmed that they maintained a position of absolute neutrality; yet, the interpretation of neutrality and impartiality was constantly in flux.

# PART II

Reconstructing the Body, Rehabilitating the Mind?

# 4

## The 'Broken' DP

### 'Remaking' the Minds and Bodies of Refugees

The Second World War triggered intense discussion about the 'rehabilitation' of Displaced Persons (DPs).[1] As Europe was reckoning with the aftermath of war and genocide, DP camps became sites of experimentation, where ideas about how best to heal the physical and mental wounds of the war were exchanged between experts and relief workers from different national, religious and professional backgrounds. In all three Western zones, DP spaces did not simply function as devices of containment and enclosure. They were also spaces of unique cultural encounters, where knowledge about the 'refugee' population was created and where gender, ethnic and social identities were profoundly remade.[2] Despite important material shortages, a significant welfare programme was developed in the French zone, as in the British and American zones. DPs were offered educational, cultural and occupational opportunities in tandem with physical treatments, medical screening, gymnas-

---

[1] See, for instance, Peter Gatrell, Population displacement and mental health after the Second World War [short version, unpublished]; Mathew Thomson, *Psychological Subjects: Identity, Culture and Health in Twentieth-Century Britain* (Oxford: Oxford University Press, 2006); Mathew Thomson, *Lost Freedom: The Landscape of the Child and the British Post-war Settlement* (Oxford: Oxford University Press, 2013); Silvia Salvatici, 'Help the People to Help Themselves': UNRRA Relief Workers and European Displaced Persons', *Journal of Refugee Studies*, vol. 25, no. 3 (2012), pp. 452–473; Michal Shapira, *The War Inside: Psychoanalysis, Total War, and the Making of the Democratic Self in Post-war Britain* (Cambridge: Cambridge University Press, 2013); Tara Zahra, 'Lost Children: Displacement, Family, and Nation in Postwar Europe', *Journal of Modern History*, vol. 81, no. 1 (2009), pp. 45–86; Tara Zahra, '"The Psychological Marshall Plan": Displacement, Gender and Human Rights after World War II', *Central European History*, vol. 44, no. 1 (2011), pp. 37–62; Tara Zahra, '"A Human Treasure": Europe's Displaced Children between Nationalism and Internationalism', *Past and Present*, vol. 210, supplement 6 (2011), pp. 332–350; Tara Zahra, *The Lost Children: Reconstructing Europe's Families after World War II* (Cambridge, MA: Harvard University Press, 2011); Henning Borggräfe, Akim Jah, Steffen Jost and Nina Ritz, *Freilegungen: Rebuilding Lives – Child Survivors and DP Children in the Aftermath of the Holocaust and Forced Labor* (Goettingen: Wallstein Verlag, 2017).
[2] Daniel Cohen, *In War's Wake: Europe's Displaced Persons in the Postwar Order* (Oxford: Oxford University Press, 2011), pp. 58–78.

tic exercises and sport.³ Some DP children were sent to open-air homes in the black forest, where they spent days in the fresh air and sun and ate an ample diet. Some DP adults were provided with vocational training and the opportunities to learn sewing, embroidery or painting. Through these activities, relief workers strove to heal, discipline and remake DPs' bodies and minds. They attempted, in particular, to re-establish the boundaries between adulthood and childhood, which they feared had been wrecked by the war, and re-impose ideal notions of femininity and masculinity.⁴ Relief workers' ideas of a successful rehabilitation were based on gendered assumptions. Welfare programmes confined DP men and women to very gender-specific spheres of activities: vocational workshops tended to assign DP men to building, metal, mechanical and leather work, carpentry, textiles, and DP women to childcare, nursery, embroidery, knitting and cooking.⁵ These programmes were also often underpinned by prejudices and received wisdom of the superiority of certain ethnic groups over others.

Much scholarship has focused on the British and American zones and on the re-masculinizing and re-feminizing purposes underpinning rehabilitation. As Tara Zahra argues, reconstructing Europe meant 're-training' DP parents, in particular DP mothers, in methods of childcare.⁶ Research into post-war rehabilitation has also highlighted that these welfare programmes were deeply political and reflected different ways of understanding the nature and needs of refugee adults and children.⁷ DPs were expected not to become burdens on German society. Some groups of DPs were thought of as potential future 'citizens' for France, Britain or other 'Western' countries. Others needed to be fit to return to their home country as quickly as possible. These contradictory drives between emigration abroad and repatriation shaped rehabilitation practices, while also creating opportunities to expand areas of expertise. Allied planners aimed to provide more than mere 'soup kitchen' charity and claimed to bring in new perspectives on relief work.⁸ A number of American relief workers had learned their professions in New Deal America and saw

---

³ On physical education, see, for instance, UNA, UNRRA, S-0438-0009-05, Conférence sur l'Education, Baden-Baden (Hotel zun Hirsch), 25 and 26 January 1946, p. 15.
⁴ Zahra, *Lost Children*.
⁵ UNA, HCRFA, S-0438-0009-05, Réunion des Welfare Officers du District Sud des Teams de l'Est, 15–16 January 1946, Wangen.
⁶ Zahra, *Lost Children*.
⁷ Pamela Ballinger, 'Impossible Returns, Enduring Legacies: Recent Historiography of Displacement and the Reconstruction of Europe after World War II', *Contemporary European History*, vol. 22, no. 1 (2013), pp. 127–138; Peter Gatrell, *The Making of the Modern Refugee* (Oxford: Oxford University Press, 2013).
⁸ *Helping the People to Help Themselves. The Story of the United Nations Relief and Rehabilitation Administration* (London: Stationary Office, 1944), p. 8.

themselves as 'professional of rehabilitation', concerned not only with material assistance but also with DPs' emotional and psychological needs.[9]

UNRRA planners' aspirations to transform humanitarianism into a 'modern profession' were hampered by its subordination to the military, its lack of uniformly trained personnel and the absence of clear definitions of what 'rehabilitation' meant. While UNRRA was widely heralded as a clear break with the past, historians have highlighted deeper continuities in ideas, personnel and practices with inter-war humanitarianism, a number of British relief workers notably drawing on practices from the British Empire and narratives of imperial responsibility.[10] As Jessica Reinisch notes, UNRRA practices represented 'old wines in new bottles'.[11] Finally, a growing literature focusing on DP communities has shifted the locus of scholarly analysis away from notions of passivity and silence on the part of DPs to demonstrate their active agency in managing their lives, resisting welfare workers' prescriptions and shaping these welfare programmes.[12] These studies have demonstrated the zealous participation of DPs in overcoming constraints, seizing economic and cultural opportunities and reconstructing politics in exile.[13] DPs did not

---

[9] For Daniel Cohen, 'International assistance provided to DPs after 1945 marked the transition, under heavy American influence between two dramatically different types of humanitarian regimes', Cohen, *In War's Wake*, p. 78. Also see Salvatici, 'Help the People to Help Themselves'.

[10] Emily Baughan, 'The Imperial War Relief Fund and the British Appeal: Commonwealth, Conflict and Conservatism within the British Humanitarian Movement, 1920-25', *Journal of Imperial and Commonwealth History*, vol. 40, no. 5 (2012), pp. 845-861.

[11] Jessica Reinisch, 'Old Wine in New Bottles? UNRRA and the Mid-Century World of Refugees', in Matthew Frank and Jessica Reinisch (eds.), *Refugees in Europe, 1919-1959: A Forty Years' Crisis?* (London: Bloomsbury, 2017), pp. 147-176. Similar debates existed about the newness of relief practices in the aftermath of the First World War. See, for instance, Peter Gatrell (ed.), 'Discussion: Humanitarianism' with Rebecca Gill, Branden Little and Elisabeth Piller', in *Encyclopedia 1914-1918 online*, November 2017, available online, https://encyclopedia.1914-1918-online.net/article/discussion_humanitarianism (last consulted 17 September 2019).

[12] Atina Grossmann, 'Trauma, Memory and Motherhood: Germans and Jewish Displaced Persons in Post-Nazi Germany, 1945-1949', *Archiv für Sozialgeschichte*, vol. 38 (1998), pp. 215-239, 116.

[13] The literature on Jewish DPs is by far the most extensive and the most varied. See, for example, Judith Tydor Baumel, 'DPs, Mothers and Pioneers: Women in the She'erit Hapletah', *Jewish History*, vol. 11, no. 2 (1997), pp. 99-110; Francoise Ouzan, *Ces Juifs dont l'Amérique ne voulait pas (1945-1950)* (Paris: Éditions Complexes, 1995); Michael Brenner, *After the Holocaust. Rebuilding Jewish Lives in Postwar Germany* (Princeton, NJ: Princeton University Press, 1997); Jay Howard Geller, *Jews in Post-Holocaust Germany, 1945-1953* (Cambridge: Cambridge University Press, 2005); Michael Meng, 'After the Holocaust: The History of Jewish Life in West Germany', *Contemporary European History*, vol. 14, no. 3 (2005), pp. 403-413; Atina Grossmann, *Jews, Germans, and Allies: Close Encounters in Occupied Germany* (Princeton, NJ: Princeton University

universally embrace relief workers' norms of gender and family nor conformed to their expectations. Instead, they advanced their own ideals of domesticity, femininity and masculinity.[14]

Building on these three strands in the recent historiography, this chapter explores how DPs' physical and mental needs were assessed in the French zone and how relief workers responded to them. As we have seen, the majority of relief workers in the French zone were French. They brought with them a specific set of assumptions and experiences, which framed how they approached rehabilitation. UNRRA was also established later in the French zone than in the other zones. As a result, no specific instruction about social work was sent to welfare workers until the beginning of 1946.[15] In this chapter, I ask: What kind of DPs did relief workers attempt to 'remake' in the French zone? What did 'rehabilitation' mean to occupation officials and relief workers and what 'therapies' and 'rehabilitative' treatments did they experiment? What hopes did they invest in the remedial effects of the nuclear family? How did they attempt to reconstruct DP bodies? And, finally, how did DPs respond to these various experiments and gendered expectations?

In answering these questions, this chapter makes three arguments. First, while existing scholarship has suggested that international organizations brought a (or several) 'psychological Marshall Plan(s)' in post-war Europe, this chapter contends that the influence of the psy-sciences in shaping discussions over the rehabilitation of DPs was more qualified than existing historical studies have maintained.[16] Histories of refugee and child welfare, notably by Tara Zahra, have illuminated the growing influence of psychology on the treatment of refugees in post-war Europe. In the United States and Britain, the 1940s marked a key moment, in which exiled continental analysts and native psychologists connected mental health to broader issues of reconstruction and citizenship.[17] The child-survivor was especially singled out for

---

Press, 2007); Avinoam Patt and Michael Berkowitz (eds.), *We Are Here: New Approaches to Jewish Displaced Persons in Postwar Germany* (Detroit: Wayne State University Press, 2010). Also see Holian, *Between National Socialism and Soviet Communism*.

[14] See, for instance, Margarete Myers Feinstein, *Holocaust Survivors in Postwar Germany, 1945–1957* (Cambridge: Cambridge University Press, 2010); Margarete Myers Feinstein, 'Jewish DPs and Questions of Gender', in Rebecca Boehling, Susanne Urban and René Bienert (eds.), *Displaced Persons Leben in Transit: Überlebende zwischen Repatriierung, Rehabilitation und Neuanfang* (Göttingen: Wallstein Verlag, 2014), pp. 159–168, 159; Katarzyna Nowak, 'Voices of Revival. A Cultural History of Polish Displaced Persons in Allied-Occupied Germany and Austria, 1945–1952', PhD thesis, University of Manchester, version submitted in July 2018.

[15] UNA, UNRRA, S-0438-0005-02, Rapport du service 'welfare' sur le district nord de la zone, R. le Goff, 11 April 1946.

[16] Zahra, 'Lost Children', pp. 45–86; Zahra, '"The Psychological Marshall Plan"', pp. 37–62; Zahra, '"A Human Treasure"', pp. 332–350; *The Lost Children*.

[17] Thomson, *Psychological Subjects*; Thomson, *Lost Freedom*; Shapira, *The War Inside*.

attention by psychologists and education specialists.[18] A number of British and American relief workers certainly approached refugee welfare armed with the psychoanalytic theories and practices of social work prevalent in the United States and the United Kingdom at mid-century. However, the overwhelming majority of French relief workers relied on different perceptions of social work rather than psychological expertise. Most of them had, in the word of an American worker working in the French zone, never heard of Freud.[19] In the French zone, the emphasis was mainly placed on vocational rehabilitation, the re-education of mothers and rest in the countryside as a means to improve mental and physical health. The range of treatment offered revealed the influence of the inter-war 'social hygiene' crusade, occupational therapy and the professional reorientation movement.[20] Relief workers also brought with them pre-war ideas about the 'return to the countryside', which linked a healthy childhood with proximity to nature. They believed that a placement in the countryside could help meet the emotional, physical and psychological needs of DP children. These influences remain largely hidden in the history of the rehabilitation of DPs in the aftermath of the Second World War. Second, this chapter illuminates the fragility of relief workers' prescriptions about the shape of 'proper motherhood' and the functioning nuclear family.[21] It traces how some DPs rejected 'welfare' injunctions in the zone, devising their own ways of rebuilding their lives. The temporary placement of children in sanatorium and children houses caused grave anxieties amongst a number of DP parents and DP children, who found these temporary separations emotionally difficult. Third, by interrogating relief workers' confidence in the 'therapeutic' nature of open-air homes, this chapter uncovers the tensions between the utilitarian (turning DPs into productive future citizens) and recreational (providing soothing and restful activities) roles of rehabilitation, between the disciplinary (controlling DPs' bodies) and empowering nature (encouraging DPs' expression and initiatives) of relief activities.

---

[18] Ivan Jablonka (ed.), *L'enfant Shoah* (Paris: Presses Universitaires de France, 2014); André Rosenberg, *Les enfants dans la Shoah. La déportation des enfants juifs et tsiganes de France* (Paris: Les Editions de Paris, 2013), pp. 435–470.

[19] UNA, UNRRA, S-1021-0085-02, Elise Zach, Informal welfare report, Fribourg, 16 June 1947. Freud's influence on French psychiatry was relatively limited. Elisabeth Roudinesco, *La bataille de cent ans: Histoire de la psychanalyse en France*, vol. 1, 1885–1939 (Paris: Seuil, 1986); Gregory M. Thomas, *Treating the Trauma of the Great War. Soldiers, Civilians and Psychiatry in France, 1914–1940* (Baton Rouge: Louisiana State University Press, 2009), p. 159.

[20] On the history on occupational therapy and rehabilitation, see, for instance, Ana Carden Coyne, 'The Art of Resilience. Veteran Therapy from the Occupational to the Creative, 1914–1945', in Leo Van Bergen and Eric Vermetten (eds.), *The First World War and Health. Rethinking Resilience* (London: Brill, 2020), pp. 39–70.

[21] On the importance of 'motherhood' and persistence of Vichyist familialism in the era of the Liberation see Adler, *Jews and Gender in Liberation France*, pp. 40–49.

## Psychological Approaches to DPs: Sex, Apathy and Immorality in Camp Life

The aftermath of the Second World War witnessed significant development in expert discourses about child trauma and the war's psychological after-effects on DPs.[22] The earliest major study on DPs' psychological problems prepared for UNRRA by an 'Inter-Allied Psychological Study Group' appeared in June 1945. Entitled 'Psychological problems of Displaced Persons', this collaborative venture was led by Dr John Rickman, editor of *The British Journal of Medical Psychology*. Rickman drew on the expertise of international psychiatrists, sociologists and social workers. During the war, Rickman had practiced group therapy with soldiers suffering from breakdown in combat. Other experts, including the Estonian-born psychiatrist and psychotherapist Henry Dicks, had been associated with the Tavistock Clinic in London.[23] These experts constructed an image of DPs as broken individuals suffering from various pathologies, which were thought to arise from the experiences of displacement, including alcoholism, delinquency and promiscuity. For these specialists, 'alcohol thirst' and 'sexual desire' were natural consequences of adult DPs' wartime traumas and 'intolerable mental pain'.[24] The authors of this report warned that 'however great the physical devastation caused by German policy, the moral and psychological disturbance is probably greater'.[25] They insisted on the remedial effects of an ample diet (considering that food is the 'primal token' of emotional security), entertainment, education, the avoidance of boredom (by the cultivation of spontaneity) and the re-establishment of personal care and cleanliness.[26]

This report reflects how the war changed attitudes towards mental health amongst experts. First, it reveals that post-war psychological discourses acquired strong political considerations, for psychologists were captivated by how democracy 'may have to be re-learned'.[27] As Peter Gatrell suggests, the psychological health of adult refugees was at the centre of a broader campaign to cultivate democratic values.[28] These discourses were not entirely new, but

---

[22] Jablonka, *L'enfant-Shoah*, p. 20.
[23] Peter Gatrell, Population displacement and mental health after the Second World War [short version, unpublished]; Pearl King, 'Activities of British Psychoanalysts during the Second World War and the Influence of Their Inter-disciplinary Collaboration on the Development of Psychoanalysis in Great Britain', *International Review of Psycho-Analysis*, vol. 16, no. 1 (1989), pp. 15–33.
[24] Ibid., p. 16.
[25] WL, HA5-4/3, Welfare Division, *Report on Psychological Problems of Displaced Persons*, 1 June 1945, pp. 1–41, 14.
[26] Ibid., pp. 1–41, 34–38.
[27] Ibid.
[28] Gatrell, 'Population Displacement and Mental Health'. We can also see this in Mary Fraser Kirsh, 'Shattered by Mental and Physical Strain'. The treatment and Assimilation

experts' aspiration to 'regenerate' and 'rehabilitate' DPs on such a large scale was unprecedented.[29] Over time these statements about DPs' amorality and disruptive behaviour gave way to a more durable concept of helplessness and apathy, a 'psychosis, which expresses itself in reluctance to face the responsibilities of a normal community life'.[30] Second, this report offers an insight into broader shifting understandings of the psychological health of children, notably the language of maternal deprivation developed by childcare experts during this period. For experts such as Anna Freud, John Bowlby and Donald Winnicott, a happy mother was essential to a child's development.[31] They considered the effects of paternal separation less detrimental than those associated with the separation from mothers.[32] The report reads 'some children ... will have been taken away from their mothers and will have suffered not only the anxiety of that separation and the loss of what little security they have known but will have experienced careful and deliberate efforts to destroy their allegiance to the mother and all that she represents'.[33] For the authors of this report, the solution rested in the recreation of a 'secure family life'.

The views of the Inter-Allied Psychological Study Group on the remedial effects of family were not, however, shared by all experts in Western Europe. In particular, the emphasis on familialism and on the notion that family was the most suitable environment for displaced children's therapy defied consensus.[34] On the one hand, the period of the 1930s to 1950s represented the 'golden age' of marriage and the nuclear family in Western Europe.[35] On the other hand, by separating children from their parents and siblings, setting

---

of 'Defective' Child Survivors' in Henning Borggräfe, Akim Jah, Nina Ritz and Stegffen Jost (eds.), *Rebuilding Lives – Child Survivors and DP Children in the Aftermath of the Holocaust and Forced Labor* (Göttingen: Wallstein Verlag, 2017), pp. 125–141, 127.

[29] Daniel Cohen, 'Un espace domestique d'après-guerre: les camps de personnes déplacées dans l'Allemagne occupée', in Bruno Cabanes and Guillaume Piketty (eds.), *Retour à l'intime au sortir de la guerre* (Paris: Tallandier, 2009), pp. 117–131, 126.

[30] UNHCR, *Final Report on the Ford Foundation Program for Refugees Primarily in Europe* (Geneva: UNHCR, 1958), p. 31. Quoted in Gatrell, *The Making of the Modern Refugee*, p. 104.

[31] See, for instance, Anna Freud and Dorothy T. Burlingham, *War and Children* (London: Medical War Books, 1943).

[32] Sara Fieldston, *Raising the World Child Welfare in the American Century* (Cambridge, MA: Harvard University Press, 2015), p. 65.

[33] WL, HA5-4/3, Welfare Division, *Report on Psychological Problems of Displaced Persons*, p. 10.

[34] Zahra, *Lost Children*.

[35] See, for instance, David I. Kertzer and Marzio Barbahli (eds.), *Family Life in the Twentieth Century* (Yale: Yale University Press, 2003); Claire Langhamer, *The English in Love: The Intimate Story of an Emotional Revolution* (Oxford: Oxford University Press, 2013).

apart husbands and wives, the war threw the ideal of the nuclear family into disarray.[36] For some experts, placement in institutions was a more effective solution for children who had lost their parents.[37] In France, in particular, 'collectivism' gained real traction. A number of education specialists and psychologists defended the therapeutic effects of institutions, rather than that of the nuclear family.[38] Psychoanalysis had made relatively little progress in the French socio-medical professions.[39] As Laura Lee Downs suggests in her comparative work on the evacuation of children in Britain and France, experts bearing psychoanalytically influenced theories about children and their relationship to their families played a far less important role in France than in Britain.[40] Further, though scientific research was carried out about the impact of war on children' psyches in France, most French UNRRA recruits did not receive any formal training that could have exposed them to such ideas.[41]

DP camps in the French zone were not the domains of experts. By 1945, the professionalization of the position of *assistante sociale* (female social worker) was far from complete in France. The legislation governing this new professional corps was only implemented in April 1946. Furthermore, faced with a severe shortage of social workers during the war, French authorities had recruited many staff lacking proper training. Even among those with specialist qualifications, there was a rift between those with 'medico-social' backgrounds and those who had been trained in 'pure social work'.[42] American workers in the zone commented on this 'lack' of expertise. According to Elise Zach, an American worker, few French UNRRA recruits understood the concept of

---

[36] See, for instance, Lindsey Dodd, 'Wartime Rupture and Reconfiguration in French Family Life: Experience and Legacy', *History Workshop Journal*, 88 (2019), pp. 134–152.

[37] Shapira, *The War Inside*, p. 1; Zahra, *Lost Children*, pp. 98–102; Jablonka, *L'enfant Shoah*, p. 59.

[38] See, for example, Daniella Doron, *Jewish Youth and Identity in Postwar France: Rebuilding Family and Nation* (Bloomington: Indiana University Press, 2015), pp. 133–137. On Anna Freud's observation of children of Theresienstadt, see Jablonka, *L'enfant Shoah*, p. 21.

[39] Laura Lee Downs, 'Aurevoir les enfants. Wartime Evacuation and the Politics of Childhood in France and Britain, 1939–1945', *History Workshop Journal*, vol. 82 (2016), pp. 121–150, 130.

[40] Ibid., pp. 121–150.

[41] See, for instance, Gustav Bychowski, 'Neuro-psychiatric Rehabilitation of Children in Post-war Europe', *American OSE Review*, vol. 3, no. 1 (1944), pp. 12–17; G. Heuyer, 'Psychopathologie de l'enfance victime de la guerre', *Sauvegarde*, vol. 17 (1948), pp. 3–30; Simone Marcus-Jeisler, 'Réponse à l'enquête sur les effets psychologiques de la guerre, sur les enfants et jeunes gens en France', *Sauvegarde*, vol. 9 (1947), pp. 3–18.

[42] Henri Pascal, *La construction de l'identité professionnelle des assistantes sociales. L'association nationale des assistantes sociales (1944–1050)* (Paris: Presses de l'EHESP, 2012), pp. 23–24.

welfare and the psychological dimension of rehabilitation.[43] She identified three main obstacles that hampered the development of the UNRRA programme. One was the scarcity of material and financial resources. Another was the shortage of personnel trained in what she called the 'modern concept of welfare'.[44] The third was the lack of agreement between relief workers of differing cultures and nationalities about the objectives sought. In Zach's eyes, '[a] considerable percentage of welfare personnel had nurses' training, very little knowledge of sociology and even less of psychology. American methods of casework and group-work were, on the whole, quite unknown'.[45] According to her, French relief workers were uninterested in the psychological dimensions of relief work, preferring to focus on providing material assistance to DPs: '[t]he main emphasis was upon concrete services and material help, the distribution of supplies'.[46]

Zach's observation reflects the discrepancy between differing Allied methods and visions of relief work, some of which drew on current psychological and psychoanalytic theories, while others remained influenced by older methods of relief work. Evidence from the archives complicates Zach's impression: her French colleagues might have understood 'rehabilitation' differently, but they did not solely focus on the distribution of supplies. As in the other zones, the French approach to rehabilitation was concerned with the reconstruction of families. Despite important material shortages, relief workers strove to retrain DP fathers to care *about* their children (breadwinning) and DP mothers *for* their children.[47] They insisted that DPs should conform to particular domestic arrangements and gendered norms, even if they were not influenced by psychoanalytically influenced theories about children and the nuclear family.

## The Fragile 'Nuclear Family'

The re-creation of a family life and of a real or imagined normality after the war was as important in DP camps as it was in other European countries.[48]

---

[43] UNA, UNRRA, S-1021-0085-02, Elise Zach, Informal welfare report, Fribourg, 16 June 1947.
[44] Ibid.
[45] Ibid.
[46] Ibid.
[47] UNA, S-0433-0001-01, Medical Officer Team 579 à Monsieur le Général-Médecin J. des Cilleuls, 25 October 1946; S-0433-0002-08, De la participation des Nurses UNRRA à l'éducation des mères de famille, August 1946.
[48] On the place of the family in the reconstruction of post-war Europe Robert Moeller, *Protecting Motherhood. Women and the Politics of Postwar West Germany* (Berkeley: University of California Press, 1993); Dagmar Herzog, 'Desperately Seeking Normality', Richard Bessel and Dirk Schumann (eds.), *Life after Death* (Cambridge: Cambridge

Many DPs and relief workers alike believed that the road to reconstruction passed through the nuclear family. However, relief workers' approaches to family were informed by specific transformations in thinking about parenthood and childhood occurring in the French domestic setting during and after the war. Research into family life and youth in France has demonstrated that the years after the Second World War were marked by deep social and cultural transformation in the ways a number of French pedagogues, social workers and psychologists thought about the proper shape of family, motherhood and fatherhood.[49] The Liberation of France was a time of reconstruction, but also of profound crises and perturbations. The young occupied a central place in the social policies and political imaginaries of post-war France. They represented both a resource to heal the 'wounds of the past' and an asset to rebuild the nation's future.[50] For many politicians and social commentators, reforming the educational system and transforming French families were essential to France's national renewal and the reconstruction of French humanist and democratic ideals.[51]

Changing moral norms about the 'proper' shape of family informed to some extent relief workers' views of DPs' domestic arrangements. The defeat of June 1940, collapse of the Third Republic and experiences of Nazi occupation led to new understandings of 'dissociated families', 'deviant' behaviours and important changes in the control of young male and female delinquents within the criminal justice system. In February 1945, the reform of the French juvenile justice system, which centred on re-education ('protection, assistance, surveillance and education') rather than punishment reflected a profound transformation of the dominant romantic view of childhood as a time of innocence.[52]

---

University Press, 2003), pp. 161-192; Pat Thane, 'Family Life and "Normality" in Postwar British Culture', in Bessel, Schuman (ed.), *Life after Death*, pp. 193-210; On the importance of 'motherhood' in DP camps see Baumel, 'DPs, Mothers and Pioneers', pp. 99-110; Grossmann, 'Trauma, Memory and Motherhood', pp. 215-239; Zahra, *Lost Children*.

[49] See, for example, Sarah Fishman, *From Vichy to the Sexual Revolution* (Oxford: Oxford University Press, 2017); Ludivine Bantigny, *Le plus bel âge? Jeunes et jeunesse en France de l'aube des 'Trentes Glorieuses' à la guerre d'Algérie* (Paris: Fayard, 2007); Richard Ivan Jobs, *Riding the New Wave. Youth and the Rejuvenation of France after the Second World War* (Stanford: Stanford University Press, 2007); Shannon Fogg, *Stealing Home. Looting, Restitution, and Reconstructing Jewish Lives in France, 1942-1947* (Oxford: Oxford University Press, 2017), esp. chapter 5.

[50] Ivan Jobs, *Riding the New Wave*; Bantigny, *Le plus bel âge?*.

[51] See, for instance, Chapman, *France's Long Reconstruction. In Search of the Modern Republic*, pp. 109-163; Jean-François Muracciole, *Les enfants de la défaite. La Résistance, l'éducation et la culture* (Paris: Presses de Sciences Po, 1998), pp. 166-173.

[52] Sarah Fishman, *La bataille de l'enfance. Délinquance juvenile et justice des mineurs en France pendant la Seconde Guerre mondiale* (Rennes: Presses Universitaires de Rennes, 2008), pp. 245-292; Bantigny, *Le Plus Bel Age?*, pp. 173-175; Anne Thomazeau, 'La clôture en question dans les internats de rééducation pour filles (1945-1975)', Clio.

And yet, these reforms took time to be implemented and, for years, juvenile courts remained a form of repressive justice, centred on surveillance and imprisonment.[53] Further, 'maternalism' continued to have a stronghold in post-war France. For many policy-elites, French women remained responsible for the well-being of the nation essentially in their role as 'mother' and, the home continued to be seen as women's ideal place.[54] By contrast, fathers were still considered as the main breadwinner and head of the family, even though they were not regarded 'as absolute or distant rulers' anymore.[55] During the war, the Vichy regime had reaffirmed fathers' legal and moral sovereignty in the family. Yet, the regime's propaganda had glorified motherhood and the absence of many fathers had undermined father's authority.[56] According to Sarah Fishman, in the late 1940s, the vision of father's authority became less absolute: from a status, fatherhood became progressively understood as a relationship.[57] These changing normative discourses shaped relief workers' assessments of DPs' domestic settings.

Despite an abundance of marriages and births amongst DPs and the faith placed in them by DP elites and relief workers' alike, the archives of the zone suggest great anxieties about the norms of intimacy and domestic life prevalent amongst the DP population.[58] In demographic terms, the post-war years were certainly a golden age for marriage in DP camps. The majority of DPs were between 18 and 45 years old in the French zone, and many aspired to create or rebuild a family.[59] In Lebach, for instance, on 30 April 1945 alone, seventeen couples were married. According to UNRRA welfare officer, 'there would have been more marriages but almost immediately after this date the Russians were instructed that there must be no more marriages except in special circumstances'.[60] In Kaiserslautern, similar problems arose, 'five Russian girls who wished to marry Italian men were refused permission by

---

*Femmes, Genre, Histoire* [online], 26 (2007), last consulted on 25 September 2019. http://journals.openedition.org/clio/6292.

[53] See, for example, Véronique Blanchard, '"Mauvaises filles": portraits de la déviance féminine juvénile (1945–1958)', PhD thesis, Université de Poitiers (2016), p. 38; Ivan Jablonka, *Les Enfants de la République. L'intégration des jeunes de 1789 à nos jours* (Paris: Seuil, 2010), pp. 209, 210.

[54] Adler, *Jews and Gender in Liberation France*, pp. 30–68.

[55] Fishman, *From Vichy to the Sexual Revolution*, p. 14.

[56] Stromberg Childers, *Fathers, Family and the State in France*.

[57] Fishman, *From Vichy to the Sexual Revolution*, p. 20.

[58] DP young were at the heart of the welfare programme and parenting was invested with a great significance. See, for instance, UNA, UNRRA, S-0438-0005-02, Rapport du service 'welfare' sur le district nord de la zone, R. le Goff, 11 April 1946.

[59] 3/5 of the population was aged between 18 and 45. PDR6/869, Note pour M. Rivain, Directeur du Cabinet de l'ambassade de France [undated].

[60] UNRRA, S-0436-0059-07, Lebach Assembly Centre welfare, Miss Dingle, 17 June 1945.

the Russian Liaison Officers and they were taken to Homburg to be returned to Russia against their wishes'.[61] In addition to this rush of marriage, a veritable 'baby boom' occurred in the French zone. In 1946 and 1947, an estimated monthly average of 120 births were registered in the French zone, the peak being reached in May 1946 with 169 births.[62] In 1948, the birth rate amounted to 23 for 1,000 in the French zone.[63] This 'baby boom' represented an important facet of the transition from the male-dominated world of wartime POW camps to the mixed environment of the DP camps. These spates of marriages, pregnancies and births also symbolized an affirmation of life after years of deprivation and fears. As Atina Grossmann suggests, for Jewish survivors, in particular, giving birth was an act of symbolic revenge.[64] It represented the reconstruction of collective and individual identity in the aftermath of the Holocaust. Katarzyna Nowak demonstrates that marriage also constituted an important aspect of the transition from war to peace for Catholic Polish DPs. Marriages were a mean to cleanse the Polish nation in exile. In this context, DP elites insisted on marriages within the Polish catholic community and opposed fiercely mixed union, even though for many Polish DP women 'marriage with a foreigner [particularly British or American soldiers] served as a ticket to a better life' abroad.[65] Some 'marriages' were clearly regarded as more valuable than others, some domestic arrangements more beneficial than others.

Welfare discussion amongst DP religious elites and relief workers reflected both the strength of the ideals of the nuclear family and anxieties about its fragility. Relief workers often feared that the war had profoundly altered motherly predispositions and gendered codes of respectable behaviour, for DP women had found themselves confronted too young to the 'difficulties of life'.[66] Concerns about DPs' maternal abilities were often complemented by doubts about their sexual morality. Welfare officers reported the same errors and misconception 'everywhere' and commented at length on the inability of young DP mothers to care for their children. They were fixated on controlling the 'deviant' DP women and calming DPs' excessive 'erotic urges', by placing

[61] UNRRA, S-0436-0059-04, C. J. Taylor, Director, John N. Wiley, Welfare Officer, Report UNRRA Team 2, Kaiserslautern, 8 July 1945.
[62] HCRFA, *Sept ans en faveur des personnes déplacées*, p. 35.
[63] PDR6/869, Note pour M. Rivain, Directeur du Cabinet de l'ambassade de France [undated].
[64] Grossmann, *Jews, Germans, and Allies*, p. 196.
[65] Nowak, 'Voices of Revival', p. 154.
[66] UNA, UNRRA, S-0438-0005-02, Rapport du service 'welfare' sur le district nord de la zone, R. le Goff, 11 April 1946; UNA, UNRRA, S-0438-0005-02, Report of Welfare Officer, Southern District, 8 June 1946, p. 5.

single mothers in collective institution, developing anti-venereal treatments and re-clothing DP mothers.[67] UNRRA reports reflected the continued importance of religious faith and morality amongst French relief workers, many of whom came from the traditions of 'social Catholicism' and the 'popular education' movement.[68]

DP religious elites also feared that conditions in camps undermined Christian marriage and familial values. For instance, the DP secretary of the Catholic Church for Polish DPs Ignacy Walczewski published a book on the 'crisis of Polish family' as an institution.[69] Drawing on priests' reports, he lamented the rise of immoral behaviour, bigamy and 'false union', arguing that the 'extreme regulation' of everyday life within camps, as well as the absence of privacy, contributed to exacerbate a crisis that had been triggered by the war and Nazi labour policies.[70] Instead of finding joy and companionship in Christian marriage, too many DPs seemed to seek pursuit of sexual pleasure for its own sake. Despite the high birth-rate amongst the DP population, Walczewski expressed deep concerns about the use of contraception and abortion in camps.[71] Both DP elites and relief workers drew heavily on Christian faith and values to 'regulate' DP mothers' life.

Enforcing traditional gender norms and Christian values was not an easy task in DP camps. While women were expected to look after their young children, they seemed absolutely ignorant to relief workers about infant's feeding, hygiene and clothing.[72] Relief workers regretted that too many sick children were presented to medical doctors too late.[73] Relief workers also deplored the numbers of illegal abortions, carried out by German doctors outside of the camps.[74] Abortion was almost unanimously condemned by relief workers in the French zone. Unlike in Britain where abortion was allowed 'for the purpose [...] of preserving the life of the mother', it remained

---

[67] Jean François Lae, *Une fille en correction Lettres à son assistante sociale (1952-1965)* (Paris : CNRS Editions, 2018), p. 32.
[68] Geneviève Perrot, 'Les savoirs en service social avant 1950', *Vie Sociale*, vol. 3, no. 3 (2008), pp. 33–43.
[69] Ignacy Walczewski, *Destin tragique des polonais déportés en Allemagne. La crise de la famille polonaise dans les camps de personnes déplacées en Allemagne. Causes, conséquences, espoirs* (Paris: Hosianum, 1951), p. 18. In the French zone, Walczeski visited the DP camp of Homburg and Landstuhl.
[70] Walczewski, *Destin tragique des polonais déportés en Allemagne*, p. 59.
[71] Ibid., p. 133.
[72] UNA, UNRRA, S-0433-0002-08, De la participation des Nurses UNRRA à l'éducation des mères de famille, August 1946.
[73] UNA, UNRRA, S-0438-0005-01, O. Despeigne, Rapport sur ma visite au team de Horb et au détachement de Freudenstadt, 30 April 1946.
[74] UNA, S-0433-0001-05, Confidentiel, A. M. Grange, Assistant Field Supervisor à Monsieur le Général, Directeur Général de l'UNRRA, 10 August 1946.

a crime and was severely punished in France.[75] In their reports, relief workers displayed very little awareness of the anxieties that pregnancy and giving birth could trigger amongst women, who might have repressed in their unconsciousness complex and non-communicable stories of prostitution, rape or 'utilitarian sex' in wartime.[76]

Pregnancy and childbirth could pose significant challenges to some DP women (and men), including feelings of guilt, nightmares, a heightened sense of vulnerability. Some DPs feared that they were unable to protect their child.[77] Relief workers noted that a number of DP women struggled to fulfil their 'motherly duties', due to manic depression and suicidal thought.[78] It is, however, difficult to assess from UNRRA and the PDR archives how far relief workers understood the concerns of DP women and men seeking to make sense of traumatic wartime experiences and struggling to envisage parenthood. In these archives, we see little traces of the tenderness, love and empathy that might have existed amongst relief workers and DPs.[79] On the contrary, a reading of relief workers' reports and correspondence suggests that rehabilitation seems to have been understood essentially as a 'disciplinary' and 'therapeutic' project aimed at reinstating pre-war social norms of 'good motherhood' that DP women had allegedly 'forgotten' during the war.

In this context, the preservation of a gendered binary of work remained important. DP mothers were perceived as the sole provider for the personal care of their infants.[80] Training for DP mothers thus included courses on how to take care of a house, prepare a meal, make a budget and take care of clothes.[81] UNRRA Health education focused essentially on women, who were deemed responsible to ensure that their husbands and children lived healthily (Fig. 4.1 and 4.2). The meaning of motherhood was mainly fixed and framed as a subordinate and dependent role.

---

[75] Anne-Marie Sohn, 'Le corps sexué', in Alain Corbin, Jean-Jacques Courtine and Georges Vigarello (eds.), *Hitoire du Corps* (Paris: Seuil, 2006), vol. 3, pp. 93–127, 116; Stephen Brooke, 'A New World for Women? Abortion Law Reform in Britain during the 1930s', *The American Historical Review*, vol. 106, no. 2 (2001), pp. 431–459.

[76] Atina Grossmann, 'La reconstruction individuelle comme projet collectif: le corps, la famille, la nation et la quête de 'normalité' chez les rescapés juifs de l'après-guerre en Allemagne occupée', in Bruno Cabanes and Guillaume Piketty, *Retour à l'intime au sortir de la guerre* (Paris: Tallandier, 2009), pp. 291–305, 296.

[77] Margarete Myers Feinstein, *Holocaust Survivors in Postwar Germany, 1945–1957* (Cambridge: Cambridge University Press, 2009), pp. 107–158.

[78] UNA, S-0433-0001-01, Medical Officer Team 579 à Monsieur le Général-Médecin J. des Cilleuls, 25 October 1946.

[79] Lae, *Une fille en correction*.

[80] UNA, UNRRA, S-0438-0001-01, Welfare Bulletin No. 1, 5 February 1946.

[81] UNA, UNRRA, S-0438-0005-05, Rapport sur l'école de formation sociale de Gutach, Miss Zach.

THE 'BROKEN' DP                213

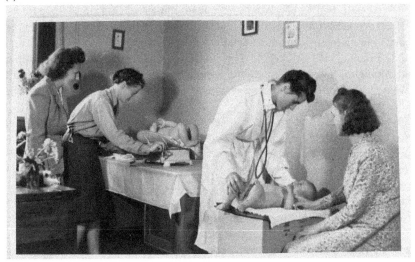

Fig. 4.1 (a and b) UNA, UNRRA, S-1021-0085-04,
Visit for young mothers, medical centre, Freiburg.

Retraining mothers to care for their children was carried out through a mixture of 'educative' and 'coercive' measures. Faced with raising infant mortality and the augmentation of illegal abortion in the camp of Mulheim, the UNRRA Medical Director decided that 'any woman that did not signal a sick child would receive a severe penalty'.[82] Most doctors deemed that children's health had to be placed under their control, even against the parents' will.[83] A special house ('*maison des mères*') was created in Lorettoberg, in the area of Freiburg, to welcome 'mentally-retarded women' ('*femmes débiles*') and their infants.[84] While UNRRA Director advocated the use of severe penalties in Mulheim, a more sympathetic approach was taken elsewhere. Pregnant women were often encouraged to attend pre-natal consultation through the distribution of extra food rations.[85] UNRRA collaborated with the Polish Red Cross, who organized visits and check-up for young and vulnerable pregnant women.[86] Polish DP religious elites viewed Polish woman in highly conservative terms, as 'nurturer of the nation'.[87] Public talks ('*Causeries de puériculture*') were also organized across the zone, educating DP women about babies' hygiene, diets, vaccination and illnesses.[88] These conferences drew heavily on practices elaborated in the inter-war period, when pro-natalist and educational films such as *La Future maman* (1925) were presented to French women, considered as 'guarantor of the health of the nation'.[89] At the end of these causeries, DP women were often rewarded with a mug of hot chocolate and a couple of biscuits.[90]

DP fathers were marginalized in UNRRA's programmes. Staffed almost exclusively by women, some of whom lived outside marriage and the domestic model, these causeries were aimed at providing both assistance and moral

---

[82] UNA, S-0433-0001-01, Zone Medical Officer Des Cilleuls à Général de Corps d'Armée Lenclud, 16 May 1946.
[83] UNA, S-0433-0001-03, Les nouvelles voies sur les notions du rachitisme [Balingen, undated].
[84] UNA, UNRRA, S-1021-0085-04, Médecin Général des Cilleuls, Exposé général de l'organisation et du fonctionnement du service médical UNRRA en zone Française, du 1er décembre 1946 au 1er mars 1947.
[85] UNA, S-0433-0001-02, Rapport d'inspection médicale, Monsieur Delrieu, Médecin Inspecteur Mobile, 17 May 1946.
[86] UNA, S-0438-0002-06, Programme général de travail fixé par la Croix Rouge Polonaise (Délégation de Schramberg) pour le mois de juillet 1946. On the importance of the inter-war Polish eugenics movement within the Polish DP population, see Nowak, 'Voices of Revival', p. 54.
[87] Nowak, 'Voices of Revival', p. 172.
[88] UNA, UNRRA, S-0433-0002-08, De la participation des nurses UNRRA à l'éducation des mères de famille.
[89] Valérie Vignaux, 'L'éducation sanitaire par le cinéma dans l'entre-deux-guerres en France', *Sociétés et Représentations*, vol. 28, no. 2 (2009), pp. 67–85.
[90] UNA, UNRRA, S-0433-0002-08, I. de Witt, Biberach, 16 September 1946. This unearths interesting parallels with the work of female nuns in the French colonies, such as '*l'oeuvre des fiancées*', aimed at preparing women to become faithful wives and caring mothers. Jean-Marie Bouron, 'Dominées ou dominantes ? Les Sœurs Blanches dans l'ambivalence des logiques d'autorité (Haute-Volta et Gold Coast, 1920–1960)', *Histoire, Monde et cultures religieuses*, vol. 30, no. 2 (2014), pp. 51–73.

guidance to DP mothers.[91] UNRRA training drew on traditional languages of femininity. This emphasis on motherhood and the promotion of breast-feeding had its roots in the eighteenth century and Jean-Jacques Rousseau's sentimental view of motherhood.[92] The Rousseauist feminine ideal of women as virtuous, faithful and self-sacrificing gained real traction in the nineteenth century, when successive French governments provided considerable financial and institutional backing to maternal societies.[93] DP women faced powerful demands that they conform to these expectations of gender roles. The role and position of single mothers in UNRRA welfare programme is illuminating here, as it reveals the prevalence of older views about respectable femininity. While UNRRA was often heralded as a clear break from the past, relief practices towards single mothers continued to draw heavily on faith-based rhetoric and religious values.

The *fille-mère* ('girl mothers') issue was a common theme in welfare reports.[94] By 1945, having children outside legal marriage had become accepted by a broader spectrum of French society, including among the upper classes. In her research on paternity outside legal marriage, Rachel Fuchs suggests that France witnessed significant changes in sexual mores and attitudes towards single mothers in the early twentieth century. While social commentators and politicians continued to hold up marriage as the ideal, they increasingly acknowledged voluntary heterosexual relationships outside of marriage.[95] Consequently, the representation of women with natural children changed. Women's sexual independence became more acceptable, as long as she only had one sexual partner and was a good mother.[96] This was followed by a change in terminology and a greater reluctance to use the disparaging term *fille-mère*.[97] In the French zone, however, relief workers drew in significant ways on discourses that pre-dated this change and continued to use the term *fille-mère* to designate single mothers. In Landstuhl, the UNRRA Welfare Officer was the wife of the former head of the Civil Cabinet of Marshall Lyautey in Morocco. She deplored the total absence of morality in the camps and the large number of *filles-mères*.[98] Some relief workers seemed surprised that many young expecting mothers were ready to keep their baby

---

[91] Bouron, 'Dominées ou dominantes?.
[92] Rachel Fuchs, *Contested Paternity: Constructing Families in Modern France* (Baltimore: Hopkins University Press, 2008), p. 8; Christine Adams, *Poverty, Charity and Motherhood. Maternal Societies in Nineteenth-Century France* (Champaign: University of Illinois Press, 2010), p. 6.
[93] Adams, *Poverty, Charity and Motherhood*, p. 5.
[94] UNRRA, S-0438-0005-02, Report of Welfare Officer, Southern District, 8 June 1946.
[95] Fuchs, *Contested Paternity*, p. 11.
[96] Ibid., p. 4.
[97] Ibid., p. 174.
[98] UNRRA, S-0438-0008-04, Vatin-Pérignon, Camp Polonais de Landstuhl [undated].

and did not seem to fear public opinion towards them.[99] This reveals both the persistence of conservative social ethics, but also the fact that DPs resisted relief workers' unwelcome interference in their lives. For DPs, camp life could offer not only romantic and sexual opportunities, but also a chance to break away or reconfigure previous family arrangements.[100] For relief workers infused with Christian values, however, the 'saving' of single mothers required finding a husband. Seeking a husband was certainly considered as the only socially acceptable solution to correct the 'sin' committed by these women.[101]

Relief workers remained mainly interested in fathers' presence or absence, rather than the role they played within family life. DP men were stereotyped as breadwinners and considered as not very involved in the everyday care of children. They were nevertheless expected to be interested in their children's future.[102] Some UNRRA Directors explicitly reported fathers who deviated from this norm. In Gutach, for instance, the UNRRA Director provided a negative evaluation of the couple Eminian, using a paternalistic pronoun to describe the man ('mon Eminian') and his relationship with his wife. According to him, their personal life constituted a 'vaudeville'. Eminian blamed his wife for being unfaithful. Incapable of finding an 'appropriate solution' with her, Eminian asked the UNRRA Director to withdraw her DP assistance and treat her as a 'German' national fed on German ration card rather than as an Allied DP, a request that the UNRRA Director refused. Desperate, Eminian attempted suicide in allegedly swallowing sulphuric acid and cutting his wrists. The UNRRA director did not believe that his intentions of killing himself were real. Soon after this incident, the couple was reunited. Yet, the UNRRA Director expressed some concerns about their ability to raise their daughter. According to him, Mrs Eminian was 'a woman of easy virtue, known in the surrounding for her promiscuous and scandalous affairs'. While he refused to withdraw her DP right, he forced her to move from the UNRRA hotel Sonne and removed the child from their custody, considering that they did not have the necessary 'parenting skills' to ensure the education of a child.[103] This story exemplifies relief workers' attempts to propose a new organization of intimate life and control of domestic sphere.

---

[99] UNA, UNRRA, S-0438-0005-02, Roberts, Rapport sur ma visite à Mulheim, 13 April 1946; Also see Rapport sur ma visite au team de Ravensburg, 13 May 1946.
[100] On this aspect of refugee camps in another context, see Jordanna Bailkin, *Unsettled. Refugee Camps and the Making of Multicultural Britain* (Oxford: Oxford University Press, 2018), p. 132.
[101] Lae, *Une fille en correction*, p. 71.
[102] This was also the case amongst DP elite. On the role of DP father, see Walczewski, *Destin tragique des polonais déportés en Allemagne*, p. 130.
[103] UNRRA, S-0421-0035-01, Durand à Directeur General UNRRA, à l'attention de Mr G. Sebille, 30 September 1946.

In the pro-natalist culture of post-1945 France, behaving responsibly towards children was considered as mark of manhood and male virility.[104] Scholars have argued that fathers' authority and power declined in the interwar years, witnessed a brief recrudescence in the 1940s and decreased again after the 1960s.[105] During the Nazi occupation of France, the absence of French POWs was regarded as harmful and blamed as the cause for juvenile delinquency. As Kristen Stromberg Childers suggests, the Vichy regime had represented the culmination of 'reactionary measures to reinstate fatherhood as the litmus test of good citizenship'.[106] According to her, the democratic impulse of the Liberation signalled the end of the age of the *père de famille*, with his 'hard mentality'.[107] As the social order anchored in the patriarchal family eroded, fathers were expected to display more tenderness towards their children.[108] This shifting understanding of family's structure based on emotional relationships originated in the period of the First World War.[109] Such transformation is, nonetheless, difficult to discern in the writings and prescriptions of relief workers in the French zone. What we see, instead, is the essentially conservative basis of UNRRA welfare prescriptions, based on the ideological importance and responsibility of motherhood rather than parenthood.

Despite the emphasis placed on retraining DPs' parents to care for their children, relief workers were prepared to undermine their authority and agency. The political culture of French republicanism was based on the idea that children were 'public beings' with a life outside of families.[110] An analysis of the placement of children in centres located in the Black Forest is particularly revealing here. The majority of French relief workers were confident that placing pre-tubercular DP children in therapeutic centres in the Black Forest would help children restore their health and develop strength and autonomy. Yet, the temporary placement of children in sanatorium and children houses caused grave anxieties amongst a number of DP parents and children.[111] In

---

[104] Fuchs, *Contested Paternity*, p. 172.
[105] Ibid., p. 4.
[106] Stromberg Childers, *Fathers, Families and the State in France*, p. 3.
[107] Ibid., p. 191.
[108] Fuchs, *Contested Paternity*, p. 241.
[109] Manon Pignot, *Allons enfants de la patrie. Génération Grande Guerre* (Paris: Seuil, 2012).
[110] Downs, 'Aurevoir les enfants'.
[111] In Landstuhl, DP parents refused to permit their tubercular children to travel by train to infant sanitary centres. In this case, UNRRA authorities accepted to provide an alternative mode of transport. UNA, UNRRA, S-0433-0002-03, Général Des Cilleuls à Monsieur l'Assistant Director, Department of Field Operations, Compte rendu des inspections des 12 et 13 mars 1947, 18 March 1947.

children's houses, some children worried that their families would leave Germany without them. In the Haldenhof children house, for instance, 'two of the nicest children' fled and were found in a nearby station, having purchased their train tickets on their own.[112] The evidence suggests that children were not alone in finding the separation emotionally difficult. In Haldenhof, parents worried that their children were beaten up.[113] In other areas, they walked kilometres to get the opportunity to see their children on Sunday. Exacerbated by such visits, which disrupted centres' life, some relief workers forbade them. This did not prevent other visits to occur.[114] Despite DP parents' anxieties, relief workers had faith in the profound benefits associated with the placement of children in the countryside and their ability to 'positively' transform DPs' ways of thinking and being. The treatment of DP children in the black forest open-air homes thus raises wider questions about the 'therapeutic' or 'coercive' nature of rehabilitation in the French zone.

### Nature Therapy: The Reconstruction of Healthy Bodies and Minds in Open-Air Homes in the Black Forest

In the aftermath of Nazi occupation, with widespread undernourishment among French children and newly rising rates of infectious diseases and infant mortality, the hygienic virtues of open-air schools gained great appeal.[115] German health institutions were requisitioned by the French military government and transformed into open-air schools for both French and DPs children alike, aged between 6 and 13 years old. These requisitions reveal the convergence between the solutions adopted for French and DP children. Here, the projects of reconstructing DP healthy bodies collided with the remaking of healthy young French bodies. Preserving and reinforcing the health of French children, whose immune systems were deemed to be weaker after years of restrictions and bad conditions of hygiene and housing, was seen as an essential prerequisite for the reconstruction of the nation.[116] This project drew

---

[112] UNA, UNRRA, S-0433-0002-01, Lettre de Mlle Chanoine à Mr Boudot-Lamotte, Haldenhof, 6 September 1946.

[113] UNA, UNRRA, S-0433-0002-01, H. P. M. J Boudot-Lamotte à Médecin Général J. des Cilleuls, 7 September 1946.

[114] In other cases, parents removed their children, convinced that their children did not receive sufficient food rations. UNA, UNRRA, S-0433-0001-07, Medical Officer Team 589 à Médecin Général Les Cilleuls, 16 March 1946.

[115] On surmortality of the infant population in France, see Gilles Ragache, *Les enfants de la guerre. Vivre, survivre et jouer en France, 1939–1949* (Paris: Perrin, 1997), pp. 241–242.

[116] UNA, UNRRA, S-0433-0001-07, De Fos, questions médicales, 11 February 1947.

heavily on inter-war social hygiene methods. Outdoor cures were an essential component of preventive social medicine for children in the preliminary stages of tuberculosis prior to the war.[117]

Since the end of the nineteenth century, concerns about tuberculous children were part of broader concerns about national degeneration in France, tuberculosis being often associated with bad housing and low morality.[118] In the French zone, all DP children were tested for tuberculosis by using Clemens von Pirquet cutaneous tests. These tests demonstrated the presence of the bacillus but did not mean that the disease was active. Those who had a positive response were then screened with X-Ray and sent to sanatoria. Treatments differed from one establishment to another, but the main principle was the same everywhere: spending as much time in the open air as possible.[119] The Black Forest, largely unaffected by aerial bombings, was an ideal setting, which was neither too populated nor too close to a major city. It became the site of healing and re-education in the open air.

The requisition of around forty rest and holiday homes (*Maisons d'enfants*) in the Black Forest reflected the persistence of educators and doctors' confidence in the benefits of open-air life and sun cures. Most of these houses, which were given new names of flowers, trees, animals and birds, welcomed French children from industrial cities such as Paris, Lille and Marseilles.[120] Instructions were provided by young French teachers, animated by the principles of the 'pedagogy of nature'. Three houses were dedicated to sick, unaccompanied or disabled DP children.[121] *Air et soleil* (Fresh air and sun), for instance, was a preventorium situated at 879 m heights near Gutach. It welcomed DP children (aged 6–13) living in Northern District DP camps and who were in generally bad health and at risk but not clearly 'tubercular', the so-called pre-tubercular.[122]

---

[117] Christian W. McMillen, *Discovering Tuberculosis. A Global History, 1900 to the Present* (New Haven, London: Yale University Press, 2015), pp. 18-19; Helen Bynum, *Spitting Blood. The History of Tuberculosis* (Oxford: Oxford University Press, 2012), pp. 128-159.
[118] Bynum, *Spitting Blood*, p. 166.
[119] Ibid., p. 138; Sandra Stanley Holton, 'To Live "Through One's Own Powers": British Medicine, Tuberculosis and "Invalidism" in the Life of Alice Clark (1874-1934)', *Journal of Women's History*, vol. 11 (1999), pp. 75-96.
[120] André Catteaux, 'Au berceau du centre de formation des maîtres des écoles de plein air (1945-1949)', in Châtelet, Lerch and Luc (eds.), *L'école de plein air*, pp. 296-304.
[121] UNA, UNRRA, S-0438-0006-02, Elise Zach, Relief services, Welfare Division, Monthly report, August 1946; Relief service, Welfare Division, Rapport mensuel de juillet 1946.
[122] UNA, UNRRA, S-0438-0006-01, R. Le Goff, District Welfare Officer à Monsieur Roquet, Field Supervisor, 22/163/208, 3 May 1946; S-0433-0002-01, Dr Bourget pour Médecin Général des Cilleuls, 18 April 1946.

Fig. 4.2   UNRRA, S-0433-0002-01, Maison d'enfants d'Haldenhof, Überlingen.[123]

In the Black Forest, days consisted of a blend of fresh air and sun, graduated respiratory exercise, ample diet and compulsory rest, on a blanket in the open air if the weather allowed it.[124] The program was not limited to hygienic practices, but also involved gardening for children and a religious service on Sunday. Relief workers commented on the difficulties in providing enough games for children.[125] Two houses were created for unaccompanied children, coming for the most part from German institutions and families, in Munderkingen and in Unterhausen.[126] Unterhausen was a beautiful villa, but according to the welfare field director, it was austere and lacked colours, flowers, art pieces and toys.[127] By June 1947, an estimated 783 children had been treated in the various sanitary centres of the zone (Fig. 4.3).[128]

[123] UNRRA, S-0433-0002-01, Maison d'enfants d'Haldenhof, Überlingen.
[124] UNA, S-0433-0002-01, Note de service relative au fonctionnement du préventorium UNRRA de Mooswaldkopf; S-0438-0006-01, Maison de repos pour enfants DPs de 6 à 13 ans située à Gutach, S-0433-0002-01, Le General Lenclud, Alimentation des Centres Sanitaires Infantiles, 15 January 1947.
[125] UNA, S-0433-0002-01, Ch. Pourchet, Field Supervisor, Rapport d'inspection du centre d'enfants de Schweigmatt, 1 October 1946.
[126] UNA, UNRRA, S-0433-0001-07, General de Corps d'Armée Lenclud à Administrateur Général Laffon, Alimentation des Centres Infantiles, 14 April 1947.
[127] UNA, UNRRA, S-0438-0005-02, Rapport, Reutlingen, O. Despeignes, 23 June 1946.
[128] UNA, UNRRA, S-0433-0002-01, Statistique des Centres Sanitaires Infantiles, 30 June 1947.

Fig. 4.3 UNA, UNRRA, S-1021-0085-04,
UNRRA Team 572, The children's meal, Centre Sanitaire Infantile, Mooswaldkopf [undated].

These open-air homes epitomized the influence of climate therapies, based on Hippocratic ideas about the influence of environment, the stars, air and water, and the development of naturism in inter-war medical circles in France.[129] Nature has long played a role in Western medical models of rehabilitation, both for physical and mental wounds. Since the nineteenth century, gardens were used as 'visual therapies' in psychiatric asylums in England.[130] Gardening was also routinely assigned to shell-shock patients in military hospitals during the First World War.[131] As Ana Carden-Coyne

---

[129] Jean-Christophe Coffin, 'Paul-Félix Armand-Delille. Vertu thérapeutique du milieu et action sociale en faveur de l'enfance', in Anne-Marie Châtelet, Dominique Lerch and Jean-Noël Luc (eds.), L'école de plein air: une experience pédagogique et architecturale dans l'Europe du XXe siècle (Paris: Recherches, 2003), pp. 222–229; Sylvain Villaret and Jean-Philippe Saint-Martin, 'L'influence du naturisme sur les écoles de plein air en France (1900–1939), pp. 230–237.

[130] Clare Hickman, Therapeutic Landscapes: A History of English Hospital Gardens since 1800 (Manchester: Manchester University Press, 2013).

[131] Ana Carden-Coyne, 'Butterfly Touch: Rehabilitation, Nature and the Haptic Arts in the First World War', Critical Military Studies, Published online First (June 2019), pp. 1–27.

Fig. 4.4 UNRRA, S-0421-0023-09, 18 April 1946, Team 572, Gutach. 'Today is Thursday. The Polish school is unfortunately closed, but we had the luck to surprise the young pupils, who, under the direction of their Polish teacher are learning gardening. These out-of-school occupation seem to please them very much.'

demonstrates, turning to nature, in particular gardening activities helped transforming horror into recovery.[132] It diverted attention from the physical and emotional pain of the war. In inter-war French Indochina, gardening was also used to inculcate the values of hard work and self-discipline and transform Vietnamese patients into productive subjects. As Claire Edington and Hans Pols note, the 'act of gardening [...] was thought to yield valuable results on account of its physical and outdoor qualities, as well as for the benign impact of repeated movements on the motor skills of the brain'.[133] In many camps of the French zone, gardening was also used to both re-train and sooth the mental and physical pains of both DP adults and children (Figs. 4.4 and 4.5).

French relief workers not only advocated gardening as therapy, but also recommended the transfer of some DP children to the Black Forest. Since the early days of the Third Republic, the 'transfer to the countryside' was a key element of state paternalism. During the French Revolution, various pedagogues and social commentators had linked education in the open-air to the demands of republican citizenship.[134] These ideas gained real tractions in the

---

[132] Ibid., p. 23.
[133] Claire Edington and Hans Pols, 'Building Psychiatric Expertise across Southeast Asia: Study Trips, Site Visits and Therapeutic Labor in French Indochina and the Dutch East Indies, 1898–1937', *Comparative Studies in Society and History*, vol. 58, no. 3 (2016), pp. 636–663, 649.
[134] Laura Lee Downs, *Childhood in the Promised Land: Working Class Movements and the Colonies de Vacances in France, 1880–1960* (Durham, NC: Duke University Press, 2002), p. 16.

*Non! Ce n'est pas une école de formation professionnelle; mais les jardiniers en herbe s'inquiètent quand même du temps qu'il fera*

**Fig. 4.5** 'No it is not a vocational school. But the young gardeners are still concerned about the weather'.

HCRFA, Service des Personnes Déplacées, *Sept ans d'activité en faveur des personnes déplacées en zone française d'occupation, 1945–1952*, rapport dactylographié et illustré [undated], [Bibliothèque du Ministère des Affaires Etrangères, Direction des Archives], p. 96.

early years of the Third Republic.[135] The transfer of abandoned children to the countryside was seen by social workers as a 'new departure', which enabled children to break away both from a shady familial past and a 'pathogenic' urban centre.[136] Concurrently, working-class children were also sent in growing numbers in *colonies de vacances* (summer camps) in the countryside or at the seashore.[137] The development of *colonies de vacances* coincided with the growth of the open-air school movement in Europe, influenced by the German model of *Waldschulen* (forest schools).[138] In the inter-war years, open-air schools were progressively imbued with greater social, pedagogical and

---

[135] Ivan Jablonka, *Ni père ni mère. Histoire des enfants de l'Assistance publique (1874–1939)* (Paris: Seuil, 2006), p. 296. Also see Jablonka, *Les enfants de la République. L'intégration des jeunes de 1789* (Paris: Seuil, 2010).
[136] Jablonka, *Ni père ni mère*, p. 296.
[137] Downs, *Childhood in the Promised Land*.
[138] Châtelet, Lerch and Luc (eds.), *L'école de plein air*.

cultural meaning.[139] Similarly, as Laura Lee Downs argues, summer camps became innovative 'pedagogic site' rather than simply 'hygienist' site of assistance to the poor.[140] These transformations certainly informed relief workers' approaches to DP rehabilitation. Yet, despite widespread agreement in the benefits of open-air life and sun cures, perspectives of relief workers differed on the effects of long session of physical exercise on DP children with poor health.

The boundaries between healthy and excessive exercises were difficult to establish. For some, DP children were too weak to do two long walks a day.[141] Many of these children were 'rachitic' or extremely fragile.[142] Furthermore, there was a shortage of drugs and physiological cards in these houses.[143] Several incidents also prompted debates about children's behaviour and appropriate methods of discipline and punishment. In Überlingen, for instance, while children were not supervised, a young girl fell in a hot tub. As a result, she suffered from severe third-degree burns.[144] In Gutach, young DP children stole goods, tore apart sleeping bags and broke the toilet seat, so much so that the welfare officer asked to avoid sending boys aged over 12–13 years old in the winter.[145] The behaviour of young boys, in particular, aroused great concerns. In the Haldenhof children house, welfare workers commented on the 'psychologically difficult personalities' of young teenagers, who suffered from 'le mal familial' (familial ill) and were leading insidiously younger and weaker boys, telling them 'stories of ghosts and witches' and disrupting their sleep.[146] A scandal erupted in Gutach when some boys were found sleeping together in the same bed.[147] The boundaries of young male friendship were

[139] Anne-Marie Chatelet, 'Le mouvement international des écoles de plein air', in Châtelet, Lerch and Luc (eds.), L'école de plein air, p. 21; Harald Ludwig, 'Les écoles de plein air en Allemagne, une forme de l'Education Nouvelle', pp. 39–48; Inge Hansen-Schaberg and Muriel Eberhardt, 'Waldschulen et écoles de plein air à Berlin (1904–1933)', pp. 257–260.

[140] Downs, Childhood in the Promised Land.

[141] UNA, UNRRA, S-0438-0005-02, Rapport, Reutlingen, O. Despeignes, 23 June 1946.

[142] UNA, UNRRA, S-0433-0001-02, J. Berger, Welfare, Rapport sur le décès de l'enfant Repotocnik Josef de la maison d'Unterhausen, 17 January 1947.

[143] In January 1947, a young Yugoslav DP died in Unterhausen, after having contracted bronchitis. UNA, UNRRA, S-0433-0001-02, J. Berger, Welfare, Rapport sur le décès de l'enfant Repotocnik Josef de la maison d'Unterhausen, 17 January 1947.

[144] UNA, UNRRA, S-0433-0001-02, Centre Sanitaire Infantile, UNRRA Medical Officer, 19 April 1947, Uberlingen.

[145] UNA, UNRRA, S-0419-0003-01, Rapport sur la conduite des enfants de Lebach durant leur séjour à 'Air et Soleil' du 5 Novembre au 17 Décembre 1946.

[146] UNA, S-0433-0002-01, Lettre de Mlle Chanoine à Mr Boudot-Lamotte, Haldenhof, 6 September 1946.

[147] UNA, UNRRA, S-0419-0003-01, Lettre P. U. Durand à Monsieur le Directeur Général de la Zone Française, rapport relatif à la conduite de certains enfants envoyés à Air et Soleil, 2 January 1947.

fluid. Although the Director attempted to smooth ruffled feathers with reassuring words, this scandal fed fears about the alleged promiscuity of young and traumatized male DPs.[148] The welfare report notes 'We have guessed that it was not only a matter of feeling warmer, the tired-looking faced of these children suggesting *something else*'.[149] This scandal reflected tensions over old and new attitudes towards 'virile friendship' and the co-existence of competing constructs of ideal young male behaviour. As Regis Revenin suggests in his work on young male delinquents in Savigny-sur-Orne, the 'norms' of social behaviour were progressively redefined in the post-war period. While 'virile friendship' (*amitié virile*) had been tolerated, the post-war period witnessed heightened concerns about the blurring of the differences between 'friendship' and love amongst young boys.[150] Faced with querulous, obnoxious and 'promiscuous' DP boys, relief workers attempted to re-inculcate self-discipline and restraint. Rehabilitation was structured as a gendered process of 're-masculinisation' from the feminized, unruly and 'un-childlike' body. It implied 'disciplining' DP bodies and minds as much as 'healing' them.

## Discipline and Play

The use of corporal punishment for educational purposes defied consensus amongst UNRRA relief workers. Complex patterns of changes and continuity emerge from the discussion about punishment. In the nineteenth century, hygienist doctors were amongst the first to oppose corporal punishment and disciplinary measures that impacted the body.[151] In the early twentieth century, however, corporal punishment was often endorsed, certainly amongst working-class individuals.[152] The post-war period witnessed a stronger current of opinion against those who employed excessively violent methods of discipline. In Schweigmatt, near Lorrach, a relief worker had a scar above her eyebrow from a projectile thrown by a young Pole.[153] In retribution, the boy was hit twice (once on his hand palm and once on his bottom) by a relief worker.[154] Discussion about this boy illuminates the uncertainty of what exactly constituted appropriate punishment for children. For the UNRRA

---

[148] Zahra, *Lost Children*, pp. 110–111.
[149] UNA, UNRRA, S-0419-0003-01, A Menereul, Rapport sur la conduite des enfants de Lebach durant leur séjour à Air et Soleil du 5 Novembre au 17 Decembre 1946.
[150] Régis Revenin, *Une histoire des Garçons et des Filles. Amour, genre et sexualité dans la France d'après guerre* (Paris: Vendémiaire, 2015), p. 156.
[151] Jean-Claude Caron, *A l'école de la violence. Châtiments et sévices dans l'institution au XIXe siecle* (Paris: Aubier, 1999), pp. 81–85.
[152] Jablonka, *Ni père ni mère*, p. 111.
[153] UNA, S-0433-0002-01, Ch. Pourchet, Field Supervisor à Monsieur le Général de Corps d'Armée, enquete au centre de Schweigmatt, 23 December 1946.
[154] Ibid.

Field supervisor, the punishment that he received was reasonable. He contended that this was a *correction* (punishment) that any father concerned about the good behaviour of his child was bound to inflict.[155] This reflected gendered understanding of punishment, for the father was regarded here as the ultimate authority in terms of discipline. By contrast, UNRRA Assistant Director condemned such practices and criticized the use of excessively strict and violent methods of discipline.[156] For him, a greater emphasis should be placed on softer disciplinary methods. He not only condemned the punishment of this boy, but also the practices employed in *Air et Soleil*, where unruly children were deprived of butter and sugar.[157] These discussions must be placed within the broader post–Second World War context of a changing educational landscape and the development of a more understanding type of discipline.[158]

Many relief workers perceived restoring discipline as an essential aspect of 'rehabilitation'. But play and recreation was also an important aspect of childhood that had been disrupted by war and exile. Child welfare practices were grounded in the belief that 'play' was important for the healthy development of DP children.[159] In this, there were important similarities across the Western zones. Relief workers placed games at the centre of the reconstruction process and shared a vision of education in which the child 'constructs him or herself as agent through various form of play'.[160] In inter-war Europe, games and play were central to educational practices across different political groups. Likewise, they were central to rehabilitation in post-war Germany.[161] In the DP camp of Rottweil, 200 toys were made by 20 DP women and a Lithuanian painter for Christmas.[162] UNRRA policy stipulated 'recreation is recognized as essential in the personal rehabilitation of Displaced Persons'.[163] Christian festivities were also celebrated along remarkably similar lines in the French, American and British zones. In Wurzach, each DP nationality had made a

---

[155] Ibid.
[156] UNA, S-0433-0002-01, G. Sebille, Assistant Director, 'Etablissement de Schweigmatt', 27 December 1946.
[157] UNA, S-0438-0006-01, G. Sebille à Directeur du District Nord, 18 June 1946.
[158] In Hinterzarten, a summer school organized by the YMCA for young DP boys, a welfare officer noted that the discipline of young DPs was far superior to that of neighbouring French children. UNA, S-0438-0006-01, S. Lau, Welfare Officer, 27 September 1946.
[159] On the importance of play theory see, for example, Thomson, *Psychological Subjects*, pp. 117–118.
[160] Downs, *Childhood in the Promised Land*, p. 8.
[161] UNA, UNRRA, S-0438-0006-01, S. Lau, Welfare Officer, rapport, Hinterzarten, La Maison des Enfants, 27 September 1946.
[162] UNA, UNRRA, S-0438-0009-05, Rapport de la Conference des Welfare Officers du District Sud, 22 and 23 January 1946.
[163] UNA, UNRRA, S-0438-0009-05, UNRRA policy on community activities for Displaced Persons in Germany.

Fig. 4.6   UNA, UNRRA, S-0418-0005-04,
UNRRA Team 211, Child's drawing, Centre de Schwenningen, Latvian colony, Kračevskis Zīmēšana [undated].

different Christmas tree. A DP noted that 'a Christmas without bomb is a beautiful Christmas' (Fig. 4.6).[164]

Over Christmas 1946, according to Elise Zach, all DP children in the zone received toys made by UNRRA or YMCA workshops. 'Each child received at least one article of clothing, as well as chocolate and candies. A number of the smaller teams were able to provide a gift for each adult DP as well.'[165] In Saulgau the Welfare Officer reported that after a Christmas dinner cooked with Russian, Polish and Baltic specialties, a polyglot Father Christmas distributed presents to all the guests. 'In our Foyer-Restaurant, lit with candles [...] we felt that our people were fulfilled and perfectly happy.'[166] For some DP children, celebrating Christmas represented a clear sign that the war was over.[167]

---

[164] UNA, UNRRA, S-0421-0086-01, Noel à Wurzach [Probably 1946], signé Blériot.
[165] UNA, UNRRA, S-0438-0006-02, Elise Zach, Care and Eligibility officer, Monthly report, 6 January 1947.
[166] UNA, UNRRA, S-0438-0007-10, B. J. Haydar, Rapport activité Team 585 Saulgau, semaine du 20–26 Décembre 1946, 30 December 1946.
[167] Nowak, 'Voices of Revival', p. 90.

Fig. 4.7   UNA, UNRRA, S-0420-0001-02,
Improvised Toys, published by arrangement with the Nursery School Association of Great Britain.

Welfare manuals produced by UNRRA headquarters were distributed in the field. UNRRA Central Welfare Division distributed pamphlets explaining how to use scrap metal in arts and crafts.[168] The British Nursery School Association and the Friends Relief service distributed a leaflet on 'improvised toys for nurseries and refugee camps'.[169] The results tended to reflect the ingenuity of UNRRA welfare personnel and DPs' particular skills (Figs. 4.7 and 4.8).

[168] UNA, UNRRA, S-0420-0001-02, Welfare Division – ERO, Leaflets on improvisation for welfare officers (Leisure time activities).
[169] UNA, UNRRA, S-0420-0001-02, Improvised Toys, NSA No. 57, published by arrangement with the Nursery School Association of Great Britain.

**Fig. 4.8**   UNA, UNRRA, S-1021-0085-08,
Lindau's toy-making workshop, UNRRA Team News, vol. 1, no. 13, 15 June 1946.

In the French zone, as in other zones, scouting also figured prominently.[170] French occupation authorities authorized DP scout groups, as long as they neither displayed national signs nor fostered nationalism.[171] Scouting was intended to encourage international entente and aimed at cultivating young boys' sense of duty, self-confidence, courage and self-respect. It was considered as a way of reinforcing the ideals of manly heroism and physical vigour through daily contact with nature. However, scouting was tainted by its association with authoritarian regimes during the war. Some relief workers

---

[170] UNA, UNRRA, S-0438-0009-05, Conférence sur l'éducation, 25 and 26 January 1946; Based on the instruction of UNRRA Central HQ, UNRRA Welfare Bulletin No. 6 was circulated to familiarise French relief workers with the principles of scouting. UNA, UNRRA, S-0420-0001-01, Welfare Bulletin No. 6, Direction Générale UNRRA, 8 July 1946.
[171] PDR6/556, Général d'armée Koenig à Délégué Général du Land Rhéno-Palatin, Wurtemberg et Bade, 16 February 1948.

feared that scout groups could foster militarism rather than peace. Official instructions insisted that military exercise should only be maintained 'in small doses', to encourage boys to act as men not sheep ('brebis').[172] It was noted that Baden-Powell disapproved of the military types of guides.[173] In Koblenz, for example, the UNRRA welfare supervisor worried that local youth movements were promoting not just discipline but militarism.[174] For young girls, the same principles of self-discipline applied, though a greater emphasis was placed on 'domestic issues'.[175] International gatherings were organized. In the summer of 1946, DP scouts from Tübingen joined a French scout troop camping around Lake Constance.[176] In 1947, a DP journalist Raimunds Caks asked whether Baltic DPs could take part in the World Jamboree in Paris.[177] During this international gathering in Moisson (Seine-et-Oise), a committee (directed by Estelle Bernadotte) was created to welcome young DPs. This committee had three main aims: bringing scouting into DP camps, establishing links with Baltic scout groups and teaching 'freedom and respect of people' to German scouts.[178] For French scouts, this large-scale international gathering called 'Jamboree de la Paix' and largely funded by French authorities was seen as a 'proof of renewal', in the aftermath of Vichy and collaboration.[179] For relief workers, scout gatherings contributed to the reconstruction of gendered bodies. Through outdoor activities, DP boys were required to exercise masculine traits of will power and determination, DP girls' feminine traits of selflessness and care.

[172] In Lebach and Gneizno, there were formation of 'Sokol', young people between 15 and 40 living in military unit. UNA, UNRRA, S-0438-0005-02, Rapport du service 'welfare' sur le district nord de la zone, R. le Goff, 11 April 1946.
[173] UNA, UNRRA, S-0420-0001-01, Welfare Bulletin No. 6, Direction Générale UNRRA, 8 July 1946.
[174] UNA, UNRRA, S-0438-0003-03, O. Despeigne à Mercier, 12 February 1946.
[175] UNA, UNRRA, S-0420-0001-01, Welfare Bulletin No. 6, Direction Générale UNRRA, 8 July 1946.
[176] UNA, UNRRA, S-0438-0006-02, Rapport mensuel d'aout 1946, relief service [August 1946].
[177] UNA, UNRRA, S-0417-0003-04, Raimunds Caks à UNRRA HQ. Haslach, 12 May 1947; Françoise de Beaulieu also asked for authorization to visit the French zone for a study of feminine scoutism in DP camps in the French zone. UNA, UNRRA, S-0416-003-03, Françoise de Beaulieu à Melle Muller, 28 November 1946.
[178] Marie-Thérèse Cheroutre, *Le scoutisme au féminin. Les guides de France 1923–1998* (Paris: Les Editions du Cerf, 2002), p. 282.
[179] The President of the French Republic Vincent Auriol came to this gathering, attracting 50,000 young people, including a fifth of French scouts. For French authorities, this gathering was a way of restoring the international image of France, while for French scouts, it was a manner to erase the fact that the federation had been an official organ of the Vichy regime during the Nazi occupation of France. Christian Guérin, *L'utopie Scouts de France* (Paris: Fayard, 1997), pp. 297–298.

## Remaking Healthy Bodies: The Fight against 'Social Scourges'

The aftermath of war was marked by an obsession for the reconstruction of healthy, well-nourished and normatively gendered bodies.[180] The war and Nazi machinery of annihilation had sought to destroy body identity: 'repairing' the emaciated and amenorrhic bodies of camp inmates and tired bodies of former POWs and soldiers, as much as soothing widespread anxieties about fertility and sterility among DP men and women were essential parts of the rehabilitation process.[181] In France, several medical theses were submitted in the spring of 1945 identifying the key medical issues that repatriation officers would confront, including tuberculosis, venereal diseases, scabies and typhus.[182] Amongst the mass of DPs, child survivors were seen as likely to suffer from the most extreme pathologies of hunger and cold, their bodies having aged prematurely and dramatically.[183] In this context, DP bodies (both adult and children) were sites of regulation, surveillance and discipline.

Welfare workers controlled how DPs took care of themselves and their living spaces. Instilling a sense of personal hygiene was a crucial part of the rehabilitation process. All DP camps were dusted with DDT powder. In some cases, though, 'DP spaces' seemed to be a hindrance to reconstruction, such as in the transit camp of Munsingen where German barracks were infested with bugs.[184] Very often, cleanliness was associated with morality and self-respect; lack of cleanliness was, on the contrary, regarded as a sign of deviancy. While DPs were considered as a population in need of protection and treatment, they were also often considered as a potential transmitter of epidemic disease.[185] As a mobile health inspector put it, the DP population was 'characterized by a

---

[180] Grossmann, 'La reconstruction individuelle comme projet collectif', pp. 291–305.

[181] Judy Tydor Baumel-Schwartz, 'The Identity of Women in the She'erit Hapletah: Personal and Gendered Identity as Determinants in Rehabilitation, Immigration and Resettlement', in Dalia Ofer, Françoise Ouzan and Judy Tydor Baumel-Schwartz (eds.), *Holocaust Survivors: Resettlement, Memories, Identities* (London: Berghan Books, 2011), pp. 16–45; Margarete Myers Feinstein, 'Jewish Observance in Amalek's Shadow: Mourning, Marriage, and Birth Rituals among Displaced Persons in Germany', in Avinoman Patt and Michael Berkowitz (eds.), *We Are Here: New Approaches to Jewish Displaced Persons in Postwar Germany* (Detroit: Wayne State University Press, 2010), pp. 257–288; Feinstein, *Holocaust Survivors in Postwar Germany*.

[182] Pierre Valette, 'L'organisation du Service de Santé du Rapatriement', Thèse pour le doctorat en médecine, présentée et soutenue publiquement le 19 février 1945, Faculté de médecine de Paris; Pierre-Jean Caplier, 'Le role du médecin dans les centres de rapatriement', Thèse pour le doctorat en médecine, présentée et soutenue publiquement le 22 mars 1945, Faculté de médecine de Paris.

[183] Rosenberg, *Les enfants dans la Shoah*, pp. 435–470.

[184] UNA, UNRRA, S-0438-0005-02, Rapport O. Despeigne, 23 June 1946.

[185] Lisa Haushofer, 'The 'Contaminating Agent': UNRRA, Displaced Persons and Venereal Disease in Germany, 1945–1947', *American Journal of Public Health*, vol. 100, no. 6 (2010), pp. 993–1003.

level of promiscuity prone to alert any epidemiologist'.[186] Poor sanitation did not necessarily imply that DPs rejected the values and hygiene standards imparted by UNRRA welfare workers. It could simply stem from a lack of soap, hot water and other hygiene supplies, which was widespread in the zone.[187] Likewise, there was a shortage of adequate clothing.[188] Yet, for many DPs, clothing was an essential mean of sustaining and performing gendered and bodily identities.[189]

Morality and medical practices often worked in tandem in French efforts at educating and regulating the bodies of DP men and women. In the French zone, UNRRA drew on practices of social medicine developed by the 'social hygiene crusade' in the inter-war years, when a network of medical doctors produced films, brochures and leaflets to educate the population about venereal diseases and their adverse effects on the family and French population more broadly.[190] During this period, the social-hygienist French state intervened in private life as never before, allowing the medical profession into the private and intimate domain of marriage, fertility and conjugal sexuality of French and foreigners alike.[191] Fertility, childbearing and sexual practices were deeply interlinked with the processes of nation building and imperial rule.[192] Policy-elites and social critics linked intimate matters to the so-called immigrant question, considering that the intimate was a site 'upon which ideas about assimilability and belonging were elaborated'.[193] These views certainly continued after the war. In the summer of 1946, an 'Ecole de Formation Sociale' (Social Work school) was set up in Gutach. As preparation for UNRRA's anticipated withdrawal, sixty-one female DPs were trained to become welfare assistants.[194] Unlike the training provided at Granville (for

---

[186] UNA, UNRRA, S-0433-0002-02, Le Dr Rellay, Inspecteur mobile au Service de Santé de la Direction des Personnes Déplacées à Médecin-Colonel Robineau, Neustadt, 19 October 1946.
[187] UNA, UNRRA, S-0433-0002-03, Rapport d'inspection du Médecin des Cilleuls, Landstuhl, 16–19 January 1946, p. 10.
[188] Walczewski, *Destin tragique des polonais déportés en Allemagne*, p. 67.
[189] Anna Andlauer, *The Rage to Live. The International DP Children's Center Kloster Indersdorf 1945-46* (CreateSpace Independent Publishing Platform, 2012) pp. 53–56.
[190] See, for example, Fabrice Cohen and Adrien Minard, 'Les mobilisations contre les 'fléaux sociaux' dans l'entre-deux-guerres', *Histoire et Mesure*, vol. 2, no. XXXI (2016), pp. 141–170; Stéphane Henry, 'Histoire et témoignages d'infirmières visiteuses (1905–1938)', *Recherche en soins infirmiers*, vol. 2, no. 109 (2012), pp. 44–56.
[191] Virginie De Luca Barrusse, 'Pro-Natalism and Hygienism in France, 1900–1940. The Example of the Fight against Venereal Disease', *Population*, vol. 64, no. 3 (2009), pp. 477–506.
[192] Elisa Camiscioli, *Reproducing the French Race: Immigration, Intimacy and Embodiment in the Early Twentieth Century* (Duke: Duke University Press, 2009), p. 6.
[193] Ibid., p. 3.
[194] UNA, UNRRA, S-0438-0009-05, Première réunion des Welfare Officers du District Nord les 20 et 21 novembre 1945.

class I recruits), the Gutach course was delivered by tutors familiar with DP fieldwork.[195] The programme (taught in French, Polish and German) was relatively comprehensive and lasted three weeks. Conditions of admissions included an 'at least average' intellectual level, a 'good morality' and clean presentation.[196] External partners from the *Service Social d'Aide aux Emigrants* (SSAE) and the YMCA were brought in for specialist classes. Lectures dealt with a wide range of topics, such as laws in the zone, the duty of confidentiality, screening, but also DP employment, child psychology and the battle against 'socials scourges' ('les fléaux sociaux').[197] Social scourges encompassed both diseases (tuberculosis, cancer, syphilis) and psycho-social infections (infant mortality, alcoholism). Such courses reinforced the connection between racial discourses, economic production and procreation.

Historians have used the concept of biopolitics, introduced by Michel Foucault to understand the ways in which state authorities exercised power through discourses of sexuality and propagation of scientific knowledge with the aim of regulating both individual bodies and populations.[198] This form of power was particularly evident in the campaign to control the spread of venereal diseases and the medico-moralizing discourse about DPs' excessive 'needs' for sex.[199] For some UNRRA directors, the transient lifestyle of many DPs not only presented physical threats, it also represented moral hazards. The medical officer of the sanatorium of Uberruh condemned, for instance, the decision to accept both male and female DPs, noting that 'erotic excesses are widespread' and threatened the good reputation of the institution.[200] French medical staff used education and isolation ('centre de triage') to prevent the spread of VD.[201] According to the French UNRRA Health Director of the zone, there was no doubt that the abnormal life, promiscuity,

---

[195] UNA, UNRRA, S-0438-0005-05, Legoff, Rapport sur l'école de formation sociale de Gutach, 13 November 1946.

[196] UNA, UNRRA, S-0438-0005-05, G. E. Sebille, Creation d'une école de formation sociale pour aides Welfare DPs, 30 July 1946.

[197] UNA, UNRRA, S-0438-0005-05, Le Goff à Zach, Rapport sur l'école de formation sociale de Gutach, 13 November 1946.

[198] See, for example, Peter Gatrell, 'From "Homelands" to "Warlands": Themes, Approaches, Voices', in Peter Gatrell and Nick Baron (eds.), *Warlands. Population Resettlement and State Reconstruction in the Soviet-East European Borderlands, 1945–1950* (Basingstoke: Palgrave Macmillan, 2009), pp. 1–22, 5–8.

[199] UNA, UNRRA, S-0433-0002-07, Dr Birietaite, Prophylaxie des maladies vénériennes, 19 March 1947.

[200] UNA, UNRRA, S-0433-0001-03, Président, Suspension de la station pour hommes de notre sanatorium pour affections pulmonaires, 27 June 1946.

[201] On educative conferences, see, for instance, UNA, UNRRA, S-0433-0002-07, Dr Scharll à Directeur General UNRRA, 28 February 1947.

general decline of morality have 'greatly contributed' to the origins and spread of venereal diseases.[202] Likewise, a chief medical officer in the Pirmasens camp noted that 'the DPs have a very active sexual life which is favoured by the fact that they live in communities and gather frequently, by the lack of occupation, the consumption of alcohol, the lack of hygiene education and of any knowledge of the consequences of these kind of diseases, factors which facilitate their spread.'[203] In place, DP women could be targeted on suspicion of being prostitutes and then subjected to compulsory medical checks.[204] In Kaiserslautern, for instance, women were unequivocally blamed for venereal diseases.[205] Scenes of public humiliation occurred when a camp nurse announced the positive results in the presence of large numbers of inmates.[206] Such practices, which according to an UNRRA relief worker recalled the 'methods applied in certain concentration camps', were, however, vigorously condemned by UNRRA authorities.[207]

Lisa Haushofer suggests that French officials saw women, and particularly DP women as 'contaminating agents' in contrast to virtuous German women.[208] The argument put forward here suggests that in some areas (such as Kaiserlautern) compulsory measures targeted DP women especially, but that the official instructions did not single out DP women. In August 1945, the hospitalization of 'all German women' who had contaminated French military men was made compulsory by French authorities. In January 1946, General Administrateur Emile Laffon recommended the creation of a 'Centre de Triage', where any 'suspected patient' and 'irrespective of their social rank' would be hospitalized for a period of eight days.[209] Though penicillin was discovered during the war and enabled a swift treatment, it remained a fairly rare commodity and doctors were instructed not to use penicillin in the treatment of venereal diseases. Penicillin was reserved for situations in which

---

[202] UNA, UNRRA, S-1021-0085-04, Médecin Général des Cilleuls, Exposé général de l'organisation et du fonctionnement du service médical UNRRA en zone Française, du 1er décembre 1946 au 1er mars 1947.
[203] UNA, UNRRA, S-0433-0001-01, Rapport du médecin chef du team 575 de Pirmasens, 11 February 1946.
[204] UNA, UNRRA, S-0433-0002-07, Examen pour les maladies vénériennes, 4 August 1946.
[205] UNA, UNRRA, S-0433-0001-05, Bayle à Lavigne, 27 June 1946.
[206] UNA, UNRRA, S-0433-0002-07, Examen pour les maladies vénériennes, 4 August 1946.
[207] UNA, UNRRA, S-0433-0002-07, Dépistage des maladies vénériennes, camp de Kaiserslautern, 22 August 1946.
[208] Haushofer, 'The Contamining Agent.' On the control of venereal disease in Four-Power Berlin see Annette Timm, *The Politics of Fertility in Twentieth Century Berlin* (Cambridge: Cambridge University Press, 2010), pp. 187–226.
[209] UNA, S-0433-0002-05, Administrateur General Laffon à Gouverneur, Lutte contre les maladies vénériennes, 2 January 1946.

the life of a patient (or one of their organs) was in danger.[210] By the spring of 1947, only 61 sick DPs had been treated with penicillin.[211]

In their efforts to ameliorate DPs' health, relief and medical workers were divided over the placement of DPs in German medical facilities, as it was impossible to assure 'that rations and medical supplies destined for sick DPs actually reached them'.[212] Only two medical centres reserved for DPs existed: one in Freiburg and one in Ravensburg. In Nordach, the Jewish Relief Unit solicited UNRRA's help to run the sanatorium Rothschild for Jewish tuberculosis patients. This sanatorium had been created in 1888 and was one of Europe's early successful elite sanatoria.[213] The Polish Red Cross also organized a Polish DP hospital in Rottenmünster with 121 beds, established in the convent of the Sisters of Saint Vincent de Paul.[214] Any sick Polish DP of the zone had in theory the right to ask to be transferred to that hospital.[215] In practice, the majority of sick DPs were sent to German hospitals, as UNRRA was in no financial position to run DP hospitals.

In German hospitals and sanatoria, DPs were sometimes isolated from German patients. In the sanatorium of Wittlich, run by Caritas, Polish DP children were clearly separated, receiving higher rations of cacao, milk and butter than German children. Their rooms were, however, not as comfortable as those of German children.[216] In other instances, however, DPs cohabited with German patients. Like in other domains, medical provision for sick DPs was hampered by severe shortages and a lack of trained personnel. By 1947, the number of DP doctors was 145. The French Zone UNRRA Medical Director found difficulty in cooperating with them, for the majority wanted to stay in the universities of Freiburg and Tübingen to finish their specialist trainings. Des Cilleuls believed that the experience of war and exodus, combined with uncertain future and linguistic barriers, had a profound impact on DP doctors' ability to perform their roles.[217] In this context, some relief

---

[210] UNA, UNRRA, S-0433-0002-05, Instruction concernant l'emploi de la penicillin, 3 September 1946.
[211] UNA, UNRRA, S-1021-0085-04, Médecin Général des Cilleuls, Exposé général de l'organisation et du fonctionnement du service médical UNRRA en zone Française, du 1er décembre 1946 au 1er mars 1947.
[212] UNA, UNRRA, S-0433-0002-02, T. S. Stallabrass to E. P. Moreland and Melle Loustalot, 12 February 1946.
[213] Bynum, *Spitting Blood*, p. 129.
[214] UNA, UNRRA, S-0433-0002-02, Plan d'Hôpital Polonais à Rottweil, Rottenmunster.
[215] UNA, UNRRA, S-0433-0002-02, le Médecin Chef Dr Zakrzewski Franciszek à Médecin Colonel Robinau, 6 August 1946.
[216] UNA, UNRRA, S-0433-0002-02, Le Sanatorium de Grunewald, Wittlich, 14 August 1946.
[217] UNA, UNRRA, S-1021-0085-04, Medecin Général des Cilleuls, Exposé général de l'organisation et du fonctionnement du service médical UNRRA en zone Française, du 1er decembre 1946 au 1er mars 1947.

workers deemed that placing DPs under German medical care was necessary. DPs would not receive bad treatment at the hands of German doctors as 'their standard of professional honour would prevent them'.[218] Others, by contrast, thought that this was highly problematic, as DPs were often extremely mistrustful of German doctors and the evidence too often suggested that German personnel fed themselves at the expenses of DPs.[219] There were other lines of fracture as well. Some DPs had a profound mistrust of DP doctors from other ethnic or national backgrounds, who did not have the same prestige as French official doctors.[220] In some cases, DP doctors neither spoke German nor Polish. In Niederlahnstein, for instance, the UNRRA director was assisted by a Russian doctor, 'very unpopular due to her nationality'.[221]

Offering DPs adequate medical care was not an easy task. Yet reconstructing healthy DPs bodies was vital for the future of 'non-repatriable' DPs, as they had to be transformed into 'useful' citizens and 'valuable migrants'.[222] According to UNRRA Health Director, the sanitary situation of DPs in the French zone was consistently satisfactory, even though a small epidemic of diphtheria broke out in Pirmasens in the winter of 1945–1946, as well as small outbreaks of pertussis, measles and mumps.[223] Admittedly, one must not take at face value this positive overview. As Chapter 6 reveals, emigration authorities rejected many DPs on the grounds of poor health, despite UNRRA's scrutiny and surveillance of DP bodies. Tuberculosis continued to be perceived as an acutely dangerous and socially stigmatizing disease by social workers and UNRRA officials.[224] The system of detection of syphilis was also particularly deficient, engendering long delays.[225] DPs were also rejected from national

---

[218] UNA, UNRRA, S-0433-0002-02, T. S. Stallabrass to E. P. Moreland and Melle Loustalot, 12 February 1946.

[219] UNA, UNRRA, S-0433-0001-07, Dr Hong-Tuan à E. J. Bastianen, Enquête sur les rations des malades dans les hôpitaux et sanatoria allemands, 10 January 1947.

[220] UNA, S-0433-0001-01, Le Dr Rellay, Inspecteur mobile au service de santé de la Direction des Personnes Déplacées à Médecin-Colonel Robineau, 19 October 1946.

[221] UNA, S-0433-0001-01, J. Bernard, Rapport à Monsieur le Directeur de District, 11 June 1946.

[222] Ada Schein, 'Medical Rehabilitation of Holocaust Survivors in the DP Camps in Germany', in Rebecca Boehling, Susanne Urban and René Bienert (eds.), *Freilegungen. Displaced Persons. Leben im Transit: Überlebende zwischen Repatriierung, Rehabilitation und Neuanfang* (Gottingen: Wallstein Verlag, 2014), pp. 81–89, 83. Also see Chapter 6.

[223] UNA, UNRRA, S-1021-0085-04, Médecin Général des Cilleuls, Exposé général de l'organisation et du fonctionnement du service médical UNRRA en zone Française, du 1er décembre 1946 au 1er mars 1947.

[224] Flurin Condrau, '"Who Is the Captain of All These Men of Death": The Social Structure of a Tuberculosis Sanatorium in Postwar Germany', *Journal of Interdisciplinary History*, vol. 32, no. 2 (2001), pp. 243–262, 48; McMillen, *Discovering Tuberculosis*, p. 23.

[225] UNA, S-0433-0001-01, Rapport du medecin-chef du team 575 de Pirmasens, 11 February 1946.

recruitment schemes on the basis of various physical 'deformity', revealing the eugenicist mind-frames of a number of doctors carrying out examinations.[226] In Emmendingen, the UNRRA Director also highlighted the 'desperate situation' of 'mad DPs' interned in the German asylum.[227] Vulnerable adults and children were kept separated from loved one. As Ruth Balint notes, old attitudes towards disability persisted, including the necessity to separate disabled children away from their family. Drawing on old traditions of workhouse and asylum, welfare workers continued to promote the institutionalization of disabled child DPs, 'where they could be kept invisible and segregated from public view'.[228] Permanently disabled DPs had little chance of being offered an opportunity to emigrate abroad, even if they had been offered educational or vocational training (usually as manual trade).

Inherent in histories of humanitarianism are questions of domination and power. DP camps were both sites of care and reconstruction, and spaces of control and surveillance.[229] Research into DP camps has demonstrated that refugee camps provided *total care*, relief workers imposing scheduled activities 'from above'.[230] They have unearthed a fundamental power hierarchy operating within these spaces, with staff feeling superior to inmates.[231] Nevertheless, the history of rehabilitation is not exclusively one of control and surveillance. Medical officers and relief workers exerted forms of social control over those who were categorized as 'vulnerable' and imposed in a coercive manner hygiene and collective discipline, but the power of relief workers greatly varied. As much as DPs developed strategies to bypass screening policies, they also reshaped 'welfare' norms that they considered alienating and circumvent prohibitions.[232] DPs, who resented the control that relief workers exercised over them, also wrote petitions and complaints letters to UNRRA and French occupation authorities.[233]

---

[226] On eugenist mindframe of Canadian doctors, see Antoine Burgard, 'Une nouvelle vie dans un nouveau pays. Trajectoires d'orphelins de la Shoah vers le Canada (1947–1952)', PhD thesis, Université du Québec à Montréal/Université Lumière Lyon 2 (2017), p. 367.

[227] UNA, UNRRA, S-0433-0002-02, Dalichampt, Directeur team 576 à Monsieur le Général de C. A. F. Lenclud, 18 September 1946.

[228] Ruth Balint, 'Children Left Behind: Family, Refugees and Immigration in Postwar Europe', *History Workshop Journal*, vol. 82 (2016), pp. 151–172, 168–169.

[229] Erving Goffman, *Asylums: Essays on the Social Situation of Mental Patients and Other Inmates* (London: Penguin Books, 1962); Tomas Balkelis, 'Living in the Displaced Persons Camp: Lithuanian War Refugees in the West, 1944–1954', in Peter Gatrell and Nick Baron (eds.), *Warlands. Population Resettlement and State Reconstruction in the Soviet-East European Borderlands, 1945–1950* (New York: Palgrave Macmillan, 2009), pp. 25–47.

[230] Balkelis, 'Living in the Displaced Persons Camp', p. 26.

[231] Ibid.

[232] PDR6/869, Lettre confidentielle, Edward Korczynski à Directeur des Personnes Déplacées, 17 November 1948.

[233] Ibid.

While it is difficult to assess is how DPs received the familial and maternal model that relief workers largely inspired by European bourgeoisies tried to impose from medical and relief reports, these sources illustrate, nevertheless, some forms of resistance to intrusive practices on the part of DPs.[234] DPs often questioned the need to vaccinate themselves or their children, despite relief workers' attempts to build faith in vaccination. DPs came from countries where vaccinations were not always compulsory, unlike in France.[235] In Pirmasens, the medical team considered that a vaccination campaign was necessary to avoid an epidemic of whooping cough (*pertussis*), but this immunization programme faced widespread opposition. A medical officer asked his superior 'To what extent can DPs oppose sanitary measures taken by UNRRA?', highlighting the difficulty of respecting the 'rights of patients', while fulfilling the duties of a doctor.[236] Compulsion could, in fact, inflame antagonism. By June 1946, medical authorities considered that the anti-typhus, anti-typhoid and anti-tetanus vaccinations were terminated in the district south: two-thirds of the DP population was vaccinated, while a third remained refractory 'despite all persuasion means employed'.[237] In Balingen, the UNRRA medical team reported that 'superstition remained a great obstacle for medical progress'.[238] Opposition to vaccination was not atypical, some degree of resistance remaining a feature in immunization campaigns through the 1940.[239] On the whole, though, DPs were extremely mistrustful of hospitals and doctors, who did not have the 'official stamp' of UNRRA and the military government.[240] Parents were extremely reluctant to leave their children in hospitals.[241]

UNRRA disciplinary power over DP bodies aroused resistance, which came in the forms of refusing treatment and rehabilitation. It could also be found in what Ana Carden Coyne has termed 'cultural agency', when DPs expressed grievances and outlet frustrations in private diaries, jokes, drawings or correspondence.[242] As Katarzyna Nowak suggests, DPs often turned to satire to

---

[234] UNA, UNRRA, S-0438-0005-02, Report of Welfare Officer, Southern District, 8 June 1946.
[235] *Sept ans en faveur des personnes déplacées*, p. 37.
[236] UNRRA, S-0433-0002-02, Le Dr Rellay, Inspecteur mobile au Service de Santé de la Direction PDR à Monsieur le Médecin-Colonel Robineau, 19 October 1946.
[237] UNRRA, S-0433-0002-06, M. Lauras, Chief Nurse, Relief Service, 25 June [1946?].
[238] UNRRA, S-0433-0001-03, La lutte contre les infections.
[239] Paul Greenough, Stuart Blume and Christine Holmberg, *The Politics of Vaccination: A Global History* (Manchester: Manchester University Press, 2017), pp. 1–16, 8.
[240] UNA, S-0433-0001-01, Le Dr Rellay, Inspecteur mobile au service de santé de la Direction des Personnes Déplacées à le Médecin-Colonel Robineau, 19 October 1946.
[241] Ibid.
[242] For the concept of 'cultural agency' see Ana Carden-Coyne, *Politics of Wounds. Military Patients and Medical Power in the First World War* (Oxford: Oxford University Press, 2015), p. 7.

attack the incompetence of relief workers and mock what they perceived as a demoralizing and patronizing regime.[243] Artistic creations, which were strongly encouraged by relief workers, could also offer a channel to vent frustrations towards infantilizing practices.[244] Artistic expression could also help DPs maintain a sense of internal integrity and 'resist' the order imposed by relief workers.

## Art Therapies

In the French zone, DPs were encouraged to create objects and keep themselves busy with artistic activities. Art and craft making was an important aspect of rehabilitation.[245] As Ana Carden Coyne suggests, artistic expression and 'haptic arts' have played a long, though hidden, role in the history of rehabilitation in Europe.[246] Since the nineteenth century, humanitarians have encouraged the production of handicrafts by wounded soldiers and displaced persons for the purposes of fundraising, as part of the rising market of humanitarian consumerism.[247] In addition to fundraising, humanitarian workers progressively came to recognize the sensory and emotional role of the act of hand-making objects for overcoming mental strains.[248] Both French occupation authorities and UNRRA officials supported numerous 'international' art exhibitions, cultural fairs and theatrical plays.[249] Baltic DPs, in particular, found an enthusiastic supporter in the military government in the person of Raymond Schmittlein, who had lived in Lithuania and Latvia between 1934 and 1940 working as a professor and as foreign correspondent for the Havas news agency.

Artistic exhibitions could both assist DPs with coping with displacement and help raise funds.[250] In Freiburg, for instance, the welfare service organized a 'charity fair' on 16 December 1945 in conjunction with the Latvian and Lithuanian DP committees, the event making significant profit.[251] Lithuanian

---

[243] Nowak, 'Voices of Revival', p. 118.
[244] Carden-Coyne, 'The Art of Resilience'.
[245] See, for instance, S-0421-0031-02, Ecole artistique de Fribourg [undated]; Exposition Artistique Baden-Baden and Paris, 25 March 1946.
[246] Carden-Coyne, 'The Art of Resilience. Veteran Therapy from the Occupational to the Creative, 1914–1945', forthcoming.
[247] Carden-Coyne, 'Butterfly Touch', p. 3.
[248] Ibid.
[249] UNA, UNRRA, S-0438-0009-05, Réunion des Welfare Officers du District Sud des Teams de l'Est, 15–16 Janvier à Wangen, 1946.
[250] UNA, UNRRA, S-0421-0031-06, Compte-rendu de la réunion du 7 Mars 1946 du Comité Artistique, Fribourg, 9 March 1946.
[251] UNA, UNRRA, S-0421-0031-09, Rapport sur la fête du 16 Décembre 1945, 19 March 1946.

children sang popular French songs such as *Sur le Pont d'Avignon* alongside Baltic folk ballads.[252] An exhibition of DP artwork was also organized in Rottweil camp in September 1945, where seventy-five art works from painters of different nationalities were exhibited.[253] The exhibition had some success and was visited by 200 people.[254] In April 1946, the orchestra of the Landstuhl camp played the *Marseillaise* and the national Polish anthem to inaugurate the opening of an exhibition of Polish handicraft. According to its UNRRA welfare officer, the exhibition was a 'success', DPs having fashioned 'marvels' ranging from wood sculpture to fine embroidery, even though the military Government had refused to disburse anything.[255] UNRRA Central Headquarters also envisaged collecting work made by DPs for inclusion in a permanent exhibition at the Archives of the United Nations, but this project never came to fruition.[256] In June 1946, a large exhibition ('Art & Travail. Personnes Déplacées') was installed in Baden-Baden, the capital of the zone. By displaying DP-produced objects, this exhibition showed the efforts, resolve and skills of industrious men and women.[257] In the summer of 1946, another exhibition of DP arts was prepared in Freiburg to '(a) publicize DP arts, (b) contribute to put DPs at work, (c) develop and encourage artistic expression amongst DPs'.[258] For relief workers, encouraging artistic expression was certainly a way to combat the lethargy of camp life.

Artistic creation could also help DPs maintain a sense of internal integrity and prevent them from 'sinking'.[259] In her work on material culture in German POW camps in Russia, Iris Rachamimov argues that POW utilized artifacts to 'bridge the temporal distance between their present existence and their previous one by recreating a sense of prewar mode of life'.[260] In the aftermath of the Second World War, some DP artists certainly found a form of

---

[252] Ibid.
[253] UNA, UNRRA, S-0438-0008-02, Rapport de la conférence des welfare officers du district sud, 22 and 23 January 1946.
[254] Ibid.
[255] UNA, UNRRA, S-0421-0066-03, G. Rouss, Principal Welfare Officer à J. J. Bernard, Field Supervisor, Team No. 2 Landstuhl, 15 April 1946; UNA, UNRRA, S-0438-0003-03, Exposition 'travaux du camp', 15 April 1946.
[256] UNA, UNRRA, S-0421-0025-04, Cyrus Greenslade, Deputy Chief of Operations, transl. M. Lardon, 6 June 1947, Headquarters DP Operations UNRRA, Instruction Technique No. 3, disposition des archives, rassemblement et conservation des échantillons des travaux faits par des personnes déplacées.
[257] See Chapter 5.
[258] UNA, UNRRA, S-0421-0031-02, Projet pour l'organisation d'une exposition ambulante 'L'art et le travail des DPs', Fribourg-en-Brigsau.
[259] J. Rozītis, *Displaced Literature. Images of Time and Space in Latvian Novels Depicting the First Years of the Latvian Postwar Exile* (Stockholm: Stockholm University, 2005), p. 118.
[260] Iris Rachamimov, 'Small Escapes. Gender, Class and Material Culture in Great War Internment Camps' in Leora Auslander and Tara Zahra, (eds.), *Objects of War. The*

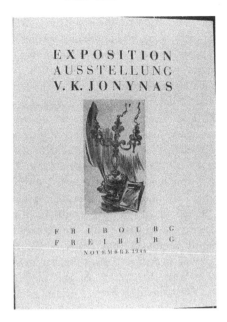

Fig. 4.9   UNA, UNRRA, S-0421-0031-02,
Exposition, Lithographs by V. K. Jonynas, November 1946, Freiburg.

'escape' in artistic creation. In Wurzach, for instance, the DP artist Kalmite painted in water colors his memories of his father's house and in particular the *rija* (traditional farm structure) in which he had grown up.[261] Some of his work was exhibited during the 'week of DP culture' in Wurzach from 3 to 10 November 1946.[262] The DP artist Jonynas also exhibited in Freiburg a series of lithographs, including some illustrations of Prosper Mérimée's *Lokys – The manuscript of professor Wittembach*, inspired by an old Lithuanian legend (Fig. 4.9).

DPs also established theatre groups and orchestras in the French zone, reviving traditional plays, folk songs and dances. These helped them soothe homesickness and create a sense of belonging, but also present cultural 'worthiness' to outsiders, as Inta Gale Carpenter shows in her work on

---

*Material Culture of Conflict and Displacement* (Ithaca, NY: Cornell University Press, 2018), pp. 164-188, p. 166.

[261] The Kalmite Story, exhibition catalogue, exhibition at Global Center for Latvian Art from 28 May 2016 to 31 December 2016. Text written by Lelde Kalmīte and Ilze Arājs.

[262] UNA, S-0418-0003-08, Semaine de Culture des DPs à Wurzach, 3–10 November 1946, Prospectus. Introduction by Janis Kalmite.

Latvian DP folklore.²⁶³ For instance, the Lithuanian Orchestra of Freiburg played a programme of folk songs and anthems, together with classical pieces written by Claude Debussy, Mozart, Frédéric Chopin or the French composer Jules Massenet in August 1946.²⁶⁴

While many UNRRA relief workers encouraged the development of recreation activities and the exhibition of DPs' arts, others condemned them. In January 1946, the UNRRA Zone Welfare Officer requested the organization in each camp of a 'high-quality' concert, a play or a music hall.²⁶⁵ UNRRA Field Supervisor Pourchet remained, however, opposed to what he decried as a policy of 'spectacular events', considering that it favoured an aristocracy of DPs while neglecting the poorest, who only received 'scraps of it and *echoes* of concerts'.²⁶⁶ If Baltic DPs found an enthusiastic supporter in the military government in the person of Raymond Schmittlein, a number of officials displayed very little interest to this public demonstration of DPs' skills. Pourchet's claim that these events only benefited an elite of DPs is not entirely true: for many 'lower-class' DPs, these cultural events offered an opportunity to engage with the culture of the DP elites. As Katarzyna Nowak demonstrates, DPs attended performances and concerts that were reserved to the upper classes prior to the war.²⁶⁷ In camps, different DP classes interacted closely with one another and shared cultural activities. These close interactions would have been unthinkable in their home countries. Rehabilitation practices and camp life prompted unique ties between DPs of different class and generations, which contributed to profoundly alter gendered, cultural and class identities.

The significance of cultural exhibitions should not be overstated, however. The fact that many DPs were dispersed throughout the countryside hampered the organization of cultural events and the development of recreational activities in some areas. Some welfare officers were disappointed to be marooned in rural areas having imagined being in charge of social activities within a large camp. In Emmendingen, for instance, the UNRRA director reported that most new welfare employees attached to his team were unhappy. As he conceded, being a part of his team, 'entails the major inconvenience of being a rural social "work of details" [*travail de detail*], admittedly interesting but rather unrewarding and not producing impressive results', when compared to the

---

²⁶³ Inta Gale Carpenter, 'Folklore as a Source for Creating Exile Identity among Latvian Displaced Persons in Post-World War II Germany', *Journal of Baltic Studies*, vol. 48, no. 2 (2017), pp. 205–233.
²⁶⁴ UNA, UNRRA, S-0421-0031-01, Invitation, comité d'entraide lithuanien de Fribourg, 10 August 1946.
²⁶⁵ UNA, UNRRA, S-0438-0003-03, Chief Welfare Officer Despeigne à Drake Brockman et Moreland, District Directors, 16 January 1946.
²⁶⁶ UNA, UNRRA, S-0421-0026-01, Ch. Pourchet à Colonel Pichot, 16 October 1946.
²⁶⁷ Nowak, 'Voices of Revival', p. 100.

cultural events organized in huge camps.[268] He urged UNRRA authorities to inform all UNRRA staff to be deployed in the French zone that the zone did not have 'model camps with between 5,000 and 10, 000 DPs, like they were told [was the case] in the theoretical training classes'.[269] DPs living in private accommodation were uninterested in communal recreational activities anyway. 'The reason behind this is not only transport and communication difficulties. It stems from the fact that private life is a much more normal way of life than camp life. Hence, DPs behave as free and independent men, that is to say, if we dare say it, in a more selfish manner.'[270] In Reutlingen, a relief worker reported that it proved difficult to encourage DPs to cultivate individual garden plots or take up language courses:

> Story of a Failure. We tried to organize language classes: English and Spanish, in view of emigration to USA, British colonies or to Spanish-speaking South America, but without success. It is difficult to get schoolbooks: we are still waiting for Hugo's Spanish, ordered a month ago in England. Very few adult DPs are interested, and those all want private and individual tuition. People do not want to leave their camps and homes in the evening, which is the only time when the welfare officer is free.[271]

In Ehingen, Frey also evoked the resistance of refugees when relief workers tried to encourage them 'to cultivate their spirit as much as their body' in the YMCA *foyer*.[272] Cultural and educational facilities were highly contingent on where DPs lived in the French zone and where they came from.

## Education and the Politics of Ethnicity

Education illuminates DP camps' competing drives between ethnic mixing and segregation.[273] DP elites tried to promote communal identities through schooling. For most relief workers and DP elites alike, it was preferable to regroup DP children by nationality and ethnicity.[274] DP elites were deeply anxious about how camp life might transform and corrupt ethnic

---

[268] UNA, UNRRA, S-0421-0015-06, Marcel Dalichampt à Germaine Loustalot, 12 February 1946.
[269] UNA, UNRRA, S-0421-0015-06, Dalichampt à Loustalot, 12 March 1946.
[270] UNA, UNRRA, S-1021-0085-08, Jean Gerbier, Rapport sur les activités de l'UNRRA ...', p. 15.
[271] UNA, UNRRA, S-1021-0085-02, Welfare Division Pr. W. O. Mme Pujos de Coudray to Mrs Zach, 2185/12/6540 [undated, 1947?].
[272] Ibid.
[273] Jordanna Bailkin argues that life in refugee camps illuminates the tensions between ethnic segregation, which was often the purpose of camp authorities – and the cross-cultural interactions that took place on the ground. Bailkin, *Unsettled*, p. 87.
[274] UNA, UNRRA, S-0438-0009-05, Conference sur l'éducation, Baden-Baden, 25 and 26 January 1946.

allegiances.[275] Polish DP elites were, for instance, deeply reluctant to place Polish children under the authority of Ukrainian teachers.[276] Welfare officers also often insisted on the importance of 'national songs, legends and national history' to re-educate DP children.[277] Yet the shortages of DP teachers meant that, in some cases, DP children from various nationalities had to be regrouped in the same classes. In these multi-national/ethnic classes, German was the most understood language, yet its use often hurt the 'national feelings' of DP parents.[278] In other cases, DP children were sent to German schools. Some parents refused categorically to let their children attend German schools. For relief workers, this could potentially have disastrous consequences: 'A few DPs did not attend school unfortunately and emigrated without knowing how to read or write ... all their lives they bore the scars of excessive nationalism.'[279] In 1948, French authorities established a 'accelerated professional school' for adult illiterate DPs.[280]

Education was seen as a crucial part of the welfare programme. It was UNRRA's stated policy 'to provide schools and educational opportunity to all displaced persons under UNRRA care, including those residing outside of Assembly Centres'.[281] Education aimed at making DP children more self-confident and helped them overcome the feeling of being 'parasite, outcast or wreck.'[282] In January 1946, at the opening of a conference on education in the zone, the Director of UNRRA in the French zone reminded his audience 'one must never forget that UNRRA is taking care of children who have suffered a great deal, as much physically as morally, and that they cannot be treated as perfectly normal children'.[283] Having been deprived of the opportunity to attend school in wartime, relief workers believed that DPs were hungry for education and eager to make up for lost time. Many young DPs from the age of 14 to 18 did not know how to read and write neither their mother tongue nor German.[284] The strong insistence on providing a good education to DP children could prove difficult for some children and teenagers, however. For all its reservoir of enthusiasm, UNRRA efforts to educate DP children were hampered by the absence of books, inadequate

---

[275] Gatrell, *The Making of the Modern Refugee*, pp. 220–221.
[276] HCRFA, *Sept ans en faveur des Personnes Déplacées*, p. 38.
[277] UNA, UNRRA, S-0438-0009-05, Conférence sur l'éducation, 25 and 26 January 1946.
[278] *Sept-ans en faveur des Personnes Déplacées*, p. 38.
[279] Ibid., p. 39.
[280] See Chapter 5.
[281] UNA, UNRRA, S-0438-0009-05, Agenda, Conference on Educational and Community Activities UNRRA French zone, 25–26 January 1946.
[282] UNA, UNRRA, S-0438-0009-05, Conférence sur l'éducation, 25 and 26 January 1946.
[283] Ibid.
[284] Walczewski, *Destin tragique des polonais déportés en Allemagne*, pp. 16–17; Also see HCRFA, *Sept ans en faveur des Personnes Déplacées*, p. 38.

facilities, various needs of DP children who had missed years of education, teacher shortages and the dispersal of DPs throughout the territory. As a result, schooling facilities varied greatly from one area to another.[285] In some camps the *Mission scolaire Polonaise* [Polish School Mission] established Polish national schools, while in other areas, DP children had to attend German schools, even though some DP parents were opposed to it.[286] According to UNRRA's figures, by November 1946, 995 children (aged 6–10) and 1,655 (aged 10–18) were enrolled in schools across the French zone.[287] In the Northern part of the zone, in April 1946, there was a 'national school' in every camp, except Niederlahnstein.[288] These schools helped foster the development of DP cultural nationalism, for teachers revisited 'Poland's history, national patriotic traditions, heritage, religion and language'.[289] French administrators and relief workers were aware that DP schools contributed to fostering nationalism amongst what they recognized as national or ethnic groups. In their views, the development of cultural nationalism could undermine the transformation of DPs into assimilated immigrants.

French authorities tried to curb the spread of DP nationalism amongst groups that were considered as potential and valuable migrants. They notably allowed some DP children to attend French schools, where they would be initiated into 'the spirit of French culture'.[290] The majority of Baltic DPs in Freiburg went, for instance, to French secondary school.[291] French authorities also created a French school in Kandel for DPs coming from the Banat, where French teachers taught children in French.[292] This school aimed to instil particular affection for France and prepare Banatais children for their future integration in France. It also formed part of wider French efforts to disseminate French culture in Germany. In German schools, French culture and history were taught in French, as were teacher-training courses. The re-education of German youth was understood as the assimilation of French values by the

---

[285] UNA, UNRRA, S-0438-0006-02, E. Zach, Assistant Eligibility and Care Officer, Monthly Report November 1946, 30 November 1946.
[286] UNA, UNRRA, S-0438-0003-04, E. J. Bastianen à Melle Roberts, 27 March 1946.
[287] Ibid.
[288] UNA, UNRRA, S-0438-0005-02, Rapport du service 'welfare' sur le district nord de la zone, R. le Goff, 11 April 1946.
[289] Anna Jaroszynska-Kirchmann, 'Patriotism, Responsibility, and the Cold War: Polish Schools in DP Camps in Germany, 1945–1951', *The Polish Review*, vol. 47, no. 1 (2002), pp. 35–66, 36.
[290] UNA, UNRRA, S-0438-0003-04, Directeur des Personnes Déplacées à Directeur de l'éducation Publique, 22 July 1946; Général de Corps d'Armée Lenclud à l'Administrateur Général, 11 December 1946.
[291] UNA, UNRRA, S-0438-0009-05, Conference sur l'éducation, 25 and 26 January 1946.
[292] *Sept-ans en faveur des personnes déplacées*, p. 44.

Germans.[293] However, and perhaps understandably, the evidence suggests that DPs, at the exception of Banatais and some Baltic DPs, proved reluctant to send their children to French schools.[294] By providing French schooling to 'rehabilitate' some (but not all) DPs, French authorities clearly differentiated between DPs that they saw as valuable 'future' citizens and those who were supposed to emigrate elsewhere. Similar lines of difference were apparent in the vocational training programme implemented in the French zone. As we will see in the next chapter, re-education and vocational training were enacted in ways that reveal the persistence of gender discrimination and ethnic prejudices.

## Conclusion

To conclude, what kind of DPs did relief workers attempt to 'remake' in the French zone? This chapter reveals that despite important material shortages, many relief workers were convinced of their ability to reshape the lives of 'broken' and 'fragile' DPs, particularly young DPs. They went beyond the simple distribution of supplies. They set up rest homes, where young DPs could engage in outdoor activities. They helped DP parents obtain education and vocational training and, in some cases, attempted to impose specific domestic arrangements onto DPs. They stressed the importance of play and nature for child's development and gardening to overcome mental turmoil of war and displacement. All together, they promulgated a highly gendered vision of relief that centred on helping DP mothers to care *for* (nurturing) their children, and DP fathers to care *about* (breadwinning) their children. This set of practices was influenced by various pre-war ideas about 'overcoming' poverty and war-induced injuries, including the inter-war 'practical education', social hygiene crusade and vocational training movement. Relief workers placed, in particular, a renewed emphasis on the 'return to the countryside' to meet the emotional, psychological and physical needs of DP children. Since the early days of the Third Republic, the 'transfer to the countryside' was a key element of state paternalism. For all UNRRA's insistence on novelty and the 'modernization' of relief, its welfare programme was enacted in the French zone in ways that reveal the persistence of conservative social ethics.

The 'successes' of rehabilitation are difficult to measure, but should certainly not be overestimated. Some DPs, including the disabled, ill and 'mentally impaired', were excluded from these programmes, while others were left in German health facilities, under the 'care' of their former oppressors. Likewise,

---

[293] Monique Mombert, *Sous le signe de la rééducation : Jeunesse et livre en zone française d'occupation, 1945-1949* (Strasbourg : Presses Universitaires de Strasbourg, 1995), p. 35.

[294] UNA, UNRRA, S-0438-0003-04, Stregels, Directeur du Team 581 à Direction Générale de la Zone Française, 15 November 1946.

we need to interrogate relief workers' confidence in the 'therapeutic' nature of open-air homes in the black forest in Germany's South West, where some DP children spent days in the fresh air and sun and ate an ample diet. The temporary placement of children in these houses caused grave anxieties amongst a number of DP parents and DP children, who found these temporary separations emotionally difficult. An examination of the range of 'treatments' available in the French zone thus reveals the tensions between the utilitarian (turning DPs into productive future citizens for emigration abroad or their home country) and recreational (providing soothing and restful activities) roles of rehabilitation, between the disciplinary (controlling DPs' bodies) and empowering nature (encouraging DPs' expression and initiatives) of relief activities.

By providing French schooling and vocational training to some (but not all DPs), French authorities clearly differentiated between DPs that they considered as valuable future citizens and those who were expected to return home or emigrate elsewhere. Rehabilitation was enacted in ways that reveal the persistence of gender discrimination and ethnic prejudices. For some DPs, rehabilitation was experienced as a deeply oppressive and infantilizing set of practices. According to Ignacy Walczewski, 'all DPs received the same food rations, clothes, duvet and bed; all DPs were asked to read the same books and newspapers; all DPs were forced to do the same leisure organised by welfare officers'.[295] Camp authorities acted as a 'providence' regulating every aspect of DP life, from their housing, food rationing and clothes to their leisure activities.[296] For others, such as DP artists who exhibited their production in the French zone, it helped them soothe homesickness, create a sense of belonging and present 'cultural worthiness' to relief workers and French occupiers alike.

---

[295] Walczewski, *Destin tragique des polonais déportés en Allemagne*, p. 59.
[296] Ibid.

# 5

## 'Rehabilitation' through Work?
### Vocational Training and DP Employment

A 1946 illustrated story published in *La France en Allemagne*, a magazine edited by the Military Government's Information Service, detailed UNRRA's efforts to instil a work ethic amongst DPs. It drew the reader's attention to the central role that employment played not only in the economy of the zone, but also in the reconstruction of each individual DP. The author of this article unequivocally maintained that DPs' conditions were unlike those of the Germans, UNRRA recognizing the DPs' victim status by granting them a (theoretical) generous daily food ration of 2,300 calories. Able-bodied DPs who refused employment were merely 'deprived of amenity supplies, in other words treats, such as chocolate or supplementary cigarette rations'.[1] The author assured readers that the overwhelming majority of DPs themselves were in fact extremely anxious to find employment, omitting that some of them were reluctant to work for their former German oppressors. According to the author, DPs organized a multitude of small workshops, including shoemaking and repairing, tailoring, dressmaking and carpentry. DP productions were even exhibited in the zone's capital in June 1946. This exhibition of DP embroidery in Baden-Baden, entitled *Art and Work*, was an impressive affair and a 'roaring success' (Fig. 5.1).[2] UNRRA archival documents concur: the exhibition had been so 'widely acclaimed' that the UNRRA Paris Mission negotiated with the French Foreign Ministry and the Ministry PDR over the possibility of transporting it to Paris.[3]

Of course, this had clear political and ideological dimensions. Whilst, during the inter-war years, Paris provided the venue for exhibitions of France's 'humanitarian achievements' in its colonies, at the Liberation, French governments strove to celebrate their country's good deeds in the German ruins towards the victims of Nazism. Indeed, French authorities

---

[1] 'Les activités de l'UNRRA dans la zone française', in *La France en Allemagne*, no. 1, July 1946, pp. 49–51, 50.
[2] Ibid., pp. 50–51.
[3] UNA, UNRRA, S-0417-0002-02, Ph. De Vomécourt à Brigadier General W. Fraser, 18 June 1946. This project was, however, later abandoned. S-0421-0031-05, Bastiaenen, Compte-rendu de la réunion du 22 Aout, Freiburg in Brigsau.

'REHABILITATION' THROUGH WORK 249

Fig. 5.1   UNA, UNRRA, S-0421-0031-01, Exhibition, 'Art and Work', 2–16 June 1946.

prided themselves in having succeeded in placing DPs in employment whereas their Western Allies had largely failed.[4] In February 1947, for example, the parliamentary mission that toured DP camps in Germany reported that French employment figures were eloquent proof of this achievement. In the British and American zones, employment rates did not reach more than 30 per cent of the employable DP population.[5] In the French zone, they attained nearly 87 per cent of the employable population: out of the 19,990 employable

---

[4] According to Malcolm Proudfoot's estimates, approximately one-half of employable DPs worked in the three Western zones. *European Refugees, 1939–1952* (London: Faber and Faber, 1957), p. 255.

[5] CAC, Fontainbleau, 770623, article 172, Rapport commun établi par les membres de la mission d'information sur le problème des personnes déplacées des trois zones d'occupation en Allemagne, 9–23 February 1947, pp. 6–7.

DPs, 17,366 were registered as being in work.[6] Highly satisfied with this result, French authorities congratulated themselves on their advancement of more individualistic and effective solutions for the DPs, in marked contrast with American methods, which, they inferred, catalyzed the development of a 'begging complex' amongst DPs.[7] And yet, the reality behind DP employment was far more grim than this self-congratulatory account suggested.

First, whilst UNRRA Central Administration rejected the compulsion to work, French authorities did not. On 5 December 1945, the commandant of the Military Government Pierre-Marie Koenig issued an order stipulating that DPs who refused work would be deprived of the privileges associated with their DP status.[8] In other words, they would lose their access to food and accommodation, and not only 'treats' as suggested in La France en Allemagne's article. Work thus became more a duty than a right in the French zone. Second, although the Administrator General Emile Laffon introduced safeguards in February 1946 to protect DPs working under German supervision, intense friction between DPs and their former oppressors persisted. As an UNRRA employment officer observed, some Germans offered DPs 'the work they [the Germans] did not want to do'.[9] In Württemberg, '[t]he situation of our workers is essentially the same as that during the war, when they were forced by Germans to do the hardest work. Coercion has stopped, but the jobs offered to them are exactly the same'.[10] While many DPs had little choice other than to accept these unattractive jobs, many Germans were disinclined to work alongside them – and some of those who did in turn mistreated them. In October 1946, for example, a DP strike broke out in the Zelstoffabrik factory in Ehingen. Amongst DPs' grievances were the brutal management methods of their German Director, an ex-Nazi official. One of the DP representatives pinpointed their resentment: 'People who wore the swastika during the war, [...] who shouted "Heil Hitler" [...] are now the direct supervisors of DPs.'[11]

---

[6] UNA, UNRRA, S-1021-0085-03, Ateliers et programmes d'éducation professionnelle, Zone Française [May 1947], p. 6.

[7] HCRFA, Service des Personnes Déplacées, Sept ans d'activité en faveur des personnes déplacées en zone française d'occupation, 1945–1952, Rapport dactylographié et illustré, [undated], [Bibliothèque du Ministère des Affaires Etrangères, Direction des Archives], p. 27.

[8] MAE, HCRFA, ADM 40, L'Administrateur Général Laffon à Président du Gouvernement Provisoire de la République, N. 5831, 30 January 1946. Also see Letter N. 5773 from Laffon to Général de Corps d'Armées, Adjoint pour le Commandement Supérieur des Troupes d'Occupation, 19 January 1946.

[9] UNA, UNRRA, S-0421-0029-05, J. Rozale à Mr E. P. Moreland et Gouverneur Délégué Supérieur pour le GM du Wurtemberg, Tübingen, 25 June 1946.

[10] Ibid.

[11] UNA, UNRRA, S-0432-0004-01, Dunst, Chef des camps du cercle de Ehingen, 7 September 1946.

Employment conditions crucially depended on where DPs lived, for whom they worked and their nationality and gender. French employment methods could be overbearing and oppressive; they frequently led to conflict as DPs refused to work for German employers. Furthermore, they contributed to the reinforcement of ethnic and gender differences amongst DPs. They often advantaged intellectual Baltic DPs and Banatais farmers, who tended to have easier access to work in camps' administration or workshops, and therefore received better rations of food and cigarettes. Polish and Ukrainian DPs, on the contrary, faced more prejudice and were more likely to be forced to work outside camps. Significant efforts were made to help a number of DPs acquire the means to learn a trade, but employment discourses often reaffirmed a hierarchical taxonomy in which productivity and desirability were explicitly linked to ethnic and gender differences. This chapter thereby contends that employment policies were deeply implicated in the mixed record of the zone: the emphasis on DP employment made at times possible the development of DPs' own initiatives and their sense of responsibility, in enabling them to run independent workshops and giving them the opportunity to live in private accommodation.[12] In this sense, it contributed to normalizing DPs' living conditions and, very occasionally, did justice to the tremendous potential of DPs' own entrepreneurialism. At the same time, actual implementation of employment policies revealed disturbing indications of brutality, unjustifiable in their cruelty and arbitrariness, as the example of the Zelstoffabrik confirms.

## Rehabilitation through Coercion?

DP employment policies aligned with the post-1945 ideology of productivism. Amid all the conflict and discord between the PDR Direction and French UNRRA Headquarters, one area of outright agreement appeared to endure: DPs were expected to work in return for the protection that France was granting them. On this, UNRRA relief workers and local PDR officials concurred with occupation officials. For French administrators, it was unthinkable to support a 'group of idle people incapable of participating in the

---

[12] Until the mid-1980s, historians tended to present the French as harsh occupiers, who exaggeratedly requisitioned German clothes and raw materials, undertook excessive, frenzied industrial removals and imposed a draconian food policy on the German population under their control. The historical reputation of the French zone has undergone a significant rehabilitation since the 1980s. For a review of this historiographical shift, see, for instance, Rainer Hudemann, 'Revanche ou parternariat' A propos des nouvelles orientations de la recherche sur la politique française à l'égard de l'Allemagne après 1945', in Gilbert Krebs and Gérard Schneilin (eds.), *L'Allemagne 1945-1955. De la capitulation à la division* (Asnières: Publication de l'Institut d'Allemand, 1996), pp. 127–152; 'L'occupation française après 1945 et les relations franco-allemandes', *Vingtième Siècle. Revue d'histoire*, vol. 55, no. 3 (1997), pp. 58–68.

reconstruction of their homeland', while French workers at home were asked to participate to the 'battle of production' and roll up their sleeves for the reconstruction of France.[13] As Charles de Gaulle maintained in 1945, '[y]esterday there was no national duty that had precedence over the duty to fight. But today there is none that can take precedence over that to produce'.[14] Leaders from the Communist Party, the *Mouvement Républicain Populaire* [Popular Republican Movement] and the *Section Française de l'Internationale Ouvrière* [French Socialist Party], all presented production as the highest duty of the French workers.

Beyond the economic demands of reconstruction, the advocacy of employment was prompted by several other factors. On the one hand, employment was, for some occupation officials and Army commanders, part of a series of measures aimed at hardening DPs' living conditions in order to encourage them to return home.[15] Many relief workers were irritated by the attitudes of occupation officials towards DP work. Too often, as an UNRRA officer notes, French Army officers forgot 'that DPs [were] our Allies, that most of them were deported or "displaced" for several years' and that not all of them were 'black sheep'.[16] Indeed, some occupation officials saw DPs as a reservoir of young, able-bodied, cheap and docile workers: they could be placed in any job, and could be reasonably expected to put up with poor wages, unregulated working hours and discrimination. The policy of compulsion to work therefore included markedly repressive elements. The Military Cabinet, a socially and politically conservative group constituted mainly of experienced military officers, craved order, stability and the rule of law.[17] Reflecting the Cabinet's views, in December 1945, its head the General Pierre-Marie Koenig announced the creation of three disciplinary camps for male DPs, located in Nonnenhof (Württemberg), the Trier-Kemmel Caserne (Rhineland) and Lörrach (Baden).[18] A month later, as anxieties about DPs' lack of discipline mounted, the Cabinet Director Henri Navarre called for vigilant policing of

---

[13] UNA, UNRRA, S-0421-0031-09, Bastiaenen à Thomasset, 11 February 1946.

[14] Quoted in Rebecca Pulju, *Women and Mass Consumer Society in Postwar France* (Cambridge: Cambridge University Press, 2011), p. 8 ; Also see Gerard Bossuat, 'The Modernization of France: A New Economic and Social Order after the Second World War ?', in Dominik Geppert (ed.), *The Postwar Challenge, 1945–1958* (Oxford: Oxford University Press, 2007), pp. 151–178.

[15] Andreas Rinke, *Le Grand retour – Die französische Displaced Person-Politik (1944–1951)* (Frankfurt am Main: Peter Lang, 2002), pp. 295–296.

[16] UNRRA, S-0421-0029-02, Zone Employment Officer à General de Marguerite dit 'Lize', 27 mai 1946; Also see S-0432-0003-01, Note de service, Travailleurs PDR employés par le centre de recuperation véterinaire de Nierderauerbach, 21 March 1947.

[17] Martial Libera *Un Rêve de Puissance: La France et le Contrôle de l'économie Allemande (1942-1949)* (Bruxelles: Peter Lang, 2012), p. 323.

[18] UNA, UNRRA, S-0421-0059-03, Note de Service, No. 6290 DGAA Dir PDR, transmis le 1 Avril 1946 par Laffon à Général Délégué Supérieur pour le Gouvernement militaire du Palatinat; refered to letter No. 1611, CAB-CC dating from 4 December 1945.

the DP population. He maintained that French authorities might achieve better results 'by shooting several culprits in each camp'.[19] For these officers, if DPs were not happy, they could return home, as the Military Governor of the Württemberg attested: '[T]hose who did not want to go home need[ed] to understand that they [could] not be stakeholders, but that they need[ed] to contribute to the economy of the Nation that protect[ed] and fe[d] them.'[20] In Niederlahnstein, a Commandant concurred: '[o]ne needs to understand that young and idle people, fed and housed in the camps, even if modestly, must in return serve the French authorities' mission through the work they perform. It is not a question of compulsory work, it is a matter of moral obligation.'[21]

Relevant here is the extent to which manual work was widely praised at the Liberation for its healing and therapeutic virtues. French relief workers and occupation officials drew substantially on the precedent set up by the Vichy regime, which had correlated manual labour with social harmony. Just as French social planners launched a veritable 'bataille du reclassement' (professional reassignment) for war veterans, repatriated prisoners and deportees on the domestic front, French relief workers embarked on a 'crusade for DP re-employment' in the zone.[22] French policy-elites and social commentators saw many virtues in productive and manual work aside from economic ones, including 're-generation, morality, patriotism, and humanism'.[23] According to the director of the PDR organization, 'among the normal activities of an individual, work is one of the most noble and commendable'.[24] Employment was perceived as the best remedy against DP apathy and idleness.[25] It was argued that acquiring a manual trade could help DPs to escape their moral suffering and restore the psychological balance disrupted by the war.

---

[19] MAE, HCRFA, Ambassade de Bonn 148, Direction du Cabinet, Fiche pour le Général Koenig signée Navarre, 11 January 1946.
[20] UNA, UNRRA, S-0421-0029-03, Le Gouverneur à Directeur de l'UNRRA Zone Sud, 9 July 1946.
[21] UNA, UNRRA, S-0421-0021-01, Cdt. J. Truchet, Note de service, 7 March 1947.
[22] For the term crusade in the French zone, UNA, UNRRA, S-0438-0003-03, De Fos à Lavigne, Field-Supervisor, 5 June 1946.
[23] Daniel Cohen, 'Regeneration through Labor: Vocational Training and the Reintegration of Deportees and Refugees, 1945–1950', *Proceedings of the Western Society for French History*, vol. 32 (2004), pp. 368–385, 384, http://hdl.handle.net/2027/spo.0642292.0032.021. On the adoption of work as therapy elsewhere, see, for example, Waltraud Ernst (ed.), *Work, Psychiatry and Society, c. 1750–2010* (Manchester: Manchester University Press, 2016).
[24] UNA,UNRRA, S-0421-0024-05, Directeur PDR à Général de Corps d'armée, 23 March 1946.
[25] UNA, UNRRA, S-1021-0085-02, Team 585, Historique du Service Welfare, 24 March 1947; Silvia Salvatici, 'From Displaced Persons to Labourers: Allied Employment Policies in Post-war West Germany', in Jessica Reinisch and Elizabeth White (eds.), *The Disentanglement of Populations: Migration, Expulsion and Displacement in Postwar Europe* (London: Palgrave Macmillan, 2011), pp. 210–228, 215.

This emphasis on the recuperative aspects of work, for the national and individual body, was also evident in charitable approaches to work. While professional reintegration had always been an important component of Jewish philanthropic activities, its importance rose in post-war France.[26] Indeed, Laure Fourtage points out that charity work, particularly when it lasted over long periods, was negatively perceived, allegedly reinforcing its recipients' feelings of humiliation, loss of self-confidence and demoralization.[27] Employment promoted a sense of dignity, freeing DPs from their 'dependency syndrome' and enhancing their sense of morality. In Germany, the American *Joint* encouraged, for instance, young Jewish DPs to work in German enterprises to learn a profession, despite DPs' reluctance to help rebuilding the German economy.[28] Some philanthropic organizations insisted on the necessity of forging new communities through labour.[29] In the French zone, the World ORT Union organized, for instance, apprenticeship and workshops for Jewish DPs in Gailingen, near the Swiss border.[30] The ORT (Organisation Reconstruction travail) was inspired by the philosophy of *productivization* set forth by socialist Zionist Russian thinkers at the end of the nineteenth century, aiming at the regeneration through manual labour and their *deghettoization* through their integration in the working class.[31] Although the Jewish population was relatively small in the French zone, it is worth recording that there were several kibboutzim in Jordanbad, Konstanz and Gailingen.[32] These

---

[26] On the 'religion of work' and 'sanctity of labour' in the inter-war period see, for instance, Daniel Lee, *Pétain's Jewish Children. French Jewish Youth and the Vichy Regime, 1940–1942* (Oxford: Oxford University Press, 2014), p. 39.

[27] Laure Fourtage, 'Les organisations juives d'aide sociale et l'insertion professionnelle dans l'immédiat après-guerre', *Archives Juives*, vol. 45, no. 1 (2012), pp. 10–26, 13. Also see Laura Hobson Faure, *Un 'plan Marshall' juif: la présence juive américaine en France après la Shoah, 1944–1954* (Paris: Armand Colin, 2013).

[28] JDC Archives, Records of the Geneva Office, GER. 68, H. Laufer, Report on the situation of the Jews in the French zone, 28 April 1947.

[29] On the *Joint* and the reconstruction of Jewish communities in post-war France see Hobson Faure, *Un 'plan Marshall' juif*, p. 141.

[30] Sarah Kavanaugh, *ORT, The Second World War and the Rehabilitation of Holocaust Survivors* (London: Vallentine Mitchell, 2008), p. 81.

[31] Daniel Cohen 'The West and the Displaced, 1945-1951: the Post-war roots of Political Refugees', PhD thesis, New York University (2000), p. 229; For an overview of the ORT work in Paris see Sophie Enos-Attali and Emmanuelle Polack, 'La contribution de l'ORT à la reconstruction de l'artisanat juif parisien dans l'immédiat après-guerre: l'exemple des métiers du textile', *Archives Juives*, vol. 39, no. 2 (2006), pp. 64–71.

[32] HA6B-2/1, Report Nr. 1 Jewish Relief Unit, Biberach, 10 June 1946, Dixi Heim; JDC Archives, Records of the Geneva Office, GER. 569, L. Kurland and Ruth Lambert, Report on the Situation and the Sanitary Needs of the Jewish Population in the French Zone in Germany, 15 August 1946; Records of the Geneva Office, GER. 68, H. Laufer, Report on the situation of the Jews in the French zone, 28 April 1947; For Jordanbad, see Reinhold Adler, 'Der schwierige Weg zur Normalität. Die UNRRA in Biberach und Umgebung

agricultural training centers were aimed at preparing DPs for immigration in Palestine and helping them imagine their future in the Jewish homeland. As Dan Stone notes, kibbutz was both a 'protector and an incubator of trauma' for Jewish DPs. In these labour groups, DPs were able to share their grief. Yet, they also became defined by it.[33] Tensions occurred between relief workers and Jewish communities on the ground. In the French zone, for instance, the representative of the American *Joint* deplored the ways these 'elite of the Jewish DPs' disappeared within 'a few hours' in the spring of 1947, selling to German population 'everything they could not take along', leaving behind debts with the German farmers and building in 'terribly filthy state'.[34] Despite this, the *Joint* pursued its efforts at encouraging DPs' work. From May 1947, the *Joint* decided to stop the distribution of supplies to any 'Jew between 16 and 38 years who d[id] not work or refuse[d] to work'.[35]

## Work Therapy

For UNRRA Employment specialists too, vocational training was an important factor in 'helping people to help themselves', by developing their skills and self-confidence.[36] They encouraged active over passive therapy.[37] UNRRA authorities recommended that each 'assembly centre' organize workshops in order to teach or refresh DP vocational skills. In the inaugural of the Gutach school, DP students were told that driving lessons, sewing courses, artistic workshop and university lectures were all intended to give 'each individual the possibility to reintegrate the position that they deserved in the global economy'.[38] Despite the difficulties in obtaining tools and raw materials in the context of French industrial removals and requisition policies, and despite the shortage of DP trained instructors, workshops and training courses flourished in many DP centres.[39]

---

1945 bis 1947', *Gesellschaft für Heimatpflege Stadt und Landkreis Biberach* (2007), pp. 36–57, 42–45.

[33] Dan Stone, *The Liberation of the Camps: The End of the Holocaust and Its Aftermath* (New Haven: Yale University Press, 2015), p. 175.

[34] JDC Archives, Records of the Geneva Office, GER. 68, H. Laufer, Report on the situation of the Jews in the French zone, 28 April 1947.

[35] Ibid.

[36] HA5-4/3, Report on Psychological Problems of Displaced Persons, 1 June 1945, pp. 1–41, 14 ; AN, AJ/43/1141, Jacques Bloch, *Problèmes de l'orientation professionnelle des enfants juifs victimes de la guerre* (Genève: OSE, 1947), p. 4.

[37] Silvia Salvatici, 'Help the People to Help Themselves': UNRRA Relief workers and European Displaced Persons', *Journal of Refugee Studies*, vol. 25, no. 3 (2012), pp. 428–451.

[38] UNA, UNRRA, S-0438-0005-05, Discours, Ecole de Formation Sociale Gutach [undated ; unsigned].

[39] UNA, UNRRA, S-0421-0029-03, Sebille à O. Gobert, 4 July 1946.

Some UNRRA directors had also made sure that DPs were given the opportunity to become apprentices in German factories.[40] In Landstuhl, for instance, the UNRRA Director launched a 'crusade for DPs' reemployment'.[41] Convinced that Allied nationals should not be forced to work in unwanted jobs in enemy country, he made considerable efforts to find tools and materials for DPs.[42] 'Without official help', he organized a forestry worksite, cabinet-work and embroidery workshops.[43] In July 1946, Landstuhl had very good carpenters and a machine workshop that was 'magnificently equipped'.[44] Vocational guidance was underpinned by gender ideologies: while DP women were actively encouraged to embrace a 'domestic role' and taught conventionally feminine skills, relief workers sought to discipline male adult DPs' behaviour through 'masculine' work and impose masculine traits of physical strength, determination and willpower. As vocational theorists had done during the inter-war period, relief workers consistently reaffirmed the maternal role as woman's true destiny and confined women to profession that were deemed 'feminine'.

'Work therapy' has a long and complex history. It was widely used as a treatment in mental asylums since the nineteenth century in both metropolitan France and the Empire.[45] It was also employed in military hospitals to heal physically and mentally wounded men during the First World War. As Jennifer Laws argues, it was part of a capitalist ideology, which aimed to transform the sick into semi-skilled worker and instil the values of self-interest and self-discipline.[46] Work therapy gained even greater salience under the influence of the Arts and Craft movement and the vocational guidance movement (*'reorientation professionnelle'*) in the inter-war period.[47] Pre-war ideas about professional re-orientation shaped both welfare discourses and the classification of employment for DPs in the French zone. UNRRA trainings

---

[40] MAE, HCRFA, PDR6/487, Rapport N. 15 Officier Léon à Directeur des Personnes Déplacées, 19 March 1946.
[41] UNA, UNRRA, S-0438-0003-03, De Fos à Lavigne, Field-Supervisor, 5 June 1946.
[42] UNA, UNRRA, S-0421-0047-02, De Fos à Field Supervisor, 18 October 1946; S-0421-0047-03, De Fos à Gobert, 29 May 1946.
[43] UNA, UNRRA, S-0421-0047-03, Directeur du District à De Fos, 18 July 1946; De fos à Capitaine Malgrat, 2 August 1946; S-0421-0041-03, De Fos à Field Supervisor N. 1, 25 January 1947.
[44] UNA, UNRRA, S-0417-0003-03, translation, raport Dorothea Greene, 30 July 1946.
[45] See, for instance, Claire Edington, *Beyond the Asylum. Mental Illness in French Colonial Vietnam* (Ithaca, NY: Cornell University Press, 2019).
[46] Jennifer Laws, 'Crackpots and Basket-Cases: A History of Therapeutic Work and Occupation', *History of the Human Sciences*, vol. 24, no. 2 (2011), pp. 65–81.
[47] J. Wolf-Machoel, *La réadaptation de la jeunesse et des déracinés de guerre* (Boudry: Les Editions de la Baconniere, 1945), pp. 186–187; Mary Louise Roberts, *Civilization without Sexes: Reconstructing Gender in Post-war France, 1917–1927* (Chicago: University of Chicago Press, 1994), pp. 184–196.

were based on the idea that an individual should be able to choose any profession for which they were suited. And yet, UNRRA insisted on manual work for DPs. During a welfare meeting in January 1946, a senior welfare officer insisted on how DPs should be helped to select a profession according to their ability, taste and the demands of the labour market, even though psycho-technic tests were not possible due to issue of language. She recommended for men, building and mechanical work, leatherwork, carpentry, textiles, metal work and, for women, childcare, nursery, embroidery, knitting and cooking.[48]

The promotion of vocational training and manual labour to assuage the effects of displacement was used in the aftermath of the First World War, when 'practical education' was employed with survivors of the Armenian Genocide. The American Near East Relief promoted, for instance, 'practical education' for children in the Near East, using earlier measures that had been employed in the United States with black Americans of the South. This education contributed, however, to maintain a socioeconomic structure in which they were at the lowest place.[49] During the 1920s, the League of Nations also advocated investment in Greece to assist the integration of refugees from Turkey.[50] In 1945, the Dutch industrialist Wolf-Machoel published *La réadaptation de la jeunesse et des déracinés de guerre*, in which he documented the psychological effects of home abandonment, including inner turmoil and paralysis of reasoning.[51] According to him, vocational training could help overcome these pathologies of displacement.

In the aftermath of the Second World War, vocational training acquired a broader symbolic meaning in the context of the politics of retribution, however. It was considered by a number of relief workers and DPs alike as a 'moral reparation'. In May 1946, the DP committees of Ravensburg (Stateless, Estonian, Latvian, Lithuanian, Hungarian, Yugoslav and Polish) protested against the fact that DPs were forced to work in Baienfurt's textile industries. Having lost the 'best years of their lives', they believed that learning a trade should be seen as a sort of moral reparation for their losses.[52] For them, it seemed only proper that the Germans who had destroyed their youth should now at least fund their training for a future that most of them intended to

---

[48] UNA, HCRFA, S-0438-0009-05, Reunion des Welfare Officers du District Sud des Teams de l'Est, 15–16 January 1946, Wangen.
[49] Davide Rodogno, 'Beyond Relief: A Sketch of the Near East Relief's Humanitarian Operations, 1918–1929', *Monde(s)*, vol. 6 (2014), pp. 45–64.
[50] Peter Gatrell, *The Making of the Modern Refugee* (Oxford: Oxford University Press, 2013), p. 201.
[51] Wolf-Machoel, *La réadaptation de la jeunesse et des déracinés de guerre*, pp. 27–28.
[52] UNA, UNRRA, S-0421-0062-02, Comités nationaux des personnes déplacées à Directeur UNRRA Team 579, 27 May 1946.

pursue outside Germany.[53] Vocational training, then, was important to both DPs and relief workers, but it tended to privilege some groups over others. Some relief workers attributed unequal value to the work performed by Baltic and *Banatais,* considered as more hard-working. Polish and Ukrainian DPs, on the contrary, faced more widespread prejudice and were more likely to be forced to work outside camps.[54] Vocational training represented a means through which older forms of gender and ethnic ordering could be re-established.[55]

In the field of vocational training, UNRRA's efforts were assisted by several voluntary agencies, which provided materials, machines and instructors. In Freiburg, the American Christian Committee for Refugees (ACCR) helped to establish sewing and knitting school.[56] The YMCA meanwhile organized a training centre in Hinterzarten, which offered correspondence courses and established a workshop in Shramberg.[57] UNRRA district employment officer nevertheless lamented that YMCA training courses remained too theoretical and insufficiently practical. The Inter-governmental Committee for Refugees (IGCR) contributed to the creation of an experimental centre in Ravensburg.[58] In the summer of 1947 nearly 100 DPs were trained in this professional centre, taking classes in electrical engineering, radio-telephony, the job of assistant topographer, civil engineering and industrial design. The YMCA also tried to promote the development of international *foyers* [centres]. In April 1946, Welfare Officers were invited for a two-day workshop on 'leisure activities' organized by UNRRA and the YMCA.[59] This training focused on how relief workers 'could help to mould these young people into leaders of their own people'.[60] During this workshop, Welfare Officers were told how to build a

---

[53] UNA, UNRRA, S-0432-0004-01, Dunst, Chef des camps du cercle de Ehingen, 7 September 1946.

[54] HCRFA, Direction générale des Affaires politiques, 116, Note pour Monsieur le Directeur du Travail, Le chef de la Section Main-d'Oeuvre, 27 March 1946. For more see Chapter 1.

[55] The inter-war hierarchy within the category of white labour and fragmentation of 'whiteness' remained powerful in the aftermath of the Second World War. Elisa Camiscioli, *Reproducing the French Race: Immigration, Intimacy and Embodiment in the early Twentieth Century* (Durham: Duke University Press, 2009), p. 7.

[56] UNA, UNRRA, S-1021-0085-06, Bastiaenen, Historique du Centre DP de Fribourg; AN, AJ/43/759, PCIRO French Zone headquarters, Rapport mensuel narratif du directeur de zone au chef des operations Juillet 1947, p. 13.

[57] UNA, UNRRA, S-1021-0084-13, Le Service aux Personnes Déplacées de l'Alliance Universelle YMCA/YWCA en Zone Française d'Occupation; S-0419-0003-05, Lettre de L. H. Hebert, Directeur YMCA, à Relief Services – Welfare Division, 27 June 1946.

[58] AN, AJ/43/594, Lettre de A. Poignant (PCIRO) à Monsieur P. Jacobsen, 4 June 1948.

[59] UNA, S-0421-0078-03, Lettre de Mrs G. M. Garvey, Principal Welfare Officer à tous les Welfare Officers du District du Sud Est du Wurttemberg, 10 April 1946.

[60] UNA, UNRRA, S-0438-0003-02, G. M. Garvey to Miss B. G. Roberts, Conference at Wurzach, 17–18 April, 7 May 1946.

foyer, based on the instructor's experience with French soldiers installed in Switzerland after the defeat of 1940. In order to enable DPs' minds to rest, welfare workers were encouraged to ban 'politics' or 'chauvinism'. They also had to ensure that no nationality dominated. Each *foyer* had to hold a library, a canteen, a radio and a room for concerts, conferences and talks. Moreover, 'to be attractive, the *foyer* [had to] be adequately decorated'.[61] As we saw in the previous chapter, voluntaries agencies, as much as UNRRA and occupation officials, drew on earlier practices developed for wounded and incarcerated soldiers to 'remake' DPs' bodies and minds.

This prevailing discourse about the 'therapeutic' nature of work explained why nobody in the French zone opposed the idea of encouraging DPs to work, even if this entailed *forcing* them to accept work. Indeed, even Administrator General Laffon's more progressive Cabinet staff endorsed the need to encourage DPs to work. Laffon did, however, set himself against abusive labour practices. On 1 February 1946, he transmitted Koenig's order dating from 5 December 1945 to the Delegates of the various military governments. But he insisted that on 'no account, unless they expressly desired it', should DPs be directly employed by Germans. If DPs were to work under German supervision, 'an employment contract or a written statement of the worker stating his desire to be employed by a German employer' was required.[62] Moreover, Laffon required that DPs' employment corresponded, as far as it was possible, to their particular skills. And, finally, he exhorted local administrators to grant the DPs preferential treatment over Germans. Their food rations were to be 'equal to those of heavy workers', and in no circumstances 'inferior to those of the German workers in the same category'.[63] As far as disciplinary camps were concerned, their role was more to 're-educate rather than punish', these DPs having been 'during five years *des épaves* [wrecks], separated by force from their homeland and thereby [now] being entitled to indulgence'.[64]

This emphasis on DP employment was not, in itself, specific to French humanitarian discourse. As Silvia Salvatici suggests, American and British humanitarian actors were also convinced about the necessity to instil a work ethic amongst DPs.[65] In May 1945, the issue of DP employment was

---

[61] UNA, UNRRA, S-0438-0007-05, Résumé d'une causerie faite à Wurzach le 17 avril 1946 au cours de la réunion de Welfare UNRRA/YMCA, William Frey.
[62] MAE, HCRFA, Bade-Sud, Délégation cercles vrac, 39, Administrateur Général Laffon à Général Délégué Supérieur pour le GM de Bade, 1 February 1946; Also see PDR6/811, Laffon's letter to the Governor of Wurttemberg, 4 April 1946.
[63] Ibid.
[64] UNA, UNRRA, S-0421-0059-03, Note de Service, No. 6290 DGAA Dir PDR, transmis le 1 Avril 1946 par Laffon à Général Délégué Supérieur pour le Gouvernement militaire du Palatinat; refered to letter No. 1611,CAB-CC dating from 4 December 1945.
[65] Salvatici insists on Allied efforts to encourage DPs employment, Nicholas Bohatiuk, on the contrary, understates them. 'The Economic Aspects of Camp life', in W. Wsevolod

introduced in the *Guide to the Care of the Displaced Persons in Germany* circulated by the Supreme Headquarters Allied Expeditionary Force (SHAEF). This guide provided for four different types of DP labour, 'inside and outside the camps, at the service of the military forces but also in the German economy'.[66] The report *Psychological Problems of Displaced Persons* issued in June 1945 by the Welfare Division of the European Regional Office also emphasized the necessity of DPs' employment. The authors of this report argued that working gave DPs a sense of purpose, restored their self-respect and transformed them from 'passive recipients' of relief into 'active participating members of a hopeful and integrated community'.[67] The fundamental difference between French, British and American employment policies lays in the compulsory nature of the work performed.

Although British and American employment policies were not without their share of ambiguities, regulations stipulating requirements for compulsory employment were only approved in January 1947 in the British zone and none were ever issued in the American zone.[68] If British military authorities approved compulsion to work, it remained contrary to UNRRA's principles.[69] For the UNRRA administration, employment should be encouraged and stimulated by every possible means, provided, of course, that it did not interfere with repatriation, but it should be voluntary and paid.[70] The Welfare Division of UNRRA European Regional Office warned that compulsion to work in sectors that did not correspond to DPs' skills and in conditions that resembled their wartime situation were unlikely to restore DPs' sense of self-respect. On the contrary, this would exacerbate their 'feelings of being unloved and isolated in strange communities'.[71] Compulsory employment was clearly anathema to the concept of 'rehabilitation' as understood by UNRRA experts, who advocated instead the careful and graduated use of incentives. According to these experts, 'contentment or even happiness are in fact inevitably bound up with use of initiative and with the acceptance of

Isajiw, Yury Boshyk and Roman Senkus (eds.), *The Refugee Experience. Ukrainian Displaced Persons after World War Two* (Edmonton: Canadian Institute of Ukrainian Studies Press, 1992), pp. 69–89, 72.

[66] Salvatici, 'From Displaced Persons to Labourers', p. 211.

[67] WL, HA5-4/3, Welfare Division, *Report on Psychological Problems of Displaced Persons*, 1 June 1945, pp. 1–41, 26.

[68] Salvatici, 'From Displaced Persons to Labourers', pp. 210–228.

[69] Georges Woodbridge, *UNRRA: The History of the United Nations Relief and Rehabilitation Administration*, vol. 2 (New York: Colombia University Press, 1950), p. 519.

[70] Central Headquarters, Germany Administrative Order 18, 'Employment Program', 24 November 1945; S-0417-0004-09, Ordre Administratif No. 28, Programme d'Emploi, signé F. E. Morgan, 26 November 1945.

[71] WL, HA5-4/3, Welfare Division, *Report on Psychological Problems of Displaced Persons*, 1 June 1945, pp. 1–41, 34.

responsibility'.[72] More fundamentally, compulsion to work tested the language of human rights articulated by UN planners. UNRRA's Central Administration called for an end to the French policy of compulsory employment and the imprisonment of those DPs unwilling to work, claiming that these measures violated international norms regarding forced labour.[73] For all that, many French occupation and UNRRA officials condoned the practice, believing that certain conditions legitimated coercion. During UNRRA council sessions in May 1946, the French delegation proposed a resolution that would have introduced the compulsion to work throughout Germany, claiming that DP idleness was both a 'breach of morale' and a source of 'physical and professional ineptitude'.[74]

Behind this insistence on the obligation to work lay some traces of a colonialist mindset. Indeed, in some significant ways, French humanitarian discourses contained elements of domination that resemble labour discourses in late colonialism. The advocacy of compulsion to work stemmed, in part, from the conviction that the French knew better what served 'apathetic' DPs' best interests than the DPs did themselves. This assumption resembled the inter-war belief that the French knew what was in the interest of 'indolent' indigenous people in the colonies, especially those reluctant to accept the regimens of waged labour. As Alice Conklin suggests, colonial administrators believed that by forcing the colonized to work they were protecting them against their own 'lazy' inclinations, and that compulsion was, therefore, justifiable as long as it was 'explained' and did not exceed colonized people's 'capacity' for understanding.[75] In the inter-war years, French psychiatrists often praised labour, in particular agricultural labour, as one of the most successful and cost-effective forms of treatment for 'insane indigenous people'. Influenced by the system of hospitals for the insane that the Dutch administration had established in the East Indies, French experts in Indochina attempted, for instance, to inculcate the values of hard work and self-discipline to transform Vietnamese patients into productive subjects and good citizens.[76]

---

[72] Ibid., p. 22.
[73] UNA, UNRRA, S-0432-0004-03, Traduction, Myer Cohen à Général Lenclud, 21 March 1947.
[74] MAE, NUOI, 294, Télégramme No. 1785, Bousquet, 17 May 1946.
[75] Alice Conklin *A mission to civilize : The republican Idea of Empire in France and West Africa, 1895-1930* (Stanford : Stanford University Press, 1997), p. 227; James Daughton, 'ILO Expertise and Colonial Violence in the Interwar Years', in Sandrine Kott and Joëlle Droux (eds.), *Globalizing Social Rights. The International Labour Organisation and Beyond* (Basingtoke: Palgrave Macmillan, 2013), pp. 85–97, 88.
[76] Claire Edington and Hans Pols, 'Building Psychiatric Expertise across Southeast Asia: Study Trips, Site Visits and Therapeutic Labor in French Indochina and the Dutch East Indies, 1898–1937', *Comparative Studies in Society and History*, vol. 58, no. 3 (2016), pp. 636–663.

Similarly, some occupation and UNRRA officials believed that they, too, were saving DPs from themselves, by compelling them to combat their 'apathetic' illness. In practice, DPs had very little say over the terms under which aid was provided.

Certainly, DPs were not forced to work in desperate conditions comparable to those of the colonies. Labour abuses and related hardships in post-war Germany were comparable neither in scope nor scale to those in the colonial world during the inter-war years. Furthermore, perceptions of DPs' psyche were different. For instance, psychiatrists attributed a specific role to Islamic religious belief in shaping a supposedly unique 'African psyche'.[77] But French official thinking about DP employment was reminiscent of the dilemmas of the late French colonial regime, which espoused 'free labour' while, in practice, often sanctioning forced labour. In French African colonies, as Frederick Cooper suggests, forced labour fitted in a conventional vision of colonial administration that had become more open by the end of the Vichy period.[78] The Vichy regime had intensified the use of forced labour, when it had the power to do so. The reformist impulse created by the war did not lead to radically different position on labour in Africa. Certainly, the Brazzaville Conference in 1944 revealed that the French wanted to demonstrate that they were taking a clear departure. Yet, as Cooper notes, the French were still ready to use colonial authority to make Africans work in their own interest.[79] In the French zone, probably only around 40 per cent of the DPs worked in jobs widely seen as unappealing or involving heavy manual labour. Nevertheless, French embrace of manual work as therapy reflected an alignment between the need to cut relief costs, the institutional discourse of rehabilitation and the general economic imperative of maintaining a positive trade balance, which relied on cheap labour. It also drew in some significant ways on practices from the empire and narratives of imperial responsibility.[80]

## Forceful Recruitment, Unattractive Jobs

Coercion to work coexisted uneasily with the desire to present French humanitarian traditions in a new light. Employment was a domain for

---

[77] See, for instance, Richard Keller, *Colonial Madness. Psychiatry in French Africa* (Chicago: Chicago University Press, 2007); Julie Le Gac, 'Haunted by Jinns: Dealing with War Neuroses among Muslim soldiers during the Second World War', in Xavier Bougarel, Raphaëlle Branche and Cloé Drieu (eds.), *Combatants of Muslim Origin in European Armies in the Twentieth Century* (London: Bloomsbury, 2017), pp. 183–203.

[78] Frederick Cooper, *Decolonization and African Society. The Labor Question in French and British Africa* (Cambridge: Cambridge University Press, 1996), p. 146.

[79] Ibid., p. 160.

[80] On how French social workers implemented a transformed civilizing mission for Algerian migrants in France, see Amelia Lyons, *The Civilising Mission in the Metropole: Algerian Families and the French Welfare State during Decolonization* (Stanford, CA: Stanford University Press, 2013).

international surveillance and judgment. Criticized by UNRRA Central headquarters for complying with this French doctrine of coercion, the French UNRRA headquarters argued that sanctions for DPs refractory to work 'were applied with great moderation'. French officials noted that 'only about a hundred DPs were sent to disciplinary camps during the year 1946'.[81] According to UNRRA officials, the overwhelming majority of internees in disciplinary camps were not DPs who refused to work. Instead, they were German *Wehrwölfes* (former members of guerrilla movement formed by the Nazi party) and DPs accused of black-market activities and thefts.[82] On 29 March 1947, UNRRA Director Lenclud maintained that coercion was never fully implemented. The insignificant minority of DPs imprisoned were incarcerated without 'the help of UNRRA'.[83] French UNRRA authorities had indeed stipulated that under no circumstances were UNRRA staff to take steps to imprison DPs who refused to work.[84] Decisions about imprisoning DPs were strictly reserved for PDR or military officials. According to French UNRRA officials, UNRRA succeeded in protecting DPs against the PDR's inclination to impose forced labour without consideration for DPs' skills.[85]

As with the instructions on repatriation and eligibility, major discrepancies persisted between official policy and local practices, however. Repressive mechanisms endured at the lower level even after they had been condemned by those higher up in the policy-making chain. For instance, the Director of the *Economats* [shops for French occupation personnel] in Balingen sent a female Estonian DP to prison after she complained about the bad working conditions in the 'vegetable section' of his shop.[86] UNRRA's Area Employment Officer condemned this action, highlighting that the method employed towards her was 'unbecoming of a French man'.[87] Rumours about bad working conditions under French supervision reached the American zone.

---

[81] UNA, UNRRA, S-1021-0085-03, Report, O. Gobert, French Zone Employment Officer March 1946–March 1947, 17 April 1947, p. 2.

[82] UNA, UNRRA, S-0438-0005-01, B. Roberts, Rapport d'une visite au camp disciplinaire de Nonnenhof, 21 June 1946. On the *Wehrwölfes*, Perry Biddiscombe, *The Last Nazis: SS Werewolf Guerilla Resistance in Europe, 1944–1947* (London: Tempus, 2004).

[83] UNA, UNRRA, S-0432-0004-04, Lettre de Lenclud à Acting Chief, Displaced Persons Operations, 29 March 1947.

[84] Ibid.

[85] UNA, UNRRA, S-1021-0084-11, Histoire de l'UNRRA, Relations avec les Autorités Militaires en Zone Française, by Sebille [undated], p. 49.

[86] UNA, UNRRA, S-0432-0002-07, Sawitzky Employment Officer (Team 574) à Pouzenc, Area Employment Officer, 16 January 1947. On the history of these French shops, see Karen Adler, 'Selling France to the French: The French Zone of Occupation in Western Germany, 1945–c.1955', *Contemporary European History*, vol. 21, no. 4 (2012), pp. 575–595.

[87] UNA, UNRRA, S-0432-0002-07, Pouzenc, Area Employment Officer à Director Team 574, Balingen, 26 January 1947.

In November 1946, at a meeting of UNRRA employment officers, the chief employment and work training officer from UNRRA central headquarters recalled that employment officers were expected to protect DP against employment abuses.[88]

The number of DPs imprisoned in disciplinary camps may have been limited, but some local officials used the threat of detention (followed by repatriation), as well as deprivation of food, to cajole DPs into accepting unattractive job offers. On the ground, sympathetic UNRRA relief workers insisted on the painful inadequacies and ironies of the DPs' situation. Germans continued to live fairly normal lives while DPs were subjected to compulsory employment and restrictions on their freedom of movement. DPs' occasional exposure to arbitrary violence, combined with shortage of soap, clothes and fresh food, contributed, in some significant ways, to confine DPs to a perceived inferior status relative to Germans.[89] Many relief workers insisted that DPs' appearance was often miserable, their clothes being 'either completely worn out or too small and their shoes without soles'.[90] In Rottweil, for instance, a PDR Officer sent two Baltic DPs to the disciplinary camp of Nonnenhof for a month after they refused to go to Saarland to work as drivers. One of them was a medical student, the other one an accountant.[91] Not surprisingly, these DPs felt aggrieved and unfairly treated. Similarly, in Friedrichshafen, DPs' placement in the *Haybach-Dernier* firm was carried out 'quite brutally under the threat of food deprivation'.[92]

The dismantlement of German factories, coupled with the disorganization of the French zone's economy, meant that there were very few possibilities to work in skilled positions, while there was great demand for manual and unskilled workers.[93] An UNRRA Team Director observed, for example, that in Sigmaringen the situation was particularly difficult due to the 'excessive requisitions' operated by occupation officials.[94] In total, France requisitioned

[88] UNA, UNRRA, S-0417-0003-03, Réunion des Employment Officers 25, 26, 27 November 1946 à Gutach, p. 6.
[89] UNA, UNRRA, S-0432-0004-04, Marchal à Chief of Operations in Germany, 13 February 1946, N.32/11; MAE, HCRFA, Bonn 150, Administrateur Général Laffon à Général d'Armée Koenig, 1 October 1946 ; AN, AJ/43/594, CPOIR et Direction des Personnes Déplacées, Rapport Général de fin d'installation du centre technique de Ravensburg, 1 August 1947, p. 3.
[90] UNA, UNRRA, S-1021-0085-06, Bastiaenen, Historique du Centre DP de Fribourg ... N. 6, p. 24.
[91] UNA, UNRRA, S-0432-0004-02, Lavau, Field supervisor à Moreland, District Director, 19 February 1946.
[92] UNA, UNRRA, S-0432-0005-04, J. Rozale, rapport de base sur le service Employment du District Sud, March 1946.
[93] Frank Roy Willis, *The French in Germany, 1945–1949* (Stanford, CA: Stanford University Press, 1962), p. 116.
[94] UNA, UNRRA, S-0421-0004-06, Sapin, Directeur du team 587 à Rodie, 22 March 1946.

'REHABILITATION' THROUGH WORK

around 40,000 machines, representing 50 per cent of those spoiled by the Germans in France between 1940 and 1944.[95] In Emmendingen, an UNRRA Employment officer admitted that '[i]n her two Kreis, sedentary or *soft* jobs [were] inaccessible to DPs. Very few DPs work[ed] in their specialities; the majority employed in agriculture and railways, a few in German industry'.[96] Working conditions in the paper and forestry industries were sometimes dreadful.[97]

In June 1946, UNRRA relief services complained about French occupation officials' arbitrary recruitment methods for the textile industries in particular.[98] DPs, even those who were studying, had no choice but to accept their work offers. In the eyes of some French officers, 'studying was not working and DPs therefore could not be students'.[99] For UNRRA Director (former resister and 'compagnon de la Libération') Jacques Bauche these 'unfair practices towards nationals from Allied countries pertained more to Gestapo methods than to the practices of representatives of an Allied Nation'.[100] Just as they perceived compulsory employment as insulting, some UNRRA relief workers interpreted DPs' lack of freedom of movement and the obligation to work as both a sign of disrespect and a lack of compassion or understanding for the trauma they had endured. DPs particularly resented the order dating from 27 September 1945, which restricted them from going further than 5 kilometres from their residence, while German inhabitants could circulate freely.[101]

On 12 July 1946, in response to the numerous written protests against brutal recruitment methods, the PDR organization issued a letter inviting local administrators to be more selective in their employment of intellectual DPs, notably those originating from the Baltic countries. French tradition, it was said, 'requires us to act with more *discernement* in the use of DPs' capacities'.[102] For its part, French UNRRA headquarters stipulated that work should

---

[95] Libera, *Un rêve de puissance*, p. 286.
[96] UNA, UNRRA, S-0421-0031-03, Detachement d'Emmendingen, rapport narratif sur la main d'oeuvre, 18 January 1947.
[97] In Ehingen, the UNRRA doctor reported the dangerous emanations of hydrochloric acid in a pulp mill. UNA, UNRRA, S-0433-0001-06, LE Directeur du Team 583 à Monsieur Roquet, 3 August 1946.
[98] UNA, UNRRA, S-0421-0028-05, Rozale, Employment officer, à Moreland, Zone Assistant Director for Relief, 3 July 1946.
[99] Ibid.
[100] UNA, UNRRA, S-0421-0040-05, Bauche (Directeur Team 676) à Moreland, 12 June 1946.
[101] UNA, UNRRA, S-0421-0062-02, Pétition, Groupements Nationaux de Ravensburg à Directeur de l'UNRRA, 27 May 1946.
[102] UNA, UNRRA, S-0421-0024-05, Employment program, documents de base provenant des autorités françaises, Lettre de la Direction PDR, 12 Juillet 1946, 284/16. Also see S-0421-0047-03, Sebille à Directeurs de Teams, 9 August 1946.

be encouraged by 'increases in food ration, the distribution of basic supplies, clothing and shoes'.[103] The evidence suggests that coercive practices persisted nonetheless. In early 1947, UNRRA relief workers raised concern about the transfers of DPs from the North to the South of the French zone. By the end of 1946, almost all employable DPs were employed in the Southern region, but UNRRA and local authorities experienced greater difficulties putting DPs to work in the North as the local job market was saturated.[104] In the Württemberg area, on the contrary, demand for manpower in agriculture, paper industries and forestry was huge.[105] DPs were therefore subject to compulsory transfers, often causing further distress to individuals who had already been uprooted from their homes. Again, it seemed unfair that Germans could remain in their usual surroundings while DPs were denied the familiarity and routine they had managed to construct. These transfers were perceived as a punishment by a number of DPs who were thus deprived of easy contact with networks of friends and family, arguably reinforcing feelings of humiliation and uprooted-ness.[106] Furthermore, the conditions under which these transfers took place seemed inhumane. For instance, it was reported that woodcutters were sent from Landstuhl to Alpirsbach in terrible transport conditions, travelling fifty-one hours with insufficient food or water.[107] Once they reached their destination, some found out that their potential employers were no longer willing to employ DPs at all.[108]

DPs working for the French forestry enterprises felt particularly cheated by their employers, who were particularly hostile to DPs. DP complaints about discriminatory practices and working conditions in forestry enterprises abound in UNRRA and PDR archives. French employers did not provide the same scale of benefits for all workers. Ingrained images of Eastern European workers as lazy did not disappear overnight. French forestry enterprises were not supposed to employ German manpower but were instead expected to take on French workers paid in francs. As DPs could not be paid in francs (they could not use this currency), they received a small amount of

[103] UNA, UNRRA, S-0417-0003-03, G. Sebille à tous les directeurs de Teams, 9 April 1947, N. 1088/16.
[104] UNA, UNRRA, S-0432-0005-03, J. de Saint Priest, Zone Employment Officer, Compterendu visite Zone Nord (17–18 avril 1947), N. 1134/16, 23 April 1947.
[105] UNA, UNRRA, S-0421-0028-05, J. Rozale à Commandant Sébille, 19 January 1946; S-0421-0029-05, Relief Services à Monsieur le Gouverneur Délégué Supérieur pour le GM de Wurtemberg, N. 353/16, 13 August 1946.
[106] UNA, UNRRA, S-0421-0047-02, Daniel de Fos à Field Supervisor No. 1, 30 October 1946.
[107] UNA, UNRRA, S-0421-0047-01, Rapport du chef de Transport, Jozef Bonkowski, Caserne Marceau, 28 March 1947.
[108] UNA, UNRRA, S-0421-0047-01, Directeur Team 2 à Détachement de Calw, 15 April 1947.

money in German marks and a sum inscribed on accounts in the General Treasury of the zone.[109] While DPs were allegedly granted the same food rations as their French colleagues, they often received considerably less.[110] Nor were they provided with adequate shoes or clothes.[111] Some DPs received more alcohol than other DPs, if their employers deemed them more 'productive'.[112] Meagre and unequal benefits and lower (if any) wages translated into low productivity and mounting hostility between DP workers and their bosses. While French employers often complained that DPs did not have the required skills and that their productivity was low, DPs actively protested against this profoundly unequal labour regime.[113] On 1 July 1948, DPs went on strike in Hohenecken against wage restraints and demanded French ration card and salaries.[114] These DPs did not win this battle and the French employer eventually prevailed. On the whole, except for DPs who emigrated in France, the majority of them were never fully paid, despite their efforts to assert their rights.[115]

## German Supervision and DPs' Discontents

Contrary to official policy, some DPs were assigned to work under German supervision without consenting to do so. For some DPs, working under German supervision revived traumatic memories of wartime abuses.[116] On 2 October 1946, the DP workers of the Zelstoffabrik in Ehingen went on strike to protest against an increase in their daily working hours from eight to ten and the methods employed by their German supervisor. This supervisor used

---

[109] MAE, HCRFA, PDR6/814, Fiche d'information à l'attention de Mr. Le Directeur chef du Service des Personnes Déplacées, 6 April 1949.

[110] MAE, HCRFA, PDR 6/813, Directeur des Personnes Déplacées à Directeur Général des Affaires Administratives, 21 May 1947.

[111] UNA, UNRRA, S-0432-0004-02, Chef Secteur Forestier du Württemberg Sud à Inspecteur des Eaux et Fôrets, 2 December 1946.

[112] MAE, HCRFA, PDR6 /814, M. Remaud, Agent PDR du cercle de Freudenstadt à M. le Gouverneur Délégué Supérieur pour le Gouvernement militaire du Wurtemberg, 9 January 1948.

[113] MAE, HCRFA, PDR6 /814, Exposé du point de vue des exploitants forestiers – instruction 20 juillet 1948. On the broader history of French businesses in Germany see, for instance, Jean François Eck, *Les Entreprises Françaises face à l'Allemagne de 1945 à la fin des années 1960* (Vincennes: Institut de la Gestion Publique et du Développent Économique, 2003).

[114] MAE, HCRFA, PDR6 /814, Le Gouverneur, Délégué pour le GM du Palatinat à Gouverneur du Land Rhéno Palatin, 5 July 1948.

[115] *Sept ans en faveur des personnes déplacées*, p. 27. Also see MAE, HCRFA, PDR6/814, Commissaire pour le Land Bade à Haut Commissaire de la République Française en Allemagne – service des Personnes Déplacées, 24 January 1950.

[116] UNA, UNRRA, S-0421-0018-08, Officier PDR situation des PDR (anciens Prisoniers, déportés et réfugiés) cercle d'Ehingen.

the threat of repatriation to force them to increase production over the longer time spent at the factory.[117] On 2 October ten men were arrested and imprisoned.[118] Thanks to the intervention of the UNRRA team director, they were released the next day. This director admitted that a minority of DPs experienced problems bending to work discipline. But he condemned the methods used by their German director, which reminded them of the oppressive atmosphere of the Nazi period. He further believed that working hours should be reduced from sixty to fifty-five per week, due to the hard nature of the work itself.[119] The area Employment Officer asked French occupation authorities to take measures against a former Nazi official.[120] Yet the evidence suggests that the problem persisted in the Zelstoffabrik. In March 1947, the local UNRRA team director warned UNRRA officials that the factory's management was gradually wearing down the DP manpower by attrition.[121]

Professional encounters between German employers and DP workers were not always so adversarial. Some DPs continued to work in the same farms or factories as they had done during the war.[122] During the Nazi period, foreign workers living and working in rural households generally experienced better conditions and less regimentation than those in factories and town.[123] Some Catholic Polish workers had developed 'reasonably cordial' relationships with their host families.[124] In the aftermath of the war, UNRRA relief workers reported mutually beneficial and relatively harmonious working relations in some areas. In the Kreis of Überlingen and Stockach, for instance, satisfying relationships between German employers and DP workers seemed to have been established.[125] The majority of DPs lived scattered in private German homes in 125 villages and worked for the same farmers 'to whom they were assigned as deported labourers'.[126] A healthy attitude towards work prevailed.

[117] UNA, UNRRA, S-0432-0004-01, Pétition Ouvriers de la Verladungskolonne et du Holzplatz de la Zelstoffabrik, 4 October 1946.
[118] UNA, UNRRA, S-0432-0004-01, Report Pouzenc attention to Zone Employment Officer, A.J.P./E.J./267, 7 October 1946.
[119] UNA, UNRRA, S-0432-0001-02, Vincent (Team 583) à Roquet, Field Supervisor du Württemberg, 10 October 1946.
[120] UNA, UNRRA, S-0432-0004-01, Report Pouzenc attention to Zone Employment Officer, A.J.P./E.J./267, 7 October 1946.
[121] UNA, UNRRA, S-0432-0002-04, Directeur (Team 583) Vincent à Directeur Général UNRRA, 11 March 1947; S-0432-0002-07, J. R.Thuraine à Director Field Operations, 14 March 1947, JRT/EJ/456.
[122] UNA, UNRRA, S-0421-0081-02, Mr Caude, UNRRA Team 30 report, 1 October 1945.
[123] Jill Stephenson, *Hitler's Home Front. Württemberg under the Nazis* (London: Hambledon Continuum, 2006), p. 279.
[124] Ibid., p. 290.
[125] UNA, UNRRA, S-0438-0007-17, Princ. Welfare Officer Travis (Team 582), 25 April 1946 to 1 November 1946.
[126] Ibid.

In some cases, DPs even demanded to work with Germans. These DPs were willing to overcome their aversion to German employers in order to develop their professional skills. In Niederlahnstein, a DP run firm 'Konstruktiva' carried out large-scale reconstruction work such as the clearing of Koblenz' ruins and the repairs of bridges.[127] In Waldsee, a Polish DP wanted to be employed as a railway worker. He had worked from February 1944 to 15 June 1945 as a *manoeuvre* [manual labourer] and then a driver's assistant on German railways. But the German Director of the railway in Karlsruhe only hired German personnel. According to the UNRRA Employment Officer, this Polish DP was very disappointed by this refusal.[128] Such an example draws attention to the active agency of DPs in managing their working lives despite the constraints placed on them by French occupiers, Allied relief workers and German employers.

DPs working in the German economy comprised the majority of DPs in full-time employment. In the autumn of 1946, among 22,000 employed DPs, 2,000 worked in agriculture, 6,000 in small industries, 4,000 in the administration of DP centres, 5,000 were artisans, 2,500 were members of the *Compagnie de Groupements Auxilliares Etrangers* (Auxiliary group of foreigners) and 2,500 occupied various miscellaneous positions.[129] These figures must be approached with caution, however. Employment figures varied considerably from one source to another. Tracking DP employment was difficult as some of them slipped in and out of work; others did not live in camps at all. The DP population was only exhaustively listed in the spring and summer of 1947, revealing the presence of an additional 5,000 DPs who had probably been in situ for a long time.[130] Furthermore, French authorities were very often at loggerheads with UNRRA team directors over questions of numbers and missing labour cards.[131] Despite their inconsistencies, figures nevertheless indicate that the largest sources of employment were the German economy followed by UNRRA. In mid-January 1947, according to UNRRA, 17,273 DPs were in employment, 4,999 were employed by UNRRA (29 per cent), 1,948 by the Military Government (11.2 per cent), 1,891 by the French Army (10.9 per cent), 6,053 within the German economy (35 per cent). Another 1,614 were

---

[127] AN, AJ/43/796, IRO rapport d'inspection du camp DP de 'Gniezno' fait les 14, 15 et 16 Septembre 1948, 27 September 1948.

[128] UNA, UNRRA, s-0432-0001-02, Guilbot, Area Employment Officer à Sebille, Waldsee, 21 August 1946.

[129] *La France en Allemagne*, No. 3, October–December 1946, p. 61.

[130] MAE, HCRFA, PDR6/467, Nombre total de DP recensés en ZFO [undated]; Général d'armée Koenig à Secrétaire d'Etat aux Affaires Allemandes et Autrichiennes, 28 July 1948.

[131] UNA, UNRRA, S-0421-0028-05, Rozale, District Employment Officer à Gobert, Zone Employment Officer, 19 June 1946'; MAE, HCRFA, PDR 3/25, 'Tableau comparatif des extraits des rapports faits par Monsieur Léon', 26 September 1946.

described as apprentices (9.3 per cent) and 768 as artisans (4.4 per cent).[132] In fact, among those working in UNRRA camps, some worked in small workshops and DP-run businesses. So, in total, a relatively small percentage of DPs were offered the opportunity to acquire the means to learn a trade during the period when UNRRA was in operation.

Overall, employment conditions greatly varied according to where DPs lived and for whom they worked. There was neither geographic uniformity nor official consistency. Working conditions also depended on DPs' gender and national affiliation. In the French zone, the proportion of women working outside camps was higher than in the rest of Germany: women represented 37 per cent of the DPs working in camps and 28 per cent of those working for the German economy.[133] Within camps, women in 'leadership role' were supposedly rare. In Reutlingen, the DP stores (food, supplies, clothing and amenity supplies) were run by a DP woman. An UNRRA Officer noted: 'this is the first place that we had found a woman in such a position'.[134] On the whole, female employment rates and salaries were considerably lower than male ones.[135] The issue of unemployed DP *fille-mère* ('girl mothers') was an important source of concern for relief workers. Very limited opportunities were open to them in terms of jobs. They were thus strongly encouraged to return to their countries of origin, where they supposedly had family networks. A relief worker noted '[i]n helping them, we have consistently worked against their interest; we have destroyed, or at least significantly diminished the solid "sense of reality" that they inherited at birth'.[136] This relief worker was a moralist: she deplored that single mothers living in camps 'did not work, were dirty and on overall letting themselves go'.[137] The strain of feeding and clothing family was also strenuous for DP widows with children. Their options for emigration were minimal. They were encouraged to let their older children take on vocational guidance and emigrate by themselves.[138]

---

[132] UNA, UNRRA, S-0432-0005-03, Monthly General Statistical report for January 1947 (16 January), Ref 07-192. For May 1947, see S-0432-0005-04, J. De Saint-Priest, Aperçu sur la situation de l'employment en zone française, 8 May 1947. For October 1947, AN, AJ/43/594, Personnes Déplacées mises au travail et disponibles, 18 October 1947.

[133] UNA, UNRRA, S-0432-0005-03, Employment of DPs, monthly general statistics report for January 1947 (16 January). In the summer of 1947, throughout Germany as a whole, women constituted some 40 per cent of the DPs working in the camps, but they amounted to no more than 10 per cent of those working in the German economy. Salvatici, 'From Displaced Persons to Labourers', p. 221.

[134] UNA, UNRRA, S-0417-0004-14, Dorothea Greene, Reutlingen, UNRRA Team 589 [August 1946].

[135] UNA, UNRRA, S-0432-0006-01, Pourchet à Monsieur le Directeur, Area Team N. 1 – Coblence, 30 May 1947.

[136] AN, AJ/43/760, Counselling, Rapport pour le mois de septembre 1948, signé E. W. D. Steel.

[137] Ibid.

[138] Ibid.

For many French administrators, the ideal was that married DP women remained confined to stereotypically feminine occupations such as providing care in the kitchen, nursery or cleaning services within their camp.[139] A number of French occupation officials explicitly defended the male breadwinner model. The Governor of Württemberg argued, for instance, that it was *normal* that most DP women did not work, as their role was to perform traditional occupations in the household.[140] At a time when citizenship rights and greater access to the paid labour force were becoming available to French women in France, DP employment reveals continuities of thought with the inter-war years and the persistence of some of the tenets of the male breadwinner ideology.[141] This question of the perceived continuities and ruptures between the wartime and liberation period can be further examined through the lens of two contested issues: DP salaries and food rations.

### DP Salaries: Fundamental Economic Right or Invitation to the Black Market?

The debates about DP salaries illustrated the tensions between compassion and coercion, moralizing paternalism and meagre material benefits. Three principles governed French official policy on DP salaries: DPs should not receive less than Germans in equivalent positions; their salaries should be determined according to local salary scales; and they should be funded by the German economy.[142] French occupation and UNRRA authorities agreed on this; they were only divided over the issue of DPs' taxes and social insurance.[143] According to the circular of 1 February 1946, DPs had to be affiliated to German social insurance (covering sickness, industrial injury and old-age

---

[139] Salvatici, 'From Displaced Persons to Labourers', p. 221.
[140] UNA, UNRRA, S-0421-0029-05, Gouverneur, Délégué Supérieur pour le GM du Wurtemberg à Directeur de l'UNRRA pour la Zone Sud, 6 June 1946; On DP women employment also see S-0432-0005-03, J. de Saint-Priest, Coblence, 26 April 1947.
[141] Laura Levine Frader, *Breadwinners and Citizens: Gender in the Making of the French Social Model* (Durham and London: Duke University Press, 2008); Hilary Footitt, '"The Politics of Political Women": Reassessing the First Députées', in Knapp, Andrew (ed) *The Uncertain Foundation, France at the Libération, 1944-1947* (Basingstoke: Palgrave Macmillan, 2007), pp. 87–102.
[142] This policy coincided with the SHAEF memorandum N. 39 which stipulated that the German economy was responsible for the costs generated by DPs. MAE, HCRFA, Bade-Sud, Délégation cercles vrac, 39, L'Administrateur Général Laffon à Général, Délégué Supérieur pour le Gouvernement Militaire de Bade, 1 February 1946; PDR6/811, Sous-Directeur des 'Personnes Déplacées' à Chef de Section des 'Personnes Déplacées' [undated]. UNA, UNRRA, S-0432-0006-01, Général de Corps d'armée Lenclud à Administrateur Général Adjoint, N.1174/16, Bareme des salaires, 9 May 1947.
[143] UNA, UNRRA, S-0417-0003-03, Réunion des Employment Officers à Gutach 25, 26, 27 November 1946.

pensions) under the same conditions as German civilian workers.[144] Yet, these contributions largely benefited German social insurance recipients, as most DPs were not supposed to remain indefinitely in Germany.[145] In September 1946, it was decided that DPs would only pay 25 per cent of the taxes due.[146] In February 1947, DPs were wholly exempted from pensions insurance, leaving them to pay only social insurance for sickness and accident benefits.[147]

In spite of these official measures, UNRRA team directors raised countless complaints about the delayed or non-payment of DPs' wages.[148] Within the same *Kreis* salaries varied markedly.[149] In the area of Ebingen, for instance, German pay scales were applied in Tübingen and Reutlingen but not in Rottweil and Balingen.[150] In Ravensburg, salaries were calculated on the basis of local German pay rates until May 1946. After that point, these tariffs were replaced by a significantly lower *Arbeitsamt* rate on the grounds that DPs should pay for their food rations.[151] In some areas DPs were simply not paid at all.[152] In others, they were asked to pay rent.[153] Delays and irregular payment caused serious disruption in DP camps' centres and undermined the credibility of UNRRA team directors.[154] In response to countless protests, the PDR

---

[144] UNA, UNRRA, S-1021-0085-03, Report O. Gobert, Zone Employment Officer March 1946 to March 1947, 17 April 1947, p. 3.

[145] MAE, HCRFA, PDR6/487, Agent contractuel de 2ème catégorie à Directeur des Personnes Déplacées, 22 March 1946.

[146] UNA, UNRRA, S-0417-0003-03, Réunion des Employment Officers à Gutach 25, 26, 27 Novembre 1946.

[147] UNA, UNRRA, S-1021-0085-03, Report O. Gobert, Zone Employment Officer March 1946 to March 1947, 17 April 1947, p. 3.

[148] UNA, UNRRA, S-0432-0001-01, E. Begleiter (Team 591 à Horb) à M. Schurmans, 27 June 1946; S-1021-0085-03, Ateliers et Programmes d'education professionnelle, Zone Française [May 1947], 4; S-0417-0002-02, Directeur de Team 579 à Général de Corps d'Armée Lenclud, 31 August 1946; S-0417-0003-05, Général de Corps d'Armée Lenclud à l'Administrateur Général Adjoint pour le GM, N.940.16.6484, 25 February 1947; S-0432-0001-01, Directeur Team 591 à M. Schurmans, 27 June 1946; S-0432-0001-02, Islert (team 581) à Délégué GM du Kreis de Wangen, 20 February 1946; Complaints about the fact that DPs were receiving less than Germans. S-0432-0005-02, J. de Saint Priest à Assistant Director, 17 June 1947.

[149] UNA, UNRRA, S-0417-0003-03, Réunion des Employment Officers 25, 26, 27 Novembre 1946 à Gutach.

[150] UNA, UNRRA, S-0432-0006-01, Visite à l'area team N.1, Ebingen, 3 June 1947. N.1234/16.

[151] UNA, UNRRA, S-0417-0002-02, Directeur (Team 579) Massip à Général de Corps d'Armée Lenclud, 31 August 1946.

[152] UNA, UNRRA, S-0432-0001-02, Lettre de Islert (Team 581) à Délégué pour le GM du Kreis de Wangen, 20 February 1946.

[153] UNA, UNRRA, S-0417-0001-07, Lt. Col Mercier, Compte-rendu d'inspection, Field Supervisor N. 3, 10 January 1947.

[154] See, for instance, Daniel De Fos' complaints: UNRRA, S-0421-0047-02, Daniel de Fos à Field Operations, 6 November 1946.

organization asked local administrators to set about, by will or by force, the full implementation of German authorities' obligations.[155]

German reluctance to honour the payment of DPs' salaries is hardly surprising. Germans had to meet the costs of French occupation at a time when their economy was at rock bottom.[156] The French zone is often presented in the historiography as the region, which, out of the four zones, suffered the least war damage.[157] But its economy was severely disorganized and its finances hobbled by French economic policies; in order to avoid inflation, French authorities had held German prices and salaries down.[158] In the context of a severe lack of financial resources, it is little wonder that some German employers and local administrators were disinclined to pay for those perceived as 'privileged' and unwelcome guests.[159] Many Germans were feeling envious of the DP population lodged and fed for 'free'. Perhaps, more surprisingly, UNRRA relief workers and occupation officials were divided over the question of DP salaries. On the one hand, some maintained that the payment of a wage was an essential economic right and a precondition for DPs' individual rehabilitation.[160] This view coincided with the developing human rights discourses and the notions that political and civil rights were inextricably linked to material entitlements. During the war, Roosevelt had indeed claimed that '[a] man in need is not a free man'.[161] On the other hand, some believed that, in the dire immediate post-war conditions, the fact that DPs were fed and lodged for 'free' was sufficient, even if this was not always true. Some DPs did pay their rents.[162] French local administrators and UNRRA relief workers often insisted that DPs' food and housing conditions were similar to those of most French workers, if not better.[163] UNRRA Assistant Director Marchal noted, for instance, that DPs

---

[155] MAE, HCRFA, PDR6/811, Sous Directeur des Personnes Déplacées à Chef de Section des 'Personnes Déplacées', GM Rhénanie, Ref. N.572 OB/MV, [probably December 1945].
[156] Richard Bessel, *Germany 1945. From war to peace* (London: Simon&Schuster, 2009), p. 343.
[157] Ibid., p. 346.
[158] Libera, *Un rêve de puissance*, p. 214.
[159] Bessel, *Germany 1945*, pp. 262–263.
[160] UNA, UNRRA, S-0421-0024-05, Copie circulaire d'application au bulletin N. 51, signé Lenclud [March 1946?].
[161] Atina Grossmann, 'Grams, Calories, and Food: Languages of Victimization, Entitlement, and Human Rights in Occupied Germany, 1945–1949', *Central European History*, vol. 44, no. 1 (2011), p. 120.
[162] On the issue of rent after the monetary reforms, see AJ/43/796, Le Directeur de la Commission CPOIR à Monsieur le Général d'Armée, Division des Affaires Administratives, 13 July 1948.
[163] UNA, UNRRA, S-0421-0018-08, Officier PDR situation des PDR (anciens Prisoniers, déportés et réfugiés) cercle d'Ehingen; Also see UNA, UNRRA, S-0421-0031-04, Bastiaenen, Directeur (Team 206) à l'attention du Comité Lithuanien, 18 November 1946.

had to understand that 'France [was] shar[ing] generously with them, the little it ha[d] left' and that they were receiving 'superior rations (in meat, fat content and bread) [relative] to the inhabitants of [French] towns, and even of the [French] countryside'.[164] According to him, DPs were more likely to get industrial workers' food allocations than were their French counterparts.[165]

A supplementary factor justified French reluctance to honour the payment of DPs' salaries prior to the monetary reforms of 1948. As the Military Governor of Wangen observed at an UNRRA meeting of Welfare Officers, an official salary where there was little possibility to spend it was simply an invitation to black-market activities.[166] In Biberach, UNRRA Team Director Levy-Duplat powerfully formulated the challenges that relief workers faced in a note entitled 'the problem of deportees':

> There is only one problem, which consists of helping deportees to restore their normal life habits. Yet, the current conditions do not facilitate our tasks. We are telling them:
> - Live according to moral standards; and we put fifteen of them in a room.
> - Be clean; and we give them 2g of soap a day.
> - Work; yet, not only is their wage of almost no interest as there is nothing to purchase but it constitutes an indirect invitation to the black market, as there are no other ways to use the money at the moment.[167]

Fears of black-market involvement, resulting from shortcomings of provision rather than the shortcomings of the individual, were also held to justify scant distribution of cigarettes. DPs who engaged in illicit trade did not necessarily do so to gain money; some simply did it to obtain essential goods. As Laura Hilton points out, the term 'black market' referred to a 'wide variety of types of economic exchanges outside the legal distribution and rationing systems', encompassing a broad range of trading activities, some more illegal and/or immoral than others.[168]

Whereas the Germans engaged in illicit trade most commonly for food or cigarettes, and occupation personnel for luxury items, DPs needed a much

---

[164] UNA, UNRRA, S-0432-0004-04, Colonel Marchal à Messieurs les Directeurs de Districts, 41/16, 14 February 1946.
[165] Ibid.
[166] UNA, UNRRA, S-0438-0007-05, Réunion des Welfare Officers du District Sud des Teams de l'Est, 15–16 janvier à Wangen, p. 8.
[167] UNA, UNRRA, S-0432-0003-02, UNRRA Team Director (209) Levy-Duplat 'le problème des déportés', Biberach, 12 March 1946.
[168] Laura Hilton, 'The Black Market in History and Memory: German Perceptions of Victimhood from 1945 to 1948', *German History*, vol. 28, no. 4 (2010), p. 483.

'REHABILITATION' THROUGH WORK 275

wider range of items, such as clothing and fresh food.[169] Many relief workers protested against irregular and at time non-existent distribution of tobacco for DPs.[170] As in the other Western zones, cigarettes often replaced money, performing 'all the functions of a metallic currency as a unit of account, as a measure of value and as a store of value', in addition to being homogeneous, durable and movable.[171] French official attitudes towards DPs' participation in the 'grey market' were ambivalent. Shoring up one's living standards by exchanging controlled goods and ration coupons was both sanctioned and condoned by French authorities.[172] The monetary reforms of 1948 ultimately led to the decline of black-market activities. Its immediate effects were, however, hard on some DPs living in private accommodation, who could not afford to pay their rents anymore.[173] It is beyond this chapter's scope to analyze in detail the problem of DPs' involvement in the black market. However, two points bear emphasis: firstly, the black market was a 'natural phenomenon'.[174] Secondly, there was a great discrepancy between perception and reality. In the French zone, the evidence suggests that, like elsewhere, rumours about DPs' involvement in the black market were widespread.[175] However, contrary to popular legend, Germans participated in illicit trading in larger numbers and higher percentages than either DPs or occupation personnel.[176] For Germans, understandings of the black market provided a framework for maintaining the categories of racial enemies that had framed the Nazi years. For DPs, it could serve as a way to gain autonomy and overcome the constraints placed on them by French occupiers.

---

[169] Ibid., p. 488.
[170] UNA, UNRRA, S-0432-0002-01, Allan à Moreland, 16 July 1946; S-0421-0047-01, De Fos à Direction Générale, 28 February 1947.
[171] Hilton, 'The Black Market in History and Memory', p. 486; Mark Wyman, *DPs: Europe's Displaced Persons, 1945–1951* (Ithaca, NY: Cornell University Press, 1998), pp. 114–116.
[172] In the summer of 1947, for instance, Poignant, who became the head of the Preparatory Commission of the International Refugee Organization (PCIRO), denounced the severity of a penalty: a DP was deprived of his rationing card and condemned to two weeks of imprisonment for trafficking five packets of cigarettes and six bars of chocolate. AN, AJ/43/760, PCIRO, Rapport Mensuel Narratif du Directeur de Zone au chef des Opérations, July 1947.
[173] AN, AJ/43/760, Health, Care and Maintenance, S. Tixier, Rapport pour le mois de juillet 1948.
[174] Paul Steege, *Black-Market, Cold War. Everyday Life in Berlin, 1946–1949* (Cambridge: Cambridge University Press, 2007); Bessel, *Germany 1945*.
[175] MAE, HCRFA, PDR6/487, Administrateur Lucien Léon à Directeur des Personnes Déplacées, 28 April 1947; S-0421-0004-05, Rodie à Moreland, Dir.RR/GF.No. 848, 12 July 1946; S-0432-0001-01, Begleiter (UNRRA team 591 Horb) à Sebille, 12 August 1946.
[176] Hilton, 'The Black Market in History and Memory', p. 490.

## The Politics of Rationing

In the French zone, much of the DPs' sense of bitterness coalesced around material entitlements and food rations.[177] Complaints about the insufficient quantity, inadequate composition or simply bad quality of the rations distributed were numerous. Bare essentials, such as sugar and flour, were missing; bread was of notoriously poor quality; vital nutrients such as vitamins were deficient.[178] The calorie counting inscribed into ration levels was deceptive. As an UNRRA Director observed, '[o]ne can indeed absorb a significant amount of calories in a single teaspoon, the fact remains that one is still hungry'.[179] In August 1946, UNRRA DP staff went on strike in Gutach. They brought their daily food rations to UNRRA's Warehouse officer: it included 22 g sugar, 23 g butter, 12 g cheese, 25 g macaroni, 30 g meat and ¼ litre of wine. The cheese and macaroni were unfit for consumption. UNRRA Welfare Officer reported to his superiors '[i]f you want to see it, just come to my office. I think it is a great shame that people who had a terrible life in Germany during the war and who are now working for UNRRA are fed so badly. I can well imagine that they refuse to work having received these rations. I would do the same' (Fig. 5.2).[180]

Many UNRRA relief workers understood DPs' grievances about food, clothing and salaries as both legitimate and the product of a deeper sense of resentment that not enough had changed since the end of the war with DPs remaining dependents to whom fundamental rights – such as access to decent food – were denied. After their experience of forced labour and precarious living, it seemed unfair that DPs were not automatically entitled to better working conditions, housing and food benefits than Germans.[181] A visiting UNRRA American training specialist strongly disapproved of the food given to DPs. She noted: '[i]n several camps, I saw rotten potatoes [...] dirty sugar containing wood residues, dirty and unusable lard. In one of the camps, an

---

[177] See, for instance, the numerous complaints of the Polish Committee of Ravensburg in UNA, UNRRA, S-0421-0061-07; the complaint of Edmond Szente Gutch in S-0432-0001-05, Edmond Szente Gutch à Durand, Directeur du Team 572, 28 October 1946; S-0421-0031-07, Compte-rendu de la réunion des Employment Officers (Gutach), 25-26-27 November 1946; MAE, HCRFA, 2Bad/39, [A2.301/1], Rapport Affaires administratives, partie personnes déplacées, 24 July 1946.

[178] UNA, UNRRA, S-0421-0031-04, Rapport spécial sur le ravitaillement des Personnes Déplacées, Bastiaenen (team 206), Freiburg, 12 July 1946. Also see S-0421-0040-05, Lettre de M. J. Bauche à M. E. P. Moreland, 12 July 1946.

[179] UNA, UNRRA, S-0421-0039-02, Bauche, Rapport mensuel (Team 676), Constance, 28 August 1946.

[180] UNA, UNRRA, S-0417-0003-03, Letter from D. A. Jansen, Chief Warehouse Officer to Mr Paulis, Adm. Officer, 13 August 1946.

[181] UNA, UNRRA, S-0432-0005-02, J. de Saint Priest à Assistant Director, visite team de Ravensburg, 17 June 1947.

Fig. 5.2   UNRRA, S-0421-0023-09,
18 April 1946, Team 572, Durand, Gutach, UNRRA Store.

analysis of the bread was made: the bread contained a high proportion of dust, and was of so poor quality that it was unfit for human consumption.'[182] In Aulendorf, '[t]he food situation [...] was nothing less than tragic. I saw a large quantity of potatoes with at least 80% spoiled, a large quantity of salt extremely dirty, and Ersatz coffee with huge solidified lumps in it. The DPs around the food store were all sullen and angry-looking'.[183]

Although DPs were officially entitled to richer food rations than Germans, many DPs were on German card rations in the French zone. These cards did not guarantee that they would actually receive the ration in question. In Freiburg, for instance, DPs living in town depended on French military supply corps (*Intendance*) while their counterparts in the villages nearby received German food rations.[184] Yet, in shops, German suppliers withheld products

---

[182] UNA, UNRRA, S-0432-0005-04, Translation, Greene à Lenclud, 'Les opérations en Zone Française', 10 August 1946.
[183] UNA, UNRRA, S-0417-0004-14, Rapport Greene, UNRRA Team 677, 10 August 1946.
[184] UNA, UNRRA, S-0421-0031-04, Bastiaenen, Rapport spécial sur le ravitaillement Personnes Déplacées, 12 July 1946.

under quota and kept many products for themselves.[185] As Paul Steege has demonstrated for Berlin, legal rationing was only one part of a multifaceted supply system, its allocation often bearing little connection with the reality of what people actually consumed.[186] In May 1946, the DP national committees of Ravensburg voiced grave concerns about the food situation in their areas, pointing out that children lacked vitamins, milk and bread. They argued that their daily allocation was smaller than that of the Germans, while Germans had easier access to non-rationed and fresh food. 'They have the advantage of being in their homeland; many of them have familial connections with people living in the countryside who help them; finally some have made savings during the war.'[187] DP representatives looked with envy to the American zone and wondered why *locally* DPs were not benefiting from the Allied regime in place in the other Western zones.[188]

As Atina Grossmann suggests, 'food was much more than a – necessary – matter of calories and physical survival'.[189] Questions of calorific content and quality of food were deeply intertwined with highly contested recognition of suffering, entitlement to human rights and issues of social justice. The authors of the *Report on Psychological Problems* noted '[f]irst things first – Food is the primal token of security. In childhood, the most potent source of reassurance that we are loved, lovable and worthwhile, is regular and friendly satisfaction of our hunger by familiar food and drink'.[190] Many DPs regarded food both as a 'reminder of what they had lost' and as a mean of preserving their identity.[191] Building on Grossmann's work, scholars have demonstrated that both Germans and DPs also used their experiences of hunger and food deprivation to present themselves as helpless and innocent victims.[192] This construction of a German 'victim mentality' was not just a political tactic; it was also a mode of

---

[185] UNA, UNRRA, S-0421-0031-04, Thomasset à Chabannes, Acting Director, Freiburg, 8 November 1945.

[186] Steege, *Black-Market, Cold War*, pp. 40–44.

[187] UNA, UNRRA, S-0421-0062-02, Comités Nationaux de personnes déplacées à Ravensburg à Directeur de l'UNRRA (Team 579), 27 May 1946. On 'hoarding as a national habit' Richard Bessel, *Germany 1945. From War to Peace* (London: Simon & Schuster, 2009), pp. 347–348.

[188] UNA, UNRRA, S-0421-0062-02, Comités Nationaux à Ravensburg à Directeur de l'UNRRA (Team 579), 27 May 1946. For a comparison with British and American ration policies, see Rinke, *Le Grand retour*, pp. 300–301.

[189] Grossmann, 'Grams, Calories, and Food', pp. 118–148, 135.

[190] HA5-4/3, Welfare Division, *Report on Psychological Problems of Displaced Persons*, 1 June 1945, pp. 1–41, 34–35.

[191] See, for instance, Jordanna Bailkin, *Unsettled. Refugee Camps and the Making of Multicultural Britain* (Oxford: Oxford University Press, 2018), p. 71.

[192] Alice Weinreb, 'Matters of Taste: The Politics of Food in Divided Germany, 1945–1971', PhD dissertation, University of Michigan, 2009, p. 28.

ascribing meaning to the dire circumstances of the post-war period and a mechanism to cope with the recent past.[193]

In the French zone, Germans often painted a very dark picture of the food situation, criticizing both French and German local administrators. In her analysis of German complaint letters addressed to German authorities, Marjorie Marquet suggests that German writers did not mention all the consequences of hunger: they insisted on its psychological and physical effects, but not on its morally dubious consequences: begging, thefts and food prostitution.[194] Scholars have demonstrated that British and American authorities were receptive to German hunger discourse.[195] In 1945, British and American occupiers were determined to impose punitive measures on the Germans, including restrictive food policies. Their resolve to do so significantly altered as the severity of the Communist threat intensified, with the result that food-aid allocations markedly increased.[196] This was not the case in the French zone.[197] An article published in the Rhineland in 1948 compared rations in Buchenwald to those of the French zone (purportedly 1,675 calories versus 805), leading a local politician to claim that Germans have 'for three years been forced to bear a level of hunger such as that known in no concentration camp in the world'.[198] Without question, these comparisons between concentration camps and the civilian rationing program had little basis in physiological fact. It remains true, however, that France imposed a drastic food rationing policy on Germans, more particularly in the Württemberg area.[199] This policy affected both Germans and DPs.

Although French authorities maintained that they were committed to comply with the 1,550 minimum calorific ration determined by the Control Commission, in autumn 1945 Emile Laffon was aware that some Germans

---

[193] Laura Hilton, 'The Black Market in History and Memory: German Perceptions of Victimhood from 1945 to 1948', *German History*, vol. 28, no. 4 (2010), pp. 479–497. On the broader issue of German as victims, see, for example, Robert Moeller, 'Germans as Victims ? Thoughts on a Post-Cold War History of World War II's Legacies', *History and Memory*, vol. 17, nos. 1–2 (2005), pp. 145–194.

[194] Marjorie Maquet, 'La lettre de doléance dans la zone française d'occupation entre 1945 et 1949', *Cahiers d'Etudes Germaniques*, vol. 71 (2016), pp. 209–219.

[195] On food relief planning during the war UNA, UNRRA, S-1021-0013-05, Memorandum Julian Wadleigh, 'Report to prepare for Food relief before the establishment of UNRRA' [August 1947].

[196] Alice Weinreb, '"For the Hungry Have No Past nor Do They Belong to a Political Party": Debates over German Hunger after World War II', *Central European History*, vol. 45, no. 1 (2012), pp. 50–78, 52.

[197] Weinreb, 'Matters of Taste', p. 83.

[198] Ibid., p. 99.

[199] For Rainer Hudemann, a 'famine' occurred in 1946 in the French zone. 'L'occupation francaise apres 1945 et les relations franco-allemandes', *Vingtieme Siecle*, vol. 55 (1997), pp. 58–68, 63.

received barely 1,000 calories.[200] Between 1945 and 1946, depending on the provinces, the size of the town and the categories of the population, some Germans received between 950 and 1,300 calories.[201] The inhabitants of Saarland were privileged, as were industrial workers. Rations progressively rose in the spring of 1946, but declined once more in the summer. Flour was in short supply everywhere; sugar and meat very were severely rationed. Germans looked with envy at the food situation in the American zone, convinced that French authorities were feeding themselves at their expense.[202] At the beginning of 1947, the food ration for the average consumer was not more than 1,000 calories.[203] German resentment was exacerbated by the fact that French administrators allowed themselves a generous and varied diet.[204] In some significant ways, as Dietmar Hüser and Karen Adler argue, this overindulgent diet, far exceeding what was provided in France, represented a symbolic expression of national strength and revenge.[205] But beyond any political or cultural motivations, this drastic food policy was also prompted by other, purely material concerns. The French zone was struggling to provide its own food. Despite its rural profile, the zone was unable to supply basic goods such as cereals, meat and milk.[206] Its economy was constituted by many small family farms, producing little or no marketable surplus. Yet the Control Commission had established that each occupier was responsible for the budget balance in their zone: in France, the idea that the French might be required to pay for Germans' food was still unthinkable.[207]

Instead of improving in the course of 1946, DP and Germans' food rations deteriorated. Before 1 August 1946, the French military supply corps was responsible for the provision of UNRRA stores: food ration rates might fluctuate but at least the distribution was regular. After August 1946, each military government assumed responsibility for providing UNRRA with 'release vouchers' (*bons de déblocages*); UNRRA authorities then directly negotiated with German producers to obtain essential foodstuffs.[208]

---

[200] Libera, *Un rêve de puissance*, p. 210.
[201] Ibid., p. 288.
[202] Ibid., p. 294 ; Weinreb, 'Matters of Taste', p. 123.
[203] Rinke, *Le Grand retour*, p. 300.
[204] This was a very divisive issue for French occupation officials; Libera, *Un rêve de puissance*, pp. 235–236.
[205] Adler, 'Selling France to the French', pp. 575–595, 584. Dietmar Hüser, 'Ventres creux, mentalités collectives et relations internationales – la faim dans les rapports franco-allemands d'après guerre', in Francine-Dominique Liechtenhan, Brad Abrams (eds.), *Europe 1946: Entre le deuil et l'espoir* (Bruxelles: Editions Complexe, 1996), pp. 142–164.
[206] Libera, *Un rêve de puissance*, p. 210.
[207] Ibid., pp. 216–217.
[208] UNA, UNRRA, S-0417-0010-06, Rapport sur l'approvisionnement des camps, 25 April 1947.

Intractable transport problems, combined with the lack of administrative flexibility, severely hampered the smooth functioning of the system.[209] As a result, the question of food allocation created many disputes between UNRRA relief workers and occupation officials.[210] In Ehingen, an UNRRA doctor raised concern about DPs' working conditions in a chemical factory and a lack of milk for DP workers.[211] Employers complained that lower food rations gave way to a feeling of discouragement and lower productivity.[212] Some authorities accused UNRRA directors of augmenting the number of *rationnaires* (food beneficiaries) in order to provide adequate rations.[213] In October 1946, Laffon officially asked the *Sous-secrétaire d'Etat aux Affaires Etrangères* to re-establish the previous system. He argued that if, in theory, the food ration had risen from 1,565 calories to 1,686 calories, in practice DPs were receiving far less:

1) In the Württemberg, for instance, spoiled meat was delivered to the DP centres
2) In the Baden Area, in Gutach, it was not possible to give potatoes to the DPs – despite the fact that the camp Director had a *bon de déblocage* for 12 tons [...]
5) In all the provinces, the order that priority should be given to DPs rather than Germans is not respected; it is no less true that one often gives to DP centres what Germans do not consume or want.[214]

Laffon contended that if they wanted DPs to stop stealing from Germans to feed themselves then French authorities should give them the minimal vital rations. And yet, the problem persisted and access to fresh vegetables was extremely difficult.[215] In February 1947, in the busy area of Lindau, the UNRRA Director noted, 'the supply situation is such that the packaging of

---

[209] UNA, UNRRA, S-0421-0038-05, Etude d'un nouveau système de ravitaillement des DPs, 17 January 1947.
[210] See, for instance, in Landstuhl: UNA, UNRRA, S-0421-0044-05, Daniel de Fos à Field Supervisor, 20 September 1946; In Freiburg: S-1021-0085-06, Bastiaenen, Historique du Centre DP de Fribourg, p. 29.
[211] UNA, UNRRA, S-0433-0001-06, le Médecin Chef du Team 583 à Médecin Général des Cilleuls, 2 August 1946.
[212] UNA, UNRRA, S-0433-0001-07, Administrateur Sequestre (Birkenhause), traduction, Ehingen, 1 August 1946.
[213] UNA, UNRRA, S-0421-0056-01, C. H. Pourchet, Field Supervisor Bade-Ouest, Note de service, 10 January 1947.
[214] MAE, HCRFA, Bonn 150, Administrateur Général Laffon à Général d'Armée Koenig, 1 October 1946.
[215] See, for instance, UNA, UNRRA, S-0421-0061-04, Lettre de J. A. Lageix, chef du détachement d'Aulendorf à F. Massip, Directeur Team 579, 31 January 1947; MAE, HCRFA, 2Bad/39, [A2.301/1], Rapport Partie Personnes Déplacées, 26 August 1947.

goods is becoming as rare in the zone as the goods themselves'.[216] Two months later, General Lenclud lodged an official complaint to the Direction PDR, highlighting DP workers' natural resentment when seeing the French working for the Army rewarded with much more abundant food for performing the same work.[217] According to the Polish chief, DPs reported that they received forty cigarettes a month while French soldiers got 480.[218]

To conclude, food rations were at the heart of contentious relations between DPs and Germans and DPs and French occupiers. French occupiers and relief workers enjoyed a comfortable material situation, often combining abundant diet with easy access to wine and luxury goods. During official receptions, lavish menus served as a potent metaphor for the apparent superiority of the French character. When the General Lenclud visited the Lindau team in November 1946, for example, the menu listed fine fattened oyster, homemade porc pâté, trout 'inspection', Roast beef and *pomme française* [French potatoes], mimosa salad, cheese, ice-creams, *pommes d'Allgau* [apples from Allgau].[219] As numerous studies have shown, French cuisine is closely linked to a sense of French national identity and superiority.[220] By eating copiously, French officials perpetuated the idea of France's 'culinary civilising mission'. DPs and Germans meanwhile bemoaned their miserable living conditions. The majority of DPs not only lacked adequate food but also clothes and shoes. Unlike Germans, their access to non-rationed food was severely restricted. And despite preferential treatment in official policy, Laffon's alarm confirms that, very often, DPs did not take precedence over Germans. The situation did not radically change after the termination of UNRRA in the summer of 1947. On paper, the average ration for DPs reached 1,438 calories.[221] Crucially, this contrast between French rich diet and DPs' poorer provision embodied social structures and marked a clear divide between French relief workers and DP recipients. DPs' social entitlements depended on local budgets, policing methods, the degree of cooperation between various occupation services and

---

[216] UNA, UNRRA, S-0421-0039-02, Jacques Bauche, Note de service, 15 février 1947.

[217] UNA, UNRRA, S-0432-0006-01, Lenclud à Délégué du GMZFO, 13 May 1947, N.1.185/16.

[218] UNA, UNRRA, S-0421-0047-01, De Fos à Direction Générale de la Zone Française, 28 February 1947.

[219] UNA, UNRRA, S-0421-0052-01, Visit of the General Lenclud in Lindau, 15 November 1946.

[220] Sylvie Durmelat, 'Introduction: Colonial Culinary Encounters and Imperial Leftovers', *French Cultural Studies*, vol. 26, no. 2 (2015), pp. 115–129.

[221] AN, AJ/43/760, PCIRO, Rapport Mensuel Narratif du Directeur de Zone au chef des Opérations, July 1947. In October 1947, the average ration reached 1,625 on average in DP centre, 1,670 when fresh vegetables were available. On the food situation during the IRO period, see the reports of the IRO nutritionist M. A. Abrahams. For example, AJ/43/796, Rapport sur les visites de la nutritioniste du 6 au 9 Octobre 1948.

DPs' own ability to establish cordial relationships with Germans. In practice, French policies protected some DPs, yet discriminated against others.

## Privilege and Prejudice: National and Gender Divides[222]

In the wake of France's full-blooded collaboration with the Nazi regime, many if not most French occupation officials and relief workers understood that it was no longer appropriate to refer to foreigners in the xenophobic terms that were ubiquitous in the late thirties and Vichy period. This did not mean, however, that well-entrenched stereotypes disappeared. In Feyen, for instance, a French captain labelled DPs as a 'group of gangsters', and he singled out the Polish race as 'dirty'.[223] More frequently, one finds contemptuous or condescending remarks. In Isny in Allgäu a welfare officer suggested that relief workers had to understand the simple-minded character of Ukrainians. In her camp DPs were characterized as being 'old and *primaires* [simple-minded]'.[224] In Neudstadt, an UNRRA employment officer reported that everyone around him was striving to get rid of uninteresting, unproductive and pitiful Poles.[225] Stereotypes of Polish DPs as morally lax, bad workers and unproductive were, it seems, endemic.[226]

In the conclusion of his book on *Hitler's Foreign Workers*, Ulrich Herbert points out that those who suffered the most after the Liberation were often, quite paradoxically, 'the very same persons who had suffered most in Germany during the war'.[227] Under Nazi rules, Eastern Europeans worked longer hours and survived on poorer diets, lower wages and less adequate housing than West European workers.[228] At the Liberation these very same unskilled workers were more likely to experience labour discrimination and

---

[222] The subtitle 'Privilege and Prejudice' refers to Mary Dewhurst Lewis's chapter four *The Boundaries of the Republic: Migrant Rights and the Limits of Universalism in France, 1918-1940* (Stanford: Stanford University Press, 2007), p. 118.
[223] MAE, HCRFA, PDR6/493, Rapport du capitaine Duvillaret, Commandant la Subdivision de Trèves, à Monsieur le Lieutenant-Colonel Griolet, Délégué Régional Rhénanie-Hesse, Section des Personnes Déplacées, Trèves, 4 January 1946. Also see Chapter 1.
[224] UNA, UNRRA, S-0421-0086-01, A. Baugnée, Welfare report, Isny im Allgäu, 5 February [1946?].
[225] UNA, UNRRA, S-0421-0029-03, Bohn à Gobert, Neustadt, 15 June 1946.
[226] UNA, UNRRA, S-0421-0018-08, Officier PDR situation des PDR cercle d'Ehingen,4; S-0421-0029-05, Lettre du Gouverneur, Délégué Supérieur pour GM du Württemberg à Directeur de l'UNRRA pour la Zone Sud, N.1995 SAA/PDR/RC/GJ, 6 June 1946.
[227] Ulrich Herbert, *Hitler's Foreign Workers. Enforced Foreign Labor in Germany under the Third Reich*, translated by William Templer (Cambridge: Cambridge University Press, 1997), pp. 376–377.
[228] Ibid., p. 391; Stephenson, *Hitler's Home Front*, p. 268.

abuses. Where they had formally been discriminated against relative to the *Westarbeiter*, after the war that discrimination persisted in new guise – relative to Baltic and Banatais DPs, both groups considered as more competent, productive and educated. In Singen, for instance, Poles were forced to work in the same factories as they had done during the war, while Latvian DP were better placed to refuse such job offers if they did not correspond to their skills. Moreover, Poles were only allocated German food rations, while Latvians typically received those of the *Intendance*. An UNRRA Employment reported that '[t]he totality of the Polish DPs of the Singen camp are simple-minded people, ill equipped to defend their interests; they did not obtain any of the advantages granted to the Latvian DPs. They suffer[ed] and protest[ed] against a striking difference in their treatment'.[229] In Ravensburg the Baltic population was composed of relatively 'wealthy' individuals, according to an UNRRA welfare officer. And, paradoxically, the wealthier DPs often received the most aid.[230] Without doubt, discrimination was not overall as striking as it was in the particular cases of Singen or Ravensburg. Yet UNRRA employment statistics show that the majority of Polish and Ukrainian DPs worked in factories, farms and forestry enterprises, while a significant number of intellectual Baltic DPs (civil servants, teachers, doctors, lawyers, entrepreneurs, students, etc.) were either unemployed or reliant on their own workshops.[231]

Unequal pay and unfair advantages amongst DPs led to many DP strikes. On 12 September 1946, for instance, twenty female DP workers from a textile factory near Lörrach went on strike. Having worked in this factory since July, they resented the fact that their comrades from the DP camp in nearby Mülheim received better food rations (including chocolate). An UNRRA Employment Officer pledged to rectify the situation.[232] But, the evidence suggests that discontent persisted.[233] A few months later, a violent strike broke out in the DP camp of Gneisenau (near Koblenz), DPs begrudging that those employed by UNRRA (team-workers) received fifteen packets of US cigarettes while everyone else were only allocated six. In a similar fashion, the food rations, clothes and children's materials were unequally distributed among the

---

[229] UNA, UNRRA, S-0421-0028-05, J. Rozale, Employment officer, à Moreland, Zone Assistant Director, 3 July 1946; S-0438-0005-01, O. Despeigne, Situation au 15 mars 1946, Freibourg.
[230] UNA, S-0438-0005-01, M. Roberts, Rapport sur ma visite au team de Ravensburg, Welfare Service, 13 May 1946.
[231] UNA, UNRRA, S-0432-0005-04, Rapport Ateliers et programmes d'éducation professionnelle, 7 May 1947.
[232] UNRRA, S-0421-0026-05, Lettre de Mlle Y. Bourguignon à Sebille, 13 September 1946.
[233] UNRRA, S-0421-0026-05, Ch. Pourchet à Desvernois, chef de la Section des Personnes Déplacées, 26 February 1947.

camp's inhabitants.[234] This strike was particularly violent, with the Polish chief of the UNRRA shop being beaten up and severely wounded.[235]

UNRRA did not always protect DPs against discrimination. On the contrary, the organization's employment policies sometimes reinforced inequalities amongst DPs. In some cases, jobs inside camps offered better food allocations and housing conditions than work outside.[236] In these cases, rather than levelling social differences by preventing the 'lower socio-economic categories from feeling the burden of material or social deprivation', as Ihor Zielyk suggests, camp employment policies contributed to social stratification.[237] In other cases, UNRRA directors could not pay their class II personnel.[238] These administrators appear to have resented the marked disparities in treatment between them and class I personnel. 'Our class II personnel proved far more valuable to the Administration than the Administration did to them' commented an UNRRA Director in Lindau. 'It is unfortunate that numerous solemn promises made to them were broken. [...] Hope being the most precious property of our DPs, it was important not to use it wrongly.'[239] The UNRRA Personnel Division in Paris meanwhile made recommendations based on their own perceptions of fairness. The Division's anonymous official historian records that '[t]he principle of equal pay for equal work is strong throughout Europe, and I believe that any future organization should reject with the greatest firmness any attempt whatever to make differentiated wage scales'.[240] It was a different story in the field, however, where attitudes of class I personnel towards class II personnel varied greatly within the zone. While some directors considered class II staffers as their equals and complained about UNRRA's official policy, others saw absolutely no contradiction between the rhetoric of human rights and the persistence of these economic

---

[234] MAE, HCRFA, Service de Liaison [SL], 52, Procès-Verbal, No. 868, Brigade de Coblence, 24 June 1947.
[235] UNRRA, S-0419-0001-07, Lettre de A. J. Pouzenc à Lenclud, 'émeute dans le camp de Gniezno', 24 June 1947.
[236] UNA, UNRRA, S-0421-0047-02, Commandant du camp Kiewlicz à Directeur de l'UNRRA, 20 November 1946; MAE, HCRFA, PDR6/487, Délégué Supérieur pour le GM du Wurtemberg à Officier de Liaison de UNRRA [Probably April 1947].
[237] UNA, UNRRA, S-0432-0004-05, G. Loustalot à Directeur Général de l'UNRRA en ZFO, 11 February 1947; Ihor V. Zielyk, 'The DP Camp as a Social System', Isajiw, Boshy and Senkus (eds.), *The Refugee Experience*, pp. 461–470, 463.
   UNA, UNRRA, S-0421-0026-05, Bourguignon à Sebille, 13 September 1946.
[238] Class I personnel were those hired internationally, class II personnel were local employees and class III personnel were volunteers attached to private voluntary relief organizations, supervised but not in the paid employ of UNRRA.
[239] UNA, UNRRA, S-1021-0085-08, Gerbier, 'rapport sur les activités de l'UNRRA', 8 May 1947, p. 26.
[240] UNA, UNRRA, S-1021-0031-07, History of UNRRA, Personnel Division [undated].

and national inequalities.[241] Not only did UNRRA employment policies entrench certain forms of social differentiation, notably between those working for UNRRA (who generally profited from more food, prestige and power) and those having to work outside; but, more importantly, it hardened differences in economic status between relief workers and DP.[242]

Questions of ethnicity and gender thus continued to prove critical to re-establishing the position of DP men and women in reconstituted post-war societies and nations. UNRRA employment officers confronted rivalries between groups of DPs. In Niederlahnstein, for instance, the welfare officer reported the difficulties experienced in running 'combined Jewish and Polish shops, owing to friction between the workers. Therefore the main camp work was done in the Polish shops, and the Jewish Committee was given a sewing machine for the express use of the Jewish community'.[243] The meanings of gender and ethnicity were not always stable, however. This was particularly evident in the discourses about vocational trainings. While vocational training sought to make career selection for men and women scientific and rational, it often reproduced the 'cultural meanings of gender difference', promoting feminine careers for DP women and reinforcing ideas about workers' masculinity for DP men.[244]

## The Accelerated Professional Training

From 1948 onwards, vocational training took centre stage because it became obvious that DP emigration depended heavily on their professional success. In April, French authorities surveyed the DP population to determine their professional attitudes. This survey revealed that many DPs did not have the skills required by most host countries and that 'professional training was the "black spot" of the French zone'.[245] To emigrate, DPs needed to be medically

---

[241] UNA, UNRRA, S-0417-0003-03, Réunion des Employment Officers 25, 26, 27 Novembre 1946 à Gutach.

[242] Gatrell, 'From 'Homelands' to 'Warlands': Themes, Approaches, Voices', in Peter Gatrell and Nick Baron (eds.) *Warlands. Population Resettlement and State reconstruction in the Soviet-East European Borderlands, 1945-1950* (New York: Palgrave Macmillan, 2009),, pp. 1–22, 10.

[243] UNA, UNRRA, S-0438-0008-07, Welfare report (25 November 1946 to 14 January 1947), 14 January 1947.

[244] Frader, *Breadwinners and Citizens*, p. 105. For the French zone: PDR9/1, Note d'information pour Monsieur le Directeur Général des Affaires Administratives, 18 March 1948; PDR9/143, Compte-rendu général du fonctionnement des cours d'enseignement ménager feminine, 30 June 1950.

[245] MAE, HCRFA, 9PDR/1, Le Secrétaire d'Etat aux Affaires Allemandes et Autrichiennes à Monsieur le Général d'Armée, Commandant en chef Français en Allemagne, Enquête sur les Personnes Déplacées en ZFO, 29 June 1948; AN, AJ/43/760, Health, Care and Maintenance, Rapport pour le mois d'octobre 1948, S. Tixier.

fit, mentally sound and adequately trained on 'papers'.[246] French occupation officials thus established eighteen vocational schools to combat the 'danger of idleness' and facilitate DPs' resettlement in a third country, training DPs for twenty-six different professions. This programme of Accelerated Professional Training [*Formation Professionnelle Accélérée*, FPA] was aimed at preparing the professional 'integration' of DPs in host countries.[247] This focus on vocational guidance was driven by broader international agendas and new funding opportunities.

Retraining DPs fitted with the changing priorities of the Preparatory Commission of the International Refugee Organisation (PCIRO). The 6 September 1947 Agreement signed by French authorities and PCIRO explicitly referred to the question of professional training.[248] As an IRO officer noted, host countries were not accepting DPs for 'what they had suffered', but rather for what they could offer.[249] Vocational training was conducted partly by FPA officials and partly by the IRO (notably for the tests). Courses were intensive and generally of short duration. Propaganda posters were distributed across the zone and 'psycho-technical tests' were organized to place DPs in a profession that best suited their existing skills and knowledge.

Prior to the establishment of the FPA, the organization of vocational trainings had often felt on DPs themselves. In Lindau, for instance, a stateless DP created a workshop of electrical appliances and trained DP apprentices.[250] In June 1946, Dr Karvelis, former Finance Minister of Lithuania and President of the Lithuanian Red Cross, contacted UNRRA to buy a factory, which he hoped to entrust to Lithuanians who would run it 'for the profit of the French Army and France'.[251] After the termination of UNRRA in the summer of 1947, the existence of workshops set up by DPs and which did not fit with the professional requirements established by host countries, became increasingly threatened. As French relief workers tried to adapt vocational guidance to the new 'emigration' climate, the focus shifted from artisanship to agricultural work and industry.[252] It was argued that there were too many artisans,

---

[246] MAE, HCRFA, 9PDR/1, Note de service, Fichier professionnel, 22 October 1948.

[247] MAE, HCRFA, PDR6/869, Note pour M. Rivain, Directeur du Cabinet de l'Ambassadeur de France Haut Commissaire de la République Française en Allemagne [undated]. AN, AJ/43/798, Directeur de l'Organisation Internationale pour les Réfugiés à Général d'Armée, Commandant en chef Français en Allemagne, organisation de la formation professionnelle des réfugiés et personnes déplacées [December 1948].

[248] AN, AJ/43/798, Compte-rendu d'une mission confiée par le Directeur des Affaires Economiques et Sociales à Guyoton, 2 November 1948.

[249] AN, AJ/43/760, Couselling, Rapport pour le mois de juin 1948, signé E. W. D. Steel.

[250] AN, AJ/43/760, Rapport concernant mon activité, A. J. Pouzenc, Zone Employment Officer, 30 June 1948.

[251] UNA, UNRRA, S-0421-0029-03, Bouchez à Bohn, 12 June 1946.

[252] MAE, HCRFA, PDR9/2, Compte-rendu de reunion, 5 May 1949.

Fig. 5.3  MAE, HCRFA, PDR9/102,
Photograph taken in the Freiburg School, Section dessin de bâtiment [undated].

professions than neither France nor other host countries needed.[253] In so doing, the FPA makeover shifted vocational training away from DPs. Just months after the termination of UNRRA, the PCIRO effectively cut support for the majority of such DP workshops. Some of these self-employed craftsmen (tailors, dressmakers, cobblers, etc.) became wholly integrated in the German economy, while others simply disappeared.[254]

The success of the FPA programme should not be overestimated (Figs. 5.3 and 5.4). Some of the training centres were notoriously inefficient.[255] By the end of 1948, 1,700 DPs only had been professionally

---

[253] MAE, HCRFA, PDR9/1, Le secrétaire d'Etat aux Affaires Allemandes et Autrichiennes à Monsieur le Général d'Armée, 29 June 1948.
[254] UNA, UNRRA, S-0432-0001-05, Rapport Field Supervisor Bade-Sud, 26 December 1946.
[255] AN, AJ/43/594, Lettre de A. Poignant (PCIRO) à Monsieur P. Jacobsen, Rééducation professionnelle, 4 June 1948; PDR6/842, Compte-rendu de l'Attaché Rebiere à l'attention de M. le Directeur, Chef du service des Personnes Déplacées, 16 January 1951.

Fig. 5.4  MAE, HCRFA, PDR9/102,
Photograph taken in the Freiburg School, Section peinture [undated].

tested by the IRO.[256] The reports written by FPA instructors made clear that the majority of DPs had very little interest for vocational training.[257] Some DP parents refused to be temporarily separated with their children, in order to enable them to attend vocational schools. After years of displacement and administrative struggle to find a stable job, DPs were often reluctant to leave their job for fear of not getting it back.[258] In relief workers' eyes, this DP reluctance was generally associated with taste for 'sedentary life' and lack of 'emigration-mindedness'. It is worth noting, though, that no matter how trained a DP was, if they were considered as medically unfit, they had little chance to emigrate.[259] Finally, training and apprenticeship occurred in areas of

---

[256] Louise Holborn, *The International Refugee Organisation. A Specialed Agency of the United Nations, Its History and Work, 1946–1952* (London: Oxford University Press, 1956), p. 276.
[257] MAE, HCRFA, PDR9/2, Compte-rendu de reunion, 5 May 1949.
[258] MAE, HCRFA, PDR9/1, L'attaché de 1. Classe Paul Orban, Délégué du Cercle de Kusel à Monsieur le Gouverneur, 30 June 1949.
[259] AN, AJ/43/760, Couselling, Rapport pour le mois de novembre 1948, signé E. W. D. Steel.

labour market that were mainly 'manual': mining, agriculture, forestry and metal work.[260]

Economic imperatives were not the only factor that governed French thinking about DP workshops. While the majority of FPA schools were aimed primarily at preparing DPs for emigration, a re-education centre was created in Lindich in late August 1949 to facilitate the integration of ill and disabled DPs (mainly male) in the German economy.[261] The administration of this centre was inefficient, however.[262] On 10 and 11 August 1950, DP trainees went on strike, as a result of delays in the payment of their bonus.[263] The Freiburg school of *Arts et Métiers* (mechanical and industrial arts) trained DPs in ceramic arts, carpet weaving, painting and sculpture.[264] The evidence suggests that there were very little professional opportunities in this domain in host countries and that the IRO threatened to close it.[265] The school was also criticized for its lack of accountability.[266] Yet, the school remained both protected and funded by French authorities, in part because it bolstered French art and cultural traditions. It was instrumental to project France's power in Germany.[267] In sum, DP training was not solely a matter of reconstructing the labour force, restoring men's position in work and rebuilding France's economy. It also intersected with broader concerns about the status and extension of France's power in the world.

## Conclusion

There is currently a debate about how to reform the present 'broken refugee system', both in terms of equipping refugees with meaningful education opportunities and empowering them economically. Some experts consider that the creation of Special Economic zones (SEZ) in neighbouring countries, where trade laws differ from the rest of the country to attract investment and jobs, constitutes the most viable option to 'repair' the system set up after the

---

[260] MAE, HCRFA, PDR9/1, Le Sécrétaire d'Etat aux Affaires Allemandes et Autrichiennes à Général d'Armée Commandant en chef Français en Allemagne, 29 June 1948.
[261] MAE, HCRFA, PDR6/484, Albert Meyer à l'Inspecteur, 21 September 1950.
[262] Ibid.
[263] MAE, HCRFA, PDR6/484, Le Commissaire pour le Land Wurtemberg-Hohenzollern à Haut Commissaire de la République en Allemagne, 19 August 1950.
[264] MAE, HCRFA, PDR9/140, Le Commissaire de la République à le Général d'Armée, 28 April 1948.
[265] MAE, HCRFA, PDR9/140, Le Général d'Armée Koenig à le Commissaire de la République, 26 July 1948.
[266] MAE, HCRFA, PDR9/140, Rapport sur l'Ecole FPA de Fribourg à la suite des contrôles de materiel effectués les 16-2-50, 3-3-50 et 16-5-50, Herrenbald, 20 May 1950.
[267] In July 1949, the director of this school went to Paris to exhibit DP work. MAE, HCRFA, PDR9/140, L'agent PDR Nury à Monsieur l'Administrateur chargé de la FPA, 4 July 1949.

Second World War.[268] Others contend that SEZ are inadequate solutions, for they foster the development of potentially exploitative and low-wage labour and distract governments from the need to offer protection.[269] They argue that encouragement for employment must be accompanied by protection, guarantee of socio-economic rights and a sense of future.[270] Without these, it is asserted that such economic enterprises can undermine labour rights and result in the development of low-waged jobs, physical abuse and environmental degradation.

While much has changed since the late 1940s, many of the themes studied in this chapter still echo in the tensions, contradictions and ambiguities of the labour policies of the West towards refugees. In the aftermath of the Second World War, French official employment and vocational policies were a product of the specific interplay between various economic considerations and cultural influences, from nineteenth century socialist utopias and the French *civilizing mission*; from the ideology of the National Revolution and the post-1945 rhetoric of production. In purely arithmetical terms, there were resounding successes. As many contemporary reports highlighted, employment rates were notably higher in the French zone than elsewhere. The official PDR leaflet proudly insisted: 'In July 1947, at the time of UNRRA's disbandment, out of 18,934 employable DPs 18,520 were employed. This success speaks for itself; when in 1951, German authorities complained that the employment of *inémigrables* DPs is not possible; one should remember these results [...].'[271] Given these successful employment rates, French officials often prided themselves in having devised a more individualist and suitable solution for the DPs in their care, hastening their return to some sense of 'normality'. Yet beneath this official self-congratulatory discourse, the reality was more complex. As a matter of fact, when French authorities entrusted the DP question to German authorities, a significant number of DPs were still not 'integrated' into the German economy. Amongst the approximate 8,000 DPs who then remained in the French zone still unable to emigrate to a third country, the majority of those living in the Baden and Rhineland-Palatinate were working; yet, for those living in Württemberg-Hohenzollern, the situation was more critical. Many of them continued to live in poor accommodation and camps, and they experienced discrimination from their German employers.[272]

---

[268] Alexander Betts and Paul Collier, *Refuge: Transforming a Broken System* (London: Allen Lane, 2017).

[269] See ODI 'Refugees: are jobs the answer ?', 11 May 2017, www.odi.org/events/4467-refugees-are-jobs-answer (last accessed 25 June 2018).

[270] See, for example, Heaven Crawley, 'Migration: Refugee Economics', *Nature*, vol. 544 (2017), pp. 22–27.

[271] *Sept-ans en faveur des personnes déplacées*, p. 28.

[272] Ibid., pp. 130–131; AN, AJ/43/797, chef du service IRO pour la Zone Sud à Directeur de l'IRO pour la ZFOA, Dir/JB/HH/2111, 13 June 1950.

Whilst official instructions stipulated that DPs should enjoy priority over local Germans, this chapter has revealed that their situation vis-à-vis their German neighbours crucially depended on local conditions and varied markedly according to DPs' nationality and gender. The revival of gender and ethnic prejudices within a climate of persistent economic difficulties translated into very different treatment for particular categories of DPs. Intellectual Baltic DPs and *Banatais* farmers were often 'privileged', while Polish and Ukrainian DPs, on the contrary, faced prejudice and were more likely to be forced to work outside camps. Over time, some relief workers protested against these blatant inequalities and helped to improve DPs' working situation and material entitlements. But, in other cases, these relief workers contributed to the very inequalities that certain DPs confronted. Crucially, DP initiatives and resiliency were often disregarded by relief workers, except for the very few DPs, whose activities aligned with French economic priorities or concerns for France's image abroad.

# 6

## Transforming DPs into French Citizens?

### The Resettlement of DPs in France

The period from the spring of 1947 to the end of 1951 witnessed the development of several schemes for the recruitment of the 'worthiest' DPs in France. After the final eviction of the Communists from the tripartite coalition in office in May 1947, these schemes enjoyed fairly wide support inside the government. They were driven by five key concerns. First, DPs constituted an enticing demographic opportunity to replenish a French population denuded by two World Wars and a declining birth rates. Policy-elites saw in DPs a valuable reservoir of manpower for the reconstruction of the French economy, which suffered from manpower shortages in the textile, agricultural and mining industries. Second, French policy-elites were eager to restore their country's place as the historical haven of political refugees, after the failure of asylum in the late thirties and the Vichy regime's suppression of elementary democratic rights.[1] As Alfred Coste-Floret, former resister and *député* of the Popular Republican Movement, put it in front of the National Assembly in August 1947: 'France, country of asylum *par excellence,* has always shown itself sensitive to the issue of refugees.'[2] Beyond this official discourse, security imperatives also motivated French attempts to recruit DPs to curb the growth of the German population. A fourth important factor behind the recruitment was the impulse given by the International Refugee Organization (IRO) and its provision of funding for the resettlement in France of certain categories of DPs. Finally, French efforts were driven by pragmatic considerations. Irrespective of official policies, DPs were seeking economic opportunities outside of Germany. It thus seemed more rational to organize their resettlement in an orderly and centralized manner with the aid of the IRO.[3]

---

[1] Greg Burgess, 'Remaking Asylum in Post-war France, 1944–1952', *Journal of Contemporary History*, vol. 49, no. 3 (2014), pp. 556–576; Jérémy Guedj, 'La France et l' "institution" des réfugiés, de l'urgence à la normalisation (1946–1951)', in Aline Angoustures, Dzovinar Kévonian and Claire Mouradian (eds.), *Réfugiés et apatrides. Administrer l'asile en France* (Rennes: Presses Universitaires de Rennes, 2017), pp. 115–125.

[2] AN, F7/16061, Alfred Coste-Floret, Rapport fait au nom de la Commission des Affaires étrangères sur le projet de loi tendant à autoriser le Président de la République à ratifier la Constitution de l'OIR signé pour la France le 17 décembre 1946, 1 August 1947.

[3] Ibid.

Despite the widespread agreement within the government, this programme was rapidly considered as a failure.[4] The various French emigration schemes were greeted with consternation in the French leftist press and circles, for the harsh selection methods adopted towards healthy workers in the German ruins recalled aspects of Nazi practices. Former Resister leader Claude Bourdet observed, for instance, in January 1948: 'the French government [...] wasted time and money to hand pick, one by one, the best workers amongst the Displaced Persons [...] dividing needlessly and inhumanly family, victims amongst victims, [...] and differentiating between those "able to work" and those "with no market value", doing exactly what Hitler did.'[5] These schemes also proved relatively unpopular amongst DPs, for whom the prospect of working in France where the communist party held a strong influence was not very attractive. DPs were often required to work in menial and strenuous occupations. Work offers largely depended on the fluctuation of the labour market: the majority of DPs neither had the choice of their profession nor of where they would be resettled in France.

In numerical terms, the recruitment was also disappointing. According to French official figures, between 15 April 1947 and 30 November 1949, 40,402 DPs and refugees entered into France: 7,324 from the French occupation zone and Berlin, 7,025 from the British zone, 11,105 from the US zone and 14,948 from Austria.[6] Significant numbers of them re-emigrated shortly after their arrival. In addition, according to the calculation of Doris Bensimon and Sergio Della Pergola, around 37,000 Jews from DP camps and Eastern European countries took up residence in France, in part because until 1948 few countries were open to Jewish refugees.[7] For many of these Jewish DPs, France was only a country of transit in their journey to Americas or Palestine. In total, Julia Maspero estimates that 15,000 Polish Jews settled in France.[8]

The failure of the French recruitment operation is, in some significant ways, paradoxical. Compared to countries belonging to the New World, France's

---

[4] AN, AJ/43/753, Relationship with government pour le mois de juin 1948, 12 July 1948.
[5] Claude Bourdet, *Personnes déplacées* (Paris: Éditions de Clermont, 1948), pp. 15–18, 18.
[6] AN, F7/16109, Réfugiés et DPs entrés en France du 15 Avril 1947 au 30 Novembre 1949; other estimates are slightly lower: in total, between July 1947 and May 1950, France drew in 37,338 DPs and refugees with the help of the IRO. AN, F/7/16061, Statistical Report with 35 Months Summary, IRO Headquarters, May 1950, p. 26.
[7] Doris Bensimon and Sergio Della Pergola, *La population juive de France: Sociodémographie et identité* (Paris: CNRS, 1984), p. 36; quoted in Maud Mandel, 'The Encounter between "Native" and "Immigrant" Jews in Post-Holocaust France. Negotiating Difference', in Seán Hand and Steven Katz (eds.), *Post-Holocaust France and the Jews 1945–1955* (New York: New York University Press, 2015), pp. 38–57, 41.
[8] Julia Maspero, 'La politique française à l'égard de l'émigration juive polonaise de l'immédiat après-guerre', *Bulletin du Centre de recherche français à Jérusalem*, 22 (2011), available at http://journals.openedition.org/bcrfj/6513 (Last consulted on 22 February 2019).

geographic position was advantageous. It offered DPs a much shorter journey than either the USA or Australia.[9] Furthermore, owing to the number of Polish and White Russian migrants who had settled in France in the interwar years, France hosted significant numbers of Polish associations, churches and welfare groups, which actively defended DPs' interests and were able to facilitate their resettlements.[10] A considerable amount of financial resources and international expertise were also invested in DPs' preparation for emigration to France. Schools and DP training centres were established in the French zone to train DPs in various trades, thereby facilitating their smooth assimilation in France. Finally, every effort was made by French Prisoners, Deportees and Refugees [PDR] authorities to stimulate interest among potential recruits.[11] On 13 January 1948, the French government signed an agreement with the Preparatory Commission of the International Refugee Organization [PCIRO], which provided for the payment of a bonus of sixteen dollars to those DPs willing to emigrate to France.[12] Later that autumn, France launched the 'Plan culture famille' [Familial Agricultural Plan], which made provision for the entry of DPs and their families. The nature of the scheme meant that many semi-skilled agricultural workers for whom other resettlement opportunities had not been found could emigrate to France together with their families.[13] In December 1948, a delegation of nine DP representatives was invited to visit France and see conditions there at first hand. According to French officials, this visit was a success.[14] The delegation on its return agreed to publicize the scheme in conjunction with the French publicity team.[15] Despite this successful official visit, by 15 January 1952, only 14,892 DPs had emigrated from the French zone to metropolitan France.[16]

Explanations for this paradoxical failure tend to fall into four broad strands. In his book *The Tyranny of the National*, Gérard Noiriel presents this episode as a blatant example of state hypocrisy. Highlighting the discrepancy between the rhetorical airs with which French government figures proclaimed human rights and the methods it employed to handpick fit and able-bodied workers in

---

[9] AN, AJ/43/628, compte-rendu de la réunion tenue le 18 décembre 1948 à Auxerre, à l'occasion de la venue en France d'une délégation de Personnes Déplacées.
[10] AN, AJ/43/628, Procès Verbal de la conférence sur le plan français 'culture famille', entre les délégué IRO, ONI et les délégués ethniques à Neuenburg, 26 October 1948.
[11] Ibid.
[12] It never, however, proved possible to distribute this grant. Louise Holborn, *The International Refugee Organization* (New York: Oxford University Press, 1956), p. 383.
[13] AN, AJ/43/628, Philip E. Ryan to Mr Tuck, 21 December 1948.
[14] AN, AJ/43/753, Rapport, délégation de l'OIR pour la France, December 1948.
[15] Holborn, *The International Refugee Organization*, p. 384.
[16] 'Tableau des effectifs DPs émigrés de zone française à la date du 15 janvier 1952', HCRFA, Service des Personnes Déplacées, *Sept ans d'activité en faveur des personnes déplacées en zone française d'occupation, 1945–1952*, p. 56.

Germany, Noiriel argues that the recruitment of DPs embodied the victors' disregard for the humanitarian values that they so recently enunciated in the Universal Declaration.[17] Alexis Spire stresses the economic factors that hindered the recruitment of DPs: after 1948, French farmers were reluctant to employ DPs in a context of worsening French unemployment and growing clandestine arrival of neo-refugees, fleeing the Soviet Bloc.[18] Other scholars demonstrate that although state intervention was significantly extended at the Liberation, administrative practices were not unified and the various services in charge of immigration control remained ill-equipped to manage incoming foreign workers. As Herrick Chapman notes, the management of immigration was marked by 'low voltage dirigisme': state officials created laws and institutions to regulate immigration, but failed to create an 'elite consensus' to 'take full advantage of them'.[19] Finally, Daniel Cohen has highlighted the role of the IRO in this transfer of 'surplus manpower' and 'surplus population'. In contrast with the interwar years, during which national immigration laws predominantly regulated the movement of migrants, the IRO employed selective procedures on a multilateral basis.[20] Admittedly, the IRO never superseded national immigration policies, but it played a decisive role in shaping emigration policies, by becoming a formidable marketing enterprise working on behalf of DPs. In this unprecedented instance of centralized international migration, France had to work hard to sell France to the DPs.

This chapter contributes a new dimension to our understanding of the transfers of DPs to France. It recognizes the importance of macro-economic factors and national politics in shaping French recruitment operations, but probes beneath the formal structure of official instructions to reconstruct the

---

[17] Noiriel, *La tyrannie du national. Le droit d'asile en Europe (1793–1993)* (Paris: Calmann-Levy, 1991), p. 135. On the absence of protection, also see Patrick Weil, 'Racisme et discrimination dans la politique française de l'immigration: 1938-1945/1974-1995', *Vingtième siècle. Revue d'Histoire*, vol. 47 (1995), pp. 77–102; On the complex interactions between the discourses of the right of man and the control of immigration flows, see Michelle Guillon, Luc Legoux and Emmanuel Ma Mung (eds.), *L'Asile politique entre deux chaises. Droits de l'Homme et gestion des flux migratoires* (Paris: L'harmattan, 2003).

[18] Alexis Spire, 'Les réfugiés, une main d'œuvre à part ? Conditions de séjour et d'emploi, France, 1945–1975', *Revue Européenne des Migrations Internationales*, vol. 20, no. 2 (2004), pp. 13–38 ; Jin-Hee Kang, 'L'accès au marché du travail des réfugiés en France entre 1945 et 1954', in Angoustures, Kévonian and Mouradian (eds.), *Réfugiés et apatrides*, pp. 153–163.

[19] Herrick Chapman, *France's Long Reconstruction: In Search of the Modern Republic* (Cambridge, MA: Harvard University Press, 2018), pp. 72–73.

[20] Daniel Cohen, *In War's Wake: Europe's Displaced Persons in the Postwar Order* (Oxford: Oxford University Press, 2011), p. 101. On the ILO and inter-war global migration policy, see Paul-André Rosental, 'Géopolitique et Etat-providence. Le BIT et la politique mondiale des migrations dans l'entre-deux-guerres', in *Annales. Histoire, Sciences Sociales*, vol. 61, no. 1 (2006), pp. 99–134.

ways in which recruitment and resettlement were put into practice in Allied-occupied Germany.[21] By unearthing French actors' contradictory requirements in the field, this chapter revisits top-down and institutional narratives to suggest that French actors in Germany articulated very different visions of the post-war nation. It also calls for a reconsideration of the dynamic relationships between foreign and domestic policies, by highlighting how French actions were held accountable to the IRO and, in turn, how the IRO agendas influenced the form that the recruitment took. More crucially, it traces how French attempts at recruiting DPs were linked to projection of power.[22] From the perspectives of French occupation officials in Germany, the issue of DP recruitment was as cultural in focus as economically determined. French occupation officials, many of whom were Gaullists, were particularly concerned about the image of France circulating in DP camps and in IRO official circles. They often associated the encouragement of immigration with French patriotism. For them, the issues posed by the recruitment of DPs were far greater than a problem of satisfying manpower needs. Their anxieties about DPs' reluctance to come to France were tied to the reformulation of French identity and the restoration of French prestige.[23]

At the centre of this centralized migration was a fascinating paradox: French officials, like other Western recruiters, often worked hard to sell France to those they considered as the *best* DPs. Meanwhile, DPs strove to present themselves as 'ideal migrants', selling their health, professional skills and probity. And yet, while French occupation officials and the PDR authorities made every effort to encourage DP recruitment, the National Immigration Office (ONI) was much more circumspect (if not hostile) in its approach to DPs until 1948. The first French ONI Selection Missions were unnecessarily harsh with DPs, rapidly gaining a reputation as arbitrary and communist-tinged. Anti-communist DPs did not fit in their vision of a post-war antifascist France. If we are to fully understand this lack of consensus on the transfer of DPs to France, we need to recognize the role played by these recruiters, which further depressed DPs' scant interest in choosing a country severely damaged by war.[24]

---

[21] On street-level bureaucracy, see, for example, Michael Lipsky, *Street-Level Bureaucracy. Dilemmas of the Individual in Public Services* (New York: Russell Sage Foundation, 1980); Vincent Dubois, *La vie au guichet* (Paris: Belin, 1999); Alexis Spire, *Etrangers à la carte. L'administration de l'immigration en France (1945–1975)* (Paris: Grasset, 2005); Sylvain Laurens, 'Les agents de l'Etat face à leur propre pouvoir. Eléments pour une micro-analyse des mots griffonnés en marge des décisions officielles', *Genèses*, no. 72 (2008), pp. 26–41.

[22] Paul Kramer, 'The Geopolitics of Mobility: Immigration Policy and American Global Power in the Long Twentieth Century', *American Historical Review*, vol. 123, no. 2 (2018), pp. 393–438, 437.

[23] Cohen, *In War's Wake*, p. 16.

[24] Andreas Rinke, *Le Grand retour – Die französische Displaced Person-Politik (1944–1951)* (Frankfurt am Main: Peter Lang, 2002), pp. 391–397.

## 'The Largest Travel Agency in the World': The IRO in the French Zone

The arrival of the PCIRO, which became the IRO on 20 August 1948, brought about important changes in the governance of DPs, with Allied policy shifting from an emphasis on repatriation to a more prominent focus on resettlement. The Soviet Union and its satellites withdrew from the organization; indeed, only eighteen of the UN's fifty-four member states participated. The IRO was rapidly dubbed 'the largest travel agency in the world'.[25] Huge sums were involved. In total, the IRO repatriated around 70,000 DPs and resettled over a million in foreign countries.[26] Between July 1947 and December 1951, the IRO spent some $430 million on resettlement alone.[27] The IRO provided support for three types of emigration: first, emigration conducted under government selection schemes (mass settlement); second, emigration through personal nomination by known sponsors in resettlement countries (individual emigration); and, third, the placement of individuals with prospective employers on the basis of specific qualifications and needs (placement service).[28]

The IRO coordinated the work of the various selection missions and compiled information about DPs' occupational skills. It published documentation and leaflets that impressed upon representatives of host countries that DPs offered 'youth as well as skills to the world'.[29] It thus became a formidable marketing enterprise working on behalf of DPs, drawing recruitment missions' attention to their wide range of skills and professional experiences. The scale of this marketing work was unprecedented. IRO Assistant Director Pierre Jacobsen observed, 'no organization prior to 1939 has attempted to put [planned international migration] into practice'.[30] In the interwar years, international organizations, such as the ILO, had already advocated supranational regulation of migratory movements and the orderly redistribution of

---

[25] Akira Irye and Pierre-Yves Saunier (eds.), *The Palgrave Dictionary of Transnational History* (London: Palgrave Macmillan, 2009), p. 876.

[26] Holborn, *The International Refugee Organization*, p. 365.

[27] Peter Gatrell and Nick Baron, 'Violent Peacetime: Reconceptualising Displacement and Resettlement in the Soviet-East European Borderlands after the Second World War', in Gatrell and Baron (eds.), *Warlands. Population Resettlement and State Reconstruction in the Soviet-East European Borderlands, 1945–1950* (Basingstoke: Palgrave Macmillan, 2009), pp. 255–268, 258.

[28] Wolfgang Jacobmeyer, 'The "Displaced Persons" in West Germany, 1945–1951', in Rystad, *The Uprooted. Forced Migration as an International Problem in the Post-War Era* (Lund: Lund University Press, 1990), pp. 271–288, 278. The individual emigration proved particularly difficult in the French zone, due to the small number of consular representatives. AN, AJ/43/760, IRO, Rapport mensuel du mois d'octobre 1948, 6 November 1948.

[29] Holborn, *The International Refugee Organization*, p. 275.

[30] AN, OIR, AJ/43/1269, Published report, 'Journée d'études de Sainte-Odile, 11 au 15 juin 1951', Secours catholique, p. 12.

excess population.[31] Yet, they had not coordinated the work of various national missions on the ground. As Daniel Cohen has demonstrated, 'orchestrated by the Cold War West under American leadership', the redistribution of 'surplus manpower' and 'surplus population' marked 'the peak of centralized international migration'.[32]

In the French zone, the IRO organized the pre-selection of DP candidates. Acknowledging that most DPs lacked adequate clothing, and yet were often judged on their physical appearance, IRO officials provided textiles and clothes.[33] Their main aim was to transform DPs into 'emigration-minded' people and 'attractive' candidates for resettlement countries. In November 1947, for instance, the IRO, helped by the YMCA, carried out a pre-selection of nurses in Ebingen for emigration to Switzerland: the candidates were then provided a short training, which included a 'moral preparation' for emigration.[34] This pre-selection was not always adequate. Out of 48 pre-selected candidates, the Swiss mission ultimately chose only 24 DPs.[35] At times, IRO medical officers proved themselves more severe than national recruiters. In August 1948, for instance, the newly arrived and inexperienced Canadian doctor appeared 'more strict than its predecessor', but more lenient than the IRO doctor.[36] As part of the preparation for DP emigration, the IRO aimed to maintain a high standard of health. Detecting incipient disease, varicosities, orthopaedic troubles and dental defects was essential, as they could all become handicaps for resettlement.[37] The medical service of the zone suffered, however, from a serious lack of supplies and shortages of staff.[38] The IRO authorities quickly realized that the rejection rates on medical grounds were higher in the North of the zone, where DPs tended to live in camps, than in the South, where DPs lived privately.[39] In order to remedy rejection on medical grounds, it toured the zone to carry out mass X-Ray survey procedures, set up centres for dentist care and arrange vaccinations prior to emigration.[40] It also set up a centre for the rehabilitation of disabled DPs.

The daily administration of DP camps was thus fundamentally altered with the arrival of the IRO. In July 1947, when it took over from UNRRA, the direct care and maintenance of DPs was entrusted to the French PDR organization.[41]

---

[31] Rosental, 'Géopolitique et Etat-providence', pp. 99–134.
[32] Cohen, *In War's Wake*, p. 101, 125.
[33] MAE, HCRFA, PDR3/35, Approvisionnement des personnes déplacées, 11 March 1949.
[34] AN, AJ/43/760, Rapport mensuel novembre 1947, 8 December 1947.
[35] AN, AJ/43/760, Rapport mensuel janvier 1948, 6 February 1948.
[36] AN, AJ/43/760, Rapport mensuel aôut 1948, 6 September 1948.
[37] Holborn, *The International Refugee Organization*, p. 240.
[38] AN, AJ/43/702, Aide memoire pour Sabatier, 5 November 1947.
[39] AN, AJ/43/760, Rapport mensuel avril 1948, 4 May 1948.
[40] AN, AJ/43/761, Rapport de la Division Santé – octobre 1949, 9 November 1949.
[41] Holborn, *The International Refugee Organization*, pp. 129–130.

Overnight, a single PDR agent was typically expected to replace a large UNRRA team in each DP centre. On 6 September 1947, an official agreement was signed between the IRO and the French government.[42] It stipulated that the IRO would support the cost of DP administration and resettlement. The PDR was supervised by the IRO, whose headquarters was established in Neuenburg, 25 miles by road from Baden-Baden (where the military government was based) and a little less from Rastatt (PDR HQ). In contrast with UNRRA, the IRO introduced a distinction between those DPs eligible for 'care and maintenance' (receiving food provision, health care, clothes and accommodations) and those to whom only 'legal and political protection' were granted. These DPs were entitled to the right of emigration, the IRO covering the costs of their travel, medical care and clothing.[43] The first months of the IRO were thus marked by intense screening operations. When UNRRA handed over the care of DPs, the numbers of DPs living in the zone varied according to the UNRRA and PDR registers. There were 32,535 DPs on the UNRRA registers, including 1,309 in the French sector of Berlin; By contrast, the PDR registers counted 40,794 DPs.[44] Determining the number of DPs eligible for care and maintenance was essential, not least because it dictated the sum that French authorities received from the IRO.[45] Between 1 July and 31 December 1947, the IRO provided 33,756 *rationnaires complets* and 11,310 *rationnaires incomplets*.[46]

The IRO preparation for DP emigration took place in a context when both the IRO and PDR faced growing pressure from the French occupation army and German local actors to hand over the buildings in which DPs were living.[47] At the end of 1947, the economic attachment of the Saarland led to the integration of 80 per cent of the DP population in the Saar economy and the transfer of the remaining 20 per cent to Ebingen, Niederlahnstein and

---

[42] AN, AJ/43/799, CPIRO-GMZFO, Organisation et fonctionnement de la commission préparatoire de l'OIR dans la ZFO, Signé A. Poignant; Cherifi, 29 October 1947.

[43] In 1949, a third category was introduced: some DPs were entitled to legal protection, but without the possibility of emigration. *Sept-ans en faveur des personnes déplacées*, p. 47.

[44] AN, AJ/43/702, Aide memoire pour Mr Sabatier, 5 November 1947.

[45] Initially, the financial terms of the 6 September 1947 Agreement seemed favourable to the French authorities. However, the IRO and French authorities disagreed about the numbers of eligible DPs. MAE, HCRFA, Ambassade de Bonn, 148, M. Cherifi, Compte-rendu d'activité de la Direction des Personnes Déplacées pour le mois de Septembre 1947, 9 October 1947, p. 1.

[46] PCIRO personnel were charged with ensuring that their agency's policies were enforced, meaning, in practice, the requirement to determine DP eligibility, to collect statistical data, to promote repatriation and, finally, to support DP resettlement. MAE, HCRFA, PDR3/35, avenant à l'accord du 6 septembre 1947 relatif à la zone française d'Allemagne.

[47] AN, AJ/43/760, Rapport février 1948, 8 March 1948.

Trier.[48] In early 1948, the caserns of Landstuhl, where many DPs were hosted, were given back to the Army and the inhabitants were evacuated to the camps in Feyen and Niederlahnstein. This transfer was operated in a hurry and resulted in overcrowded camps.[49] In February 1948, the French Director of the IRO sent a damning report to the head of the military government condemning these transfers and deploring the living conditions in many DP camps, including Münsingen, Ebingen and Tuttlingen. The IRO director was particularly concerned about Tuttlingen, designed as recruitment centre for the Canadian mission, and which was in a filthy condition. He insisted on the 'deplorable effects' that this camp would have on foreign missions and observers.[50] After April 1948, the PDR faced more pressing demands of restitution, which intensified even further in 1949. In addition to this growing pressure, the monetary reform of June 1948 imposed severe budgetary restriction, which limited its 'rehabilitative' actions and provisions.

While all IRO officials understood the importance of DP emigration, conflict and institutional rivalries hampered the development of DP emigration. The Division of Resettlement, directed by an 'autocratic' chief, was at loggerheads with the Department of Care and Maintenance, supervised by a 'newcomer' and 'a woman'.[51] On the whole, though, the relation between officials within IRO and with the PDR was considerably smoother than that between the UNRRA and the PDR. IRO interests aligned more closely with that of the French PDR Service: the IRO favoured the emigration of DPs in European countries, in particular France and Britain considered as cheaper.[52]

## International Competition

Foreign recruitment missions competed with each other to obtain the best DPs. Recruitment standards varied from one country to another, but most governments were initially interested in healthy DPs able to fill specific fields of economic activity. DPs were fully conscious of the importance of a 'clean bill of health'.[53] The severity of the medical selection varied according to the selection missions: one of the missions went so far as to disqualify any DP who

---

[48] Some of the DPs who stayed in the Saar in 1947, then decided to move to the zone in 1949. MAE, HCRFA, PDR6/485, General Koenig à Monsieur le Délégué Général pour le GM de l'Etat Rhéno-Palatin, 17 May 1949.
[49] AN, AJ/43/796, Gouverneur Hettier de Boislambert à Général, 16 March 1948.
[50] MAE, HCRFA, PDR3/35, Directeur de la CPOIR à Général d'Armée Commandant en chef français en Allemagne, Neuenbürg, 19 February 1948.
[51] AN, AJ/43/702, Internal memorandum, Lane, Report on Visit to French zone, 23 December 1948.
[52] AN, AJ/43/760, Report Resettlement, signé Poignant, October 1947.
[53] Holborn, *The International Refugee Organization*, p. 241.

had ever suffered from a venereal disease.[54] Other recruiters identified flat fleet or varicosities as ground for rejection, implicitly resorting to eugenic convictions.[55] DPs' emigration choices were thus largely determined by how healthy their bodies and minds appeared to recruiters. As an IRO counselling officer noted, '[o]f all the victims that have survived the 1939–1945 cataclysm, the situation of mental patients was by far the most tragic'.[56] They were offered no opportunity for emigration and were condemned to live far away from their families. Not only did emigration procedures stigmatize the ill, elderly and illiterate, but for many DPs the administrative formalities were very long and confusing. The time that lapsed between the emigration demand and the departure was never shorter than several months and could last several years.[57]

Like all Western policies, French DP recruitment policies initially focused on the 'fit' body and economically *useful* migrant. On 10 June 1947, French authorities signed agreements for the recruitment of DPs with the American, the British and the Inter-Governmental Committee on Refugees' authorities.[58] The first French scheme was designed to attract 14,000 single men to work in coalmines. DPs were offered an initial contract of one year, renewal at yearly intervals, with permanent settlement in mind.[59] They were to be paid at the same rate as French workers and were entitled to join the trade union of their choice. Provisions to return to Germany were made for those who rescinded their contract for a valid reason; the scheme also allowed the forced return of DPs who proved not to have the aptitude to work in France or DPs who 'by action or propaganda became a danger to public order.'[60] Arrangements were made for certain dependents (wife, mother, father, children) to join the workers in France, after a period of probation.[61] The French impressed upon their Allies the necessity of very 'thorough medical examination', including blood tests and X-Ray screening.[62]

When the scheme was implemented in the British and American zones, it faced the competition of the Belgian 'Operation Black Diamond' scheme,

---

[54] Ibid., p. 249.
[55] Antoine Burgard, 'Une nouvelle vie dans un nouveau pays. Trajectoires d'orphelins de la Shoah vers le Canada (1947–1952)', PhD thesis, Université du Québec à Montréal/Université Lumière Lyon 2, September 2017, pp. 336–367.
[56] AN, AJ/43/760, Counseling, Rapport du mois d'aout 1948, signed by E. W. D. Steel.
[57] *Sept-ans en faveur des personnes déplacées*, p. 55.
[58] NA, FO/945/470, Telegram from the British Embassy, Duff Cooper, N. 523, 12 June 1947.
[59] AN, AJ/43/793, Control Commission for Germany (B.E.) Prisoners of War and Displaced Persons Division, 'Technical Instruction No. 26 DPs for France', 21 August 1947.
[60] NA, FO/945/470, Agreement between the French government and the IGRC regarding the recruitment and the establishment in France of DPs originally in the American zone of Germany and Austria.
[61] AN, AJ/43/793, Control Commission for Germany (B.E.) Prisoners of War and Displaced Persons Division, 'Technical Instruction No. 26 DPs for France', 21 August 1947.
[62] AN, AJ/43/793, Incoming cable, PWDP LEMGO to P. C. IRO LEMGO, 31 July 1947.

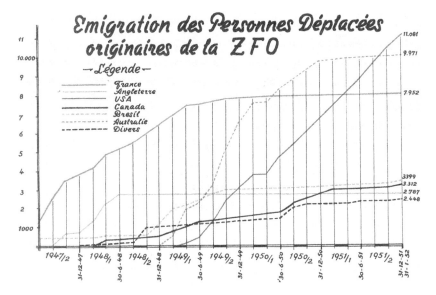

Fig. 6.1 'Emigration of DPs from the French zone', in Haut Commissariat de la République française en Allemagne, Service des Personnes Déplacées, *Sept ans d'activité en faveur des personnes déplacées en zone française d'occupation, 1945–1952*, rapport dactylographié et illustré [undated], [Bibliothèque du Ministère des Affaires Etrangères, Direction des Archives], p. 54.

which had started earlier and targeted able-bodied miners. After the intensive recruiting for Belgium, few DPs were left in the camps who wanted to go into mining, and even fewer who were skilled coal miners. The Belgian mission had been fairly liberal in its medical criteria and had benefited from the fact that it was the first scheme open to refugees looking for resettlement opportunities.[63] French recruiters also contended with British recruiters, who had launched the 'Westward Ho!' scheme, aimed initially at workers without dependents due to housing shortages in Britain. In the French zone, both the PDR and the IRO gave priority to the recruitment of labour to France.[64] Until the opening of the Australian, American and Canadian schemes, French recruiters did not face significant competition, except from the British scheme (Fig. 6.1).

The French scheme was then covered retroactively by a further agreement concluded on 15 January 1948, which provided for recruitment in mining, farming, factory and domestic work.[65] In April 1948, the age limits of workers

---

[63] Holborn, *The International Refugee Organization*, p. 378.
[64] AN/AJ/43/702, Report of Field Representative, French zone, Germany, 10 August 1947.
[65] Holborn, *The International Refugee Organization*, p. 383.

were established: DPs had to be 18–35 years old for mining work and 14–45 years old for agricultural and industrial work. The minimum age of 14 was only applicable to dependents of adult workers. The age limits for unaccompanied workers were 18 for men and 21 for women.[66] After 1948, the French realized that other missions were more successful in capturing DPs' imagination than theirs. DPs preferred emigrating overseas in the belief that the New World provided better security in the event of renewed international conflict.[67] Rumours circulated in DP circles about conditions in host countries.[68] DPs compared wages, housing and life opportunities. In the French zone, for instance, although 'everyone knew in the DP world that the Canadian mission was one of the most selective', Canada was a very attractive destination.[69] DPs were hesitant to resettle in Europe and preferred to flee beyond the oceans the communist threat. The US, which passed the 'Displaced Persons Act of 1948' on 24 June, was also one of the favoured destinations of DPs. The main inconvenience of the US scheme, however, was that preference was accorded to relatives of US citizens or aliens permanently residing in the US, which was not the case of many DPs living in the French zone.[70] Many DPs also saw their entries to the US rejected because of convictions for petty theft committed in 1945 in the euphoria of victory.[71] Polish American relief organizations were crucial in shaping this recruitment: they carried out a severe unofficial screening amongst DPs, in collaboration with the DP elites and the Polish clergy.[72]

French authorities tried to limit the promotion of very popular schemes. In August 1948, for instance, the French IRO HQ decided not to promote the Australian scheme, Australia being extremely popular, particularly amongst Baltic DPs.[73] In the other zones, the Australian teams spend considerable time and efforts selling Australia as a welcoming and exciting destination and promoting the 'Australian way of Life'.[74] As Ruth Balint shows, the Australia teams produced films, such as *Men Wanted in Australia* (1947) and *This is the Life* (1947), radio programs, booklets, posters and lectures, all presenting

---

[66] AN, AJ/43/793, Schleswig Holstein, Employment & Resettlement Bulletin N. 14, 5 April 1948.
[67] AN, AJ/43/760, IRO, Rapport mensuel juillet 1948, 2 August 1948.
[68] AN, AJ/43/760, Counselling Service, Rapport juillet 1948, E. W. D. Steel, 11 August 1948.
[69] AN, AJ/43/760, Rapport mensuel avril 1948, signé Poignant, 4 May 1948.
[70] AN, AJ/43/702, M. A. Grimaud, Mission des 18/19 aout 1949, 29 August 1949.
[71] *Sept ans d'activité en faveur des personnes déplacées en zone française d'occupation*, p. 55.
[72] Katarzyna Nowak, 'Voices of Revival. A Cultural History of Polish Displaced Persons in Allied-Occupied Germany and Austria, 1945–1952', PhD thesis, University of Manchester, version submitted in July 2018, p. 79.
[73] AN, AJ/43/760, Rapport mensuel Aout 1948, 6 September 1948.
[74] Jayne Persian, '"Chifley Liked Them Blond": DP Immigrants for Australia', *History Australia*, vol. 12, no. 2 (2015), pp. 80–101, 92.

Australia as a 'prosperous homeland of sunshine, industry, freedom and opportunity'.[75] Despite French efforts to initially limit the promotion of this scheme, the evidence shows that Australia was a popular destination. Australia favoured the migration of North Europeans, accepting only Baltic DPs at the beginning of its scheme.[76] The Australian schemes were highly gendered: the men came as 'labourers' and the women as 'domestics'. By the late 1948, larger family groups were permitted to enter Australia as well as widows and unmarried women. In total, on 15 January 1952, 9,939 DPs from the French zone emigrated to Australia and 10,903 to the USA.[77]

## The ONI Selection: A Communist Sabotage?

Throughout the period, DPs faced disproportionally harsh, unfair and arbitrary selection processes. The IRO recorded a 30 per cent rejection rate for Canada, 33 per cent for the United States and up to 40 per cent for Australia.[78] Recruiters segregated disabled and unfit DP bodies. They also identified certain sexual behaviours and gender traits as ground for exclusion. In the French zone, some DPs suspected of effeminacy were rejected: the simple fact of having well-manicured hands could result in rejection.[79] This concern for keeping 'undesirable' out of the country on the ground of sex and gender nonconformity was not new. In her work on the American 'straight state', Margot Canaday has, for instance, highlighted how 'federal interest in homosexuality developed in tandem with the growth of the bureaucratic state'.[80] As the American state expanded in the early twentieth century, it increasingly developed 'conceptual mastery over what it sought to regulate'.[81] This culminated in the late 1940s when the state devised tool to *explicitly* target homosexuality. Even so, in post-war Germany, French ONI bureaucrats acquired a particularly awful reputation. They distinguished themselves by their discourteous, condescending attitudes towards DPs. The early excesses of French selection teams casted a shadow over the rest of the French recruitment. Not without reason, French occupation officials fretted about the presence of these

---

[75] Ruth Balint, 'Industry and Sunshine. Australia as Home in the Displaced Persons' Camps of Postwar Europe', *History Australia*, vol. 11, no. 1 (2014), pp. 102–127, 104.
[76] Persian, '"Chifley Liked Them Blond"', p. 91.
[77] 'Tableau des effectifs DPs émigrés de zone francaise à la date du 15 janvier 1952' in *Sept ans d'activité en faveur des personnes déplacées*, p. 56.
[78] Ibid, p. 55.
[79] MAE, HCRFA, PDR6/818, Rapport confidentiel sur le fonctionnement du Centre de Fribourg, 19 November 1947. Transmis par Koenig aux Ministères des Affaires Etrangères, 26 November 1947.
[80] Margot Canaday, *The Straight State: Sexuality and Citizenship in Twentieth-Century America* (Princeton, NJ: Princeton University Press, 2009), p. 2.
[81] Ibid., p. 3.

ONI communists in the three Western zones, worrying that they adversely affected recruitment rates while tarnishing the reputation of France.

The French recruitment scheme seemed, at least initially, relatively popular. In June 1947, an ONI delegation, headed by a Labour Inspector, arrived in Baden-Baden to take charge of the recruitment process. It was made up of two ONI representatives and a delegate of the International Labour Organization (ILO) who, in turn, oversaw nearly 200 agents.[82] Three recruitment centres were created, one in each zone (in Freiburg for the French zone, Paderborn for the British zone and Karlsruhe for the American zone).[83] By October 1947 the PDR authorities reported that nearly 20 per cent of the DP population, accounting for nearly half of the able-bodied male population, had presented themselves to French recruiters.[84] Yet, as rumours about ONI communist recruiters and strikes in France circulated, DPs' enthusiasm fell away. The fear that poor vetting had excluded many suitable candidates prompted PDR and IRO officials to urge the French government to bring ONI personnel to heel. These recruiters were accused of ideologically motivated 'political sabotage'.

In October 1947 a local administrator from Freiburg lamented the atmosphere in which the recruitment was carried out: 'It is disheartening to see people full of eagerness to start a new life and willing to accept hard and unpopular labour, who sacrificing their current situation and considering France as their last hope to live freely, are brutally condemned to remain in a country where they have suffered so much, either as prisoners of war or as deportees.'[85] General Koenig informed the Foreign Ministry in November 1947 that the organization PDR was being 'bombarded' with complaints originating from local authorities about arbitrary selection processes at the Freiburg centre.[86] Koenig claimed that ONI agents considered any 'Polish or Yugoslav citizen who expresses a wish to work in France' to be politically suspicious and rejected them due to 'unfitness'.[87] Failed candidates far outnumbered successful applicants: over 700 candidates had been turned down in

---

[82] MAE, HCRFA, PDR6/821, Fiche d'information, 6 June 1947; PDR6/846, Report from Préfet Roger Gromand, p. 4.

[83] MAE, Bonn 148, Compte-rendu d'activité de la Direction des Personnes Déplacées pour aout 1947.

[84] MAE, HCRFA, Ambassade de Bonn, 148, M. Cherifi, Compte-rendu d'activité de la Direction des Personnes Déplacées pour Septembre 1947, 9 October 1947, p. 4.

[85] MAE, HCRFA, PDR6/818, attaché de 2ème classe Ponty à Commissaire de la République, Délégué Supérieur pour le GM de Bade, le 2 octobre 1947; PDR6/846, Fiche secrète pour Colonel, chef du Cabinet Militaire du Commandement en chef Français en Allemagne, 30 juin 1948. Signé Meillon.

[86] MAE, HCRFA, PDR6/818, Rapport confidentiel sur le fonctionnement du Centre de Fribourg, 19 November 1947. Transmis par Koenig aux MAE, 26 November 1947.

[87] Ibid.

under three weeks.[88] By the end of December only 5,309 DPs had been recruited from the French zone, alongside 525 dependents, figures that fell well short of the government's minimum expectations.[89] On 15 February 1948, Henri Fesquet used the pages of *Le Monde* to exhort the French government to rid the ONI of its political and syndicalist influences.[90]

In Freiburg, a Polish worker was rejected on the grounds that he could not harness a horse *à la mode française*.[91] Elsewhere, DPs were faulted for not knowing how many teeth a cow had or that tractors usually ran on diesel.[92] The Münsingen area delegate raised the case of Stefan Mazur, 'best of all the Poles of Münsingen'. He failed his professional test, despite being 'strong, calm, intelligent and meticulous at work', and his determination to work in France.[93] The reason? Mazur was told that he was a *'fumiste* [shirker] who only wanted to go to France in order to be with his family'.[94] In Reutlingen, a Hungarian DP was failed because his hands were too well-kept, an observation taken to prove that he was lazy and a bad worker.[95] According to a PDR official, 'certain nationalities', such as Hungarians and Yugoslavs, were systematically turned away.[96] Arbitrary rejections were sometimes tied with outright racial discrimination and anti-Semitism. The Director of the American *Joint* complained about the exclusion of three Jewish families that had been sent from Berlin to the Freiburg's recruitment centre. 'After having abandoned everything, these families were denied entry in France having learned that the fact of being Jews [allegedly] prevented them from performing manual work.'[97]

In the American zone, US authorities became increasingly frustrated at the costs of the French scheme, the disproportionate number of ONI agents involved and their archaic administrative methods.[98] In Karlsruhe, Polish

---

[88] Ibid.
[89] AN, AJ/43/628, Statistiques des DPR introduits en France comme travailleurs, 19 January 1948 [Gouverneur V. Valentin-Smith].
[90] AN, AJ/43/628, Henri Fesquet 'L'immigration individuelle donne de meilleurs résultats que l'immigration collective', 15 February 1948.
[91] MAE, HCRFA, PDR6/491, Berge à Colonel, Directeur des Personnes Déplacées, 17 November 1947.
[92] MAE, HCRFA, PDR6/822, H. L. Chaplain à Chef de Mission, 3 December 1947.
[93] MAE, HCRFA, PDR6/818, Délégué de cercle de Münsingen à Délégué Supérieur pour le GM du Wurtemberg, signé Blanc.
[94] Ibid.
[95] MAE, HCRFA, PDR6/818, Rapport confidentiel sur le fonctionnement du Centre de Fribourg, 19 November 1947.
[96] MAE, HCRFA, PDR6/818, administrateur Estrade, Rapport concernant l'immigration en France de Travailleurs DPs volontaires, 31 December 1947.
[97] MAE, HCRFA, PDR6/818, Rapport confidentiel sur le fonctionnement du Centre de Fribourg, 19 November 1947.
[98] MAE, HCRFA, PDR6/803, Gouverneur V. Valentin-Smith to MAE, 30 December 1947.

DPs formally complained about the ONI recruiters' bad behaviour. According to them, they were treated as cattle and not as 'allied and voluntary workers'.[99] They quoted the case of a Polish DP, called Midler, originating from a village near the German border. Arriving equipped with his DP identity papers and evidence of prior IRO screening, he was nonetheless rejected because he had a German-sounding name.[100] In the same camp, another DP was turned away on the grounds that he was 'a bigmouth'.[101] DPs' newspapers meanwhile continued to circulate stories about French communist recruiters. On 25 January 1948, the *Ukrainian gazette*, related the story of a former soldier who was asked to answer political questions by a French bureaucrat after undergoing a demanding medical test: 'The employee, who was busy reading *L'Humanité* [the French communist party newspaper], refused my return to France, where I had been a soldier for several years. And yet I presented him my certificates.'[102]

Rumours that ONI agents were Soviet fifth-columnists also spread.[103] On 2 October 1947, Officer Ponty bemoaned that the Professional Reorientation Commission comprised '50% naturalized agents'. He pleaded for the hiring of agents who would put the interest of France above party politics.[104] Faced with rising complaints, the State Secretariat for German and Austrian affairs ordered an inquiry in January 1948. Carried out by the prefect Roger Gromand, it drew the attention of senior French governmental figures to the irregular activities of the ONI agents: 'Numerous reports have signalled that the recruitment was the target of a veritable sabotage, motivated by political reasons.'[105] Without doubt, Gromand concluded, 'DPs were asked to answer questions by [politically motivated] recruiters who had no other aim than to oust candidates that were hostile to the Soviet regime.'[106] Recruiters justified their decision by arguing that official instructions required appraising whether 'the ideas of the candidate were not in complete opposition with the social beliefs prevailing in the *milieux* where they were bound to live in France'.[107] Extracts from Gromand's report offer a sense of its flavour:

---

[99] MAE, HCRFA, PDR6/822, l'attaché H. L. Chaplain à Chef de Mission, 3 December 1947.
[100] Ibid.
[101] Ibid.
[102] MAE, HCRFA, PDR6/818, traduction d'un article extrait de la *Gazette ukrainienne* du 25 janvier 1948.
[103] MAE, HCRFA, PDR6/491, Berge à Colonel, Directeur des Personnes Déplacées, 17 November 1947.
[104] MAE, HCRFA, PDR6/818, Ponty à Commissaire de la République, Délégué Supérieur pour le GM de Bade, 2 October 1947.
[105] MAE, HCRFA, PDR6/846, Report from Préfet Roger Gromand, p. 4.
[106] Ibid.
[107] Ibid., pp. 4–5.

We deplore the case of Senesse, agent from Karlsruhe, former ONI driver, employed by the OIR, accused of carrying a prohibited weapon and falsifying money; the case of Jonis, CGA delegate at Paderborn, former Latvian member of Parliament, not naturalized, having only lived a year in France, completely oblivious about agricultural matters; the case of Hourdeaux, former chef of the Donaueschingen center who has just been sent back to France due to accusations of false declarations, falsification of food rations cards, unlawful wearing of decoration, abusive use of police cards, illegal possession of weapons.[108]

In Berlin, French Political Advisor Jacques Tarbé de Saint-Hardouin urged the *Quai d'Orsay* to act, noting that American authorities had a 'very bad opinion of the French recruitment mission'. According to him, this constituted 'bad propaganda in our zone whose political colours you know as well as in the American zone'.[109] As this quotation subtly indicates, the opposition to ONI agents emerging from within the military government was intrinsically linked to the broader conflict between communist leaders and Gaullist followers.

## Selling France to the DPs

The Gaullist party-cum-movement, the *Rassemblement du peuple français* (RPF), formally launched in 1947, certainly benefited from the unofficial support of numerous occupation officials in the zone.[110] As Fourth Republic President Vincent Auriol observed, '80% of the *Quai d'Orsay* is Gaullist. Same in Germany'.[111] In the context of the Cold War and the opposition to the newly established Fourth Republic, RPF activism in the zone combined ardent anti-communism with a defiant, unapologetic imperialism. It was, according to Emmanuel Droit, 'perceived by many RPF servicemen as the expression of a specific political culture based on a continuity of practices and values that arose during the Resistance period'.[112] To illustrate the point, a confidential information note from the Brigade de Bad-Kreuznach reported on 16 October 1947 :

---

[108] Ibid., p. 5.
[109] CAC, Versement 770623, article 172, Saint-Hardouin à Bousquet, Berlin, 20 October 1947.
[110] Emmanuel Droit, 'Le RPF dans les Zones Françaises d'Occupation en Allemagne (1947–1958)', in François Audigier and Frédéric Schwindt (eds.), *Gaullisme et gaullistes* (Rennes: Presses Universitaires de Rennes, 2009), pp. 187–201, 197.
[111] Auriol, *Journal*, quoted in Dietmar Hüser *Frankreichs 'Doppelte Deutschlandpolitik.' Dynamik aus der Defensive – Planen, Entscheiden, Umsetzen in gesellschaftlichen und wirtschaftlichen, innen- und außenpolitischen Krisenzeiten 1944–1950* (Berlin: Duncker & Humblot, 1996), p. 168.
[112] Droit, 'Le RPF dans les Zones Françaises d'Occupation en Allemagne (1947–1958)', p. 188.

Over the last two weeks, several gendarmes of the Brigade have been 'contacted' in order to join a Gaullist group [...]. Gendarmes who gave evasive answers to these requests were told 'if you are not Gaullists, you are Communists. After the taking of power, if you did not go along us, you will be dismissed. If you disclose that we spoke to you, *il vous en cuira* [you'll pay for it].' According to these gendarmes, the garrison's officers are eager to act and firmly believe that the occupation troops should march into France.[113]

PDR efforts to sell France to the DPs must be placed in the broader context of French Gaullist occupation authorities' attempts to promote French culture in post-war Germany. The analysis of the PDR archives unveils the cultural – as well as the economic – aspect of DP emigration to France. The symbolic linkage between encouragement to emigrate and the post-war recasting of French patriotism reveals how anxieties about DPs' reluctance to emigrate to France were tied to the restoration of French prestige.

The French PDR executive was bedevilled by the rapid deterioration in France's reputation. It informed local PDR agents that creating a 'pro-French movement' in Germany was more than an economic necessity; it was a 'national duty'.[114] PDR Administrators were asked to work in close collaboration with DP priests to propagate Francophile sentiments in the zone. French language courses were to be provided whenever possible.[115] And, finally, in order to increase DPs' pro-French affinities, PDR administrators were required to live inside DP camps. 'Live [with DPs], think with them, get to know each of them personally, pay them loving attention.'[116] The French PDR Director, according to the dictates of one briefing, 'must be assisted, if not by a French doctor or social worker, at least by a DP with Francophile sentiments. The priests [...] will also be devoted to the cause of France. The teachers, the physical trainer [...] will be the emanation of France and its spirit.'[117]

Despite the countless efforts of the PDR administrators and other French officials to counteract it, the image of Communist France had enormous potency. This may be gauged from the testimony of Anne-Marie de la Morlais, a social worker from the *Union Nationale des Associations*

---

[113] MAE, BONN 148, Fiche de renseignements, origine: brigade de Bad-Kreuznach, 16 October 1947.

[114] MAE, HCRFA, PDR6/556, Extrait du procès verbal de la réunion de Section 'Personnes Déplacées' du 13 juillet 1948.

[115] MAE, HCRFA, PDR6/556, Administrateur Reclus, chef de section des personnes déplacées, Land Rhéno-Palatin à chefs de camp de Niederlahnstein, Gniezno, Feyen, 19 February 1948.

[116] MAE, HCRFA, PDR6/556, Extrait du procès verbal de la réunion de Section 'Personnes Déplacées' du 13 juillet 1948.

[117] Ibid.

*Familiales* (UNAF) charged with female recruitment in the American zone.[118] A well-known figure in the IRO circles as well as within the French military government, she was highly critical of ONI management.[119] Convinced that female recruitment was not the business of men, she arrived in Karlsruhe on 28 August 1947 and set up a 'specific plan' for women's recruitment.[120] De la Morlais repeatedly complained about the 'organized apathy of the ONI'.[121] According to her, France's survival depended on the entry of healthy, *assimilable* DP women.[122] Despite France's obvious demographic needs, the ONI direction was, in her words, 'botching recruitment'.[123] Not only did it take more than two months for work contracts to arrive, but the propaganda leaflets that de la Morlais meticulously designed were not printed. In a note entitled *sabotage des contrats,* she drew French authorities' attention to the unprofessionalism of ONI Direction management: 'Work contracts are used to send anyone, anywhere. The ONI's main concern [...] is to get rid of the maximum number of contracts.'[124] While some medical officers were told to recruit women aged between eighteen and thirty-five, others were informed that women up to forty-five could be selected.[125] This administrative *pagaille* was all the more deplorable because the number of foreign recruitment missions was steadily increasing and thereby the competition between them was worsening. When she first arrived, only six nations were recruiting. But, by February 1948, seventeen nations were competing with France.[126]

De la Morlais spent a considerable amount of her time touring DP camps, reassuring their residents about the supposed 'communist threat' in France:

> Many questions about communism – political life in France – DPs' rights in France – their situation regarding the Soviet embassy etc.
>
> Two miners from neighbouring camps returned from France – at the time of the general strikes – because they could not work and therefore stayed without money. They asked to return to Germany because life was impossible in France. I try to minimize the incident in presenting it as

---

[118] Jérome Minonzio and Jean-Philippe Vallat, 'L'union nationale des associations familiales (UNAF) et les politiques familiales', *Revue française de science politique*, vol. 56, no. 2 (2006), pp. 205–226, 206.

[119] MAE, HCRFA, PDR6/846, Madame de la Morlais à Inspecteur du Travail, Délégué Général de l'ONI, 20 January 1948.

[120] MAE, HCRFA, PDR6/846, Rapport du Travail de Mme de la Morlais sur le recrutement et le placement féminin, 4 February 1948.

[121] MAE, HCRFA, PDR6/846, Anne M. de la Morlais, note [24 May 1948].

[122] MAE, HCRFA, PDR6/846, de la Morlais à Inspecteur du Travail, 20 janvier 1948.

[123] MAE, HCRFA, PDR6/846, de la Morlais à Président de l'UNAF, 11 February 1948.

[124] MAE, HCRFA, PDR6/846, Anne M. de la Morlais, 'Sabotage des contrats' [undated].

[125] MAE, HCRFA, PDR6/846, Rapport du Travail de Mme de la Morlais sur le recrutement et le placement féminin, 4 February 1948, p. 2.

[126] Ibid., p. 2.

'perhaps plausible' but certainly exceptional! The DPs understand and become less dubious about France – very good atmosphere at the end.[127]

De la Morlais also stressed the breadth of French welfare provision when compared with other, more popular destination countries:

> I am being asked to present life in France, its social legislation etc. ... Then a noisy heckler says that 'it is better to go to Australia or Canada, as they are superior countries.' My answer disconcerted the noisy hecklers 'no social legislation in America comparable to France – nor family support'.[128]

French approach to DP immigration was thus contradictory: while many officials, like Anne-Marie de la Morlais, tried to sell France to the DPs and delivered propaganda talk, organized language courses and set up vocational trainings to facilitate their integration in France, many ONI agents looked askance at DP immigration as an anti-communist peril and a threat to French workers' bargaining power.

In January 1948, though, the ONI was restructured and the majority of the ONI communist recruiters were dismissed.[129] A month later, CGT representatives were also forced off the ONI Board of Directors.[130] This heralded a drift to the political right for the ONI administration, which matched the recent end of centre-left coalition government in France.[131] These punitive measures were followed by a reform of the recruitment procedures, with the creation of IRO-directed prospecting missions.[132] These changes were aimed at depoliticizing the recruitment by evincing anti-DP local recruiters.[133] Until June 1948, recruitment was based on the number of work contracts available for DPs. After June, it was decided to adopt the procedures followed by the British, Canadian and Belgian missions: DPs were to be selected first by representatives of the *General Confederation for Agriculture and Les Houillères* (coal mining) and then attributed work in France. More importantly, DP families were to depart at the same time as the DP worker, rather than joining them later.[134]

---

[127] MAE, HCRFA, PDR6/846, Anne De La Morlais, Report, Region de Amberg, 19 April 1948.

[128] MAE, HCRFA, PDR6/846, Anne De La Morlais, Région de Stuttgart, 3 May 1948.

[129] MAE, HCRFA, PDR6/846, Report from Préfet Roger Gromand, p. 4. On the restructuration of the ONI see, for instance, Chapman, *France's Long Reconstruction*, pp. 70–71.

[130] Léon Gani, *Syndicats et Travailleurs immigrés* (Paris: Editions Sociales, 1972), p. 45.

[131] Ibid., p 44.

[132] AN, AJ/43/760, IRO, Rapport mensuel mai 1948, 3 June 1948. In the spring of 1948, the IRO supervised for instance the recruitment of DPs for Citroen factories; AN, AJ/43/760, IRO, Rapport mensuel avril 1948, 4 May 1948.

[133] AN, F/7/16038, Direction de la Réglementation et des étrangers, Note pour Monsieur le Ministre de l'Intérieur, 9 June 1948.

[134] AN, F/7/16038, Direction Générale des Affaires Administratives et Sociales, Opérations spéciales d'immigration de personnes déplacées, 2 June 1948.

For all that, the impression left by *communist* ONI agents lasted. Coupled with the effects of the strikes of the winter of 1947, they helped cement a negative view of France as a poor country rapidly falling under Communist influence. In April 1948 Général Koenig highlighted France's dismal recruitment figures when compared with Britain, Belgium, the United States and, to a lesser extent, Canada:

> Host countries [...] are in order of diminishing importance: Great Britain (47,635 without counting the soldiers of the Anders Army), Belgium (26,000), the United States (24.000), France (21.500 but one needs to deduct 14.500 *Israélites* who are only transiting via France); so France ranks in fact behind Canada (10.500) and just in front of Palestine (5000), Holland (3.500), Brazil (2.700), Paraguay (2.300), Australia (2.200), Venezuela (1.223), Switzerland (1.142), Bolivia (750) and Morocco (500). France has barely benefited from its geographical proximity to supplant overseas countries.[135]

Despite the reorganization of the ONI and French governmental efforts to simplify recruitment procedures and improve administrative coordination, the road to emigration either to France or French colonies was still strewn with bureaucratic hurdles in the summer of 1948. The departure of the forty-six candidates selected by the Moroccan mission during its visit to the zone in July and August was, for instance, delayed by nearly a month because the visas for DPs' families were not sent to the French Consul at the same time as those of the workers.[136] The IRO authorities were unimpressed with the Moroccan mission, which they decried as being made up of a handful of incompetent businessmen whose visit was costly and unproductive.[137] Recruitment for France was also delayed by the June 1948 monetary reform and the resulting non-payment of DP salaries.[138] The majority of unpaid DPs preferred to wait in the zone before being resettled in France or elsewhere.

### From Single Workers to Families

France introduced the 'Plan Culture-Famille' [Familial Agricultural Plan] in November 1948, a scheme designed to recruit agricultural workers with their families. The launch of the Plan Culture-Famille followed on previous attempts to improve France's attractiveness.[139] This policy of enhancement

---

[135] MAE, Bonn 148, Etude d'ensemble sur les personnes Déplacées, Lettre secrète Général d'Armée Koenig à Secrétaire d'Etat aux Affaires Allemandes et Autrichiennes, 14 April 1948.
[136] AN, AJ/43/760, IRO French zone, narrative report, November 1948, p. 3.
[137] AN, AJ/43/760, Rapport mensuel aout 1948, 6 September 1948.
[138] AN, AJ/43/760, IRO, Rapport mensuel juillet 1948, 2 August 1948.
[139] CAC, Versement 770623, 173, Ministère des Affaires Etrangères à Ministre du Travail, 11 June 1948 (signé Bousquet).

of familial immigration was also in affinity with the Christian values of the new Ministry of Population, Germaine Poinso-Chapuis.[140] A practising Catholic, she was a strong advocate of familial immigration. The scheme was started by a visit of nine DP delegates to France, who brought back a favourable impression from France with them. During a meeting in Auxerre, chaired by the IRO chief of Mission in France, DP delegates raised several concerns 'which were studied point by point with a view to improving conditions for the emigration of DP farm-workers'.[141] IRO officials welcomed the project, particularly its recognition that heads of families could be up to fifty years of age. They also valued the further concession that, in special cases, where the individual's physical condition was exceptionally good or where their children were already of working age, the age limit might be increased to fifty-five.[142] The plan generated considerable expectation among DPs and IRO officials, as it meant that semi-skilled agricultural workers for whom other resettlement opportunities had not been found could emigrate to France together with their families.[143]

By offering emigration opportunities to DP families, some welfare workers also hoped that one would combat the issue of parents' abandonment of their offspring. The problem of young men emigrating alone while leaving behind unmarried mothers with their abandoned children was acute.[144] This issue caused mounting anxiety among IRO and PDR officials, who worried about the increasing number of 'forgotten' children in camps as well as the proliferation of illicit abortions.[145] While it was men who more commonly abandoned their offspring, some women did too.[146] These concerns were echoed among certain ethnically based support agencies. The Association of Ukrainian Women complained that DP men and women bore children with different partners, asking emigration committees to insist that male DPs take responsibility for their illegitimate children.[147] For all their emphasis on the preservation of the family unit, however, welfare workers advised parents of disabled or

---

[140] Spire, *Les étrangers à la carte*, p. 126.
[141] AN, AJ/43/753, IRO, Paris Office, Narrative Report, December 1948.
[142] Holborn, *The International Refugee Organization*, p. 384.
[143] AN, AJ/43/628, Philip E. Ryan to Mr Tuck, 21 December 1948.
[144] MAE, HCRFA, PDR6/790, Présidente pour la Zone Française et représentante pour l'Allemagne de l'Association des Femmes Ukrainiennes, à la Direction des PDR, 21 October 1950.
[145] MAE, HCRFA, PDR6/483, Gouverneur Hettier de Boislambert à Général d'Armée, 12 August 1948.
[146] MAE, HCRFA, PDR6/556, l'administrateur Griolet, Directeur PCIRO à Administrateur Chef de Service des Personnes Déplacées, No. CM/ti/800, 7 April 1948.
[147] MAE, HCRFA, PDR6/790, Présidente pour la Zone Française et représentante pour l'Allemagne de l'Association des Femmes Ukrainiennes, à la Direction des PDR, 21 October 1950.

sick children to separate from them in order to emigrate. As Ruth Balint notes, those who insisted on keeping their family together were considered as selfish and unrealistic.[148] An IRO counselling officer noted, for instance, that DPs' unhealthy attachment to their families was one of the symptoms of their 'refugee complex'. According to her, DPs were 'removed from reality' and in a state of permanent anxiety.[149] Just as unmarried mothers with children were offered little, if any, opportunity to emigrate, people aged over forty-five had little prospect of passing through the screening of labour migrants. In Ravensburg, a group of older DPs were denied official authorization to create an association to aid DPs aged over forty-five to emigrate.[150] Young people with elderly dependents were also advised to separate from them, a suggestion that, quite understandably, revived traumatic memories of wartime separations.[151]

Normative conceptions of gendered order lay at the heart of the French recruitment schemes. The French selection mission discriminated against those who transgressed gendered moral norms: the welfare-dependant single mother and child, or those with sexually transmitted infections. For the French, like for all Western countries, the ideal DP family was patriarchal and nuclear. The gendered notion of the *useful* citizen profoundly shaped what constituted the ideal DP family in the eyes of recruiters.[152] Women with children were considered as dependent on male workers. Those without husbands were excluded from resettlement or were expected to be childless and to accept to work in gender-specific activities. Several countries had female-specific recruitment schemes, including Britain (domestic work), Switzerland (nurses) and Canada (domestic work).[153]

The hopes initiated by the Farm scheme were soon disappointed. The implementation of the Plan depended on the Ministry of Foreign Affairs, the Ministry of Work, the Ministry of Finance, Agriculture, Health and Population and Overseas France.[154] Despite intense IRO propaganda activities in favour of the recruitment, DPs still remained reluctant to emigrate to France. International competition was, if anything, intensifying. In June 1948 the US congress passed the DP Act, authorizing the admission of 205,000 DPs over a period of two years.[155] For Jewish DPs the formation of

---

[148] Ruth Balint, 'Children Left Behind: Family, Refugees and Immigration in Postwar Europe', *History Workshop Journal*, vol. 82 (2016), pp. 151-172, p. 153.
[149] AN, AJ/43/760, Counselling service, E. W. D. Steel, Rapport juin 1948, 12 July 1948.
[150] MAE, HCRFA, PDR6/484, Général d'Armée Koenig à Gouverneur Délégué Supérieur pour le GM du Wurtemberg, 27 May 1949.
[151] AN, AJ/43/760, Counselling Service, Rapport juillet 1948, signed by E. W. D. Steel.
[152] Balint, 'Children Left Behind', p. 155.
[153] AN, AJ/43/760, Rapport mensuel janvier 1948, 6 February 1948.
[154] AN, AJ/43/753, Relationship with government pour Janvier 1949.
[155] Holborn, *The International Refugee Organization*, p. 367.

the State of Israel in May 1948 was also of central importance, transforming the outlook for emigration to the newly established country. Even for Banatais DPs, the Familial Agricultural Plan proved disappointing. In their efforts to 'sell France' to the refugees from the Banat, the PDR organization had lulled Banatais into thinking that they would benefit from more advantageous resettlement conditions than other DPs. In particular, refugees from the Banat believed that they would be granted individual parcel of land to cultivate. Instead, the French resettlement scheme only allowed them to emigrate as 'agricultural worker' to work for French farmers and landowners like other DPs.

According to IRO Director Poignant, camp life was also detrimental to emigration. Not only were DPs in poorer health, but DPs were more likely to be influenced by DP leaders and changed their minds quickly about resettlement.[156] To remedy the situation, the IRO started publishing a monthly bulletin containing practical information about the various emigration schemes.[157] In April 1949 Bulletin No. 9 published an official complaint about DPs refusing resettlement after having signed up for a recruitment scheme. 'Do they realise that [...] their enrolment to a recruitment scheme generated many costs (involving several travels, costly medical examinations and a waste of time for the IRO personnel) and, far worse, that it prevented the IRO examining more serious candidates, due to the quota being reached?[158] Exasperated, the IRO Counselling officer noted that it was about time that DPs learned to become individuals 'able to think and reason with themselves'.[159] IRO officials were not alone in despairing at DPs' lack of enthusiasm for resettlement. PDR officials also wished that DPs showed greater eagerness to re-emigrate, particularly to France. Abiding mistrust of Communist influence in France remained problematic.[160]

These problems were compounded by the steady trickle of dissatisfied DPs returning from France. In August 1948, A. C. Dunn, IRO acting chief of Operations noted,

> [D]espite repeated promises, French authorities are still sending returnees back to the US Zone without following the legal procedure outlined by EUCOM [United States European Command] Headquarters. It appears from reports reaching this Headquarters that many workers recruited for France arrive in that country only to find that the jobs for which they

[156] AN, AJ/43/760, IRO, A. Poignant, Rapport mensuel avril 1948, 4 May 1948.
[157] AN, AJ/43/760, S. Tixier, Rapport septembre 1948, Public Information.
[158] AN, AJ/43/799, Bulletin de l'OIR, ZFOA, Neueuburg, April 1949, No. 9.
[159] AN, AJ/43/760, IRO, E. W. D. Steel, Counselling service, Rapport juillet 1948, 11 August 1948.
[160] AN, AJ/43/628, Procès Verbal de la conférence sur le plan français 'culture famille', 26 October 1948.

signed a contract are not available, or that living accommodation promised for families is not obtainable.[161]

As Dunn's report suggests, many DPs who went to France in 1947 and 1948 found reception arrangements defective. Housing was substandard, food rations unsatisfactory and many DPs were rejected by their employers, leaving them in desperate circumstances. In addition, there were often considerable lapses of time before family dependants were admitted into France. In 1950, reflecting on immigration and French public opinion, Professor Joanny Ray admitted that 'living conditions, which used to attract immigrants in the past, have changed considerably: real wages have not yet returned to the pre-war level [...] housing conditions were still very precarious'.[162]

## *We Are Behind Barbed Wire*'[163]

The IRO provided DPs with a platform to raise concerns about national selection missions and, in so doing, transformed them from 'passive recipients' to 'actors' in their resettlement. Scholarship on DPs has emphasized how DPs exhibited agency by presenting themselves as 'ideal migrants' to selection missions: DPs showed their strength, muscles and work ethic, hid diseases and erased any traces of wartime collaboration.[164] In the French zone, some DPs organized vocational groups to enhance their skills and present their students to the IRO testing commission. Two groups were particularly successful: the electricians of Salgau and the industrial designers of Freiburg.[165] Writing letters against recruiters could also provide a framework through which DPs articulated grievances about how expectations raised in the camps were frequently ill met.

If we are to fully understand DPs' reluctance to emigrate to France, we need to recognize the importance of anti-French rumours in DP camps and protest letters. In January 1948, a French administrator toured the DP camps of Northern Bavaria in the hope of stimulating DPs' interest in France. Dissatisfaction with the French scheme reigned:

---

[161] AN, AJ/43/628, A. C. Dunn, Acting chief of operations to Executive Secretary, PCIRO Headquarters, 20 August 1948.

[162] AN, AJ/43/1269, Prof. J. Ray, 'Les problèmes actuels de l'immigration face à l'opinion publique française', in *Pages documentaires. Un problème social: émigration et immigration,* April–May 1950, pp. 261–277, 273.

[163] AN, AJ/43/628, Translation, Letter from Chabeniok Stefan, 26 November 1947.

[164] Laura Hilton, 'Cultural Nationalism in Exile: The Case of Polish and Latvian Displaced Persons', *The Historian*, vol. 71, no. 2 (2009), pp. 280–317; Inta Gale Carpenter, 'Folklore as a Source for Creating Exile Identity among Latvian Displaced Persons in Post-World War II Germany', *Journal of Baltic Studies*, vol. 48, no. 2 (2017), pp. 205–233; Nowak, 'Voices of Revival', p. 222.

[165] AN, AJ/43/594, A. Poignant, Rééducation professionnelle, 4 June 1948.

As in all the other DP camps, those of the Bayreuth area are unfavourably impressed by France's high cost of living, governmental instability, political troubles and the bad reception that DPs often receive at their arrival in Karlsruhe. Everyone knows that these rumours, either true or false, circulate very rapidly in all the DP camps and often appear in DP national gazettes.[166]

This administrator reported the tragic odyssey of Rudolf Uzanicki, a former legionnaire who was awarded the French Legion of Honour.[167] Lodged in a rabbit hutch in Montpellier, he was forced to strike with other agricultural workers:

In this place were only Communists, and they strike weekly. During this strike, I didn't dare to work, for they threatened to kill me or to return me back to Yugoslavia. Not only the workers were communised, the same authorities and police was communised too. I have been permanently hungry and very afraid of communists.[168]

Constantly suffering from hunger and cold, he returned to Germany, where he was placed in the Brombach centre, a 'veritable concentration camp'. Before emigrating to France, Uzanicki was allegedly amongst the loudest advocates of the French cause. After his unfortunate experience, he became one of its severest critics. This administrator urged the French government to stop sending DPs to French departments whose local administration was either overwhelmingly communist or otherwise hostile to DPs.[169] *Meurthe et Moselle* was one such. There, French farmers refused DP workers with dependents:

You can imagine the strong emotion caused by this decision, a decision backed up by *les services départementaux de la main d'oeuvre*. Obviously, many DPs cannot accept the idea of a long separation from their family, who remains in the precarious DP situation in Germany. And, here, things get worst. Returned to the French zone, the 'réfractaires' (If one dares using this word) are sent in special camps. They often call these camps 'concentration camps' in their correspondence.[170]

DPs' grievances were magnified by their camp representatives, who circulated letters and stories from DPs in France. In December 1947, for instance, an American Zone Camp Director passed on a series of letters sent by DPs to

---

[166] MAE, HCRFA, PDR6/818, Paul E. Gobe à Capitaine R. Schultz, 21 January 1948.
[167] MAE, HCRFA, PDR6/818, Paul E. Gobe à R. Schulz-Leclerc, chef du service de l'immigration, 27 January 1948.
[168] MAE, HCRFA, PDR6/818, Declaration of Uznanicki Rudolf, transcripted by the camp Leader, Blazo Cetkovic, 13 January 1948.
[169] MAE, HCRFA, PDR6/818, Gobe à R. Schulz-Leclerc, 27 January 1948.
[170] MAE, HCRFA, PDR6/846, Commissaire de Police G. Alexinsky à Directeur de la Réglementation et des étrangers, Fribourg (Bade), 22 January 1948.

their wives.[171] 'We are here behind [barbed] wire [...] we do not know how long we shall stay here.'[172] 'The contract which we signed in Karlsruhe is a valueless scrap of paper [...] French authorities failed to check employers' offers before recruiting people for France.'[173] Another letter read:

> We left for France, but we were not permitted to work because we have families. The *Arbeitsamt* (Labour Office) sent us back to Nancy in order that we might return to Germany; we went to Camp Offenburg and then to a concentration camp in Brombach. We do not know why we are behind wire – we fear we are in some danger, the nature of which is well known to you. We are asking you most sincerely to get us out of this miserable position; we have not offended against the law – everything happened in the way I have told you. This is pure truth, and we can swear to it. God help us![174]

Another DP related his arrival in a camp near Paris: '[t]he walls were full of holes and it was as cold as a dog's kennel. We were given something to eat but it was awful – dried snails and peas.'[175] The experience of hunger is central in this testimony, which ended in almost apocalyptic terms: 'Dear Father, ... I would not even advise my worst enemy to come to this country. Please write and tell me what I have to do – am I to be lost without a trace, as in Siberia?[176] These multiple allegations of 'concentration camp'-type conditions and of comparisons with Stalin's gulag recurred time and again in such letters exchanged with loved ones. DPs also sent appeal letters to the IRO HQ, insisting that there were in 'critical position in regard to clothing and shoes'.[177]

In spite of protracted negotiations, it proved impossible to establish procedures for the return of DPs to the satisfaction of the British and American occupation authorities.[178] A large number of those who returned made their own way back to Germany. Alerted by IRO officials and the French Ministry of Foreign Affairs, the Ministry of Labour nevertheless ordered an investigation into the inadequacies of DPs' reception arrangements in France.[179] French observers conceded in response that returning DPs should be sent to a

---

[171] AN, AJ/43/628, G. G. Roberts, Camp Director, IRO Stuttgart Centre to Miss C. Trimble, Resettlement Division [December 1947].
[172] AN, AJ/43/628, Annex to G. G. Roberts to Miss C. Trimble [December 1947].
[173] AN, AJ/43/628, Extract from letter written by the Lettonian DP Zanis Marka and his wife Alma Marka who immigrated to France with their two children, 3 December 47. Translation from Latvian.
[174] AN, AJ/43/628, Chabeniok Stefan to Magister Sojko Wasyl, 26 November 1947 [Translation].
[175] AN, AJ/43/628, Translation of letter from Bernard Kosarynski, 28 November 1947.
[176] Ibid.
[177] AN, AJ/43/702, Aleks Ziakin to Headquarters, IRO, 15 June 1948.
[178] Holborn, *The International Refugee Organization*, p. 383.
[179] MAE, HCRFA, PDR6/818, Paul E. Gobe à R. Schultz, 21 January 1948.

disciplinary camp, the Brombach camp, for security reasons. For French officials these disciplinary measures were justifiable, necessitated by the need to prevent contact between returnees and other DPs still considering emigration to France, and in order to avoid counterpropaganda. They believed that DPs' complaints were exaggerated. First, they insisted that the conditions in this camp had significantly improved, and barbed wire had been cut off.[180] Second, they argued that Italian migrants were satisfied with the situation they encountered in France.[181] Commissioned by the Ministry of Labour, an official concurred. 'These persons who have experienced multiple forms of deceit during their internment in Germany are now suffering from a veritable psychosis of propaganda and broken promises.'[182] According to him, conditions in France were as good as the economic situation allowed them to be. What bears emphasis, though, is that many French employees remained reluctant to provide DPs with the same wage as French workers as they considered them less productive.[183] Although French authorities made substantial efforts to sell the DP population to French employees – through radio broadcasts and articles in newspapers – they never really succeeded. In the summer of 1949 the *refoulement* centre of Toul-Bautzen was still full of DPs rejected by French employees.[184]

### Historical Land of Liberty or Impoverished Communist Enclave?

The recruitment of DPs revealed that France had lost appeal as a prosperous nation with a proud tradition of asylum and hospitality to European DPs. In early 1949, the first signs of job market saturation appeared, and by May, the Ministry of Labour recorded a significant decrease in employers' demand for foreign workers.[185] In the face of worsening unemployment, French local authorities opposed the circulation of materials advertising DP labour.[186] As a result, the inter-ministerial commission and the ONI decided in August to

---

[180] AN, AJ/43/628, Rapport sur les enquêtes effectuées à la suite de la communication par le Délégué pour la France de la CPOIR de lettres émanant de 'Personnes Déplacées' recrutées en qualité de travailleurs pour la France, 1 March 1948.

[181] Ibid.

[182] MAE, HCRFA, PDR6/818, Rapport confidentiel sur le fonctionnement du Centre de Fribourg, 19 November 1947.

[183] AN, AJ/43/628, Report signé Samson, Ministère du Travail et de la Sécurité Sociale, sent to the Ministry of Foreign Affairs, 2 April 1948.

[184] CAC, Versement 770623, 173, compte-rendu de la réunion du 8 aout 1949 du comite mixte charge de suivre l'application des accords relatifs a l'immigration directe.

[185] CAC, Versement 770623, 173, Ministère du Travail et de la Sécurité Sociale, Note pour Monsieur le Sous-Directeur de la Main d'œuvre étrangère, sous direction de l'emploi, 21 May 1949.

[186] CAC, Versement 770623, 173, Section de la Main d'œuvre, note pour Monsieur le Directeur, 3 August 1949.

temporarily suspend direct immigration, reducing the quota for farm families.[187] Three months later, in October, all French selection of DPs was suspended owing to seasonal unemployment in agriculture and the consequent overcrowding of DPs' reception centres.[188] Not only could France barely absorb those DPs already accepted, but the various recruitment schemes were proving increasingly expensive.[189]

The ONI, which depended on French employees' financial contributions, confronted a severe financial crisis.[190] Cost varied depending on whether DPs were recruited on contracts or through the family scheme.[191] But French officials complained that IRO participation only reduced overall costs by a tenth.[192] Meanwhile, continuous French efforts to obtain additional funds from the IRO, by arguing that sending DPs to France was cheaper than to Australia or South America, infuriated their British counterparts.[193] As British officials observed, labour demands were not the only factor that governed French thinking about the resettlement of DPs. The French saw in the IRO an opportunity for funding.[194] This was clear during inter-allied discussions about what to do with the 'hard core', those whose claims of resettlement had been rejected on grounds of age, physical or mental disability or having a criminal record.

> [The] IRO may be able to provide a stick and a carrot to induce the French to take larger numbers and hence more 'marginal hard core' DPs

---

[187] CAC, Versement 770623, 173, compte-rendu de la reunion du 8 aout 1949 du comite mixte charge de suivre l'application des accords relatifs a l'immigration directe.

[188] Holborn, *The International Refugee Organization*, p. 384.

[189] In January 1949, representative of the Ministry of Labour Guerard estimated that DP entry to France cost 17,250 frs to the French government. CAC, Versement 770623, 173, compte-rendu de la réunion du 31 janvier 1949 du Comité mixte chargé de suivre l'application des accords relatifs à l'immigration directe.

[190] CAC, Versement 770623, 173, Compte rendu de la réunion du 25 octobre du comité mixte chargé de suivre l'application des accords relatifs à l'immigration directe; Boris Dänzer-Kantof, *Immigrer en France. De l'ONI à l'OFII, histoire d'une institution chargée de l'immigration et de l'intégration des étrangers, 1945-2010* (Paris: Cherche-midi, 2011), pp. 45–47.

[191] CAC, Versement 770623, article 173, Lettre du Ministre des Affaires Etrangères à Ministre des Finances, 21 July 1948.

[192] AN, AJ/43/628, Procès verbal de la conférence sur le plan français 'Culture-Famille' le 26 octobre 1948 à Baden-Baden. As far as the general ratio is concerned, France's overall contribution to the IRO budget was almost equivalent to the sum of the subsidy it received from it. MAE, NUOI, Secrétariat des conférences 1944–1959, 296, Rapport confidentiel de R. Pointe, chef du Cabinet de M. Jacobsen, 'La France et l'organisation internationale pour les réfugiés', 6 April 1951.

[193] NA, FO 371/78198, Confidential telegram of the United Kingdom Delegation to the IRO General Council, Geneva, 29 June 1949.

[194] See, for instance, AN, F/7/16061, Réunion chez M. Serres au sujet du 'hard-core', 22 December 1950.

by increasing the grant for each additional 5,000 DPs, e.g. 50 dollars a head for the first 5,000, 70 dollars for the next, 90 dollars for the next, and so on. Thus the last to be taken on (who would, of course, be those who had been rejected by everyone else) would repay the French so much more that the first, or better class recruits, that they would be under a mounting temptation to accept sub-standard DPs for the sake of their immediate dollar-earning capacity, rather than their ultimate social value.[195]

By early 1949, French interest in taking in large numbers of DPs had dissipated. An unanticipated phenomenon had overturned demographic projections: in only four years a post-war baby boom had produced an additional 3 million live births.[196] As Paul André Rosental points out, demographers first believed that the birth rate increase was a short-term, circumstantial phenomenon.[197] After the First World War, the French birth rate had risen sharply but then immediately dropped, a reflection, it was thought, of child-bearing deferred during the conflict. Yet, throughout 1948 and 1949, the rising birth rate continued to prove demographers wrong.

As the IRO prepare to wound up its operations and find solutions for the 'hard core' problem, French authorities accepted a small contingent of elderly or disabled DPs for re-establishment in France.[198] This was not disinterested act of generosity. Political interests coincided with economic one. IRO funding enabled French authorities to renew the facilities in place for ill refugees established in France.[199] The creation of sanitary houses for old, disabled and ill refugees was an integral part of the re-imagination of France as 'historical land of asylum' in the wake of Vichy and Nazi collaboration.[200] In the post-war years, as we have seen, the French embarked on an important mission to re-imagine France both at home and abroad. As France committed to offer protection to this small group of elderly DPs, it nevertheless

---

[195] NA, FO 371/78198, Confidential telegram of the United Kingdom Delegation to the IRO General Council, Geneva, 29 June 1949.

[196] AN, AJ/43/1269, Prof. J. Ray, 'Les problèmes actuels de l'immigration face à l'opinion publique française', *Pages documentaires. Un problème social: émigration et immigration* (1950), pp. 261–277, 269.

[197] Rosental, *L'intelligence démographique*, p. 202.

[198] AN, F/7/16038, by October 1951, 538 elderly DPs had been resettled in 54 asylums. Le Ministre de l'Intérieur à Préfet des Alpes Maritimes, 18 September 1950; L'Inspecteur divisionnaire du Travail et de la Main-d'œuvre à Monsieur le Ministre du Travail, 11 October 1951.

[199] A 1952 illustrated IRO leaflet presented the 27 rest-homes created in France and Algeria for these refugees. AN, F/7/16061, OIR, Un aspect de son oeuvre en France, 1952.

[200] Greg Burgess argues that the paragraph on asylum in the Preamble to the 1946 Constitution of the Fourth French Republic was one of the foundation principles of post-war republicanism. *Refugees and the Promise of Asylum in Postwar France, 1945–1995* (London: Palgrave Macmillan, 2019).

abandoned around 1,700 'hard core' DPs to the care of German authorities – the future of which was particularly uncertain in the Württemberg.[201]

## Conclusion

Considering how French recruitment schemes were implemented on the ground complicates the dynamics of state-led immigration control. The selection of DPs was influenced both by the *domestic* dynamics of French politics of national recovery and the *external* agendas of the IRO, which provided funding and shaped the ways the recruitment took place in the field. Originally, conceived as a plan to attract single workers, the scope of the French recruitment scheme was enlarged in 1948 to encompass DP families. The ideal DP family remained, however, healthy, patriarchal and nuclear. In recruiting DP workers and families, French recruiters were not solely interested in attracting *productive* DP and *assimilable* migrants. Rather, French occupation officials were also concerned about the image of France abroad. The issue of France's unpopularity was particularly salient, in a context when French officials strove to restore France's prestige. The presentation of France through Anne de la Morlais' conferences and the PDR material demonstrates the desire of a post-war generation to rebuild the image of the nation as an industrious and generous state. In the battleground for DP labourers, France suffered severely in comparison with other competitor countries. Despite French IRO officials and PDR administrators' efforts to publicize the attractions of France, DPs proved understandably cautious about emigrating to what they regarded as an impoverished and, for some, a quasi-Communist country. New World Countries and Britain remained far more popular. In total, between July 1947 and May 1950, France drew in 37,338 DPs and refugees with the help of the IRO, while Britain attracted more than the double this number: 83,399.[202] For their part, the United States absorbed nearly 300,000 DPs, Israel accepted 132,109 DPs and Australia admitted 182,159.[203]

Following French recruitment teams through the selection centres also illustrates the extent to which DP bodies and minds were appraised and monitored in a completely new way. The verification of DPs' identification papers was not the sole component of the selection process. Rather, DPs were subjected to intensified international and state intervention. DPs were put through many tests, several times, by various national recruiters, all obsessed with 'healthy bodies' and 'sound minds'. This was not simply a French phenomenon: across the zones, the notion of the *useful* citizen shaped the

---

[201] HCRFA, *Sept-ans en faveur des personnes déplacées*, pp. 76–81.
[202] AN, F/7/16061, Statistical Report with 35 Months Summary, IRO Headquarters, May 1950, p. 26.
[203] Holborn, *The International Refugee Organization*, p. 415.

political and social construction of the 'DP family'. Recruiters and medical doctors drew heavily on assumed norms of patriarchal breadwinner and obligation. They wanted to avoid the recruitment of those who could be considered as a 'burden' for the host community. In categorizing *able* and less *abled bodies,* they often implicitly resorted to moralist, eugenist and hygienist considerations. Arbitrary bureaucratic practices often took precedence over humanitarian feelings. Selecting migrants was a source of power that some recruiters, in particular ONI agents, abused. This chapter thus exposes the exploitative business of migrant transport and the dark side of the state as an institution of restriction and exclusion. Crucially, this troubles us because it is a potent reminder of the long history of both the transformation of refugee into *useful* citizen and the professional culture of arrogance and condescension of today's *asylum counters* [guichet d'asile].[204]

---

[204] Alexis Spire, 'L'asile au guichet. La dépolitisation du droit des étrangers par le travail bureaucratique', *Actes de la recherche en sciences sociales*, vol. 169, no. 4 (2007), pp. 4–21.

# Conclusion

## Reinventing French Aid?

This book has illuminated the multiple and complex encounters between French officials, members of new international organizations, relief workers, DPs and defeated Germans, as they tried to reckon with the aftermath of war and genocide in the territory of the French zone of occupation. It has demonstrated that DP camps did not simply function as device of enclosure, but that they were also spaces of unique cultural encounters, where various actors attempted to propose a new organization of DPs' intimate life and 'positively' transform their ways of being and thinking. By examining the forgotten history of refugee relief in the French zone, this book reveals that 'caring' for DPs became a political and moral project, overseen by the French state, international organizations and occupation authorities. This project was influenced by the dynamics of French national recovery and the international rivalries of the Cold War.

Refugee relief provides a fascinating lens through which to view French aspirations to reassert national identity and play a leading international role in the aftermath of Vichy and Nazi occupation afresh. *Reinventing French Aid* unearths, in particular, the active, and often bottom-up nature of the restoration of France's prestige. Reconstructing France's 'grandeur' was not the exclusive domain of government officials, occupation administrators, technocrats, members of cultural institutions and businessmen. It involved a larger and more diverse cast that historians of post-war France have recognized, including relief workers. Not only were the latter concerned about the image of France circulating in DP camps, but they also drew a number of DP artists into the orbit of French cultural diplomacy in Germany. For French occupiers and relief workers, exhibiting French cultural richness and selling the 'French way of life' was considered as a tool to express and project French political power.

In paying close attention to French relief workers' everyday responsibilities and practices, along with DPs' connections to France, it is possible to embed refugee relief in the history of French foreign relations. This in turn raises questions about historians' tendency to emphasize narratives of American exceptionalism, especially those underlining the rehabilitative role of New-Deal–influenced humanitarian workers. As Adam Davis and Betrand Taithe argue, French humanitarian aid also 'constituted an explicit and material development of the meaning of being French in the world'.[1] This book does not argue, however, that the French succeeded in their efforts at 'rebranding' France as a welcoming nation in the aftermath of Vichy. Presenting France as a hospitable and humanitarian nation proved challenging. Over the course of the occupation, UNRRA and (later) the IRO became important forums for DPs to raise concerns about French provisions of aid and publicize French failures.[2] Further, in the battleground for DP labourers, France suffered severely in comparison with other Western competitor countries. Despite French efforts to publicize the 'French way of life' after 1947, DPs proved understandably cautious about emigrating to what they regarded as an impoverished and, for some, a quasi-Communist country.

If we are to fully understand this period, we thus need to recognize that the story of DP aid was marked by acute uncertainties: in 1945, it was neither clear to French occupation officials nor relief workers what post-war France would look like or where 'non-repatriable' DPs would end up. Nobody knew how long DPs' life in limbo would last or how to handle the emotional consequences of surviving Nazi terror and genocide. Very few people had anticipated the problems that would arise when trying to establish DPs' legal identities and provide professional certificates, 'translatable' in different countries. And yet, these uncertainties also gave rise to visionary aspirations around individual and collective reconstruction. In paying close attention to the dynamic relationships between prescription and practice, diplomats and occupation officials, experts and field workers, this book challenges the dominant view of the French as 'harsh occupiers' and little else. Certainly, DPs were often expected to fulfil unskilled and menial jobs. Likewise, humanitarian provisions embodied social structures and created a clear divide between French donors and DP recipients. Despite this, some relief workers genuinely believed they could make a difference and change DPs' ways of being. For French occupiers and relief workers, rehabilitation and vocational training were not solely a matter of reconstructing the labour force, restoring DP women's role within the 'home' and DP men's position in work or rebuilding France's economy. Their genuine belief in the therapeutic nature of work and

---

[1] Adam Davis and Bertrand Taithe, 'From the Purse and the Heart: Exploring Charity, Humanitarianism and Human Rights in France', *French Historical Studies*, vol. 34, no. 3 (2011), pp. 413–432, 414. Also see Nicolas Duvous, 'Philantropies et prestige d'Etat en France, XIXe-XXe siècles', *Genèses*, vol. 109, no. 4 (2017), pp. 3–8.

[2] See, for instance, the numerous complaints of the Polish Committee of Ravensburg in UNA, UNRRA, S-0421-0061-07; the complaint of Edmond Szente Gutch in S-0432-0001-05, Edmond Szente Gutch à Durand, Directeur du Team 572, 28 October 1946; S-0421-0031-07, Compte-rendu de la réunion des Employment Officers (Gutach), 25–27 November 1946; MAE, HCRFA, 2Bad/39 [A2.301/1], Rapport Affaires administratives, partie personnes déplacées, 24 July 1946.

vocational training intersected with broader concerns about the status and extension of France's power in the world.

By integrating DPs and international actors into the history of the French zone, this book revisits a long-established historiographical question concerning the specificity of French occupation policies. In doing so, it expands understandings of the ways in which French occupiers approached the occupation of Germany more broadly. French occupiers thought through relief in very different ways than the British and Americans. This book uncovers, in particular, a deep-seated link between French individual and community experiences and memories of the war and their approaches to the DP question. The trauma wrought on France by three wars with Germany in the space of three generations affected the way in which French authorities and relief workers addressed the occupation. Ever conscious of Germany's physical proximity, the French Foreign Office's attempts to secure the political or economic detachment of the Ruhr and Rhineland region as well as measures taken to ensure German industrial disarmament were devised to prevent Germany from regaining its economic power and thereby its military potential.[3] Security concerns also motivated French attempts to recruit the 'most worthy' DPs and German refugees to curb the growth of the German population. DP and German children were particularly coveted, their youth promising better prospects for seamless integration into French society. Finally, security issues influenced official thinking about vocational training. French officials feared that vocational training could be detrimental to France's interests, if 're-trained' DPs did not emigrate. The development of a skilled and specialist labour force was seen as a potentially dangerous economic asset for a future newly independent Germany. This book thus calls for a reconsideration of the intersection of French foreign relations, occupation policies and immigration politics. The characterization of immigration as essentially a matter of 'domestic politics' is false.[4] On the one hand, the pursuit of labour power depended on diplomatic agreements reached between French authorities, Allied governments and the IRO. The recruitment of DPs was also established, enforced and fought over with other countries' recruitment missions. On the other hand, the search for 'useful' DPs was linked to French international politics of legitimation.[5] French efforts to increase DPs' pro-

---

[3] Jessica Reinisch, *The Perils of Peace. Public Health Crisis in Occupied Germany* (Oxford: Oxford University Press, 2013), p. 292.
[4] For a review of the literature examining the intersections between US immigration and foreign policies, see, for example, Paul A. Kramer, 'The Geopolitics of Mobility: Immigration Policy and American Global Power in the Long Twentieth Century', *American Historical Review*, vol. 123, no. 2 (2018), pp. 393–438.
[5] Kramer, 'The Geopolitics of Mobility', p. 420.

French affinities were tied to the reformulation of French identity and the restoration of France's prestige.

The French had distinct priorities and a different style of occupation compared to the British and Americans, but they worked with the same international organizations: first the United Nations Relief and Rehabilitation Administration and then the International Refugee Organisation. These organizations' experts and norms helped to influence the framing of the DP question as well as the implementation of DP policies. While histories of these organizations focus overwhelmingly on the perspectives of the United States and Britain, this book exposes the varied character of French visions of international cooperation and the ways in which these organizations transformed the implementation of DP policies on the ground. In Paris, policy-elites initially viewed UNRRA as an intermediary to forge better relations with governments of Eastern Europe, where most DPs came from. They did what they could to make sure that the majority of UNRRA personnel were French. In the French zone, conflicts with this organization arose when French occupation officials and PDR administrators perceived their activities as a threat to their authority.

Despite these tensions, UNRRA and the IRO participated in some ways in the reinvention of French humanitarianism, by exhibiting DP arts, displaying French 'medical prowess' and carefully monitoring the information about DPs' living conditions that was circulated outside the zone. By providing funding opportunities to create 'modern' sanitary centres in France and publicizing it, the IRO also helped the French to capitalize on their humanitarian actions. In the French Empire too, the United Nations played a critical role in the reimagining of France's project overseas. In post-war French Africa, as Jessica Pearson shows, the UN prompted the French to re-conceptualize the colonial project as one of development and move away from more traditional concept of the civilizing mission.[6] As colonial administrators and medical doctors attempted to turn a long relationship based on violence and subordination into something resembling community and labelled the 'French Union', they tried to find new ways to speak about France's project overseas, from 'civilizing mission to international development'. In practice, however, the project was not fundamentally altered. The study of French involvement in the nascent UN thus reveals the widening of the notion of French 'propaganda' beyond the cultural sphere.[7]

---

[6] Jessica Lynne Pearson, *The Colonial Politics of Global Health France and the United Nations in Postwar Africa* (Cambridge: Harvard University Press, 2018).

[7] Charlotte Faucher and Laure Humbert, 'Introduction – Beyond de Gaulle and beyond London: The French External Resistance and Its International Networks', *European Review of History: Revue Européenne d'Histoire*, vol. 25, no. 2 (2018), pp. 195–221.

By integrating state and non-state actors in the analysis of DP policies, this book also offers a productive way of rethinking the view that French pollicymaker were able to influence post-war international developments and shape the reconfiguration of post-war Europe.[8] There is a good deal of truth in this, but it is a view, which stands in need of qualification. Internal rivalries, coupled with a complex decision-making process and the lack of coherent direction from Paris, fed political and jurisdictional conflicts between political planners, experts and relief workers in the field. As a result, decision-making was fractured and susceptible to changing circumstances. Metropolitan debates about the recruitment of DPs revealed how deep and multifaceted the divisions created by the war were. The DP problem not only pitted East against West; it also divided French against French. The bitterness of the debates over DP recruitment mirrored the nascent Fourth Republic's internal divisions. On the one hand, some French planners saw DPs as a rich source of human capital for economic and social reconstruction at home. The philosophy behind their approach was strongly nationalist and republican. On the other hand, Communist decision makers and their ideological fellow travellers on the French left remained strongly opposed to the recruitment of what they regarded as *fascist* DPs. These debates resulted in contradictory instructions from the Foreign Ministry and Parisian ministries, affecting the implementation of DP policy inside occupied Germany.

This book thus challenges dominant assumptions about French 'pro-Soviet' occupiers. It acknowledges that French officials were certainly remarkably reluctant to openly confront Soviet Repatriation Officers. French officers had to make concessions in their dealings with the Soviet Union, in order to guarantee the return of the French *Malgré-nous*. But this book argues that contradictory instructions and jurisdictional disputes between French authorities and international organizations opened spaces for DP leaders hostile to repatriation to make claims of their own and to develop strategies to avoid forced repatriation, hiding behind false identities or taking up job opportunities offered by French occupiers. Strategies for repatriating and screening DPs on the ground were more varied and ambiguous than most historians have recognized. By highlighting these discrepancies between official policies and practices, this book stresses that DPs exhibited agency in managing their lives despite the constraints placed on them by French occupiers and German employers.

Perhaps no example illustrates better DPs' ability to seize opportunities than that of the Banatais' activities to downplay their own participation in the Nazi war and gain the favour of French authorities. Banatais refugees

---

[8] See, for instance, Talbot Imlay, 'A Success Story? The Foreign Policies of France's Fourth Republic', *Contemporary European History*, vol. 18, no. 4 (2009), pp. 499–519, 500.

instrumentalized the past to present themselves as 'ideal migrants'. They reclaimed, in particular, their eighteenth-century French roots, their ancestors having been transferred from Alsace-Lorraine to colonize the Banat by Empress Maria Theresa. In doing so, they challenged accusations of their collaboration with the Nazis, portrayed themselves as hard-working, highly moral and law-abiding migrants and were allowed to emigrate to France. Likewise, a number of Baltic DPs were able to gain the support of Raymond Schmittlein and exhibit their creations in the French zone. For instance, the Baltic DP-run school of *Arts et Métiers* (mechanical and industrial arts) in Freiburg remained both protected and funded by French authorities. DP schools and exhibitions were not for DPs' sake alone, but also for French occupiers and the public to appreciate. DPs' art bolstered French cultural traditions and was instrumental to project France's power in Germany. For these DPs who exhibited their production in the French zone, artistic expression helped them soothe homesickness, create a sense of belonging and present 'cultural worthiness' to relief workers and French occupiers alike. But by providing French schooling and cultural activities to some but not all DPs, French authorities clearly differentiated between DPs that they considered as valuable future citizens and those who were expected to return home or emigrate elsewhere. Rehabilitation was enacted in ways that reveal the persistence of gender discrimination and ethnic prejudices.

Relief workers' ideas of a successful rehabilitation were based on gendered assumptions. They insisted that DPs should conform to particular domestic arrangements and gendered norms. They tried to 'retrain' DP mothers to care *for* (via nurturing) their children, and DP fathers to care *about* (via breadwinning) their children. Welfare programmes confined DP men and women to very gender-specific spheres of activities: vocational workshops tended to assign DP men to building, metal, mechanical and leather work, carpentry, textiles, and DP women to childcare, nursery, embroidery, knitting and cooking.[9] In practice, however, the gender culture of DP spaces was more fluid and the ideals of the 'nuclear family' more fragile than relief workers' prescriptions suggested. Life under occupation suspended some of the gendered expectations of respectable femininity. In the intimate atmosphere of the DP camps, some female relief workers engaged in romantic relationships with DPs outside the bond of marriage. These 'transgressive' and immoral conducts of a minority of female relief workers were not only the subjects of criticisms amongst French occupation and PDR officials. It also tarnished UNRRA's reputation in DP religious elites' eyes, who condemned the low morality of French relief workers.

---

[9] UNA, HCRFA, S-0438-0009-05, Réunion des Welfare Officers du District Sud des Teams de l'Est, 15–16 January 1946, Wangen.

Certainly, much more remains to be discovered about how DPs responded to relief workers' injunctions and attempts to influence their behaviours. As French relief workers rarely spoke DPs' languages, they could only effectively liaise with the elites of the DPs who communicated in French or German. DP initiatives and resiliency were often disregarded by relief workers, except for the very few DPs whose activities aligned with French concerns for France's image abroad. As a result, DP voices and agencies appear sporadically in relief workers' reports. Some voices (such as those of the Banatais or Baltic artists) were heard more by French relief workers than others because they fitted with their visions of the occupation. Further research into DP diaries and personal narratives may tell us a different story about how 'ordinary' DPs overcame constraints placed on them by French occupiers and Allied relief workers and develop strategies for self-protection.

Fundamentally, this book nuances the view that the Second World War was a radically 'modernizing' and 'internationalizing' moment in the history of humanitarianism. For all UNRRA's rhetorical insistence on novelty and the 'modernization' of relief, its welfare programme was enacted in the French zone in ways that reveal the essentially conservative basis of post-war humanitarianism. The French UNRRA Director drew upon French military discourses of efficiency, discipline and practices of military relief predating the Second World War. Perhaps no example illuminates the conservative nature of UNRRA welfare programme better than the familial and maternal model largely inspired by the European bourgeoisie that relief workers tried to impose upon DPs. As we have seen, UNRRA female relief workers built on a tradition that had long constructed women as 'natural educators' and penetrated DP camps to instruct DP women how to fight the social diseases of alcoholism, tuberculosis and infant mortality.[10] In doing so, French women participated in the promotion of a gendered and conservative conception of compassion.

Today, these two organizations appear virtually forgotten in France.[11] Apart from a handful of specialist historians, most French people are unaware that they ever existed, including direct successor institutions. Most studies of French humanitarian aid have focused on the period of the creation of the French organization *Médecins Sans Frontières* (Doctors Without Borders)

---

[10] Sarah A. Curtis, *Civilizing Habits: Women Missionaries and the Revival of French Empire* (Oxford: Oxford University Press, 2010); Amelia Lyons, *The Civilising Mission in the Metropole: Algerian Families and the French Welfare State during Decolonization* (Stanford: Stanford University Press, 2013), p. 5.

[11] UNRRA recently appeared in a TV documentary 'Après Hitler' (2016) directed by David Korn-Brzoza.

from the Biafra crisis onwards.[12] Yet, this history of French DP aid resonates deeply with challenges that face the twenty-first century world. Despite the United Nations High Commissioner for Refugees (UNHCR)'s authority to exercise its supervisory role to enforce legal obligations to the Refugee Convention, asylum remains today mainly a matter of national sovereignty, rather than common European policies decided in Brussels or Geneva. Since the summer of 2015, the arrival of refugees from the Middle East and Africa gave way to increasing political and public anxieties about people seeking refuge in Europe. Across Europe, public discourses have flourished about a 'crisis of migrants', which allegedly 'threatened' the security defences and democracies of Europe. Rather than a 'crisis of migrants', refugees are confronted with a 'crisis of Europe'.[13] In 1950, Robert Schuman affirmed that a solution to the problem of refugees and population surplus was 'a precondition to the success of European integration'.[14] In June 2018, as I am writing this conclusion, European leaders are struggling to find solutions to manage displacement (the Dublin accords proving ineffective and absurd) and fight populist appeals against migrants. The Italian minister refused to let the *Aquarius*, a boat transporting 629 migrants rescued in the Mediterranean, dock in Italy; debates about the 'refugee question' have placed the German coalition of Angela Merkel at risk and strained French–Italian diplomatic relations after French President Emmanuel Macron's reactions to the Italian government's decision. 'Identity nationalism' is flourishing in so-called 'illiberal democracies' in Europe, where very few asylum seekers have arrived. In this context, Emmanuel Macron has made a series of high-profile speeches on the international stage presenting migrants as 'symbol of our times' and recalling France's and Europe's traditions of asylum. As Didier Fassin notes, Macron's idea of Europe and France is at odds with his actions.[15] In France, the security forces are harassing asylum seekers and undocumented migrants, children are held in detention centres and NGOs are repeatedly accused of being 'agents of smugglers'. The French Constitutional Council has recently ruled against the French state policing attitudes towards those who

---

[12] See, for example, Davis and Taithe, 'From the Purse and the Heart'; Eleanor Davey, *Idealism Beyond Borders. The French Revolutionary Left and the Rise of Humanitarianism, 1954–1988* (Cambridge: Cambridge University Press, 2015); Marie-Luce Desgrandchamps, *L'humanitaire en guerre civile. La crise du Biafra (1967–1970)* (Rennes: Presses Universitaires de Rennes, 2018).

[13] Colloque de rentrée du Collège de France 'Migrations, refugiés, exil', 12–14 October 2016. Programme available at www.college-de-france.fr/site/colloque-2016/p1675254353854300_content.htm (last consulted on 5 November 2019).

[14] Daniel Cohen, *In War's Wake: Europe's Displaced Persons in the Postwar Order* (Oxford: Oxford University Press, 2011), p. 122.

[15] Dider Fassin, 'Sure Looks a Lot Like Conservatism', *London Review of Books*, vol. 40, no. 13, 5 July 2018, pp. 15–17.

help them – arguing that helping undocumented migrants and asylum seekers is not a crime.

In this context, it has been tempting for today's observers to read the period of the immediate aftermath of war backwards, as a moment of successful and compassionate management of displacement.[16] The Western Allies, including war-torn France, repatriated millions of DPs and helped thousand resettle. In the French zone, alone, an estimated 47,586 DPs were resettled, for the most part in France, the USA and Australia.[17] In doing so, though, they turned the majority of refugees into economic migrants. Wartime Nazi collaborators escaped retribution, while 'real' victims of the Nazi regime were denied access to international aid.[18] DPs were not protected on account of their wartime experience, but on how convincing their account of this was. Then, as much as now, refugees were confronted to the arbitrariness of the state and the power of local bureaucrats. As Peter Gatrell notes, history is thus a resource to question states' rhetoric about 'traditions of hospitality' and commentators' claims about the 'increasing scale and "complexity" of refugee crisis'.[19] The continual reference today to France's 'humanitarian traditions' points to the enduring power of the notion that France is a *land of asylum*, but in the late 1940s as now there were sharply divergent ideas over what this meant and who was 'worthy' of France's assistance.

---

[16] See, for example, Angelina Jolie Pitt and Arminka Helic, 'Don't Blame Refugee for Seeking a Better Life', *Times*, 7 September 2015.

[17] 'Tableau des effectifs DPs émigrés de zone française à la date du 15 janvier 1952 par nationalité et pays de destination', HCRFA, Service des Personnes Déplacées, *Sept ans d'activité en faveur des personnes déplacées en zone française d'occupation, 1945-1952*, Rapport dactylographié et illustré [undated], p. 56.

[18] Catherine Gousseff, 'L'Est et l'Ouest entre consensus et divergence face aux DPs d'Allemagne', in Defrance, Denis and Maspéro (eds.), *Personnes déplacées et guerre froide en Allemagne occupée*, pp. 37-60, 38.

[19] Peter Gatrell, 'Refugees – What's Wrong with History?', *Journal of Refugee Studies*, vol. 30, no. 2 (2017), pp. 170-189, 184.

# SELECT BIBLIOGRAPHY

The following represents a sample of the works I have cited, those central to understanding the administration of Displaced Persons in French-occupied Germany. Further publications, websites, theses and newspapers used are located in the footnotes alongside detailed archival references.

## Archives Consulted

### Archives Nationales [AN], Pierrefite

F/17/28771: Dossier Alfred Poignant
Série AJ/43: Organisation Internationale des Réfugiés
Série AJ/72: Archives de la Commission d'Histoire de la Deuxième Guerre mondiale
Série F1/a: Commissariat à l'intérieur de Londres (septembre 1941–juin 1943) et délégation à Londres du Commissariat à l'Intérieur d'Alger (juin 1943–aout 1944)
Série F7: Police Générale
Série F9: Commissariat aux Prisonniers, Déportés et Réfugiés (Alger) et Ministère des Prisonniers, Déportés et Réfugiés (Paris)

### Centre des Archives Contemporaines [CAC], Fontainebleau

Versement 770623: Ministère de l'Intérieur, Direction générale de la Sureté nationale

### Service historique de la Défense, Vincennes

Série 8P: Mission de Liaison auprès des Alliés

### Centres des Archives diplomatiques [MAE], La Courneuve

Administrateur Général (ADM)
Administration d'occupation en Autriche (AUT)
Affaires Culturelles (AC)
Affaires Economiques et financières, Affaires Allemandes et autrichiennes, 1944–1949
Cabinet, 1945–1955 (HC)

Délégation provinciale pour la Rhénanie-Palatinat (RP)
Délégation provinciale pour le Bade (BAD)
Délégation provinciale pour Wurtemberg – Hohenzollern (WH)
Direction Générale des Affaires Politiques (DGAP)
Europe 1949–1955, Allemagne
Europe, Généralités, 1949–1955
Europe, Pologne, 1944–1949
Europe, URSS, 1944–1949
Europe, URSS, 1949–1955
Groupe Français au Conseil de Contrôle (GFCC)
HCRFA, Haut Commissariat de la République française en Allemagne
NUOI, Nations Unies et Organisations Internationales, Secrétariat des conférences 1945–1959
Personnes Déplacées et Réfugiés (PDR 1): Mission française de rapatriement (MFRA)
Personnes Déplacées et Réfugiés (PDR 2): Cabinet
Personnes Déplacées et Réfugiés (PDR 3): Organisation et fonctionnement du service
Personnes Déplacées et Réfugiés (PDR 6): Administration des PDR
Personnes Déplacées et Réfugiés (PDR 9): Formation Professionnelle Accélérée
Service de liaison (SL)
Y Internationale

## National Archives [NA], Kew Garden

FO 371: Foreign Office General Correspondence

## Wiener Library [WL], London

H46A-3/2, HA5-3/6, HA5-4/5, H46A-1, H46A-1/6, HA16-4/5, HA6B-2/1, HA16-1/3.
HA5-4/3: Report on Psychological problems on Displaced Persons, June 1945.

## International Tracing Service [ITS], Bad Arolsen (Germany)

Digitized Collections
1 Incarceration and persecution
1.1 Camps and Ghettos
1.1.29 Concentration camp Naztweiler (Struthof)
1.1.29.0 General Information on Natzweiler Concentration camp
2.2.2 Forced Labor
2.2.0.1 Correspondence and records on forced labor (information about administrative districts of the French Occupation zone only)
2.3 Post-war Evaluations of Various organizations

2.3.3 Haut-Commissariat de la République Française en Allemagne
2.3.3.5 French catalogue on concentration and forced labour camps in Germany and on German-occupied territory
6. Records of the ITS and its predecessors
6.1 Administration and organization
6.1.1 Predecessor organizations
8323001: Historical Survey of Central Tracing Activity in Germany 1945–1951; Study by UNRRA Administration; Study by IRO Administration
8323034: French zone 29.6.1945–21.5.1947
8323044: British zone 28.6.1947–10.1.1951 / French zone: 6.9.1947–16.3.1949
8323081: Conferences of Representatives of National Tracing Bureaus I 1945–1947
8323082: Conferences of Representatives of National Tracing Bureaus II 1948
8323083: Conferences of Representatives of National Tracing Bureaus III 1949
8323084: Documents of ITS Liaison Missions and National Tracing Bureaus France 10.6.1945–30.12.1948
6.1.2 Child Tracing Service field under UNRRA and IRO

*UN Archives [UN], New York*

Office of the Historian

**Germany Mission**
Central Headquarters – French Zone
Enquiries – Privileges and Immunities of UNRRA in Germany
European Regional Office
French Agreement
French Red Cross
French Zone – Employment Division
French Zone – Field Operations of Welfare Services
French Zone – Haslach (Administrative Orders, General Bulletins)
French Zone – Office of the Director
French Zone – Office of the Director of Field Operations
French Zone – Repatriation Division
French Zone – Reports
French Zone – Reports Division
French Zone – Team and Camp Files
Offices in France
United States Zone – District, Team and Camp

*JDC Archives, Records of the Geneva Office of the American Jewish Joint Distribution Committee*

GER.68
GER.347
GER.569

## Printed Primary Sources

### Official Documents

Haut Commissariat de la République française en Allemagne, Service des Personnes Déplacées. *Sept ans d'activité en faveur des personnes déplacées en zone française d'occupation, 1945–1952*, Rapport dactylographié et illustré [undated], [Bibliothèque du Ministère des Affaires Etrangères, Direction des Archives].

*Helping the People to Help Themselves: The Story of the United Nations Relief and Rehabilitation Administration* (London: His Majesty's Stationary Office, 1944).

Ministère des prisonniers, déportés et réfugiés. *Bilan d'un effort* (Paris: Imprimerie Busson, 1945).

### Medical Theses

Horrut, Jean-Marie. 'Le Goitre endémique dans la population infantile DP', thèse pour le doctorat en médecine, Université de Bordeaux, 1947, [Bibliothèque Nationale, Site François Mitterand].

Mora, Henri. 'Dix sept mois de travail médico-social dans l'UNRRA en Allemagne occupée', thèse pour le doctorat en médecine, Université de Bordeaux, 1947, [Bibliothèque Nationale, Site François Mitterand].

### Articles and Books

Anold-Foster, William. 'UNRRA's Work for Displaced Persons in Germany', *International Affairs*, vol. 22, no. 1 (1946), pp. 1–13.

Berge, François (ed.). *Personnes déplacées* (Paris: Éditions de Clermont, série chemin du monde, January 1948).

Blanchard, Francis. 'Le problème des réfugiés devant l'opinion', *Politique étrangère*, vol. 14, no. 2 (1949), pp. 167–172.

Davis, George. 'Handling of Refugees and Displaced Persons by the French MMLA (Section féminine)', *The Social Service Review*, vol. 22, no. 1 (1948), pp. 34–39.

Ginesy, Robert. *La seconde Guerre mondiale et les déplacements de population. Les organismes de protection* (Paris: Éditions A. Pedone, 1948).

Howard, Donald. 'UNRRA: A New Venture in International Relief and Welfare Services', *The Social Service Review*, vol. 18, no. 1 (1944), pp. 1–11.

Jacobsen, Pierre. 'L'oeuvre de l'Organisation Internationale pour les Réfugiés', *Population*, vol. 6, no. 1 (1951), pp. 27–40.

Nourissier, François. *L'homme humilié. Sort des réfugiés et personnes déplacées (1912–1950)* (Paris: Spes, 1950).

Sekutowicz, Jean. 'La participation française à l'administration de l'Allemagne occupée (1945–1949)', *Revue administrative*, vol. 41, no. 42 (1988), pp. 109–112.

Walczewski, Ignacy. *Destin tragique des polonais déportés en Allemagne. La crise de la famille polonaise dans les camps de personnes déplacées en Allemagne. Causes, conséquences, espoirs* (Paris: Hosianum, 1951).

Weintraub, Philipp. 'UNRRA: An Experiment in International Welfare Planning', *The Journal of Politics*, vol. 7, no. 1 (1945), pp. 1–24.

Wolf-Machoel, J. *La réadaptation de la jeunesse et des déracinés de guerre* (Boudry: Les Éditions de la Baconnière, 1945).

## Published and Unpublished Memoirs

Bradley, Jean. *Jours Francs* (Paris: Julliard, 1948).

De Coquet, James. *Nous sommes les occupants* (Paris: Librairie Arthème Fayard, 1945).

Klemme, Marvin. *The Inside Story of UNRRA: An Experience in Internationalism* (New York: Lifetime Editions, 1949).

Welty, Joel Carl. *The Hunger Year in the French Zone of Divided Germany* (Beloit, WI: Beloit College Archivist, 1993).

## Secondary Sources

### PhD Theses

Burgard, Antoine. 'Une nouvelle vie dans un nouveau pays. Trajectoires d'orphelins de la Shoah vers le Canada (1947–1952)', Université du Québec à Montréal/Université Lumière Lyon 2, 2017.

Edington, Claire. 'Beyond the Asylum: Colonial Psychiatry in French Indochina, 1880–1940', PhD thesis, Columbia University, 2013.

Miot, Claire. 'Sortir l'armée des ombres. Soldats de l'Empire, combattants de la Libération, Armée de la Nation : la Première Armée française du débarquement en Provence à la capitulation allemande (1944–1945)', PhD thesis, Paris Saclay, 2016.

Nowak, Katarzyna. 'Voices of Revival: A Cultural History of Polish Displaced Persons in Allied-Occupied Germany and Austria, 1945–1952', PhD thesis, University of Manchester, version submitted in July 2018.

Torriani, Riccarda. 'Nazis into Germans: Re-education and Democratisation in the British and French Occupation Zones, 1945–49', PhD thesis, University of Cambridge, 2005.

Sękowski, Paweł. 'Les Polonais en France dans l'immédiat après-guerre (1944–1949)', PhD thesis, Université Paris 4, 2015.

Sharpe, Charles Wesley. 'The Origins of the United Nations Relief and Rehabilitation Administration, 1939–1943', PhD thesis, University of Pennsylvania, 2012.

### Published Books and Articles

Adler, Karen. *Jews and Gender in Liberation France* (Cambridge: Cambridge University Press, 2003).

'Selling France to the French: The French Zone of Occupation in Western Germany, 1945–c.1955', *Contemporary European History*, vol. 21, no. 4 (2012), pp. 575–595.

Adler, Reinhold. 'Der schwierige Weg zur Normalität. Die UNRRA in Biberach und Umgebung 1945 bis 1947', *Gesellschaft für Heimatpflege Stadt und Landkreis Biberach*, (2007), pp. 36–57.

Die UNRRA in Saulgau und Sigmaringen und Umgebung 1946/47 – Aus den Wochenberichten des UNRRA-Teams 585', *Zeitschrift für Hohenzollerische Geschichte*, vol. 49/50 (2013/2014), pp. 251–290.

Angoustures, Aline, Kévonian, Dzovinar and Mouradian, Claire (eds.). *Réfugiés et apatrides. Administrer l'asile en France (1920–1960)* (Rennes: Presses Universitaires de Rennes, 2017).

Antons, Jan-Hinnerk. 'Displaced Persons in Postwar Germany: Parallel Societies in a Hostile Environment', *Journal of Contemporary History*, vol. 49, no. 1 (2014), pp. 92–114.

Armstrong-Reid, Susan and Murray, David. *Armies of Peace: Canada and the UNRRA Years* (Toronto: University of Toronto Press, 2008).

Arnaud, Patrice. *Les STO. Histoire des Français Requis en Allemagne Nazie* (Paris: CNRS Éditions, 2010).

Aslander, Leora. 'Coming Home? Jews in Postwar Paris', *Journal of Contemporary History*, vol. 40, no.2, Domestic Dreamlands: Notions of Home in Post-1945 Europe (2005), pp. 237–259.

Balint, Ruth. 'Children Left Behind: Family, Refugees and Immigration in Postwar Europe', *History Workshop Journal*, vol. 82 (2016), pp. 151–172.

Ballinger, Pamela. 'Impossible Returns, Enduring Legacies: Recent Historiography of Displacement and the Reconstruction of Europe after World War II', *Contemporary European History*, vol. 22, no. 1 (2013), pp. 127–138.

Baumel, Judith Tydor. 'DPs, Mothers and Pioneers: Women in the She'erit Hapletah', *Jewish History*, vol. 11, no. 2 (1997), pp. 99–110.

Bernou-Fieseler, Anne and Théofilakis, Fabien (eds.). *Dachau. Memoires et Histoire de la déportation. Regards franco-allemands* (Paris: Éditions Tirésias, 2006).

Bessel, Richard. *Germany 1945: From War to Peace* (London: Simon & Schuster, 2009).

Bessel, Richard and Haake, Claudia. *Removing Peoples: Forced Removal in the Modern World* (Oxford: Oxford University Press, 2009).

Bessel, Richard and Schumann, Dirk (eds.). *Life after Death* (Cambridge: Cambridge University Press, 2003).

Bezias, Jean-Rémy. *Georges Bidault et la politique étrangère de la France, Europe, Etats-Unis, Proche-Orient, 1944–1948* (Paris: L'Harmattan, 2006).

Boehling, Rebecca, Urban, Susanne and Bienert, René (eds.). *Displaced Persons Leben in Transit: Uberlebende zwischen Repatriierung, Rehabilitation und Neuanfang* (Göttingen: Wallstein Verlag, 2014).

Borggräfe, Henning, Jah, Akim and Schwabauer, Elisabeth (eds.). *Freilegungen: Rebuilding Lives – Child Survivors and DP Children in the Aftermath of the Holocaust and Forced Labor* (Göttingen: Wallstein Verlag, 2017).

Bories-Sawala, Helga. *Dans la gueule du loup: les Français requis du STO* (Paris: Presses Universitaires du Septentrion, 2010).

Brown-Fleming, Suzanne. *Nazi Persecution and Postwar Repercussions: The International Tracing Service Archive and Holocaust Research* (London: Rowman & Littlefield, 2016).

Bruttmann, Tal, Joly, Laurent and Wieviorka, Annette (eds.). *Qu'est ce qu'un déporté? Histoires et mémoires des déportations de la Seconde Guerre mondiale* (Paris: CNRS Éditions, 2009).

Burgess, Greg. *Refuge in the Land of Liberty: A History of Asylum and Refugee Protection in France since the Revolution* (London: Palgrave Macmillan, 2008).

*Refugees and the Promise of Asylum in Postwar France, 1945–1995* (London: Palgrave Macmillan, 2019).

Burgard, Antoine. 'Retranscrire la violence et le traumatisme: Mises en récit administratives de la persécution dans l'immédiat après-Shoah', *Vingtieme Siecle*, vol. 139, no. 3 (2018), pp. 165–176.

Cabanes, Bruno and Piketty, Guillaume (eds.). *Retour à l'intime au sortir de la guerre* (Paris: Tallandier, 2009).

Carpenter, Inta Gale. 'Folklore as a Source for Creating Exile Identity among Latvian Displaced Persons in Post-World War II Germany', *Journal of Baltic Studies*, vol. 48, no. 2 (2017), pp. 205–233.

Chapman, Herrick. *France's Long Reconstruction: In Search of the Modern Republic* (Cambridge, MA: Harvard University Press, 2018).

Cochet, François. *Les exclus de la victoire. Histoire des Prisonniers de guerre, déportés et STO 1945–1985* (Paris: Kronos, 1992).

Cohen, Daniel. 'Naissance d'une nation: Les personnes déplacées de l'après-guerre, 1945–1951', *Genèses*, vol. 38 (2000), pp. 56–78.

'Remembering Post-War Displaced Persons: From Omission to Resurrection', in König, Mareike and Ohliger, Rainer (eds.), *Enlarging European Memory: Migration Movements in Historical Perspective* (Stuttgart: Thorbecke Verlag, 2006), pp. 87–97.

*In War's Wake: Europe's Displaced Persons in the Postwar Order* (Oxford: Oxford University Press, 2011).

Corni, Gustavo, Kochanowski, Kerzy, Schulze, Rainer, Stark, Tamas, Stelz-Marx, Barbara and Stark, Tamás (eds.). *People on the Move. Forced Population Movements in Europe in the Second World War and Its Aftermath* (Oxford: Berg, 2008).

Coudry, Georges. 'Le rapatriement des ressortissants soviétiques de 1945 à 1947: avatars de la réciprocité', *Guerres mondiales et conflits contemporains*, vol. 178 (1995), pp. 119–140.

*Les camps soviétiques en France* (Paris: Albin Michel, 1997).

D'Abzac-Epezy, Claude. 'La France face au rapatriement des prisonniers de guerre allemands', *Guerres mondiales et conflits contemporains*, vol. 223, no. 1 (2009), pp. 93–108.

Dänzer-Kantof, Boris. *Immigrer en France. De l'ONI à l'OFII, histoire d'une institution chargée de l'immigration et de l'intégration des étrangers, 1945–2010* (Paris: Cherche-midi, 2011).

Davis, Adam and Taithe, Bertrand. 'From the Purse and the Heart: Exploring Charity, Humanitarianism and Human Rights in France', *French Historical Studies*, vol. 34, no. 3 (2011), pp. 413–432.

Defrance, Corine. *La politique culturelle de la France sur la rive gauche du Rhin* (Strasbourg: Presses Universitaires, 1994).

'La mission du CNRS en Allemagne (1945–1950): entre exploitation et contrôle du potentiel scientifique allemand', *La revue pour l'histoire du CNRS*, vol. 5 (2001), Online version, http://histoire-cnrs.revues.org/3372.

Raymond Schmittlein (1904–1974): médiateur entre la France et la Lituanie *Cahiers Lituaniens*, no. 9 (2009).

Defrance, Corine and Pfeil, Ulrich (eds.). *Entre guerre froide et integration européenne. Reconstruction et rapprochement, 1945–1963* (Villeneuve d'Ascq: Presses Universitaires du Septentrion, 2012).

Defrance, Corine, Denis, Juliette and Maspero, Julia (eds.). *Personnes déplacées et guerre froide en Allemagne occupée* (Frankfurt am Main: Peter Lang, 2015).

Denéchère, Yves. 'Des adoptions d'Etat: les enfants de l'occupation française en Allemagne', *Revue d'Histoire Moderne et Contemporaine*, vol. 57, no. 2 (2010), pp. 159–179.

Denis, Juliette. 'Identifier les "éléments ennemis" en Lettonie. Une priorité dans le processus de resoviétisation (1942–1945)', *Cahiers du monde russe*, vol. 49, no. 2-3 (2008), pp. 297–318.

'Complices de Hitler ou victimes de Staline? Les déplacés baltes en Allemagne de la sortie de guerre à la guerre froide', *Le Mouvement Social*, vol. 244, no. 3 (2013), pp. 81–98.

Dombrowski Risser, Nicole. *France under Fire: German Invasion, Civilian Flight and Family Survival during World War Two* (Cambridge: Cambridge University Press, 2015).

Doron, Daniella. *Jewish Youth and Identity in Postwar France. Rebuilding Family and Nation* (Bloomington: Indiana University Press, 2015).

Droit, Emmanuel. 'Le RPF dans les Zones Françaises d'Occupation en Allemagne (1947–1958)', in Audigier, François and Schwindt, Frédéric (eds.), *Gaullisme et Gaullistes dans la France de l'Est sous la IV République* (Rennes: Presses Universitaires de Rennes, 2009), pp. 187–201.

Dufoix, Stéphane. *Politiques d'exil* (Paris: Presses Universitaires de France, 2002).

Dyczok, Marta. *The Grand Alliance and Ukrainian Refugees* (London: Palgrave Macmillan, 2000).

Eder, Angelika. 'Perspectives of Displaced Persons in West Germany after 1945. A Comparison of Jewish, Baltic and Polish Non-Repatriates', in Steinert,

Johannes-Dieter and Weber-Newth, Inge (eds.), *Beyond Camps and Forced Labour* (Osnabrück: Secolo, 2005), pp. 79–89.

Elliot, Mark. *Pawns of Yalta: Soviet Refugees and America's Role in Their Repatriation* (Urbana: University of Illinois, 1982).

Fauroux, Camille. 'L'etiquette infamante de volontaire'. Genèse administrative d'une catégorie de l'histoire de l'occupation', *Revue d'histoire moderne et contemporaine*, vol. 2, no. 66 (2019), pp. 96–115.

Feinstein, Margerete Myers. 'Jewish Women Survivors in the Displaced Persons Camps of Occupied Germany: Transmitters of the Past, Caretakers of the Present and Builders of the Future', *Shofar*, vol. 24, no. 4 (2006), pp. 67–89.

Fleury, Antoine and Frank, Robert (eds.). *Le rôle des guerres dans la mémoire des européens* (Berne: Peter Lang, 1997).

Fishman, Sarah. *The Battle for Children World War II, Youth Crime and Juvenile Justice in Twentieth Century France* (Harvard: Harvard University Press, 2002).

*From Vichy to the Sexual Revolution Gender and Family Life in Postwar France* (Oxford: Oxford University Press, 2017).

Fogg, Shannon. *Stealing Home. Looting, Restitution, and Reconstructing Jewish Lives in France, 1942–1947* (Oxford: Oxford University Press, 2017).

Footitt, Hilary. *War and Liberation in France. Living with the Liberators* (Basingstoke: Palgrave Macmillan, 2004).

Forcade, Olivier, Duhamel, Emmanuel and Vial, Philippe (eds.). *Militaires en République, 1870–1962. Les officiers, le pouvoir et la vie publique en France* (Paris: Publication de la Sorbonne, 1999).

Forcade, Olivier and Nivet, Philippe. *Les réfugiés en Europe du XVI$^e$ au XX$^e$ siecle* (Paris: Nouveau Monde Editions, 2008).

Forsythe, David. 'On Contested Concepts: Humanitarianism, Human Rights, and the Notion of Neutrality', *Journal of Human Rights*, vol. 12, no. 1 (2013), pp. 59–68.

Fourtage, Laure. 'Les organisations juives d'aide sociale et l'insertion professionnelle dans l'immédiat après-guerre', *Archives Juives*, vol. 45, no. 1 (2012), pp. 10–26.

Frank, Matthew and Reinisch, Jessica (eds.) *Refugees in Europe 1919–1959: A Forty Years' Crisis?* (London: Bloomsbury, 2017).

Franck, Christiane (ed.). *La France de 1945. Résistances, retours, renaissances* (Caen: Presses Universitaires de Caen, 1996).

Gani, Léon. *Syndicats et Travailleurs immigrés* (Paris: Editions Sociales, 1972).

Gatrell, Peter and Baron, Nick (eds.). *Warlands. Population Resettlement and State Reconstruction in the Soviet-East European Borderlands, 1945–1950* (Basingstoke: Palgrave Macmillan, 2009).

Gatrell, Peter. *The Making of the Modern Refugee* (Oxford: Oxford University Press, 2013).

'Refugees – What's Wrong with History?', *Journal of Refugee Studies*, vol. 30, no. 2 (2017), pp. 170–189.

*The Unsettling of Europe* (London: Penguin Books, 2019).
Gay, Ruth. *Safe among the Germans: Liberated Jews after World War Two* (New Haven, CT: Yale University Press, 2002).
Geller, Jay Howard. *Jews in Post-Holocaust Germany, 1945–1953* (Cambridge: Cambridge University Press, 2004).
Geppert, Dominik (ed.) *The Postwar Challenge, 1945–1958* (Oxford: Oxford University Press, 2007).
Gerbet, Pierre. *Le relèvement, 1944–1949* (Paris: Imprimerie Nationale, 1991).
Girault, René and Frank, Robert (eds.). *La puissance française en question (1945–1949)* (Paris: Publications de la Sorbonne, 1988).
Gousseff, Catherine. 'Des migrations de sorties de guerre qui reconfigurent la frontière: ouverture et refermeture de l'URSS avant la guerre froide (1944–1946)', in Coeuré, Sophie and Dullin, Sabine (Eds.), *Frontières du communisme* (Paris: La Découverte-Recherche, 2007), pp. 428–442.
Grandhomme, Jean-Noel. 'Tambov et autres camps. Le lent retour d'URSS des "Malgré-nous" d'Alsace-Lorraine (1944–1955)', *Revue d'Allemagne et des Pays de Langue Allemande*, vol. 39 (2008), pp. 551–568.
Grossmann, Atina. 'Victims, Villains and Survivors: Gendered Perceptions and Self-perceptions of Jewish Displaced Persons in Occupied Postwar Germany', *Journal of the History of Sexuality*, vol. 11, no. 1/2 (2002), pp. 291–318.
  *Jews, Germans, and Allies: Close Encounters in Occupied Germany* (Princeton, NJ: Princeton University Press, 2007).
  'Grams, Calories, and Food: Languages of Victimization, Entitlement, and Human Rights in Occupied Germany, 1945–1949', *Central European History*, vol. 44, no. 1 (2011), pp. 118–148.
Grynberg, Anne. 'Des signes de résurgence de l'antisémitisme dans la France de l'après-guerre (1945–1953)?', *Les Cahiers de la Shoah*, vol. 1, no. 5 (2001), pp. 171–223.
Halamish, Aviva. *The Exodus Affair: Holocaust Survivors and the Struggle for Palestine* (2nd edn., Valentine Mitchell, 1998).
Hand, Seán and Steven, T. Katz (eds.). *Post-Holocaust France and the Jews 1945–1955* (New York: New York University Press, 2015).
Haushofer, Lisa. 'The Contaminating Agent: UNRRA, Displaced Persons and Venereal Disease in Germany 1945–1947', *American Journal of Public Health*, vol. 100, no. 6 (2010), pp. 993–1003.
Herbert, Ulrich. *Hitler's Foreign Workers: Enforced Foreign Labour in Germany under the Third Reich* (New York: Cambridge University Press, 1997).
Herzog, Dagmar. *Sex after Fascism. Memory and Morality in Twentieth-Century Germany* (Princeton: Princeton University Press, 2007).
Hillel, Marc. *L'occupation française en Allemagne* (Paris: Balland, 1983).
Hilton, Laura. 'The Black Market in History and Memory: German Perceptions of Victimhood from 1945 to 1948', *German History*, vol. 28, no. 4 (2010), pp. 479–497.

'Who Was "Worthy"? How Empathy Drove Policy Decisions about the Uprooted in Occupied Germany, 1945-1948', *Holocaust and Genocide Studies*, vol. 32, no. 1 (2018), pp. 8-28.

Hitchcock, William. *France Restored. Cold War Diplomacy and the Quest for Leadership in Europe, 1944-1954* (Chapel Hill: The University of North Carolina Press, 1998).

*The Bitter Road to Freedom: A New History of the Liberation of Europe* (New York: Free Press, 2008).

Hobson-Faure, Laura. *Un 'plan Marshall' juif: la présence juive américaine en France après la Shoah, 1944-1954* (Paris: Armand Colin, 2013).

Holborn, Louise. *The International Refugee Organisation. A Specialed Agency of the United Nations, Its History and Work, 1946-1952* (Oxford: Oxford University Press, 1956).

Holian, Anna. 'Displacement and the Post-war Reconstruction of Education: Displaced Persons at the UNRRA University of Munich', *Contemporary European History*, vol. 17, no. 2 (2008), pp. 167-195.

'Anticommunism in the Streets: Refugee Politics in Cold War Germany', *Journal of Contemporary History*, vol. 45, no. 1 (2010), pp. 134-161.

*Between National Socialism and Soviet Communism: Displaced Persons in Postwar Germany* (Ann Arbor: University of Michigan Press, 2011).

'The Ambivalent Exception: American Occupation Policy in Postwar Germany and the Formation of Jewish Refugee Spaces', *Journal of Refugee Studies*, vol. 25, no. 3 *Special Issue: the Refugee in the Postwar World, 1945-1960* (2012), pp. 452-473.

Holman, Valerie. 'Representing Refugees: Migration in France, 1940-1944', *Journal of Romance Studies*, vol. 2, no. 2 (2002), pp. 53-69.

Hudemann, Rainer. 'Revanche ou parternariat' A propos des nouvelles orientations de la recherche sur la politique française à l'égard de l'Allemagne après 1945', in Krebs, Gilbert and Schneilin, Gérard (eds.), *L'Allemagne 1945-1955. De la capitulation à la division* (Asnières: Publication de l'Institut d'Allemand, 1996), pp. 127-152.

'L'occupation française après 1945 et les relations franco-allemandes', *Vingtième Siècle*, vol. 55, no. 3 (1997), pp. 58-68.

Hüser, Dietmar. 'Ventres creux, mentalités collectives et relations internationales – la faim dans les rapports franco-allemands d'après guerre', in Francine-Liechtenhan, Dominique and Abrams, Brad (eds.), *Europe 1946: Entre le deuil et l'espoir* (Bruxelles: Editions Complexe, 1996), pp. 142-164.

*Frankreichs 'doppelte Deutschlandpolitik'. Dynamik aus der Defensive-Planen, Entscheiden, Umsetzen in gesellschaftlichen und wirtschaftlichen, innen- und aussenpolitischen Krisenzeiten 1944-1950* (Berlin: Duncker und Humblot, 1996).

Jacobmeyer, Wolfgang. *Vom Zwangsarbeiter zum heimatlosen Ausländer: Die Displaced Persons in Westdeutschland, 1945-1951* (Gottingen: Vandenhoeck & Ruprecht, 1985).

Janco, Andrew Paul. '"Unwilling": The One-Word Revolution in Refugee Status, 1940–1951', *Contemporary European History*, vol. 23, no. 3 (2014), pp. 429–446.
Jaroszynska-Kirchmann, Anna. *The Exile Mission* (Athens: Ohio University Press, 2004).
Judt, Tony. *Postwar: A History of Europe since 1945* (New York: Penguin, 2005).
Kevonian, Dzovinar. *Réfugiés et diplomatie humanitaire: les acteurs européens et la scène proche-orientale* (Paris: Publication de la Sorbonne, 2004).
'Les réfugiés européens et le Bureau international du travail: appropriation catégorielle et temporalité transnationale (1942–1951)', in Aglan, Alya, Feiertag, Olivier and Kévonian, Dzovinar (eds.), *Humaniser le travail. Régimes économiques, régimes politiques et Organisation international du travail (1929–1969)* (Bruxelles: Peter Lang, 2011), pp. 167–194.
Klein-Gousseff, Catherine (ed.). *Retour d'URSS. Les prisonniers de guerre et les internés français dans les archives soviétiques, 1945–1951* (Paris: CNRS Éditions, 2001).
Knapp, Andrew (ed.). *The Uncertain Foundation, France at the Libération, 1944–1947* (Basingstoke: Palgrave Macmillan, 2007).
Kochavi, Arieh. *Post Holocaust Politics Britain, the US and Jewish Refugees 1945–1948* (Chapel Hill: The University of North Carolina Press, 2001).
Konigseder, Angelika and Wetzel, Juliane. *Waiting for Hope: Jewish Displaced Persons in Post-World War II Germany* (Evanston: Northwestern University Press, 2001).
Koreman, Megan. *The Expectation of Justice: France, 1944–1946* (Durham, NC: Duke University Press, 1999).
Lagrou, Pieter. *The Legacy of Nazi Occupation: Patriotic Memory and National Recovery in Western Europe, 1945–1965* (Cambridge: Cambridge University Press, 2000).
Lalieu, Olivier. *La zone grise? La résistance française à Buchenwald* (Paris: Tallandier, 2005).
Lane, Thomas. *Victims of Stalin and Hitler: The Exodus of Poles and Balts to Britain* (New York: Palgrave Macmillan, 2004).
Lattard, Alain. 'A propos de l'occupation française en Allemagne 1945–1949: le conflit Laffon– Koenig', in *Sept décennies de relations franco-allemandes 1918-1988* (Paris: Publication de l'Institut d'Allemand, Université de la Sorbonne Nouvelle, 1989), pp. 227–262.
Lavsky, Hagit. *New Beginnings. Holocaust Survivors in Bergen-Belsen and the British Zone in Germany, 1945–1950* (Detroit, MI: Wayne State University Press, 2002).
Lazar, David. *L'opinion française et l'Etat d'Israël, 1945–1949* (Paris: Calmann-Lévy, 1972).
Le Bras, Hervé. *Marianne et les lapins. L'obsession démographique* (Paris: Hachette, 1991).
Lee Downs, Laura. *Childhood in the Promised Land: Working Class Movements and the Colonies de Vacances in France, 1880–1960* (Durham, NC: Duke University Press, 2002).

'Aurevoir Les Enfants: Wartime Evacuation and the Politics of Childhood in France and Britain, 1939–1945', *History Workshop Journal*, vol. 82, no. 1 (2016), pp. 121–150.

Lefèvre, Sylvie. *Les relations économiques franco-allemandes de 1945 à 1955. De l'occupation à la coopération* (Paris: Comité pour l'histoire économique et financière de la France, 1998).

Lesur, Adolphe. 'Le droit d'option nationale des citoyens polonaise établis en France, nés à l'Est du Bug: les positions méconnues du Gouvernement provisoire de la République française d'après les archives du Quai d'Orsay (octobre 1944–février 1946)', *Revue des etudes slaves*, vol. 75, no. 2 (2004), pp. 321–332.

Lewin, Christophe. *Le retour des prisonniers de guerre français: naissance et développement de la F.N.P.G., 1944–1952* (Paris: Publication de la Sorbonne, 1986).

Lewis, Mary Dewhurst. *The Boundaries of the Republic: Migrant Rights and the Limits of Universalism in France, 1918–1940* (Stanford: Stanford University Press, 2007).

Libera, Martial. *Un Rêve de Puissance: La France et le Contrôle de l'économie Allemande (1942–1949)* (Bruxelles: Peter Lang, 2012).

Loescher, Gil. *Beyond Charity. International Cooperation and the Global Refugee Crisis* (Oxford: Oxford University Press, 1996).

Luciuk, Lubomyr. *Searching for Place. Ukrainian Displaced Persons, Canada and the Migration of Memory* (Toronto: University of Toronto Press, 2000).

Ludi, Regula. *Reparations for Nazi Victims in Postwar Europe* (Cambridge: Cambridge University Press, 2012).

Macardle, Dorothy. *Children of Europe – A Study of the Children of Liberated Countries* (Boston: Beacon Press, 1951).

Maelstaf, Geneviève. *Que faire de l'Allemagne? Les responsables français, le statut international de l'Allemagne et le problème de l'unité allemande (1945–1955)* (Paris: Direction des Archives, MAE, 1999).

'Le "facteur soviétique" dans la politique allemande de la France, 1945–1954', in Soutou, Georges-Henri and Robin-Hivert, Emilia (eds.), *L'URSS et l'Europe de 1941 à 1957* (Paris: Presses Universitaire de la Sorbonne, 2008), pp. 341–356.

Malkki, Liisa. 'Refugees and Exile: From "Refugee Studies" to the National Order of Things', *Annual Review of Anthropology*, vol. 24 (1995), pp. 495–523.

Manfrass, Klauss and Rioux, Jean-Pierre (eds.) *France-Allemagne 1944–1947* (Paris: Cahier de l'IHTP No. 13/14, 1990).

Mankowitz, Zeev. *Life between Memory and Hope: The Survivors of the Holocaust in Occupied Germany* (London: Cambridge University Press, 2002).

Maquet, Marjorie. 'La lettre de doléance dans la zone française d'occupation entre 1945 et 1949', *Cahiers d'Etudes Germaniques*, vol. 71 (2016), pp. 209–219.

Marbau, Michel. 'La France et les organisations internationales 1939–1946', *Matériaux pour l'histoire de notre temps*, vol. 65, no. 1 (2002), pp. 75–83.

Marès, Antoine and Milza, Pierre. *Le Paris des étrangers depuis 1945* (Paris: Publication de la Sorbonne, 1994).
Marrus, Michael. *The Unwanted: European Refugees in the Twentieth Century* (New York: Oxford University Press, 1985).
Martens, Stephan (ed.). *La France, l'Allemagne et la Seconde Guerre mondiale. Quelles mémoires?* (Bordeaux: Presses Universitaires de Bordeaux, 2007).
Maspero, Julia. 'Les autorités françaises d'occupation face au problème des personnes déplacées en Allemagne et en Autriche, 1945-1949', *Revue d'Allemagne*, vol. 40, no. 3 (2008), pp. 485-500.
'La question des personnes déplacées polonaises dans les zones françaises d'occupation en Allemagne et en Autriche: un aspect méconnu des relations franco-polonaises (1945-1949)', *Relations internationales*, vol. 138 (2009), pp. 59-74.
'La politique française à l'égard de l'émigration juive polonaise de l'immédiat après-guerre', *Bulletin du Centre de recherche français à Jérusalem* [Online], 22 | 2011, Online since 25 March 2012, connection on 29 September 2013. http://bcrfj.revues.org/6513.
'Sur les traces des camps de personnes déplacées dans les anciennes zones françaises en Allemagne et en Autriche: une mémoire effacée ou déplacée?', in Jean-Frédéric de Hasque and Clara Lecadet (dir) *Après les camps. Traces, mémoires et mutations des camps de réfugiés* (Paris: Academia Harmattan, 2019), pp. 171-198.
Matard-Bonucci, Marie-Anne and Lynch, Edouard. *La Libération des camps et le retour des déportés* (Bruxelles: Complexe, 1995).
Mazower, Mark. *Dark Continent: Europe's Twentieth Century* (New York: Alfred A. Knopf, 1998).
Ménudier, Henri. *L'Allemagne occupée 1945-1949* (Paris: Publication de l'Institut d'Allemand, Sorbonne Nouvelle, 1989).
Moeller, Robert. 'Germans as Victims? Thoughts on a Post-Cold War History of the Second World War's Legacies', *History and Memory*, vol. 17, no. 1-2 (2005), pp. 147-194.
Moullec, Gaël. 'Alliés ou ennemis? Le GUPVI-NKVD, le Komintern et les "Malgrés-nous". Le destin des prisonniers de guerre français en URSS (1942-1955)', *Cahiers du monde russe*, vol. 42, no. 2-4 (2001), pp. 667-678.
Mühle, Eduard. 'Resettled, Expelled and Displaced: The Baltic Experience 1939-1951. Some Observations on the Current State of Research', in Angermann, Nobert, Garleff, Michael and Lenz, Wilhelm (eds.), *Ostseeprovinzen, Baltische Staaten und das Nationale* (Münster: LIT Verlag, 2005), pp. 565-589.
Myers Feinstein, Margarete. *Holocaust Survivors in Postwar Germany, 1945-1957* (Cambridge: Cambridge University Press, 2009).
'All under One Roof: Persecutees, DPs, Expellees, and the Housing Shortage in Occupied Germany', *Holocaust and Genocide Studies*, vol. 32, no. 1 (2018), pp. 29-48.

Nicault, Catherine. *La France et le sionisme, 1897–1948. Une rencontre manquée?* (Paris: Calmann-Lévy, 1992).
 'La Shoah et la creation de l'Etat d'Israel: où en est l'historiographie?', *Les Cahiers de la Shoah*, vol. 1, no. 6 (2006), pp. 161–204.
Noiriel, Gérard. *La tyrannie du national. Le droit d'asile en Europe (1793–1993)* (Paris: Calmann-Lévy, 1991).
 *Réfugiés et sans-papiers. La République face au droit d'asile XIXe-XXe siècle* (Paris: Hachette, 2006).
Nolan, Mary. 'Germans as Victims during the Second World War; Air Wars, Memory Wars', *Central European History*, vol. 38, no. 1 (2005), pp. 7–40.
Nord, Philip. *France's New Deal from the Thirties to the Postwar Era* (Princeton: Princeton University Press, 2010).
Notin, Jacques. *Les vaincus seront les vainqueurs* (Paris: Perrin, 2004).
Nourrissier, François. *L'homme humilié. Sort des réfugiés et 'personnes déplacées 1912–1950* (Paris: Spes, 1950).
Ouzan, Françoise. *Ces juifs dont l'Amérique ne voulait pas (1945–1950)* (Paris: Editions Complexe, 1995).
 'La reconstruction des identités juives dans les camps de personnes déplacées d'Allemagne (1945–1957)', *Bulletin du Centre de recherche français de Jérusalem*, vol. 14 (2004), pp. 35–49.
Patt, Avinoam and Berkowitz, Michael (eds.). *We Are Here: New Approaches to Jewish Displaced Persons in Postwar Germany* (Detroit, MI: Wayne State University Press, 2010).
Persian, Jayne. 'Displaced Persons and the Politics of International Categorisation(s)', *Australian Journal of Politics and History*, vol. 58, no. 4 (2012), pp. 481–496.
 *Beautiful Balts – From Displaced Persons to New Australians* (Perth: New South Books, 2017).
Polian, Pavel. 'Le rapatriement des citoyens soviétiques depuis la France et les zones françaises d'occupation en Allemagne et en Autriche', *Cahiers du Monde russe*, vol. 41, no. 1 (2000), pp. 165–190.
Ponty, Janine. *Polonais méconnus. Histoire des travailleurs immigrés en France dans l'entre-deux-guerres* (Paris: Publications de la Sorbonne, 1988).
 'Les rapatriements d'ouvriers polonais (1945–1948)', in *L'impact de la Seconde Guerre mondiale sur les relations franco-polonaises* (Paris: INALCO, 2000), pp. 125–137.
Proudfoot, Malcolm. *European Refugees, 1939–1952* (London: Faber and Faber, 1957).
Reinisch, Jessica. 'Introduction: Relief in the Aftermath of War', *Journal of Contemporary History*, vol. 43, no. 3 (2008), pp. 371–404.
 'Internationalism in Relief: The Birth (and Death) of UNRRA', *Past and Present*, supplement 6 (2011), pp. 258–289.
 '"Auntie UNRRA" at the Crossroads', *Past and Present*, vol. 218, supplement 8 (2013), pp. 70–97.
 *The Perils of Peace. Public Health Crisis in Occupied Germany* (Oxford: Oxford University Press, 2013).

'Old Wine in New Bottles? UNRRA and the Mid-Century World of Refugees', in Matthew Frank and Jessica Reinisch (eds.), *Refugees in Europe, 1919–1959: A Forty Years' Crisis?* (London: Bloomsbury, 2017), pp. 147–176.

Reinisch, Jessica and White, Jessica. *The Disentanglement of Populations: Migration, Expulsion and Displacement in Post-War Europe 1944–1949* (Basingstoke: Palgrave Macmillan, 2011).

Rinke, Andreas. *Le Grand retour – Die französische Displaced Person-Politik (1944–1951)* (Frankfurt am Main: Peter Lang, 2002).

Ristelhueber, René. *Au secours des réfugiés. L'oeuvre de l'Organisation Internationale pour les Réfugiés* (Paris: Plon, 1951).

Robin, Antony, Kushner, Jeremy and Knox, Katherine. *Refugees in an Age of Genocide: Global, National and Local Perspectives during the Twentieth Century* (London: F. Cass, 1999).

Rosental, Paul-André. *L'intelligence démographique: sciences et politiques des populations en France (1930–1960)* (Paris: Odile Jacob, 2003).

'Géopolitique et Etat-providence. Le BIT et la politique mondiale des migrations dans l'entre-deux-guerres', *Annales. Histoire, Sciences Sociales*, vol. 61, no. 1 (2006), pp. 99–134.

Rossy, Katherine. 'Faceless and Stateless: French Occupation Policy toward Women and Children in Postwar Germany (1945–1949)', in Muehlenbeck, Philip E. (ed.), *Gender, Sexuality and the Cold War. A Global Perspective* (Nashville, TN: Vanderbilt University Press, 2017), pp. 15–34.

Rystad, Goran (ed.). *The Uprooted. Forced Migration as an International Problem in the Post-War Era* (Lund: Lund University Press, 1990).

Salomon, Kim. *Refugees in the Cold War: Toward a New International Refugee Regime in the Early Postwar Era* (Lund: Lund University Press, 1991).

Salvatici, Silvia. 'Le gouvernement anglais et les femmes réfugiées d'Europe après la Seconde Guerre mondiale', *Le mouvement social*, vol. 225, no. 4 (2008), pp. 53–63.

'Help the People to Help Themselves': UNRRA Relief Workers and European Displaced Persons', *Journal of Refugee Studies*, vol. 25, no. 3 (2012), pp. 452–473.

'Sights of Benevolence. UNRRA's Recipients Portrayed', in Fehrenbach, Heide and Rodogno, Davide (eds.), *Humanitarian Photography: A History* (Cambridge: Cambridge University Press, 2015), pp. 200–222.

'"Fighters without Guns": Humanitarianism and Military Action in the Aftermath of the Second World War', *European Review of History: Revue Européenne d'Histoire*, published online first, October 2017.

Sanderson, Claire. *L'impossible alliance? France, Grande-Bretagne et defense de l'Europe 1945–1948* (Paris: Publication de la Sorbonne, 2003).

Seipp, Adam. 'Refugee Town: Germans, Americans, and the Uprooted in Rural West Germany, 1945–52', *Journal of Contemporary History*, vol. 44, no. 4 (2009), pp. 675–695.

Seipp, Adam and Sinn, Andrea. 'Landscapes of the Uprooted: Displacement in Postwar Europe', *Holocaust and Genocide Studies*, vol. 32, no. 1 (2018), pp. 1–7.

Shapira, Michal. *The War Inside: Psychoanalysis, Total War and the Making of the Democratic Self in Postwar Britain* (Cambridge: Cambridge University Press, 2013).
Shennan, Andrew. *Rethinking France. Plans for Renewal 1940–1946* (Oxford: Clarendon Press, 1989).
Shepard, Ben. *The Long Road Home. The Aftermath of the Second World War* (London: Bodley Head, 2010).
Silverman, Maxim. *Deconstructing the Nation: Immigration, Racism and Citizenship in Modern France* (New York: Routledge, 1992).
Sjöberg, Tommie. *The Powers and the Persecuted: The Refugee Problem and the Intergovernmental Committee on Refugees* (Lund: Lund University Press, 1991).
Skran, Claudena. *Refugees in Inter-war Europe. The Emergence of a Regime* (Oxford: Clarendon Press, 1995).
Sluga, Glenda and Clavin, Patricia (eds.). *Internationalisms a Twentieth-Century History* (Cambridge: Cambridge University Press, 2016).
Smouts, Marie Claude. *La France à l'ONU* (Paris: Presses de la Fondation Nationale des Sciences Politiques, 1979).
Soutou, Georges-Henri. *La guerre de cinquante ans. Le conflit Est-Ouest 1943–1990* (Paris: Fayard, 2001).
Spire, Alexis. *Etrangers à la carte. L'administration de l'immigration en France (1945–1975)* (Paris: Grasset, 2005).
Steege, Paul. *Black Market, Cold War. Everyday Life in Berlin, 1946–1949* (Cambridge: Cambridge University Press, 2007).
Steinhouse, Adam. *Workers' Participation in Post-Liberation France* (London: Lexington Books, 2001).
Stern, Frank. 'The Historic Triangle: Occupiers, Germans and Jews in Postwar Germany', in Moeller, R. G. (ed.), *West Germany under Construction: Politics, Society and Culture in the Adenauer Era* (Ann Arbor: University of Michigan Press, 1997), pp. 199–230.
Stone, Dan. *The Liberation of the Camps: The End of the Holocaust and Its Aftermath* (New Haven, CT: Yale University Press, 2015).
Théofilakis, Fabien. 'Les autorités françaises face aux prisonniers de guerre allemands SS (1944–1948)', *Guerres mondiales et conflits contemporains*, vol. 223, no. 3 (2006), pp. 93–107.
Thomson, Mathew. *Psychological Subjects: Identity, Culture and Health in Twentieth-Century Britain* (Oxford: Oxford University Press, 2006).
Thonfeld, Christoph. 'Memories of Former World War Two Forced Labourers – An International Comparison', *Oral History*, vol. 39, no. 2 (2011), pp. 33–48.
Tolstoy, Nicholas. *The Secret Betrayal* (New York: Charles Scribner's Sons, 1977).
Torriani, Riccarda. '"Des bédouins particulièrement intelligents"? La pensée coloniale et les occupations française et britannique de l'Allemagne (1945–1949)', *Histoire et Sociétés. Revue européenne d'histoire sociale*, vol. 17 (2006), pp. 56–66.

Ulrich-Pier, Raphaële. *René Massigli (1888–1988) Une vie de diplomate* (Paris: Peter Lang, Direction du Ministère des Affaires étrangères, 2006).
Vaïsse, Maurice (ed.). *8 mai 1945. La victoire en Europe* (3rd edn., Paris: Editions Complexe, 2005).
Viet, Vincent. 'Les politiques de la main-d'oeuvre en Europe à l'heure de la reconstruction' *Les reconstructions en Europe 1945–1949* (Bruxelles: Complexe, 1997) pp. 191–212.
'La politique de l'immigration entre main d'oeuvre et population', in Bernstein, Serge and Milza, Pierre (eds.), *L'année 1947* (Paris: Presse de Sciences Po, 1999), pp. 461–485.
Virgili, Fabrice. *Naître ennemi. Les enfants de couples franco-allemands nés pendant la Seconde Guerre mondiale* (Paris: Payot, 2009).
Vultur, Maranda. 'De l'Ouest à l'Est et de l'Est à l'Ouest. Les avatares identitaires des Français du Banat', in Diminescu, Dana (ed.), *Visibles mais peu nombreux. Les circulations migratoires roumaines* (Paris: Editions de la Maison des sciences de l'homme, 2003), pp. 99–105.
Wall, Irwin. *The United States and the Making of Postwar France, 1945–1954* (Cambridge: Cambridge University Press, 2002).
Wambach, Julia. 'Vichy in Baden-Baden – The personnel of the French Occupation in Germany after 1945', *Contemporary European History*, vol. 28, no. 3 (2019), pp. 319–341.
Weidling, Paul. 'Belsenitis: Liberating Belsen, Its Hospitals, UNRRA and Selection for Re-emigration 1945–1948', *Sciences in Context*, vol. 19, no. 3 (2006), pp. 401–418.
'"For the Love of Christ": Strategies of International Catholic Relief and the Allied Occupation of Germany, 1945–48', *Journal of Contemporary History*, vol. 43, no. 3 (2008), pp. 477–492.
Weil, Patrick. 'The Return of Jews in the Nationality of in the Territory of France', in David Bankier (ed.), *Jews Are Coming Back: The Return of the Jews to Their Countries of Origins after WWII* (New York and Oxford: Bergahn Books, 2005), pp. 58–71.
*How to Be French: Nationality in the Making since 1789* (Durham, NC: Duke University Press, 2008).
Weinreb, Alice. '"For the Hungry Have No Past nor Do They Belong to a Political Party": Debates over German Hunger after World War II', *Central European History*, vol. 45, no. 1 (2012), pp. 50–78.
Weiss, Petra. 'Die Koblenzer Lager für Displaced Persons 1945–1947', *Jahrbuch für westdeutsche Landesgeschichte*, vol. 29 (2003), pp. 467–507.
Wetzel, Juliane. 'Les camps pour personnes déplacées en Allemagne de 1945 à 1957', *Vingtième Siècle*, vol. 54, no. 1 (1997), pp. 79–88.
Wieviorka, Annette. *Déportation et Génocide: Entre la mémoire et l'oubli* (Paris: Hachette, 2003).
Willis, Roy. *France, Germany and the New Europe 1945–1967* (Stanford: Stanford University Press, 1968).

Woodbridge, Georges. *UNRRA: The History of the United Nations Relief and Rehabilitation Administration* (New York: Colombia University Press, 1950) 3 volumes.
Wyman, Mark. *DPs: Europe's Displaced Persons, 1945-1951* (Ithaca: Cornell University Press, 1998).
Zakić, Mirna. 'The Price of Belonging to the Volk: Volksdeutsche, Land Redistribution and Aryanization in the Serbian Banat, 1941-1944', *Journal of Contemporary History*, vol. 49, no. 2 (2014), pp. 320-340.
Zahra, Tara. 'Lost Children: Displacement, Family, and Nation in Postwar Europe', *Journal of Modern History*, vol. 81, no. 1 (2009), pp. 45-86.
  'Enfants et purification ethnique dans la Tchécoslovaquie d'après-guerre', *Annales. Histoire, Sciences Sociales*, vol. 66, no. 2 (2011), pp. 449-477.
  '"A Human Treasure": Europe's Displaced Children Between Nationalism and Internationalism', *Post-war Reconstruction in Europe. Past and Present*, vol. 210, supplement 6 (2011), pp. 332-350.
  *The Lost Children: Reconstructing Europe's Families after World War II.* (Cambridge, MA: Harvard University Press, 2011).
  '"The Psychological Marshall Plan": Displacement, Gender and Human Rights after World War II', *Central European History*, vol. 44, no. 1, *Human Rights, Utopias and Gender in Twentieth-Century Europe* (2011), pp. 37-62.
Zertal, Idith. *From Catastrophe to Power: The Holocaust Survivors and the Emergence of Israel* (Berkeley: University of California Press, 1998).

# INDEX

abortion, 211, 213
*Absents*, 3, 14, 77–78, 99, 133
Allied Control Council, xiii, 15, 167
American Christian Committee for Refugees (ACCR), 258
American Joint, 29, 254, 307
anti-communism, 64, 192, 309
antifascism, 297
Anti-Semitism, 29, 92
Australia, 10, 65, 295, 304–305, 312–313, 321, 323, 333
  recruitment policies, 305
Austria, 38, 40, 52, 55–58, 72, 146, 152, 181, 187, 294, 302

baby boom, 210, 322
Bad Arolsen, 101, 195
Baden, 7–8, 22, 31, 60, 79, 85, 87, 89, 101, 103, 128, 166, 172–173, 195, 230, 240, 248, 252, 281, 291
Baden-Baden, 22, 31, 60, 79, 85, 101, 105, 128, 166, 195, 240, 248, 300, 306
Balingen, 90, 190, 214, 238, 263, 272
Baltic art, 133, 240, 331
Baltic DPs, 13, 64, 69, 95, 109, 132, 141, 147–148, 151, 155–156, 158, 164–165, 184, 193–194, 230, 239, 242, 245–246, 251, 258, 264, 284, 292, 304–305, 330
Baltic States, 7, 132, 147–148, 151, 179, 187, 265
Banat
  Banatais, 40, 52–58, 69, 72–75, 245–246, 251, 258, 284, 292, 316, 329, 331
  Region, 40, 53–57, 73, 245, 316, 330

Bauche, Jacques, 119, 265
Belgium, 115, 187
  Belgians, 1, 47, 118
  Labour recruitment policies, 68, 302, 313
Bergen-Belsen, 5, 82
Berlin, 8, 15, 43, 51, 60, 69, 86, 95, 166, 187, 278, 294, 300, 307, 309
Biberach, 87, 90, 93, 165, 169, 176, 274
Bidault, Georges, 42–43, 67, 151
Black Forest, 126, 217–220, 222
black market, 31, 62, 80, 103, 108–109, 111, 159, 177, 274–275
Buchenwald, 4, 49, 146, 174, 279
Bulgaria, 56, 146

calories, 248, 276, 278–279, 281–282
Canada, 58, 301–302, 304–305, 312–313, 315, 338
Cartier-Bresson, Henri, 133
Catholicism, 25, 112, 211
child welfare, 14, 50, 202
Churches, 93, 135, 163, 211
citizenship, 7, 14, 57, 73, 144, 146–148, 155, 160, 164, 180, 183, 202, 217, 222, 271
civilizing mission, 291, 328
Cohen, Daniel, 28, 179, 296, 299
collaborators, 4, 8, 10, 37–38, 68, 74, 128, 133, 144, 150, 172, 178–181, 187–188, 333
Communist Party, 38, 66, 78, 83, 121, 252
communists, 38–39, 75, 318
criminality, 30, 63, 92, 158
Croizat, Ambroise, 59, 66, 72
Curzon Line, 160

353

Czechoslovakia, 147, 168, 178, 181
  Czechoslovak Republic, 150
Czechs, 1, 8, 47, 91, 175

de Gaulle, Charles, 4, 42, 105, 252
de la Morlais, Anne, 51, 310–312, 323
Debré, Robert, 47
democratization, 16–17
denazification, 181, 186
deportation, 19, 53, 57, 77, 79, 99, 134, 193
des Cilleuls, Jean Lambert, 120, 127, 235
DP artists, 12, 132, 240, 247, 325

Estonia, 155
  Estonians, 1, 8, 138, 155–156, 257, 263
Ethnic Germans
  Reichsdeutsche, 21, 71
  Volksdeutsche, 21, 52, 55–56, 71–72, 181, 185, 187
expellees, 21, 38, 52, 56, 147

familialism, 205
fascist, 10, 37, 61, 65, 69, 72, 74, 190, 329
fatherhood, 25, 208–209, 217
femininity, 27, 112, 118, 120, 135, 200, 202, 215, 330
Feyen, 90, 283, 301, 310
First World War, 17, 26, 40, 49, 53, 107, 130, 144, 146–147, 181, 188, 217, 221, 256–257, 322
food protests, 30
Freiburg, 87, 90, 95–96, 101, 110, 133, 175, 184, 194, 214, 235, 239, 241, 245, 258, 277, 290, 306–307, 317, 330
Freiburg, University of, 235
Frenay, Henri, 3, 77, 81

Gailingen, 94, 254
Gatrell, Peter, x, 56, 70, 200, 204, 233, 237, 244, 257, 286, 333
Gaullists, 10, 58–59, 132, 297, 309–310
gender
  gender anxieties, 124
  gender culture, 27, 135, 330

gender discourses, 7, 24, 27, 32, 126, 141
gender identities, 6, 232
gendered bodies, 230, 305
norms, 24, 27, 32, 80, 108, 120–121, 200, 207, 211, 215, 256, 330
General Secretariat for German and Austrian Affairs, 155
Gerbier, Jean, 90, 98, 119, 182
Gneisenau, 88–90, 168, 284
grandeur. *See* prestige
Granville, 116, 232
Great Britain, 67, 153, 313
  authorities, 68, 71–72, 82, 107, 145–146, 148, 151, 166, 175, 260, 319, 321, 327–328
  British zone, 72, 118, 139, 143, 168, 180, 186–187, 190–191, 199–201, 226, 249, 260, 279, 294, 302, 306
  London, 4, 43, 79, 82, 101, 105, 151, 153, 166–169, 195, 204, 298
  recruitment policies, 68, 303, 312
  relief workers, 114–115, 117, 119, 203, 259
Gutach, 97, 121, 173, 184, 216, 219, 224, 232, 255, 276, 281

Hilton, Laura, 92, 110, 194, 274–275, 279, 317
hospitals, 64, 132, 221, 235, 238, 256, 261
Hungarian, 53, 127, 171, 181–182, 184–185, 257, 307
Hungary, 146, 178, 181, 185

Israel, 95, 316, 323, 348
Italy, 60, 72, 146, 187, 332
  Italians, 1, 175, 179, 187

Jeunesse Ouvrière Chrétienne (JOC), 48
Jewish community, 94, 286
Jewish DPs, 8, 46, 64, 94, 179, 193, 254, 294, 315
Jewish Relief Unit, 93, 235

Kaiserslautern, 109, 157, 183, 209, 234
Karlsruhe, 101, 269, 306–307, 309, 311, 318–319

## INDEX

Koblenz, 20, 90, 184, 230, 269, 284
Koenig, Pierre, 22, 43–44, 54, 59, 105, 158–159, 188, 250, 252, 259, 306, 313
Konstanz, 95, 97–98, 102, 155, 254

labour conscripts, 2, 62, 77, 79, 99
Laffon, Emile, 22, 54, 85, 100, 103, 112, 156–158, 160–161, 163, 165, 171, 173, 178, 181, 194, 234, 250, 259, 279, 281–282
Landstuhl, 89–92, 122, 124, 168, 215, 240, 256, 266, 301
languages, 1, 28, 64, 82, 112, 310
Latvia, 133, 155, 181, 195, 239
  Latvian diaspora, 96
  Latvian folklore, 242
  Latvian novels, 184
  Latvians, 1, 8, 96, 138, 155–156, 193–194, 239, 257, 284, 309
Lebach, 89–90, 209
Lee Downs, Laura, 123, 206, 222, 224, 226
Lenclud, Fernand, 29, 81, 101, 103–108, 111, 153, 164, 168–169, 172–176, 187, 263, 282
Lithuania, 132, 239, 287
  Lithuanian art, 133, 226, 241
  Lithuanian diaspora, 189
  Lithuanian Orchestra of Freiburg, 242
  Lithuanian Red Cross, 287
  Lithuanians, 1, 8, 127, 138, 156, 193, 195, 239, 257

Mainz, 13, 20, 110
Malgré-nous, 9, 40, 73, 75, 149, 329
Marshall Plan, 68
masculinity, 200, 202, 286
  virility, 123–124, 217
Maspero, Julia, 19, 23, 39, 43–44, 64, 71, 85, 93, 95, 98, 166, 294, 341
maternalism, 209
  maternalist discourse, 27, 120
Mauco, Georges, 46
military credentials, 104, 106
Military Mission for German Affairs, 41
Minister of Agriculture, 62
Ministry of Agriculture, 42, 62, 68
Ministry of Foreign Affairs, 43–45, 51, 58, 63, 67–68, 71, 78–79, 83, 87, 103, 143, 150–151, 153–154, 156, 163, 195, 248, 306, 315, 319, 327, 329
Ministry of the Interior, 45, 69
Ministry of Justice, 150
Ministry of Labour, 10, 37–38, 42, 45, 59–62, 66, 68–69, 71, 74–75, 319–320
Ministry of Public Health and Population, 45–47, 61, 68, 71, 75, 314
Mission Militaire de Liaison Administrative (MMLA), 11
monetary reforms (1948), 273–275
Monnet Plan, 44, 65–68, 74
Morin, Edgar, 11
motherhood, 25, 27, 203, 208–209, 212, 215, 217
Mülheim, 90, 172, 190, 193, 213

Nansen passport, 160
Neustadt, 101, 159
New Deal, 200
Niederlahnstein, 89–90, 236, 301
Nordach, 235
nutrition, 28, 102

Offenburg, 90, 319
Office National d'Immigration, ONI, 10, 37, 39, 61, 68, 71, 74–75, 297, 305–309, 311–313, 321, 324
ORT (Organisation Reconstruction travail), 254

Palestine, 64, 94–95, 255, 294, 313
Parodi, Alexandre, 42, 59
patriotism, 10, 253, 297, 310
photography, 29, 125–126, 141
  photographs, 28–29, 126, 128–129, 137–139, 141–142
Pirmasens, 89–91, 93, 103, 169, 176, 234, 236, 238
Poignant, Alfred, 46, 85–87, 107, 158, 161, 167, 182, 301, 316

Poland, 43–44, 60, 67, 88, 94, 129, 147, 163, 166, 175–176, 178, 181, 183, 187, 190, 192, 245
Poles, 1, 7, 47–48, 52, 60, 62–64, 69, 89, 91, 99, 137, 172, 174–175, 191–192, 194, 283–284, 307
Polish DPs, 7, 38–39, 42–48, 50, 55, 59–67, 71, 75, 78, 84, 88, 91, 94, 97, 99, 127, 135, 137, 154–156, 160–162, 165–169, 171–173, 175, 177, 184–185, 189–193, 196, 210–211, 214, 227, 233, 235–236, 240, 244–245, 251, 257–258, 268–269, 282–286, 292, 294, 304, 306–307
Potsdam Conference, 20–21, 56, 67, 166, 181
POWs, 1–2, 7, 9, 44, 62, 66–67, 119, 137, 145–146, 148–149, 151, 171, 179, 182, 193, 210, 217
prestige, 11–13, 58, 80, 107–108, 123, 125, 127, 130, 135, 150, 158, 236, 286, 297, 310, 323, 325, 328
Prigent, Robert, 48
psychoanalysis, 206
psychology, 14, 117, 202, 207–208, 224, 233, 246, 253, 257, 260, 278

radiance, *See* prestige
Rastatt, 22, 85, 101, 166, 300
rationing, 30, 110, 122, 247, 274, 276, 278–279
food rations, 31, 93, 102, 139, 214, 247, 259, 267, 271–272, 276–277, 280–282, 284, 309, 317
Ravensburg, viii, 13, 63, 90, 96, 127, 129, 164, 169, 184, 190, 193–194, 207, 235, 257–258, 264–265, 272, 276, 278, 284, 315, 326
Red Army, 9, 55, 64, 78, 147–149, 184, 193–194
rehabilitation, 6, 14, 19, 24–26, 33, 125–126, 135, 141, 199–202, 207, 212, 218, 221, 224, 226, 231, 237–239, 246–247, 260, 262, 273, 299, 326, 330
Reinisch, Jessica, 11, 17, 20, 27, 144, 147, 201, 327
religious faith, 25, 211

Resistance
experiences, 4, 77
former members, 22, 32, 81, 83–84, 105, 114, 119
legacies, 33, 39, 49, 59, 83, 130, 309
myths, 128, 130, 145
Resnais, Alain, 5
Reutlingen, 165, 193, 243, 270, 272, 307
Rhineland, occupation of, 12, 131
Rhineland-Palatinate, 7–8, 87, 89, 291
Romania, 56, 146
Romanian Parliament, 57
Romanians, 7, 91, 182, 187
Rottweil, 87, 90, 95, 226, 240, 264, 272
Ruhr, 17, 22, 66, 327

Saar, 7–8, 17, 20, 87, 89, 300
Saarbrücken, 20
Salvatici, Silvia, 64, 100, 104, 116, 126, 139, 255, 259–260, 270–271
Saulgau, 90, 194, 227
Sauvy, Alfred, 47
Schmittlein, Raymond, 132–133, 239, 242, 330
Schuman, Robert, 332
scoutism, 230
screening, 7, 33, 47, 61, 88, 103, 127, 138, 142–143, 176, 178–185, 187–188, 195, 199, 233, 237, 300, 304, 308, 315, 329
sexuality, 32, 118, 122, 232–233
Socialist Party, 252
Soviet Union, 9–10, 38, 41, 43, 57, 142, 147, 149–150, 152–157, 159, 161, 163, 166, 195–196, 298, 329
Franco–Soviet Agreement, 155, 157–158, 165–166
Russians, 1, 89, 138, 191–192, 209
Soviet authorities, 138, 148, 151–152, 155, 161, 164, 194
Soviet citizen, 148, 150, 171
Soviet embassy, 311
Soviet nationals, 7, 42–43, 137, 147–149, 152, 160
Soviet occupation, 181
Soviet Repatriation Officers, 143, 148, 156–158, 164, 169, 176, 194, 329
Spaniards, 91

Spanish refugees, 61
stateless, 8, 127, 155, 160, 169, 176, 179, 181, 184, 187, 287
strikes, 284, 311, 313
summer camps, 223
Supreme Headquarters of the Allied Expeditionary Forces, SHAEF, xiii, 2, 42, 82, 90, 117, 146, 260
Switzerland, 259, 299, 313, 315

Third Republic, 208, 222, 246
Tirard, Paul, 131
trade unions, 39, 59–61, 72
Trier, 91–92, 169, 301
Tübingen, 20, 95, 101, 111, 161, 184, 193–194, 230, 272
Tübingen, University of, 183, 235
Tuttlingen, 30, 95, 139, 141, 175, 301

Ukraine, 160
Ukrainians, 1, 7, 55, 63, 69, 75, 91, 138, 147, 155, 158, 160–161, 164, 179, 192, 244, 251, 258, 283–284, 292, 308, 314
United States, 304
American authorities, 66–67, 92, 148, 151, 166, 181, 186, 279, 309
American relief workers, 113–115, 117–119, 122, 124
American zone, 32, 42, 55, 67, 72, 92, 94–95, 118, 139, 143, 148, 155, 168, 174, 179, 183, 186–187, 190–191, 194–195, 260, 263, 278, 280, 302, 306–307, 309, 311
relief workers, 276
Washington, 79, 101, 105, 195

vaccination, 214, 238
venereal diseases, 231–234

Vichy, 13–14, 31, 40, 46, 61, 83, 105–106, 114, 128, 150, 209, 217, 230, 253, 262, 283, 293, 322, 325–326
Vichy regime, 61, 83, 105–106, 129, 209, 217, 253, 262, 293
victimhood, 193
Vlasov Army, 149–150, 157
vocational guidance movement, 256
vocational training, 15, 24, 200, 203, 237, 246–247, 255–258, 270, 286, 288–289, 326–327

Wangen, 87, 90, 96, 141, 159, 162, 164, 169, 194, 200, 239, 257, 272, 274, 330
Wehrmacht, 2, 9, 84, 90, 149, 179, 181, 184–185, 187
Women
DP mothers, 24–25, 200, 207, 210–212, 215, 246, 330
female relief workers, 11, 27, 121, 135, 330–331
World War One, 52
Württemberg, 7–8, 24, 87, 89, 103, 139, 155, 184, 194, 250, 252–253, 266, 271, 279, 281, 291
Wurzach, 95, 226, 241

Yalta Conference, 148–149, 151
YMCA, 226–227, 233, 243, 258–259, 299
Yugoslavia, 56, 139, 147, 178, 318
Yugoslavs, 1, 8, 60, 69, 89, 137, 175, 179, 191, 307

Zach, Elise, 206–207, 212, 227, 233, 243, 245
Zahra, Tara, 14, 48, 200, 202
Zionism, 64, 94–95, 254

CPSIA information can be obtained
at www.ICGtesting.com
Printed in the USA
LVHW011048030821
694401LV00005B/350